Colin Wilson is one of the most prolific, versatile and popular writers at work today. He was born in Leicester in 1931, and left school at sixteen. After he had spent years working in a wool warehouse, a laboratory, a plastics factory and a coffee bar, his first book *The Outsider* was published in 1956. It received outstanding critical acclaim and was an immediate bestseller.

Since then he has written many books on philosophy, the occult, crime and sexual deviance, plus a host of successful novels which have won him an international reputation. His work has been translated into Spanish, French, Swedish, Dutch, Japanese, German, Italian, Portuguese, Danish, Norwegian, Finnish and Hebrew.

By the same author

MYSTERIES

AN INVESTIGATION INTO THE OCCULT, THE PARANORMAL AND THE SUPERNATURAL

COLIN WILSON

WATKINS PUBLISHING
LONDON

First published in the UK in 2006
Reprinted 2006

Distributed in the USA and Canada by Sterling Publishing Co., Inc.
387 Park Avenue South, New York, NY 10016

Watkins Publishing, Sixth Floor, Castle House,
75–76 Wells Street, London W1T 3QH

First published in hardback by Hodder and Stoughton in 1978
Published by Granada Publishing Ltd in Panther Books
in paperback in 1979

3 5 7 9 10 8 6 4 2

Printed and bound in Great Britain

Library of Congress Cataloging in Publication Data Available

ISBN 13: 978-1-84293-185-1
ISBN 10: 1-84293-185-7

www.watkinspublishing.com

For information about custom editions, special sales, premium and
corporate purchases, please contact Sterling Special Sales
Department at 800-805-5489 or specialsales@sterlingpub.com

Acknowledgments

It would have been impossible to write this book without the help of many friends who have kept me supplied with material, or drawn my attention to cases that I might otherwise not have seen. Chief among these has been Ira Einhorn, who is virtually a one-man liaison service for parapsychologists and scientists interested in various aspects of the paranormal. My old friend June O'Shea has also provided me with invaluable material, including Walter Prince's original articles on the Doris case. Lawrence Leshan spoke to me of the Philip case, and put me in touch with Dr George Owen, who not only sent me his wife's book on the subject, but provided equally fascinating material on Matthew Manning, Uri Geller and on poltergeist phenomena. I am also indebted for material to C. L. Tilburn, Hugh Corbett, Walter Williams, Robert Turner, Joyce Carol Oates, Doris Cerea, Kathie Schlichting, Angelica de St. Prix, Jerry Neff, John Comley, Sir Robin Mackworth-Young, Jacquetta Hawkes, Arthur Young, Martin Gardner, Nigel Morland, Jesse Lasky jnr, Carol Davies, Anita Gregory, Wilson Knight, Theo Brown, Andrew Green, Idries Shah, Linda Woolery, Arthur Guirdham, Geoffrey Ashe, Björn Sjöval, Sheila Clarkson, Stephen Skinner and Robert Temple. The *National Enquirer* was kind enough to send me photostats of various items that I had otherwise been unable to trace. The Society for Psychical Research, represented by its Librarian Miss Eleanor O'Keefe, has been equally generous in lending me otherwise unobtainable books, as has the Harry Price Library of London University. The staff of the London Library has shown incredible patience and ingenuity in tracing dozens of obscure books and references that would otherwise have been unavailable to me. (Their particular triumph was the details of the career of Benoit de Maillet.)

Finally, I wish to offer my warmest thanks to my English and American editors, Rivers Scott and Anne Freedgood, for their truly enormous labours in getting this book into its final shape.

Colin Wilson

FOR EDDIE CAMPBELL
WITH AFFECTION

Contents

PART
THREE

Analytical Table of Contents

———◆———

PART
ONE

1 Ghosts, Ghouls and Pendulums

Tom Lethbridge moves into Hole House. Lethbridge and dowsing. The 'witch' who lived next door. Her astral projections. She teaches Tom how to throw pentagrams. How to use the pendulum. Locating buried silver. Lethbridge studies 'rates' of length. Searching for truffles. The problem of ghosts. The invisible porter of Trinity. The ghoul on the stairs. The apparition of Hole Mill. Was she a tape recording? The suicide in the wood. The 'blanket of depression' on Ladram beach. Mina is urged to jump over the cliff. The common denominator: water. Lethbridge's 'field' theory of ghosts and ghouls. Bill Lewis and Leonard Locker. Are ghosts intelligent? Beverley Nichols' story of the haunted house of Torquay. Arthur Guirdham's theory of houses that induce illness. Lethbridge's poltergeist on Skellig Michael. A ghost steals the sandwiches. Vanishings and apports. Sir Oliver Lodge's 'tape recording' theory. Andrew Green and the house in Ealing. The haunting of the Ma Barker house in Florida. Unusual powers of animals: the cat's 'second sight'. Are cats' whiskers divining rods? The behaviour of the hawk moth. Is dowsing 'electrical'? Sexual electricity. Freida Weisl, whose orgasms made ornaments jump off the mantelpiece. Electrical theory of the paranormal. Lethbridge and 'other dimensions'. Can the pendulum reveal what is beyond death? 'The second whorl of the spiral.' The timeless zone. Robert Leftwich and the 'superconscious' theory of dowsing. Jung's 'other selves'. The concept of 'promotion'. Our inborn passivity. Lethbridge's last days. Lethbridge's four areas of study.

2 Giants and Witches.

The owner of Skellig Michael suggests a theory. Lethbridge disagrees. The white dog of Hole. The tile with the white hare. The search for the giant of Wandlebury Camp. The legend of the ghostly knight. The mystery of the giant hill figures. The Cerne Abbas giant. The Long Man of Wilmington. The white horses of England. Dragons? Lethbridge locates the Wandlebury giant and discovers three figures. The Celts and their gods. Lethbridge's theories cause controversy. He leaves Cambridge. Frazer and *The Golden Bough*. Andrew Lang's criticisms. Margaret Murray and the god of the witches. Leland's *Aradia*. 'The old religion.' Lethbridge's theories of the Great Mother. The sun god Lugh becomes St Michael. Gerald Gardner and the witchcraft revival. Norman Cohn's criticisms of Margaret Murray. Michael Harrison's *Roots of Witchcraft*: the phalluses hidden in the altar. The Bishop of Exeter catches the monks worshipping 'the pagan Diana'. Sheila-na-gigs. Michael Dames's theory of the purpose of Silbury Hill: a giant fertility figure? My own investigations into the 'Old Religion' in Cornwall. The Helston furry dance; the Padstow 'Obby 'Oss. The Hungerford tuttimen. The horned dancers. Lethbridge on magic. Are the stone megaliths storage batteries? Levi and Crowley on magic: the 'Astral Light'. Robert Graves and the moon cult.

3 The Path of the Dragon

The modern 'occult revival'. Gerald Gardner, *The Morning of the Magicians*. The Piri Reis maps. Kenneth Arnold sights the first flying saucers. George Hunt Williamson and the Great Pyramid. Kubrick's *2001*. Lethbridge reads von Däniken. Von Däniken's inaccuracies. His literary offences. Lethbridge's theory of 'space men'. Who were the 'giants in the earth'? The 'war in heaven'. Lethbridge on Stonehenge. Geoffrey of Monmouth's account. Where did the stones come from? Lethbridge's investigations. Were the stones intended to guide space craft? Robert Temple's *Sirius Mystery*. How did the Dogon know Sirius was a double star? Lethbridge at the Merry Maidens. My own experience of dowsing. Alfred Watkins discovers ley lines. Are leys ancient trade routes? Guy Underwood and his theory of aquastats. The 'earth force'. White horses and dragons. John Michell's theory of leys. The *feng-shui* lines. The currents of the earth force. Does this explain the 'Old religion'? Man and the earth. Leys and acupuncture. The coiled serpent. Hermes as god of the leys. The earth as a living being. Its forces can interact with the human mind. Poltergeists and ley lines. Black dogs. Animal ghosts. Colin Godman's story of the white dog of Blaize House. Ancient man as a nomad. The theories of Alexander Thom and Gerald Hawkins: the megaliths as astronomical observatories. The new Carbon 14 dating of Stonehenge. Euan MacKie's theory of a 'theocratic élite caste' in the late Neolithic. Evidence that the Great Pyramid was an observatory. Why was ancient man so

Neither science nor religion have a monopoly of truth. Kuhn's *Structure of Scientific Revolutions*. Gertrude Schmeidler's 'sheep and goats' experiment. Charles Fort and his ideas. An ice-covered meteorite. The father of Ufology. Early UFO sightings. The aim of science. The visual distortion experiment of Dr Anton Hajos. The need for security and the hankering after insecurity. Jung and alchemy.

2 How Many Me's Are There?

Jung's first case: the girl with dual personality. 'Ivenes' speaks of past incarnations. Jung's poltergeist experiences. The case of Mary Reynolds. Janet's case of Leonie. The case of Doris Fischer. First appearance of 'Ariel'. Emergence of three more sub-personalities. Walter Prince's cure of Doris. The Douglass Deen case of 'demoniacal possession'. Janet's case of Achille. Janet's discovery about the 'contracted field of attention of the hysteric'. The case of Christine Beauchamp. Wilder Penfield's discovery of 'memory playback'. Eric Berne on the Adult, the Child and the Parent. Sybil Dorsett and her sixteen personalities. Janet's nine levels of consciousness. Michael Polanyi and his objection to 'nothing butness'. George Sully's experience of 'inner voices'. William James's 'threefold dream'. The inhibition of personality. The 'hierarchy of possible beings'. Depth psychology and magic.

3 In Search of Faculty X

Crowley on Magick. The 'lifting experiment'. A demonstration of 'will pressure'. Joire's experiments in telepathy. J. B. Priestley and the poetess. A schoolgirl levitates. The control of psi power—J. B. Rhine's experiments. Nina Kulagina and psychokinesis. Geller's spoon-bending. Felicia Parise and psi. Frankl's law of reversed effort. How does psi work? Magic and the 'true will'. The four laws of magic. Importance of will and imagination. MacGregor Mathers and the 'vampire'. The art of visualisation. Robert Graves on seduction. Alexandra David-Neel's story of the 'hat that walked'. How to make a knife commit murder. The Huna concept of the higher self. 'Man dictates his own future.' Glanvill's scholar gypsy: thought reading at a distance. What is imagination? Cro-Magnon man exterminates the Neanderthals. He invents a primitive form of writing. The impor-

6 Revelations

Jullian's explanation of their experience. Criticism of the explanation. The 'undoubted queerness of time'. Janet and the 'reality function'. Jane O'Neill's experience of retrocognition in Fotheringhay church. Rayner Garner's glimpses of the past. Bergson's theory that the nervous system is a filter. How does perception work? 'The psychic faculty does more harm than good.'

7 Worlds Beyond

Ouspensky on dreams. The half-dream state. Lucid dreams. Use of dreams by *shamans*. Charles Leland on dreams. His dream in Homburg. Van Eeden on lucid dreams. Oliver Fox and his discovery of 'astral travel'. Fox and his friends meet in a dream. My own experience of dreams. Out-of-the-body experiences. Ingo Swann has his tonsils removed. Tests at Stanford. William Gerhardie's experience of astral travel. Sylvan Muldoon's experience. Ed Morrell's out-of-the-body experience in prison. Robert Cracknell's 'lucid dream' of the Orderly Officer. The Verity case. St Anthony of Padua. Alphonse de Lignori. Goethe's experience of döppelgängers. The case of Emilie Sagée. Vardøgers and forerunners. Dr Charles Féré observes the 'neuropathic halo'. Baron von Reichenbach's discovery of 'odic force'. Radiations of crystals. Braid's criticism of Reichenbach. J. Rhodes Buchanan discovers psychometry. William Denton and his geological specimens. Kilner and the 'health aura'. The invention of Kilner goggles. Burr and Northrop's *Electrodynamic Theory of Life*. The electrical blueprint of life. Discovery of Kirlian photography. Lichtenburg figures. Thelma Moss's results. Acupuncture. Max Toth's survey of 'human storage batteries'. Spontaneous combustion. D. H. Lawrence's 'out-of-the-body experience' on his deathbed. Keith Boland's phantasm of the living. Is the mind a 'private place'? Are Jews descended from Neanderthals? The Cabbala. *The Book of Enoch*. Merkabah mysticism. Ascent to the throne. *The Zohar*. The holy names. Dion Fortune on the Cabbala. The four worlds. The Cabbala as a psychological system.

8 Ancient Mysteries

Amory's *John Buncle*. The antiquarian Thomas South and his daughter. The Mysteries of Eleusis. Boehme and 'mystical alchemy'. Mary

9 The Great Secret

telepathy. The Gurdjieff method and the Houdini method. The powers of Matthew Manning and Uri Geller. Are they 'controlled poltergeist activity'? Manning's theta activity when using his psychic powers. Geller's experiment with Nitonol wire. He 'de-materialises' a piece of vanadium foil. Does Geller's energy come from the earth? Did Geller and Manning 'blow a fuse'? The dowser who tracked down murderers. The secret of the alchemists.

10 Powers of Evil?

Bill Slater fights off 'possession'. The 'witch' of St Leonards on Sea. Donald Omand and 'psychic pressure'. Barrett's *Magus*: the nine varieties of demon. My dream of de Sade. Joachim Kroll, the cannibal. The 'bewitched' armchair. Has evil an objective existence? Robert Morris's experiment with animals in a haunted house. The 'T-field'. Travels with Ho-tei. Unlucky ships: the *Great Eastern*, the *Hinemoa*, the *Scharnhorst*. Jinxed cars and aircraft. Archduke Ferdinand's car. The James Dean car. Jung's haunted house. Multiple personality and poltergeists. The Wesley Poltergeist case. The Cock Lane ghost: was it genuine after all? The discovery that frustrated adolescents 'cause' poltergeists. The case of Esther Cox. Poltergeist or demon? The Rosenheim case. Human batteries: Caroline Clare, Jennie Morgan, Frank McKinistry. Strindberg's 'electric shocks'. The role of shocks in inducing paranormal powers. Ghosts associated with ley lines. Stephen Jenkins' experience of disorientation. The phantom army of Mounts Bay. The phantom Roman legions of Wroxham. The ghosts of Edgehill. The Merlin Stone. My experience of disorientation at Boscawen-un. Are UFOs visitors from other dimensions? The Ardachie haunting. The leys at Ardachie. 'Astral monsters'—Robert Monroe's experience. Elementals. Oliver Fox's elemental. Henry James Snr's experience of an 'invisible monster'. My investigation of the case. Herne the Hunter and Windsor Park. The ley lines of Windsor. Was Windsor Park a site of the 'ancient religion'? Geoffrey Hodson's 'elemental'. The spirits of the Slippery Hills. Van der Post apologises, and the jinx ceases. Parallel universes? The Michael Taylor case of possession. Powers of mind. Thomas Castellan, the 'wicked magician'. The Franz Walter case. Gurdjieff and Rasputin. Crowley's hypnotic powers. Sexual magic used in seduction. Castellan, Walter, Rasputin, Gurdjieff, were all healers. The structure of the self. The mechanism of poltergiest energies. Colonel Olcott performs miracles in Ceylon. Our hidden powers.

PART
THREE

1 Evolution

The 'dream-like' quality of life. Our need for permanence. Mental breakdown. The meaninglessness of human existence: nausea and absurdity. Jouffroy's experience of disillusion. The fallacy of the 'nausea' experience: Bennett at Fontainebleau. Passive consciousness. Consciousness is 'constructed'. The need for 'filters'. Mechanical evolution versus 'inner' evolution. Man is a god who has forgotten his own identity. The Fall theory. Some calculating prodigies. Nicola Tesla and his power to 'visualise'. What is wrong with Darwinism. The purpose of the pyramids. Mendelssohn's theory of the Meidun pyramid. The Alpbach symposium. The Kammerer scandal. Was Kammerer right after all? Stan Gooch's theory of evolution. The ego and the self: the new brain and the old. The conflict between passion and reason. Why did the new brain develop so quickly? Gooch's theory of 'potential responses'. Gooch's experience of mediumship. Elmer Green and theta rhythms. Charlotte Bach's sexual theory. Sexual deviation as the driving force of evolution. The eight 'types'. The anomaly of transvestitism. The zebra finch and ten-spined stickleback: displacement activities. The desire to become the opposite sex. Classification of types. Neotony: is man an immature ape? The axolotl lizard. The eight-hour orgasm. Are great creators always unbalanced? Charlotte Bach's insistence on human freedom. The 'outsider' theory of evolution. Ornstein's theory of the brain hemispheres. The problem of 'insight'. The sleeping areas of the brain. The robot theory of evolution. Man has become over-automatised. The notion of the Fall. The need to achieve 'normal consciousness'. The reason for irrational behaviour. The need for de-conditioning. The concentrative mechanism. The danger of 'de-programmed' behaviour. The wider horizon of values. The robot as jailer. The de-programming of sex. The need for inner freedom. The futility of mere activity. The outsider as an evolutionary force. The reappearance of outsiders.

2 Messages from Space and Time.

The Parascience Conference of 1976. Ted Owens, the PK Man. Owens' power over the weather. His UFO contacts. Space Intelligences. Susanne Padfield's theory of 'psychic support figures'. Nicholas Roerich's UFO sighting of 1926. Men in black. The career of Andrija Puharich. The case of Harry Stone: reincarnation of Ra Ho Tep? The sacred mushroom: John Allegro's theory. *Beyond Telepathy*. The theory of psi-plasma. Adrenergia and cholinergia. Puharich meets Uri Geller. His UFO contacts. Arigó, the psychic surgeon. Geller's tests at Stanford. Puharich's 'contacts' after the break with Geller. Phyllis Schlemmer and Tommy Wadkins. 'Tom', the representative of The Management. *Messages from the Aeons*. Tommy Wadkins at Brunel University. Can plants transmit healing energy? The philosophy of The Management. The Jews as 'the Chosen People'. Abraham and the space intelligences of Hoova. Puharich averts a Middle East war. Can Puharich be taken seriously? An evening with Puharich. The new race of children. Criteria for acceptance of paranormal phenomena. John Keel's *Mothman Prophecies*. The West Virginia sightings of 1966. Keel is persecuted by space men. Accurate prophecies of space intelligences. The Pope escapes assassination. UFO contacts: Barney Hill and Herb Schirmer. Keel's 'fear zone'. A Lethbridge 'ghoul'? Ted Holiday's theory that the Loch Ness monster is a ghost. Dragons and discs. Ghost sightings on ley lines. Ted Holiday's 'man in black'. Sightings at Loch Ness. Review of evidence. Are UFOs *tulpas*? The mind's power to create psychic manifestations. Dr George Owen's case of Philip, the 'invented ghost'. Alexandra David-Neel's *tulpa*. Dion Fortune's werewolf. Thomas Bearden's theory of UFOs as creations of the collective unconscious under stress. UFOs and the Cold War. UFOs and the cattle mutilations. Ed Sanders on the mutilations. John Keel talks to 'Mr Apol'. Is Mr Apol a disembodied spirit? New interpretation of the history of spiritualism. Are 'spirits' the tramps and con-men of the spirit world? Chesterton and the ouija board. Hawthorne on D. D. Home. The wave of vampirism in the eighteenth century. Jacques Vallée's theory of UFO phenomena as a heuristic 'game'.

3 The Mechanisms of Enlightenment

William James's case of the man who fell out of love. Andreyev's

Abyss, and its implication that 'man's higher nature' is a delusion. The 'negative revelation'. Peter Kürten and Carl Panzram. An 'outside' power? Mystical revelation from Raynor C. Johnson's *Watcher on the Hills*. Bucke's glimpse of 'cosmic consciousness'. Consciousness of 'eternal life'. Man's 'other selves'. Gilbert Ryle's reductionist view of man: the 'ghost in the machine'. Julian Jaynes' theory of 'the bicameral mind'. Did Homeric man possess consciousness? Auditory hallucinations. The left and right sides of the brain. Mystical revelation in a railway carriage. Was the sense of 'great power' an illusion? Louis Jacolliot's experiences with Indian holy men. Miracles of Sai Baba. Theory of the Oversoul. Case from *A Drug Taker's Notes*. 'Something mounting up.' The *chakras* and the *kundalini* serpent. Gopi Krishna's experience of *samadhi*, 'immersed in a sea of light'. He comes close to insanity and death. The Hindu belief that life lies outside the physical body, and that the *chakras* are the 'connecting points'. Acupuncture points. *The Boy Who Saw True* and his visions of human auras. Shafica Karagulla's investigations: energy fields. Does our energy come from outside the body? John Humphrey Noyes and the *karezza*: intercourse without orgasm. Rodney Collin's glandular theory of cosmic influence. New evidence for astrology: Krafft and the Gauquelins. Collin's theory of birth patterns. Is the 'ladder of selves' purely physical? Case of a student in the overturned tractor: 'All my life flashed before me.' My own experience in North Devon. The complexity of the brain. Intentionality—the key to mystical consciousness. Cancer as information underload. Myth of the Golden Age and the Fall. Evelyn Underhill on the basic mystical 'trick'. C. S. Lewis and his experiences of 'joy'. Lewis's fallacy of 'pure objectivism'. His failure to grasp importance of intentionality. The *relationality* of consciousness. Perception itself is a creative act. The career of Fechner: from atheism to mysticism. His breakdown and recovery. The soul life of plants. His anticipations of Cleve Backster. Gurdjieff's breakdowns. Loss of control and the draining of energy. Yeats's theory of inner crisis: Dante and Villon. My weekend at Bennett's school at Sherborne. My objections to Bennett and Gurdjieff. The need for control of the robot. My insight into 'panic attacks'. The planaria method. Why human beings are like 'grandfather clocks driven by watchsprings'.

4 *Other Dimensions*

A comprehensive theory of the paranormal? Where did 'the computer' come from? The Galapagos finch and its reaction to hawks. Bennett's theory of 'the fifth dimension'. Is the fifth dimension human freedom? Defining an event in four dimensions. Charles Tart's investigations into precognition. His theory of 'the second dimension of time'. The 'channel for psi information'. Lateral inhibition. Arthur Young's *Reflexive Universe*. The Cretan paradox. Young's theory of 'the fall'. Life as seven levels. Wittgenstein on intentionality. 'Using our freedom to increase our freedom.' Science and the paranormal. The problem of death. Stan Gooch's views on the evidence for survival. The Fox case as evidence: Margaret's confession of fraud. The 'cross correspondences' case. The case of Nils Jacobsen's uncle. Dr George Ritchie's experience of 'dying'. My mother's experience in hospital. The researches of Dr Karlis Osis into pre-death hallucinations. William Blake's visionary powers; his deathbed experience. Tolstoy's Ivan Ilyich. Why do so many Christians doubt the evidence of Spiritualism? Irrelevance of 'survival' as a solution of the existential problem. The 'seed of destiny'. The problem of time. Steve Rosen's theory of time. The development of consciousness. The danger of self-consciousness. The prison of concepts. The mechanism that steals human freedom. Analysis of my panic attacks: 'closing the windows'. The problem of human longevity. My 'Gita period'. The trick of inducing 'inner expansion'. My *Philosopher's Stone*. The wider and the narrower personality. 'Unproductive tension.' The importance of 'focusing'. Art as an aid to 'focusing'. The basic drive of evolution: to raise the pressure of consciousness. The concept of 'the feedback point'. Human evolution has not yet reached 'the feedback point'. Consciousness as an 'aid to survival'. Evolution as a flight from pain and inconvenience. The need for inner freedom. The nineteenth century as a turning point in the evolution of consciousness. The 'Outsider problem'. Modern 'Romanticism'. Man is approaching the 'feedback point'. The need for more consciousness. The 'recycling' of evolutionary energy. Conclusion.

Appendix: Electromagnetic Induction of Psi States, by Peter Maddock
    Bibliography, Notes and Index.

Introduction to the New Edition

———————◆———————

In the new Introduction to this book's predecessor, *The Occult*, I have described how I became interested in the subject almost by pure chance. It was towards the end of the '60s, when a book called *The Morning of the Magicians (Le Matin des Magiciens)* had become a world bestseller, and other publishers hastened to cash in. When my American agent asked me if I would like to write a book called *The Occult*, I accepted, because I needed the money. It was not a subject in which I took a deep interest, for I had started out in life intending to become a scientist, and had only abandoned the idea because I decided when I was sixteen that I would prefer to become a writer instead.

I was lucky. After seven years of drifting from job to job, I started to write a non-fiction book called *The Outsider*, about people who felt themselves to be misfits in society, focusing on such figures as Van Gogh, Nietzsche and Lawrence of Arabia. Published in 1956, when I was still twenty-four, it amazed me by becoming a bestseller and making me famous. But being bracketed with writers like John Osborne and John Braine as an 'Angry Young Man' alienated the serious critics who had praised the book, and its sequel, *Religion and the Rebel*, was received with such hostility that my publisher advised me to give up writing and get myself an office job. I declined the suggestion, bought a house in a remote part of Cornwall, and went on writing and lecturing to support my family.

Which is why, in 1969, I was quite ready to write a book to order, even though I regarded the occult as mostly superstitious nonsense. But as soon as I became absorbed in research, I realised I was wrong.

The change of mind began when my wife, Joy, showed me a passage in a book she was reading. It was a volume of autobiography by Osbert Sitwell, telling how, in the summer of 1914, he and some brother officers visited a famous palmist. As she studied their hands, she became obviously upset and distracted. When Sitwell asked afterwards what had disturbed her, she said: "There was nothing in their hands—they were empty." These officers were killed in the first months of the World War I in the same year.

I was impressed because I knew Sitwell was a sceptic, and as soon as I began serious research on the book, I realised that such things cannot be dismissed as superstition. The evidence for 'hidden powers' like telepathy, second sight, and precognition, was overwhelming, and only a dogmatic materialist could deny them. Precognition—the ability to catch glimpses of the future—struck me as particularly important because my common sense as well as my scientific training told me that it should be simply impossible. Yet there were dozens of well-authenticated examples of its genuineness.

I was so fascinated by all this that the book became huge—a quarter of a million words long—and its English publisher asked me to cut it by half. I refused, and my British agent found me another publisher who was less timid. When *The Occult* came out in England and America—then a dozen other countries—in 1971, it soon restored health to my finances.

Naturally, the publishers wanted a sequel. I was perfectly willing, but how could I write another book about the occult without repeating myself?

It was Joy who once again handed me the solution. Ten years earlier I had bought a second-hand copy of a book called *Witches: Investigating an Ancient Religion* by T. C. Lethbridge, and so liked his casual, breezy way of writing that I had bought several more of his books since. Busy with other work, I left them unread on my shelf. But Joy began reading them, and one day started to tell me about Lethbridge—how, as an archaeologist, he had taught himself to dowse with a pendulum, and later found that it could not only detect buried artefacts, but many different substances like iron and copper, according to its length. It would even respond to abstract ideas such as evolution, anger and death.

Fascinated, I also began to read Lethbridge, and found him just as extraordinary as Joy had said. Lethbridge was an archaeologist and a Cambridge don, by inclination a sceptic, but his involvement in dowsing had drawn him deeper and deeper into the realm of the paranormal, until his interests extended to ghosts, telepathy, precognitive dreams and the nature of time. I suddenly saw that by tracing Lethbridge's own story I could cover an enormous range of subjects relating to the paranormal.

Then chance came to my aid again, but this time in a more alarming manner. In July 1973, I was working for a crime magazine publisher helping to plan and launch a 'part work'—that is, a work that can be bought in weekly instalments then bound up as an encyclopedia. The backers were in a hurry, and I found myself—as a contributing editor—working at a terrifying pace, and forced to churn out thousands of words a week. Finally, sheer overwork induced a series of panic attacks. It was a frightening experience that made me think I was on the brink of a mental breakdown. For months, I felt like someone who has fallen into a swollen river and is clinging to an overhead branch, trying not to be swept away. But learning to master the attacks taught me that our minds are not as unified as we think (all this is described at the beginning of this book). Since I had also become fascinated by the strange subject of multiple personality—people whose bodies can be 'taken over' by a series of different 'selves'—it brought me a glimpse of a new possibility: that we all contain many selves, arranged in the form of a ladder.

This, I realised, implied a vision of the mind that differed fundamentally from that of most psychologists. Abraham Maslow, a psychologist I admired deeply, objected that Freud has 'sold human nature short', overlooking the possibility of 'further reaches of human nature'. My own vision of a 'ladder of selves' seemed to me an important step in creating a psychology that could take the occult in its stride.

It was when I was writing the second part of the book that I had another of those strokes of serendipity that opens up a range of new ideas. A friend named Ira Einhorn came to visit me, and had with him a copy of a recently published book called *The Origin of Consciousness in the Breakdown of the Bicameral Mind* by Julian Jaynes. It was from this

I first learned of a subject that has been around since the 1950s, but had only become widely known in the past ten years: split-brain physiology. I had been aware of the fact that the left and right halves of the brain have completely different functions, the left being concerned with logic and reason, the right with feeling and intuition—in other words, that the left is a scientist while the right is an artist. But what I had not realised—and what I learned from Jaynes—is that we literally have two different people living in our heads, and that what you call 'you' lives in the left, while a few inches away there is a total stranger. As it struck me that this stranger is responsible for the reaction of the dowsing rod, and for most of what are described as 'psychic powers', I suddenly realised that I had discovered a new key to this whole realm of the occult.

Once I began to write the book, I had the same experience as with its predecessor. New material flooded in so fast that it seemed to write itself. It ended by being even longer than *The Occult*.

Once again I encountered the same problem—except that when a self-assertive female editor demanded that I cut it by half, I objected; she refused to give way, and so again I was forced to find another publisher.

The reception of *Mysteries* was not quite as enthusiastic as that of *The Occult*, but that would have been too much to ask. As it was, the book was widely reviewed, and I took great satisfaction in watching it going through many editions in subsequent years.

I should mention one central point upon which I have changed my mind. In this book I attempt to account for the whole field of the paranormal in terms of unknown powers of the human mind—what Maeterlinck called 'the unknown guest'. This included the poltergeist or 'noisy ghost', which, like most students of the paranormal, I at the time regarded as 'recurrent spontaneous psycho kinesis', or mind over matter, caused by the unconscious energies of a disturbed teenager. But when, in 1980, I went to investigate a case of poltergeist haunting in Pontefract, I came to a quite different conclusion; that poltergeists are mischievous spirits who simply borrow their energy from human beings, mostly teenage.

But to speak about that, and what it implies, would require more space than I have room for in this Introduction.

Colin Wilson

The Ladder of Selves

At the time when I was still collecting materials for this book, I had a nasty but curiously fascinating experience: a series of attacks of 'panic anxiety' that brought me close to nervous breakdown. What surprised me most was that I was not depressed or worried at the time. I was working hard, and therefore under a certain amount of strain, but I seemed to be taking it all in my stride. For the past eighteen months I had been involved on the editorial board of a kind of encyclopedia of crime; but as every meeting ended in disagreement, it began to look as if the whole project would have to be abandoned. Then, at short notice, the publisher decided to go ahead. Suddenly, everything had to be completed in a few months; and I, as co-ordinator, was asked to produce around a hundred articles—3,000 words each—at a rate of seven a week. I began to work at the typewriter for eight or nine hours every day and tried to unwind in the evenings with a bottle of wine and a pile of gramophone records.

One day, a couple of journalists came to interview me. In fact, they did most of the talking. They were young and enthusiastic, with a tendency to interrupt one another. When they left, at about two in the morning, my eyes were glazed with boredom, and I felt as if I'd been deafened with salvos of cannon fire. This, I later realised, was the trouble. When you become bored, you 'let go'; you sink into a kind of moral torpor, allowing your inner-pressure to leak away as if you were a punctured tyre. The next day they came back for another session with the tape recorder. When they left I felt too dull to do any work; instead I took the opportunity to perform a number of routine household chores.

That night, about 4 a.m., I woke up feeling unrested and lay there thinking about all the articles I still had to write, and the books I ought to be writing instead. Anxiety hormones began to trickle into my bloodstream, and my heartbeat accelerated. I actually considered going to my workroom and starting another article—then realised that if I did *that*, I'd really be letting things get on top of me. Lying there, with nothing else to think about, I felt my energies churning, like a car being accelerated when the engine is in neutral. It was rather like feeling physically sick, except it was the emotions that were in revolt. When it was clear that I was not going to improve the situation by ignoring it, I tried making a frontal assault and suppressing the panic feeling by sheer will power. This proved to be a mistake. My face became hot, and I felt a dangerous tightness across the chest, while my heartbeat increased to a point that terrified me. I got up, went to the kitchen and poured myself a glass of orange juice. Then I sat down and tried to soothe myself as I might try to calm a frightened horse. Gradually, I got myself under control and went back to bed. As soon as I was in the dark, the process started again: rising panic, accelerating heartbeat, the feeling of being trapped. This time I got up and went into the sitting-room. I was inclined to wonder if I was having a heart attack. Quite clearly, *something* had gone wrong. The panic kept rising like vomit; the calm, sane part of me kept saying that it was absurd, some minor physical problem that would resolve itself within twenty-four hours. Like nausea, it came in waves, and between each wave there was a brief feeling of calm and relief.

The attack differed from nausea in that there was no point in giving way to it and making myself sick. This panic caused energy to disappear, like milk boiling over in a saucepan. There was a vicious-circle effect; the anxiety produced panic, the panic produced further anxiety, so the original fear was compounded by a fear *of* fear. In this state, it seemed that any move I made to counter the fear could be negated by more fear. In theory, the fear could overrule every attempt I made to overrule it. Like a forest fire, it has to be somehow contained before it destroyed large areas of my inner-being.

I *had* experienced something of the sort in my teens, but without this sense of physical danger. One day at school, a group of us had been discussing where space ended, and I was suddenly shocked to realise that the question seemed to be *unanswerable*. It felt like a betrayal. It suddenly struck me that a child's world is based on the feeling that 'Everything is OK.' Crises arise, apparently threatening your existence; then they're behind you, in the past, and you've survived. Or you wake up from a nightmare, and feel relieved to realise that the world is really a decent, stable sort of place. The universe *looks* baffling, but somebody, somewhere, knows all the answers . . . Now it struck me that grown-ups are, in this respect, no better than children; they are surrounded by uncertainty and insecurity, but they go on living because that's all there is to do.

For years after that insight, I had been oppressed by a sense of some terrible, fundamental bad news, deeper than any social or human problem. It would come back with a sudden shock when life seemed secure and pleasant—for example, on a warm summer afternoon when I saw a ewe feeding her lambs, looking a picture of motherly solicitude, unaware that both she and her lambs were destined for someone's oven.

Now, as I sat in the armchair and tried to repress the panic, I realised that it was important *not* to start brooding on these fundamentals—our total ignorance, our lack of the smallest shred of certainty about who we are and why we are here. That way, I realised, lay insanity, a fall into a kind of mental Black Hole.

I suppose that what seemed most ironical was that I had always felt that I understood the cause of mental illness. A couple of years before I had written a book called *New Pathways in Psychology* in which I had argued that mental illness is basically caused by the collapse of the will. When you are making an effort, your will re-charges your vital powers as a car re-charges its battery when you drive it. If you cease to will, the battery goes flat, and life appears to be futile and absurd. To emerge from this state, all that is necessary is to maintain *any* kind of purposeful activity—even without much conviction—and the batteries will slowly become re-charged. That is what I had said. And now, struggling with the panic, all the certainty had vanished. Instead, I found myself thinking of my novel *The Mind Parasites*, in which I had suggested that there are creatures that live in the depths of our sub-conscious minds, draining our vitality like leeches. That seemed altogether closer to what I was now experiencing.

Finally, I felt sufficiently calm—and cold—to go back to bed. I lay there, staring at the grey square of the window to keep my mind from turning inward on itself; some automatic resistance seemed to have awakened in me, and I suspected that the daylight would make the whole thing seem as unimportant as a bad dream. In fact, I woke up feeling low and exhausted, and the 'bad-news' feeling persisted at the back of my mind as I worked. But the effort of writing another article made me feel better. In the evening I felt drained, and the fear began to return. I suspected myself of wanting to ignore something frightening and felt myself sinking into depression as into a swamp. I would make an effort, rouse myself to mental activity, and suddenly feel better. Then something on television or in what I was reading, would 're-mind' me of the fear; there was a kind of inner jerk, like a car slipping out of gear, and the panic was back.

The articles still had to be written; in fact, a few days later, the editor rang me to ask if I could produce ten during the next week instead of the usual seven. An American backer was waving his chequebook and demanding speed. Since I had decided against the temptation to back out of the project, I stepped up my production to an article and a half a day. I was treating myself like a man with snake-bite, forcing myself to keep walking. Gradually, I was learning the tricks of this strange war against myself. It was rather like steering a glider. An unexpected flash of fear could send me into a nose dive; a mental effort could turn the nose upward again; sometimes this could happen a dozen times in an hour, until continued vigilance produced a feeling of inner-strength, even a kind of exhilaration. It was likely to be worst when I let myself get over-tired. Three months later, on a night-sleeper from London, I woke up with a shock, and the panic was so overpowering that I was afraid I might suffer cardiac arrest. At one point, I seriously considered getting off the train at the next stop and walking—no matter where. Then, in one of the periodic ebbs of panic, I forced myself to repeat a process I had taught myself in previous attacks: to reach inside myself to try to untie the mental knots. While I was doing this, it struck me that if I could soothe myself from panic into 'normal-ity', then surely there was no reason why I shouldn't soothe myself *beyond* this point, into a still deeper state of calm. As I made the effort to relax more and more deeply, I felt the inner turmoil gradually subside, until the spasms ceased; then I pressed on, breathing deeply, inducing still greater relaxation. At the same time, I told myself that I was sick of being bullied by these stupid attacks, and that when I got home the next day I was going to do a perfectly normal day's work. My breathing became shallow and almost ceased. Suddenly, it was as if a boat had been lifted off a sandbank by the tide; I felt a kind of inner jerk and floated into a state of deep quiescence. When I thought about this later, it struck me that I had achieved a state that is one of the basic aims of yoga: Rilke's 'stillness like the heart of a rose'.

Slowly, I began to understand the basic mechanism of the attacks. They began with a fatigue that quickly turned into a general feeling of *mistrust* of life, a loss of our usual feeling that all is (more or less) well. Then the whole thing was compounded by the old problem of self-consciousness. If you think about itching, you begin to itch. If you brood on a feeling of sickness, you feel sicker. Consciousness directed back on itself produces the 'amplification effect' which is the basis of all neurosis (i.e. the harder a stutterer tries not to stutter, the worse he becomes). If I woke in the middle of the night and tried *not* to feel tense, my heartbeat would accelerate and the panic would begin. I had to develop the trick of turning my attention to some everyday problem, as if saying to myself, 'Ah yes, how interesting'. Once I had learned to do this, the attacks became easier to avert. It was a great comfort to me when a friend who had been through the same kind of thing told me that, even without treatment, the condition cures itself after eighteen months.

When I tried to think out the basic reasons for the panic, I had to acknowledge that my trouble was a certain 'childishness.' When a child is pushed beyond a certain limit of fatigue or tension, its will surrenders. Some instinctive sense of fair-play is outraged, and it declines to make any further effort. An adult may also feel like surrendering to a problem, but common sense and stubbornness force the will to further effort. As an obsessive worker, I am accustomed to drive myself hard. Experience has taught me that when I get over-tired, the quickest way to recovery is often to drive myself on until I get 'second wind'. But to do this effectively, you need the full support of your subconscious mind, your deep sense of inner-purpose and meaning. In this case, I was trying to push myself beyond my normal limits—by writing the equivalent of a full-length book every three weeks—and some childish element in my subconscious had gone on strike. It was sitting with folded arms and a sullen expression, declining to do its proper work of re-charging my vital batteries. And so, when I passed a certain point of fatigue, I would discover that there was no more energy to call on. It was like descending a ladder and discovering that the last half dozen rungs are missing. At which point I would force my conscious will to interfere; a thing it is reluctant to do, since the subconscious usually knows best. I had to tell myself that I was being bloody stupid; that in my younger days, I worked far harder as a navvy or machine operator than I have ever worked as a writer, and that writing for a living has made me lazy and spoilt.

The panic, then, was caused by a lower level of my being, an incompetent and childish 'me'. As long as I identified with this 'me', I was in danger. But the rising tension could always be countered by *waking myself up fully* and calling upon a more purposive 'me'. It was like a schoolmistress walking into a room full of squabbling children and clapping her hands. The chaos would subside instantly, to be succeeded by a sheepish silence. I came to label this 'the schoolmistress effect'.

I had always known that Gurdjieff was right when he said that we contain dozens of 'I's'. The aim of his method is to cause some of these 'I's' to fuse together, like fragments of broken glass subjected to intense heat. As it is, consciousness passes from one to the other of our 'I's' like the ball in a Rugby game. Under these conditions, no continuity is possible, and we are at the mercy of every negative emotion.

The schoolmistress effect made me recognise a further fact about these multiple 'I's'—that they exist inside me not only on the 'Rugby field', or horizontal plane but also at different *levels*, like a ladder. All forms of purposive activity evoke a higher 'I'. William James pointed out that a musician might play his instrument with a certain technical virtuosity for years and then one day enter so thoroughly into the spirit of the music that it is as if the music is playing *him*; he reaches a kind of effortless perfection. A higher and more efficient 'I' takes over. Gurdjieff's 'work' is based on the same recognition. His pupils were made to drive beyond their normal limits until the moments of 'effortless perfection' became everyday occurrences.

J. G. Bennett gives an interesting example in his autobiography

Witness. He was staying at Gurdjieff's Fontainebleau Institute for the Harmonious Development of Man, and Gurdjieff himself was in charge of the 'exercises', based on Dervish dances. The aim of these exercises is to arouse man to a higher degree of alertness, to enable him to gain total control of his 'moving centre'; they involve an incredibly complicated series of movements—sometimes doing quite different things with the feet, the hands and the head. (To get an idea of the problem involved, try the old trick of rubbing your stomach in a circular motion with one hand and patting yourself on the head with the other.) Bennett was suffering from dysentery and feeling physically exhausted. One day, he found himself shaking with fever. 'Just as I was saying to myself: "I will stay in bed today," I felt my body rising. I dressed and went to work as usual, but this time with a queer sense of being held together by a superior Will that was not my own.' In spite of extreme exhaustion, he forced himself to join in a new and particularly difficult series of exercises. They were so complicated that the other students dropped out one by one; Bennett felt that Gurdjieff was willing him to go on, even if it killed him. And then: 'Suddenly, I was filled with an influx of an immense power. My body seemed to have turned into light. I could not feel its presence in the usual ways. There was no effort, no pain, no weariness, not even any sense of weight.'

The exercises were over, and the others went off for tea. Bennett went into the garden and began to dig.

> I felt the need to test the power that had entered me, and I began to dig in the fierce afternoon heat for more than an hour at a rate that I ordinarily could not sustain for two minutes. I felt no fatigue, and no sense of effort. My weak, rebellious, suffering body had become strong and obedient. The diarrhoea had ceased and I no longer felt the gnawing abdominal pains that had been with me for days. Moreover, I experienced a clarity of thought that I had only known involuntarily and at rare moments, but which was now at my command. I returned in thought to the Grand Rue de Péra and discovered that I could be aware of the fifth dimension. The phrase 'in my mind's eye' took on a new meaning as I 'saw' the eternal pattern of each thing I looked at; the trees, the plants, the water flowing in the canal and even the spade, and lastly my own body. I recognised the changing relationship between 'myself' and 'my pattern'. As my state of consciousness changed, 'I' and my 'pattern' grew closer together or separated and lost touch. Time and eternity were the conditions of our experience, and the Harmonious Development of Man, towards which

Gurdjieff was leading us, was the secret of true freedom. I remember saying aloud: 'Now I see why God hides Himself from us.' But even now I cannot recall the intuition behind this exclamation.

This vision of the 'eternal pattern' behind trees and plants brings to mind Boehme's mystical experience when he walked in the field and saw 'the signature of all things', as if he could see the sap rising in the trees and plants. But Bennett went one stage farther still. He went for a walk in the forest and met Gurdjieff; Gurdjieff told him:

The real complete transformation of Being, that is indispensable for a man who wishes to fulfil the purpose of his existence, requires a very much greater concentration of Higher Emotional Energy than that which comes to him by nature. There are some people in the world, but they are very rare, who are connected to a Great Reservoir or Accumulator of this energy. This Reservoir has no limits. Those who can draw upon it can be a means of helping others. Suppose a man needs a hundred units of this energy for his own transformation, but he has only ten units and cannot make more for himself. He is helpless. But with the help of someone who can draw upon the Great Accumulator, he can borrow ninety more. Then his work can be effective.

Farther in the forest, Bennett recalled a lecture of Gurdjieff's leading disciple, Ouspensky.

He had spoken about the very narrow limits within which we can control our own functions and added: 'It is easy to verify that we have no control over our emotions. Some people imagine that they can be angry or pleased as they will, but anyone can verify that he cannot be astonished at will.' As I recalled these words I said to myself: 'I will be astonished.' Instantly, I was overwhelmed with amazement, not only at my own state, but at everything I looked at or thought of. Each tree was so uniquely itself that I felt I could walk in the forest forever and never cease from wonderment. Then the thought of 'fear' came to me. At once I was shaking with terror. Unnamed horrors were menacing me on every side. I thought of 'joy', and I felt that my heart would burst from rapture. The word 'love' came to me, and I was pervaded with such fine shades of tenderness and compassion that I saw that I had not the remotest idea of the depth and range of love. Love was everywhere and in everything. It was infinitely adaptable to every shade of need. After a time, it became too much for me; it seemed that if I plunged any more deeply into the mystery of love, I would cease to exist. I wanted to be free from this power to feel whatever I chose, and at once it left me.

Bennett's experience is a particularly striking example of what, in *The Occult*, I have called 'Faculty X'. When we say we *know* something to be true, we are lying. 'Ten people died last night in an air crash.' 'Yes, I know.' We *don't* know. The rescuers trying to free the bodies from the burning wreckage knew. For the rest of us, this knowledge is a poor carbon copy. And how can I claim to 'know' that Mozart wrote the Jupiter symphony? I cannot even grasp that Mozart really existed. If I walk into a room in Salzburg in which Mozart actually played, I might, if I were in the right mood, come a little closer to grasping that he actually lived. But I would still be a long way from 'knowing' it.

There are two ways in which I might 'know' that Mozart existed. I might sit in a room where he had played and deliberately induce a mood of deep calm, perhaps by some form of 'transcendental meditation'. *Then* I could grasp it, for I would have slowed my senses down, arrested their usual frantic forward rush. Or I might grasp it in a sudden flash of intuition, as I run my fingers over the keyboard he actually touched. To do this requires intense concentration; it is the mental equivalent of leaping a six-foot fence. And there is a third method, rather less satisfactory than those two, yet also less difficult. I might immerse myself in Mozart's music, read books about his life, study his letters. Art has the power of inducing a degree of Faculty X. This is why human beings invented it. As we immerse ourselves in some composer's creative world, those inner 'leaks' that drain so much of our energy gradually close up, and our inner-pressure rises. We experience the 'magic carpet' effect, floating up above our own lives, seeing human existence as a panorama spread out below. The main problem with this kind of consciousness is that it makes it hard to come back to earth, and we find everyday reality futile and disgusting. Undiluted Faculty X has the reverse effect; it strengthens our power to cope with everyday reality by raising our inner-pressure.

Gurdjieff clearly possessed some curious ability to arouse hidden powers in other people. I have quoted elsewhere the episode in which Ouspensky describes how Gurdjieff began to communicate telepathically with him in Finland.[1] There can be no doubt that Gurdjieff had achieved some degree of control over his Faculty X. Yet this control seems to have been only partial. This becomes plain from an anecdote in *Gurdjieff Remembered* by Fritz Peters, who knew Gurdjieff from boyhood. During the war, Peters was an American GI, and in 1945 he was experiencing severe strain and depression. In Paris, he called on Gurdjieff in a state verging on nervous breakdown. Gurdjieff persuaded him to lie down, but after a few minutes Peters went to look for Gurdjieff in the kitchen. Gurdjieff refused to give him aspirin but began to make coffee.

> He then walked across the small room to stand in front of the refrigerator and watch me. I could not take my eyes off him and realised that he looked incredibly weary—I have never seen anyone look so tired. I remember being slumped over the table, sipping at my coffee, when I began to feel a strange uprising of energy within myself—I stared at him, automatically straightened up, and it was as if a violent electric blue light emanated from him and entered into me. As this happened, I could feel the tiredness drain out of me, but at the same moment his body slumped and his face looked grey as if he was being drained of life. I looked at him, amazed, and when he saw me sitting erect, smiling and full of energy, he said quickly: 'You all right now—watch food on stove—I must go. . .'
>
> He was gone for perhaps fifteen minutes while I watched the food, feeling blank and amazed because I had never felt any better in my life. I was convinced then—and am now—that he knew how to transfer energy from himself to others; I was also convinced that it could only be done at great cost to himself.
>
> It also became obvious within the next few minutes that he knew how to renew his own energy quickly, for I was equally amazed when he returned to the kitchen to see the change in him; he looked like a young man again, alert, smiling, sly and full of good spirits. He said that this was a very fortunate meeting, and that while I had forced him to make an almost impossible effort, it had been—as I had witnessed—a very good thing for both of us.

Gurdjieff's whole 'method' depends on forcing people to make unusual efforts, to release their 'vital reserves'. The effort of helping Peters apparently *reminded* Gurdjieff of something he had partly forgotten—how to call upon his own vital reserves. After his efforts to help Peters he looked exhausted: 'I have never seen anyone look so tired.' Being forced to help Peters awakened his own vital energies. So it would seem that Gurdjieff—in spite of the tremendous vitality that impressed everyone who met him—was not in permanent and habitual control of his own 'strange powers'.

It seems clear that, as Peters believed, Gurdjieff knew the secret of transmitting his energy directly to other people. Many 'healers' seem to possess this ability. There is a well authenticated story concerning the 'monk' Rasputin and the Tsarina's friend Anna Vyrubova. In January 1915, Anna Vyrubova was involved in a railway accident; her head was trapped under an iron girder and her legs badly crushed; in hospital, the doctor declared that there was no hope for her life. Rasputin heard of the accident twenty-four hours later—he was in disgrace at the time—and rushed to the hospital. Ignoring the Tsar and Tsarina, who were by the bedside, he went over to the unconscious woman and took her hands. 'Annushka, look at me.' Her eyes opened and she said: 'Grigory, thank God.' Rasputin held her hands and stared intently into her eyes, concentrating hard. When he turned to the Tsar and Tsarina, his face looked drained and exhausted. 'She will live, but she will always be a cripple.' As he left the room, he collapsed in a faint. But Anna Vyrubova's recovery began from this moment.

The question we have raised here is of central importance in the life of every human being: the question of how to gain access to our 'vital reserves'. The tensions of modern life mean that most of us suffer from a constriction in the pipeline that carries our vital energy supply. My experiences of panic attack made me aware that it can become a matter of life and death. The panic tends to feed on itself and I was like the driver of a car whose accelerator has jammed at top speed. In this condition I was aware of the frightening possibility of hypertension leading to 'exhaust status' and cardiac arrest. As I learned the basic tricks of controlling the attacks, I also gained a certain insight into the problem of vital reserves.

One of our highest human attributes is our power of concentration. But it involves a major disadvantage. When I concentrate on something, I *ignore* everything else in the universe. I lock myself into a kind of prison. If I stay in this prison too long, I begin to suffocate. This is what happens when we overwork or become obsessed by some trivial worry. We forget the universe that exists outside us until it becomes only a distant memory. Even when the task is finished, we often forget to re-establish contact and open the windows. The inner watchspring can get so overwound that we become permanently blind and deaf.

This is one of the worst habits we have developed in the course of our evolution. There is a parable of two Zen monks who encounter a girl waiting at a ford; one of them picks her up and carries her across the river, then sets her down on the farther bank. Ten miles farther on, the other monk bursts out: 'How could you do that? You know we're not allowed to touch women.' 'Put her down,' says his companion, 'You're still carrying her.' Most human beings carry a dozen invisible burdens.

The tendency is dangerous because our mental health depends on the 'meaning' that comes from the world around us. Meaning is something that walks in through the senses on a spring morning, or when you arrive at the seaside and hear the cry of the seagulls. All obsession cuts us off from meaning. My panic attacks began when I had overwound the watchspring and lost the trick of unwinding it. I was like a man slowly suffocating to death and, what is more, suffering because I was gripping my own windpipe.

It is important to realise that this throttling effect is quite automatic. It is the result of an aspect of the mind that I have called 'the robot', that unconscious servant who performs all the automatic tasks of everyday life. The 'robot' is now typing this page for me, while the 'real me' does the thinking. When I am feeling energetic and cheerful, the robot stays in the background, and I walk around with my senses wide awake. As I get tired, the robot takes over more and more of my functions, and the reality around me becomes less and less real. If I become nervously exhausted, the robot takes over completely and life becomes a permanent unreality. If, in this state, I am subjected to further pressures instead of being allowed to unwind, anxiety escalates into panic. It is the robot whose accelerator is jammed in the top-speed position.

I have always been fascinated by the way that shock or crisis can release us from the 'suffocation', bursting open the locked windows and often producing an almost mystical vision of meaning; my first book, *The Outsider*, discussed many such cases. There was, for example, the experience of Nietzsche on a hill called Leutsch; he describes it in a letter to his friend von Gersdorff:

> Yesterday an oppressive storm hung over the sky and I hurried to the top of a nearby hill . . . At the summit I found a hut, where a man was killing a kid, while his son watched him. The storm broke with tremendous force, gusting and hailing, and I had an indescribable sense of wellbeing and zest, and realised that we actually understand nature only

when we must fly to her to escape our cares and afflictions . . . Lightning and tempests are different worlds, free powers, without morality. Pure will, without the confusions of intellect—how happy, how free!

Even more significant is the experience of the modern Hindu saint Ramakrishna. He describes his first mystical ecstasy:

> I was suffering from excruciating pain because I had not been blessed with a vision of the Divine Mother . . . life did not seem worth living. Then my eyes fell on the sword that was kept in the Mother's temple. Determined to put an end to my life, I jumped up and seized it, when suddenly the Mother revealed herself to me . . . The buildings . . . the temple and all vanished, leaving no trace; instead there was a limitless, infinite shining ocean of consciousness or spirit. As far as the eye could see, its billows were rushing at me from all sides . . . I was panting for breath. I was caught in the billows and fell down senseless.

From this time onward, the mere name of the Divine Mother could send Ramakrishna into *samadhi*, a trance of ecstasy.

In both these cases, the release was preceded by a sense of oppression and narrowness, the 'overwound watchspring' effect. Their senses were closed, so that both were suffering from 'meaning starvation'. Human beings accept lack of meaning with stolid fatalism, as an animal accepts illness and pain. So the release comes like a thunderclap, like a sudden reprieve from death, bringing a sense of overwhelming joy and gratitude, and the recognition that meaning is always there. It is we who close our senses to it.

Once a man has experienced this revelation, he can never wholly forget it. He may still be subject to moods of fatigue and depression; but always, at the back of his mind, there is the memory of a paradoxical truth: *that men are far stronger than they suspect.* Their energies seem limited, their powers circumscribed, only because in some strange, unconscious way, they set the limits themselves.

As my own energies became more constricted by the panic attacks, I had to learn to become conscious of these mechanisms. I was particularly intrigued by the 'schoolmistress effect'. The 'schoolmistress' seemed to be a higher level of my being, which became operative when I shook off my panic and forced myself into a state of vigilance and wakefulness. It reminded me of the experience of an academic friend who was subject to moods of depression and self-doubt. One summer holiday, he came to see us looking completely transformed; he had lost weight and radiated vitality. I asked him what had happened. He explained that his doctor had ordered him to lose weight and the thought had filled him with a sense of defeat. However, he tried eating less and walking to the university, and to his astonishment found it less difficult than he had expected. As the weight melted away his optimism increased; he began to feel that *all* problems could be solved with a little common sense and determination. He looked back on his earlier self with pitying condescension. A 'higher level' had taken control, and he felt it to be realer and truer than the old self.

Obviously, Ramakrishna's attempt at suicide had produced a more powerful version of the 'schoolmistress effect' and raised him to a higher level still. On the other hand, boredom and lack of purpose tend to produce the opposite effect: surrender to a conviction of weakness and general unworthiness. (As all sociologists know, this condition incubates crime.) If we revert to the image of a whole series of 'selves', arranged like the rungs of a ladder, we may say that consciousness can move up or down the ladder, identifying with different 'selves'.

But reflecting on this image, it struck me that the ladder is unusual in one respect: it is shaped like a triangle, so that the higher rungs are shorter than the lower ones. When I move up the ladder, I experience a sense of concentration and control. When I move down—through depression or fatigue—my being seems to become diffused, like a cloud, and I begin to feel at the mercy of the world around me. In this state, it seems obvious that 'I' am weak, selfish and incapable of doing anything worthwhile.

The interesting question, of course, is: what lies at the top of the ladder? Some ultimate 'me'? A mystic would say, God. Edmund Husserl talked about the 'transcendental ego', the being that presides over all consciousness, and defined philosophy as the attempt to uncover the secrets of the transcendental ego. Gurdjieff agreed, except that he doubted the value of philosophy. He insisted that the only way to explore the ladder is to climb it.

When I decided to write a sequel to *The Occult*, I considered restricting it to the question of human survival of death. But these insights introduced new complications into the project. To begin with, what precisely *is* it that dies? Biologically speaking, I am more like a city than an individual. I am full of colonies of bacteria called mitochondria, which are quite separate from 'me', yet are essential to my vital maintenance. Then, of course, my body is made up of billions of cells, all of which die off and are replaced every eight years, so that there is not now a single atom left of the person I was eight years ago. When a man is decapitated, every cell in his body goes on living as if nothing had happened—this is why the hair and nails continue to grow. Then what actually dies as the blade severs his neck? Clearly, some higher principle of organisation, one or more of the 'higher selves'. But the higher selves do not die if a man falls into depression or takes to crime; they remain dormant or latent. Is there any logical reason to believe that they die with the death of the body?

This approach seemed to throw new light on all kinds of questions connected with the 'occult' or paranormal. For example, since I wrote *The Occult*, I have become fascinated by the subject of dowsing, particularly when I discovered that I could use a divining rod, and that it produced powerful reactions around ancient standing stones. But I have seen dowsers suspending their pendulums over a map and accurately locating hidden streams. They can even ask the pendulum questions—'When was this stone circle erected?'—and get precise answers. The ancients knew about these effects, and assumed that the answers were given by spirits. It seems to me more logical to suppose that one of the 'higher selves' has access to the information and can transmit it through the pendulum, or the yarrow stalks, or the Tarot pack, or whatever method of divination is being used.

Then there is the curious mystery of 'multiple personality'. In *The Occult* I wrote briefly about Morton Prince's case of 'Miss Beauchamp', who was periodically 'possessed' by a totally different personality called Sally. In 1973, I worked on a series of BBC television programmes on the 'paranormal' and had a chance to study the case more closely, which in turn led me to re-examine the whole phenomen of multiple personality. Dr Flora Schreiber's 'Sybil' exhibited no less than sixteen different personalities. The psychiatric view is that the personality becomes fragmented by shock, but that, like a broken mirror, each fragment retains a kind of identity. I found myself wondering whether that may not apply to all of us—that our everyday selves are a mere fragment of some ultimate personality towards which we are all striving. Professor Ian Stevenson, a parapsychologist of the University of Virginia, reported a case of reincarnation which has even stranger implications. A three-and-a-half-year-old Indian boy, Jasbir Lal Jat, apparently died of smallpox, but revived a few hours later with a totally new personality. The 'stranger' identified himself as a man from another village who had died after eating poisoned sweets, and his detailed knowledge of the man's life convinced his parents—and later Stevenson—that he was telling the truth. The strangest feature of the case was that the man had died at about the same time the child went into his 'death trance', suggesting the complete transfer of the personality from one body to another.[2]

I was struck by the parallels between cases of multiple personality and those involving poltergeist activity. Another of the television programmes dealt with one of the best authenticated poltergeist cases on record, the 'Rosenheim spook'. The poltergeist played havoc with the electronic equipment in a lawyer's office; the culprit turned out to be a young clerk named Annemarie Schaberl. Yet Annemarie was clearly ignorant that she was the cause of the trouble. And this is so in the majority of poltergeist cases. (Professor Hans Bender, who investigated the Rosenheim poltergeist, emphasises the importance of 'breaking it gently' to the children who are the unconscious cause of the disturbances, to avoid frightening them.) 'Miss Beauchamp's' alter-ego, Sally, was mischievous and given to practical jokes; it is easy to imagine a disembodied Sally behaving exactly like the Rosenheim poltergeist.

I was intrigued when the producer of the programmes, Anne Owen, told me that she had been through a period when she could predict the future. Before a concert with a celebrated cellist, she had a premonition that he would break a string and asked the producer what they should do if this happened; he dismissed it as unlikely. But the string broke eight minutes before the end of the concert. (The cellist, hearing about her prediction, jumped to the conclusion that she had somehow made it happen, and refused to speak to her.) At a race meeting with her husband and some friends, she suddenly knew with certainty which horse would win the next race. Everyone rushed off and backed the horse, which won. But her husband had somehow mis-heard her and put the money on the wrong horse. Her conclusion was that such powers cannot be used for one's own profit. The number of famous psychics and 'occultists' who have died in poverty seems to bear out that judgment.

I found myself looking around for evidence that might link powers of prediction with my 'ladder of selves' theory. Dowsers have told me that the pendulum can answer questions about the future, and I have seen convincing evidence that this is true; but dowsers rely on the divining rod or pendulum, not upon some mystical illumination. Then I came across Alan Vaughan's book, *Patterns of Prophecy*, and found the example I was looking for. Vaughan describes how, in 1965, he bought an ouija board to amuse a friend who was convalescing. When the radio announced the death of newspaper columnist Dorothy Kilgallen from a heart attack, they asked the board if this was correct; the board replied that she had died of poison. Ten days later, an inquest revealed this to be true.

One of the 'spirits' who made contact through the board identified herself as the wife of a Nantucket sea captain; she was called Nada. 'Then, both to my fascination and fear, "Nada" got inside of my head. I could hear her voice repeating the same phrases over and over again.' Asked about this, the board replied: 'Awful consequences—possession.'

In the presence of a friend who understood such matters, another spirit called 'Z' made Vaughan write out the message: 'Each of us has a spirit while living. Do not meddle with the spirits of the dead.'

> As I wrote out this message [writes Vaughan] I began to feel an energy rising up in my body and entering my brain. It pushed out both 'Nada' and 'Z'. My friends noted that my face, which had been white and pinched, suddenly flooded with colour. I felt a tremendous sense of elation and physical wellbeing. The energy grew stronger and seemed to extend beyond my body. My mind seemed to race in some extended dimension that knew no confines of time or space. For the first time, I began to sense what was going on in other people's minds, and, to my astonishment, I began to sense the future through some kind of extended awareness . . .

Vaughan's brief glimpse of 'extended powers' led him to embark on a programme of research into powers of 'prevision', whose results are described later in the book.

The phrase 'a tremendous sense of elation and wellbeing' brings to mind Nietzsche's 'indescribable sense of wellbeing and zest' and Bennett's 'influx of an immense power'. Here, then, we have a case in which the orgasmic upsurge of energy not only brings the typical sense of power and illumination, but also seems to trigger psychic faculties—telepathy and knowledge of the future.

This raises an interesting point. Most recorded instances of telepathy and prevision have taken place without the surge of heightened consciousness. The same goes for mediumship, thaumaturgy, second sight, telekinesis and the rest. So it would seem that if such powers depend upon our 'higher centres', then there are two ways of establishing contact: either clambering up the ladder, or through some form of short circuit that connects the higher self and the everyday self without the everyday self being aware of it. The first is Gurdjieff's way, the second Rasputin's.

Faculty X seems to be a combination of the two: a flash of extended awareness without the surge of energy. Proust's famous flash of 'remembrance of things past' occurred when he was tasting a cake dipped in tea and was suddenly made aware of the *reality* of his childhood. He writes: '. . . an exquisite pleasure had invaded my senses . . . And at once, the vicissitudes of life had become indifferent to me, its disasters innocuous, its brevity illusory . . . I had now ceased to feel mediocre, accidental, mortal.' William James, describing a similar experience, also says that it began when he was suddenly reminded of a past experience, and that this 'developed into something further . . . this in turn into something further still, and so on, until the process faded out, leaving me amazed at the sudden vision of increasing ranges of distant fact. . .' James makes it sound almost as if he had been snatched into the air, to a height where he could see reality spread out panoramically below him. Something similar happened to the historian Arnold Toynbee when he sat in the ruined citadel of Mistra and had a sudden vision of the *reality* of the day it was destroyed by barbarians; the experience produced a sense of history as a panorama, and led to the writing of *A Study of History*.[3] Gibbon's *Decline and Fall* seems to owe its origin to the same kind of experience in the Capitol.

Perhaps the most interesting thing about these experiences is the sense of security, the feeling that 'all is well'. Which brings us back squarely to the central problem, not only of this book, but of human existence itself. A sense of security is essential to all conscious life. The happiest moments of childhood are filled with it; John Betjeman writes about a security that 'holds me as I drift to dreamland, safe inside my slumberwear'. Life gradually erodes this blissful security—but not the belief that security *is* achievable. This is why we work and scheme and buy houses on mortgage and furniture on hire-purchase; this is why we open savings accounts and accumulate possessions. And although we know about earthquakes and disasters and sudden death, the world around us still has a comforting air of permanence; if I fall asleep watching television, everything is still going on as usual when I wake up.

But then, if we are honest, we have to admit there is something wrong with this basic assumption. The child views the universe from the security of his mother's arms, and things look pleasantly reasonable. It may be puzzling, of course, but all puzzles can be solved. And puzzles are the grown-ups' problem. Some people manage to pass their whole lives in this undisturbed state of mind. Others become aware that life is not as rosy as it looks. People die of disease or accident, or of old age after years of slow decay. Worse still, there seems to be something fundamentally queer about the universe. It contradicts our assumption that there are no questions without answers. The greatest questions are not only unanswered; they seem to be unanswerable. We cannot form even the *concept* of an answer to the question, 'When did the universe begin?' or, 'Where does it end?' On earth, everything has a beginning and end; space and time seem to have neither. The same riddle confronts me when I think about myself. My birth certificate tells me I had a beginning; but the idea violates my sense of logic, so that I am naturally inclined to think of *something* before my birth: perhaps a disembodied existence in some kind of heaven, or a whole series of previous incarnations. I also know from observation that I shall die in due course. I *can* imagine simply 'fading out', because it happens to me every night in bed; yet again, my logic rejects the idea of extinction. It demands *some* kind of continuation.

How is it possible for people to go through life without seriously thinking of such questions? The answer is again disturbing. Because my thought is *tied down* to familiar things. As absurd as it sounds, the human mind does not seem to be really made for thinking. You realise this if you try to think about some fairly simple abstract problem, such as why a mirror reverses your left and right sides, but not your head and feet. The mind tries to grasp the problem, then skids, like a car on ice. It is as if some gravitational force pulled your mind back to the here-and-now as the ground pulls us back when we jump. You try to focus on big, universal problems, and a moment later find yourself wondering if you posted a letter. Philosophers who are aware of these problems are inclined to take the view that human life is brutal and meaningless. It is hard for a logical mind to disagree.

This explains why most intelligent people are suspicious of the idea of reincarnation, or of life after death. They see such ideas as another symptom of the human inability to face up to reality. We are hopelessly drugged by the biological sense of security—as sheep and cows are until they get to the slaughterhouse and smell blood. We like to soothe ourselves with the tacit assumption that things will always go on as they are now. And so most religions promise their followers an afterlife that bears all the signs of wishful thinking—from the Elysian Fields of the Greeks to the Happy Hunting Ground of the American Indians. Philosophers can see through the daydream, but they have no convincing alternative to suggest.

If we can drag our mind away from everyday trivialities and think honestly about these problems, we have to admit that the pessimists inspire no more confidence than the 'true believers'. Most of them use their pessimism as an excuse for not thinking. At first sight, this seems a reasonable attitude, since they believe that thinking only leads back to the conviction that life is meaningless. But then, some deep instinct tells us that when a man ceases thinking, he has thrown away his greatest advantage. There is an odd feeling of arrested development about most of the total pessimists, as if they had ceased to evolve as human beings.

Besides which, none of the pessimists—Schopenhauer, Andreyev, Artsybashev, Beckett, Sartre—has really come to grips with the central question about human existence. All right, I have no idea where I came from or where I am going to, and most of the meanings that I see around me are mere conventions. I am little more than a blinkered horse, plodding along patiently, doing more or less what I did yesterday and the day before, and I see all the human beings around me behaving in the same way. Yet there *does* seem to be a certain logic about human existence, particularly when I am gripped by a sense of purpose. When I experience a feeling of intensity, I catch a glimpse of meanings that seem far greater than the 'me' I know. But then, I get the feeling that the 'me' I know is some kind of temporary half-measure. On top of all this, I begin to believe that the pessimists are making a fundamental mistake about the rules of the game. 'Meaning' is revealed by a kind of inner-searchlight. (This is just another way of stating Husserl's insight: Perception is intentional.) The greater the intensity of the beam, the more meaning it reveals. So a man who stares at the world with a gloomy conviction of defeat is going to see as little meaning as he expects to see.

There *is* something absurd about human existence. You find yourself surrounded by apparently 'solid' meanings—which are all comfortingly trivial. But when you try to raise your eyes beyond them, all certainties dissolve. It is as disconcerting as walking through the front door of a magnificent building and finding that it is just a façade, with nothing behind it. The odd thing is that the façade seems solid enough. This world around us certainly looks consistent and logical. It is hard to believe it is part of a bad joke or a nightmare.

Which brings us back to this most fundamental of all questions. Is it possible that the ladder-of-selves theory is the key not only to 'psychic powers', but also to the basic question of human existence, the riddle that has always tormented philosophers and theologians and 'existentialist' thinkers? Mystics have declared that in flashes of revelation the answer to the mystery of the universe suddenly becomes obvious. And again and again, they have expressed the essence of this revelation in words like 'All is well' or 'Everything is good'. This is hard—in fact, impossible—to conceive. But that is not necessarily an ultimate objection. We cannot conceive infinity, yet Georg Cantor created a mathematics of infinity which has proved to be a valuable tool. We cannot conceive the notion that future events have somehow already taken place; yet cases of precognition seem to demonstrate that, in some baffling sense, this is true.

The ladder-of-selves theory certainly throws light on some other basic problems of human existence: for example, the problem of absurdity or meaninglessness. The world around us seethes with endless activity, and this normally strikes us as quite reasonable. But there are certain moments of fatigue or depression when this meaning seems to crack under us, like thin ice. Camus compares it to watching a man gesticulating in a telephone booth, but being unable to hear a word he is saying. We suddenly wonder if our whole relationship with the world is based on a misunderstanding. Man likes to think he has a symbiotic relation with the universe, but perhaps the universe has never heard of him? Sartre calls this same feeling 'nausea'; it comes if you stare at something until your sense of 'knowing' it dissolves, and it seems to become alien and strangely hostile. According to Sartre, this is because man has suddenly recognised the truth about his own nothingness. Simone de Beauvoir expressed it in a passage of *Pyrrhus et Cinéas*: 'I look at myself in vain in a mirror, tell myself my own story, I can never grasp myself as an entire object, I experience in myself the emptiness that is myself, I feel that I am not.'

According to the ladder-of-selves theory, this is precisely what one would expect in a state of low inner-pressure. But it is *not* an inescapable part of the human condition, still less a fundamental truth about the universe. In moments of intensity, of excitement, of creativity, I move up the 'ladder', and instantly become aware that the meaninglessness was an illusion. For I *can* 'tell myself my own story' and grasp it as a reality; I *can* look in a mirror and experience myself as an entire object. This is what is meant by Faculty X.

Another way of expressing the same conclusion would be to say that when my inner-pressure is low, consciousness is dominated by the robot, and life becomes unreal. The sense of the uniqueness of the present moment is lost, and you find it difficult to distinguish between something you have experienced and something you have only read about or dreamed. In this state, I become separated from my own life, as if by a glass wall; if I listen to music, it is the robot who hears it; if I eat, it is the robot who tastes the food. The higher I move up the 'ladder', the more I am able to experience my own life.

It is important to recognise that meaning can *draw* us up the ladder, and that when this happens, we feel revitalised and re-energised. Sex provides an obvious example: a state of boredom and fatigue can be instantly dissipated by a sudden sexual stimulus. The result is a kind of *invasion* of meaning that lifts us to a more concentrated and purposive state. A man who has discovered this simple trick—like Casanova—may spend his whole life repeating it. He believes it is the sex he is interested in; in fact, it is the 'intensity experience', the momentary glimpse of a less mediocre self. But since he fails to grasp the meaning-content of the insight, he continually falls back to a lower level.

On the other hand, when the meaning content *is* grasped the 'trick' can be used to tap vital energy reserves. This is clearly something Gurdjieff understood. Others—like Uri Geller and Matthew Manning seem to be able to achieve contact with another form of energy that can be used for bending spoons or deflecting compass needles. The nature of this energy is still not understood, but of its existence there can be no doubt.

It seems too much to hope that any single theory could cover the whole field of the 'paranormal'. In 1784, the Puységur brothers—disciples of the notorious Dr Mesmer—stumbled on the phenomenon of hypnotism when they were making 'magnetic passes' over a young shepherd, and he fell into a trance. Ever since then, hypnosis has been widely used in medical treatment; but still no one understands its nature. In 1848, mysterious rappings in the house of the Fox family in Hydesville, New York, led to a nationwide interest in the subject that became known as Spiritualism. The rappings always took place in the presence of the two daughters of the family—aged twelve and fourteen—and were probably some kind of poltergeist activity. But other 'mediums' went into trances and were apparently able to communicate with the spirits of the dead; they were usually taken over by a 'guide' from the other world. The Society for Psychical Research was set up to investigate the phenomena scientifically, and eminent investigators—like Professor Ernest Bozzano, Professor Charles Richet, F. W. H. Myers—attempted to construct theories that would serve as a foundation for 'psychic science'. None of them came even remotely near to succeeding. And this, on the whole, still remains true today.

But it is worth noting that many of the phenomena—from hypnotism to mediumship—seem to involve 'other levels' of the personality.

Of course, the notion of a ladder of selves is not even a theory. It is simply a convenient description of what happens when we feel 'more alive'. But since this sense of increased vitality and heightened awareness also involves a feeling of 'expanded powers', it may be worthwhile to see how far the 'ladder' hypothesis can be made to tie in with the known facts.

This raises another problem. In the past ten years or so, there has been such an 'information explosion' in the psychic field that it is difficult to know where to begin. Any comprehensive book on the paranormal is now expected to cover such subjects as plant telepathy, psychic surgery, transcendental meditation, bio-feedback, Kirlian photography, multiple personality and synchronicity, as well as such optional fringe topics as possession, UFOs, leys and the 'ancient religion'.

I have chosen an approach which has, for me, the virtue of straightforwardness. When he died in 1971, Tom Lethbridge was the author of nine books on 'occult' subjects, one of them still in typescript. His books cover an immense range; at one time or another he thought about all the major subjects that concern modern paranormal research.

When I wrote *The Occult*, I was familiar only with his early book *Witches: Investigating an Ancient Religion*. It was not until later that I discovered books like *Ghost and Divining Rod* and *ESP*, and experienced the excitement of encountering a first-rate intelligence that combined scepticism with imagination and a sense of humour. When I learned that he lived fairly close to me, in Devon, I wrote him a letter and sent him a copy of *The Occult*. His wife Mina replied, saying that he had died the previous year.

The more I read of Lethbridge, the more I became convinced that he is the only investigator of the twentieth century who has produced a comprehensive and convincing theory of the paranormal. Because this is scattered over nine books, it is still insufficiently known to the general reader. That is why I have devoted the first long section of this book to his work and ideas. It will serve the dual purpose of introducing him to readers who have not yet made his acquaintance and raising most of the topics that will be discussed in the rest of this book.

It will also enable me to pay a debt of gratitude to one of the most wide-ranging and original minds in modern parapsychology.

PART

ONE

1

Ghosts, Ghouls and Pendulums

———◆———

In the autumn of 1957, a bulky, powerfully-built Cambridge don moved into a fourteenth-century house at Branscombe, on the south coast of Devon. For most of his life, Tom Lethbridge had been an archaeologist. He had lived in Cambridge—with a few interruptions—since the end of the First World War, and had been for many years Honorary Keeper of Anglo-Saxon Antiquities in the University Museum of Archaeology and Ethnology.

Lethbridge was emphatically no 'occultist'. His interest in the supernatural was minimal. Yet there was one branch of the paranormal that aroused his interest: dowsing. Any archaeologist will understand the reason. Archaeology consists mainly of digging for things that are buried under the ground. Some of the great archaeologists—Schliemann and Evans, for example—have apparently possessed a kind of sixth sense that led them to dig in precisely the right spot. Less gifted workers have to make do with trial and error, and everyone wishes there was some simple method of looking straight through the soil. Dowsing seems to be such a method. For some unknown reason, the dowser's forked twig twists in his hands when he walks over underground water. What is stranger still is that most dowsers can 'programme' their minds to look for almost anything. Lethbridge had discovered this when he was on an archaeological expedition to the island of Lundy and decided to try dowsing for volcanic dykes, now hidden under centuries of earth. A friend had led him blindfolded along the cliff path, so there was no chance of visual clues. Periodically, the hazel rod would twist in his hands. As he removed the blindfold, his friend told him that he had accurately located every one of the dykes.

Lethbridge was fifty-six when he retired to Devon. The past few years had been hectic and soured by controversy; now he looked forward to a time of peace and relaxation—country walks, a little archaeology, perhaps some fishing and boating.

It was not to be as simple as that. To begin with, he and his wife quickly discovered that their neighbour, the old lady who lived down the hill, was a witch. This is not as alarming as it sounds. In most country areas in England, you can find old ladies—or men—with certain curious powers—to charm warts, heal sick cattle, foretell the future, and so on. It has always been so throughout history. In primitive tribes such people are revered as *shamans* or priestesses; nowadays, most country people take them for granted, and ask their help on occasions. The Lethbridge's neighbour was not a particularly frightening specimen—a good humoured, eccentric, talkative lady who enjoyed relaxing in the local pub over a glass of gin and occasionally had difficulty in navigating her way home. She told them she was able to leave her body—the technical term is 'project her astral body'—and travel around at night, making sure that her friends were safe. They were at first inclined to treat these claims as fantasy, but a curious event convinced them that there could be more to it than that. Their neighbour one day explained to Tom how to 'throw pentagrams'—an ancient magical ritual for protecting oneself; she mentioned that it was useful for keeping away unwelcome visitors. All that was necessary was to draw a pentagram—a five-pointed star—in your head, and imagine it on your gate. That night, before he fell asleep, Lethbridge lay in bed, practising drawing a mental pentagram round their two beds. A few nights later, his wife woke up in the dark to see a faint glow of light moving around the foot of their beds; then it vanished. Shortly thereafter, they met their neighbour, who asked them if someone had been 'putting protection' on them. 'Why?' asked Tom. 'I came to your bedroom the other night and I couldn't get near the bed because there were triangles of fire around it.' (I assume that Lethbridge drew the pentagram in the form of interlocked triangles:)

But what intrigued Lethbridge even more than her talk of ghosts and astral projection were her comments on the use of the pendulum. Lethbridge had known for years that a pendulum could be used for divining and had even performed a few simple experiments, locating coins that were hidden under a pile of books. But he had treated it as a simple alternative to the divining rod—and of rather less use outdoors because it blows in the wind. Their neighbour assured him that it was altogether more accurate, and could convey far more complex information than a forked twig.

At this point, I suggest that the reader should spend five minutes deciding for himself whether this assertion is an old wives' tale or piece of wishful thinking, or not. Almost anything will do for a pendulum—a button or wooden bead on a thread, a locket on a chain. Shorten the thread to about three inches and hold it about an inch above your left hand. If nothing happens, give it a gentle forward swing to start it off. After a few seconds, the pendulum will cease to oscillate backwards and forwards and take up a circular motion. Try the same thing over the other hand. This time, the motion will probably be in the opposite direction. For most people, it swings in a clockwise direction over the right hand, and anticlockwise over the left. The sceptical reader will, of course, bear in mind that he may be unconsciously causing the movement himself—if so, the experiment simply demonstrates the power of suggestion. A few readers may get no reaction at all—I found this to be so the first time I tried it. In which case, it is worth keeping the pendulum in your pocket and repeating the experiment at intervals. When I was trying it rather absent-mindedly one day, I suddenly seemed to 'tune in', and the pendulum began to revolve unmistakably in circles. A majority of people seem to 'tune in' the first time they try it.

Most dowsers use a short pendulum; Lethbridge decided it might be more interesting to experiment with a longer piece of thread. He made a ball of hazelwood, with a hole through the middle, and attached it to the end of several feet of string. The other end of the string was wound round a pencil, so its length could be adjusted. Next, he placed a silver dish on the floor, held the pendulum over it, and carefully proceeded to lengthen the string. When it reached twenty-two inches, the pendulum stopped swinging back and forth and went into a circular motion. So it seemed that twenty-two inches was the 'rate' for silver. Then, following the neighbour's instructions, he stood in the court-yard, where he suspected there might be some buried silver coins, with the pendulum in one hand, while holding the other arm straight, with the first finger outstretched. He slowly moved the pointing arm across the courtyard. At a certain point, the pendulum in the other hand began to circle. This suggested he was pointing in the direction of buried silver. Noting the direction of the line, he went to another point in the courtyard and did it again. The place where the two lines crossed should be where the silver was buried. He stood over it and tried it again; the pendulum immediately went into its circular swing.

He cut out a square of turf with the spade and proceeded to dig cautiously. He soon came upon two pieces of old pottery. Tested again, the empty hole gave no reaction. That meant, presumably, that he had already dug out the silver, and that it must be in the pile of earth. He tried the pendulum over this; it went into a circular swing. He sifted carefully through the heap, using a small trowel, but found nothing. At this point, he concluded the pendulum was a fraud, and prepared to refill the hole. But as he shovelled the earth back in, he paused periodically to test it with the pendulum. Finally, with only a tiny pile of earth left, the hole was still giving a negative reaction and the earth a positive one. He broke it up with his fingers—and found a fragment of pottery that his trained eye recognised as seventeenth-century Rhineland stoneware. He tried the pendulum over it, and it went into a circular swing. So this was the 'silver coin'? What had gone wrong? *Some* early stoneware was glazed with lead salts, and old lead might well contain silver. Was that the solution? He tried the pendulum over a piece of lead, and it went into a circular swing. So that was the solution: lead was on the same 'rate' as silver, twenty-two inches. And German seventeenth-century stoneware, unlike English medieval pottery, was glazed with lead. The pendulum had revealed a useful piece of historical information.

Lethbridge tried again, and located another piece of lead in the courtyard—a bit of an Elizabethan window. He tried the pendulum over a copper pot and discovered that it responded to a rate of thirty and a half inches. Using the same technique of establishing cross-bearings by pointing, he quickly unearthed a small copper tube. It was very tiny, yet the pendulum had located it without any trouble.

Lethbridge was understandably excited. 'The pendulum was absurdly accurate', as accurate as the finest voltmeter. And if it could find copper, silver and lead, it could probably find anything. In a burst of scientific enthusiasm, he spent days testing different substances to discover their 'rates': sulphur, aluminium, gold, milk, apples, oranges, alcohol, sand, garlic, diamonds . . . There seemed to be no limit to its uses. He even tried locating truffles. An enthusiastic naturalist, he found a rare beetle that lived on truffles—an underground fungus of great scarcity. How could you find the rate for truffles? He remembered that this culinary delicacy is contained in *pâté de foie gras*. He opened a small and expensive tin of this, and picked out the tiny shreds of truffle. With considerable labour he extracted enough to make a small pile and tried the pendulum over it. The pendulum gave the rate for truffles as seventeen inches.

Truffles are usually found in woods. Lethbridge stood outside the front gate, the pendulum in one hand, the other arm pointing at the wood. Half an hour later, he and his wife had dug up a small dark object the size of a pea. They sent it to the South Kensington Science

Museum for identification. Two weeks later the reply came back: they had found an exceedingly rare type of truffle.

Lethbridge had expected an uneventful retirement; instead it now looked as if he had launched himself on a new career. Of course, the science of radiesthesis—detecting things with pendulums—has been known since ancient times; but most people are inclined to regard it as a crank subject, like newspaper astrology or the reading of tea-leaves. Besides which, research into every branch of parapsychology—telepathy, clairvoyance, ghosts and poltergeists—has been going on now for at least half a century and there is still a lack of the kind of solid evidence that would silence every doubter. There *have* been plenty of exciting results in carefully controlled experiments, but not the kind other scientists could duplicate in their laboratories. Now Lethbridge was convinced that his own experiments with pendulums were not only incredibly accurate; they were also infinitely repeatable. Although he is too modest to say so in his books, there must have been moments in the course of his explorations when he felt like a combination of Columbus and Isaac Newton.

The next step was to ask what was causing the reactions. The obvious explanation would seem to be that each substance—water, gold, garlic—gives off a vibration of definite wavelength, and that the pendulum somehow responds to this. But many eminent dowsers reject this view. Sir William Barrett conducted experiments that seemed to show that dowsers could read messages inside sealed envelopes.[1] He concluded that dowsing is basically a form of cryptesthesia—a term invented by Professor Charles Richet, the pioneer psychical researcher, meaning hidden perception or second-sight. That is to say, the pendulum is not responding directly to water or gold, but to *the mind of the dowser,* which is, in turn, reacting to the substance.

In which case, thought Lethbridge, the pendulum ought to react to thoughts and emotions as well as to things. He set out to test this idea. He had brought a number of sling stones from his last major excavation in the Cambridge area; they came from an Iron Age fort called Wandlebury camp, where Lethbridge had been engaged in uncovering a giant figure cut into the turf. (We shall have more to say of this in the next chapter.) It seemed likely that the stones had been used in a battle. He tested them with the pendulum; they reacted strongly at twenty-four inches, and also at forty. He went to a nearby beach and collected a bucketful of stones—picking them up with a pair of coal tongs to avoid 'influencing' them. These stones showed no reaction, either at twenty-four inches or forty. Then he and Mina took them one by one and hurled them against a wall. Then they tested them again. The stones Tom had thrown now reacted to a twenty-four inch pendulum; those Mina had thrown reacted at twenty-nine inches. This seemed to suggest that the rate for maleness was twenty-four inches, and that for femaleness, twenty-nine inches.

But what of the forty-inch rate? This time the stones showed no reaction to forty inches. Could it be something to do with the possibility that the stones had been used in war? Could forty inches be the rate for war or anger? Lethbridge set the pendulum at forty inches, and thought about something that annoyed him. It instantly began to gyrate. So forty inches *was* the rate for anger. Which also meant that the pendulum could respond not only to substances, but to ideas. He now began a new series of experiments, altering the length of the pendulum inch by inch and thinking about abstract qualities. Provided the thought was clearly formulated, the pendulum would respond at the appropriate rate. When he thought of evolution—envisaging the evolution of fishes into amphibians—the pendulum responded at thirty-six inches. The rate for sex was sixteen inches; for life, twenty inches; for death, forty inches, the same as anger.

Two basic facts had now emerged. The first was that many things had the same rate, but they often seemed to be interconnected. For example, forty is the rate for black, cold, anger, deceit, sleep and death. Twenty-two is the rate for grey, lead, silver, sodium and calcium—all grey or grey-ish. Predictably, life, at twenty, is associated with the colour white, and also with the earth and electricity.

Surely this introduces an element of ambiguity? If thirty inches is the rate for west, water, hydrogen, green, sound, moon and age—and perhaps for a hundred more things—how can you tell which the pendulum is responding to? Lethbridge soon discovered that there is another coordinate—the *number* of times the bob swings in a circle. For greyness, it gyrates seven times; for lead, sixteen times; for silver, twenty-two. If he had known this when he was trying to find the silver coin, there would have been no confusion when he found lead-glazed pottery.

Although Lethbridge was a man of exceptional persistence, he was by no means of a one-track mind. All the time he was studying the pendulum, he was also thinking about various related problems. One of these was ghosts.

In his early twenties he had seen a ghost. He had been about to leave the rooms of a friend in Trinity when a man dressed as a college porter came in. Lethbridge said good evening to him as he left the room. The next morning, he asked his friend what the porter wanted; his friend flatly denied that anybody had walked into the room as Tom left. It was only then that it struck Lethbridge that the man had not been dressed as a porter, but in some kind of hunting kit—and had probably been a ghost.

Then there was a curious event that had occurred in 1924 at a Choristers' School. Lethbridge describes it in his book *Ghost and Ghoul*. He and a friend entered the common room to find a master looking thoroughly depressed. 'The ghoul is on the stairs again,' he explained. So Lethbridge and his friend went to see for themselves. Sure enough, there was a strange, icy presence at the bottom of the stairs.

> There was more to it than cold. It was actively unpleasant. I have only met such a sudden cold in Melville Bay on the west coast of Greenland, when the motor boat in which I was sitting passed from sunlight into the shadow of an iceberg. At one moment the sun was streaming on to you and you were enjoying the glittering beauty of the bergs; at the next, an icy hand seemed to grip the whole of your body. This feeling at the bottom of the stairs was much like that, but there was a feeling of misery with it too.

With the confidence of youth, Lethbridge and his friend grinned at one another and advanced up the first step. The 'ghoul' retreated before them. They went on up the stairs, and it continued to move ahead of them. By the time they had pushed it up two flights of stairs to the top of the house, they were both feeling frightened—what if some horror materialised in front of them? They linked arms and took the last step; the 'ghoul' reappeared behind them. They lost their nervousness and pushed it back downstairs, where it again assumed its vigil.

The school was later exorcised, with the exception of a single bathroom. A new master who slept in the bedroom next to this bathroom had an appalling dream of a hairy figure emerging from the bathroom. Worse still, it was friendly. The bathroom was exorcised which apparently had the effect of driving whatever it was into the passageway outside where the servant girls kept their bicycles.

These two experiences led Lethbridge to differentiate roughly between a ghost and a ghoul. A ghost was something you saw—or perhaps heard; a ghoul was a kind of 'nasty feeling' that sometimes hangs around old houses. (The traditional ghoul is a demon that feeds on corpses.)

Two years after Tom and Mina moved into Hole House at Branscombe, an odd experience revived his interest in ghosts. On February 22, 1959, a Sunday, he was sitting on the hillside above the home of their neighbour, the 'witch'. Looking down on the mill, he saw her and waved to her. Then he noticed another woman behind her. She seemed to be in her sixties, dressed in a dark skirt, with a wide-brimmed hat on her head. The style of her clothes reminded Lethbridge of the clothes worn by his aunts before the First World War.

A few minutes later, Tom and Mina strolled down the lane and leaned over their neighbour's gate. The 'witch' walked across the yard to join them, and Lethbridge enquired about her guest. 'What guest?' she asked. When he explained, she said, 'You're seeing my ghosts now.' The Lethbridges recalled that she had mentioned seeing the figure of an unknown man at the spot where he had just seen the woman. On another occasion, some invisible person wished her good morning.

This event so intrigued Lethbridge that he decided to see if it would repeat itself on the same day the following year—ghosts are supposed to be fond of anniversaries. Accordingly, one year later, he and his wife waited at the same spot; both noticed an electric tingling in the air, but no ghost appeared.

Still, it led him to begin thinking seriously about the problem. He even decided to write a book about it. He had written nothing since *Gogmagog*, describing his excavations at Cambridge; this had been so poorly received by academic colleagues that he had abandoned writing for several years. Now, in *Ghost and Ghoul*, he wrote about his experience with the 'huntsman' at Trinity, the 'ghoul' at the Choristers' School, and the lady in Hole Mill, and came up with the theory that they might all have been some kind of television projections. That is to say, someone might have been thinking about the man, and Lethbridge had picked up his thought telepathically. This 'telepathic' theory is by no means new. In 1886, Gurney, Myers and Pod-more—three founders of the Society for Psychical Research—published a massive two-volume work entitled *Phantasms of the Living*, dealing with hundreds of cases in which 'apparitions' of living people have been seen, often when the person in question had been *imagining* being there. In a case recorded by Tyrrell, a lady deliberately 'projected' her apparition to a house in Kew by sitting and concentrating on it; a lady in the house saw the experimenter walking along the corridor in Kew at the moment she began making the attempt.

But in such cases, the 'apparation' seems to be a mental projection of the person who is seen—so presumably this explanation would not cover a ghost—i.e. someone who is dead. And what about the 'ghoul' on the stairs? Lethbridge was at first inclined to the theory that this also had been some kind of mental projection. The school *had* a room that was supposed to be haunted and someone had hung a crucifix in it. Perhaps somebody in the house had been afraid that the ghost would be driven out of the 'haunted room', and had somehow projected the fear on to the Queen Anne staircase?

Yet there was something about this 'projection' theory that left him rather unsatisfied. He recalled an event that had happened when he was eighteen. He and his mother had been on a walk through the Great Wood near Wokingham when they had both experienced a sudden acute depression. A few days later they heard that the body of a suicide had been found close to the spot where they had felt the atmosphere of gloom. If the man had been lying there dead when they passed the spot, it could hardly have been his 'thought projection'.

Then, not long after publication of *Ghost and Ghoul* (in 1961), Lethbridge stumbled on the vital clue he had been looking for. One grey afternoon in January, he and Mina drove down to Ladram Bay to collect seaweed for Mina's asparagus bed. 'As I stepped on to the beach,' writes Lethbridge, 'I passed into a kind of blanket, or fog, of depression, and, I think, fear.' Mina went off to look for seaweed at the other end of the beach. A few minutes later she hurried back. 'I can't stand this place any longer. There's something frightful here . . .'

That evening, Mina spoke to her mother on the phone and mentioned what had happened; her mother commented that she had experienced the same depression on the beach on Christmas day, five years earlier. The following day, Mina's brother came to the house and remarked that he and his wife had encountered a similar feeling of horror and depression in a field near Avebury. Lethbridge was suddenly struck by an idea. 'What kind of weather was it?' 'Very warm and muggy.' It had been warm and muggy on the day when he and his mother had encountered the 'ghoul' in the wood. And again when he and Mina went to Ladram Bay.

The following Saturday, another warm, drizzly day, Tom and Mina again set out for the Ladram beach, carrying sacks for seaweed. 'The same bank of depression greeted me at the same place as before.' And he noted that it was close to a place where a tiny stream ran on to the beach. The depression occurred in a definite place around this stream-let, like a bad smell. Mina pointed out the spot where she had experienced the 'ghoul' the previous week. 'Here the feeling was at its worst. It was so strong as to make me feel almost giddy. The nearest I can get to a description is that it felt not unlike one feels with a high temperature and when full of drugs. There was definitely a sensation of tingling to accompany it.' They went to the clifftop, and Lethbridge began to make a sketch. Mina wandered off and stood at the clifftop; there she experienced another unpleasant sensation, and a feeling as if someone was urging her to jump.

Thinking it over at home, Lethbridge saw another clue. Their local 'witch' had died in the meantime, and the circumstances were rather odd. She had quarrelled with a local farmer and told Tom she intended to put a spell on his cattle. Tom warned her that 'black magic' has its own special danger; if it fails to work, it is likely to bounce back on the magician. She ignored him—and died suddenly. No harm came to the cattle of the farmer with whom she had quarrelled, although the cattle on the farms on both sides began to suffer from foot and mouth disease. For some time after her death, there was a definite unpleasant feeling hanging around her house. Lethbridge noted another interesting fact: that it had a quite definite limit. It was possible to step beyond it, as if stepping over an invisible wall.

And now, suddenly, all these ideas coalesced. He and Mina had experienced a tingling sensation as they waited for the old woman's ghost to appear at Hole Mill in 1960. Dowsers notice a tingling sensation in their hands as they approach water. They had experienced tingling again on Ladram beach. Now Tom took his divining rod to the spot above the mill where he and Mina had waited; a stream ran close by and vanished into the grass. He traced its course, and, just as

he had suspected, it curved and passed directly below the spot where
he had seen the 'ghost'.

Water! That, it seemed, was probably the answer. A tingling sensation suggests a force-field—like that around an electric wire. If a stone
can somehow 'record' the emotions of a man who threw it more than
two thousand years ago, is it not equally possible that the 'field'
of water can somehow record emotions, like a magnetic tape? Or
perhaps the field acts like the low current in the head of a tape recorder
and somehow causes events or emotions to be imprinted on their
surroundings? Or like the flash of a camera that imprints a picture on
the photographic plate? As a dowser, Tom was sensitive to the force-
field of water, so he might well 'pick up' a recording that was invisible
to non-dowsers. In the case of the old woman at Hole Mill, the spot
where she had appeared and the spot where Tom was standing had
been connected by the force field of the water, like a telephone wire.

The ancients believed that there were supra-normal powers associated with streams; they were called naiads or water nymphs. Then
there were wood nymphs or dryads, mountain nymphs or oreads and
sea nymphs, the nereids. A classical dictionary defines a nymph as 'an
inferior divinity of nature'. Is it possible that man was personifying
real forces of nature—forces that he recognised 'in his bones', and
assumed to be supernatural in the same way as he assumed the thunder
and lightning to be deities? Perhaps, suggests Lethbridge (in *Ghost and
Divining Rod*) there are various kinds of fields connected with water,
woods, mountains, open spaces, and he suggests calling these 'naiad
fields', 'dryad fields', 'oread fields', and so on. The emotions of the
man who committed suicide in the Great Wood were imprinted on a
'dryad field', and played back two days later when Tom and his
mother passed near the spot. When Mina felt someone urging her to
jump over the cliff, she may simply have been picking up the emotions
of someone who stood there and contemplated suicide; but, as Lethbridge remarks, this does not mean the suicide actually happened. The
man may have gone home, had a large whisky and felt much better.[2]

The 'field theory', of course, contradicts—or at least modifies—Sir
William Barrett's cryptesthesia theory. Barrett was inclined to the
'second sight' theory because there are many cases in the history of
dowsing when the diviner has been able actually to *see* the underground water. Barrett cites a Miss Miles, who located a lost underground cistern and was able to describe its exact appearance. Presum-

ably second-sight, like ordinary sight, does not require 'fields' for its operation. This room I am sitting in does not need a 'field' in order for me to see it; just light bouncing off the walls. But Lethbridge's experience of being able to walk in and out of 'ghouls' led him to test various objects with a pendulum. He concluded that every object has a field that extends around it. Its radius is the 'rate' for that object. So, for example, a copper penny would have a field exactly thirty and a half inches wide, extending around it, as well as upward and downward in the form of a cone.

Presumably, then, emotions can impress themselves on any kind of field (or be recorded by it.) Water, however, seems to have a peculiarly active field. Dowsers insist that much illness is caused by sleeping above an underground stream and will often advise people to change the position of their beds. I have known at least one person who benefited considerably from changing the position of her bed, after two dowsers had independently advised her that she was directly above a stream. (Significantly, the first dowser, Bill Lewis of Abergavenny, diagnosed the underground stream from five hundred miles away by dangling his pendulum over a sketch of her bedroom; the second dowser, Leonard Locker, located the same stream on the spot—although he had not seen or been told of the earlier result.) It seems that long-term exposure to the radiation of water can be as harmful as long-term exposure to radioactivity.

My own original reaction to Lethbridge's theory of ghosts was that it fails to cover the many cases in which ghosts have behaved as if they were intelligent beings. A case I remembered that seemed to support this objection was the one described by Beverley Nichols in his autobiography *Twenty-Five*.[3] This took place at a house called Castel Mare in Middle Warberry Road, Torquay. Beverley Nichols, his brother and an Oxford friend, Lord Peter St Audries, decided to investigate the 'haunted house' one Sunday evening in the late 1920s. It was said to be haunted by the ghost of an insane doctor who had murdered his wife and the maidservant there.

The three young men found the place oppressive, but in no way frightening. Nichols was standing alone in the upper hall, waiting for his companions, when he had a sensation as if his thoughts were going in slow motion; a black film seemed to cover the left side of his brain, as if he were being anaesthetised. He managed to stagger outside before fainting. He came round feeling oddly tired and low. The other two went on exploring, then Nichols was joined by his brother, while Lord St Audries continued to investigate alone. Every few seconds he would whistle, to show that all was well. Then the whistles stopped. The brothers had a sensation as if something had rushed past them out of the house. At the same time, Lord St Audries screamed. They rushed to the window and heard thuds, and sounds of a struggle, with more cries. Then Lord St Audries came out, dishevelled and coated with plaster dust. He explained he had gone to the room where Nichols had felt faint and noticed a patch of greyish light. As he was about to return, something had rushed past him, and he was knocked to the ground; he experienced a sense of overwhelming evil and had to struggle with all his strength to crawl down the stairs and into the garden. The oppression seemed to vanish when he reached the foot of the stairs.

When I re-read this story, I realised that, far from contradicting Lethbridge's theory, it supports it in many ways. Lethbridge said that the 'ghoul' on Ladram beach made him feel disconnected and giddy, as one feels 'with a high temperature and when full of drugs': precisely what Nichols describes. My original impression of the struggle with the ghost was that Lord St Audries had actually wrestled with it. On re-reading it, I see that what happened is that the ghost drained Lord St Audries of energy as it had drained Beverley Nichols, and that the struggle was against the feeling of fear and oppression.

The fact that St Audries was knocked down seems to contradict the 'ghoul' theory—until one asks what *happened* to the energy that was drained from Beverley Nichols? One explanation could be that the Castel Mare ghost was not a ghoul but something more like a poltergeist. Yet why do so many accounts of apparitions mention a sudden drop in temperature? Could it be that 'negative emotions'—like fear and misery—record themselves by draining energy from a magnetic field; and when someone 'tunes in' to the recording, it has the effect of stealing his energies and blurring his faculties? Dr Arthur Guirdham, chief Psychiatric Consultant to the Bath Medical Area, has stated that he knows several houses in Bath that have a history of mental illness and suicide; that is, where one tenant after another has become ill with depression. Guirdham (of whom I shall speak later) accepts the reality of some 'evil influence'. When patients were removed from these houses, the depression promptly vanished.

Lethbridge himself was far from convinced that all 'supernatural' manifestations are mere recordings. He had encountered something altogether more active on the island of Skellig Michael, off the coast of Kerry in 1924. He had climbed a hill to look at the ruins of an eighth-century monastery when he noticed the remains of a rubbish dump a hundred feet below, on the cliff face. He decided to go down and investigate. Halfway down, he was overtaken by an odd conviction that somebody wanted to push him off the cliff. The unpleasant sensation finally became so strong that he changed his mind and climbed back up. Shortly afterwards, as he walked down the low hill below the monastery, something made him want to turn round. Before he could do so, he was knocked flat on his face. When he sat up, the hillside was deserted.

Back on the mainland, a telegraph operator asked him if he had seen any ghost on the island. The lighthouse there was apparently haunted; since a shipwreck the previous winter, doors had slammed, sea-boots had trampled through the sleeping quarters, and there had been loud screams; two lighthouse keepers had gone insane as a consequence. Lethbridge did not believe that his experience was connected with the shipwreck; he thought that it was, quite simply, some kind of poltergeist activity associated with the ancient religious site. The interesting point to observe about the Skellig Michael experience is that, like Beverley Nichols' ghost, it seemed to *combine* the characteristics of the 'ghoul' and the poltergeist: the 'nasty feeling' followed by some form of attack.

In this connection, it is worth mentioning another of Lethbridge's speculations concerning these forces. In 1922, he was one of a group from Cambridge who visited the Shiant Islands, in the Hebrides. One man placed his coat and lunch on a deserted hilltop and on returning found that they had vanished. The others laughed and said it must be seagulls—the island was otherwise uninhabited. But Lethbridge points out that a gull would not be interested in a macintosh and that few gulls are courageous enough to investigate a white paper parcel. The victim of the inconvenience believed that some supernatural force was responsible—a view that Lethbridge's later experience on Skellig Michael inclined him to accept. (The Shiants are probably named after the 'shee'—a spirit related to the banshee of Irish legend.) 'Sometimes, we are told, things vanish', says Lethbridge. 'At other times, things appear from nowhere. They are technically known as "apports" . . .' And, in fact, 'apports'—objects that fall from the air—*are* frequently associated with poltergeist activity. (Vanishings are reported less often than 'apports' because we are usually convinced that there could be a natural explanation; Lethbridge himself was convinced that supernatural 'vanishings' occur more frequently than we think.) His point may be worth bearing in mind later when we discuss poltergeist activity.

Ghost and Divining Rod (1963) represents a crucial point in Lethbridge's development, with its recognition that ghosts and dowsing may amount to fundamentally the same thing. (It might be more accurate to say 'ghouls' and dowsing, since genuine hauntings may involve more complex phenomena: footsteps, bangings, cries, 'apports', smells, movements of furniture, and apparently 'solid' ghosts.) Lethbridge was not the first to conclude that ghosts may be 'recordings'. That distinction may belong to Sir Oliver Lodge, who wrote as long ago as 1908: 'Take, for example, a haunted house . . . wherein some one room is the scene of a ghostly representation of some long past tragedy. On a psychometric hypothesis, the original tragedy has been literally *photographed* on its material surroundings, nay, even on the ether itself, by reason of the intensity of emotion felt by those who enacted it.'[4]

Andrew Green, one of the most active of modern investigators of hauntings, holds the same view. He has described a haunted house in Montpelier Road, Ealing, where at least three people have died by falling or jumping from the tower; Green himself experienced a strange urge to jump when he stood on the tower.[5] Again, the American writer on psychical research, Susy Smith, has described the haunting of the house at Oklawaha, Florida, where the notorious gangster Ma Barker and her son Freddie were shot to death in 1935; the haunting consisted mainly of footfalls and sounds of voices in conversation, often quarrelling. Many voices were involved. Yet oddly enough, Ma Barker and her son had been alone when they were surrounded by police; the rest of the gang had fled. Susy Smith concludes: 'It seems . . . logical that some kind of memory image has been left there because of the violence they generated.'[6]

But Lethbridge has the distinction of being the first to speculate on whether hauntings may not be connected with the 'field' of water. (He would have been interested to note that the Ma Barker house stands on the edge of Lake Weir.) He was also the first to recognise that, if dowsing *is* some form of cryptesthesia or second-sight, then the faculty for seeing ghosts and the faculty for divining water—or any other substance—may be identical.

His next step was a logical one. Lethbridge had always been an enthusiastic naturalist—as a young man, he had intended to take it up as a profession, until he discovered that it involved dissecting dead animals. Like most animal lovers, he had often observed that his pets appeared to possess a 'sixth sense'. Sitting on the terrace at Branscombe, he was intrigued when Mina's cat woke from sleep and sat bolt upright, staring at the wall. The terrace looked out across the valley. Tom fetched the field-glasses and looked in the same direction as the cat; he saw a black and white cat hunting among the bushes about 450 yards away. Mina's cat was staring at it *through* the brick wall that bounded the terrace.

On other occasions, the cat would leap to its feet and stare at the corner of the bedroom, its fur bristling, then rush outdoors and return shortly afterwards with a mouse or vole. Lethbridge worked out that the grassy bank where the cat caught the rodents was on the other side of several walls, as well as the courtyard; yet its sleeping mind had picked up the signal of the animal.

Staring at the cat's whiskers, Lethbridge was struck by an idea. Could they be divining rods? He tried testing them with the pendulum. The longest and farthest back had a rate of sixteen inches—the rate for sex. The next hairs had a rate of twenty inches, the rate for time, human beings, love and life; the smallest group are farthest forward and react to twenty-four inches—the rate for mice. The eyebrows react to the ten-inch rate—the rate for heat; Tom speculated that this may explain why the cat invariably finds its way to the warmest place in the house. He concluded that the longest whiskers are for sexual detection and the shortest for detecting food; the medium ones are probably connected with the cat's emotional life. (Cat owners will have noticed that cats always jump in the laps of people who can't stand them—as if they were a more interesting challenge than cat-lovers; presumably the middle whiskers explain how this unerring selection is made.)

Lethbridge was inclined increasingly to the belief that the forces involved in dowsing, ESP and ghosts are electrical. He was intrigued by the behaviour of a privet hawk-moth, which on two successive evenings flew in through the window and settled on the seventeenth-century plate hanging on the wall. Lethbridge observed that it always stayed in the same spot on the plate. Turning it over the next day, he discovered that it had been riveted at some point, to strengthen it, and one of the rivets had gone right through the plate. It was on this that the moth had settled. The plate was held in a coil of iron wire, and it now struck Lethbridge that he was looking at a primitive electric coil, with the rivet as its core. The answer, then, could be that the rivet produced a tiny electrical signal, equivalent to the signal used by female moths to attract the male, which suggested to him that the nature of sexual attraction may be basically electrical.

This, I should admit, has always been my own theory. I arrived at this conclusion through an incident that happened in my early twenties. My wife and I had been separated for some time, and I had been largely celibate. The first night we came together again, I was particularly tired and fell into a deep sleep as soon as I climbed into bed. In the middle of the night I woke up in a state of intense sexual excitement. It seemed to be emanating from my thigh. After a moment, I realised that my wife's fingertip was resting against the thigh and that a tingling, electrical sensation was running *from* her finger and into my skin. I observed with interest that this seemed to be a physical phenomenon—like the faint tingling you experience if you apply the tip of your tongue to a torch battery. Her breathing convinced me that she was fast asleep, that this flow of 'sexual electricity' was quite unconscious.

It may also be significant that poltergeist activity is usually associated with teenagers who are passing through a period of sexual disturbance. In *The Occult* I cited the case of the Austrian medium Frieda Weisl, whose sexual excitement when engaged in lovemaking would cause objects to jump off the mantelpiece. Many mediums have been most brilliant in puberty and lost their powers later. All of which suggests that there could be a close link between sex and paranormal powers and that the energies involved in cases of ghosts, 'ghouls' and poltergeists may be some form of electrical energy. Damp conditions would obviously be more propitious than dry ones. (This could explain why England, with its notorious climate, also has more ghosts per square mile than any other country in the world.) That ghosts involve *some* form of energy seems to be clear from the 'refrigeration effect' that so often accompanies manifestations—suggesting that the ghost manifests by 'borrowing' energy from the surrounding air. If the nature of these energy fields was understood, there seems to be no reason why ghosts should not finally become as observable and measurable as any other physical phenomenon.

Towards the end of *ESP: Beyond Time and Distance*, it becomes clear that Lethbridge is increasingly inclined to accept a quasi–electrical theory of the paranormal; he even suggests that the relation between mind and body may be electrical: 'This mind is apparently linked to our body by an electromagnetic field and its signals can be recognised as minute electric shocks.' In which case, dowsing would be simply a matter of the interaction of two electric fields. But if that is so, what becomes of the second–sight theory? How can an electric field explain how a map dowser can accurately trace the course of an underground stream in a place that he has never visited? Or, for that matter, how Lethbridge's pendulum could answer questions like 'How old is this standing stone?' The Abbé Mermet, author of a famous book on dowsing, accepts the view that thought waves can travel round the earth at the speed of light—in about one seventh of a second—and that therefore it is as easy to dowse for something on the other side of the world as in your own back garden; but even this would not explain how the pendulum can answer questions about the past or future.

In the Preface to *ESP*, Lethbridge recalls a time in Greenland when the ice suddenly collapsed under his feet and he found himself floundering in the sea; he remarks that he now has much the same sensation: 'From living a normal life in a three dimensional world, I seem to have suddenly fallen through into one where there are more dimensions. The three dimensional world goes on as usual, but one has to adjust one's thinking to the other.' This can be sensed in the books he wrote in the last ten years of his life. He is intensely aware that there is something false about the 'real world' around us, he can see through it, as if it was glass, and catch glimpses of something beyond. Yet there is no sign of the personality change that often accompanies such conversions, no tendency to abandon 'tough mindedness' and adopt a softer attitude. He remains cheerful, practical, rather agnostic, a natural doubter. The universe simply appears to be a bigger and stranger place than he had thought.

Clearly, it is the words 'other dimensions' that strike him as the key. And this notion became increasingly important in the succeeding books. In *ESP* he remarked that while the rate for death seems to be forty inches, the pendulum also responded to dead creatures at the rate of twenty inches, which led him to speculate that forty inches 'may represent life force on a higher plane'. In all probability, he was making a simple error; dead creatures probably respond to the 'life' rate because they are still swarming with living organisms. Still, the observation led him to think more closely about the various rates, and it struck him that the rates for ten, twenty, thirty and forty inches all seem to carry special significance. At ten inches, the pendulum responds to light, sun, fire, red, east, graphite and truth. At twenty inches we find life, heat, earth, white, south and electricity. At thirty, sound, moon, water, green, west and hydrogen. At forty, death, cold, air, black, north, sleep and falsehood.

Lethbridge drew a circle, and marked on it all the qualities and substances he had measured by the use of the pendulum. The result was interesting: opposite qualities seemed to occur where you would expect to find them, on opposite points of the compass: danger at twenty-nine, safety at nine, pleasant smells at seven, unpleasant smells at twenty-seven. Curiously enough, male and female are *not* opposites, lying respectively at twenty-four and twenty-nine, and suggesting—what medical knowledge confirms—that there is only a thin dividing line between the two. (Significantly, the rate for thought —twenty-seven—is exactly between the two; so is art: suggesting that successful intellectual and artistic activities require a balance of male and female qualities.)

He also tried another arrangement of the 'qualities'; on the twenty diameters he had drawn across the circle, he arranged the various rates at their appropriate distance from the centre: i.e. sulphur at seven inches along line seven, chlorine nine inches along line nine, and so on. He then joined up the dots. Staring at the resultant spiral, it struck him as odd that it should stop abruptly at forty; in theory, a spiral goes on. This led him to see if the pendulum could register rates above forty. What he discovered made him thoughtful. A heap of sulphur not only caused a seven-inch pendulum to rotate; it had the same effect on a forty-seven-inch pendulum. There was one slight difference. The strongest reaction with a forty-seven-inch pendulum was not directly over the heap—as you might expect—but a little to one side. And everything he tested confirmed the result. Silver reacted at twenty-two inches, and at sixty-two inches—forty, plus twenty-two. But when tested with a sixty-two inch pendulum, the reaction was again slightly to one side. In short, everything seemed to react to its 'normal' rate, and to its normal rate *plus forty*.

What Lethbridge deduced from this may be regarded as quite arbitrary; it is certainly highly controversial. Since forty inches is the rate for death, he assumed that the rates beyond forty are the rates beyond death. We have moved into another dimension; the object continues to exist, but apparently in another position. Or the difference may be due to some natural effect—like a pencil appearing to be bent when you put it into water.

Stranger still, if the pendulum is extended yet another forty inches—to eighty plus the normal rate—it once again registers the same rates for objects; sulphur is now eighty-seven, silver, a hundred and two. And once again, there is a false position for the object—the 'parallax effect'.

In short, Lethbridge came to the astonishing conclusion that when you lengthen it beyond forty, the pendulum registers another 'dimension' beyond death—presumably the 'spirit world'. Lengthened beyond eighty, it seems to indicate yet another world beyond that one, suggesting—Lethbridge thinks—that the 'next world' is merely another level. There is no reason why there should not be any number of levels beyond these two: the difficulty of confirming them with a pendulum is that a pendulum with a ten-foot string is difficult to handle, and shows poor response. (The shorter the pendulum, the more easily it responds—hence the popularity of the 'short pendulum'.)

His pendulum experiments with rates beyond forty also led him to a curious discovery about time. A normal pendulum—shorter than forty inches—will not register the idea of time. Lethbridge assumed that this is because our world is *in* time, and time is on the move, so to speak. (If you were drifting down a river in a boat, unable to see the banks, you would not be able to test the speed of the river.) Using a pendulum that was more than forty inches, Lethbridge discovered that time appears to exist in this 'next world'—at sixty inches—but that it seems to be static. He admits that he does not understand this. Time in the 'next world' is a perpetual 'now', according to the pendulum. In his final book, Lethbridge speculates that this next world is a kind of museum, in which all events in history are somehow preserved, as in the BBC's Sound Archives. But the world beyond that—beyond the eighty-inch rate—seems to have a 'flowing time', like ours. And when Lethbridge succeeded in testing a pendulum with a 120-inch string—by mounting a flight of stairs and leaning over the banister—he discovered that there *is* another 'dimension'; but, as in our world, there is no reaction for time.

He concludes in *A Step in the Dark*:

> Our earth life compares with the larval stage [of an insect] and contains time and movement. The next phase is like that of a chrysalis, which remains for a while apparently dead and completely inert. Then comes the stage of the perfect insect, when time and movement not only return again, but are much accelerated. Here we must stop until more work has been done; but at least we can leave this study with a greater conviction of the survival of the individual human mind.

And so Lethbridge's experiments led him to the conclusion that various worlds—including the state of life-after-death—exist parallel with this one, and will even respond to a pendulum. An object that exists here also, apparently, exists there—an interesting sidelight on the mystical formula: 'As above, so below.'

To some, this may sound absurd. Yet anyone who reads Lethbridge's books consecutively can see that he reasons slowly and carefully, step by step. Anyone who performed the same experiments and obtained the same results would probably reach very similar conclusions. Once he had established that the pendulum told him the truth about buried fragments of pottery or copper pipe, everything else followed logically. It became simply a matter of believing the pendulum.

Which brings us back to the basic question: how can a piece of wood and string 'tell the truth' about anything? And by what mechanism does a divining rod react to the presence of underground water?

There are three schools of thought. The most pragmatic maintains that water emits some kind of radiation, and that we possess some organ that can detect it. It is no more mysterious than detecting a piece of gorgonzola cheese with your nose. The adherents to this view argue that our prehistoric ancestors needed such a sense in order to survive in the great droughts, and that it has probably lain dormant in us for millions of years.

The second school inclines to the view that the dowser *emits* a radiation, as bats emit a high-pitched squeak. This radiation—perhaps some form of radio wave—bounces back off objects in the manner of radar. Lethbridge believed that this is how the 'sixth sense' of animals operates—for example, how Mina's cat picked up the presence of a mouse or vole through several thicknesses of wall.

The third view is that dowsing depends on an unknown faculty, a kind of 'superconscious mind' that can answer questions whose answers are unknown to the conscious self. This view is widely held among dowsers nowadays. I have elsewhere[7] described my own experiments with the dowser Robert Leftwich, in one of which Leftwich used me as a kind of living dowsing rod. He stood with his back to me, holding his divining rod. I walked away from him, towards an underground water pipe, the position of which I knew but he didn't. After I had gone twenty or thirty yards he called: 'Stop —you're on it.' And, in fact I was.

He also demonstrated fairly convincingly that his ability did not depend on my conscious knowledge. I was told to shuffle a pack of cards—my own, not his—and to place them, one by one, face downward on the table; he said he would stop me when I got to the ace of clubs. He stood on the other side of the room, so that it would have been impossible for him to see the cards. After a while he called: 'Stop.' I had just thrown down the ace of clubs. We repeated the experiment several times; he was successful about four out of seven. Leftwich was dissatisfied, feeling that he had failed to 'tune in'; but I found the result impressive.

Understandably, Leftwich subscribes to the 'superconscious mind' explanation of dowsing: that there is some part of the mind that can be 'elsewhere'—like Prospero's Ariel. The Abbé Mermet, as we have seen, believed that this was thought itself.

Lethbridge tends to accept all three views. Since individual substances have their own 'rates', they must give off some form of radiation. The 'sixth sense' that warns us of danger seems more akin to radar. But the 'message' of the signal is not picked up by the conscious mind. In *The Occult* I cited the story of the tiger hunter Jim Corbett, who developed a high degree of 'jungle sensitiveness'. One morning, absent-mindedly retracing his own footprints (made the night before), he was intrigued to find that they crossed the road at a certain point, then returned to the original side. He had no memory of why he had crossed the road there. Searching nearby, he found the pug marks of a tiger, which had been lying in wait. His subconscious mind had made him cross the road at that point, while his conscious remained unaware.

And so the radar theory itself already implies that some *other level* of the mind is involved, and that this level can command the body without the knowledge of the conscious mind.

Freud would have had no doubt that it was simply a question of the subconscious mind, meaning a level of the mind related to instinctive or sleeping consciousness. It was Aldous Huxley, in his introduction to Myer's book *Human Personality and Its Survival of Bodily Death* who pointed out that the subconscious mind hardly seems a satisfactory explanation for the powers of men of unusual genius—a Leonardo, a Mozart, an Einstein. The flash of *insight* that has enabled men of genius to solve difficult mathematical and scientific problems seems to contradict the notion of the Freudian subconscious, with its sub-human characteristics. Huxley suggested that the notion of a superconscious mind would be a less contradictory hypothesis.

The idea of a superconscious mind has the disadvantage of being unprovable; it may or may not exist. On the other hand, the ladder-of-selves hypothesis, which I outlined in the Introduction, has a foundation in our everyday experience. We all know what it is to feel bored and listless, incapable of facing the world. Consciousness seems to diffuse and spread, like oil poured on the floor. We make an effort to focus an idea, but the mind refuses to grasp it. In this state, any humiliation or disaster makes us worse still. It plunges us into a state in which no effort seems worth making.

By contrast, when something seizes our interest or we suddenly see the chance of getting something we want badly, the 'oil' ceases to spread and unexpectedly begins to contract of its own accord. We refer to this 'contraction effect' when we speak of a man being 'galvanised' by a sense of purpose; the application of an electric current to a frog's leg causes it to contract. 'Meaning' suddenly becomes self-evident; it is all around us for the asking. And if we look back on our moods of defeat, there is a distinct impression of contemplating a *lower self*. We experience a mixture of condescension and pity, as if thinking about a weaker and less mature personality, a kind of dissipated younger brother.

The psychologist Jung attached considerable importance to this notion of 'selves', and the notion seems to have been based on his own youthful experience of being two distinct personalities: an immature, awkward schoolboy, and an old man of great authority and power. At one point, Jung actually believed the latter to have been an eighteenth-century manufacturer. In later life, Jung taught himself a kind of self-hypnosis in which he was able to hold conversations with a 'higher self' whom he called Philemon, and who seemed to him to be independent human being rather than a figment of his imagination.

I have elsewhere coined the term 'promotion' to refer to this sense of leaving behind a 'lower' self, and becoming a more controlled and authoritative personality. It is instructive to observe the actual mechanisms of 'promotion'. If, for example, I am reading a book that I have been trying to get hold of for a long time, it is easy to observe the 'contraction effect'. My mind tries to absorb its meanings in the same way that a python kills its prey: by crushing them into a smaller and smaller compass. If there is something I do not quite grasp, I concentrate harder; my brows contract. And if I succeed in understanding, it is because I have succeeded in 'compressing' the meaning until I can get it 'into' my consciousness. When this happens, I experience the flash of 'insight'.

The interesting thing is that meaning *summons* energy and a sense of purpose. A simple example would be a man glancing casually through a doorway and seeing a girl removing her clothes. Or an old warhorse responding to the sound of the trumpet. Conversely, when I am feeling *de*pressed (as opposed to *com*pressed), my lack of a sense of meaning is reflected in my lack of energy and purpose.

And here we come to the heart of the matter. In states of low energy, I fail to activate the 'compression mechanism' because I do not believe it will lead to any result—that is, will awaken my 'appetite for life' and my sense of meaning. In states of intensity I can see, quite simply, that this is a short-sighted error. The only *certain way* to a sense of meaning is through the effort of compression. And the meaning seems to be infinite. There is no point at which my effort becomes subject to the law of diminishing returns. On the contrary, the wider the area of meaning I am able to grasp, the less effort it costs me to enlarge it. I glimpse dazzling, immense vistas of meaning.

The basic trouble seems to lie in our inborn passivity, in our tendency to allow 'the robot' to do our living for us. And this is partly because meaning is often obliging enough to present itself to us without any effort on our part. 'A certain odour on the wind', a smell of burning autumn leaves or of mince pies in the oven, and we are suddenly flooded with a sense of the sheer sweetness of life, and its incredible multiplicity. A few men of genius—like Beethoven, Goethe, Balzac—discover that there *is* another way to meaning, the way of activity and purpose. But most of us sit around passively, waiting for fate to offer us meaning on a plate. At best, we get used to relying on the predigested meanings of works of art. At worst, we become passive spectators—of television, of football matches, of the quarrels of the next-door neighbours.

Low energy delivers us to the robot, who hastens to take over when he sees we are tired. Then we lose all sense of freedom, and life takes on a curiously dull, muted quality. Keats described it as 'living a post-humous' existence'. Because of its sense that 'nothing is worth doing', the state can easily become self-perpetuating. Moreover, the over-all state of unreality may deliver you into the hands of your fears, so that consciousness takes on a nightmare quality. The answer, as I dis-covered during my own panic attacks, is to shake yourself into a state of wakefulness, so the process is taken out of the hands of the robot. Beyond that, any act that causes the mind to *focus upon meaning* will serve. *Any* discipline will activate the 'compression mechanism'. (I stumbled on this discovery as a schoolboy when I found that half and hour in the gymnasium—which I always anticipated with loath-ing—made me feel more alive.)

The effort of compression leads to 'promotion', to a deeper level of perception of meaning. Or, in terms of our previous image, to the next (and slightly shorter) rung of the ladder. But if the whole process can be described in terms of freedom from 'the robot', why do we need the ladder image? Because the process seems to take place in definite stages. I may spend weeks in a state of fatigue and depression before I suddenly 'fall' to a lower level. Conversely, I may struggle for a long time to achieve a higher state—as Ramakrishna struggled to achieve the vision of the Divine Mother—and then achieve it in a single leap. The inside of the mind seems to be shaped like a ladder or a flight of steps, not like a continuous slope. And each new level seems to be a revelation of an unknown part of ourselves.

Everyone has noticed that in these states of intensity or 'aliveness', we seem to achieve a new degree of efficiency. We become less accident-prone. Difficult feats are achieved with less effort. (While playing darts, I have occasionally experienced a state when I found it difficult *not* to score whatever I aimed for.) Problems are solved with ease. Memory unhesitatingly furnishes us with names or facts that we haven't thought about for years. Moreover, we experience an intuitive certainty that we are *still* calling on only a fraction of our latent capacities. This vast computer we call the brain was *meant* to operate at a far higher level of efficiency.

In states like this, we feel altogether less troubled about the 'insoluble mysteries' of the universe and the 'accursed questions' of human existence. It is all very well to talk about the limitations of the human mind; but if you can see perfectly well that the mind normally operates at only about one thousandth of its proper capacity, you are more likely to lay the blame on human timidity, laziness and mediocrity.

In short, whether or not there is such a thing as the superconscious mind, there can be no doubt that what we accept as everyday consciousness is thoroughly sub-normal. In which case, it seems a fair guess that such faculties as dowsing, second-sight, precognition and divination may simply be latent in some higher level of the computer.

Lethbridge wrote in *The Power of the Pendulum*: 'It [the superconscious] knows far more than we do because . . . it does not have to use the brain to filter out everything . . . It lives in a timeless zone . . .' All of which may possibly be true—and probably is—but is also incomprehensible to us. But everyone has experienced 'melting moods', moods of excitement and heightened vitality, flashes of sudden ecstasy. And, armed with our memories of such moments—as well as our power to re-create them—the power of everyday reason can carry us a considerable distance into these realms of mystery.

As a result of sending a copy of *The Occult* to Hole House, I learned of Tom's death and became acquainted with his wife Mina Lethbridge. She believed that too much experimentation with the pendulum had depleted him, and may have been responsible for his final heart attack. His health had never been good, possibly because he was considerably overweight. I was surprised to hear that the use of the pendulum could be exhausting, but Mina assured me that this was so, and that she had given it up herself for the same reason.

She told me another curious story of Tom's last days. He had been in correspondence with—but never met—a woman of strong psychic powers, another 'witch'. One night she rang up to speak to Tom; Mina explained that he was ill in bed. 'Tell him not throw pentagrams at the time of the waning moon', said the witch. 'It's bad for the health.' Mina said she thought Tom was sufficiently versed in occult tradition not to do such a thing. Nevertheless, she repeated the message to Tom, who looked sheepish. 'You *haven't* been throwing pentagrams, have you?' Tom admitted that he had.

When I settled down to the systematic study of Lethbridge's books, it became clear that they fall into four groups. There are the books on archaeology and primitive religion, and the books on pendulums and related matters. *Legend of the Sons of God*, that remarkable anticipation of the findings of Erich von Däniken and John Michell about 'visitors from other worlds' and the magnetic forces of the earth, belongs in a group on its own. The same is true of the final (posthumous) book *The Power of the Pendulum*, in which he seemed about to embark on a new line of enquiry about dreams and the nature of time.

I must admit that, as I picked my way among his strange theories, I was reminded of some of the weird cults described in Martin Gardner's *Fads and Fallacies in the Name of Science*. Yet the shrewdness and humour—and a breezy willingness to admit that he may be quite wrong—remained basically reassuring.

So let us now plunge into the curious mystery of the giant pagan goddess and her consort . . .

2

Giants and Witches

Lethbridge never forgot that inexplicable episode of the 'poltergeist' that hurled him on his face near the ruins of the ancient church on Skellig Michael. A decade later, after he had given a radio talk, he received a letter from the owner of the island, who told him that Skellig Michael had once been a pagan sanctuary before the monks took it over; his theory was that the 'powers of darkness' had again taken control after the departure of the holy men. Lethbridge disagreed; apart from his unwillingness to equate paganism with the devil, he had an inkling of a stranger and more complex explanation. He suspected that the force that threw him down might be connected with the place itself. Many Christian churches are built on the site of pagan temples. And the ancients believed that such places are permeated by certain non-human forces. Dowsing itself is a response to energies that are unrecognised by science. Could the poltergeist be such a force—perhaps triggered by the violent emotions of the shipwreck? Lethbridge felt the dim outlines of an explanation begin to take shape.

Shortly after the Lethbridges moved to Devon, another curious episode seemed to point in the same direction. They saw a large white dog looking at them through the gate. Tom asked a local farmer who owned it, and the farmer told them there was no such dog for miles around. They learned later that the lane outside Hole House is reputed to be haunted by the ghost of a white dog—at least four other people had seen it.

The story has a sequel. Clearing the undergrowth in the slope below the house, Tom found that someone had dug a trench as the foundation for a shed. With the natural instinct of an archaeologist, he clambered into it and examined its sides; sticking out of the earth, he found a fragment of a glazed floor tile dating from the fourteenth century. Further excavations produced most of the rest of the tile. It had probably come from the floor of a small chapel and it contained pictures of a white hare and a white dog, as well as symbols of the sun and moon. By this time, Lethbridge had reason to believe that these symbols were associated with ancient pagan religion. So again there seemed to be a tenuous connection between this religion and a 'supernatural' occurrence, the 'ghost' of a white dog.

In order to understand the reasons for Lethbridge's absorbing interest in the ancient religion of pre-Christian Britain, it is necessary to go back to 1954, three years before Tom and Mina left Cambridge for Devon. It was on a damp autumn afternoon of the year that Tom began his search for a giant. The search was the beginning of a curious detective story, and of a train of events that led him to abandon his academic career.

The giant was called Gog, and Tom was fairly certain that he lay beneath the turf of Wandlebury Camp, an Iron-Age hilltop fort built by the Celts about 400 BC.

He first came across his trail in a legend recounted by a dubious cleric named Gervase of Tilbury, who was born around 1150. For a priest, Gervase was an unpleasant character—in one of his works he boasts that he told lies about a girl who spurned his advances and got her burnt as a heretic. In 1212, Gervase wrote a book to flatter his patron, the Emperor Otto IV. In this book, he describes Wandlebury Camp ('Wandlebiria'), and tells the legend of a ghostly warrior on horseback. If a knight should ride up to the entrance of Wandlebury Camp on a moonlit night, and shout a challenge, the phantom guardian of the camp would appear, also on horseback, and engage him in battle. Gervase goes on to tell how Osbert, son of Hugh, conquered the phantom knight and led away his magnificent black horse. As the sun rose, the horse broke its tether and galloped away, never to be seen again. But the spear wound made by the phantom knight re-opened every year on the anniversary of the fight.

A century ago, historians would have dismissed such a legend as a fairy tale invented by superstitious countrymen. Nowadays, students of folklore realise that most of them are based on some core of historical fact. And in this case, Lethbridge had a clue to what it was. One of his colleagues at the Museum of Archaeology was an old man called Sammy Cowles, an expert in restoring broken pots. And when Sammy was a child—say around 1870—he had met an old man who told him that there used to be a giant cut into the hillside near Wandlebury. Sammy knew nothing about a horse, or, for that matter, a legendary chariot of gold that is supposed to be buried in the same area. But about the giant he was positive.

Significantly, the range of hills that includes Wandlebury is called the Gogmagog hills. Magog was a legendary giant, and his story is told in the *History of the Kings of Britain* by Geoffrey of Monmouth, a bishop who died in 1155. Geoffrey's *History* is best known as one of the chief sources of the legends of King Arthur and the knights of the round table. It begins by explaining how, when the Trojan War came to an end, Aeneas and his companions fled to Italy, and became the founders of Rome. Another Trojan warrior named Brutus came to an island in the western ocean, 'twixt Gaul and Ireland', and named it after himself—Britain. The island was shared out among his companions, among whom was one called Corineus. He became lord of the peninsula that forms the westernmost tip of Britain, which became known as Corinea, or Cornwall. Cornwall was peopled with giants, and the largest and fiercest was Goemagot, or Gogmagog, who was twelve cubits tall (about eighteen feet). All the giants were killed in a great battle, and Gogmagog was slain by Corineus, who hurled him from a clifftop on to the rocks below. Later tradition turns Gogmagog into two giants, Gog and Magog, who were brought to London, and forced to work as porters at the royal palace. Their effigies can still be seen outside the Guildhall. And the giant figures of Gog and Magog were once carved into the turf at Plymouth Hoe—between Devon and Cornwall—although they vanished in the time of Queen Elizabeth I.

Now the giant Gogmagog may or may not have existed. But the giant hill figures are certainly one of the great historical mysteries of

Britain. I possess a pleasant illustrated book, published in the 1920s, called *Lovely Britain*, and the article on Dorset contains the following comments: 'On the hill slope north of Cerne Abbas, outlined in the turf, sprawls the famous giant. A mighty man is he, 180 feet high, carrying in his hand a massive club nearly as tall as himself. He was there before the Romans came; but who carved him there, and for what purpose, no one knows, though many have made guesses.' These statements reflect the current state of knowledge about the giant. What the author of the piece—a Miss Joyce Reason—omits to mention is that the Cerne Abbas giant displays a monstrous erect penis. Not far away are the immense earth ramparts of Maiden Castle, site of a Stone-Age town that was used as a fort until Roman times. Taken in conjunction, these facts suggest that the giant could be a fertility figure whose origin may stretch back far beyond the fall of Troy. Significantly, the Benedictines built a monastery at the foot of the giant.

Near Wilmington, on the Sussex downs, there is an even larger figure carved into the chalk. His anatomy displays no embarrassing features; he simply stands upright, his arms spread apart, between two parallel lines that seem to suggest he is opening a vast pair of doors. Again, the Benedictines built an abbey by his feet.

Then there are the white horses. The Berkshire White Horse, near Westbury (actually in Wiltshire), is supposed to have been carved in 878, to celebrate King Alfred's victory over the Danes. It looks like a good, solid cart horse; but then, it has been changed in recent centuries by interfering landscape gardeners, and we do not know what it looked like originally. But the immense White Horse of Uffington, 374 feet long, retains its primitive shape, and there can be no doubt that it looks more like a dragon; in fact, a nearby hill is called Dragon Hill. Local legend insists that the Uffington Horse was also cut to celebrate King Alfred's victory, and G. K. Chesterton's long narrative poem *The Ballad of the White Horse* describes King Alfred's battle with King Guthrum. But Chesterton knew—or guessed—that this white horse was far older than Alfred:

> Before the gods that made the gods
> Had seen their sunrise pass,
> The White Horse of the White Horse Vale
> Was cut out of the grass.

Within easy walking distance is Wayland's Smithy, actually a Neolithic burial chamber, more than five thousand years old. Wayland (or Wieland) was also a giant who was lamed and made to work as a blacksmith. Altogether, it seems a safe guess that giants and white horses—or dragons—played a considerable part in the beliefs of the primitive occupants of the British Isles.

When Lethbridge announced that he intended to look for the Wandlebury giant, he encountered a certain scepticism among his colleagues. To begin with, no one was certain where to start looking. The giant had been mentioned by various long-dead historians, but none of them specified which hill. Sammy Cowles had told him that it was visible from the village of Sawston. But beech woods had been planted on the lower slopes of Wandlebury Hill. And there were buildings inside the earthwork of the Iron-Age site, where one Elizabethan historian said the figure was located. It might well be inaccessible. But even if it hadn't been covered over, how could it be located once the turf had grown over it?

Tom reasoned that if the figure had been exposed and re-cut for many centuries, then its chalk must be eroded. In that case, the turf above would be deeper than elsewhere on the slopes of the hill. This is why, on that autumn afternoon in 1954, he carried a stainless steel bar as he investigated the hillside below Wandlebury Camp. Above the beech trees there was a space of about two hundred yards of exposed hillside. He walked across this in a straight line, pausing every nine inches to drive the heavy bar into the wet turf. On average, it proved to be about a foot thick. Mina walked behind him, carrying a bundle of sticks of equal length, and pushing one into each hole. Some of the soundings were almost two feet deep, and they showed that there were two hollows in the chalk. That seemed to be promising.

In fact, with the incredible luck that seems to attend certain archaeological ventures—or perhaps with his instinctive dowsing ability—Lethbridge had not only selected the right patch of hillside, but had traced his line straight across the missing giant. His luck did not end there. He decided to concentrate on the second hollow area, and proceeded to make soundings around it. A few more days of patient work revealed that *two* different outlines passed through this second hollow. There was not one 'giant', but two. And if Lethbridge had concentrated on the first hollow, he would have discovered only one of them.

It was a long, slow business. His hands became blistered from driving the bar into the turf; winter rains turned the hillside into squishy mud, after which it froze solid. Covering five thousand square yards with sticks at nine-inch intervals requires over a hundred thousand sticks; fortunately intelligent guesswork was able to reduce the number considerably. And it gradually became clear that Lethbridge was dealing with at least three separate figures. The central one was a woman on horseback, with a chariot behind her, and the symbol of the waning moon above her. To the right of the chariot there was a giant warrior, a sword raised above his head. To the left was another giant figure of a man, with white rays emanating from his forehead—Lethbridge assumed him to be the sun god. An object like a giant cloak billowed behind him.

And so the investigation had justified the assumption that old 'fairy stories' may contain a core of truth. Here was the origin of the legend of the buried golden chariot, and the warrior with his phantom horse. Careful excavation of the turf soon brought to light the face of the 'goddess'—a great round moon-face, with goggling eyes and perfunctory nose and mouth. Her 'horse' is a curious monstrosity, not unlike a dragon with a bird's beak. In fact, both the goddess and her mount look like science fiction monsters. The White Horse of Uffington has this same stylised, surrealistic quality.

Understandably, the excavations became one of the chief subjects of gossip in Cambridge, and Lethbridge became aware that he had achieved a kind of dubious celebrity. Most of his academic colleagues seemed to feel that the whole thing was a hoax, or at least, a piece of unconscious self-deception. To Lethbridge, the outlines in the chalk were perfectly clear; there was an obvious difference between the eroded chalk of the figures and the untouched chalk around them. Some of his colleagues professed to be unable to see the difference—or they suggested it had been made by Lethbridge himself as he excavated the figure. Fortunately, he was not the type to be unduly worried by hostility. He disliked what he called 'academic trade unionism', and his private income had allowed him to remain aloof from university rivalries. He had always gone his own way; the few colleagues he respected regarded him as a brilliant archaeologist, and these were the only opinions he cared about. So he continued to excavate the giants, and to ponder on the problem of who made them, and why.

To begin with, the answer looked as if it might be fairly straight-forward. At an early stage in the investigation, his colleague, Sir Cyril Fox, had suggested that the female figure was Epona, the Celtic horse goddess, said to be the result of a union between a man and a super-natural mare. This was a logical guess, for the style of the figures was Celtic, and all the evidence suggested that the people who carved them were the Celtic invaders who came to Britain sometime after 600 BC.

The Celts were one of the most remarkable races in European history—as remarkable, in their way, as the Greeks and Romans; if historians have shown less interest in them, it is because of the absence of written records. (The Celts acquired writing only around 500 AD.) They originated somewhere in central Europe, probably in the reg-ions that are now Czechoslovakia and Bavaria. It has been suggested that they may have settled in Ireland as early as 1500 BC. But the great Celtic 'explosion' occurred after 500 BC, at the end of the Bronze Age. In fact, it was the Celts who were responsible for the end of the Bronze Age, since they brought the use of iron to the countries they con-quered. They invaded Gaul (France), Italy, Greece, Asia Minor, and spread along the Danube as far as the Black Sea. Their warriors were tall and fair, although another variety of Celt was dark-haired and round-headed. The historian Lewis Spence describes them as 'that race of artists, poets and aristocrats'. They were formidable fighters but, as the Greek historian, Strabo, pointed out, 'boasters and threateners, and given to bombastic self-dramatisation'. They were also dreamers, intelligent, temperamental and pessimistic; Plato mentions that they were inclined to drunkenness. It can be seen that the Celtic character has changed very little in three thousand years.

The religion of the Celts was Druidism. This seems to have been a form of nature worship; their sacred places were groves of trees. Wells and rivers were also worshipped. Their chief deities were Lug, prob-ably a fertility god, and Matrona, the nature goddess and earth mother. But there were some four hundred gods and goddesses in all, including Epona (or Eoponos), the horse goddess, Moccos, the boar god, Taruos, the bull god, and Cernunnos, the horned stag god. The oak was their sacred tree (the word druid probable comes from the Greek *drus*, an oak). So was the mistletoe. The latter is, of course, a parasite that usually grows on apple trees; when Druids found mistletoe growing on an oak, they regarded it as a gift of the gods, and cut it with a golden sickle. It was then used in their religious rituals.

One of the great linguistic discoveries of the nineteenth century was that most European languages had their origin in Sanskrit, the language of the primitive tribes of India, who began to break up around 2000 BC. Celtic is in many ways close to Sanskrit, and the Celts belong to the racial group known as Indo-Europeans. So it is highly probable that the gods of the Celts derive from the gods of India, and that Druidism is a descendant of the old Hindu religion expressed in the Vedic hymns. The archaeologist Sir Flinders Petrie points out in his book *Hill Figures* that India also has its giants carved on hillsides. Like the Hindus, the Druids firmly believed in life after death and in the transmigration of souls.

Lethbridge reasoned that the female giant of Wandlebury with her golden chariot is the mother goddess Matrona; and since the hills are traditionally known as the Gogmagog hills, it seemed a reasonable assumption that she was locally known as Magog, or Ma-God, mother god. The cloaked figure on her right is therefore likely to be her consort Lug, here presumably called Gog. As to the sword-waving warrior, Lethbridge concluded that he is the god Wandil, after whom Wandlebury is named. An ancient legend declares that Wandil stole the spring time, so that the winter became longer and longer; the gods finally compelled him to give it back, and threw him into the sky, where he became the constellation Gemini. And what is Wandil doing in the picture with Gog and Magog? The answer, Lethbridge thought, is that he was the local Druidic equivalent of the devil. (Celtic religion is full of local deities.) What is more natural than that the devil should appear with mother goddess and her consort?

Now if Lethbridge had confined himself to these theories about the meaning of the figures, it is probable that his book *Gogmagog* would have been politely received, and the controversy would have died away. But he had a feeling that he was on to something far bigger, something of greater importance than a few local deities drawn on a hillside. The Celts were pantheists; they worshipped Nature and the universe. Their Druids were skilled in philosophy and astrology. Perhaps Lethbridge's own dowsing ability predisposed him in favour of a people who worshipped the forces of the earth and the universe.

In brief, Lethbridge was inclined to accept the theory of his friend

Margaret Murray, that the pre-Christian world was permeated with a fertility religion known as 'wicca', which has descended to modern times in the form of witchcraft. According to Margaret Murray, this religion was far older than the Celts. Lethbridge believed that his Wandlebury giants were living symbols of this religion, and that sacred rituals were probably performed within their outlines.

At this early stage, he had still not made a connection between this religion and his own experiences of the 'paranormal', such as the Skellig Michael poltergeist. This would have to wait another five years, until he wrote *Witches: Investigating an Ancient Religion*. Even so, the views he put forward in *Gogmagog: The Buried Gods* (1957) struck his colleagues as wildly speculative and caused a small-scale intellectual war in Cambridge. Lethbridge was startled by the bitterness he aroused. For many years his attitude to Cambridge had been ambivalent; he disliked the cliquishness, and hated the gradual erosion of old traditions. The Gogmagog controversy settled his decision to leave. The results of that decision have been recounted in the previous chapter.

In order to understand the development of his later views, it is necessary to digress for a moment, and say something about the origin of this theory of the 'Old Religion'.

In 1890, the science we now know as anthropology was hardly out of its infancy. Henry Rowe Schoolcraft's monumental study of the American Indian appeared in 1851. Sir Henry Maine's *Ancient Law*, McLennan's *Primitive Marriage*, Sir Edward Tylor's *Primitive Culture*, Robertson Smith's *Religion of the Semites*, were all early classics of this new science. But in 1890, there appeared a two-volume work wider in scope, bolder in conception, more startling in its implications, than anything that had gone before. It was written by a small, neatly dressed Scotsman of conservative tastes, James Frazer, and its title was *The Golden Bough*.

The bough referred to in the title is the mistletoe—which turns golden after it has been plucked. Frazer begins with a famous description of Turner's painting 'The Golden Bough', showing the woodland grove at Nemi in Italy. In Roman times, a man with a sword walked around a tree in this sacred grove. He was the priest of Diana, the earth and moon goddess, and he held the title of King of the Wood. He had achieved this position by killing the previous holder, and he would, in due course, be killed by his successor. A runaway slave could achieve a precarious kind of freedom by fleeing to the sacred grove above Lake Nemi. If he could pluck a branch from the sacred tree, he could fight the priest; if he killed him, he himself became sacred and ran no risk of incurring the usual penalty for runaway slaves—crucifixion.

Frazer started with the apparently modest aim of wanting to know how this curious custom came about. *The Golden Bough* eventually expanded into thirteen large volumes, and they constitute an elaborate treasure hunt, a search through the mythologies and religions of the whole world. (Frazer did little 'field work', but he kept up a vast correspondence with hundreds of missionaries, traders and travellers in remote parts of the globe.)

Frazer's central explanation sounds plausible enough to us; but in 1890, it was as disturbing as the theories of Freud. Frazer was one of the first anthropologists to lay major emphasis on the element of fertility in primitive religions. His friend and mentor, Robertson Smith, had written of early Semitic fertility gods in *The Religion of the Semites*, and other anthropologists had discussed this element in primitive religion; but for Frazer, the desire to induce fertility was the mainspring of all such religions. The king, he said, embodied the powers of nature; one of his chief tasks was rain-making. Since he was an intermediary of the gods, it was important that his powers should not weaken, otherwise the harvest might fail. Ancient man was accustomed to offer sacrifices to the gods to ensure their favour. And if the king's powers began to fail, what better sacrifice could be offered? Then he could go to intercede directly for his people. It followed that if the king was killed in his prime, before his powers began to fail, the sacrifice would be even more effective.

The chief problem here, of course, is that the king himself can be expected to take a dim view of the custom. In primitive tribes, the basic sense of unity would over-rule his objection. But as civilisation progressed, the sacrifice would become symbolic. In Babylonia, there was an ancient custom of dethroning the king for one day and killing his substitute king. Then there were the many gods and heroes of mythology who must be sacrificed ritually to ensure good harvests—the Babylonian Tammuz, the Egyptian Osiris, the Greek Attis and Adonis. In these cases, the god—or hero—is resurrected, symbolising the spirit of nature, which revives every spring. In the Lebanon, the River Adonis became red every autumn as the red soil was washed down by the rains; this, said his followers, was because Adonis had been slain by the wild boar. They went into the mountains looking for the 'corpse', and, having found a figure like a man, held funeral lamentations in which they sobbed with genuine grief. When the hero was resurrected, this was celebrated by wild orgies.

With examples like this—literally hundreds of them—Frazer built up his case. John Barleycorn is cut off at the knees and buried in the earth, yet he appears again in the spring, bearing no resentment. Frazer even pointed out that the Christian rituals involving the death and resurrection of Jesus have much in common with these pagan festivals and may derive from them—the kind of observation that struck the Victorians as blasphemous. (Frazer's friend Robertson Smith had been deprived of his chair at the University of Aberdeen for suggesting that the Bible should be examined with the same critical detachment as any other historical document; his opponents declared that his writing 'tended to create the impression that Scripture does not present a reliable statement of truth and that God is not the author of it'.) Frazer's implication was clear, even if he never stated it in so many words: we think of ourselves as highly civilised, but our religious beliefs are probably as unsophisticated and absurd as those of any primitive tribe. It was this unstated suggestion that was responsible for the impact of *The Golden Bough*. It is significant that *The Golden Bough*, and Jessie L. Weston's *From Ritual to Romance* (an anthropological study of the Grail Legend) play a central part in T. S. Eliot's *Waste Land*, the poem that expressed the religious despair of the 1920s.

Frazer went on to point out the importance of fire in these myths of sacrifice. The Druids burned their human sacrifices—criminals or enemies—alive in wicker baskets. Midsummer fires—in which John Barleycorn is burnt—are a worldwide custom. People leap through the flames for good luck. The flames represent the sun, the power that arouses life from the earth.

In the thirteenth volume, Frazer moves towards the conclusion of his argument. He examines the myth of Baldur, the Scandinavian god who is killed by a sprig of mistletoe. Most schoolchildren have heard the story and been troubled by it. The goddess Fricka made all creatures promise they would not harm Baldur the beautiful, but she overlooked the mistletoe. The mischievous god Loki noted the omission. When the gods held a celebration, in which they all pelted Baldur with every conceivable object to demonstrate his immunity, Loki handed the mistletoe to the blind god Hodur, who threw it at Baldur and killed him. This sounds slightly illogical; if the sprig would not harm Baldur normally—being too light—why *should* it kill him? Frazer's guess is that the mistletoe is supposed to embody the *life* of Baldur—in fact, is a symbol of life and fertility. Its milky berries have the colour of male semen. We all know the custom of kissing girls under the mistletoe at Christmas—which probably originated in something altogether more orgiastic. And this may also explain the second of the two mysteries connected with the sacred grove at Nemi—why the challenger had to pluck a branch from the tree before he could challenge the priest-king to battle. Could it be that the branch was the mistletoe, and that the ancients thought it embodied the life of the god or priest? So the challenger had made the priest mortal by plucking the bough; now he was allowed to kill him in combat.

Anyone who has ever tried to read *The Golden Bough*—even in its abridged one-volume edition—must have felt that it is ultimately unsatisfactory. The descriptions of the various folk beliefs and customs are fascinating, but the whole thing seems to spread out sideways in both directions, until you are no longer sure what is being argued. Frazer has remained a tremendous influence, because of the imaginative scope of his work, but few anthropologists now regard his central arguments as sound. Andrew Lang pointed out that Frazer is able to produce only one example of an actual king who was slain as a sacrifice—the Babylonian 'king for a day'. And this is a poor example, since he was really a slave.

Another of Lang's criticisms is perhaps more important. Tylor and Frazer both treated magic as crude superstition. But as a child in Scotland, Lang had known people with second sight, and people who had seen ghosts. He pointed out that most such people are not imaginative hysterics, but 'steady, unimaginative, unexcitable people with just one odd experience'. He quotes Professor Charles Richet: 'There exists in certain persons, at certain moments, a faculty for acquiring knowledge which has no relation to our normal faculties of this kind.' And this may be stronger in savages than in civilised men. 'We hold that very probably there exist human faculties of unknown scope: that these conceivably were more powerful and prevalent among our very remote ancestors who founded religion; [and] that they may still exist in savage as in civilised races . . .' These words were written in 1898, at the height of the age of rationalism, and they led some critics to conclude that Andrew Lang had an old-fashioned streak of Celtic superstition. Nearly a century later, it is Lang who strikes us as balanced and open-minded, and the critics who seem old-fashioned.

At the end of the first section of *The Golden Bough*, Frazer wrote: 'Reviewing the evidence as a whole, we may conclude that the worship of Diana in her sacred grove at Nemi was of great importance and immemorial antiquity; that she was revered as the goddess of woodlands and of wild creatures, probably also of domestic cattle and of fruits of the earth; that she was believed to bless men and women with offspring and to aid mothers in childbed . . .' Diana is, of course, also the moon goddess—the Roman equivalent of the Celtic goddess on the Wandlebury hillside.

In 1894, four years after Frazer's book appeared, an upper-class young Englishwoman named Margaret Alice Murray decided to go to University College, London, to attend lectures on Egyptology by the famous Sir Flinders Petrie. It was not her own choice; her elder sister made up her mind for her. In due course, Margaret Murray would become even more controversial than James Frazer; all her later work would develop from the paragraph quoted above.

Margaret Murray was fairly old to begin university studies; at the age of thirty-one, she had already made two false starts in life—first as a nurse, then as a social worker. Neither appealed to her as a vocation. Egyptology was a different matter. It seems probable that Flinders Petrie became a kind of father figure to her (although only ten years her senior). He was already famous as the explorer of the Valley of the Kings and had actually lived in a pyramid while he conducted his researches. Now, with Petrie's encouragement, Margaret Murray studied the language of the ancient Egyptians and learned to read hieroglyphics. By the outbreak of the First World War, when she was fifty, she had become a well-known archaeologist in her own right, and was the author of half a dozen books. In 1915, during a period of illness, she stayed in Glastonbury and became—inevitably—interested in the legend of the Holy Grail. She turned from the archaeology of the Middle East to write a paper on *Egyptian Elements in the Holy Grail Romance*. Then, feeling at a loose end, she decided to devote the war years to the study of witchcraft. In her autobiography *My First*

Hundred Years, she explains that someone once told her that witches had their special form of religion, and that they danced around a black goat.

> I had started with the usual idea that witches were all old women suffer-
> ing from illusions about the Devil and that their persecutors were
> wickedly prejudiced and perjured. I worked only from contemporary
> records, and when I suddenly realised that the so-called Devil was simply
> a disguised man I was startled, almost alarmed, by the way the recorded
> facts fell into place, and showed that the witches were members of an old
> and primitive form of religion, and the records had been made by
> members of a new and persecuting form.

Unfortunately, she fails to explain how this revelation came about. All we know is that she became increasingly convinced that the witches were members of Frazer's 'immemorial fertility-cult' of Diana, the moon goddess, and that ritual sacrifices of kings and priests had continued well into the Christian era, the victims including William Rufus, King John, Edward II, Richard II, Thomas à Becket, Joan of Arc, Gilles de Rais, and two wives of Henry VIII. When she wrote *The Witch Cult in Western Europe*, which appeared in 1921, some of her more startling views were undeveloped; even so, the book caused a sensation. What is perhaps more surprising is that it convinced a large number of serious scholars and historians. Her theory quickly became 'respectable', and for the next four decades the article on Witchcraft in *Encyclopaedia Britannica* was by Margaret Murray, and stated her theories as if they were proven fact.

Her views were not entirely original. Since 1739, when an Italian cleric named Tartarotti-Servato had written *Nocturnal Meetings of Witches*, many scholars had pointed out that certain witch prac-tices—notably the Witches' Sabbath—bore some resemblance to pagan religious rituals. Yet, oddly enough, Margaret Murray never mentioned the book that is by far the most convincing piece of evidence for her theory. In Italy in the 1880s, a swashbuckling Ameri-can lawyer named Charles Godfrey Leland became friendly with an Italian fortune-teller named Maddalena, a hereditary witch. In Italy, witchcraft is often referred to as *'la vecchia religione'*—the old relig-ion—and Maddalena confirmed that it was precisely that. She gathered together various fragments of poetry and witch-lore, which Leland published in 1899 in a book called *Aradia: the Gospel of the Witches*. This book bears all the hallmarks of authenticity, and it is difficult to see why anyone *should* have concocted it; it is short, unsensational, and its material would be of interest only to a folklorist. In fact, it went out of print almost as soon as it was published and has remained out of print until recent years. And if *Aradia* is genuine, then it would be fair to say that Margaret Murray's theory rests on a very solid foundation.

According to *Aradia*, the goddess Diana had an incestuous affair with her brother Lucifer—the light-bringer—and gave birth to a daughter named Aradia, or Herodias. There came a period of great social oppression, when many slaves were treated so cruelly that they fled to the wilderness and became robbers. Diana thereupon ordered Aradia to go down to earth and teach these oppressed people the arts of poisoning, ruining crops and casting spells on the aristocracy and the priests. And if the priests anathematised her in the name of God, Jesus and Mary, she was to reply: 'Your God, Jesus and Mary are Devils.' Obviously, the Italian witches saw themselves as revolutionaries, the equivalent of today's left-wing guerrilla organisations; or at least, as a peasant's protest movement. (The French historian Michelet had stumbled on the same idea. He suggested that witches were poor peasants who came together at night to perform pagan rituals as a protest against the Church and the aristocracy.) The remainder of the book is a compilation of rituals, legends and witch-lore.

Like Frazer—and unlike Andrew Lang—Margaret Murray had no belief in the supernatural as such. She tried Frazer's explanation on her witchcraft material, decided that it fitted, and wrote her epoch-making book. Her thesis is simple. Old religions are never totally replaced by new ones: they continue to exist, often side by side with the new religion. She cites many laws against pagan practices that prove that it still existed long after the coming of Christianity, and that the Church regarded it as a menace. She considers various witch trials and insists that the magical practices described are not nightmares of a fevered imagination but perfectly credible descriptions of pagan fertility ceremonies, in which the high priest dressed up like the nature god Pan, with goat's feet and horns. (This, she says, is the origin of the Christian idea of the Devil.) Perhaps the most startling assertion in the book is that Joan of Arc and Gilles de Rais, the sadist executed for the murder of more than a hundred children, were both leaders of a witch cult and died for their faith. Gilles' murders were the human sacrifices of the 'old religion'. (In fact, both Joan and Gilles were accused of witchcraft.)

Margaret Murray's second book on the subject, *The God of the Witches*, appeared in 1933; it aims at presenting a popular account of her theory. In this book she lays rather more emphasis on 'the horned god', pointing out that ancient *shamans* dressed up in animal skins, and that there are many modern survivals of ancient fertility dances in which the men wear horns or antlers. This book was largely ignored when it appeared; there were more pressing problems to think about in the mid-thirties than witches and fertility cults. Republished after the war, it became a best-seller—an early sign, perhaps of the 'occult revival' that became so widespread in the sixties.

Perhaps emboldened by her sudden fame, Margaret Murray produced her third and most controversial volume in 1954. *The Divine King in England* offers a bewildering list of English kings and substitute victims who have been killed as ritual sacrifices. She manages to give the general impression that practically every famous murder in English history was connected with the witch cult. The book was generally dismissed as a crank aberration (after all, she was over ninety years old when it appeared), but the first two books continued to be highly regarded by scholars.

Tom Lethbridge knew Margaret Murray at Cambridge; he liked her personally, and was inclined, on the whole, to accept her views on the 'ancient religion'. His attitude was not shared by many of his colleagues—he has described how various petty indignities were visited on her at Cambridge. *Gogmagog*, like the later *Witches*, takes it for granted that Margaret Murray is fundamentally correct. This was why the controversy around *Gogmagog* became so acrid.

Lethbridge concludes that the central figure on the Wandlebury hillside—the woman surmounted by the crescent moon—was the moon goddess *and* the earth mother. Gog, her consort, is the sun god. (In Leland's *Aradia*, the moon goddess's consort is Lucifer, the light-bringer.) He goes on to argue that in Celtic and many other ancient religions, the oak tree is the symbol of the sun. Hence its importance for the Druids. The berries of the mistletoe symbolise the moon, because they look like small moons. The Druids cut them with a golden sickle, symbolising the sun, when they found them growing on an oak tree. What could be a better augury of fertility than the symbol of the earth goddess growing on the tree of the sun god?

Although Druidism came to England around 600 BC with the Celts, Lethbridge believed that other forms of the 'ancient religion' existed here for centuries before that. We know that the Druids on the Continent sent their novices to study with the English Druids, which suggests that an older and purer form of the religion existed in England. We know the Druids claimed magical powers, to foretell the future, change bodily shape, cast spells to cause death and lunacy ('moon-sickness'), and induce invisibility, in fact, most of the powers that witches were later believed to possess. The human sacrifices were almost certainly fertility rituals, with the firelight symbolising sunlight, as Frazer suggested. For the ancients, sunlight was all important, the source of fertility. Darkness was evil. When eclipses of the sun and moon occurred, primitive man believed the powers of darkness were attempting to destroy the powers of light, and the earliest religious rituals were intended to aid the sun against his enemy. (Some African tribes still beat pots to aid the sun during an eclipse.)

This explains why the 'old religion' was so indestructible in country areas. It was not simply a matter of loyalty to old gods, but of genuine belief that if they ceased to perform the fertility ritual, there would be no crops. Even today, many country folk believe that crops can be improved or blasted by witchcraft.

Gogmagog is the only one of Lethbridge's later books that contains no reference to 'occult' matters; he seems tacitly to accept Margaret Murray's view that the magical side of witchcraft is pure superstition. If he had remained at Cambridge, he might well have continued to accept this view, in spite of his experience of ghosts, 'ghouls' and poltergeists. But when the Lethbridges moved to Hole House in Devon, the first person they met was the 'witch' who lived next door.

Then there was the interesting coincidence that the moor above Hole House was called Lugmoor. Lug, or Lugh, was the Celtic sun god, whose name is obviously related to Lucifer. Even the name 'Bran' in Branscombe was another name for Lugh, after he had changed himself into a raven (that famous witches' bird).

It is interesting to wonder why Lucifer, the angel of light, should have been identified with the devil. The story is not—as most people assume—in the Bible. Isaiah 14 contains the well-known lines: 'How are you fallen to earth, O day star, son of the dawn' (in Hebrew, *helel ben shahar*), but Isaiah is jeering at the King of Babylon, and the legend of a falling star on which the insult is based obviously refers to a meteor. Milton's story of the war of the rebel angels against God is based on a short reference in Revelation 12 to the 'Dragon' who raised an army to challenge God. It was the early Christian theologians who identified this beast—Satan—with Lucifer or Lugh, the sun god. Even more significant, in the next chapter of Revelation, Gog and Magog are referred to as the enemies of the kingdom of God. (Ezekiel also has a reference to the 'hordes of Gog and Magog'.) There can be little doubt that Lethbridge is correct when he says that when a new religion conquers, the gods of the old religion are turned into devils. Even the word devil is derived from the Hindu *deva*, meaning a god. When Christianity ousted the religion of Lugh and Matrona, the old gods were promptly demoted to the rank of unsuccessful rebels.

When Saint Augustine landed in England in 597 AD, he found an island covered with pagan temples dedicated to the sun god and the earth mother. We know that many churches are built on pagan sites. What names, Lethbridge wondered, would the Christians choose in re-dedicating these sites? A tenable assumption is that Magog—or Matrona—would be replaced by Mary, the Mother of God, and Lucifer by his legendary adversary, the Archangel Michael. By way of checking this hypothesis, Lethbridge looked through Crockford's clerical directory, and picked out all churches dedicated to the Virgin and to St Michael in the south-west, and marked them on an ordnance survey map. The result was as he had expected. Where there were old Iron-Age forts, there were plenty of Michaels and Marys; where there were no Iron-Age forts, Michaels and Marys became infrequent. He also observed a high percentage of St Andrews in these areas, which seemed to confirm another of his theories—that St Andrew had ousted the Welsh sun god Mabon.

According to Lethbridge, Mary, Michael and Andrew not only replaced Magog, Lugh and Mabon; they finally *became* these gods. Pope Gregory the First advised St Augustine to 'accommodate the Christian ceremonies as much as possible to those of the heathen'. The result was that many pagan ceremonies—such as slaughtering oxen on feast days—were simply incorporated into the Christian religion. (The mistletoe under which we kiss at Christmas is another example.) And in country areas, where the old religion was still observed, St

Michael was worshipped as the bringer of light and fertility, and Mary as the earth mother herself.

Lethbridge was also a step nearer to explaining the force that knocked him down on Skellig Michael. It was at least, a fair assumption that the monastery of St Michael had been built on a site dedicated to the pagan sun god, a spot in which the forces of the earth had been invoked for centuries in pagan ceremonies. Ten years later, in one of his most controversial books, *Legend of the Sons of God*, he was to carry the argument a significant stage further.

When *Witches* appeared in 1962, Margaret Murray's theory of witchcraft had been losing ground for more than two decades. But the turning point seems to have been the year 1954. Even her most devoted followers were embarrassed by *The Divine King in England*. In the same year, she wrote an approving introduction to Gerald Gardner's *Witchcraft Today*, a book that quickly acquired an unsavoury notoriety. Gardner was an eccentric masochist and voyeur who not only claimed to be a member of a witch coven, but insisted that such covens still flourished all over Europe. The book inaugurated the modern 'witchcraft revival', with its emphasis on sexual rites. Gardner identified the modern cult of 'wicca' with Margaret Murray's ancient fertility religion of Diana. And Margaret Murray apparently agreed with him. Understandably, historians began to feel she could no longer be taken seriously.

But guilt by association is no argument against the basic soundness of her views. The question that concerns us here is: how far are these views supported by historical evidence?

The most devastating—and carefully documented—attack so far appeared in Norman Cohn's book *Europe's Inner Demons* (1975). Professor Cohn seemed to have no doubt that Margaret Murray either distorted or invented most of her 'evidence'. He reached this conclusion after studying the original documents that she cites in her books. Her main argument was that nothing very extraordinary happened at the Witches' Sabbaths, and that the descriptions of the witches themselves fitted the view that the Sabbaths were pagan fertility rites. Cohn quickly discovered that where she had left rows of dots, to indicate something left out, there were often descriptions of the most wildly improbable events—such as the devil having sex with all the women present, who in due course gave birth to toads and serpents. In a subsequent chapter, Cohn demonstrates that some of the most con-vincing documents about early witchcraft were forgeries—a brilliant display of historical detective work. He concludes that the witch craze of the late Middle Ages began with the persecution of the heretical sect called the Waldenses, and snowballed from there.

Cohn's personal assessment of Margaret Murray seems correct. He says:

> Her knowledge of European history, even of English history, was superficial, and her grasp of historical method was non-existent. In the special field of witchcraft studies, she never seems to have read any of the modern histories of the persecution; and even if she had, she would not have assimilated them. By the time she turned her attention to these matters she was nearly sixty, and her ideas were firmly set in an exaggerated and distorted version of the Frazerian mould. For the rest of her days (and she lived to be a hundred) she clung to these ideas with a tenacity that no criticism, however well informed or well argued, could ever shake.

All of which leaves untouched Lethbridge's central thesis: that there was an ancient fertility religion, probably far older than Druidism, which, in spite of the persecution of the Christian Church, survived into modern times. Lethbridge rightly felt that Leland's *Aradia: The Gospel of the Witches* was the most convincing evidence for his argu-ment. Cohn doesn't even mention *Aradia*. His chief aim is to prove that the witch craze grew from the persecution of the Waldenses—which began in 1487—and not, as many scholars have always believed, from the persecution of another heretical sect, called the Cathars, two centuries earlier. This matter is hardly as crucial as Cohn seems to think; it scarcely matters which outbreak of persecution triggered the witch craze, and there is no good reason why both the Cathars *and* the Waldenses should not have been involved. (In the Pyrenees, witches are called *gazarii*, which sounds as if it derives from Cathar.)

Cohn's own position is less unbiased than it looks. He is the author of two earlier books on irrational cults: *Warrant for Genocide*, dealing with a notorious forgery called *Protocols of the Elders of Zion* that has inspired many anti-Jewish pogroms, and *The Pursuit of the Millennium*, a study of various strange sects of the Middle Ages. Cohn is centrally concerned with persecution and with the persistent myth that society at large is threatened by a small secret society that rejects its laws and practises horrible abominations: the accusation that has so often been brought against the Jews. He is naturally inclined to see the witch craze in similar terms—an irrational outbreak of hysteria against innocent people—and tends to ignore evidence that fails to fit his thesis—like Leland's *Aradia*.

So if we decline to be sidetracked by Margaret Murray's sins as a historian, the evidence for the existence of the witch cult is surprisingly convincing, considering that we are dealing with bits of broken tile and pottery, old coins, and gods who change their names every hundred years or so. The evidence lies all around us—particularly in country districts—in old churches, in curious festivals associated with May Day, Midsummer Eve and harvest time. In his book *The Roots of Witchcraft*, Michael Harrison mentions a discovery made by Professor Geoffrey Webb, when he was Secretary of the Royal Commission on Historical Monuments. After the Second World War Webb was assigned the task of surveying ruined churches with a view to restoration. Looking inside an altar whose top slab had been removed by a bomb blast, he found a male sexual organ carved in stone. This led him to look in other altars. Webb concluded that similar phalluses could be found inside the altars of ninety per cent of churches built up to the time of the Black Death (1348)—that is, shortly before the great witch craze.

Harrison also mentions an event documented in the Bishop's Register of Exeter in the fourteenth century: it states that the Bishop of Exeter caught the monks of Frithelstock Priory (in Devon) worshipping a statue of 'the unchaste Diana' in the woods, and made them destroy it. No punishment is mentioned. The monks themselves probably knew so little about theology that they were hardly aware that Diana was a pagan goddess.

Again, anyone who has studied old churches will have seen examples of the curious carvings known as *Sheila-na-gigs*, showing a female squatting with her thighs open, exposing her genitals. Many *Sheila-na-gigs* were placed in prominent positions—above church doors or windows—suggesting that there was a time when churchgoers took them as much for granted as they took statues of the Virgin. *Sheila-na-gig* is usually translated 'lady of the breasts', but many such figures have hardly any breasts; Lethbridge suggests it should be *Sheila-na-gog*—lady of the god, or mother goddess.

This view is convincingly argued by Michael Dames, a senior lecturer at Birmingham Polytechnic, in his book *The Silbury Treasure*,[1] and subtitled *The Great Goddess Rediscovered*. Silbury Hill, near Avebury in Wiltshire, is a vast prehistoric mound whose purpose has puzzled historians for centuries. The most popular theory is that it is a Bronze-Age barrow—a mound of earth raised above a burial site—although it is vastly larger than any known barrow. And careful excavations have revealed no grave inside it. The legend that it was the grave of a certain King Sil, who was entombed upright on his horse, clearly has no foundation.

A flint discovered inside the hill suggested that it was far older than the Bronze Age (1000–2000 BC). Since then, radiocarbon dating has proved that the hill is some 5,000 years old, pre-dating the oldest part of Stonehenge by a century or more. Yet the most recent excavations (1967) still revealed no clue to its purpose.

Michael Dames concluded that the mystery of Silbury can be explained only when we recognise that the hill itself is intended to represent the womb of a pregnant woman. Seen from above, with its oddly-shaped surrounding moat, Silbury resembles a *Sheila-na-gig* seen in profile—a woman squatting in the birth position, with her legs open. (Many primitive people still give birth in this position.) Dames believes that Silbury was the scene of a Stone-Age religious rite. At harvest time, when the corn was ready to be cut, country people would climb to the terrace just below the summit of the hill, to watch the spectacle of the goddess giving birth, with the aid of Diana, the moon. At eight o'clock on Lammas Eve (August 7th), the moon rises over Waden Hill; it falls across the thigh of the mother and indicates the vulva; at ten o'clock it touches the left knee, and at eleven thirty, the baby's head—the reflection of the moon in the moat—appears to emerge from between the mother's legs. A few hours later it falls on the breast, and the reflection of moon in the water simulates flowing milk. (A legend reported by Aubrey says that the hill was raised 'while a posset of milk was seething'.) The child held on the belly is now feeding, and the corn can be cut. The earth mother has given birth.

Predictably, Dames's theory has aroused bitter opposition from the 'experts', who nevertheless admit that they have no idea of why Silbury Hill was raised. But it supports, in every particular, the views advanced by Lethbridge. The *Sheila-na-gigs* are images of a religion far older than Christianity, older than the Druids and the warriors who beseiged Troy. And no clear distinction was made between the earth goddess and the moon goddess; like the Italian Diana, they blended into one. This is the religion of Magog, whose symbols are carved into the Wandlebury hillside.

At this point, I should admit that my own attitude towards these matters was distinctly sceptical, until I began to look into it for myself. Cornwall, where I live, is full of survivals of the 'old religion', and a little research soon revealed many more.

At Helston, in Cornwall, the May Day celebration takes placed on May 8 (the date has probably been displaced over the centuries because of changes in the calendar). The people of Helston dance through the streets to a tune called the Floral Dance. But the dance itself is called the Furry, not the Floral, Dance. From the time of the Stone Age *shamans*, fertility ceremonies have been performed by men dressed up as animals. The other song that is sung during the celebrations concerns Robin Hood and Maid Marian; Robin Hood has been shown by the folklorist Lord Raglan to be a Celtic horned god. Even the name of the town, Helston, seems to be a version of Hele stone, the stone of the sun god. (The same is true of the Heel Stone of Stonehenge.) Its patron saint is, of course, St Michael.

The ceremony that takes place at Padstow, in Cornwall, on May Day is generally acknowledged to be a survival of an ancient fertility rite. It is known as the Festival of the Hobby Horse (pronounced Obby Oss). The horse is the most important of Celtic animal gods, hence the various white horses portrayed on hillsides. In Padstow, the horse parades through the streets surrounded by dancers. Claude Berry has described the scene in *Portrait of Cornwall*: 'Although the Hobby Horse is the principal figure in the festivities, scarcely less important is the man who, with mask and club, "dances before" the horse the day long through . . .' The 'horse' occasionally darts at a girl and bumps her, or takes her under its skirts; custom has it that the girl will become pregnant within the year.

The article on 'Curious Customs and Ceremonies' by I. O. Evans in *Romantic Britain* is full of reference to rites involving fertility and animals. The ceremony of the Deermen is held at Abbots Bromley in Staffordshire every September 4. The Deermen, dressed in antlers, escort Robin Hood and Maid Marian across the town; Robin Hood sits astride a hobby horse. The Deermen carry clubs with deers' heads on them. And—significantly—the antlers are kept in the local church, like the stone phalluses discovered by Professor Webb.

At Hungerford, in Berkshire, two men known as Tuttimen parade through the streets on the second Tuesday after Easter, demanding a kiss from every girl and a coin from every man. They knock on doors and demand a kiss from every woman in the house. Again, this seems to be a survival of a fertility ritual whose origin was less restrained: the girls are made to give themselves, the men to offer tribute. Like the Deermen, the Tuttimen carry wands or staffs of office. Lethbridge suggests that the ceremonial staffs (like the Mace in the House of Commons) originate in Gog's club. (The discoverer of 'leys', Alfred Watkins, had another explanation, as we shall see in the next chapter.)

The name Tuttimen puzzled me until I consulted a dictionary of non-classical mythology, and discovered that Teutates was the Celtic god of war. The ceremony takes place at Hocktide, which suggests Hogtide. The Gogmagog Hills were known until a century ago as the Hogogmagog Hills, and Hog is one of the many forms of Gog discovered by Lethbridge in his researches.

A photograph in Evans' article shows the Christmas mummers in the village of Marshfield, in Oxfordshire; they are dressed in strange, shaggy garments, with masks over their faces and again look like the *shamans* in Palaeolithic drawings. Evans mentions that in Wales, mummers carry a horse's head, and the plays they perform include one about Robin Hood. He suggests that the term 'horse play' originates in the rough antics around the hobby horse.

Evans notes of the Morris dancers:

> Dressed in white, girt with brightly coloured ribbons on which tiny bells jingle, their heads covered with braid-brimmed or flower-decked hats, the Morris dancers stamp and kick and bound, wave their handkerchiefs or clash with their staves . . . So they danced long ago, it is said, to influence the corn and make it grow . . .

He also speaks of 'Bale fires' that used to burn at the four seasons of the year to mark the turning of the sun in the heavens. And here again, we are plunged into Druidic mythology. Lethbridge devotes a whole chapter of *Witches* to the god Baal, or Bel, who became Beelzebub or the Devil in Christian mythology. Bel actually means beautiful, as in

Baldur. What everyone remembers about the priests of Baal in the Bible is that they performed human sacrifice by throwing their victims into a fire—the method of the Druids. Baal was a fertility god who originated in Palestine; he wore bull's horns, and his wife was Astarte (or Ashtoreth) the moon goddess. (She became Diana of the Ephesians.) Here again we have an example of the conquering religion turning into the gods of the old religion into devils. The four seasons at which Bale fires are burnt are the four Druidic festivals. May 1st is actually called Beltane.

In connection with Cornish giants, Evans quotes an interesting little rhyme:

> Here I am, old Hub-bub-bub,
> And in my hand I carry a club,
> And on my back a frying pan,
> Am I not a valiant man?

Hub-bub-bub sounds like the giant Gogmagog, formerly portrayed on Plymouth Hoe. Evans' chapter was written in 1920, before publication of *The Witch Cult in Western Europe*; yet most of it sounds as if it had been written specifically to support Margaret Murray and T. C. Lethbridge.

All this discussion of witch cults, pagan gods and legendary giants may strike the reader as a diversion. What has it to do with Lethbridge's theories of ghosts, ghouls and other dimensions? The answer begins to emerge towards the end of *Witches*. Speaking of Aradia, queen of the witches, he observes that she was sent to earth to teach men magic, and comments: 'Magic has an ugly name to those who have seen black magic at work among primitive people. Others think that it is completely bogus and no such powers exist. But magic is simply the use of powers of the mind that are not yet understood by science.' And by way of illustration, he cites his own ability to locate volcanic dykes on Lundy while blindfolded.

In the last chapter of *Witches* he writes:

> Magic was the great object to be obtained through the witch ritual, and their way to obtain it was by the simple expedient of working up mass excitement. The stone rings on our hills and the wild dances of the witches were all designed for this great purpose. All over the ancient

world it was the same. The magic power was generated, or so it was thought, by these dances, and it was kept in and directed to its object by the stone circles, which were put there so that the power should not drift away and be lost in the countryside.

In short, Lethbridge became convinced that the stone circles that can be found all over the British Isles were some kind of storage battery for this power. His experiments with pendulums had convinced him that a stone could hold an impression made on it three thousand years ago by the anger of the man who used it in his sling. So why should it not be used as a storage battery for some kind of 'mind power'?

Lethbridge's view of magic is close to that of two of the most important representatives of the modern magical tradition: Eliphaz Levi and Aleister Crowley. Both believed that 'magic' is simply an unexplored power of the mind, and that the purpose of ritual magic is to direct the will, to focus the 'true will'. In his everyday life, man scarcely makes use of his will; he seldom wants anything sufficiently long or sufficiently intensely to summon his 'true will'. But when a man wants something deeply, and believes he can achieve it, he directs all his will towards it; this is the basic act of summoning 'magical' powers. Levi wrote: 'Would you reign over yourselves and others? Learn to will. . .' And, like most magicians, Levi believed that there is some form of intangible 'ether' that carries the impulses of the will in the way that the 'luminiferous ether' carries electromagnetic vibrations. (It is difficult to see how the poltergeist can be explained without some such assumption.) Levi called this ether 'the Astral Light', and explains that it is a plastic medium upon which thoughts and images can be imprinted. (This is why the training of the imagination is so important in ritual magic.) Theosophical tradition speaks of an 'akashic ether' which serves the same function, and asserts that everything that has ever happened is imprinted on the 'akashic records', some form of cosmic memory. The astral light and akashic ether are obviously related to Lethbridge's 'fields' that can record strong emotions, and play them back in the form of ghosts and ghouls. Lethbridge took no interest in occult tradition, and deliberately avoided reading books on parapsychology, so he was unaware that he had discovered for himself some of the basic principles and traditions of the Hermetic Art.

What is perhaps more surprising is that he seems to have been unaware of Robert Graves's theories of the moon cult, outlined in *The White Goddess*. Graves had been pondering a series of riddles in a medieval Welsh poem, and concluded that the answers were connected with a secret Druidic alphabet—an alphabet whose letters were the names of trees. It also served as a sacred calendar describing positions of the sun. This calendar, Graves believed, had been in use since the New Stone Age, from Palestine to Ireland. Further research into the Druidic religion led him to the conclusion that the moon goddess is central to a whole range of pre-Christian cultures and mythologies; that it is, in fact, the fundamental Ur-religion of the whole world. The moon goddess was the goddess of poetry and magic and the irrational; and she was gradually supplanted by the sun god, the god of light and rationality. As the mystical Druidic alphabet gave way to the commercial Phoenician alphabet, the age of magic gave way to the age of science, with its emphasis on the physical world and 'daylight' knowledge.

But the white moon goddess stands for a different kind of knowledge, a knowledge as real and logical in its way as our intellectual rationalism. Science is based on man's view of himself as a curiously limited creature, trapped in a purely physical universe; 'Lunar knowledge' recognises that the universe of mind intersects the physical universe at right angles, and stretches into a different dimension. Lunar knowledge is concerned with what we would now call magic or the 'supernatural'. Primitive people make no such distinction; for them, such things are as natural as harvest or childbirth—or as mysterious. Lethbridge's study of the mother goddess, and his recognition of the power of the pendulum led him to the same conclusion.

After *Witches*, he wrote no more about the 'old religion'. But he continued to meditate on the problems it had raised, particularly in the storage of 'mind power'. These reflections were to lead him to some of his most bizarre and original conclusions.

3

The Path of the Dragon

———————◆———————

Lethbridge was always a loner. The 'occult' books, starting with *Ghost and Ghoul*, received scant attention from reviewers, and sales were modest. Working away quietly at Branscombe, he had no reason to suppose that the world was becoming more receptive to the ideas that excited him so much. It is a pity he paid so little attention to the weekly reviews and current literary fashions; he might have realised that he was less of an 'outsider' than he supposed.

By the late 1950s, Gerald Gardner's *Witchcraft Today* had achieved a *succes de scandale* and led to the formation of dozens of witch covens; but it reached only those who were already predisposed to an interest in the subject. Then, in 1960, there appeared in Paris the first book on 'magic' to reach a mass audience: *Le Matin des Magiciens*, by Louis Pauwels and Jacques Bergier. The authors were an oddly assorted pair: Pauwels, a journalist who had edited a hostile book on Gurdjieff, denouncing him as a charlatan, and Bergier, a physicist, a student of Kabbalism, and a practising alchemist. Almost single handed, these two inaugurated the modern 'occult revival'.

The Dawn of Magic became a best-seller largely because of its startling suggestion that Hitler was a psychic, possibly a practising 'occultist', and that the Nazis were basically a magical movement. But this was only a small part of the astonishing material that the authors gathered together. The basic thesis of the book is that science is too narrow-minded, and that 'there are more things in heaven and earth . . .' They discuss UFOs, alchemy, astrology, the world-ice theory, the Great Pyramid, Atlantis, black magic, mediumship, telepathy and the ideas of Charles Fort. The book is full of strange odds and ends of information and curious anecdotes; for example, it tells of a German engineer who discovered in a Baghdad museum electric batteries manufactured ten centuries before Volta. It speaks of the mysterious markings on the desert plain of Nazca, in Peru: gigantic drawings of flowers and spiders, tremendous intersecting patterns of lines, some of them miles long, and all made by moving small stones on the surface of the desert—and, the authors point out, all of them invisible *except from the air*. They discuss the mystery of the Piri Reis maps. Admiral Piri (Reis means admiral) was a Turkish pirate of Greek nationality who was beheaded in AD 1554. Some of his maps found in Istanbul in 1929 seemed to indicate a knowledge of trigonometry and geography far beyond that of the sixteenth century. They show Antarctica— which was not discovered until 1818—and, moreover, seem to show it *before* it was covered with ice. Another map of the same period shows a land bridge across the Bering Strait, between Siberia and Alaska, a bridge that geologists believe existed many thousands of years ago. The inference seems to be that Piri's maps were based on far older maps that were made from space craft or aeroplanes by alien visitors to our planet. The authors mention legends of tribes being transported to the north by great metallic birds.

Critics pointed out that the book is full of inaccuracies. Typical of its misinformation is the statement that Piri Reis was a nineteenth-century naval officer who presented his famous maps to the Library of Congress. Still, in spite of its faults, the sheer range of its conjecture is exciting. There are few subsequent works of 'occult' speculation that are not in some way indebted to it.

In suggesting that the gods of ancient man were beings from outer space, Pauwels and Bergier were almost—but not quite—the first to give a new twist to the curious saga of the flying saucers. This saga had begun on June 24, 1947, when a businessman named Kenneth Arnold, piloting his private plane near Mount Rainier, in Washington State, saw nine shining discs travelling against the background of the mountain. He estimated their speed as being about a thousand miles an hour. The incident was widely publicised in *Fate* magazine, and during the next few years there were thousands of sightings of flying saucers—now called Unidentified Flying Objects or UFOs—from all over the world. One investigator, Dr George Hunt Williamson, was convinced that the space men were contacting him through automatic writing; in his book *The Secret Places of the Lion*, published in 1958, he explains that visitors from space arrived on our earth as long ago as eighteen million years, and that they have since been devoting themselves to the evolution of mankind. The Pyramid of Cheops was one of their creations; it was built 24,000 years ago (and not around 2500 BC, as historians believe), and a space ship is concealed in its foundations. Most of Williamson's book is taken up with Biblical exegesis, which may explain its lack of impact on first publication. It was Pauwels and Bergier who first captured the public imagination with speculations about visitors from remote galaxies.

In 1968, Stanley Kubrick's film *2001: A Space Odyssey* transformed the idea into a part of the intellectual mythology of the twentieth century. Criticised at first as a monument of obscurity and dreariness (angry customers wrote to Kubrick asking for their money back), it quickly became a cult among the young, who may have been attracted by its 'psychedelic' visual effects. The film was scripted by Arthur C. Clarke, and it popularised the notion that 'visitors from space' had played an active part in man's evolution. There seems to be no obvious and agreed explanation for man's sudden appearance on the evolutionary stage at the beginning of the Pleistocene era, some three million years ago. In Clarke's version of the myth, unseen aliens place a crystal monolith on earth near the cave dwellings of primitive ape men; it probes their minds and stimulates their intelligence, enabling them to discover the use of tools and weapons.

Now at this time, Lethbridge was also meditating on the problem of human evolution, and explaining his objections to the Darwinian version in *The Monkey's Tail* (his last book to be published in his lifetime). When this was completed, he turned his thoughts to the problem of flying saucers, and whether our planet might have been visited by aliens in the remote past. Because of his illness, the new book—*Legend of the Sons of God*—progressed slowly, and was not completed until 1971. Lethbridge felt that it contained some of his most important and exciting ideas. And then, while the book was still in typescript, he had the devastating experience of realising that he had been anticipated. Someone sent him Erich von Däniken's *Chariots of the Gods?*—a book that had first appeared in Germany in 1967 under the title *Memories of the Future*, and had since become an international best-seller. Lethbridge was at first tempted to destroy his own manuscript. Then he read Däniken and decided that this sacrifice was unnecessary. 'I saw that there were points of difference and that this was an interesting example of the often observed phenomenon of a particular idea occurring to people in different parts of the world at the same time.'

Lethbridge was typically—but unnecessarily—charitable. Däniken's book is an expansion of the ideas already put forward by Pauwels and Bergier (although neither are acknowledged in the text). Däniken has added a great deal of speculation, a mass of unassimilated facts, and some downright inventions. He takes from George Hunt Williamson the idea that the pyramids were built by space men—on the grounds that they are too massive to have been built by human beings; but he somehow manages to multiply their weight by five. He explains that the engineering problems would have been beyond men who knew nothing about the use of rope—although there are rope-making scenes on the walls of Egyptian tombs dating long before the building of the great pyramid. He suggests that the Nazca lines are giant runways, without pausing to reflect that the most powerful modern aircraft does not need a runway several miles long. (And if modern reports of UFOs are anything to go by, they land vertically, as our own space craft do.)

At times, his information seems to be wilfully distorted. Chapter Five of *Chariots of the Gods?* begins with an account of the Assyrian *Epic of Gilgamesh*—'a sensational find [that] was made in the hill of Kuyundjik around the turn of the century.' (In fact, the *Epic* was discovered by Hormuzd Rassam, an assistant of the great archaeologist Layard, in 1853, and further missing portions were unearthed twenty years later.) The aim of Däniken's re-telling is to demonstrate that the ancient races of Mesopotamia knew about space ships; so he describes how the sun god seized the hero Enkidu in his claws and bore him upward with such velocity that his body felt as heavy as lead—which, as Däniken rightly observes, seems to show an astonishing knowledge of the effect of acceleration. A visit to the tower of the goddess Ishtar (Innanis) is described, implying that it is a space vehicle, and then 'the first eye-witness account of a space trip' in which Enkidu flies for four hours in the brazen talons of an eagle and describes the earth as seen from the air.

Anyone who takes the trouble to check the Gilgamesh *Epic* will discover that all these episodes appear to have been imagined by Däniken; nothing remotely resembling them is to be found in it. The sun god (Shamash) does not seize Enkidu in his talons; there is no visit to the tower of the goddess Ishtar (she makes only one appearance in the *Epic* as the attempted seductress of Gilgamesh); there is no four-hour space trip in the claws of an eagle.

Däniken also tells us that 'the door spoke like a living person', and that we can unhesitatingly identify this with a loudspeaker; he goes on to say that Gilgamesh asks whether Enkidu has been smitten by the poisonous breath of a heavenly beast (i.e. has breathed in the fumes of a space ship), and asks how Gilgamesh could possibly know that a 'heavenly beast' could cause fatal and incurable disease. The answer is that he couldn't, for he does not ask the question; neither does the loudspeaker doorway make any kind of appearance in *Gilgamesh*.

Däniken's books provide, to put it kindly, plenty of examples of intellectual carelessness combined with wishful thinking and a casual attitude towards logic. In *Gold of the Gods*, he offers a photograph of a skeleton carved out of stone and wants to know: 'Were there anatomists who dissected bodies for the prehistoric sculptor? As we know, Wilhelm Conrad Röntgen did not discover the new kind of rays he called X-rays until 1895!' It never seems to have occurred to him that every graveyard must have been full of skeletons.

Perhaps the most irritating thing about Däniken's books is their hectoring, table-thumping style. He spends a great deal of time abusing the experts and railing at imaginary objectors. Whole pages seem to consist entirely of 'unanswerable' questions. 'Why are the oldest libraries in the world secret libraries? What are people really afraid of? Are they worried that the truth, protected and concealed for thousands of years, will finally come to light?' The answer to which is that the oldest libraries in the world are not secret.

Altogether, it seems a pity that the theory of 'ancient space men' should have become identified with Däniken's name. He is by far its least plausible advocate.

Lethbridge's work differs from Däniken's in one basic respect: it is based on the down-to-earth research of a practising archaeologist, and when he is merely presenting imaginative speculation, he says so frankly.

The starting point of *Legend of the Sons of God* is the passage about giants in the Book of Genesis: 'There were giants in the earth in those days . . .' And this is followed by a statement that has intrigued so many students of the Bible, declaring that when the sons of God 'came unto the daughters of men, and they bare children to them, the same became mighty men which were of old, men of renown'—in short, heroes. Of course, the ancient Greeks conceived their gods in human terms, and saw nothing incongruous in the idea of a god having an affair with a mortal. Clearly, it never struck them that a god would find a human being as unattractive as an intelligent man would find a female ape. But the Biblical angels seem altogether less anthropomorphic, and it is correspondingly more difficult to imagine them as rakish seducers.

Lethbridge always approached legends in the spirit of *The Golden Bough*: that is, with the belief that they may contain memories of things that actually happened, and that if the pattern is scrutinised closely enough, it is possible to glimpse this kernel of reality.[1]

Lethbridge was also intrigued by the legend of the 'war in heaven' in which Michael and his angels fought against the 'dragon'. Although he does not say so, it is probably safe to assume that Lethbridge was originally interested by the mention of the giants and the dragon, wondering if there was any connection between these and the giants and dragons of the great chalk carvings. In this case, the war might symbolise the clash between the old religion and the new. In the event, he was to come to a totally different conclusion.

Typically, Lethbridge begins his investigation with Stonehenge, the giant circle of megaliths on Salisbury Plain. The great uprights of Stonehenge—the sarsens—weight fifty tons each, and are more than thirteen feet high. Thirty of these, surmounted by massive lintels, were originally arranged in a thousand-foot circle. Inside this there was another circle consisting of sixty 'bluestones', each weighing about five tons; and inside these, a horseshoe, also of bluestones. Between these was another horseshoe of five vast 'trilithons'.

Most people are aware that, as an engineering feat, Stonehenge compares with the Great Pyramid. Yet it requires an effort of imagination to grasp the sheer magnitude of the conception, and the effort of willpower it represents. Even today, it would tax the ingenuity of a construction engineer to transport the fifty-ton sarsens. The builders of the outer circle had to rely on manpower, ropes and wooden rollers. The megaliths were cut from outcrops of rock on the Marlborough Downs, twenty-four miles from Stonehenge. Then the stones were dragged—on rollers or sleds—by a workforce of about fifteen hundred men. Each stone must have taken more than two months to transport. Since these men were farmers, who would not be able to spare more than a few months each year for these immense labours, it probably took most of two generations—forty or fifty years—to move all sixty stones. But even when they were finally on the site, the labour had only just started. Sarsen is so hard that it is impervious to most modern steels. The great stones had to be shaped and smoothed by being pounded with other stones. It would have taken a dozen masons, pounding away steadily through the daylight hours, three months to shape each stone. Then came the dangerous task of erecting them into position. The uprights would be tilted into holes that had been dug for them, and slowly levered into the vertical position with the aid of solid platforms of treetrunks. The lintels were then raised inch by inch on ramps, and slid over onto the uprights, held securely in place by mortice and tenon joints, a stone nipple on the top of the uprights fitting into a hole in the lintel.

The labour of transporting the five-ton bluestones—sixty in the outer circle, nineteen in the horseshoe—must have been even greater; the nearest quarry from which they could have been cut is 135 miles away; again it must have taken hundreds of men and decades in time.

In his *History*, Geoffrey of Monmouth states that Stonehenge was built by a certain King Ambrosius in the fifth century AD, as a memorial to earls and princes who were treacherously slain by the Saxons. According to Geoffrey, the wizard Merlin—the same one who appears in the King Arthur legends—told the king of a stone circle known as the Giant's Dance, near 'Killaraus', in Ireland; these stones, said Merlin, originally came from Africa. An expedition fought the Irish and brought back the Giant's Dance to Salisbury Plain with the aid of Merlin's magic.

A few centuries later, the Jacobean chronicler John Aubrey expressed the opinion that Stonehenge was built by the Druids, which places its date around 500 BC—a thousand years earlier than Merlin. By the mid-twentieth century, more accurate historical—and scientific—techniques had suggested a new set of dates which came to be generally accepted by scholars. The original great ditch that surrounds Stonehenge was constructed around 1900 BC by Neolithic farmers. A century later came the invaders we call the Beaker people; they brought the Bronze Age to England and also constructed the double bluestone circle (no trace of which now remains above ground), and the avenue leading to the monument. Finally, around 1500 BC, the merchant aristocracy we call the Wessex people erected the great ring of sarsens and the inner horseshoe. In fact, new methods of radiocarbon dating have since shown most of this to be incorrect—but this is a story that can be left until later in the chapter.

Most books on Stonehenge state dogmatically that the bluestones were brought from the Prescelly mountains of North Pembrokeshire, in Wales; some writers believe they were already part of a sacred circle. Transporting them would have been a tremendous task. The favourite modern theory is that they were floated down the Bristol Channel on rafts, then brought to Salisbury Plain by means of rivers, dragging them across intervening tracts of land on sledges. (Another theory, that they were carried close to their present site by glaciers, is now generally rejected.)

Lethbridge was inclined to wonder if there was any foundation of truth in Geoffrey of Monmouth's story about 'Killaraus' in Ireland. It is true that the Prescelly mountains are the nearest site from which the bluestones could have been obtained, but there is no actual proof that they came from there. On the other hand, Killaraus can be translated 'the church on the River Ary', and there *is* a River Ary in Ireland; the town of Tipperary stands on it. And not far to the west of Tipperary there is an area of diorite, the stone of the bluestones. The River Ary joins a larger river, the Suir, which in turn flows into the sea at Waterford; so the stones *could* have been transported from Ireland as easily as from Wales.

Lethbridge decided to check his theory with the pendulum. He borrowed some fragments of the Stonehenge bluestones from an archaeologist friend; the pendulum gave a date of 1870 BC.

Next, he conducted an experiment in map-dowsing. This is certainly one of the most controversial aspects of divining, and one that provides most ammunition for sceptics. Yet, for some reason, it works. (Doctor C. E. M. Joad, himself something of a sceptic, once described on a BBC Brains Trust Programme how he had seen a map–dowser tested; he was given a map on which there were no rivers or ponds marked; with the aid of the pendulum, he traced them all accurately.) Lethbridge himself had no difficulty coming to terms with it; a map is an abstraction, and he had discovered that the pendulum responds to abstractions as easily as to physical objects. He now used a large map of the British Isles, on which he placed a chip of bluestone (to 'tune in'), and held the pendulum over Stonehenge. It proceeded to gyrate. He tried it over the Prescelly mountains. There was no reaction. But when he tried the pendulum over the beds of diorite near Tipperary, there was a strong and unmistakable reaction. He concluded that Geoffrey of Monmouth had probably been correct; the original Giant's Dance was near Tipperary. The pendulum even gave a precise age for the setting up of the Irish stone circle—2650 BC.

In fact, Lethbridge's theory provides a simpler explanation of how the bluestones were transported. One of the main arguments against the Prescelly theory is that the stones would have to sail on the open sea, which would have been dangerous. (Rafts are difficult to navigate—particularly when carrying a five-ton load.) But Lethbridge points out that an extremely heavy type of anchor, known as a kedge, is easily carried slung *between* two ships, so that the sea bears most of its weight. The bluestones could have been taken by sea all the way to the south coast of England—near present-day Christchurch—then up the River Avon to within three miles of Stonehenge with a minimum of effort. (His guess about how the lintels were placed on the sarsens is equally logical; the snow on Salisbury Plain is deep in the winter, and the lintels could have been dragged up long ramps of snow.)

Which brings us to the question: *why* were the stones erected? Not just Stonehenge, but many other monuments in Western Europe: in Sweden, Spain, Portugal, Malta, France, Italy, Ireland and the Hebrides. France alone has no less than 6,000 such monuments, including the immense avenues of standing stones at Carnac, in Brittany—a thousand of them set up in lines amounting to four miles. Cornwall is full of stone circles, including one—Boscawen-Un—which is probably the oldest in Britain; it also has hundreds of solitary monoliths. There has always been a vague assumption that they are pagan religious sites (with the result that the villagers of Avebury have systematically destroyed one of the greatest ancient monuments in Europe over the centuries). But, apart from that vague guess, they have always remained a mystery.

In 1934, a forty-year-old Scots engineer named Alexander Thom anchored his sailing boat in Loch Roag, near Callanish, in the Outer Hebrides. He had always been vaguely interested in the great stone circle—a kind of miniature Stonehenge—that stands on a hilltop there. Looking along the avenue of menhirs, he realised that it was pointing at the pole star—and therefore ran north–south. But in megalithic times, the pole star was not in its present position; so the builders of Callanish must have aligned the stones without its help. 'It struck me,' said Thom, 'that these boys were engineers, like me.' And as he examined megalithic sites all over the British Isles and Europe, he became increasingly certain that they had been constructed with pains-taking accuracy by men who knew all about geometry and engineer-ing. The key to the construction was a measure that Thom discovered by comparing hundreds of measurements: the megalithic yard, 2·72 feet. It seemed to have been in use from Scotland to Spain. But why were the stones erected? Thom reached the conclusion that they had been vast calculating machines, whose chief purpose was to predict eclipses of the moon. There were so many, says Thom, because obsolete 'observatories' were always being replaced with new ones. On the question of why ancient man had erected these vast seasonal calendars, Thom had little to say; he seemed to feel that they were merely huge clocks. Yet his theory remained startling enough, for it implied that the men of nearly four thousand years ago had a civilisa-tion sufficiently complex to require a standard unit all over Europe. (The implications are even more startling since carbon dating has pushed back the dates by about a thousand years.) Professor Gerald Hawkins was later to popularise Thom's ideas in his best-selling *Stonehenge Decoded*.

Now Lethbridge produced an even stranger hypothesis. Since most of the megaliths are not visible from the sea—where they might serve as landmarks for sailors—could they have been intended to be visible *from the air*—to serve as guides to some kind of aircraft? Which would seem to suppose that our earth was visited in prehistoric times by men in flying machines. Unlike Däniken, Lethbridge is not convinced that the answer is yes; he subtitled the book *A Fantasy?* Yet he had always been struck by the similarity of ancient objects from Europe and America. Easter Islanders believe that certain planets are inhabited and that there are people living on the moon. Our space probes have proved that this is unlikely—but then, primitive people would simply know that the visiting aliens came from 'up there'. The ancient inhabitants of Easter Island certainly seem to have known the difference between the planets and the stars, and that the sun is the centre of the solar system. (They say: 'All the planets worship the sun.') They also believe that an invisible race of people live among us. As to the mysterious statues of Easter Island—whose erection is as much a mystery as Stonehenge—Lethbridge finds the most interesting tradition that the statues were transported from far away and set up in their present position by a king who could command magical power —'mana'.

If Lethbridge had lived another five years, he would have found exciting confirmation of his ideas in the researches of Robert Temple, an Oriental scholar who was intrigued by the astronomical knowledge of an African tribe called the Dogon. Modern astronomers know that the dog star Sirius, the brightest star in the sky, is actually a double star; it has an invisible companion, known as Sirius B, which is a white dwarf, a star in which the atoms have collapsed in on themselves, giving it enormous density. The Dogon not only have a tradition that says that all creation originated in Sirius B (which they call the Digitaria star); they also know that it is 'the smallest and heaviest of all stars', that it rotates on its axis, has an elliptical orbit, and revolves around Sirius A every fifty years. Temple rightly feels that such accuracy of information is incredible for a primitive tribe. In *The Sirius Mystery*, he argues skilfully that their knowledge probably came from the ancient Egyptians. An Egyptian treatise attributed to Hermes Trismegistos—the legendary founder of magic—asserts that Hermes landed on earth to teach men the arts of civilisation, then returned to his home in the stars.

Temple also has an interesting observation about Stonehenge. He notes that, like the Rollright stones of Oxfordshire, it had sixty stones in its outer circle.[2] Temple cites evidence to support the view that this is related to the sixty-year cycle in the astronomy of the Dogon, the Hindus and the Chaldeans, the founders of astronomy. The cycle is based on the fact that Jupiter and Saturn—the father planets—came into close alignment once every sixty years. The Hindu sixty-year cycle is known as Brihaspati, the Hindu name for Jupiter. We may recollect Lethbridge's belief that the religion of the great mother originated in India.

But Lethbridge was not thinking of Stonehenge merely as some kind of astronomical calculator, although he was aware of the theories of Professor Thom and Gerald Hawkins. What intrigued him was the power in the stones—the force to which a pendulum or dowsing rod will respond. Why was Stonehenge originally called the Giants' Dance? Why are legends of dancing associated so persistently with stone circles? (One of the most frequent is that the megaliths were men and women who were changed to stone as a punishment for dancing on the Sabbath.) We have seen that in the final pages of *Witches* he suggests that stone circles were 'accumulators' that could be charged—like batteries—by the activity of dancing. And in *Legend of the Sons of God* he suggests that this activity was not simply connected with religious ritual, but was intended to enable a space craft to home-in on the stones. He calls the energy 'bio-electricity'.

As to the 'war in heaven', Lethbridge advances his theory—which he properly admits to be little more than a fantasy—in the ninth chapter of the book. Why are the moon and Mars so heavily cratered? It suggests either a level of volcanic activity far beyond that of earth, or millions of years of bombardment by meteors. Of course, we know that earth's atmosphere has protected it from meteors, most of which burn up before they reach the surface. Even so, some of the craters on Mars and the moon are so vast that meteors of that size would certainly have reached the surface of the earth. Is it not possible, he asks, that the moon and Mars suffered a real bombardment with atomic weapons? He goes on to suggest that the war took place between the inhabitants of Venus and Mars, perhaps for the mineral resources of the earth. The Martians had bases on the moon.

Lethbridge evolves his theory to explain the origin of the alien visitors. Elsewhere in the book, he makes the equally plausible suggestion that the aliens came from 'another dimension'. In fact, if there is anything in Temple's Sirius theory, this suggestion is rather more plausible than the Venus-Mars theory. Distances in space are so vast—it takes light almost nine years to reach us from Sirius—that voyagers would need some less pedestrian method than travel in our own space-time continuum.

But Lethbridge is less concerned with these cosmic speculations than with more down-to-earth problems. The notion that the megaliths could be giant accumulators had come to him when he and Mina visited the prehistoric stone circle known as the Merry Maidens, a few miles west of Penzance, in Cornwall. It consists of nineteen upright stones, mostly about four feet high. The legend asserts that they were maids who were turned to stone for dancing on the Sabbath; in a nearby field are two tall stones known as the Pipers. Lethbridge took his pendulum, set it at thirty inches (the length for age), and allowed it to swing. He stood with the other hand resting on one of the stones. After a few moments, the hand on the stone began to tingle, as if a mild electric current were flowing through it, and the pendulum began to swing so strongly that it became almost parallel with the ground. The stone felt as if was moving. He counted precisely 451 gyrations before it stopped and returned to its normal swing. Allowing ten years for each turn, this gave the date of the circle as 2540 BC. Mina tried it the next day and got the same result. He also tried his pendulum on the Pipers; they gave a date of 2610 BC, which makes them more than a century older than the maidens. In this case, it was a perfectly normal response without the tingling and violent gyrations.

At this point I should speak of my own experience of the Merry Maidens, which are a ninety-minute drive from where I live. At Easter, 1975, a friend—Gaston St Pierre—suggested that I ought to test the stones for myself. I agreed to go, but without much expectation. When investigating the powers of Robert Leftwich, I had tried to use both the pendulum and the divining rod, and obtained no result with either. (My wife, on the other hand, obtained immediate results with both and proved to be a natural dowser.) We drove down on a windy, rather dull day; the entrance to the field was muddy and the grass waterlogged.

Gaston produced two dowsing rods, and handed one to me. It was made of two thin strips of whalebone from an old corset bound together at one end with cotton. When I took hold of the two ends between my thumbs and forefingers, he explained I was holding it wrongly. The ends have to be bent outwards at an angle of about ninety degrees, so the rod is in a state of tension, like a spring.

I now walked between two stones on the west side of the circle; the rod suddenly jumped upwards. Suspecting that I had caused this myself, I readjusted it, and walked back; again, the rod twisted upwards. Gaston said: 'Ah, you are an upper.' 'What's that?' 'For some people it points up, for others, down. I am a downer.'

Subsequent experiments have led me to wonder if it is as simple as that. If I walk along our kitchen holding the rod, it dips over a spot where I know there is an underground water pipe. But near the standing stones, it invariably twists upwards. (Many dowsers find that the rod twists upwards when held above the solar plexus, and downwards when held below it.) The next time I visited the Merry Maidens, I was accompanied by the writer David Cornwell (John Le Carré) who lives nearby. Like me, he was expecting that it wouldn't work. ('These things never do for me.') In fact, he proved to be a natural dowser, the rod twisting upward so strongly that it almost turned itself inside out. But although he seemed to be an 'upper' for most of the time, there were places near the circle where his rod dipped downward. More recently, I took the psychic Matthew Manning to the Merry Maidens. As he walked towards them from the stone stile at the western edge of the field, the rod rose and fell as regularly as a metronome every four paces.

At first I suspected that I was causing the rod to twist upwards by unconsciously changing the pressure—this is easy to do. Two simple experiments convinced me this was not so. Walking up to the stones, I tried to make it move downwards instead; it refused. Again, I tried a different way of holding the whalebone strips, twisting the ends inward, so that all the natural tension of the rod points downward, at an angle of a few degrees from the horizontal. Approaching the stones, the rod still twists upward *against* its natural tension.

The force seems to be in the stones themselves, and in between them. It also extends in a line from the stone circle to an outlying stone which lies half buried in the ground. The centre of the circle also gives a powerful response. It is possible to walk across it with the eyes tightly closed, and to know when you are over the centre by the response of the rod. When I first did this, I had the impression that the response was somehow connected with my solar plexus.[3]

What is this force to which the rod is responding? It seems to be magnetic or electrical in nature. The Welsh dowser Bill Lewis is convinced that it is produced by underground streams, and that two or more of them cross underneath all major standing stones. He believes, further, that the standing stones act as some kind of amplifier for this force and that it circles the stone in a spiral, with two 'coils' hidden underground and five above. In his book *Earth Magic,* Francis Hitching has described how two physicists from London University —Professor John Taylor and Dr Eduardo Balinovski—decided to check the theory with their electrical measuring instruments. They took a gaussmeter—which measures magnetic fields—to a twelve-foot megalith near Crickhowell, in South Wales. As soon as the probe was pointed at the stone, the needle on the meter swung across the dial. In a later experiment, the two physicists constructed a kind of wooden lift-pulley that would raise the gaussmeter up and down the stone; as it moved up, the needle again revealed that the magnetic field of the stone had different strength at different points. Bill Lewis made chalk marks to indicate where he felt the spiral to be, and again, these areas of the stone showed a strength about double that of the rest of the stone. All this seemed to prove conclusively that, for some unknown reason, the stone had a far more powerful 'charge' than the land around it.

Lewis made another curious observation: that the direction of the spiral changes once a month—so the stone changes its polarity. He has no idea why this should be so. (But it may be worth pointing out that the astrological tradition also asserts that the heavens change their polarity once a month, as a result of which half the signs of the zodiac—Aries, Gemini, Leo, Libra, Sagittarius, Aquarius—are linked to extraversion, while the other half—Taurus, Cancer, Virgo, Scorpio, Capricorn, Pisces—are regarded as introvert.) Professor Taylor has pointed out that none of Bill Lewis's theories can be regard as *proved* scientifically.

Lethbridge was aware that there was a contradictory element in his assumption that the megaliths were set up as 'accumulators' or beacons; stone circles may look like induction coils, but what about great avenues of stones, like those at Carnac in Brittany? So he introduced an alternative assumption. He had studied similar rows of stones on Dartmoor, and made the observation that Black Tor, when projected, cuts another row at Warren House. He writes: 'It may be coincidence, but these two lines could have given you a cross bearing on rich deposits of tin . . .' He goes on:

> The two rows mentioned are not the only suggestive ones. That at Sharp Tor when produced runs very close to Avebury itself. Those at Fernworthy, Chagford and Higher White Tor hit the great monolith on the summit of Exmoor near the Chains . . . It has been hinted that Carnac might be the most important place in the whole system. If so, and if there is anything in the idea at all, one at least of the stone rows on Dartmoor

should give an approximate bearing on Carnac. Actually, three do, the double row on Headland Warren, and the single ones at Dartmeet and Butterdon.

Now if Lethbridge had spent more time reading other people's books, he might have discovered that his idea was less wildly eccentric than he supposed. Half a century earlier, on June 30, 1921, a Hereford businessman was riding his horse across the hills near Bredwardine when he was suddenly struck by a kind of revelation. The English countryside is criss-crossed by various footpaths and farm tracks. But as Alfred Watkins looked down from his hilltop, it struck him that there seemed to be another network of lines connecting up old churches, standing stones, hilltops and ancient mounds (known as tumps). In some cases, there were still remains of such 'old straight tracks'. But it seemed clear to him that such tracks had once existed, forming a network of straight lines across the landscape.

Alfred Watkins was not an 'occultist', or a member of any esoteric or magical group. He was sixty-five years old, a brewer, and a local magistrate. In his youth he had been a brewer's representative working for his father, which involved riding all over Herefordshire. He was a lover of the countryside and became an enthusiastic photographer; many of his plates of countryside scenery can still be seen in Hereford Museum. And, like most lovers of the English landscape, Watkins was fascinated by ancient sites. He was familiar with a book called *The Green Roads of England* by R. Hippesley Cox (1914), which opposed the view that hill forts (like Wandlebury) were merely local defences, thrown up wherever they happened to be needed, and argued that they were part of a highly developed system of travel ways—staging posts, as it were. Long before Alexander Thom, Cox had suggested that megalithic circles like Stonehenge were astronomical observatories, which implied that Stone-Age—or Bronze-Age— man was more sophisticated than had generally been supposed. So Watkins was not entirely unprepared for his sudden vision of a system of old straight tracks criss-crossing England.

He called them 'leys' or 'leas', borrowing the word from the archaeological writer Williams-Freeman, who had also pointed out that ancient landmarks seem to be connected by invisible tracks. Many place names end in 'ley' or 'leigh', and etymological dictionaries declare that it means an enclosed field; Watkins pointed out that there are dozens of 'ley' names to which this explanation cannot apply, and suggested that it simply meant a grassy track across the country.

Watkins attached no mystical significance to his leys. He took the straightforward view that they were simply roads. Some of them may have had a certain religious significance, in that they joined old churches—and probably old pagan sites—and others may have had some astronomical use, connected with sunrise and sunset. But most of them, Watkins thought, were simply trade routes. In a wild, heavily wooded, sparsely populated country, these routes would tend to move from hilltop to hilltop. When they descended into the valleys, their course would be marked by standing stones, crosses, man-made mounds, gaps in hedges, and so on.

And how was all this accomplished by Stone-Age man? By a simple method still used by modern surveyors. If a man wishes to mark a straight line from where he is standing to a distant hilltop, he needs only three long staves. He sticks one of them in the ground, closes one eye, and looks past the staff towards the hilltop; an assistant then places another staff in a straight line from the first. (The surveyor, of course, has to signal exactly where to place the staff.) Then the third staff is placed further along still, in such a position that it is blotted out by the second staff. The first staff is pulled out of the ground, and the whole process is repeated. The result is a perfectly straight line.

This led Watkins to an interesting explanation of such monuments as the Long Man of Wilmington, who seems to be opening a pair of vast doors—or holding a long staff in either hand. Surely the man who was entrusted with the work of constructing the leys would be of priestly rank? In which case, it would be natural to represent him in drawings at sacred sites? The same explanation could apply to the staves carried by mummers, tuttimen, even morris dancers (who often carry two short sticks in either hand). They could be the staff of office of the priest-surveyor who drew the leys.

Surprisingly, Watkin's harmless suggestion provoked violent hostility. The editor of *Antiquity* magazine declined an advertisement for *The Old Straight Track* (1925) on the ground that it was a crank work. But the book also found many friends—not cranks, but serious-minded country lovers who enjoyed searching for the remains of leys, and reporting their finds to Watkins at the Straight Track Postal Club. The qualifications for the recognition of a ley were fairly strict—it had to be acknowledged by several independent observers. Watkins died in 1935, but ley-hunting continued, although interrupted by the war.

In the late 1930s, a leading ley-hunter, Major F. C. Tyler, made an observation that puzzled his fellow enthusiasts: that leys often consist of *two* parallel tracks. This hardly seemed to make sense; why make two tracks close together when one would suffice? It seemed to suggest that Watkins could have been mistaken about the whole trade-route theory. Many ley hunters were also discouraged and disconcerted by theories about the alignments of ancient sites. In 1909, the astronomer Sir Norman Lockyer had observed that Stonehenge, Old Sarum (the ancient Salisbury) and Grovelly Castle lie at the angles of an equilateral triangle. A ley-hunter named Arthur Lawton began to note similar alignments, and he and his followers soon covered the ordnance survey map with dozens of squares, triangles and other geometric figures. Ley-hunting seemed to be getting a bit out of hand.

Yet at this time, when there was a certain confusion and disarray among the members of the Old Track Club, a dowser named Guy Underwood was rediscovering the leys by his own methods. Underwood, like Watkins, was a respected figure in a small country town—Bradford on Avon, in Wiltshire. He was a solicitor, a JP and a local councillor; he was married with one son (who was killed in the war).

Underwood had been intrigued by theories of two British dowsers, Captain Robert Boothby and Reginald Smith of the British Museum. Boothby asserted that barrows and other prehistoric sites were crossed by underground streams, and that long barrows had a stream running along their full length; Smith stated that at the centre of every prehistoric site a spot could be found from which a number of streams radiated; he called these 'blind springs'. When he retired—at the end of the war—Underwood decided to devote his days to exploring prehistoric sites with a dowsing rod. He quickly reached the conclusion that Boothby and Smith were both correct about underground streams and blind springs; his rod detected these without difficulty. He found that the rod responded 'negatively'—that is to say, the left hand seemed to take most of the 'pull'. And then, to his surprise, he found another type of force that caused a pull on the right hand. This did not seem to be water, but some magnetic force under the earth. In fact, there seemed to be two types of magnetic force, one at least twice as wide as the other. Underwood called the narrower type 'track lines';

they seemed to consist of two parallel lines of magnetic force, between one and two feet apart. He called the other, more powerful, type 'aquastats'; these consisted of *two* sets of parallel lines, like two railway tracks running parallel. Sometimes, the 'negative' water lines and the positive aquastats ran along the same course. These he found particularly significant because they seemed to explain why certain sites were chosen as holy. Because he found so many of these 'double lines' on sacred sites, he named them 'holy lines'.

Track lines, he discovered, seemed to be used by animals for their regular perambulations; moreover, all old roads seemed to be aligned on them, arguing that early man also recognised them instinctively. But such lines could not be identified with Watkins' 'old straight tracks', because neither they nor the roads aligned on them ran straight for long. The same applied to the other two types of line. They might meander like the track of a drunken man, or proceed in a series of loops or S-bends. Sometimes they formed whorls or whirlpools, and such shapes seemed to have a particular significance on sacred sites. He found that all 'lines' cross one another at regular intervals, so that a drawing of a track line or aquastat looks rather like a string of sausages.

Underwood had no doubt that he had discovered 'a principle of Nature . . . unidentified by science'.

> Its main characteristics are that it appears to be generated within the Earth, and to cause wave motion perpendicular to Earth's surface; that it has great penetrative power; that it affects the nerve cells of animals; that it forms spiral patterns; and is controlled by mathematical laws involving principally the numbers 3 and 7. Until it can be otherwise identified, I shall refer to it as the earth force . . . [It] manifests itself in lines of discontinuity, which I call geodetic lines, and which form a network on the surface of the earth.

So Underwood's geodetic force is undoubtedly related closely to Watkins' leys. He adds:

> The philosophers and priests of the old religions seem to have believed that—particularly when manifested in spiral forms—it [the earth force] was involved with . . . the generative powers of Nature; that it was part of the mechanism by which what we call Life comes into being; and to have been the 'Great arranger'—that balancing principle which keeps all Nature in equilibrium, and for which biologists still seek. Plato gave this force the name of 'Demiurge' . . .

Such assertions may sound highly speculative; yet Underwood started from scratch, without preconceptions. He began by assuming that dowsing is an electrical response, because all streams have a weak electric current.[4] Yet dowsers react only to *underground* streams, which seems to dispose of the notion that the rod responds to electricity. Underwood thought the answer lay in the negative nature of the dowser's response to water, which suggests that an underground stream somehow *interrupts* a positive force in the earth itself, 'in the same way that a wire over a candle casts a shadow on the ceiling'.

Many dowsers, he discovered, are wholly negative: that is to say, they can dowse only for water. Such men may show extreme sensitivity to water. Underwood cites the well-known French dowser Barthelemy Bleton who discovered his abilities accidentally at the age of seven because he always felt sick and faint when he sat on a certain spot. Digging at this spot revealed an underground spring powerful enough to drive a mill wheel. (Similarly, I have watched a Cornish water diviner who dowsed by interlocking the fingers of both hands; above water, his hands rose and fell with a violent pumping motion that left him perspiring and breathless.) These negative dowsers seem unable to pick up track lines or aquastats. 'Positive' dowsers, on the other hand, can pick up underground streams *and* track lines, and their response is altogether more delicate. A negative dowser would not be aware that an underground stream had a zigzag course because he would be reacting too strongly to the total field; a positive dowser could trace the course of the stream with precision.

Underwood spent the last years of his life investigating various 'sacred sites' with his divining rod; the results were published after his death in *The Pattern of the Past* (1969). He was particularly fascinated by Stonehenge, and his investigation showed that it was the centre of geodetic lines. The great outer ditch, the earliest part of Stonehenge, is defined by the enormous loop of an aquastat which forms an almost complete circle; one end of this aquastat runs northward and curls in a double loop around the Heel Stone. Underwood concluded that Stonehenge is a kind of whirlpool of geodetic lines, with dozens of minor eddies. It is hardly surprising that it should have been chosen as sacred by the Neolithic priests of the moon cult.

An examination of the White Horse of Uffington—the one that looks like a dragon—revealed that its weird outline is almost wholly defined by geodetic lines. Dragon Hill, below the horse, has two bare patches of chalk where the grass never grows; legend says that dragon's blood was spilled there. Underwood found that the two bare patches covered blind springs, 'which themselves mark the terminations of right-handed multiple spirals—a phenomenon of great sanctity and rarity'. The Cerne Abbas giant again is defined almost wholly by geodetic lines. Underwood believed that the ancient priests—who were, of course, also dowsers—traced these lines, noted their resemblance to a human figure, or a horse, as the case may be, and so decided that the site was sacred. This would explain the rather weird drawings of many of the hill figures—for example, Lethbridge's Wandlebury giants.

Underwood extended his researches to medieval churches and cathedrals, and concluded that they were also aligned on geodesics. 'With few exceptions, the naves of churches and cathedrals are aligned on a geodetic line running along the central aisle and terminating in a blind spring enclosed at the chancel step by one or more spirals.' This, of course, is hardly surprising, since we know that most old churches and cathedrals were built on pagan sites. But the precise alignment of the nave, chancel, altar and so on implies that the builders of cathedrals—traditionally, the Freemasons—also knew about the forces of the earth and continued the ancient tradition of the priests of the old religion.

Underwood made no attempt to publicise his findings; probably he anticipated derision. At the same time, he had no doubt whatever of the revolutionary importance of what he had discovered. In the last chapter of *The Pattern of the Past* he writes with uncharacteristic immodesty: 'By stating that I have written this book for posterity I risk being thought presumptuous, but because that is exactly what I have felt compelled to do, the fact must be admitted without apology.' He felt that he had discovered an unrecognised force that had been the basis of all ancient religion—Oriental as well as Western. (The spirals, he felt, explained the universality of the serpent symbol.)

> For a long time I was unwilling to believe that I was on to something, if not new, at least unwritten. But as I delved into books and papers, and as I questioned and corresponded, I was to discover that in a great many spheres of learning the effects of the Earth Force were accepted without recognition of the Force itself. Biologists, naturalists, archaeologists, historians and many other practitioners of the -ologies and -isms have

observed anomalies of growth and construction, and a world-wide code of symbols, without looking further.'

But he also felt that he had only begun to scratch the surface of the mystery. It was interesting to know that the great avenues of stone at Carnac were built on parallel underground streams. But why should that make the site sacred? How did the ancients *use* the force? 'The question must arise as to what use geodetic lines are to man. As yet I do not know enough to answer.' And, regrettably, he died before he was able to come to any decision.

Underwood several times makes the interesting observation that the patterns of great temples like Stonehenge could be comprehended only from the air. Yet he never entertained Lethbridge's wild hypothesis that perhaps they were *intended* to be seen from the air.

This same idea had occurred independently to another student of antique monuments named John Michell. In fact, Michell published the idea in a book that appeared in 1967, before Lethbridge or Underwood—or even von Däniken—had committed their speculations to print. The book received less attention than it deserved, perhaps because its title—*The Flying Saucer Vision*—made it sound as if it was merely another addition to the voluminous literature on UFOs. In fact, Michell was not primarily a 'ufologist'; he was a retiring, slightly eccentric scholar with an enthusiastic devotion to Plato, and wide knowledge of ancient historians, philosophers and mystics.

His rather curious erudition led him to discover that the ancient Chinese had their equivalents of leys, which they called 'dragon paths' or Lung Meis; lines from hilltop to hilltop that were supposed to be the routes of dragons flying between their nests. Michell also wrote of the Chinese science of *feng-shui*, 'the science of wind and water' (or geomancy) which is basically a philosophical (or religious) system concerned with the harmony between man and nature. *Feng-shui* treats nature as a living entity, and believes that man must learn to conform to it if he is to be happy. According to *feng-shui*, the surface of the earth is a 'dim mirror' of the powers of the heavens (i.e. the stars and planets of astrology). 'Wherever there is nature's breath pulsating, there will be visible on earth some elevation of the ground.'[5] It seems to differ from Watkins' theory of leys in certain basic respects—for example, *feng-shui* holds that benevolent powers usually reside in crooked, wandering lines, and that straight lines are associated with negative forces. Yet it is remarkably close to Underwood's theory of geodetic lines. Basically, as Michell points out, the ideas of the ley-hunters are a rediscovery of principles that have been recognised in China for thousands of years.

Speaking of Watkins, Michell observes: 'Whereas Watkins supposed that the leys were ancient footpaths, modern ley explorers are inclined to see them as having some meaning as lines only to be seen from above.' And he remarks that ancient religious sites, hilltops and artifical mounds (like Silbury) are linked by a system of ley lines. He also notes that there have been an unusual number of sitings of flying saucers above Cley Hill, near Warminster, where several leys intersect. Yet, at this point, Michell seems inclined to regard the leys as markings on the surface of the earth, not as lines of force running below its surface.

But in his next book, *The View Over Atlantis* (1969), Michell takes this conclusive step. 'It was as if some flow of current followed the course of these man-made alignments', he says, summarising Watkins. But, in fact, Watkins never went this far, even though, towards the end of his life, he was inclined to abandon the view that the leys were trade routes. Michell has stumbled on Underwood's discovery, the earth force. The Atlantis referred to in his title is not the legendary lost continent of Plato, but the 'ancient knowledge system' that underlies the 'old straight tracks'. Michell now boldly identifies the leys with the 'dragon paths' of China, and quotes a nineteenth-century traveller, W. E. Geil, who was informed: 'The positions of [the Great Mound of Ching] was fixed by men of magic as being auspicious. The dragon pulse, meaning the magnetic currents with which the dragon is supposed to be connected, is good. The mountain south is a dragon at rest. The river north is a dragon in motion.'

This leads Michell to one of his most exciting ideas. He points out that the whole face of China is heavily 'landscaped' in accordance with the laws of *feng-shui*, even to the extent of building an artificial hill on which to place a city. He elsewhere[6] quotes Ernst Börschmann's book on Chinese landscape: 'Certain summits of the neighbouring mountains, often the main summit, are crowned with pagodas, small temples or pavilions to harmonise the magic forces of heaven and earth. The thought is akin, for instance, to our conception of the outflow of a magnetic force from a pointed conductor. And the Chinese geomancer also regards the forms of nature as a magnetic field.' This knowledge of the harmony of heaven and earth, Michell believes, existed all over the ancient world, and was the foundation of the religion of the earth mother and the sky god. Man recognised that the harmony of society depended on the harmony of the earth force. And so in ancient China, ancient Greece, ancient Britain and Gaul, men built their temples where the forces of the earth were most powerful. Legends of the 'Golden Age' were not an invention; there *was* once a kind of golden age on earth. It was not the kind of golden age depicted by the creators of Utopias, with their various political systems, but a time when men lived in harmony with the forces of the earth and made use of these forces to supply their simple needs. Nowadays this concept of harmony has vanished; men tear up the earth and leave it scarred and disfigured with slag heaps, or build ugly skyscraper blocks. Consequently, man lives in an increasingly claustrophobic civilisation, endlessly beset with problems of poverty and violence.

Michell's observations on Chinese geomancy are confirmed by the scientist and historian Joseph Needham in a section on geomancy in his monumental *Science and Civilisation in China*.[7] *Feng-shui* is defined as 'the art of adopting the residences of the living and the dead so as to cooperate and harmonise with the local currents of the cosmic breath'. Needham adds that the force and nature of the invisible currents 'would be from hour to hour modified by the positions of the heavenly bodies', so that these also had to be taken into account. The earth force consisted of two currents, Yin and Yang, the negative and the positive. (These obviously correspond to Underwood's negative and positive lines.)

There is only one point at which the Chinese idea seems to conflict with those of the ley hunters. Leys are straight lines. But Needham says of the Chinese: 'There was in general a strong preference for tortuous and winding roads, walls and structures, which seemed to fit into the landscape rather than to dominate it.' Here Underwood may serve as intermediary to reconcile the two views. His track lines seldom ran for any great distance in a straight line. But lines of earth force may nevertheless run for long distances in various forms, track lines alternating with water lines and the whorl-like aquastats. Lines of earth force cannot be expected to run absolutely straight, any more than streams do; yet streams run for long distances and connect distant places. Moreover, streams may be deepened and straightened by skilful engineering, or even connected together by canals. (Perhaps the standing stones played some part in canalising the forces.) This was also part of the art of *feng-shui*.[8]

Michell writes:

> A use of *feng-shui* that became even more important with the growth of the Chinese empire was to assist the concentration of the power in the imperial capital by diverting the natural, serpentine streams of earth energy into long straight channels and directing them towards the emperor at the seat of government in Peking. These channels were the imperial dragon paths (*lung mei*) of China, carefully preserved even into the present time by the Government Board of Rites; on their course, no buildings or tombs other than those of the emperor and his family were allowed to be sited.

And he mentions a case of a Japanese student who had committed suicide and was buried on a *lung mei*; as soon as the authorities found out, the grave had to be moved.

In ancient Europe, Michell believes, man also learned to make use of the earth forces. In the Chinese science of acupuncture, pins are placed in the skin at the junction of certain lines of vital energy that criss-cross the body. The great menhirs and dolmens serve the same function on the surface of the earth. This is what Börschmann meant when he described pagodas and temples as 'pointed conductors'.

Why 'dragon lines'? The answer probably lies in Underwood's observation that the whorls of his aquastats look like coiled serpents. The dragon and the serpent symbol tend to be interchangeable. The whorls are the positive form of the earth force. This speculation seems to be supported by the prevalence of the whorl (or spiral) symbol in ancient Celtic monuments. Evan Hadingham's book *Ancient Carvings in Britain* contains dozens of illustrations of these Celtic spirals and concentric circles. Speaking of the 'crude circles, entwined spirals and meandering zigzags' carved in Lhwyd's cave in Ireland, he comments: 'The vision behind these patterns seems quite different from the vivid representational art of the European cave painters.' And to understand what is being represented in the whorls and zigzags, it is necessary only to look at Underwood's drawings of the forces he detected under Stonehenge or Dragon Hill. Radiocarbon dating revealed that the Lhwyd's cave drawings date from about 2500 BC, the period of the Neolithic farmers who raised Silbury Hill and the first circle of

Stonehenge. John Michell's *Earth Spirit* book contains an illustration showing similar enormous carvings on a rocky hillside at Routing Lynn, in Northumberland. Michell speculates that drawings showing St Michael driving his lance into the dragon symbolise the tapping of the earth force by the 'acupuncture' system of standing stones.

He also observes that many hills and mounds named after the dragon 'stand at the junction of well-marked leys, and in one case, at least, the straight line between them is of the highest precision, elaborately engineered and of obvious astronomical significance'. He is referring to the 'great ley' that runs from St Michael's Mount—the beautiful island off the coast of Cornwall—through stone circles on Bodmin Moor and Dartmoor, the 'Mump' at Burrowbridge, Glastonbury Tor and the Avebury circle, along a ridge that marks the edge of the Midland Plain, and across the east coast above Lowestoft. The two greatest abbeys of medieval England, Glastonbury and Bury St Edmunds, lie on it; so do a remarkable number of churches dedicated to St Michael (who, as we may recall, Lethbridge believed to be Lugh, the sun god).

Michell makes another interesting observation that throws a new light on the problem of the tuttimen of Hungerford (near the Vale of the White Horse). He writes: 'Watkins compared the straight track leading to the Greek cities with the leys of Britain, and found in both cases an association with Hermes, known to the Egyptians as Thoth, to the Gauls [Celts] as Theutates, the name surviving in the numerous Tot or Toot hills all over England.' This comment brings many things into focus. Hermes is the Greek god of fertility—he is responsible for making the corn grow—and is credited with inventing animal sacrifice, another basic part of the Druidic ritual. He is the god of roads, and heaps of stones were raised at crossroads in his honour. In Egypt he was Thoth, the god of learning, who later became transformed into Hermes Trismegistos, the legendary founder of magic and alchemy, to whom is attributed the most famous of magical sayings: 'As above, so below.' In Celtic mythology he is Theutates, after whom the tuttimen are named. The tuttimen carry staves; Hermes carries a *caduceus*, a staff with two serpents twined around it; the serpent is one of the basic symbols of alchemy as well as of ancient religion. The Reverend W. Stukely, one of the early writers on Avebury—a prehistoric temple even older than Stonehenge—discerned the design of a vast serpent in the landscape. Both Lethbridge and Michell have speculated on the purpose of the great Serpent Mound of Adams County, Ohio, pointing out that its shape—a writhing snake—would be visible only from the air.

What begins to emerge is a complex yet astonishingly integrated theory of 'the occult'. Lethbridge came very close to grasping the whole picture, even though he was unacquainted with the work of Underwood, Michell or even *The Dawn of Magic*. His inspiration came from dowsing. He guessed that the earth has its lines of force, and he felt that force as a tingling sensation in the palms of his hands at the Merry Maidens. He guessed the importance of alignments and worked out for himself a considerable portion of the 'great ley' that crosses Dartmoor. He even stumbled on the significance of Hermes; he quotes Caesar on a number of occasions to the effect that Mercury (Hermes) is the chief of the Celtic gods.

The earth itself is, in a certain basic respect, a living being, and its surface is permeated with magnetic forces that are influenced, like the tides, by the heavenly bodies, particularly the moon. But these forces are not purely magnetic or electrical. The most important thing about them is that they can interact with the human mind. A 'negative dowser' can be shaken by them so violently that he falls down or feels faint. Moreover, the human mind itself can affect these earth forces, somehow causing them to 'record' strong emotions—as Lethbridge realised on Ladram beach.

Ancient man understood these forces, and knew something of how to harness them. The standing stones served two purposes: to canalise the force, and to act as outlets. They could be compared to the needles placed at acupuncture points in the human body, which serve to stimulate and direct the vital energies. They also made the energy available to human beings—perhaps even (if Bill Lewis is right) acted as amplifiers. But the chief clue to their actual use comes from Standing Rock, in South Dakota, a megalith against which Sioux Indian medicine men used to press their spines to revitalise their powers of telepathy, healing and second sight. It would seem that these powers of the earth can be used by human beings to activate their psychic forces. Moreover, many of the stones and the wells standing on ley lines are reputed to have powers of healing and fertilisation. According to the thirteenth-century poet Layamon, Stonehenge was a healing centre where all kinds of people went to cure their ills; in Brittany, peasant women still embrace the standing stones to ensure fertility; the holed stone called Men-an-tol in Cornwall is still used to cure children of rickets (they have to crawl through the hole nine times). But the force can also be dangerous; as has been mentioned earlier, most dowsers believe that streams running underneath houses can cause illness—even cancer. Dowsers can be drained and exhausted by the force; Bill Lewis remarked to Francis Hitching: 'If I feel it building up in my body, I back away very quickly.' Like electricity, it must be treated with respect. And these effects are not confined to underground streams; many ley-hunters claim that leys can produce dizziness and disorientation.[9]

Lethbridge's experience on Skellig Michael seems to suggest a connection between these earth forces and poltergeists. He was standing on a spot where the earth forces were exceptionally powerful, and where they had been 'used' by human beings in religious worship. Dion Fortune, the occultist, writes: 'Whenever a place has had prayers and concentrated desires directed towards it, it forms an electrical vortex that gathers to itself a force . . . that can be felt and used by man.' Skellig Michael had been the scene of a shipwreck tragedy the previous winter, which may or may not have been connected with the 'ghoul' Lethbridge felt as he clambered down the cliff. Then the force was unleashed, perhaps triggered by his own uneasiness, knocking him on his face.

This would also seem to suggest that poltergeists in general are connected with the earth forces—earth forces that have been affected by human negativity. In fact, Lethbridge came to exactly this conclusion, mentioning the case of a poltergeist on the Isle of Mull that caused all the bells in a house to start ringing. If he is correct, then a poltergeist is a kind of active 'ghoul'. This is not as strange as it sounds. Mina felt as if someone were urging her to jump over the cliff at Ladram. Dowsers can be shaken by the presence of water. A human being can apparently become a conductor of the earth force, in its positive or negative forms. Underwood pointed out that nearly all children can dowse, which means that they are sensitive to the earth forces. When children reach adolescence, they fall victim to forces of depression and confusion, which may well trigger the negative earth force.

And surely, if the force of water—or a ley line—can cause a dowsing rod to twist, it could also, when concentrated, move far heavier objects? Lethbridge actually suggests this: 'If such power can be utilised, surely that is how Stonehenge and other monuments must have been moved and erected?' 'Mana' is the name given to this power of the earth by the Milanesians, and Lethbridge mentions the legend that the stones of Easter Island were erected by a king who used the force of mana. The suggestion will strike rationalists as preposterous; yet rationalists find it difficult to explain how monuments like Stonehenge were raised by Neolithic farmers. One menhir in Brittany, now fallen and broken, was over *sixty feet* high, while any number of standing stones in Brittany are between ten and twenty feet high; it baffles the imagination to conceive how they could have been erected.

Both Michell and Lethbridge also mention that ghosts and other supernatural occurrences seem to be associated with ley lines. Michell writes: 'Traditionally they are also paths of psychic activity, of apparitions, spirits of the dead or fairies, particularly on one day of the year.' In Ireland, leys are known as fairy tracks, and *The Earth Spirit* has a photograph of an Irish cottage whose corner has been removed because it had been built across a fairy track. It also contains a photograph of a church path at Bishop Cannings in Wiltshire (not far from Stonehenge) where a black dog is often seen to run across the road. The apparition of a black dog is associated with the Rollright stone circle in Oxfordshire—a site linked persistently with witchcraft, even in modern times; the dog was actually seen by detectives investigating the savage 'witchcraft murder' of Charles Walton in a nearby field in 1945. Lethbridge devotes several paragraphs in *Witches* and subsequent books to apparitions of dogs, both black and white, and he recognised them as a manifestation of the site itself. (We already know that Hole House—where the white dog was seen—was associated with a Celtic religious site, and that the moor above was sacred to the sun god Lugh.) He would have been fascinated by the researches of Ivan Bunn, a collector of black dog legends in the East Anglia area. Bunn noted that almost all apparitions of black dogs—and he collected over forty from the same fairly small area—were seen near water, either the sea or rivers, and on low-lying (i.e. damp) ground. 'In about fifty per cent of these accounts, the witnesses state that shortly after their encounter with the black dog a close relative has died suddenly.'[10] Another researcher, Phil Grant, noted that in the Bournemouth area, over ninety per cent of the UFO and supernatural phenomena, including black dogs and pumas, were sited on ley lines.[11]

But why black dogs—or any other kind of dog? Lethbridge's explanation is typically original. Anyone who thinks hard enough about something, he believes, can imprint the thought—or emotion—on the surrounding 'field'. This is particularly so in damp places. So supposing a young man, sitting on the banks of a stream, indulges in auto-erotic fantasies about a naked girl. Because of its intensity, the thought imprints itself on the 'naiad field' of the stream. And later, some casual visitor to the spot, thinking about nothing in particular, is astonished to see a naked girl hovering around the stream . . .

Black dogs were associated with Diana, the witch goddess, whose cult was particularly strong in country areas. It is easy to see why their image should be associated with such areas. But why as harbingers of death? Because some level of the mind *already knows* about the future; this is its method of conveying the information symbolically. Similarly, Carl Jung believed that flying saucers are a production of the subconscious mind, a 'projection' of modern man's desire for a saviour, and 'intervention from heaven'.

All this suggests that there is a close interaction between the human mind and the earth forces. When this occurs spontaneously it is called a poltergeist; when it happens deliberately, it is called magic or psychokinesis.

John Michell speculates that in ancient times, man was a nomad who moved from one religious site to another. Even today, some primitive people live like this; Charles Mountford has described a journey with Australian aborigines, travelling along the earth lines that join sacred centres, in order to re-animate their forces. Each tribe looks after its own stretch of line. They believe that each centre can bring about the fertility of a particular plant or animal. Rocks at these places show the symbol of the serpent; but the aborigines say that the power does not reside in the drawing, but in the rock itself. Michell suggests that ancient European man—perhaps 5,000 years before Christ—led a similar existence. There were no monuments at the sacred sites then, for man was directly aware of their earth forces. Then the tribes began to settle; they became farmers. They erected monuments on the sites—huge stones to facilitate the flow of energy. 'Magi' and priests became necessary. Monuments like Carnac and Stonehenge were not only 'markers' of the lines of force, but were also aligned to the stars, since the earth force varied with the heavens. People who live near the sea—as I do—keep a tide table handy. I know that there is no point in taking the coast road past Portmellon in winter because it will probably be flooded, and if a high tide combines with an inshore wind, the resulting waves may knock down sea walls and wash slates off rooftops. Primitive people who lived close to nature needed to know about earth power. Michell has pointed out that a map showing ancient dwellings is almost the reverse of a modern map. You would expect ancient man to choose sheltered valleys and forests; instead he seemed to prefer bleak hilltops and moorlands. He made dew ponds on the tops of hills by lining hollows with an insulating material so that they were colder than the surrounding land and would precipitate dew. But why bother when there must have been more convenient streams in the valley? The usual answer is: because he was afraid of enemies, and wanted a good defensive position. This hardly seems likely in a sparsely populated land; besides, as Michell points out, some of the hill forts were so vast that it would have taken an army of thousands to man them; the Dorsetshire cursus, for example, is over six miles long. Primitive man lived on hilltops because they were holy places and centres of natural power. He travelled along the ridgeways for the same reason, which is why so many dew ponds and stone circles are found on these roads that ran against the sky-line.

Primitive religious observances were an *interaction* between man and nature, between the human mind and the earth forces. You could say that their purpose was to propitiate the gods, or to keep the earth 'sweet'. If bad vibrations can pass into the earth and cause a site to be accursed, good vibrations can have the reverse effect. (It is horrifying to think what the earth's 'field' must be like after the wars and disasters of the twentieth century.) 'In this way,' says Michell in *The Old Stones of Land's End*, 'the earth, understood as a living creature, were made fertile and contented, a mood which it communicated to all living things inhabiting its body.'

When I visited the Merry Maidens, and later, the nearby Boscawen-un circle (one of the oldest in England), I found myself wondering why both contained nineteen stones—it seemed a curious number. Similarly, Hawkins found himself puzzled by the fifty-six 'Aubrey holes' in the outer ditch of Stonehenge—its oldest part. He fed astronomical data about the second millennium BC into a computer, and made the interesting discovery that an eclipse of the moon or sun occurred every nineteen years, when the winter moon rose over the Heel Stone. It was not quite every nineteen years—the exact figure was 18.61. A nineteen-year interval would have been inaccurate; the simplest way to calculate correctly would have been with two lots of nineteen years plus an eighteen. The total is fifty-six—the number of the Aubrey holes. By simply moving a stone every year from one hole to the next, the priests would have had an accurate computer of lunar eclipses. The Merry Maidens and Boscawen-un are slightly less accurate computers. In his book *Megalithic Lunar Observatories*, Alexander Thom has shown how many other stone circles could have been used in the same way.

We have no way of knowing precisely how primitive man made use of his knowledge of eclipses. Did the eclipse of the moon increase the earth forces in some way so they could be used for 'magical' purposes? We know that even now the moon affects the human mind; police forces all over the world report a rise in crime at the time of the full moon, and mental homes take care that violent patients are in strait-jackets. It is conceivable that the priest—or shaman—was somehow able to unite the forces of his own mind with those of the earth at such times, and perhaps even transmit the power straight along the leys, as a modern engineer could transmit an electric current along a cable. At all events, there seems little doubt that the ancient Celts—and their forerunners—had a reason for wanting the sources of earth force joined together.

At this point, let us pause to enquire: how much solid *evidence* is there for these extraordinary theories?

The question of what constitutes evidence is controversial; for Lethbridge, it meant what he had seen and tested for himself. As a dowser, he had no doubt that some powerful force resides in the ground at places like the Merry Maidens, or possibly in the stones themselves. Underwood, another cautious and pragmatic investigator, reached the same conclusion. I am a worse dowser than either, but I certainly entertain no doubts on this particular matter. The sites were chosen because there was 'something there'—perhaps merely blind springs, as Underwood and Bill Lewis both believe.

We know next to nothing about the ancient religion of the earth mother, except that one of its main concerns was fertility—this is still apparent in modern survivals like the Furry Dance and the hobby horse. Connect together these two known facts—that the sites were chosen for their 'power', and that the rituals held there were concerned with fertility—and you have a glimpse of a religion that regards the earth as a living being in the most literal sense.

All this, we must admit, proves only that ancient man had his own unique form of religion: not that he was visited by aliens from Sirius, or that he somehow managed to acquire a higher level of civilisation than historians admit. Here again, the question of evidence depends upon what the individual finds convincing. Robert Temple writes in *The Sirius Mystery*:

> Arthur Clarke introduced me to one interesting professor after another—each with a pet mystery all his own. Derek Price, Avalon Professor of the History of Science at Yale University, had discovered the true nature of the now famous mechanical computer of approximately 100 BC found in the Anti-Kythera shipwreck at the turn of the century and unappreciated until it was dropped on the floor in Athens, cracked open and they saw what it was. He also found traces of Babylonian mathematics in New Guinea and talked a lot about 'the Raffles shipwreck'. Then there was Dr Alan McKay, a crystallographer of Birkbeck College at the University of London, who was interested in the Phaistos Disc of Crete, in a mysterious metal alloy found in a Chinese tomb, and in the wilder stretches of the Oxus River . . .

The passage is a reminder that interest in such matters is not confined to Däniken and his followers.

Lethbridge was an archaeologist; what intrigued him was the universality of ancient culture. Irish goldwork found in Palestine, Greek and Egyptian ornaments in Bronze-Age tombs, Phoenician glazing on Saxon pottery. Early Welsh settlers in America remarked that the language of the Mandan Indians had a number of Welsh words; it seemed to lend support to a legend that the Welsh Prince Madoc had led an expedition to America about AD 1170. Then there is Geoffrey of Monmouth's assertion that the megaliths of Stonehenge originated in Africa.

Most modern archaeologists take a highly sceptical view about such matters. Jacquetta Hawkes, for example, dismisses the 'astronomical' theories of the megaliths as wholly untenable. Professors Richard Atkinson and Glyn Daniel lost no time in condemning Michael Dames's great mother theory of Silbury Hill as a fairy-tale. Yet Atkinson's book on Stonehenge—a standard work—contains a chapter entitled: 'Was there a Mycenaean Architect?' He explains that among the Wessex-period graves found at Stonehenge, small ribbed beads of blue faience were discovered. 'Careful examination leaves no doubt that these beads are of Egyptian manufacture, and their sporadic occurrence both in Crete and on the Atlantic coasts of Iberia and France suggests forcibly that they reached Britain by sea . . . Is it then too fanciful to regard this handful of trinkets . . . as the tangible relics of some unsung Odyssey?' He points out that the postern gate at Mycenae in Greece is very similar to the trilithons at Stonehenge, with mortice-and-tenon joints to hold the lintel in place. Atkinson suggests that the architect of the trilithons may have travelled from Bronze-Age Greece at the behest of some powerful British king, and speculates that the king may be buried in Silbury Hill—a guess we now know to be unfounded. The objection to the 'great king' theory is that such a man is unknown to history; surely a British Charlemagne or Alexander the Great would have left some traces behind, in legend if nothing else. Why, however, assume the existence of such a king? Because he provides an alternative hypothesis to the theory that there was more intercourse between Bronze-Age civilisations than is generally supposed. The great-king theory suggests that one man was powerful enough to send to North Africa or Greece for his architect. The alternative theory is that there was already a two-way traffic between England and the Mediterranean.

One of the most interesting parts of this story is still to come. In speaking of the modern dating of Stonehenge, I indicated that this has subsequently been corrected. What happened, in fact, was that certain historians and scientists began to have their doubts about the accuracy of radiocarbon dating. This depends on the discovery that all living creatures absorb a radioactive isotope of carbon known as C-14 from the atmosphere, and that when they die, the C-14 decays into nitrogen at a fixed rate. So provided an archaeological site has a few bones, the 'carbon clock' enables scientists to check its date within a decade or so.

The method of carbon dating depends on the assumption that the amount of C-14 in the earth's atmosphere has remained constant. In the late 1960s, scientists devised a method of checking this by examining the rings in Bristlecone pine trees—many over 4,000 years old—in California. This revealed the startling information that only fairly recent C-14 datings can be relied on at their face value—say within 500 years. Beyond that, the dating becomes increasingly inaccurate, and greater allowances must be made. And when the C-14 dating was corrected, it was revealed that the original ditch around Stonehenge was *not* built in 1900 BC, but a full thousand years earlier, in 2900. In fact, at the same time as Silbury Hill. The double bluestone circle was built some time after 2400 by the Beaker people, who thus must have arrived in England some six hundred years before anyone had supposed. The sarsen circle was constructed soon after this; an antler-pick in one of the sarsen holes has been dated around 2150 BC. This clearly rules out the possibility of a Mycenaean architect. On the other hand, the inner horseshoe, and various holes intended for bluestones (known as the X and Y holes) *were*, apparently, constructed by the Wessex people sometime between 1550 and 1450 BC, and there is no reason why a Mycenaean architect should not have supervised the task.

The implications of these discoveries are startling. To begin with, they offer strong support to Michael Dames's theory about Silbury Hill. He assumed that the priests of the Neolithic fertility cult must have had an exact knowledge of astronomy—a contradiction of the generally accepted view that the Neolithic people were simple farmers and agriculturalists. But the outer ditch and Aubrey holes of Stonehenge reveal the same astronomical knowledge as the later parts; and if they were constructed at the same time as Silbury Hill, this points to the existence of a caste of priest-astronomers in that 'primitive' time.

This is a conclusion that has been carefully examined by Dr Euan MacKie, of the Hunterian Museum at the University of Glasgow.[12] Dr MacKie is a supporter of the Thom-Hawkins theory that the megalithic circles were astronomical observatories. This leads him to conclude that 'by about the twenty-ninth century BC an élite class had appeared in Wessex . . . and had reached a stage in which they commanded considerable prestige, power and authority . . . The two sites [Silbury Hill and Stonehenge I] seem to symbolise the start of a new era in which theocratic rulers had established themselves to the extent that they were able to control men and supplies to a degree never before achieved in Britain.' This power was not achieved through wealth derived from the metal trade, for that lay 500 years in the future. 'We may conclude that somehow the astronomical and magical expertise of these wise men had given them this power . . .' In other words, in England around 3000 BC, at a time when there was supposed to be only a scattered rural community, there was actually a powerful caste of magician–priests who could organise vast numbers of people to construct immense public works, much as in Egypt at the time of the building of the pyramids. The scale of the pyramids is, of course, far greater; but then, the population of Egypt in 2500 BC was far greater than of England in 3000 BC.

Comparison with the pyramids raises another interesting point. For many centuries scholars assumed that the Great Pyramid of Cheops (Khufu) was built as a tomb; yet when Arab workmen, under the direction of the Caliph Abdullah Al Mamun, succeeded in breaking into the pyramid in AD 820, they discovered the 'King's Chamber' to be empty except for a lidless granite sarcophagus; seals indicated that the pyramid had never been entered by robbers. And instead of being riddled with passages and chambers—as everyone had expected—the structure proved to be very nearly solid. There was an ascending passage, a descending passage, and a mysterious well joining the two. But the Roman historian Proclus makes the interesting remark that the pyramid was used as an astronomical observatory before its completion. In the late nineteenth century, a British astronomer, Richard Proctor, saw that this provided the likeliest theory to explain the pyramid. In the days before telescopes, the Egyptian priests constructed a vast observatory, with its descending passage aligned on the meridian, and a pool of water at the bottom of the 'well' to act as a reflector. Proctor showed in detail how the pyramid could be used as a combination of computer and observatory—like so many other ancient monuments.

In more recent years, Professor Livio Stecchini has shown that the ancient Egyptians had calculated the size of the earth—which they knew to be a sphere—its circumference, and even the fact that it is flattened at the poles. His study of the temples of Karnak and Luxor revealed that Egyptian mathematics was 2,000 years in advance of the Greeks, who knew less than the Egyptians about the subject in the time of Plato. Advocates of the Atlantis theory have suggested that this knowledge came from the great submerged continent. Däniken would argue that it proves that ancient Egypt was visited by space men. But if MacKie is correct—and it is difficult to see how he can be faulted—the explanation is rather less bizarre: late-Neolithic man had evolved a sophisticated fertility religion in which the study of the heavens played a major part and the priests possessed a high degree of 'magical' and astronomical knowledge. The evidence suggests that their interest in the heavens was the direct outcome of their interest in the earth. Otherwise, it is difficult to explain why they took so much interest in the sky. Apart from its astronomy, their civilisation seems to have been extremely crude and practical; the only 'astronomy' needed by a farmer is a knowledge of the seasons. The Chaldeans, who are generally regarded as the founders of astronomy (and astrology) appeared on the scene much later. In his history of astronomy, *Watchers of the Skies*, Willy Ley remarks: 'Early astronomy, with written records . . . comprises approximately the period between 800 BC and the time of Pythagoras of Samos [530 BC].' And he makes the interesting observation: '[Chaldean] astronomy did not end because of a specific political event such as a war . . . It just petered out; the last tables . . . dealt with the year 10 BC, and later an astronomical table from AD 75 was found. And after that, nothing.' But then, towards 800 BC, civilisation was nearing the end of the Bronze Age; the religion of the earth mother was more than half forgotten. The astronomers of Mesopotamia and Persia studied the heavens because they were looking for omens, for methods of predicting the future. The astrology of the Babylonians and Assyrians seems to have been basically a jumble of superstitions: 'When [Mercury] approaches [Aldebaran] the king of Elam will die'; 'When Mars is dim, it is lucky, when bright, unlucky.' Chaldean astronomy petered out because it had lost its *raison d'être*: its contact with the earth, and its power to predict the fluctuations in its forces.

We can say, then, that the carbon dating of Stonehenge seems to provide a certain basis of support for Lethbridge's theory of the ancient religion, as well as for Michell's belief that Neolithic religion was more sophisticated than anyone realised. It also disposes of some of the chief objections to the Thom-Hawkins theory of the megalithic monuments: for example, why the Wessex people—whom Hawkins describes as 'great lords and international financiers'—should have troubled to build a vast computer like Stonehenge III (the sarsens). Nature worship hardly seems to fit in with an artistic merchant aristocracy. Now we know that the major part of Stonehenge was not erected by the Wessex people, but by the far more energetic and warlike Beaker people, not long after the construction of the Great Pyramid. Although the Beaker people were warriors and traders, they were also wanderers. Professor Gordon Childe comments: 'They roved from the Moroccan coasts and Sicily to the North Sea coasts, and from Portugal and Brittany to the Tisza and the Vistula.' And, like their Neolithic predecessors, they worshipped the earth mother. If we can attach any credence to the notion that the Great Pyramid was built as an observatory, then the picture that emerges is of a religion as universal as Christianity—although with many local variations—that covered most of Europe and the Mediterranean.

Such a notion raises another historical problem. It seems to suggest that the civilisation of 3000 BC had a fairly sophisticated communication system, not only by land but by sea. And this runs counter to the views held by most historians. Although we know that the Sumerians were sailing the Persian Gulf as long ago as 4000 BC, and that the Egyptians often made the 400-mile voyage to Byblos, in Lebanon, around 2600 BC, there is a generally held view that real 'seafaring' began in the Bronze Age, some time after 2000 BC. It is true that there are drawings of boats with many oars on Aegean pottery of 3000 BC, but they are believed to have been used only for voyages between islands.

In 1973, these views were challenged by an amateur historian and archaeologist, James Bailey, in a closely argued book, *The God-Kings and the Titans*. Studying at Oxford immediately after the Second World War, Bailey had become intrigued by references in various classical writings to the possibility of land on the other side of the Atlantic ocean. In the *Timaeus* and *Critias*, Plato seems to describe a great sea battle involving men from the other side of the Western ocean. Diodorus Siculus, writing about 21 BC, describes how Phoenician sailors were driven off course by strong winds, and eventually reached a fertile island far out in the Atlantic; this could have been the Azores or even one of the islands of the Caribbean.

In 1967, an essay by a retired Nigerian judge, M. D. W. Jeffreys, revived Bailey's interest in the subject; Jeffreys contended that Africans had reached the New World long before Columbus. Bailey undertook a detailed study of the evidence of South American arahaeology for contact between the Old World and the New in pre-Biblical times. A rock inscription in Brazil, three thousand feet above the ground, mentions Tyre and Phoenicia; it dates from 900 BC. Another Brazilian inscription—which some authorities think a forgery—describes how a ship from Sidon was separated from its companions and crossed the Atlantic. Bailey was particularly impressed by a great body of evidence linking the Sumerians with Brazil and Mexico as early as 2370 BC.

The evidence that Bailey assembles in *The God-Kings and the Titans* is not easy to digest; much of it is concerned with the similarity between artifacts—and language—in the Old World and the New; and he is frank enough to admit that some of his speculations lack a solid foundation. (For example, that the Sargasso Sea was named after the Sumerian king Sargon.) But the total weight of evidence is impressive, particularly when he speaks of universality of symbolism. (The Egyptian serpent symbol is a spiral, like Underwood's aquastats.)

Bailey's views failed to reach a wide audience. His argument is too complex for the general public, and serious scholars were inclined to dismiss him as an eccentric amateur. Yet if MacKie is right in believing that the Britons of 3000 BC had a sophisticated culture, then Bailey is certainly right in believing that exploration by sea began far earlier than historians have assumed.

Oddly enough, Bailey makes far less than might be expected of some of the most convincing evidence that Westerners arrived in South America long before Columbus. When Hernan Cortes arrived on the shores of Mexico in 1519, he was welcomed by the Indians because they took his men for white gods who had promised to return; by coincidence, Cortes landed close to the spot where they were expected. The Indian legend told how fair-skinned men with blue eyes had come by sea in the remote past; they wore ornaments like snakes on their heads (snakes were associated with the earth goddess from Europe to India). They brought knowledge of science, engineering and the law, and their leader was finally worshipped as a god throughout the continent. To the Toltecs he was Quetzacoatl, the plumed serpent, to the Mayans, Kukulcan, to the Aymaras of Peru, the blue-eyed Hyustus. After defeat in battle, he flew away on a magic carpet, promising to return one day.

Däniken, writing in the 1960s, takes the predictable view that the white gods were space men, in spite of the fact that they arrived in ships. But a decade earlier, a German-speaking Frenchman named Pierre Honoré had studied the legends and had reached the slightly less preposterous conclusion that they were Cretans. His study of the Mayan script convinced him that it bears fundamental resemblances to the ancient Cretan pictorial script, and to the later—and more symbolic—script known as Linear A. There is not much resemblance to the late Cretan script known as Linear B, which is closer to Greek, and which persisted in Greece as late as 1100 BC. There *are* differences between Mayan script and ancient Cretan, but this is to be expected, since Mayan civilisation began about 300 BC, and its hieroglyphs were presumably taken from some earlier civilisation. Honoré describes a journey into the Amazon jungle, near the town of Manáos, Brazil, where he was able to see many stones carved with symbols, submerged in the river. A rubber planter named Ramos had investigated the stones during the First World War, and wrote a book about them, with many illustrations, which Honoré saw in the Sâo Paolo Library; Ramos assumed that the language on the stones was Phoenician. In his book *In Quest of the White God*, Honoré details his reasons for believing it to be Cretan (for example, he mentions seeing the Cretan symbol of the double-headed axe). He concluded that it reached Brazil around 1500 BC, the date Atkinson believes his Mycenaean architect came to Stonehenge.

It is obviously unnecessary to assume that the white gods reached South America in flying saucers. It is startling enough that the culture of Crete—or Mycenae—could penetrate as far as England in 1500 BC; it would be even more astonishing if it could be established that it reached South America. The problem is not simply a matter of seamanship; Crete had a fine navy before it was destroyed by the tremendous volcanic explosion of Santorini, which occurred around 1500 BC. The real question is how primitive people, whose world was the Mediterranean, dared to sail so far. *If* Honoré is correct—and his parallels of Mayan and Cretan are certainly impressive—this would be one of the most convincing arguments so far in favour of a visit by space men to our earth in the remote past. Mariners would not have dared to face the Atlantic—or Pacific—in wooden ships unless they knew what land lay on the other side; and the likeliest source of this information would have been someone who had seen it from the air.

Lethbridge himself maintains a balanced attitude towards these speculations. He admits that the legends of the white gods—Quetzacoatl and so on—are thought-provoking. But he maintains that they may have reached South America as late as AD 1100, about the same time that Prince Madoc reached North America. And he believes that Prince Madoc probably learned of the existence of America from earlier Norse voyagers who had reached it via Greenland. As far as he is concerned, the visitors from outer space are simply an interesting hypothesis. And he finds the alternative hypothesis just as intriguing: that our remote ancestors may have been more inventive and more adventurous than anyone has given them credit for.

But then, Lethbridge was centrally concerned with other, and even stranger, matters.

4

The Timeless Zone

———————◆———————

In May 1964, BBC television in Bristol arranged to come to Branscombe to film Lethbridge; he was to give a demonstration of dowsing. At eleven in the morning, Lethbridge heard a car arrive and went down to meet it. A young man, who proved to be the cameraman, climbed out, looking a little dazed. Something in his manner as he stared at the house made Tom ask: 'You aren't going to tell me you've been here before?' And the cameraman, whose name was Graham Tidman, admitted that he had—at least, in a dream. 'Are there any other buildings behind the house?' Lethbridge admitted there were and took him to see. They came to a place where there had been a garden wall, which Tom had knocked down and rebuilt. 'It used not to be like that,' said the young man. 'There used to be buildings against the wall.' There *had* been pigsties and cowsheds there, but not in Tom's time. They walked into the courtyard, in which Tom had conducted his first experiments in finding silver coins; with a bewildered expression, the young man admitted that it was all as he had seen it in his dream. When they came into the herb garden, he remarked: 'There were buildings here. They were pulling them down and someone said: "Now we will be able to see the sea." ' Again, it was true—but many years before; now a row of trees in the distance made the sea practically invisible.

Graham Tidman had never been to Hole House or anywhere near it; he had no friends or relatives in the area. Yet on five occasions he had dreamed of the house—not as it was in 1964, but as it was shown on a set of plans that Tom had found attached to the deeds. The plans were dated 1896. Graham Tidman had dreamed of the house as it was before he was born.

Ian Stevenson, the author of *Twenty Cases Suggestive of Reincarnation*, might well regard this as evidence that Graham Tidman had lived in Hole House in a previous existence. Predictably, Lethbridge had a simpler explanation. The house itself was full of 'tape recordings' of past events; somehow, the cameraman's mind had 'tuned in' to these while he was asleep. But this in itself fails to explain how Tidman's mind—residing in Bristol with the rest of his body—succeeded in touring a place he had not yet visited.

A few years later, Tom's publisher asked him if he would consider researching a book about dreams. Tom was not enthusiastic; he was convinced that he seldom dreamed. However, he was willing to make the attempt. He recalled the curious episode of Graham Tidman, and he began making notes of his own dreams, to see if they produced any similar items of 'paranormal' information. In fact, the procedure had already been worked out by J. W. Dunne, the celebrated author of *An Experiment With Time* (1927); Dunne had realised that some of his dreams were about future events, and he made a habit of keeping a notebook by his bed, and quickly noting down his dreams as soon as he opened his eyes. Lethbridge now used the same technique. And the results, while not spectacular like Dunne's dreams of earthquakes and erupting volcanoes, confirmed quite distinctly that his dreams often provided knowledge of future events. In 1969, he woke up seeing the face of a man he did not know looking at him through some kind of frame, as if from a mirror; he seemed to be making movements with his hands in the area of his chin, and Tom assumed he was soaping his face prior to a shave. The next day, as Tom and Mina were driving to the local market town, they turned a bend in the road, and Tom found himself looking into the face of the man he had seen in his dream. It was looking out at him from behind the windscreen of the car, and his hands *were* moving in the area of his face—as he moved the steering wheel. Lethbridge had mistaken the frame of the windscreen for the frame of a mirror.

Other 'dreams of the future' were equally unsensational, yet just as oddly convincing. He lists them in the appendix to his last—posthumous—book, *The Power of the Pendulum*. Many of them were simply of items—or pictures—seen in newspapers the day after the dream: a man on a penny-farthing bicycle, a conductor signing programmes. After dreaming of a steamship against a stone jetty, he woke up to hear the news on the radio that the *Queen Elizabeth* was being withdrawn from service. After dreaming of an Arab in a dhow, he received a picture postcard from a friend in Africa showing Arabs in a dhow. Correspondents provided him with some rather more remarkable examples. In November 1968, someone sent him a letter describing a dream about the burning of a square-looking Edwardian building with many chimneys; three days later, the Lethbridges saw the hotel—or one very like it—being burnt down on a television newsreel. A female correspondent dreamed of the collapse of a building as the side was blown out; she heard someone say: 'Collapsed like a pack of cards.' A month later, a gas explosion blew out the wall of a block of flats at Ronan Point, in East London; a newspaper report contained the subheading: 'Collapsed like a pack of cards.' In both cases, it seems that his correspondent dreamed of seeing the news report rather than the disaster itself.

With a little research, Lethbridge could have uncovered far more spectacular examples of dream prophecy. One of the best authenticated of recent years is the case of John Godley, later Lord Kilbracken, who succeeded in realising every punter's dream and predicting the winners of horse races.

On the morning of March 8, 1946, Godley, who had gone to bed exceptionally late the night before, woke up with the names of two horses running in his head: Bindle and Juladdin. He had dreamed he read them in a list of winners in a newspaper. Godley, who was at Balliol College, Oxford, went to the Randolph Hotel and told his friend Richard Freeman; they checked the newspapers and found that Bindle *was* running in the one o'clock at Plumpton, and Juladdin at Weatherby. A group of them decided to risk a bet. Godley rang his London bookmaker and backed Bindle; it won at six to four. He transferred his winnings to Juladdin, which duly won at ten to one, netting Godley over £100.

A few weeks later, back home in Ireland, he again dreamed of looking at a list of winners in the newspaper. The only one he could recall when he woke up was a horse called Tubermor. A check with the local postmistress (who placed bets) revealed that a horse called Tuberose was running in the four o'clock at Aintree. Godley and his brother and sister managed to scratch together a few pounds to back it (they were not a rich family.) The horse won at a hundred to six, making them over sixty pounds between them.

In late July, 1946, Godley dreamed that he went into the telephone box of the Randolph Hotel and called his bookmaker to ask for the winner of the last race; he was told that it was Monumentor. The only horse with a similar name was Mentores, running that afternoon at Worcester. The odds—as he had dreamed—were five to four. Godley backed it. Later that day, he went into the Randolph Hotel, into the call box—which, as in his dream, was stuffy, and called his bookmaker. Mentores had won.

Another year went by before he had another dream of horses. This time he dreamed he was at the races and recognised the colours of one winner as those of the Gaekwar of Baroda; it was ridden by a jockey he recognised as Edgar Brett. He also heard the crowd shouting the name of another winner—'The Bogey'. The next day, he rushed to see his girlfriend Angelica, and told her what had happened. They checked in the racing news; Edgar Brett was riding a horse belonging to the Gaekwar of Baroda—it was called Baroda Squadron. They could find no horse called The Bogey, but there *was* a horse called The Brogue running at Lingfield. Godley placed a five-pound win double on the two horses—so that if Baroda Squadron won, the winnings would be placed on The Brogue. Once again, both horses won.

This kind of thing obviously could not continue forever. Godley *did* dream two more winners; but he also dreamt several losers. The only consolation was that his fame as a 'psychic punter' launched him into a career of journalism—as the racing correspondent of the *Daily Mirror*.

Ten years later, in 1958, he dreamed that the Grand National had been won by a horse called What Man? The only horse with a similar name was Mr What, and the odds were not the same as in his dream—sixty-six to one instead of eighteen to one. But on the morning of the Grand National, when Godley happened to be in Paris, he checked *The Times* and found that Mr What was now eighteen to one; he rang his bookmaker and placed a bet of twenty-five pounds to win. Later that day, he heard that Mr What had won, bringing him

£450—the largest sum he had so far won. Since that time, his powers have apparently deserted him.

The case strongly supports Lethbridge's view that we regularly glimpse the future in dreams, but can remember only things that interest us deeply. Although not a 'racing man', Godley was sufficiently interested to have an account with a London bookmaker and to recognise the colours of the Gaekwar of Baroda. As a hard-up undergraduate, he also had a strong motivation for wanting to dream winners.

When I presented the case on BBC television in 1977, I was struck by two points that I had overlooked when I read about it. The first was that Godley made so little money from his dreams. After that first double win, one might have expected him to try to raise a large sum of money to back his next dream winner. The other was that he felt he had somehow to work to 'make' the horses win, by concentrating hard and carefully repeating the ritual he had followed in his dream—looking it up in a newspaper or ringing his bookie from the same call box as in his dream. This could have been mere superstition, the desire not to tempt fate. It could also have been an unconscious feeling that it wasn't entirely 'right' to win money in this way without any kind of effort. This could also explain why he placed so little money on the horses. Most psychics believe that it brings misfortune to try to profit from their powers, which is why many refuse to be paid for their services. It is a curious fact that few psychics (or 'magicians') have ever become rich through the use of their powers, and that a large percentage have died in poverty. They seem to feel that using psychic powers for self-advancement is not playing the game according to the rules. But no one has yet succeeded in defining either the rules or the game.

One of the most interesting problems raised by such cases is what *conditions* have to be satisfied before a precognitive dream can take place. After John Godley's first win, his friends tried duplicating the conditions of his dream: taking him to the same restaurant for dinner, ordering the same food, putting him to bed at exactly the same time. Predictably, it had no effect.

If Lethbridge is correct about 'levels' of reality, the crucial factor may be the *depth* of the dream. In the past half century, our knowledge of sleep has increased enormously. In the early 1930s, Dr Hans Berger of Jena University tried testing dreamers with an electroencephalograph machine, which measures 'brain waves'. He discovered that we have different levels of sleep. When we first fall asleep we plunge quickly to the deepest level; then gradually, over the next hour and a half, we gradually 'surface' through at least three more distinct levels. After that we plunge back into deep sleep—but for a briefer period; and so on throughout the night.

In 1953, a student of Professor Nathaniel Kleitman, at the University of Chicago, noticed that a baby's eyes moved rapidly during sleep. Kleitman tried attaching his EEG machines around the area of the eyes and discovered that we all have 'rapid eye movements' (REMs) during the shallowest part of sleep. People who were awakened at this stage usually said they had been dreaming—even people who were convinced they never dreamed.

Yet it is hard to accept the scientist's conclusion that dreams are limited to Stage 1 (shallow) sleep. To begin with, we begin to experience a form of dream—known as hypnogogic visions—on the edge of sleep, while still half awake. It seems unlikely that these cease abruptly as we fall asleep. Moreover, anyone who has been awakened suddenly after a few minutes of sleep can recall dream images that fade almost immediately. In my own experience, there is a definite impression of having been 'absorbed' in something.

This view seems to be supported by a remarkable case of 'dream prophecy' that was investigated by Professor Hans Bender of Freiburg University. In April 1960, Frau Johanna Bravand went to bed much later than usual—she and her husband ran a hotel. After a brief sleep, she woke from a nightmare, which she was able to recall in detail. She and her sister had been climbing a mountain—the Recken-berg—accompanied by their husbands; near the top she saw a drinking trough that was filled by a spring. She ran to drink, then noticed that the water had a pink tinge. Looking more closely, she saw a woman's body in the water; it was wearing one of her own dresses. At that moment, she realised that her sister was no longer with them, and had a conviction that something terrible had happened. At that moment, she woke up, sweating and alarmed.

The dream upset her so much that she woke her husband and told him about it; but he was tired and told her to go back to sleep. The next morning she had another dream to tell. She had been running onto a bridge over a river as she felt someone was chasing her. To her right and her left, she could see two more bridges. Again there was a strong sense of something being wrong. She also told this dream to her husband and several other people in the hotel.

During this period, Frau Bravand's sister—Mina—lived about ten miles away at Augst with her husband and two young daughters. She and Johanna had always been close. Now both were experiencing marital problems and turned to one another for moral support. But Johanna's problems ended in divorce; she married again—Dr Max Frölicher—and moved to his estate in the Canton of Bern. Mina was left alone to cope with her own troubles which she did with the aid of drugs.

One day, Johanna's brother-in-law phoned to ask if Mina was with her; she had vanished the previous evening. Johanna hurried towards Augst but decided to turn aside en route and search the woods near Gotisberg, their birthplace. They had a hut in the forest, but there was no sign of Mina. She walked around the town, looking in their favourite spots—and then suddenly recognised the scenery of her dream. She was standing on a bridge, with two more bridges on either side and with the same feeling of deep foreboding.

In Augst, there was still no news of Mina. Then Johanna recalled a dowser, Edgar Devaux, who was famous for tracing missing persons. He lived in the village of Pery Reuchenette, in French-speaking Switzerland. It was about an hour's drive from Basel. Mina's husband flatly declined to go on such a wild-goose chase, so it was Johanna's husband, Max Frölicher, who went with her.

Devaux is an ex-schoolmaster with a figure like a barrel—not unlike Lethbridge. They arrived to find him waiting on his front doorstep holding his pendulum. He had dowsed their progress from the railway station.

In Devaux's study, Johanna offered him a photograph of Mina and one of her slippers. Devaux took only the photograph and suspended his short pendulum over it. He shook his head. 'I am sorry, but this person is no longer alive.' The pendulum, he explained, had swung north-east to south-west, which indicated death; if she had been alive, it would have swung from east to west. He was also able to tell Johanna that he felt Mina was in the water.

Johanna produced a map showing Basel and Augst. Devaux suspended his pendulum over the map, and with the other hand traced a pencil line along the river. He made a cross. 'She is there. And I have a feeling she is being held down by a piece of metal.'

Johanna and Max Frölicher were not entirely convinced; but then, the Rhine ran only a few hundred yards behind Mina's flat. It seemed worth checking. The police declined to help. They were convinced Mina had run away. But a diving club in Basel was more accommodating. Their leader, Hans Engler, thought it was probably a waste of time; there had been a lot of rain and melting snow that spring and the river was high and fast. But to oblige the Frölichers, his frogmen went to the spot indicated by Devaux. Devaux himself went along to help.

At first it seemed hopeless; it was like swimming in coffee. Then one of the divers found a stocking—the same size and brand used by Mina. They continued to search. Then one of the frogmen struggled out of the water looking sick and shocked. He had touched a body, but as he made a grab for it, it floated away in the current.

Devaux did not seem unduly worried; he said it would be quite easy to trace the progress of the body with his pendulum. But farther along the towpath, their way was blocked by factories. The search had to be abandoned.

Fortunately the corpse was not likely to float more than a few miles. Across the river at Birsfelden there is a barrage, where the current is used to drive the power station that supplies Basel's electricity. The water is sieved through grids to protect the turbines from damage. The engineer in charge found Mina's body, badly decomposed after ten days in the water, and notified the police. They contacted Johanna, and told her to go to the mortuary at Birsfelden to identify the body.

When Johanna walked into the mortuary, she received a shock. Mina's body had been placed in a special metal-lined coffin that is used for drowning cases. The coffin looked like the trough that Johanna had seen on the mountainside in her dream. The body lay in pinkish water—the flesh had been torn pulling her out of the river—and she was wearing the dress that Johanna had seen on the corpse. Johanna had totally forgotten that she had given it to Mina some time after her dream.

From the parapsychological point of view, the most interesting thing about the case is the amount of verification that Bender was able to obtain—from the many witnesses to whom Johanna had told the dream and from the diving club who searched for the body under Devaux's guidance. (Its leader, Hans Engler, has ceased to disbelieve in the power of dowsers.) From our point of view, the main interest lies in the question of the 'mechanism' of prophetic dreams. Johanna's dream had one interesting thing in common with John Godley's. Both had gone to bed much later than usual, after exceptionally hard work. Laboratory tests show that when someone goes to bed very late, the period between deep and shallow sleep is contracted; the sleeper 'comes up' much faster. Johanna describes waking suddenly after a fairly brief period of sleep. According to Lethbridge, certain dreams are simply glimpses of the 'second whorl of the spiral', the timeless world beyond the one we live in every day. But this hardly seems to apply to the kind of shallow dreaming that we find comparatively easy to remember. If Lethbridge is right, the kind of dreaming he means should belong to one of the deeper levels, perhaps even Level 4. In normal cyclic sleep, any such insights would have been long forgotten by the time the dreamer has 'surfaced' slowly to Level 1. In 'foreshortened' sleep, it is possible that they may be retained. Which in turn seems to suggest that the practical way to investigate precognitive dreams is to awaken the sleeper *before* he reaches the stage of rapid eye movements.

The Frölicher case also raises the interesting question of the parallel between Johanna's precognitive dreaming and Devaux's dowsing. Johanna foresaw her sister's death; Devaux located the body from a distant village. (Bender checked that Devaux could not have been influenced by the radio appeal for Mina; Pery-Reuchenette is beyond the range of the German radio network that broadcast the appeal.) How much difference is there between the two psychic faculties involved? Devaux declares that the pendulum is merely an amplifier that picks up radiations; yet it must be far more than that, or it could not answer questions about the remote past. It is the dowser's subconscious—or superconscious—mind that can travel in time. Lethbridge would say that dowsing and precognitive dreaming both involve the 'second whorl of the spiral'. Again, this is easy enough to grasp in the case of dreaming, since we can accept the possibility that some part of the mind is in contact with this level of existence. Then does it not follow that the same could be true of the dowser, and that he somehow exists *simultaneously* in two worlds?

If we consider *The Power of the Pendulum* as a study in precognitive dreams, it must be admitted that its range is less wide than one might have hoped. On the other hand, much of Lethbridge's observation is totally original. He was intrigued, for example, by 'backward dreams'. He woke up dreaming of a furry, snake-like object coming to the room, and recognised it as the tail of their Siamese cat walking backwards. Bedroom furniture was also reversed in a looking-glass effect; he noticed this reversal of objects in space in a number of dreams. His female correspondent, Mrs Beresford, reported two reversed dreams. In one, she saw a couple she knew walk backwards from the door, enter the garage and drive the car backwards down the lane; then the car reappeared, came to the house, and the couple got out in the normal way and entered the house. She said that it was like a film, shown backwards, then the right way round. Another dream is even more curious; she saw a number of men, walking backwards, carrying a coffin, and one of them said: 'Burnt be to enough good woods any.' It was only when she woke up that she realised that the sentence had also been reversed, and should have been: 'Any wood's good enough to be burnt.' When she woke up, she had a letter from Tom mentioning an inquest on his brother-in-law, who was cremated three days later.

What struck Lethbridge so forcefully was the apparently *impersonal* content of so many dreams. He was particularly interested in what he called 'flash dreams', dreams which occurred almost instantaneously before waking, and which seemed literally like a brief glimpse of a film—a face, a beach, a laughing girl, a ship seen through trees. In most cases he had never seen the person or place involved, and did not see them in the future; it was as if they were pictures from somebody's else's mind.

Lethbridge had already spoken about dreams in earlier books. He recognised, of course, that most dreams are compounded of memories, that they are, in fact, the sleeping equivalent of a daydream. But he also believed that precognitive dreams are a glimpse of that 'other world', which exists at the next level of the 'spiral'—the world to which the pendulum responds when it is stretched beyond forty inches.

This 'next level', it will be remembered, appears to have *no time*—if the pendulum can be relied on. Lethbridge also concluded that its energy vibrations are four times the speed of those on earth. This, he thinks, is why we cannot perceive it, although it exists among us; in the same way, you cannot read the name on a station if the train flashes though it at seventy miles an hour. (By the same analogy, people on this next level ought to be able to perceive us, but as more-or-less static objects, as we perceive trees, or the hour hands of a clock.) He was inclined to think this explained the Polynesian belief that invisible people live among us.

In *The Power of the Pendulum*, Lethbridge expresses the view that the 'spirit'—or astral body—is able to visit this next level in sleep. He speculates that we may simply pass through it, en route to a higher level still. This could also explain the 'reverse' effect of certain dreams. You would be entering the second level—the dream world—from a higher level where time goes faster still. The result would be like a fast train passing a slower one; although the slower one is actually moving forward, it appears to be going backwards.

Lethbridge was also inclined to regard 'out of the body experiences' as a confirmation of his theory; he noted that in a large number of such experiences, the person seemed to view his body from above and slightly to one side—in fact, about six and a half feet above and two feet to one side—the false position effect. He quotes a correspondent who describes an out-of-the-body experience when under anaesthetic at the dentist: 'I seemed to be floating in a corner near the ceiling, slightly to the left of the chair where my "body" sat. I could see the back of my head and the dentist bending over . . .'

Perhaps the most impressive confirmation of Lethbridge's theories about 'other levels' appeared a year after his death, in a book called *Out of the Body*. The author was an American business man, Robert Monroe; he was studied by the parapsychologist Charles Tart, author of the classic work on 'altered states of consciousness', who had no doubt of Monroe's genuineness.

Monroe's experiences began in the late 1950s. One Sunday afternoon, when he was lying on the living-room couch, he suddenly felt as if he had been 'struck by a beam of warm light', which caused his body to vibrate. Physical checks revealed nothing wrong with him, but the experience kept on recurring. One day, lying in bed in this condition, with his hand hanging over the side of the bed, he had the curious sensation of being able to push his fingertips through the rug and then on through the floor beneath. Four weeks later, there was a 'surge that seemed to be in my head'; when he opened his eyes, he found that he was floating close to the ceiling; down below, on the bed, was his body. With a shock of desperation he plunged down towards his body and dived into it.

Slowly and cautiously, Monroe began to explore this strange ability to leave his body. He quickly discovered that it was not as abnormal as he had first supposed; there have been many books describing the experience, notably three classic volumes by Sylvan Muldoon and Hereward Carrington.

At first, Monroe used his power simply to explore the world around him, call on friends, and so on. He confirmed, to his own satisfaction, that it was not some kind of hallucination or dream. He called on a friend who was supposed to be ill in bed and found him leaving his house with his wife. Later the friend confirmed that he had decided that he felt well enough to get up and take a walk. Monroe actually pinched one woman friend, who reacted sharply; later, she showed him the bruise at the spot where he had pinched her.

Monroe explains that he was able to explore three distinct realms of locales; he calls them Locale I, II and III. Locale I is 'this world', and he found astral travel in this realm more difficult than might be expected. To begin with, the world is seen from a thoroughly unfamiliar perspective—from overhead, so that there are navigational difficulties. Monroe asserts that the 'astral body' was never intended to travel in Locale I; it presents the same kind of problems that a diver without a face mask would encounter in diving to the bottom of the sea. It *can* be done, but only with considerable strain.

Locale II is—as you might expect—Lethbridge's timeless world of the 'next whorl' of the spiral. 'Time, by the standards of the physical world, is non-existent.' 'Locale II is a non-material environment with laws of motion and matter only remotely related to the physical world. It is an immensity whose bounds are unknown . . . In this vastness lie all the aspects we attribute to heaven and hell.'

Monroe explains that in Locale II, 'thought is the wellspring of existence . . . As you think, so you are.' In that sense, Locale II sounds like a dream world. But 'the interesting aspect of this thought world (or worlds) . . . is that one does perceive what seems to be solid matter as well as artifacts common to the physical world'. Locale II is the natural environment of the astral body, and the realm to which the body moves after death. It is also visited by the astral body of sleepers.

Our traditional concept of place suffers badly when applied to Locale II. It seems to interpenetrate our physical world, yet spans limitless reaches beyond comprehension . . . The most acceptable theory [of the whereabouts of Locale II] is the wave vibration concept, which presumes the existence of an infinity of worlds all operating at different frequencies, one of which is this physical world. Just as various wave frequencies . . . can simultaneously occupy space, with a minimum of interaction, so might the worlds of Locale II be interspersed in our physical matter world.

All this is not merely close to Lethbridge's concept; it is practically identical on every major point. And Monroe's descriptions enable us to understand the most baffling thing about the 'next whorl', its 'timelessness'. Monroe says: 'There is a sequence of events, a past and a future, but no cyclical separation.' This sounds obscure, particularly when he says: 'Both [past and future] continue to exist coterminously with "now".' Yet if we think for a moment about the nature of time, we see that it is tied up with the *solidness* of our world. A solid object has inevitable processes; you wind up a clock and it runs down. If it were made of gas, it could not be wound up. Because our world is relatively solid and unchanging, we can make a clear distinction between yesterday and the day before. Our history books tell about the Battle of Waterloo, and we can go and visit the place if we want to, and see all the landmarks described in the histories.

Yet even in our world, there is a timeless realm. I can play a record of Caruso, who died decades ago. I can see films acted by long-dead movie stars. Above all, when I have finished a novel that ends with the death of the hero, I can turn back fifty pages, and he is alive again. In a perfectly understandable sense, the world of imagination—or thought—is timeless. It has a kind of time: a novel or a film goes on from beginning to end. But it has no past or future in our sense; you can even run the movie backwards.

These observations are of tremendous importance. They explain, for example, that basic sense of security that is so vital to human existence. We ought to feel horribly insecure as our bodies age steadily and we see the death of those around us. And we *do* feel momentarily insecure if we witness some violent accident or narrowly avoid being knocked down by a bus; for a moment, we are confined to the purely physical world in which, as Hemingway says, men die like animals, not men. But a half of our being inhabits another world, the world of thought, the world in which all things are reversible; the result is that we decline to take the physical world too seriously. (Some people have so little sense of inevitability that they waste their lives, which seems to argue in favour of a certain degree of pessimism.) In the past two centuries, we have learned to spend so much of our time in an imaginary world—of novels, films, television programmes—that we find it increasingly hard to distinguish between dream and reality; we have become forgetful of existence, and live in a strange world of double exposures.

All of which should enable us to understand what Lethbridge and Monroe mean by saying that Locale II is a timeless zone; it is timeless because it is a zone of thought. Monroe says: 'In Locale II, reality is composed of deepest desires and most frantic fears. Thought is action, and no hiding layers of conditioning or inhibition shield the inner you from others; where honesty is the best policy there can be nothing less.' He explains how, when he first visited Locale II, he was embarrassed as his repressed emotional patterns exploded into reality. 'In conscious physical life, this conditioning would be considered psychotic.' Understandably. In real life, you may want to hit someone in the face, or unzip a pretty girl's dress, but unless you express the feeling in action, no one will ever know. In Locale II, according to Monroe, the desire would instantly become apparent to everyone. The lesson seems to be that one of the most important things we can learn on this level is self-discipline—to be the master of emotions rather than their slave. 'If it doesn't happen during physical life, it becomes the first order of business upon death.' And he goes on: 'This implies that the areas of Locale II "nearest" the physical world (in vibratory frequency?) are peopled for the most part with insane or near-insane, emotionally-driven beings. They include those alive but asleep or drugged and out in their Second Bodies, and quite probably those who are "dead" but still emotionally driven.' Monroe found that he had to pass through this area each time he ventured into Locale II, and that it could be a terrifying experience, like passing through a shark-infested sea.

Here again, Monroe was able to obtain a certain amount of corroboration for his 'visions'. On one occasion, he visited—in his astral body—a boy who seemed to be seriously ill. He was able to comfort him. Some weeks later, about to enter Locale II, he saw the boy, who was looking bewildered; apparently he had just died. The boy asked 'What do I do now?' Monroe was again able to comfort and reassure him. The next day, he saw in the newspaper an item about the death of a ten-year-old boy from a lingering illness. He tried to think of an excuse to go and see the parents, but could think of none.

It is worth noting, in passing, that many things in Monroe's book seem to confirm the teachings of that other eccentric visionary, Emanuel Swedenborg, who also claimed to be able to leave his body at night and converse with beings in the 'other world'. On at least two occasions, Swedenborg carried a message from someone still alive to a dead relative, and brought back the required answer. The relevance of Swedenborg's insights must be discussed in the second part of this book.

Monroe emphasises many times the importance of thought in Locale II.

> Like attracts like. I didn't realise there was such a rule that acted so specifically. It had been to me nothing more or less than an abstraction. Project this outward, and you begin to appreciate the infinite variations to be found in Locale II. Your destination seems to be grounded completely within the framework of your innermost *constant* motivations, emotions and desires. You may not consciously want to 'go' there, but you have no choice. Your Supermind (soul?) is stronger and usually makes the decision for you. Like attracts like.

By the use of the pendulum, Lethbridge concluded that the zone on the other side of the 'second whorl' was altogether more like our world. It had time, for example. Monroe's experiences seem to confirm this. The word 'seem' is necessary, for his chapter about Locale III sounds, as one commentator has remarked, rather like *Alice in Wonderland*. Monroe discovered Locale III when his Second Body turned over in bed, facing downwards. Below him there seemed to be a hole in a kind of wall, with blackness on the other side. When he reached through, he felt his hand shaken by a warm hand. Two months later, he had made the discovery that the 'hole' was populated. There was a physical world there, rather like our world, which he was at first inclined to think might be the past or future of our world. There was no electricity, although old-fashioned wagons were drawn by a kind of steam engine. The people seemed to get around in small vehicles that sound like a cross between a bicycle and a child's go-cart. Monroe says that he was able to merge with a man—his 'I' in this world of Locale III—and that his intrusions caused his alter-ego some embarrassment, since he knew so little about the manners and customs of Locale III. In fact, Monroe's description of Locale III inclines one to question his whole book. It sounds like a weird dream. Monroe hazards the suggestion that it may be some kind of anti-matter counterpart of our world, but this is no more convincing than his description of Locale III itself. The likeliest hypothesis—which seems to be supported by many other events in the book—is that Monroe's out-of-the-body experiences were partly objective, partly subjective, and that he had no power to distinguish between them.

Monroe has nothing to say on the subject of time-reversal, but he has an interesting passage on space-reversal. In February 1963, he tried returning to his body immediately after leaving it, and touching it with his hands. (It seems clear that his sight is impaired when he is in Locale I—perhaps, again, like an underwater swimmer.) His body was reversed—the head where the feet should be, the left foot where the right one should be. (A distorted nail that should have been on the left foot had transferred to the right.) 'Everything was reversed, like a mirror image.' He makes no attempt to explain this reverse effect, nor does he refer to it elsewhere.

One of the most curious observations in Monroe's book is that he was often able to speak to living people, who apparently had no memory of the conversation. In May 1961, he 'projected' himself into the study of Dr Andrija Puharich, the eminent parapsychologist. Puharich spoke to him, apologised for neglecting their project, and said he understood Monroe's need for caution. Later, checking with Puharich, he discovered that his memories of the study were correct, and that Puharich *was* writing on a sheet of paper at the time of Monroe's 'visit'; but Puharich had no memory of speaking to Monroe. Similar situations occur elsewhere in the book. The inference seems to be that Monroe's 'astral body' could communicate with the 'astral body' of other people, but that their physical memory retained no record of the communication. (Elsewhere, Monroe explains that there is a 'barrier' between Locale II and the physical world, the same screen that lowers when you waken from sleep, blotting out the last dream—or your memory of your visit to Locale II.) What he says seems consistent with the theory of the 'hierarchy of selves' advanced in the Introduction to this book; Monroe communicated with a 'higher' level of personal consciousness, and the everyday self was either unconscious of the communication, or promptly forgot it. Most people can find parallels in their personal experience: sudden intuitions, forebodings, warnings. These occur most often when the mind is in a state of calm and relaxation. Such intuitions are normally drowned by the noisy machinery of the conscious will. So it is easy enough to understand that the 'everyday self' is normally incapable of receiving communications from other parts of the mind—whether or not we decide to label these 'subconscious' or 'superconscious'.

And what of precognition? Monroe has nothing to say about this in connection with his explorations of Locales II and III. But he had interesting precognitive experiences on the verge of 'separating' from his physical body. 'There would be a hissing sound, localised in the forebrain, and I would get a sensation of a small rectangular door, hinged at one end, swinging downward to an angle of about forty-five degrees. This exposed a perfectly round hole. Immediately thereafter, I would see and semi-experience an event or incident like a dream, except that I retained all my consciousness and sense awareness.' In early July 1959, Monroe dreamed—or saw—himself taking an aeroplane trip, and the plane flying under wires and then crashing; he himself survived. Less than three weeks later he went on a flight to North Carolina, and recognised the various passengers of his dream. Nevertheless, he decided to stick it out—an apparently rash decision that was justified by the sequel. The plane flew into a thunderstorm—Monroe felt that this had been symbolised by the wires—but finally landed safely. Four days later, Monroe suffered a heart attack and had to spend some months in hospital. He concluded that the precognition had actually been about his heart attack, but that since he was so certain that his heart was sound (two doctors had told him: 'You'll never have to worry about your heart') his subconscious mind had totally rejected the possibility of a coronary and fixed on the plane trip as a possible source of his foreboding. Which would seem to suggest that even the higher levels of the mind have communication problems.

Other precognitions on the point of separation were more accurate. He 'saw' a house in a southern city two years before he and his wife moved into it; just at the beginning of a recorded programme he 'saw' the tape snapping—and it did; he 'saw' the oil pressure warning light in his car flash on an hour before it actually did so. (In this case, he points out, it was not subconscious worry; it was a new car, that turned out to have an oil leak.) There were some eighteen more similar instances.

Monroe also describes a series of apocalyptic 'glimpses' that are altogether more disturbing: a city being destroyed by aircraft, a city in which all the inhabitants are fleeing. 'There is principally a feeling of doom and the break-up of civilisation as we know it due to something momentous having taken place . . .' This sounds ominously like Nostradamus's prophecy about the 'great king of terror' who will descend from the sky in July 1999. On the other hand, many prophets—like Edgar Cayce—have foretold great upheavals in the last quarter of the twentieth century, and Monroe is certainly familiar with Cayce; we may take comfort in the notion that his 'glimpses' may have been influenced by what he has read. He comments: 'There are many more [glimpses], personal, general, specific, local, worldwide. Only time will bring confirmation. I hope some of them *are* hallucinations.'

Lethbridge's view was that such 'glimpses' are precognitions of the future seen as the astral body makes the transition from our world to the 'second whorl' of the spiral. And again, the literature of precognition and prophecy offers much support for the view. A typical example is cited in Alan Vaughan's *Patterns of Prophecy*. (Vaughan, we may recall, experienced a state of telepathy and precognition when he was 'dispossessed' of some invading entity, and thereafter devoted his time to the study of powers of prophecy.) During the Second World War, Mrs A. M. Kaulback attempted to use telepathy to keep in touch with the activities of her sons, who were in the armed forces overseas. She soon concluded that her successes were not due entirely to her own powers, but often to the intervention of 'discarnate entities', including her deceased husband. On November 4, 1942, her husband informed her—through automatic script—that their son Bill was at that moment being given command of a battalion. The scene was described in some detail. Mr Kaulback's description proved to be incredibly accurate, except for one small detail: the scene he described took place *a month later*, on December 1. Such confusions of time sequence happened so often that Mrs Kaulback asked one of her 'communicators'—'Uvani', who was also the spirit 'guide' of the famous medium Eileen Garrett—to explain it. The reply was that it was difficult to grasp time between two planes: the discarnate entities on the next level were aware of the future as well as the past, and could easily get them mixed up.

In attempting to explain such paradoxes, Lethbridge frequently invokes the name of J. W. Dunne; as already noted, Dunne and Lethbridge share the same starting point. This is a convenient moment to examine Dunne's theory of 'serial time', and his belief that it somehow 'proves' human immortality.

John William Dunne was an aeronautics engineer who wrote his most famous book, *An Experiment With Time*, when he was past fifty. What he did *not* explain in *An Experiment With Time*—although he was more forthcoming in the posthumously published *Intrusions?*— is that ever since childhood, he had been possessed by a certainty that he would bring an important message to mankind. The 'intrusions' were moments when some supernatural power—or perhaps merely the hand of coincidence—intervened to remind him of his destiny. A Cape Town medium had told him at a seance that he was to become the greatest medium the world has ever seen; certain dreams and semi-mystical experiences seemed to confirm this.

In 1899, when Dunne was twenty-four, he dreamed that his watch had stopped at half past four, and as he woke up, a crowd seemed to be shouting in unison: 'Look, look . . .' Accordingly he lit a match and looked at his watch; it *had* stopped at half past four. He rewound it, and the next morning, discovered that it was only a few minutes slow; he had awakened at the moment the watch stopped. Understandably, Dunne felt that his period of 'mediumship' was beginning. Then began the series of 'dreams of the future' which he described a quarter of a century later in *An Experiment With Time*.

In that book, he significantly omitted the detail about the voices shouting 'Look'; at that stage, he was unwilling to talk about the 'intrusions'. But it is worth bearing in mind that Dunne not only stumbled on the phenomenon of 'dreams of the future', but believed that his ability was connected with mediumship. Towards the end of his life, he concluded that it had been his destiny to bring to the world the great theory of 'serial time'—and his conviction that it somehow proved human immortality and the existence of God, or a Universal Mind. A final example of an 'intrusion' was his dream that an angel was scolding him, and warning him that it would be a 2,000-year calamity for mankind if he failed to clear up his theory of serialism; his right arm then developed severe neuritis, so that he was unable to work at his drawing board and had no alternative but to finish his last book.

The basic idea of serialism is best expressed in a short book called *Nothing Dies* (1940). Classical science, he points out, has tried to picture the world 'from outside'—as if the scientist were a detached observer, a kind of ghost standing outside the real universe. This, says Dunne, is an impossibility—as Einstein and Heisenberg recognised; the scientist alters the universe in the act of observing it.

Far from being 'outside' the world, says Dunne, 'you' and the universe are opposite ends of a stick. And if you start by examining the other end—the world—and then try working inward, towards 'yourself', you soon realise that your goal is unattainable; you never reach the end of the stick that is 'you', because in some weird way, you keep on *regressing*.

In order to explain this concept, he uses the image of a man painting a picture. The painter looks at the world in front of him and tries to transfer it on to canvas. Having done that, it strikes him that his picture of the world is incomplete, because he has failed to include himself. So he paints a second picture, this time showing himself painting the first picture. But that is incomplete too. For it now strikes him that in order to paint this second picture, he had to 'get outside' himself, and regard himself as a physical object, a part of the world. This means that another 'him' has somehow risen above the first one, a 'Self No. 2'. So he paints another picture showing Self No. 2 observing Self No. 1 painting the picture. Yet the fact that he can think detachedly about Self No. 2 means surely that once again he has risen above it to become a Self No. 3? And so on, ad infinitum.

We all experience this on a practical level; everyone has experienced this sense of splitting into two, the 'I' to whom something is happening, and another 'I' who looks on coldly from above.

Dunne goes on to suggest that each of these different 'Selves' lives on a different level of time. When we say 'Time flows', it follows that we are measuring it *against* something. And that something must be another kind of time, 'Time No. 2'. And this in turn is measured against Time No. 3 . . . This, Dunne thinks, explains how we can foresee the future in dreams. Self No. 1 exists in 'this world', stuck in the flow of Time No. 1. But Self No. 2 exists in another kind of time, a more flexible time; he can rise above the time of Self No. 1 and foresee the future. Dunne even gave some practical meaning to the first three Selves. Self No. 1 is the 'me' who looks out through my eyes when I stare blankly out of a window; he is a mere observer, nothing more. Self No. 2 takes over when I sit up and pay attention, selecting what interests me and ignoring other things. This is undoubtedly a higher self than Self No. 1, as I realise if I try to write in a room full of children; it requires tremendous effort to focus on what interests me, and prevent Self No. 1 from taking over again. Then there is Self No. 3, the detached 'I', who seems to be able to look down coldly on the 'observer' *and* the 'selector'. It is even more difficult to preserve this Olympian attitude for more than a split second at a time.

In his book *Man and Time*, J. B. Priestley summarises Dunne's theory, and tells a story that seems to illustrate the difference between Self No. 1 and Self No. 2. A young mother had a dream that she was on a camping holiday and left her year-old son by the river while she went to get soap; when she returned, he was drowned. She forgot the incident, but some time later, on a camping holiday, suddenly recognised the scene of her dream as she was about to go and get soap. She took the child with her and so—presumably—a tragedy was averted. The mother had dreamed of herself—Self No. 1—in Time No. 1; but by paying attention, taking thought, she had become Self No. 2, and so had risen to Time No. 2, where a degree of free will is possible. But Priestley goes on to reject Dunne's 'infinite series' of 'Selves', arguing that we need only the first three 'I's' to cover most of our everyday experience. Dunne's infinite regress of selves, he argues, is just an abstract hypothesis.

A similar objection can be applied to Dunne's infinite regress of times. To say 'Time flows' is only a manner of speaking. We really mean 'Process happens'. So all this talk about measuring one time against another is also a misunderstanding.

Yet while it is true that Dunne's theory contains many flaws, the basic structure remains sound. The image of the painter painting a picture expresses a truth about consciousness. Man *is* capable of infinite regress; it is impossible to catch him. If I look at a great portrait by Rembrandt, I may say: 'Ah yes, he has caught the very essence of the sitter.' But I know this is not true. The sitter contains a rich, deep complexity of emotions and impulses that no painter could ever catch.

We can even imagine a god, who can see into a man's heart, and who would *still* be incapable of grasping the 'whole man'. For man is capable of evolution; he seems to contain some principle that is capable of re-arranging all his basic elements. The job of transformation may be unbelievably arduous; yet it is always possible.

Priestley is undoubtedly right when he says that our everyday experience can be described in terms of the first three Selves ('the seeing I', 'the willing I' and 'the comprehending I'). And it is certainly true that these three 'I's' seem to experience time in a different manner. When I am staring blankly out of a window, time goes slowly. When I exert my will, it accelerates. If, as I get older, I identify more and more with my 'detached self'—the Jamesian observer of life—the days go faster still. But none of these three Selves is capable of seeing into the future. Which suggests that the Self who is responsible for precognition is higher still—a Self No. 4, perhaps.

Dunne is convinced that Time No. 1 flows inevitably to its appointed end, carrying Self No. 1 along with it to his death. (Dunne calls Time No. 1 'pseudo-time'.) But there is a higher 'you', to which you refer when you speak of '*my*self'. And there is no evidence that *this* self dies. We may call it Self No. 2, or perhaps Self No. 3 or 4; at all events, it seems to be the Self that is capable of precognition.

And what happens if you pursue the 'Selves' far enough? In Chapter 26 of *An Experiment With Time*, Dunne asserts that you would eventually reach a 'superlative general observer, the fount of all self-consciousness', a Universal Mind, a tree-trunk of which individual observers are branches. He concludes that life is a play in which the actor is also, in some strange sense, the dramatist. Hence precognition.

Lethbridge's own view of the problem differs precisely where you might expect it to differ from Dunne's. For him, Self No. 1 is our living body and personality—in other words, what Dunne means by the first three Selves. Self No. 2 exists on the second whorl of the spiral, the next level. He writes: 'There appears to be a series of observers (if you can so describe a succession of degrees of mental awareness) but they are not counterparts of the original observer. The time succession is quite unlike his, for the second observer finds himself on a mental plane where there is succession but no movement of time. On the third plane, time begins to move once more . . .' And, if the pendulum is correct, then there is no death on this plane.

Like Dunne, Lethbridge believes that the meaning of the whole drama lies in some kind of evolutionism. Our purpose is creative thinking, the development of the mind; he even suggests that 'those who cannot be bothered to develop their minds will have to return to earth again after death and do the whole business again'. Man is provided with a series of 'clues' (Dunne's 'intrusions'?) and it is his business to make the best of them. 'When looking back over the past sequences of my life, I have observed that whatever one undertook invariably had a relationship to something one was going to do, perhaps many years afterwards. Something in some archaeological investigation would explain what was found in a completely different bit of work decades later.' This, he feels, 'must surely imply the existence of some kind of plan for each individual'.

Yet this, like Dunne's evolutionism, leaves many questions unanswered. The most basic is the problem of time and free will. The common-sense view of time tells us that the future has not yet happened, and that therefore there is no possible way of foreseeing it in any detail. Which means that we must dismiss all the 'prophets', from Nostradamus to Dunne, Edgar Cayce and Jean Dixon, as self-deceivers or liars. But if we are willing to admit even the slightest doubt—if we are willing to admit that *perhaps*, on one single occasion, Dunne or Lethbridge actually dreamed of something that had not yet taken place—then we have admitted the possibility that the common-sense view of time is as crude and simplistic as the flat-earth theory. And we have also committed ourselves to the view that in some sense, the future is already predetermined. To say 'it has already taken place' is a logical contradiction—and there is no sense whatever in abandoning logic—but we are certainly admitting the suggestion that history may be somehow sketched out in advance, like the rough draft of a play script. Dunne occasionally used the analogy of a film in which some kind of 'loop' occurs; but that is altogether too deterministic. The characters in a film have no freedom; they are mere shadows. On the other hand, the characters in a play are only roughly determined by the script; they are free to improvise 'business' as much as they like. In an experimental play, they may even be free to alter the lines and the course of the action.

Another kind of analogy may clarify the issue. If I drive from London to Brighton, or Lausanne to Geneva, the scenery along my route is fundamentally predictable, and if I make the journey more than once, one trip will be much like another. Yet although the journey is more-or-less predetermined, all the minor decisions remain free: what I think en route, where I stop for lunch, whether I listen to the car radio or not. The day may be sunny or rainy; *that* is not predetermined. I may have an easy journey or crawl for hours in a traffic jam. I may decide to leave the main road and take side roads. In *that* sense, every journey is a mixture of 'freedom and necessity'.

And what determines my degree of freedom? The answer lies in the word 'alertness' or attention. If I am tired or bored, I drive automatically—that is to say, my robot does the driving. 'I' go into a kind of trance, and my will goes to sleep. And unless I encounter some problem or obstacle, the journey will go exactly 'according to plan', for the robot is a creature of habit. If, on the other hand, I am wide awake, intensely enjoying the scenery, the journey will become far less predictable. I may slow down as I pass some historic monument; I may decide to take a side road; I may even turn the car and go back, to look more closely at something that has interested me. I am now exercising my freedom of choice.

According to Dunne—and Lethbridge—our foreknowledge of the future can be only of the scenery along the road, so to speak. The 'you' of the dream is your 'automatic' self. In the actual event, you may arouse yourself to a new level of effort and attention, and behave in a completely different manner, like the mother who averted the drowning tragedy. The whole concept could be compared to one of those films that are used in driving schools; the driver sits at a steering wheel, looking at a screen on which a road has been projected, with cars moving towards him. The image on the screen responds to his steering wheel, so that he has a sensation of driving down a real road; if he drives carelessly, he may cause an accident—but only on the screen.

Dunne also makes the point that when a film is slowed down, it seems to become more real. An aeroplane flashing by at the speed of sound has the quality of illusion; a racehorse that is slowed down so that it floats slowly over a hedge seems to become solider. But when we are bored or tired, time seems to slow down; this is why the watched pot never boils. This has the paradoxical effect of making the world around us oppressively real. Boredom and misery seem far more real than happiness and excitement. A man suffering from mental exhaustion is likely to experience fits of 'nausea' or 'absurdity', a sudden sense of meaningless: 'What am I doing here?' Everyone who has experienced nervous depression knows the feeling. It is important to recognise that this is a kind of optical illusion, a mirage, associated with the slowing-down effect.

And so we can say that the Dunne-Lethbridge theory of time is fundamentally optimistic. It avoids both extremes: the kind of idealism that regards life as ultimately an illusion, and the kind of realism—typified by Sartre—that regards it as brutally meaningless. Their view is not based simply upon precognitions or other 'psychical' experiences, but upon the much more common recognition that we seem to know far more 'deep down' than we know on the surface. St Augustine made the same observation: 'What is time? When I do not ask myself the question, I know the answer.'

It must be admitted that this view of time—as a kind of illusion—has a deep appeal to most human beings. Things that happen in space are reversible; if I walk to the end of the street and discover I have forgotten my wallet, I can walk back again. But if I realise I have forgotten an important letter that should have gone last week, I cannot return to last week and send it. Writers and artists who have come to accept this one-way flow of time tend to become deeply gloomy about it; their works take on a melancholy, autumnal atmosphere, as in Arnold Bennett's *Old Wives' Tale* or the music of Elgar and Delius.

But most of us tend to take a more optimistic view, accepting—consciously or instinctively—some form or another of the illusionist view. That is, we live and behave as if we will still be here in a thousand years. We live as if we were spectators of life, sitting in a cinema, and as if nothing that happens on the screen can really affect us. For more than three thousand years, philosophers have noted this strange sense of security that pervades the human psyche. Most of them have put it down to stupidity and short-sightedness. From childhood on, we all love stories that end 'And they lived happily ever after'; they satisfy our need to believe in an 'ever after'. (The truth is that the Prince and Princess lived on for another fifty years or so, then died like everyone else.) On the other hand, the mystics have always insisted that our sense of security *is* justified, that in some ultimate, universal sense, 'all is well'.

There can be no doubt that various philosophies of life after death are popular because they confirm our feeling that nothing is 'inevitable'. It is also fairly obvious that there is an element of absurdity in such a belief. We find ourselves living in a universe that seems to be incomprehensible and inscrutable. The real mystery, as William James remarks, is why anything exists at all. To say: 'Ah, but we continue to live after death' is a *non sequitur*. Belief in life after death may comfort our purely human emotions, the desire to see our loved ones, and so on; but where the basic mystery of the universe is concerned, it is a total irrelevancy.

In this sense; the approach of Lethbridge and Dunne is rather more satisfactory. In recognising that human beings may exist on many levels, and that everyday consciousness may be only one of these levels, they have at least made a frontal assault on the problem; their approach takes into account the 'absurdity', the incompleteness of the world as presented to everyday consciousness. Lethbridge himself deserves the credit for inventing a completely original and pragmatic method of investigating the problem of life after death.

In retrospect, cheerful pragmatism seems to be Lethbridge's most memorable quality. No one who reads his work continuously—from *Ghost and Ghoul* to *The Power of the Pendulum*—can help feeling that it was a tragedy that he died when he did. All his books are pervaded by an underlying feeling of excitement. He believed he was on the point of some important breakthrough, a discovery that would revolution- ise paranormal research as Einstein revolutionised classical physics. And the reader of his books also seems to catch glimpses of that discovery. It is basically a feeling that the answer lies somehow in *rates of vibration*. A mere eighty years ago, scientists still believed that matter consists ultimately of small indivisible lumps called atoms; it was not until 1897 that Rutherford demonstrated that atoms can be made to emit electrons. And it was not until well into the twentieth century that physicists finally recognised that the electron is not a particle but a unit of energy—a kind of vibration. Since the dropping of the atomic bomb on Hiroshima, every child in the world knows that matter consists basically of energy: of vibrations. What is vibrat- ing? No one seems quite sure; scientists used to believe it was some- thing called the luminiferous ether, a jelly-like medium that pervades all space and sounds oddly like the 'astral light' (or akasic ether) of the occultists. At all events, it now seems clear that our common-sense picture of the world has to be totally revised. If you cover a comb with a piece of cellophane and blow against it, it will emit a buzzing note, and you will experience a tickling, vibratory sensation in your lips and in the fingers holding the comb. If you put your finger in an electric point, you will experience the same kind of vibrations, but intensified to the point of painfulness. When you lay your hand on a solid surface, you are again experiencing the same vibrations, but now held in some sort of equilibrium, so that, like tethered horses, they are forced to go round in circles.

Lethbridge knew little modern physics; but he knew enough to know that if matter can be explained in terms of vibrations, then the same thing probably applies to the world of 'paranormal' phenomena—such as telepathy, dowsing and ghosts. What really excited him was that his own investigations seemed to be somehow connecting up with those of modern physics. Everything in the universe seemed to have a 'rate'—just as the elements all have their atomic weights. Moreover, the pendulum seemed to make no distinction between the world of things and the world of ideas. It could even, apparently, detect some *other* world. He seemed to be catching a glimpse of a theory of the universe that went beyond relativity and quantum physics. First matter had dissolved into energy; now energy seemed to be somehow dissolving into mind stuff—or at least, to be in some way dependent on it.

His natural pragmatism inclined him to the belief that one day all this would be accepted as casually as radio or television. In *Legend of the Sons of God* he writes:

> If scientists could get rid of the mental block which prevents them investigating a vast subject right under their noses, they could soon learn a great deal more than my wife and I are capable of doing. The block no longer seems to restrain scientists in America and Russia . . . Let us assume that in a hundred years' time the block will have gone completely and what is now known as the 'odd' will have become a commonplace of bio-electronics. By then it will be possible, no doubt, to get on to the second mental whorl at will, using some elaborate electronic machine to alter the vibrational rate.

The reference to American and Russian scientists suggests that he may be referring to the experiments in telepathy that are described in *The Dawn of Magic* (although Mina Lethbridge assures me that he never read the book). But his following paragraph indicates another possibility:

I should imagine this would necessitate some kind of dynamo to produce a field of force around the experimenters, and this would be contained in a hemispherical type of housing. Having altered your personal bio-electronic field of force from that of your earth body to the vibrations of the next whorl, you would be in the timeless zone and could go backwards and forwards in time. It would probably be possible also to move the whole machine instantly in any direction by the power of thought. This hypothetical machine is not at all unlike what is reported of the flying saucers.

What Lethbridge may have had in mind—in the reference to scientists—is the curious legend of the Philadelphia Experiment, which has become part of modern UFO folklore. According to Dr Morris K. Jessup, a machine such as Lethbridge describes *has* been constructed, by US Navy scientists. Jessup wrote one of the earliest books on flying saucers—*The Case for the UFO* (1955)—and was a teacher of astronomy and mathematics at the University of Michigan, an eminent scientist whose researches led to the discovery of thousands of binary stars. After investigating Inca and Maya ruins, Jessup arrived independently at Lethbridge's notion that they might have been set up by some 'levitating power'. Soon after publication of *The Case for the UFO*, Jessup received two letters from a man who signed himself Carlos Allende (or Carl Allen), who described the 'experiment'.

Allende claimed that in October 1943, the Navy had tried inducing a tremendously powerful magnetic field on board a destroyer in Philadelphia, presumably on the Delaware River. 'The "result" was complete invisibility of a ship. Sailors on board the ship became semi-transparent to one another's eyes ('vague in form'). The ship itself vanished from its Philadelphia dock and reappeared at its other regular dock at Newport, Virginia. Half the crew became insane. Some went into a semi-comatose state which Allende calls 'deep freezing'. They had to be exposed to another piece of electronic equipment to 'unfreeze' them. One man walked through the wall of his cabin in the sight of his wife and children, and vanished. Two more burst into flame as they were carrying compasses and burned for eighteen days. Other 'frozen' crew members were restored by 'laying on of hands'.[1]

The story sounds preposterous enough, and is made more so by Allende's claim that he read it in a Philadelphia newspaper. It is full of inner contradictions—in one paragraph, Allende says the experiment took place at sea, and a page later, in Philadelphia—and seems to be the work of a crank. But according to Jessup's friend, Dr Manson Valentine (quoted in Berlitz's book on the Bermuda Triangle), Jessup was asked to go to the Office of Naval Research in Washington, and was there shown a heavily annotated copy of his book on UFOs and asked if he recognised the handwriting. Some of it resembled Allende's, and Jessup gave them the Allende letters, which included his address in New Kensington, Pennsylvania. Subsequently, Allende vanished, and the Office of Naval Research went to the trouble of having Jessup's book mimeographed, together with all the written comments.

Three years later, in April 1959, Jessup was found dead in his parked station wagon in Dade County Park, Miami; a hose connected the exhaust with the interior of the car. Many 'ufologists', including John Michell, have suggested that Jessup's death was not suicide, but this claim is unsupported by a shred of evidence. Jessup was depressed by his failure to make a living as a writer and by the collapse of plans to investigate UFO evidence in Mexico.

Valentine asserts that Jessup 'had a theory that the power of magnetic fields could transform and transport matter from one dimension to another'. He also states that in the last year of his life, Jessup was approached by the Office of Naval Research to work on 'the Philadelphia Experiment on similar projects' but had declined 'because he was worried about its dangerous ramifications'. No doubt the Allende letters *are* from a crank, yet it still seems possible that Jessup had stumbled on to something that Naval scientists felt worth investigating.

It is worth mentioning another version of the Philadelphia Experiment story, as reported (allegedly) by the Russians; it was told to the writer Robert Charroux by Professor Doru Todericiu, who claimed to have derived his information from behind the Iron Curtain. The Russian version asserts that the Americans were experimenting with a magnetic field in the shape of a Moebius Strip. A Moebius Strip is a geometrical figure with only one side. It can be constructed easily by taking a long strip of paper, giving it a twist, and gluing the ends together. The resulting circle of paper has only one side—as can be verified by tracing a pencil line down its centre; the line connects up with its own beginning without having to change sides. If the circle is cut into two with a pair of scissors—cutting along the pencil line—the result is one large circle, and not, as you might expect, two interlinked circles.

According to the Russian version, the powerful magnetic field was in the shape of a Moebius Strip, and a submarine (not a destroyer) traced its course, turning over once in the course of every revolution. Some electronic device was then used to cut the field in two. At this point, the submarine vanished from Philadelphia, to reappear in Newport. The chief interest of this version—which is at least as preposterous as Allende's—is that again, a powerful magnetic field is alleged to have been involved.

Now Lethbridge's—and Jessup's—belief in the properties of such a field is less absurd than it sounds. There was a point in the late 1920s when the British government was willing to finance research into the matter. In the 1920s, Dr W. E. Boyd became convinced that high-frequency electric currents could increase man's telepathic powers, and he constructed a machine which he called an emanometer. A team of government investigators was deeply impressed by the high scores consistently attained by subjects in card-guessing experiments, and reported favourably on the emanometer. Then came the Depression and the coalition government; funds were no longer available, and the idea was dropped. In recent years it has been revived again by Peter Maddock, head of the Parascience Institute, who presented a paper on Boyd's ideas and on his own experiments to a Parascience Conference held at City University, London, in August 1976. Maddock pointed out that Russian scientists seem to have stumbled upon the same discovery; in *Psychic Discoveries Behind the Iron Curtain*, Sheila Ostrander and Lynn Schroeder mention that Russian scientists have improved telepathic communication and ESP by surrounding subjects with an artificial magnetic field. They also mention the report that a Washington electronics engineer told the Parapsychology Foundation that 'working with high frequency machines, my colleagues and I have found that we are on occasion telepathic'. This would not have surprised Lethbridge. He believed that telepathy takes place via the intermediary of the 'second whorl', so that his high frequency 'time machine' would also have the effect of amplifying man's telepathic abilities.

Lethbridge's aim was to make a comprehensive 'table of vibrations' with the use of the pendulum, a table that would include ideas as well as material substances. In his last years, he was beginning to formulate a notion of the universe in which mind and matter—or ideas and objects—were no longer opposites, but were somehow aspects of a broader continuum.

The works of Lethbridge's last five years show no falling off, either in liveliness of style or variety of ideas. Yet this was the period of a slow decline in his health. It began in the spring of 1966, when he had a painful chest infection, which was diagnosed as a bronchitic infection; Mina suspects that it was the beginning of the heart trouble that finally killed him, and that if it had been diagnosed in time, he might have lived longer. A strenuous week with the BBC television team that August brought on another attack, and this time it was recognised as a heart ailment. Nevertheless, he finished *A Step in the Dark*, and went on to write *The Monkey's Tail*, his own attempt to suggest a less mechanistic form of evolutionism than orthodox Darwinism. In the Introduction, he wrote: 'Orthodox science has cut itself off from investigating these things with its own self-imposed terms of reference, and only the very boldest, such as Sir Alister Hardy and Raynor Johnson, dare to step over the barrier.' The result is one of his liveliest and most aggressive books. Lethbridge never ceased to worry about the way that so many scientists seem determined to actively hinder any attempt to widen the boundaries of science. (This is a subject we shall consider at length in the next chapter.)

In 1971, he seemed to realise he was dying; Mina Lethbridge mentions: 'He gradually taught me to take over all the jobs he had previously done.' In August, both of them caught a virus infection, and Tom had to be moved to an Exeter hospital. There he fascinated the nurses with his discourses on the pendulum and ESP. His kindness and good humour made him a favourite with everyone.

Mina records that he was slightly disappointed not to have had out-of-the-body experiences when he was semi-delirious. But his interest in dreams continued, and he told Mina of a series involving 'lively small people' who declared they were busy preparing things for the 'Show Biz' world. Lethbridge had never been interested in the theatre, so Mina felt that his concern for the subject was out of character.

Towards the end of August, 1971, Mina had a clear dream in which a friend told her that Tom was dying. There were also odd portents: a bell rang violently when there was no one outside; the side mirrors fell off her car at different times, although they seemed to be firmly fixed on. Tom died peacefully in the nursing home on September 30, 1971.

Understandably, Mina found life difficult without him. She had known him since she was a child and had been with him for more than thirty years. Her first reaction was a total loss of interest in everything to do with dowsing or the paranormal. Then, gradually, she began to feel as if he were still present. She was forced to leave Hole House—which belonged to the Lethbridge trustees—and at first the thought was traumatic. Then, by good fortune, she came upon another house at Ottery St Mary, which suited her perfectly. She wrote to me: 'When I left Hole House, I felt then, and still feel, that he had a hand in finding my present home. It is just right for me and the sort of thing he would have liked too.'

Since his death, Lethbridge's books have continued to be read, and his reputation has grown steadily. Mina has continued to receive letters from readers who were not aware of his death. But she has resisted a suggestion to help in the formation of a Tom Lethbridge Society. 'I don't think he would have approved of this. The whole point of his work was to make people think for themselves.' Lethbridge could not have had a better epitaph.

PART

TWO

1

The Curious History of Human Stupidity

When the educational psychologist Sir Cyril Burt died in 1971, at the age of eighty-eight, he was one of the most highly respected men in his field. Five years later, that reputation was in ruins. What had happened was simply that Burt had been caught cheating. He had been one of the most influential advocates of the view that we inherit intelligence from our parents, and that our upbringing has relatively little to do with it. And this apparently harmless conclusion became a matter for bitter controversy when it was used to argue that blacks are genetically inferior to whites. Professor William Shockley in America and Professor Hans Eysenck in England, were denounced as racialists; Eysenck was actually attacked by left-wing students at one of his lectures. Both defended themselves—as scientists should—by replying that science is completely non-political, and that their views were true, whether they happened to suit the leftists or not.

Then Burt died. And two of his colleagues noticed simultaneously that there was something wrong with his figures. One of his best-known pieces of research concerned identical twins. When raised together, said Burt, their intelligence tended to be almost identical—a correlation of over ·90. Now if the 'environmentalists' are correct, there ought to be a large and dramatic difference if the twins are separated, and one is raised in a far less favourable environment than the other. This, said Burt, did not occur; there *was* a difference, but it was fairly small—a drop from ·90 to ·77.

Burt's colleagues found one outstanding inconsistency. In different papers, Burt mentioned a different number of twins—between twenty-one and fifty-three. Yet the intelligence correlation was *identical*—even to three decimal places— ·771 for twins raised separately, ·994 for twins raised together. *That* kind of accuracy was impossible with a varying sample unless Burt had started with the result and worked backwards. Once this suspicion had dawned, there were further investigations, and it was soon being suggested that Burt had invented two of the colleagues with whom he was supposed to have collaborated on scientific papers.

But why should a famous and highly esteemed scientist risk his whole reputation on a careless piece of skulduggery? In a letter to a Sunday newspaper, Professor Eysenck suggested charitably that the answer lay in carelessness rather than dishonesty, and reasserted his view that science is concerned with *facts*, not opinions and prejudices. But another newspaper probably came closer to expressing the general view when it commented that Grand Old Men of science tend to become increasingly possessive about their theories as they get older, and defend their work with force of personality rather than scientific argument. In short, that 'facts' often matter far less than personal prestige.

And why do I drag this sad cautionary tale into a book about the 'paranormal'?

Because it touches on a fundamental problem of human nature and raises some disturbing questions about man's attitude to events beyond his everyday experience. Men have a deeply ingrained habit of starting with the 'facts' they want to believe, and then working backwards to find the evidence to support them.

I am not now suggesting—what every crank would like to believe—that all scientists are involved in a conspiracy to suppress unpalatable 'facts'. I was trained as a scientist, and I firmly believe that most scientists do their level best to face the facts as they understand them. Eysenck himself is a good example; although he is a tough-minded behaviourist, with a deep suspicion of all forms of 'occultism',

he was open-minded enough to allow Michel and Françoise Gauquelin to persuade him to examine their statistics on astrology. And
when, contrary to all his expectations, these proved to be indisputable,
Eysenck caused dismay among his colleagues by publicly acknowledging his finding, and admitting that, for some odd reason, astrology
really seemed to work.

But the problem goes deeper than this. We are probably being naïve
if we imagine that Burt *consciously decided* to be dishonest. If he had
intended to cook the figures, he would have taken more care to make
them convincing. What almost certainly happened is that he became
totally convinced of the correctness of his early findings, and unconsciously 'adjusted' the later figures to demonstrate what he saw as a
foregone conclusion.[1] If he noticed any small discrepancies, he probably dismissed them as 'experimental error'. So Eysenck was right: it
was a kind of 'carelessness'—but a carelessness unconsciously directed
at increasing his personal prestige, at proving that *he* knew best.

This is the problem that most scientists prefer to ignore: the sheer
voracity of man's appetite for recognition and self-esteem. The late
Abraham Maslow has pointed out that man is swayed by three basic
appetites: for security, sex, and self-respect. All three produce irrational behaviour; but the appetite for self-esteem causes more damage
than the other two put together. At its worst, it can produce a form of
insanity accompanied by delusions. And in spite of their ideals of
honesty and fair-mindedness, scientists are as prone to this appetite as
anybody else.

Satirists and philosophers have always recognised the intensity of
man's craving to be 'in the right'. Alfred Adler even formulated a
'psychology of self-esteem', based on the recognition that man's most
dominant urge is his will-to-power. But the first man to recognise the
disturbing implications of this curious defect of human nature was
neither a philosopher nor a psychologist: he was the writer of science
fiction, A. E. Van Vogt.

It was in the 1950s that Van Vogt became interested in what would
now be called 'male chauvinist piggery', and began to study examples
of it in divorce cases. He observed that there is a type of man who
demands one code of conduct for himself and another for his wife.
And it dawned on him that he had stumbled on an aspect of human
nature that had been overlooked by orthodox psychology.

The chief characteristic of this type of male was an obsession with *being right*. Under no circumstances would he ever admit that he might be wrong. If something upset him, he would tend to look for somebody to blame and pour his irritation on the head of the nearest person, particularly if it happened to be a member of his own family. He could never admit that *he* might be to blame. With strangers, or colleagues at work, he would usually seem to be a perfectly reasonable human being. Where his family was concerned, he was a kind of miniature Hitler. He was prone to pathological jealousy and could behave like the most puritanical of Victorian fathers. Yet he was often a philanderer and a seducer; sexual conquest was one of his most important sources of self-esteem. He made a habit of indulging every emotion without regard to the rights or wrongs of the matter. If contradicted, he was likely to become violent. Van Vogt labelled him 'the Right Man', or the Violent Male.

Understandably, such conduct often led to family conflict and divorce. One Right Man went into business five times, using money that his wife had inherited; each time he went bankrupt. When his wife went to work to support the family, the husband talked about divorce and asked the children to live with him. To his surprise, they refused. At this, he called them together and told them that their mother had not been a virgin when he married her, twenty years earlier. His wife was stunned by this treachery, and pointed out that *he* had constantly had affairs *since* they were married. At this, the husband fell into a violent rage, asserting that she had no right to reveal his weakness to the children.

This kind of thing sounds comic; but anyone who has ever lived in a house with a Violent Male (or a Violent Female, for that matter) knows that it can be a long-drawn-out tragedy, a ruthless attempt to force other people into one's own mental moulds. All human beings have a tendency to daydream, to indulge in fantasies that flatter the ego. The Right Man tries to act out his fantasies and uses his authority to force others to support the charade. If, as occasionally happens, he manages to achieve a position of authority, he is likely to become utterly corrupted by self-indulgence, like so many tyrants and dictators of history. He can now indulge his fantasy of being omnipotent; he regards anyone who opposes his will as a criminal who deserves to suffer. Stalin and Hitler were Right Men; so, probably, was Mao Tse Tung. When, shortly before Mao's death, the Chinese demonstrated in the Square of Heavenly Peace in Peking against the downfall of the moderate Teng Hsiao-Ping, many were arrested; these were all shot or sentenced to long terms in prison. Mao was old and sick but he could still be roused to murderous rage by the least sign of contradiction or opposition.

But the tendency to live in a fantasy world can be the Right Man's downfall. He has constructed an edifice of self-delusion, a sandcastle that can be kicked down by reality at any moment. The total submission of his wife—real or apparent—is often the foundation stone of the fantasy. Van Vogt discovered that if the wife summons up courage to desert the Right Man, he often undergoes total collapse; he may suffer nervous breakdown or even commit suicide.

Now Van Vogt emphasises that the Right Man is not simply an habitual liar. 'He has a strong desire for truth, but the story of his life is an unconsciously distorted version, which shows him to have been a hundred per cent right and everyone else to have been wrong.' And, paradoxically enough, this 'strong desire for truth' may make the Right Man a good scientist or philosopher. It is only where *he* is concerned that his perception of truth is distorted; besides, which, the pursuit of abstract knowledge provides a welcome relief from his obsession with himself.

An example will serve to underline the point. The late C. E. M. Joad was an evolutionist philosopher and a disciple of Bergson and Shaw. During the Second World War, he became famous as a member of the BBC's Brain's Trust team. His manner was waspish, erudite and overbearing, the kind of man the audience 'loves to hate'. In private life he was a philanderer. He once said he had no interest in speaking with a woman unless she was willing to sleep with him. His wife apparently accepted these *affaires*.

On April 12, 1948, readers of the evening newspapers were startled by a headline: 'Dr Joad Fined for Common Ticket Fraud.' On a train from Waterloo to Exeter, Joad had attempted to save himself seventeen shillings and a penny by telling the ticket inspector that he had boarded the train at Salisbury. It was revealed later that Joad made a habit of defrauding the railway. The BBC dropped him from their programmes and the scandal ruined his career; he died four years later of cancer.

The case has obvious parallels with the Burt scandal; but where Joad is concerned, we are fortunately in possession of some of the answers.

His personality emerges clearly in his books, and in the testimony of acquaintances.[2] Even the titles reveal his obsessive self-preoccupation: *The Book of Joad, The Testament of Joad, The Pleasure of Being Oneself*. Most friends agree that he was a touchy man who could be thrown into a towering rage by any affront—real or imagined—to his dignity. But an appeal to his vanity could bring instant and magnanimous forgiveness. Like most Right Men he was not very deeply interested in the personality of other people; he preferred to impose his own over-simplified notions on them—even to calling all his mistresses Maureen.

Why, then, should he risk his career for this silly offence? When a friend later asked him this question, he admitted ruefully: 'Hubris.' But this tells us nothing. What we really need to know is that the Right Man lacks all sense of personal morality because he can always find a thousand reasons for believing that anything he does is correct. He is a spoilt child, who believes that his desires ought to be laws of nature. Joad actually wrote some perceptive books on moral philosophy, and there can be no doubt that, where mankind in general was concerned, his sense of morality was acute and profound. And anyone who believes that a Right Man cannot be a good philosopher should look at Joad's books; the best of them are witty, intelligent and stylish. Joad's moral blindness applied only to himself. His 'Rightness' was something he had to live with, like a lifelong illness.

The really disturbing implications of the Right Man theory begin to emerge when we try to draw the line between 'unbalanced' people like Joad and normal, decent people like ourselves. For it proves impossible to do it. The need for self-esteem is a fundamental appetite of human nature; to lack it would be as serious as lacking white corpuscles in the blood. All healthy, normal human beings dislike being in the wrong; we all feel embarrassed about making mistakes and being *seen* to make them. What is wrong with the Right Man is that he has never conquered a childish desire to have everything his own way, to have the universe bow to his wishes. But is there anyone who is totally free of this attitude? For example, anyone who doesn't swear when he hits his finger with a hammer? Or who doesn't feel furious when the taxi he has hailed stops a few yards away and someone else jumps in? But the hammer is an inanimate object. The other person has as much right to the taxi as you have. Nevertheless, the frustration arouses a flood of anger that would have made our Neolithic ancestors reach for their stone axes.

We accuse Joad of being basically uninterested in other people; but again, the cap fits any of us. We never, for example, fall in love with a *whole* person—simply with a pleasant smile, a musical voice, an attractive mannerism. These provide the basis for a kind of portrait; we add the rest ourselves, drawing the other qualities from some mental image of the kind of person we would like to fall in love with. Many people are married for a lifetime to a person they never really *know*, because they experience no real curiosity as to what the other person is actually like. Hundreds of wives of murderers have assured the police, with total sincerity, that their husband would be incapable of harming a fly. Provided the other person conforms to our mental image, we ask no questions.

Van Vogt points out that there are far more Right Men around than we ever realise. They are adept at concealing it from other people and from themselves. And again, the same thing applies to the rest of us. People who strike us as selfish or egocentric are the exceptions; yet as soon as we get to know them well, we become aware that even the nicest people are full of their own little vanities and delusions and bigotries. As to myself, I freely confess that I can detect some nasty pockets of Rightness in my own personality, although I doubt whether my friends are aware of them. Like certain butterflies, we have learned to adapt our coloration to the environment. It helps us to feel we are living in a society of normal, balanced people like ourselves.

It is when we begin to grasp its implications that this insight becomes truly alarming. Freud made us recognise that sex plays a far greater role in human life than the Victorians cared to acknowledge (although it now seems clear that he carried it to the point of absurdity). Van Vogt's achievement is equally striking; he has shown that egoism can produce a form of mild insanity, and that we all suffer from this to some extent. This immediately undermines one of our basic assumptions about human nature: that men can be relied on to behave sensibly out of 'rational self-interest'. Rightness overrules self-interest; it can make a man blind to his own destruction provided he can inflict damage on his enemy—or, better still, make him beg for mercy. And we are living in a society where practically everyone suffers from some degree of 'Rightness'. Good manners and social conventions have been developed to minimise the friction. But whenever these fail, the conflict comes out into the open. Governments issue ultimatums and threaten war, and whole nations are willing to agree that a few million dead is a small price to pay for avenging an insult.

In discussing the paranormal, all this turns out to be highly relevant. There is no subject that arouses more extreme reactions than 'the occult' (I use the term as a convenient label). The majority of scientists seem to feel that 'occultists' are mildly insane and should be locked up. The 'occultists' reply that scientists are conceited, prejudiced and intellectually dishonest. Both sides talk about reason, logic and evidence, and neither believes that the other side knows what these terms mean.

On the whole, the scientists seem to be in the stronger position. They point out that science is simply an attempt to understand the universe by asking intelligent questions. The scientist has no axe to grind; he sits down before fact like a little child, in the famous words of T. H. Huxley, and follows humbly wherever she leads. It is the religious people and the 'occultists' who distort the facts to accord with their own wishful thinking. They shrink from reason because it threatens their superstitions and dogmas. The whole shameful story can be read in Andrew White's remarkable *History of the Warfare of Science with Theology*, published as long ago as 1894, but still the classic account of the clash between superstition and reason. Seen in this light, the modern 'occultists' are simply the last lingering remnants of the forces of the Inquisition, who burnt Giordano Bruno and forced Galileo to recant by threats of torture.

It is a powerful and convincing argument. But we are in a position to see its basic weakness. Most good scientists are fairly dominant individuals, and dominant individuals are inclined to like to have their own way. This picture of the scientist as a detached investigator, pursuing truth with a humble and pure heart, is too good to be true. He may have the best intentions in the world; but unless he is aware of his innate tendency to 'Rightness', he will never achieve scientific detachment.

When we read *The History of the Warfare of Science with Theology* in the light of this recognition, it seems to change into a completely different book. White tells a harrowing story of the persecution of honest scientists by dogmatic churchmen; but when we read between the lines, or take the trouble to study the biographies of men like Bruno and Galileo, it ceases to be the story of reason versus superstition, and becomes a tale of Right Men locked in violent conflict.

Giordano Bruno, burnt at the stake in 1600, is usually regarded as a martyr in the cause of reason. Francis Yates's book *Giordano Bruno and the Hermetic Tradition* reveals not only that he was boastful, thin-skinned and paranoid, but also that he was the advocate of a sinister anti-Christian form of magic. Galileo was not the gentle, dedicated scientist portrayed in the play by Bertolt Brecht; he was conceited, bad-tempered and sarcastic. And, unfortunately, both of them came into head-on collision with an ecclesiastical opponent who was another Right Man. Bruno locked horns with Cardinal Robert Bellarmine, Jesuit consultant to the Inquisition, who was canonised in 1930. Bellarmine is described by a sympathetic biographer—Giorgio de Santillana—as 'immensely ambitious, direct, prompt to flashing anger . . . conceited about his intellectual gifts'—in fact, very like Bruno himself. Even so, had he been the gentlest and most compassionate soul in the world, he would have been unable to save Bruno. In order to escape the stake, Bruno would have had to recant and admit that he was—theologically speaking, anyway—in the wrong. He refused to recant, and left Bellarmine with no legal alternative to the death sentence.

Galileo's case has been the subject of even more misrepresentation. In fact, the Catholic Church was not doctrinally opposed to the belief that the sun is the centre of the solar system. This had first been proposed in 1543 by Copernicus, who was a canon of the Church; his book *On the Revolutions of the Heavenly Spheres* was actually dedicated to Pope Paul III. Protestants disliked it because it seemed to cast doubt on Holy Scripture. Catholics might suspect that it was ultimately nonsense, but no one seemed to regard it as a danger to the faith. In the normal course of events, the new ideas about the solar system would have flowed quietly into the Church until they were generally accepted, and no one would have made a fuss.

This 'normal course' was interrupted by the clash of two Right Men, Galileo and Pope Urban VIII. This is Jacob Bronowski's description of Urban VIII: 'He had a confident, impatient turn of mind: "I know better than all the cardinals put together . . ." he said imperiously. But in fact, Barberini as Pope turned out to be pure baroque: a lavish nepotist, extravagant, domineering, restless in his schemes, and absolutely tone-deaf to the ideas of others. He even had the birds killed in the Vatican gardens because they disturbed him.' It would be difficult to find a better description of a Right Man. But so was Galileo, although certainly to a lesser extent than Bruno. He was a man who refused to suffer fools gladly, and he had alienated his colleagues at the University of Pisa by writing satirical verse about them. In 1616, Galileo heard rumours that the Church was about to prohibit the teachings of Copernicus, so he went to Rome and talked to Cardinal Bellarmine. Bellarmine told him that he could not, in fact, teach that the system of Copernicus was a *proven fact*; but he *could* use it as a hypothesis. When Barberini became Pope Urban VIII in 1623, Galileo hurried along to see him. The Pope was sympathetic, but unwilling to go further than Bellarmine (who was now dead). Galileo was welcome to discuss the ideas of Copernicus in the form of a dialogue, putting the opposite case as well as his own, but he must not state dogmatically that Copernicus was right. He was also particularly insistent that Galileo should state in print that it would be absurd for anyone to limit God's power and wisdom to his own conjectures. He also made various other suggestions about the dialogue, which Galileo promised to include.

Eight years later, in 1632, the Pope saw a copy of the printed book *Dialogue on the Two Chief World Systems*, and was infuriated to find that Galileo had not stuck to his side of the bargain; he had come down squarely in favour of the system of Copernicus. But the crowning insult was that he had put one of the Pope's suggestions into the mouth of a fool (*in bocca di un sciocco*) who was actually named Simplicio. This was not only defying the Pope, but twisting his tail. Understandably, Galileo was summoned to Rome and ordered to retract. When he did so, there was no stake, or even prison. He was allowed to return home and remain under house arrest; he was also made to promise not to write any more. He ignored this and wrote a book on physics, which was printed in the Netherlands; but the Holy Office made no attempt to punish him for breaking his word.

What is perfectly clear is that Galileo *could* have published all his arguments in favour of the heliocentric system if he had ended it by saying: 'Of course, only God knows if all this is true.' It would have had precisely the same effect as the book he actually wrote and would probably have been accepted by the Church within a decade or so.

Instead, he went about it with the tactlessness and stubbornness of a Right Man and infuriated the Pope to whom he had given his word. And since the Pope was the stronger of the two, Galileo was rapped on the knuckles and ordered to apologise. The Pope emerges from it without much credit, but so does Galileo.

In the long run, of course, Galileo triumphed. Before the end of the century, Newton's *Principia* had placed the Copernican theory beyond argument, and the Church had considerable difficulty explaining why it had ever opposed it. From then on, it was a great deal more circumspect about interfering in matters of science. In fact, the Galileo affair was its last major intervention.

According to *A History of the Warfare of Science with Theology*, the Church continued to fight a vigorous rearguard action for the next two centuries, doing its best to slow down the advance of geology, astronomy and the theory of evolution. But when we turn to the history books, we again discover that this is a curiously one-sided account. What White somehow refrains from mentioning is that it was the scientists themselves who, as often as not, dug in their heels against some new discovery, and opposed it with all the force of deep-seated prejudice. White mentions, for example, that the potter Bernard Palissy was charged with heresy for suggesting that fossils are the bones of long-dead animals (he died in the Bastille in 1589). But he fails to add that when an amateur geologist, Johann Scheuchzer, defended the same notion in a pamphlet in 1708, the Church found no fault with his views; it was the scientists who dismissed the idea, citing Aristotle to support their view that fossils are merely rocks that happen to look like living creatures. The arch-rationalist Voltaire took a hand in the controversy on the side of the scientists; he conceded that bones might turn into stone but argued that the fossilised bones found on mountains were probably dead fishes thrown away by travellers.

The theory of evolution was not invented by Charles Darwin, or even by his grandfather Erasmus Darwin. The credit should probably go to a French diplomat named Benoît de Maillet, born in Lorraine in 1656. Around 1715, Maillet wrote a book called *Telliamed* (his own name spelt backwards), which propounded a remarkably accurate view of evolution. The germ of life came from space, said de Maillet, and gradually developed into simple marine organisms in the primeval ocean. Fishes crawled up onto the land and developed into animals and birds. This happened, he said, over vast spans of time.

Maillet decided against publishing his book during his lifetime; it might have endangered his job as a government official. It appeared in 1749, eleven years after his death. But many people had read the manuscript, and the idea of evolution was being widely discussed by the 1730s. Again, it was almost unanimously rejected by the scientists, led by the greatest palaeontologist of the eighteenth century, Karl Linnaeus, who began his monumental *System of Nature* (1735) with the assertion: 'There are as many species now as at the beginning of creation.' (He also dismissed fossils in a single page on minerals.) Voltaire also poured scorn on Maillet's theory in the name of reason and common sense.

The Church was not entirely out of the running. In 1750, the naturalist Count Buffon, superintendent of the royal gardens, wrote *Theory of the Earth*, in which he asserted that the earth was originally a fragment of the sun and that fossils were the remains of primitive ancestors of present-day creatures. The Church was shocked, and the censors pointed out that Buffon's views did not accord with the Biblical account of creation. In a subsequent volume of the *Natural History*, Buffon was obliged to explain that nothing was farther from his thoughts than contradicting the Holy Scriptures. But he went on expounding his theory of evolution, and he suffered no further persecution.

Unfortunately, the one element in Buffon's theory that made a general impact was his explanation of why these earlier species had become extinct. The materialist philosopher Lamettrie had stumbled on the correct answer: because they failed in the battle for survival and died out. Buffon rejected this; instead, he suggested that the earth had been subject to a series of violent catastrophes—floods and earthquakes—that had destroyed all life. Then 'spontaneous generation' had occurred, and it started all over again. This theory of 'catastrophism' was to become another dogma that would cause endless trouble during the next fifty years or so.

The poet Goethe also ventured into evolutionary theory and instinctively came up with most of the right answers. In the 1780s, living at Weimar as a minister of the ducal court, Goethe became interested in palaeontology. He was particularly intrigued by the statement of the Dutch palaeontologist Peter Camper to the effect that man differs from the lower animals in having no intermaxillary bone (the bone in the upper jaw that contains the incisors). Goethe declined to believe that man is fundamentally different from other animals; so he proceeded to study as many skulls as he could borrow from the Weimar museum. In March 1784 he announced to his friend Herder that he had found the intermaxillary bone in man; it was barely visible, but it existed. He wrote a paper about it and sent it to Camper; Camper was duly respectful to the famous poet and friend of the Duke Karl August; but he explained patronisingly that Goethe could not have discovered traces of the intermaxillary bone in man because it didn't exist. Goethe tried sending his essay to Buffon's follower Blumenbach, whom he knew to be open-minded; he was baffled and irritated when Blumenbach was equally dismissive. Goethe was having his first taste of the peculiar conceit of scientists. He failed to understand that they regarded him as an interloper, a clumsy amateur. So he pressed on alone to develop his own theory of evolution, including a speculation that the multiplicity of living creatures had originally developed from a few basic forms or archetypes. The scientists continued to ignore him until a century later, when it was safe to hail him as an inspired forerunner of Darwin.

Perhaps the saddest casualty of Buffon's catastrophe theory was his friend and pupil, Jean-Baptiste Lamarck. Understandably, Lamarck was an enthusiastic advocate of the theory of evolution developed by Maillet, Lamettrie and Buffon. But he could see no reason for the 'catastrophes'. Surely the diversity of species could be explained by the diversity of conditions on earth? A bear in a snowy climate would need to develop a white coat to conceal it from its prey; a forest bear would need to blend into the trees.

In 1794, a young man named Georges Cuvier applied for a job at the Jardin des Plantes; he became a special favourite of Lamarck. In fact, Cuvier proved to be another born palaeontologist like Linnaeus, with a natural genius for comparative anatomy. His bold theories earned him a reputation as something of a revolutionary. Yet in the essentials, he was far more conservative than Lamarck. He accepted Linnaeus's view that species are immutable, although Linnaeus himself changed his mind towards the end of his life. He also felt that Buffon's catastrophe theory was a matter of common sense. After all, our eyes tell us

that many species are now extinct; they have not evolved into something else. He concluded that creation must have taken place in a series
of steps—first for vertebrates, then insects, then molluscs, then
worms.

His incredible learning lent authority to his views. He was famous
for being able to reconstruct a whole prehistoric animal from a single
bone; he argued that nature is totally consistent and that animal
characteristics come in sets (he called this the Law of Correlations).

Cuvier finally used his Law of Correlations to destroy the reputation and the livelihood of his old friend and patron. One day, Cuvier
came to Lamarck's lecture to heckle. He challenged Lamarck to prove
that fossils are ancestors of present-day species. Lamarck replied that
this was impossible. Then Cuvier led the students back to his own
lecture room and announced that he would prove he knew more about
fossils than Lamarck. He identified a prehistoric fossil from a single
bone protruding from a slab of rock. Then, with careful deliberation,
he chiselled away the rock until the students could see that his identification was correct. The students carried him out in triumph, and from
then on, Lamarck's lectures were deserted. He died a few years later,
discredited and forgotten. No one noticed that Cuvier's 'proof' was a
non sequitur; the correct identification of a fossil from a single bone
neither proves nor disproves the theory of evolution.

Understandably, Andrew White has no mention of this incident.
But he *is* compelled to acknowledge that Cuvier was a dogmatic bully.
His manner of doing so is rather interesting. He explains that Cuvier
took up the warfare 'avowedly for science, but unconsciously for
theology', and he goes on to explain that 'there was in him, as in
Linnaeus, a survival of certain theological ways of looking at the
universe'. White is committed to the view that all theologians are
dogmatic and superstitious, and all scientists are open-minded and
reasonable; so if Cuvier and Linnaeus were dogmatic and unreasonable, they must be disguised theologians. Van Vogt's view at least has
the advantage of removing the contradiction. We would expect a
scientist who was a Right Man to behave very much like a theologian
who was a Right Man, and vice versa.

Even in death, Cuvier was lucky; he died in 1832, just before the
catastrophe theory was finally discredited by the discoveries of
geologists like Charles Lyell. And science had a quarter of a century to

recover from the result of Cuvier's wrong-headedness before Charles Darwin sounded the trumpet for the next major battle in the 'warfare of science with theology'.

The Darwinian controversy enables us to see what had started to go wrong with science and what has continued to go wrong ever since. At first sight, it appears to be simply a battle between the forces of progress and the forces of reaction. Darwin's chief opponent, Bishop Wilberforce (known as Soapy Sam because of his unctuous manner) was so obviously a pompous bigot that he played straight into the hands of the scientists. When someone told him that Darwin had spent twenty years proving his theory of evolution, Wilberforce replied crushingly: 'A person of intelligence needs only ten minutes' reflection to see that the theory is utterly imposible.' In a debate at Oxford, he was deservedly pulverised by T. H. Huxley, after he had enquired whether Huxley was descended from a monkey on his father's or his mother's side of the family. Huxley retorted: 'I would not be ashamed to have a monkey for an ancestor, but I *would* be ashamed to be connected with a man who used his great gifts to obscure the truth.'

But the story spotlights the inaccuracy of the usual view of the controversy. It was not really about whether man is descended from a monkey. If it had been, we would now have to acknowledge that Wilberforce was right and Huxley was wrong; for we now know that the hominids (man-stock) separated from our mutual ancestor at least thirty-five million years ago. The present-day monkey is no more than a very distant cousin—as distant, say, as the horse and the camel.

But this is *not* what the controversy was about. What really alarmed the Church was Darwin's implication that there is no such thing as free will, and that we are living in a godless and meaningless universe. A century earlier, the philosopher Julien de Lamettrie had caused a similar scandal with a book called *Man the Machine* (1748), in which he had argued that the soul does not exist and man can be explained purely in mechanical terms. The rage aroused by this view was not so much based on religious conviction as a feeling that Lamettrie was talking outrageous nonsense, which nevertheless defied all attempts to *pin down* its basic fallacy. Darwin himself was an orthodox Christian who never suggested that man was a machine or that nature was purposeless. But his theory of Natural Selection seemed to make free will superfluous. Lamarck had believed that species evolve because they *want* to; the giraffe developed its long neck and the ant-eater its long nose by trying to reach into inaccessible places. Darwin did not deny that; but he also pointed out that there was no need for any effort. In times of food shortage, short-necked giraffes or brown polar bears would die out, and only long-necked giraffes and white polar bears would live to continue the species. Samuel Butler went straight to the point when he said that Darwin had 'banished mind from the universe'.

The monkey issue enabled the Darwinians to score an easy victory over the Church, and over men like Wilberforce and Disraeli (who raised a laugh by saying that he was 'on the side of the angels'). It made it look as if such people were merely standing on their dignity, unwilling to be classified with the 'lower animals', when what they really objected to was being classified with lumps of rock and clods of earth. And this was not a matter of dignity, but of common sense. The quickest way to destroy a man is to take away his sense of freedom and meaning; and the same thing applies to civilisations. If Wilberforce had been intelligent enough to go to the heart of the matter, he would have pointed out that science had involved itself in a basic contradiction, and that if it was not careful, it would end by tying itself in knots. Men become scientists for the same reason they become explorers: for the joy of discovery, the excitement of new vistas, the sense of unknown possibilities. If, out of sheer mischievous delight in upsetting the Church, the scientists insist that there is no such thing as free will and that the universe is meaningless and purposeless, they are doing more harm than a dozen Torquemadas. It is preposterous to destroy man's sense of freedom in the name of freeing him from the dogmatism of wicked theologians; it is stupid to try to convince him that he is a machine in order to free him from the superstition that he possesses an immortal soul and the power to decide his own fate.

The scientists were too delighted to be allowed to shake their fists at the Church and get away with it to bother their heads about such matters. In fact, what had really happened was that science had 'come to power', as the *sans culottes* came to power in France in 1789 and the Communists in Russia in 1917. The old régime was being swept away, and the scientists had no intention of giving it the slightest foothold in their new world of ideas.

In retrospect, we can see that science had no right whatever to pronounce on matters of free will and purpose, any more than Pope Urban VIII had any right to pronounce on the solar system. Darwin was concerned with scientific facts, and these are undeniable. But his demonstration of the mechanism of evolution did not 'prove' materialism, any more than Lamettrie's demonstration that man is a machine disproves free will. Anyone has a right to state that the universe is made of matter; no one has a right to state that it is made of nothing but. Anyone has a right to point out that man is a machine (Gurdjieff did it repeatedly); no one has a right to assert that he is *merely* a machine and incapable of being anything else.

A few scientists and philosophers were worried by this totalitarian trend; some of them even had the courage to try to correct it. A young biologist named Hans Driesch, who worked in the Marine Zoology Station at Naples in the last decade of the nineteenth century, began to have his doubts about the orthodox mechanistic position. He was not bothered by its philosophical aspect but by purely practical considerations. He tried repeating an experiment on a fertilised ovum that had been performed by Wilhelm Roux. It consisted in waiting until a frog's egg divided and then killing off one half with a hot needle. The remaining half developed—as one might expect—into a mere half-embryo. This, said Roux, is because an egg is a kind of machine, and the surviving part develops automatically, unaware that half its parts is missing. Driesch tried performing the same experiment with the eggs of a sea urchin. To his surprise, the surviving half developed into a perfect but half-sized embryo. Each half of the egg apparently contained a 'blueprint' of the whole. Driesch found himself wondering how a 'machine' could rebuild the same organism if it is chopped in two. It sounded oddly like a sense of purpose.

He tried flattening an egg between glass slides; when the pressure was removed, it reshaped itself into a ball. If he pressed two eggs together, they fused and produced a double-sized larva. Roux had obtained his result with frog's eggs because they tend to be far less adaptable than most other kinds; yet even frog's eggs would show 'purposive' behaviour if handled carefully. In other words, it was important not to 'discourage' them. And the very notion of discouragement again raises the notion of free will.

Driesch concluded that the living cell aims at some kind of 'wholeness'. And if it can 'aim', he argued, it cannot be wholly mechanical. From this, he went on to suggest that organisms can only be understood as functioning *wholes*; physics and chemistry can never tell us everything about a living organism. And finally, almost ten years after he had begun to feel his first misgivings, he took the plunge and announced his conviction that the vital, purposive part of a living creature is somehow *completely separate* from its chemistry, acting from another dimension, as it were. His critics lost no time in pointing out that Driesch's 'vitalism' was no more than a return to the old religious notion of body and soul. Driesch disagreed; he felt that what he had to say was far more complex and interesting. In 1908, he made the mistake of abandoning science for philosophy. As far as the scientists were concerned, he had now shown himself in his true colours; a philosopher was little more than a theologian in disguise. He could be safely ignored. And the scientists continued to ignore Driesch until his death in 1941. What had happened is what we would have expected from Van Vogt's Right-Man theory. The scientists had simply stepped into the shoes of the theologians.

The full irony of the situation can be appreciated in the strange history of the rise and fall of Trofim Lysenko. In Russia in the late 1920s, a form of Lamarckism was championed by the agriculturalist I. V. Michurin, whose work with fruit trees gained Stalin's approval. Michurin believed that acquired characteristics *can* be passed on to future generations; a case in point, he believed, was winter wheat, which could become 'vernalised'—adapted to spring sowing—by treating it with water and refrigeration. T. D. Lysenko, another skilled horticulturalist, adopted this method for large-scale use, with beneficial results on the Russian harvests in the early 1930s. Lysenko became Stalin's favourite scientist, not simply because he had improved wheat production (a point that is sometimes disputed), but because his philosophy seemed ideally suited to propaganda purposes. Lysenko believed that heredity counts for nothing, environment for everything. So all the Communists had to do was improve the environment, and within a couple of generations they would breed a new type of Russian.

The optimism was certainly Lamarckian; Bernard Shaw had been saying something of the sort since 1900. But Lysenko was in a peculiar position, living in a society that was based on dialectical materialism and preaching a philosophy based on free will and purpose. And at a scientific congress in 1936, the contradiction began to seem absurd. Lysenko announced that the genetic theory of evolution—based on Darwin and Mendel—was nonsense, nothing more than a Fascist plot to justify oppression. Soviet 'materialist' biology, he said, contemptuously rejects all such 'idealistic' absurdities. So the chief exponent of Mendelism, N. I. Vavilov, was arrested and charged with spying and planning to wreck Russian agriculture; he died in prison. The war intervened to prevent the further decimation of Russian biologists, but at the 1948 meeting of the Lenin Academy of Agriculture five more biologists were accused of the Mendelian heresy and forced to apologise and confess their error.

The confusion was now complete. Soviet 'materialists', who believed in free will, denounced Western 'idealists' who rejected it. And Western 'idealists', who believed in freedom of expression, denounced their Soviet colleagues for jailing people who disbelieved in free will. It was as if all the labels had come off, and then been stuck back on the wrong people.

Finally, Stalin died and was denounced by Khrushchev as a tyrant; Lysenko shared his master's disgrace. And Russian biologists turned thankfully from optimistic 'materialism' to the pessimistic 'idealism' of the West. They are again free to think what they like—provided, of course, this does not include a belief in Lamarckism or free will.

Obviously neither science nor religion possesses a monopoly on truth. Ideally, science is the impersonal pursuit of truth; but then, so is religion—as all the saints and mystics have recognised. And to pursue truth requires some of the qualities of a saint and mystic. Ordinary human beings are too easily swayed by the appetite for power and recognition and self-esteem.

For the past four centuries, science has been victim of the delusion that all that is necessary to pursue truth is the 'scientific method'. The history of science reveals that this view is false. Scientists squabble as bitterly—and as frequently—as theologians, and are just as prone to use personal authority to suppress their opponents.

Does this mean that scientific truth is unattainable? Obviously not. Newton was probably the most neurotic and paranoid of all great scientists; he was so suspicious of others that he refused to publish his discoveries lest they be stolen. Yet the *Principia* is a monument to 'scientific truth'. This proves that a Right Man can be a great scientist; but it does not prove that paranoia is a desirable intellectual quality. The problem, clearly, is that most scientists are not sufficiently self-critical to recognise when they are behaving like theologians.

In his important study *The Structure of Scientific Revolutions* (1962),

Thomas S. Kuhn has a story that goes to the heart of the matter. In 1949, J. S. Bruner and Leo Postman devised an interesting experiment in perception. Subjects were asked to call out the names of playing cards that were shown to them. Some of these cards had been specially made, and included deliberate 'freaks' such as black hearts and red clubs. When exposures were brief, the subjects would call 'hearts' or 'clubs' without noticing anything wrong. When the exposures were longer, they became puzzled; they knew there was something amiss, but couldn't tell what. If exposures were long enough, most of them finally saw what was wrong. But there were a few who never fathomed what was going on, and these experienced 'acute personal distress'.

Kuhn argues that once scientists have become comfortably settled with a certain theory, they are deeply unwilling to admit that there might be anything wrong with it. If small facts contradict the theory, they tend to ignore them. If the contradictory facts grow larger, they become distressed and angry. But they are totally unaware that there is anything unreasonable about this reaction; they feel that it is the natural annoyance of a reasonable man in the face of time-wasting absurdities.

Kuhn might also have cited one of the most significant experiments in the history of scientific research; it was conducted at Radcliffe College in 1942 by Dr Gertrude Schmeidler, and has become known as 'the sheep and the goats experiment'. Dr Schmeidler was testing a group of students for evidence of extrasensory perception by asking them to guess cards. Before the experiment, she asked which of them believed in the possibility of ESP. Those who said yes she classified as sheep; those who said no were goats. The results of the test showed that the sheep scored significantly above chance, which was interesting enough. What was even more extraordinary was that *the goats somehow managed to score significantly below*. That is to say, they were quite unconsciously 'cheating' to support their view that there was no such thing as extrasensory perception. They must have been ignoring their genuine 'hunches' about the correct identity of the cards. In doing so, they were revealing as much ESP as the sheep, but using it negatively. They were being influenced by their determination *not* to believe in ESP.

Kuhn was not the first to analyse this unconscious negativity.

William James had already put his finger on it in an essay with the significant title 'On a Certain Blindness in Human Beings'. And James's recognition of this deliberate 'blindness' formed the basis of the work of another New Yorker who spent his life haranguing the scientists on their lack of open-mindedness. His name was Charles Hoy Fort, and, by a peculiar irony, this rigidly methodical collector of 'awkward facts' has become known as a kind of patron saint of cranks.

Fort was the eldest son of a wealthy and bad-tempered businessman; he grew up with a smarting sense of injustice and a dislike of both his parents. At the age of twenty-two, he supported himself by writing stories in a style that owed something to Mark Twain. He also cultivated a taste for oddities—books about the Great Pyramid, Atlantis and the canals of Mars. His first non-fiction book, written in his mid-thirties, was called simply *X* and argued that our civilisation is controlled from Mars. In his next book *Y*, he espoused the hollow-earth theory and described a civilisation inside the South Pole. After many rejections, both manuscripts were lost. They seem to have been an anticipation of the kind of thing that was to make Erich von Däniken famous in the 1960s. The reason for their rejection was fairly certainly Fort's atrocious style—a disability that obviously bothered publishers more in 1910 than it did in the 1960s.

In 1916, when Fort was forty-two, a small legacy enabled him to devote his days to writing another book, originally to be called *Z*. He began to spend his days in the public libraries of New York, searching the periodicals for reports of strange and unexplained events. It struck him that although scientific journals often *reported* curious happenings, no one seemed to want to explain them. Particularly numerous were reports of things falling from the sky: not just meteorites, but showers of stones, coal, fishes, frogs, sand, even blood. They sounded too silly to be significant. But Fort pointed out that in September 13, 1768, French peasants in the fields near Luce heard a violent crash like a thunderclap and saw a great stone object hurtle down from the sky. The French Academy of Sciences asked the great chemist Lavoisier for a report on the occurrence; but Lavoisier was convinced that stones never fell out of the sky, and reported that all the witnesses were mistaken or lying. It was not until the nineteenth century that the Academy finally accepted the reality of meteorites.

The Book of the Damned was a collection of hundreds of unexplained events, and it made Fort's reputation among literary men. It failed to reach a wider public because Fort wrote in an almost unreadable style, hopping from subject to subject. But the facts are certainly astonishing enough. He describes, for example, a strange series of events that took place in the early 1860s. In July 1860, a great meteorite covered with ice crashed down in Dhurmsalla, India, and was described by the British Deputy Commissioner in the area. But how could a meteorite—which becomes red hot as it falls through our atmosphere—be covered with ice? The following evening, the Commissioner saw lights moving in the sky like fire balloons. At the same time, a Benares newspaper carried a circumstantial report of a shower of live fish, while at Farrukabhad a red substance rained from the clouds. In 1861 there was an earthquake at Singapore, followed by days of torrential rain; in the pools left in the streets, live fish were found swimming. The popular theory that the rain had caused a river to overflow seemed to be contradicted when fish were found in a courtyard surrounded by a high wall.

Fort suspected that these curious phenomena were somehow connected with space; there were luminous effects in the sky like an aurora borealis at the time of these curious events, a period of darkness during daylight hours, a dark spot on the sun, and an earthquake. We may know a great deal about the surface of our planet, but we know very little about the billions of miles of space that the earth travels through. Fort's biographer Damon Knight was inclined to take the same view after he had gone to the trouble of making a vast card index of all the odd events described in Fort's books, then making graphs showing the times of their occurrence. He discovered an immediate correlation between storms, things seen in the sky, things falling from the air, and things seen in space (like sunspots and comets). For example, all of them reached a peak in 1887 and again in 1892. Knight suggests tentatively that such events could be connected with forces exerted by heavenly bodies—the forces astrologers believe in. But Fort makes no attempt to present a coherent argument, in either *The Book of the Damned* or the three volumes that followed it. He is capable of suggesting on one page that there was some sort of floating continent hovering in the sky over India in 1860, and on the next, that there is a sort of universe parallel to ours but in another 'dimension'. You get the feeling that he takes neither idea seriously. His aim was to provoke 'anger and distress' in the scientists, and to force them into examining their assumptions. He succeeded in neither object; the scientists ignored him.

After his death in 1932, Fort's work was largely forgotten, except by a small circle of admirers who formed a Fortean Society. It began to attract attention again in the late 1940s, after the curious affair of Kenneth Arnold and his sighting of nine Unidentified Flying Objects near Mount Rainier in Washington State.[3] As the flying saucer cult gained momentum, somebody remembered that Fort had been talking about such things for years. For example, in *The Book of the Damned* he had cited the experience of the astronomer E. W. Maunder, of Greenwich Observatory; in November 1882, Maunder had observed a kind of aurora, and in the midst of it, a great circular disc of greenish light that passed across the moon. In the same book, he suggests that there have been many 'visitors' to earth, and even —probably his most famous idea—that mankind might be the 'property' of such aliens. But Fort had never committed himself to any single Däniken-type theory about gods from the stars. Fort's attitude to data could be described as sitting on a fence with both ears to the ground.

All the same, the increasing discussion of UFOs, the moon landings, the speculations about life on other planets, suddenly made Fort's work relevant to a wider public than ever before. He became known as the Prophet of the Unexplained. This was, in a sense, a misrepresentation. After all, if scientists should finally discover that UFOs *are* visitors from other planets or other dimensions this would qualify as a scientific discovery, and Fort would be simply a far-sighted pioneer. But that is not what really concerned him; he had no desire to join the scientists. His books are so irritating and repetitive because he was struggling to enunciate a basic criticism of the whole idea of science. And it was, fundamentally, the criticism we have examined in this chapter: the feeling that no matter how honest scientists *think* they are, they are still influenced by various *unconscious* assumptions that prevent them from attaining true objectivity. Expressed in a sentence, Fort's Principle goes something like this: people with a psychological need to believe in marvels are no more prejudiced and gullible than people with a psychological need *not* to believe in marvels.

So let us conclude this chapter by re-stating Fort's basic argument—which also happens to be the basic argument of this book.

Science is a method of investigating the universe. Any good investigator begins by trying to *take his bearings*. He attempts to form a mental map of the kind of universe he thinks he is investigating (Ptolemy's 'map' showed the earth at the centre of the universe and the stars and planets all revolving round it). Such a mental map is called a 'paradigm'.

When we look at the history of science, we see that paradigms are always being scrapped and replaced by new ones, but this is not quite the automatic process one might expect. Scientists seem to hate to abandon their old paradigms and cling to them as long as possible, determinedly ignoring or dismissing the new evidence that is trying to push them into reconsidering.

We all have a basic need to believe that the universe is a stable and orderly place, as was interestingly demonstrated in an experiment conducted by Dr Anton Hajos at Innsbruck University in the early 1960s. Hajos constructed a pair of spectacles that made everything look distorted. Straight lines became curved, angles were twisted out of shape, and outlines were fringed with prisms of colour. Objects were not where they were supposed to be and made abrupt movements when the subject turned his head. Yet when people were made to wear these spectacles all the time, they quickly became used to them. Lines straightened out, prismatic colours disappeared, and after six days, the world once again looked perfectly normal. When the spectacles were taken off, the trouble began all over again, and it took several days for things to return to normal.

Human beings possess a powerful stabilising mechanism, which operates on the psychological as well as the physical level. This explains why they can accomplish such an apparently impossible feat as riding a bicycle and why people whose lives have been shattered by some appalling disaster—like an earthquake—can pick up the pieces and start anew. A person who feels deeply insecure is afraid to begin living. *That* is why we tend to ignore things that upset our basic sense of normality—or to forget them as quickly as possible. It is not 'choice' but a subconscious mechanism.

Admittedly, a world full of 'exceptions' would become a kind of nightmare. We can all remember the difficulties of the first day at a new school, or the emotional upheavals of adolescence, when the certainties of childhood seemed to cave in beneath our feet. Nobody could stand too many of these 'revolutions'. But a world with *no* 'exceptions' would either turn us into vegetables or drive us insane with boredom. Poets have been known to become alcoholics or drug addicts to escape too much 'stability'.

The problem is to strike a balance between the two extremes. We need a world with enough strangeness and 'newness' to keep us awake but not enough to produce a feeling of insecurity. And here we have to recognise that different people can stand different degrees of uncertainty. As we have seen, most scientists seem to have a strong compulsion to cling to their old paradigms. By contrast, people like Fort and Lethbridge take pleasure in the fact that the world is bursting with anomalies. It is true that Lethbridge compared his discoveries to a feeling of ice collapsing beneath his feet; but he never seemed unduly alarmed at the coldness of the water.

Both Lethbridge and Fort, however, failed to offer a new paradigm. Lethbridge tried hard, but there is nothing in his books to make an open-minded scientist start revising his view of the universe. Fort openly admitted that he had no new theory of the universe to offer. His major contribution was to repeat, over and over again, that the paradigms of the scientists were totally inadequate. Both men could be accused of not being sufficiently conversant with the sheer *extent* of the field of the 'paranormal'.

For example, Lethbridge's observations of the behaviour of the pendulum clearly imply that there is some 'other' part of the mind that knows the answers to all kinds of questions. He writes in *ESP: Beyond Time and Distance*: 'Although this influence may well be Jung's psyche, it seems unlikely that it is unconscious. In fact it appears to be very much awake and much more knowledgeable than the brain.' He recognised Jung as one of the chief pioneers of these unknown areas of consciousness; yet he seems never to have taken the trouble to read Jung systematically and find out what he had to say about the collective unconscious. In fact, Jung's studies in multiple personality—with which he began his career as a psychologist—were anticipated by Pierre Janet, whose insights into the structure of the psyche explain how a part of the mind can be 'unconscious' and yet 'more knowledgeable than the brain'. Until we begin to study these actual *mechanisms* and how they relate to ESP, precognition, and the strange energies that produce poltergeist activity, we cannot hope to begin to produce a paradigm that will satisfy the scientists.

The same kind of criticism could be directed at Jung. At a fairly early stage in his career, he recognised instinctively that the parts of the mind that interested him were also connected with 'paranormal' cognition, second sight, and so on. He also came to recognise that the half-forgotten science of alchemy is full of clues to these areas of the psyche. Yet, although he wrote three large books on alchemy, he made no attempt to connect his interest in alchemy with his interest in the paranormal, presumably because he had no idea of how to go about it. He might have found his clues in the work of Gurdjieff, who referred to his method as a form of alchemy; but apparently he never took the trouble to investigate.

There is no reason why we should not take our clues wherever we can find them—in Lethbridge, Jung, Janet, Gurdjieff, alchemy, astrology, even ritual magic. Let us see, therefore, if we can at least supply some of the missing parts of Lethbridge's paradigm.

2

How Many Me's Are There?

—————◆—————

When Carl Jung was still a university student at Basle, he was intrigued by the behaviour of a female cousin aged fifteen and a half who began to exhibit signs of multiple personality. She would become suddenly pale, sink slowly to the ground (or a chair), then begin to speak in a manner completely unlike her everyday self. Instead of her usual Swiss dialect, she spoke literary German in a smooth and assured manner. Various spirits claimed to speak through her mouth, and her mannerisms changed completely as different ones 'took over'. One of them claimed to be her grandfather who had been a banal and sanctimonious clergyman. Another was an inane chatterer who flirted with the ladies who came to the 'séances'. Another, who claimed to be a nobleman, was an amusing gossip who spoke High German with a North German accent.

Jung began to attend his cousin's Sunday evening séances. The group would join hands around the table, and the table would immediately begin to move. His cousin would then go into a trance. Sometimes the 'spirits' spoke through her—mostly rambling and unimportant material that might have come from second-rate books. Sometimes the girl seemed to go into an ecstatic sleep; when she woke up, she would tell them how she had left her body and moved into a realm of spirits. In this 'other world' she became a mature, rather saintly personality called Ivenes. Sometimes Ivenes spoke during the séances; she was intelligent, confident, modest and self-possessed and claimed to be the 'real' S.W. (the initials with which Jung concealed his cousin's identity).

All this was the more surprising because S.W. herself sounds like a singularly dreary girl. Jung describes her as being of mediocre intelligence, with no special gifts, shy, hesitant and poorly educated. Her father was dead, and her mother treated her—and her brothers and sisters—so badly that she spent as little time as possible at home. Physically, she was pale and unattractive, with a rachitic skull. Yet in séances, says Jung, 'she could talk so seriously, so forcefully and convincingly, that one almost had to ask oneself: Is this really a girl of fifteen and a half? One had the impression that a mature woman was being acted out with considerable dramatic talent.'

Ivenes disclosed that Jung's female cousin was only the latest of her incarnations; she had been a Christian martyr at the time of Nero, a French countess called de Valours who had been burnt as a witch, a clergyman's wife who had borne Goethe an illegitimate child, and Frederika Hauffe, the 'seeress of Prevorst', about whom the poet Justinus Kerner had written a well-known book. (Jung's cousin read this book some time after she began to experience trance states; it was after this that Ivenes declared that the seeress had been one of her previous incarnations.)

Jung took many notes at the séances and later expanded them into the thesis he submitted for his doctorate, his first published work. At this time, he had no thought of becoming a psychiatrist. But while staying in the house of a fellow medical student, he came upon books on spiritualism, and began to wonder if this had any bearing on his cousin's fits of 'somnambulism', as it was then called. Later, a book by Krafft-Ebing, author of the famous *Psychopathia Sexualis*, convinced him that psychiatry held the key to the mystery.

He found his cousin's subsequent history less interesting. In her early twenties, she took up dressmaking and designing, and the 'mature' personality took over; she became a considerable success and employed many assistants. She continued to hold séances but after one of these admitted to Jung that her trance had been simulated; as her 'psychic powers' waned, she felt the need to fake results. Jung stopped seeing her. She developed tuberculosis and died at twenty-six. Jung suspected that she had an unconscious knowledge that she would die young, and that the personality of Ivenes was an attempt to compensate for her lack of full maturity. She had often said that her soul hung on to her body by a thin thread and that her body could scarcely go on living. In *Memories, Dreams, Reflections*, Jung records that 'during the last months of her life her character disintegrated bit by bit, and . . . ultimately she returned to the state of a two-year-old child, in which condition she fell into her last sleep'.

When Jung wrote his thesis 'On the Psychology and Pathology of So-Called Occult Phenomena' in 1902,[1] he had no doubt that there was nothing supernatural about his cousin's attacks. The trance personalities displayed no knowledge that his cousin could not have acquired normally, and they tended to be evasive when asked direct questions about themselves. The sexual adventures of her previous 'incarnations' seemed to be typical of a pubescent girl's fantasies. In spite of this, there was the plain fact that his cousin was a dull, stupid girl, while Ivenes showed mature intelligence. Moreover, Ivenes had propounded a mystic-philosophic system about the purpose of the universe, which Jung regarded as a remarkable intellectual achievement—at least, for his cousin. Jung later read widely in occult literature in search of parallels, and found many, particularly in Gnostic systems. But his cousin certainly never had access to these books.

Jung's conclusion was that his cousin's strange behaviour was basically nothing more than a vivid fantasy life—that she was a kind of Walter Mitty who threw herself into her daydreams with such conviction that she actually 'lived' them. Her chief difference from 'pathological dreamers' was that 'her dreams came up explosively, suddenly bursting forth with amazing completeness from the darkness of the unconscious'. As a young man, Jung had been impressed by *The Philosophy of the Unconscious* by Edouard von Hartmann, so he was already familiar with this concept. The case of his cousin brought it home to him as a reality, a realm of mystery like the depths of the sea; he later spoke of 'this dark side of the soul [that] does not come within the purview of consciousness'. In 1900, while still attending séances at his cousin's house, he had read Freud's book *The Interpretation of Dreams* but gained nothing from it. When he read it again three years later, he had had time to digest and reflect on the séances, and the book struck him as a revelation. The result was that for the next ten years,

Jung was basically a Freudian (in spite of the reservations about Freud's emphasis on sex); the questions he had posed at the end of the paper on his cousin's multiple personality remained unanswered.

When Jung speaks of his cousin in *Memories, Dreams, Reflections*, he mentions two events that were omitted from the earlier paper. A few weeks before he heard of his cousin's 'illness', the dining-room table suddenly split with a loud report. There was no heat in the vicinity, and it had split not along a joint but through the solid wood. Two weeks later, another deafening report came from an old sideboard. Jung looked inside; in the bread basket, he found that the bread knife had snapped into several pieces. It had been used shortly before, and no one had been near it since. A cutler who examined it said that it must have been carefully snapped into pieces, possibly by inserting the blade in a crack in a drawer.

When Jung heard about his cousin's trances, he immediately suspected that her multiple personality might have something to do with the curious occurrences—that is, that the explosions were some form of 'poltergeist activity' connected with his cousin. But he either abandoned this hypothesis, or made no attempt to pursue it.

In fact, the more closely we look into the mystery of 'multiple personality', the more difficult it becomes to interpret the facts within a Freudian—or even Jungian—framework. Jung made his own chosen interpretation easier to impose by citing parallel cases in which the subject had experienced total amnesia. In 1811, a girl named Mary Reynolds, who lived in Pennsylvania, fell into a deep sleep for twenty hours; when she woke up, she had lost every vestige of memory—not only of her identity but even of language. She had to re-learn everything like a child, although this took only a few weeks. Five weeks later, she woke up one morning and took up her life where she had left it off previously; she had no memory whatever of the past weeks. For the next sixteen years, the two personalities alternated, until finally, the 'number two' personality became fairly constant. She died quite suddenly, at the age of sixty-one, after a pain in the head which sounds like a brain haemorrhage.

What Jung fails to emphasise—and what can be seen very clearly in the original account[2]—is that the two 'Mary Reynoldses' were virtually different persons. The original was a dull girl, subject to fits of depression, and never very lively; her 'secondary personality' was merry, mischievous and vivacious. The first Mary Reynolds was a stay-at-home; the second loved nature and went for long rides and walks. The 'final' Mary Reynolds was also gay and lively, but also serious and practical, with no trace of her earlier melancholia.

From this account, a shadowy explanation seems to emerge. 'Mary Number 1'—the melancholiac—had fallen into what William James calls 'a habit of inferiority to [her] true self'. Because her *attitude* towards life was negative and gloomy, she had fallen into a permanently devitalised state; it was almost as if her subconscious mind said at some point: 'Look, you're wasting your life—and mine. You've got to snap out of this'—and then proceeded to administer a kind of shock treatment. The immediate result was highly inconvenient—a Mary without memory, like a new-born baby. It was even dangerous. On one occasion, riding in the woods, Mary Number 2 encountered a black bear, which reared up and growled at her. Mary Number 2 seemed immune to fear; she assumed the bear to be a black hog. When her horse refused to go forward, she advanced on the bear fearlessly, brandishing her riding crop, whereupon it turned and ambled off, growling. Similarly, Mary strode through the woods oblivious of the danger of rattlesnakes, copperheads and even panthers. Yet the risky 'shock treatment' worked. The irresponsible, flighty Mary 2 blended slowly into Mary 1, and the result was an altogether more satisfactory Mary 3.

Assuming this explanation to be correct, why did the subconscious have to play the game so dangerously? If it had the power of waving a magic wand and wiping out Mary's memory, why did it not produce Mary 3 at once?

The answer that suggests itself is that it had to use elements that were *not* present in Mary 1. It is almost as if the personality is made up from a kind of construction kit. Since Mary 1 had used up the seriousness and caution, Mary 2 had to make do without these attributes.

The psychologist Pierre Janet cites an equally curious case of a woman he called Leonie. From childhood on, Leonie had been subject to attacks of 'somnambulism'. She was a poor peasant woman with a husband and two children. Under hypnosis, she became a lively and vital character, noisy, gay and sarcastic. Leonie 2 flatly denied that she was the same person as Leonie 1, saying that Leonie 1 was too stupid. She admitted that Leonie 1's children were hers but refused to acknowledge the husband—a significant distinction, since children are from the body, while a husband 'belongs' to the personality. Finally, a 'Leonie 3' began to emerge whose character was much superior to the other two. She referred to Leonie 1 as 'a good and stupid woman, but not me', and to Leonie 2 as 'a crazy creature'. When she returned from her hypnotised state, Leonie 1 knew nothing whatever about her two alter egos, although they knew all about her. This, again, is typical of such cases.

There is nothing in either of these cases that fails to fit into the Freudian picture of 'unconscious repressions'. Mary 1 and Leonie 1 were bored and frustrated; their fantasies finally took on a life of their own, fuelled by the explosive energies of the *libido*. (In Freud, *libido* refers to repressed sexual energy; in Jung, it has the more general meaning of unconscious psychic energy.) So Mary 2 and Leonie 2 were basically a kind of supercharged wishful thinking.

Yet the more we study cases of multiple personality, the less satisfactory this explanation seems. The 'secondary personalities' so often appear to be distinct human beings with their own identity. If they are not really separate personalities—perhaps explainable by possession or reincarnation—then they suggest that personality has a definite and highly complex structure, quite different from what 'common sense' has assumed in the past—like a crystal or a DNA molecule.

The following case makes this very clear. In 1910, the wife of a Pittsburgh psychiatrist, Walter F. Prince, became acquainted with a sweet, good-natured girl named Doris Fischer,[3] who lived with her drunken father. Mrs Prince became fond of her and invited her to come and live in their home. In due course, Dr Prince discovered that Doris was no less than *five* distinct personalities.

Her family background was unfortunate. Her mother, who had been brought up in pleasant, fairly affluent surroundings, eloped with a man of whom her parents disapproved. Her father never spoke to her again. Her parents' misgivings proved to be correct; although her husband had a good executive job, he became an alcoholic and finally had to work as a labourer. He was bad-tempered, brutal, utterly oblivious to anyone's feelings but his own—a typical Right Man. Understandably, Doris's mother—a patient, sweet-tempered woman—was unhappy, and often dreamed of the life she had left behind.

Doris was born in 1889. The first sign of 'dual personality' appeared when she was three years old and her father hurled her to the floor in a drunken rage. The girl who sat up was no longer Doris but another personality, who later claimed to be a spirit; for that reason we shall refer to her as Ariel.[4] As Doris started to go upstairs to bed, yet another personality suddenly took over—Margaret. It was Margaret who went upstairs and went to sleep, and the next morning came down the stairs. As she reached the foot of the stairs, there was a slight snap of the neck, as if an electric current had been turned on, and Doris reappeared. She had no memory of what had taken place since her father snatched her out of her mother's arms on her way to bed.

From then on, Mrs Fisher witnessed a peculiar—although not necessarily distressing—change in her daughter. Sometimes Doris was the normal, quiet child she had always known. At other times, she became a mischievous sprite—noisy, tomboyish, witty and amusing, an excellent mimic and generally lovable. Mrs Fischer had no way of knowing that this was not Doris but Margaret.

Doris had no knowledge of the existence of Margaret. All she knew was that she would periodically 'blank out'; and often, when she came back to consciousness, she found herself in trouble for some mischievous prank. If she was reaching out for cake, Margaret might suddenly take over and gobble it down; Doris would return to consciousness as she was licking her lips. Yet on the whole, Margaret was not ill-disposed to her. Later she told Doris all about herself using Doris's mouth. The two of them would hold conversations, and Doris had no idea of what Margaret would say until it actually came out of her mouth. If Margaret wanted to speak to her when there were other people present, she simply put the words into Doris's mind, so that no one suspected that Doris was two people. One day when Doris was five, she was playing with a rubber ball, which Margaret felt belonged to her. Margaret made her pick up the ball, to draw her attention to it, and then made her scratch herself on the cheek until she bled; it was Margaret's way of telling Doris to let her toys alone.

In spite of these complications, Doris's childhood was not too unhappy. Both her personalities were lovable, her relationship with her mother was a close one, and Ariel appeared only at night, when Margaret was asleep. (Doris continued to blank out as she reached the stairs on the way to bed and to reappear the next morning.) It was rather as if Doris had a mischievous twin sister, who was always getting her into trouble—and sometimes helping her out of it. Margaret often did her school work for her. But her recklessness was sometimes dangerous; Mrs Fischer could never understand why Doris would go swimming in the docks, after solemnly promising not to. On the whole, however, the relationship was tolerable, even affectionate.

The first real conflict occurred when Doris was in her mid-teens. She graduated almost at the top of her class and decided to go on to high school. Margaret flatly refused. The conflict would have made life impossible; so Doris left school and went to work as a seamstress.

When she was seventeen, she one day had several visual hallucinations of her mother while she was at work. She rushed home to find her mother dying, although she had been well that morning. It was sudden acute pneumonia. By two the following morning, her mother was dead. Her father staggered home drunk while she sat by the bedside of her dying mother, and slumped into the bed fully dressed. As Doris drew the sheet over her mother's face, she experienced a sudden pain in her head—and another personality was looking out through her eyes. This new person had no memory at all. She suddenly came to birth sitting by a bed that contained a dead woman in her nightgown and a fully dressed man. She was not afraid or worried, because she had no idea of what death was. In the next room, Doris's sister Trixie—also ill—woke up and called 'Doris', but the new personality had no idea who this name referred to.

Although Doris had attended to her dying mother, Margaret was also there, 'underneath', watching it all, and sympathising with Doris's splitting headache. When Doris had finished laying out the corpse, Margaret made a brief appearance, immediately felt the headache and beat a quick retreat. Then, to Margaret's surprise, the 'other' person suddenly appeared in Doris's body. 'What a *dumb* thing that new one was,' she later told Dr Prince. 'She didn't seem to know *anysing*.' Margaret had a kind of childish lisp.

Margaret found herself sharing Doris's body with another inmate who was unable to read, write or talk—who was basically a new-born baby. She decided to make the best of it and teach the newcomer to speak. This was slightly easier than it would have been in the case of two separate people, for even when the newcomer was in control of the body, Margaret could make her lips move to repeat words. She taught her the names of objects by pointing at them, and the newcomer repeated the names after her.

Prince called the newcomer 'Sick Doris'. Even when she had

learned to speak, she was obviously an inferior personality. Her face was wooden and dull; she was afraid to meet people's eyes; her voice was montonous; she was shy, nervous and incapable of affection, although she could sustain a doglike friendship. She was religious in a stupid kind of way, literal-minded and inclined to hysteria and various aches and pains. Since Prince emphasises that she was a completely separate personality, we will refer to her as Mary Anne.

When Doris was eighteen, she slipped and fell on the back of her head. This brought into existence another personality on a lower scale than any so far, a partial individuality who appeared only when Doris was asleep. Margaret, who observed the appearance of this newcomer one night, referred to her as 'Sleeping Real Doris', but this is a misnomer, since she was not 'real Doris' in any sense; we will call her Jane. Jane was basically little more than a tape recorder; she would accurately 'replay' whole conversations dating back to Doris's childhood, with all the changes of facial expression of a seven-year-old girl. Prince quotes a conversation between Doris and her mother—recited by Jane—in which Doris spoke only her own part, and left silences as her mother replied.

So by the age of eighteen, Doris was a walking compendium of personalities: herself, Margaret, Ariel, Mary Anne and Jane. In the following year, she met Mrs Prince and began to go to the Princes' for meals. Finally, she moved in with them and became a kind of adopted daughter. In these new and delightful living conditions, with the constant attention of Dr Prince, her mental health began to improve steadily, so that it is possible that even without 'treatment', she would have recovered. By 1914, Doris was back in sole control, although Margaret continued to pay occasional visits, simply out of friendliness.

When she first moved in, Doris had almost disappeared; the chief personality was Margaret—a pleasant girl whose development had ceased, unfortunately, at the age of ten—who alternated with the lumpish Mary Anne.

The first thing Prince observed was that he was dealing with two completely different girls. This is apparent even from their photographs, which appeared with Prince's paper about the case in *The Journal of Abnormal Psychology* in 1916. There is only a family resemblance. On her very occasional appearances, Doris was different from both. Even their physical characteristics were different. Doris had little or no sense of taste or smell; Prince says she suffered from anaesthesia in the bladder, by which he means, presumably, that she was unaware of the normal sensations when her bladder was full and inclined to wet herself. Mary Anne seemed to have no nerves in her skin below the waist, and not many above it. Margaret, on the other hand, not only had unusually sharp hearing but could also see in the dark.

The different personalities would take over with the slight 'click' in the neck. It really looked as if there were several persons making use of Doris's body, as several members of a family might make use of one car. The various personalities even talked about being 'in' and 'out'. Margaret would often remark that she was allowing Doris to rest while she took over. Margaret also told Prince that she could 'duck under'—that is, abandon Doris's body while Doris was not yet in control. She did this occasionally by way of demonstration; then Doris's body would lie still, hardly breathing, apparently in a cataleptic trance.

Prince observed that the various personalities seemed to be in a definite hierarchy of 'higher' and 'lower'. At the bottom of the ladder (my phrase, not his) was the 'tape recorder', Jane. Next came Mary Anne, then Margaret, then Doris—then Ariel. Ariel, who appeared when Doris was asleep, seemed to know more than any of them and claimed that she was a spirit who had come in answer to fervent prayers of Doris's mother to protect her daughter.

Doris knew nothing about any of the other personalities, at least, by direct insight or memory. Margaret could 'read the minds' of Doris and Mary Anne but was unaware of the existence of Ariel. This led to some minor tension between Prince and Margaret. If Margaret had been in Doris's body too long, Ariel got annoyed and gave her a blow on the forehead—or at least produced the hallucination of giving her a blow. The startled Margaret would imagine that Prince had hit her and shrink away from him; his denials were obviously regarded as lies. These 'jolts' (as Ariel called them) failed to achieve the desired effect—understandably, since Margaret had no idea why she was being hit—and Ariel finally promised to stop it. Thereafter the 'jolts' ceased.

Margaret finally realised that there must be some personality of whom she was unaware. One day, when Doris was 'in', Margaret suddenly took over and started to talk to Dr Prince. Ariel grabbed

Margaret by the scruff of the neck and dragged her back 'into the depths', allowing Doris to reappear. Later, the round-eyed Margaret told Dr Prince: 'Papa, there's another Sick Doris [Mary Anne], there's another Sick Doris! There must be, 'cause I was yanked in just the way I used to yank Sick Doris in.' But Ariel kept her interference to a minimum; apparently she found it an exhausting effort.

The relationship between the various personalities was, on the whole, what one might expect. Margaret could read Doris's and Mary Anne's mind. Ariel could read both these and also Margaret's. Sometimes Doris would be watched by all three alter egos, although only Ariel was aware of the full situation. Each personality—except Jane—had a mind of its own. Occasionally, something like a quarrel would develop. Mary Anne would think wistfully that if Doris stayed away for good, she and Margaret could share the body, and Margaret might come to like her as much as she liked Doris. Margaret would read this thought and get angry with Mary Anne. Ariel in turn would feel irritated with Margaret—Ariel apparently felt protective towards Mary Anne. Doris, vaguely disturbed by these tensions, would 'vanish' and leave either Margaret or Mary Anne to take over.

To complicate matters, the relationships altered according to Doris's mental health; at times, Ariel could read Doris's thoughts only by reading Mary Anne's mind. There were also occasions when two personalities were in control at once. Prince could converse with Margaret *and* Doris, who took turns speaking. Or sometimes Margaret and Mary Anne shared the 'driving seat'. And on rare occasions, Margaret and Ariel shared. Since Margaret was unaware of the existence of Ariel, Prince had to devise a method of talking with Ariel 'behind Margaret's back', getting Ariel to signal the answers to questions by movements of her feet, while Margaret was oblivious of what was going on. This interesting technique had earlier been developed by Pierre Janet, and we shall refer to it again.

When Doris came to live with the Princes in 1910, the cure began. Doris began to spend more and more time in control, and Mary Anne began to fade out. To encourage Mary Anne's departure, Prince prevented her from doing needlework, which had previously been her chief occupation. Without this aid to concentration, her mind began to wander; in effect, she became an idiot. She realised that she was going to die and went for a last walk with Dr Prince. Then she wrote a letter to Margaret (the various personalities often communicated by leaving notes for one another), full of advice, and telling Margaret what do do with her few possessions. After then Mary Anne ceased to recognise the Princes. She began 'growing backwards', reverting to infancy, like Jung's cousin, until she could only prattle and gurgle. She 'died' on June 28, 1911.

Jane, the 'tape recorder', stayed around longer. Prince was curious about her; he wondered whether she could become a real person and tried to 'bring her out'. Jane proved to be so responsive that Prince decided to stop, since ultimately he wanted to get rid of her. Jane simply faded away, making her last appearance in April 1912.

As Doris's health and confidence increased, Margaret began to get younger and younger. She began using the German pronunciations that she (and Doris) had used in early childhood. Her visual field gradually narrowed—something that had also happened to Mary Anne—so that she could see only things a little more than a foot from her face. Light stung her eyes, and if no shade was interposed, they began to weep. Finally Margaret went blind. Two years after Jane had 'died', Margaret appeared one evening, laughed and made a few remarks, then fell asleep. That was her last appearance.

There was no question of trying to 'freeze out' Ariel; she had no intention of hanging on. Prince refers to her as 'the maturest, wisest and most prescient of the quintet'. In the evenings, after Doris had gone to sleep, Ariel would occasionally chat with Dr Prince. She would also occasionally interfere while Doris was awake, to warn her of some emergency. Prince makes the extraordinary statement: 'If I had not the experience of the first-hand study of [Ariel] for years I would certainly be of the opinion that she represents a slight or deeply-seated remaining dissociation of personality; as it is, I have my doubts.' That is to say, Prince was half-inclined to believe her claims that she was some sort of independent guardian spirit, not a 'splinter' of Doris's personality.

In 1916, another doctor suggested that Prince should take Doris to New York to sit with a well-known medium, Mrs Chenoweth. At first Prince refused; he had now moved to California and could not leave his practice. Ariel pointed out that *she* could look after Doris and suggested that Doris should go 'alone'. And Prince had so much trust in Ariel that he agreed.

The séances that followed are reported in full by Dr Prince in *The Proceedings of the American Society for Psychical Research*, volume 17;

Prince had no doubt that it was one of the most remarkable and convincing cases of 'communication with the dead' on record. Doris's mother—or someone claiming to be Doris's mother—wrote out long messages in which she showed close knowledge of Doris's background and childhood. A 'spirit' who appeared to be Margaret also put in an appearance; when asked about her after-life, she replied drily: 'I never had a before life; how can I have an after life?' And a 'spirit' that identified itself as Dr Richard Hodgson appeared and made some interesting comparisons between the Doris case and Morton Prince's famous Christine Beauchamp case. Hodgson had actually worked with Morton Prince on this case. Perhaps the most interesting assertion made at these sittings was the claim of Doris's mother that Doris's illness was a case of 'benevolent possession'—a suspicion that is bound to occur repeatedly to anyone who reads Walter Prince's long report on the case.

However, no great importance can be attached to these séances. The medium could have been unconsciously reading Doris's mind (although she was absent from many of the séances in which important information was given), or even the mind of Dr Hyslop, the doctor who had invited Doris to New York. Fundamentally, the sittings add nothing to what we know of Doris. Ariel failed to put in an appearance—probably bored by the endless verbiage. And so the last we hear of Doris is of her return from New York to California, none the wiser about the nature of her own strange illness.

On the evidence provided by Dr Prince, most readers will probably agree that it sounds remarkably like possession. We all know about fantasy, and we have all met people who seem unable to draw a clear line between fantasy and actuality. Such people usually have a difficult time trying to avoid being mauled by actuality. The fantasy habit is like trying to keep yourself covered with a blanket that is too small; reality keeps freezing the extremities. Yet there was apparently no element of fantasy in Doris's complex mental existence. Ariel and Margaret simply appeared out of the blue, as independent entities. So, later, did Mary Anne.

The possession hypothesis cannot be lightly dismissed. The success of the film *The Exorcist* brought the subject into the news, and it soon became clear that, far from being an old-fashioned superstition, exorcism is still widely practised by members of the clergy of many denominations. And this is not simply because of outdated credulity. The majority of people engaged in paranormal research are willing to admit at least the possibility of the existence of 'discarnate entities'—and that some of them might be ill-disposed. Robert Monroe[5] is only one of many 'astral projectors' to describe encounters with mischievous entities, who sound oddly like the traditional 'evil spirits', when in an out-of-the-body state.

It seems equally certain, however, that many famous cases of 'diabolic possession' can be explained in terms of hysteria or (more rarely) poltergeist phenomena. The Douglass Deen case, on which *The Exorcist* was based, seems to belong to both categories. It began when scratching noises were heard in the walls of the room occupied by the fourteen-year-old Douglass Deen in Washington DC; then the boy's bed began to move violently when he was in it. The minister of the local church, called in to investigate, moved the boy from the vibrating bed to an armchair, whereupon the chair began to move around the room, and finally tilted and threw the boy on the floor. A makeshift bed on the floor slid around the room with Douglass in it. Attempts were made to 'cure' the boy by psychiatric treatment; when these failed, a Jesuit was called in. He performed rites of exorcism for six months before the evil spirits were 'driven out'. During the rites, Douglass cursed and screamed obscenities in a shrill voice; he also allegedly recited in Latin, a language he had never studied. (On the other hand, if the priest recited the exorcism in Latin, it would not be difficult for the boy to pick it up.) These phenomena lasted for most of the year 1949, then ceased. There is nothing here that needs to be explained in terms of 'discarnate entities'.

The classic case of hysterical possession was recorded by Pierre Janet in 1894 and seems even more conclusive. Janet encountered his patient, whom he calls Achille, at the Salpêtrière hospital in 1890. Achille was a businessman in his mid-thirties, son of a family of French peasants. Although he had been brought up in an atmosphere of peasant superstition, Achille professed to hold few religious beliefs. Although inclined to be 'oversensitive'—brooding over conflicts and humiliations—he had no history of mental illness.

In the winter of 1890, Achille returned from a short business trip depressed and taciturn, then suddenly went dumb. One day, after embracing his wife and children, he sank into a coma, which lasted for two days. When he woke, he sat up and uttered a strange laugh, crying

out that 'they' were burning him. The next morning he was worse,
asserting that the room was full of demons and the Devil was inside
him, forcing him to utter horrible blasphemies. After running away
from home several times and making a number of suicide attempts, he
was placed in the Salpêtrière under Charcot, who handed the case over
to Pierre Janet.

Janet observed all the signs of possession as described in the Middle
Ages. In a deep voice Achille cursed God, then in a shrill voice
protested that the Devil had made him do it. He held endless exhausting arguments with this 'Devil'.

Janet had earlier made an interesting discovery about hysteric subjects. Many psychologists had noted that a hysteric's field of attention
becomes 'contracted' so that he can pay attention to only one thing at
a time. Most of us notice it if we are holding a conversation and
someone else comes into the room; the hysteric would fail to notice
even if the newcomer shouted in his ear. What Janet discovered was
that hysterics noticed things *at a subconscious level*. If a hysteric was
absorbed in a conversation and Janet whispered 'Raise your hand', the
patient would obey without even noticing.

All open attempts to persuade the patient to co-operate were failures; the 'Devil' sneered and mocked. But while Achille was raving,
Janet found that he could insert a pencil in his fingers and cause it to
sign Achille's name. Janet tried ordering the patient—in a whisper—to
make certain movements. To his surprise, the pencil wrote: 'I won't.'
'Why?' whispered Janet. 'Because I am stronger than you.' 'Who are
you then?' asked Janet. 'The Devil.'

Janet now decided to try one of the classic tricks to outwit the Devil.
Bearing in mind the tradition that the Devil's chief weakness is vanity,
Janet asked Achille's Devil to prove its power by raising Achille's arm
without his knowing it. This was easy. Achille's arm rose; Janet
pointed it out to the patient, who was astonished. 'That demon has
played another trick on me.' Janet used the same method to make
Achille dance, put out his tongue and kiss a piece of paper. He asked
the Devil to make Achille think he saw a bunch of roses and to imagine
that he pricked his finger. Achille cried out with astonishment as he
apparently saw the roses and then winced as he pricked his finger.

Janet now cunningly asked the Devil if he would demonstrate his
power by sending Achille to sleep. All earlier attempts to hypnotise
Achille had failed; now he quickly became drowsy and slept. When

Janet addressed him softly, he answered the questions without hesitation. At last, Janet was able to get to the root of his illness.

In the spring before his illness, on one of his business trips, Achille had committed a 'grave misdeed'—presumably some rather unusual act with a prostitute, the nature of which filled him with guilt. 'There are some weak-minded people,' remarks Janet, 'who can do nothing by halves, and constantly fall into curious exaggerations.' Achille brooded on his guilt. No doubt he felt that he had been possessed by an evil spirit when he committed the misdeed. Like someone who thinks about itching and begins to itch all over, Achille began to suffer from various aches and pains which he felt he deserved as punishment. A desire to confess the guilty secret led to psychosomatic dumbness.

He dreamed of death, said goodbye to his wife and children and sank into a deep sleep in which he dreamed he was in hell. He could smell sulphur and burning flesh. The Devil took possession of his wicked heart. He woke up blaspheming, convinced that he was dead and damned.

Once he was able to hypnotise Achille, Janet was able to control his hallucinations, transforming the memory of his original misdeed into something less serious and finally producing Achille's wife at a critical moment in the hallucination to pronounce complete forgiveness on her husband. Achille's consciousness slowly took a more active role; although at night he still dreamed of hellish torments, during the day he laughed at his superstitions. Within a short time, Achille was completely cured; at the period of Janet's paper,[6] three years later, he had shown no sign of a relapse.

In this case, we can see clearly the role that 'self-consciousness' plays in mental illness. Janet mentions a parallel case of a weak-minded girl who became so obsessed by guilt about some fault and the attempt to keep it secret that she began to lie gratuitously about everything. One day, she forgot herself and allowed an admission of the fault to slip out; she obtained pardon and immediately ceased to lie. The psychologist Viktor Frankl also reached the conclusion that many neuroses are caused by brooding on some minor problem until it has been blown up out of all proportion; he advocated a method called 'the law of reverse effort', whereby the patient stops trying to avoid the calamity and goes to the other extreme (i.e. a stammerer is cured by being told to *try* to stammer). Anyone can observe the same phenomenon when he wakes up in the middle of the night and begins to worry about some minor problem; the problem expands like a balloon.

The Achille case offers another interesting clue to the mystery of multiple personality. Even before Janet succeeded in hypnotising Achille, the latter's personality was in a state resembling hypnosis. When someone is hypnotised, his 'everyday self' goes to sleep or becomes passive, and the hypnotist is able to communicate directly with another 'self'—what used to be called the subliminal self. Janet was communicating with Achille's subliminal self—the Devil—even before he hypnotised the patient.

One of the most famous of all cases of multiple personality confirms this observation: the Christine Beauchamp case referred to by the 'spirit' of Dr Hodgson. Christine Beauchamp was the name given by Dr Morton Prince to a student who came to him for treatment in 1898. Prince was a professor at the Tufts Medical School in Boston. Christine was suffering from 'bad nerves'—abulia (inhibition of will) and ataxia (uncontrolled movements of the body). Prince decided to try hypnotherapy. Christine proved to be a good hypnotic subject, and Prince referred to the relaxed, truthful Christine who emerged in light trance as B-2. He tried putting her into deeper trance. To his astonishment, another personality emerged, a girl who referred contemptuously to Christine Beauchamp as 'she'. 'But you are she,' said Prince. 'No, I am not,' said the new personality, very positively.

The new personality—whom Prince called B-3—told him he could call her Sally. And she seemed totally unlike Christine—a mischievous, fun-loving, high-spirited girl who sounds like Doris's 'Margaret' personality. Sally was utterly contemptuous of Miss Beauchamp, regarding her as a vacillating weakling and a 'goody fool' (i.e. too conventional). But although Sally obviously knew all about Christine, Christine had no suspicion of the existence of Sally.

Prince had apparently given Sally a life of her own by placing Miss Beauchamp under deep hypnosis. At first, Sally was unable to open her eyes (since Christine closed them when she went into a trance), but when she finally succeeded, she began to indulge her highly individual sense of mischief. She loved shocking Christine with 'unladylike' behaviour. Christine would wake up with her feet on the table, a cigarette in her mouth and a glass of wine in her hand. Sally was also contemptuous of Christine's poor health—she herself was sturdy and tireless—and enjoyed taking walks to distant places, then vanishing and leaving the exhausted Christine to walk home.

One day Prince called on Miss Beauchamp to discover that she had become yet another personality, an adult, responsible, self-controlled girl whom he called B-4. But B-4 seemed to be under the illusion that Dr Prince was someone called William Jones and warned him that it was foolish of him to come, that he risked breaking his neck by climbing in through the window.

Sally and B-4 loathed one another. Christine accepted Sally's practical jokes with passive fatalism; B-4 hated them and often repaid in kind. On one occasion, Christine set out for New York to find a job. Sally got off the train at New Haven and took a job as a waitress. Christine found the work exhausting; B-4 hated it as being below her dignity. One day B-4 walked out of the job, pawned Christine's watch and returned to Boston. Sally took over and decided to spite B-4 by refusing to return to her old lodging; instead she took a new one. Christine 'came to' in a strange bed, having no idea of where she was or how she got there.

William Jones eventually proved to be the key to the mystery of Christine's disintegration. Christine's father had been an unreliable alcoholic who made her childhood miserable; she concentrated her admiration on William Jones, a family friend who treated her kindly. Jones, said Christine, was an upright, godly man, all that her father should have been. When Christine was thirteen, her mother died under circumstances that were horrible to her; she became depressed and tearful and began to sleepwalk.

At sixteen, she left home to escape her drunken father; she took a job as a nurse in a Providence hospital and continued to see William Jones. One night, Jones came to see her when he had been drinking. He found a ladder and decided to play a joke; he placed it against the second-floor window of the nurses' recreation room. Christine, looking at the window, was shocked to see the distorted face of her substitute father leering at her through the glass. She went downstairs to talk to him, and he tried to kiss her. It was from then on, said Sally—who told Prince the story—that Christine became 'queer and moony'.

Oddly enough, B-4 also remembered that traumatic evening. *But she remembered nothing since*. It was as if the shock of losing her father-figure had caused a part of Christine's personality to go into sudden eclipse, leaving her timid, fearful and incompetent.

Prince made a peculiar decision. He decided that Christine and B-4 were Miss Beauchamp's 'true selves', and that Sally would have to be suppressed. Sally struggled fiercely, crying: 'I won't—I won't be dead. I have as much right to live as she has.' Prince secretly agreed; Sally was the nicest and brightest of the family. Nevertheless, he performed a series of hypnotic 'exorcisms', ordering Sally to return to the place she came from. Then he used the same hypnotic techniques to integrate Christine and B-4. When he published his classic book on the case in 1905,[7] Christine was again a fairly normal person. Yet Prince was not wholly successful. In the 1920s, in a second edition of the book, he related Christine's subsequent history; she had been able to take up nursing again, but Sally still put in occasional appearances, playing her usual practical jokes.

This case is clearly less complicated than that of Doris. We may theorise that Sally was Christine's childhood self suppressed by her catastrophic home background and B-4 the adult, responsible part of her personality, which was suppressed by the sudden loss of her father substitute. The Christine who was left was only one-third of a 'normal girl'. Morton Prince's great mistake was in not trying to integrate Sally into the final Miss Beauchamp. Of course, this was partly Sally's own fault; she often declared that she was a 'spirit' and sometimes hinted that she was in league with the Devil. But this may have been simply to alarm Christine.

If that is true, the consequences would be, to say the least, of considerable interest for the science of psychology. It would imply that all of us are made up of a series of 'selves', each complete and independent. These selves, it would seem, are *already there*, inside the new-born baby, as the caterpillar, the chrysalis and the butterfly are present in the new-born grub.

This view is consistent with Janet's observations on hysterics. Hysteria is fundamentally a 'narrowing' of the personality as a result of fear or anxiety. If I am deeply worried, I tend to grit my teeth and concentrate frantically on whatever worries me. I ignore or 'forget' everything else. If I continued to do this over a long period, one part of my personality would become over-developed, while the rest remained static. But even though I have narrowed my consciousness down to a narrow wedge, the remainder is *still there*, as Janet showed.

A useful way of envisaging this is to imagine that the 'total personality' (whatever that means) is like one of those Japanese fans that you can open out until it has turned into a circle. Such a degree of completeness has probably never been achieved by any human being. Let us imagine a fairly normal, healthy, fulfilled human being as being half the fan—a semi-circle. This is how we feel when we are in a state of happy relaxation—for instance, at the weekend. Then Monday morning arrives; we have to get up and prepare to concentrate our attention on routine tasks. We can no longer afford to be 'wide open'. The fan closes until it is only a quarter of a circle. When we have finished the day's work, we relax, put our feet up, and the fan expands—perhaps not to a whole semi-circle (that state is reserved for moods of great happiness and relaxation, perhaps during holidays) but at least to more than a mere quarter.

The 'neurasthenic' person distrusts life. Not only does he feel unable to relax and expand; he has a compulsion to contract further, so that he becomes a mere eighth of a circle. He is like a person who has closed the rest of the house and tries to live in one room. Understandably, this 'cramped' position causes his health to deteriorate and his energies to sink. This was the state of the Christine Beauchamp who first came to see Morton Prince. Light hypnosis released a more relaxed Christine—B-2—but under deeper hypnosis, the long-suppressed Sally emerged. She knew all about Christine because Christine was *part* of her. Sally was a semi-circle while Christine was only an eighth of a circle.

Significantly, while Sally could not at first read B-4's mind, she quickly learned to do so; B-4 was part of the original Christine—say a quarter of the circle.

This explains why Miss Beauchamp's health became abruptly better as Sally took over. In effect, Christine was abusing her body and her mind by keeping them in corsets. Sally took off the corsets. Frankl's 'law of reverse effort' cured patients through the same mechanism.

Doris's 'Jane' personality seems to confirm this analysis. Jane was the tape recorder who could report past conversations. We now know that all human beings are capable of such accurate 'playback'. During the Second World War, doctors discovered that soldiers suffering from battle neurosis could be cured by making them *re-live* the experience that had caused the trauma. The technique became known as abreaction therapy. The patient was placed into a trance-like state by means of a drug. Then the doctor suggested that the soldier was back in a burning tank or buried alive in a shell hole, and watched as the experience was re-enacted in detail. The patient often went into a state of emotional shock, slept heavily, and woke up feeling relieved and purged.

In 1951, Dr Wilder Penfield, a neuro-surgeon at McGill University, Montreal, was performing a brain operation when he touched the patient's temporal cortex with a wire carrying a mild electric current. The patient proceeded to 'replay' a scene from his past. The brain stores 'tapes' containing every second of our lives; Penfield had discovered accidentally how to replay the tapes.

Eric Berne, the founder of Transactional Psychology, pursued a parallel discovery. He came to the conclusion that we all contain three basic 'persons' whom he called the Child, the Adult and the Parent. Interviewing certain patients, he could actually watch the three taking over, one after the other. The Child was often boisterous, mischievous and naïve. The Adult was responsible, balanced, concerned with adjusting successfully to reality. The Parent seemed to be part of the personality that we derive from one of our parents by imitation: usually the parent of the same sex as ourselves. A lawyer whose father was philanthropic gave away large sums of money in his 'father' phase. An ex-seaman whose father was a boastful drunk slipped into an imitation of his father's personality at certain moments.[8]

This seems to come even closer to explaining the Christine Beauchamp case; presumably Sally was the Child, while B-4 may well have been an 'imitation' of Christine's mother.

But this simple and convenient hypothesis seems to be contradicted by the Doris case. If Margaret was the Child, Ariel was the Parent, and Jane the tape recorder, what was Mary Anne? She was duller and narrower than Doris herself. And if we reply that Mary Anne was the equivalent of the neurasthenic Christine Beauchamp (Walter Prince actually called her Sick Doris), then who was Doris? We seem to have one personality too many.

In the case of Sybil Dorsett, recorded by Flora Rheta Schreiber, we have no less than thirteen personalities too many.[9] The 'alter-egos' who had been taking over Sybil's body since she was three years old included a two-year-old baby ('Ruthie'), two boys, two girls, and a host of grown women. The blame for Sybil's fragmentation was finally traced to her mother, who was so eccentric as to be virtually insane. She had practised every kind of abuse on the child, including suspending her from the light flex and inserting all kinds of objects into her vagina. In spite of this, the mother had preserved an image of puritanical respectability in the small New England town where they lived. Sybil had developed a habit of 'splitting'; each new shock caused further fragmentation. The child's problems were complicated by her unwillingness to admit, even to herself, that she hated her mother.

The resulting entities had an amazing cross-section of personalities. One was a writer and painter, another a musician, another deeply religious, another a builder and carpenter, another a giggling teenager. The writer and the musician liked each other so much they often did things together like any other friends—attending plays and concerts, holding conversations. Again, we get an incredible sense of *possession* rather than of some psychological illness. The Adult personality, who called herself Vicky, played roughly the same role as Ariel in the Doris case; on one occasion she rang up the doctor—Cornelia Wilbur—and said: 'Sybil was going to throw herself in the Hudson River, but I didn't let her.'

Dr Wilbur eventually cured Sybil—after more than a decade of treatment—by using the same technique as Morton Prince. The various personalities were 'integrated' by hypnotherapy. Dr Wilbur concluded that the fragmentation of the personality is basically a form of hysteria. She pointed out that most cases of multiple personality can be traced back to a restrictive and hysterical family background. But she goes on to admit that the mechanics of multiple personality remain elusive. Every parent has observed that a baby seems to be born with its own distinct personality, which begins to emerge before it can walk or speak. But multiple personalities often seem to be as different as brothers and sisters in the same family. Flora Schreiber ends her books by mentioning various tests carried out on two other cases of multiple personality. One was tested with word associations and showed four quite distinct sets of responses and associations. Another was subjected to neurological and psychological tests and revealed four totally distinct personalities; even their electro-encephalograms were different.

Dr Wilbur could often tell which of Sybil's sixteen personalities was waiting for her when she saw her sitting in her outer office. We may as well admit frankly that the evidence seems to suggest that Sally and Ariel were telling the truth when they asserted that they were 'spirits'.

In fact, we seem to be back to Hans Driesch's notion that the living part of us—the 'entelechy' or 'psychoid'—operates from outside space and time, and has its independent existence. Which in turn seems to suggest—as Myers concluded in his best-known book—that there is some part of human personality that can survive the body's death. But it would be rash to jump to such a conclusion while there are more down-to-earth explanations.

If Berne's hypothesis of Parent, Adult and Child seems too simplistic, we can turn to a more complex theory suggested by Janet.[10] Janet's studies led him to believe that he could distinguish nine distinct levels of consciousness in living creatures. First the reflex level, which is probably the level on which an amoeba operates or a very young baby; then simple consciousness of objects, as when a baby's eyes follow a bright toy; then response to other people, recognising them as separate entities; then elementary intelligence, as when the first men learned to make tools; then the level of language, which involves a new level of intelligence and foresight—the level at which belief comes into being; then 'deliberate belief'. The zoologist Louis Leakey once suggested that men became warlike when they had discovered fire and could sit in their caves in the evening and tell stories of past exploits; it was at this stage, he thought, that men developed the notions of 'us' and 'them'. If true, this is a good illustration of Janet's sixth stage of consciousness. The seventh level, what Janet calls the rational-energetic level, is when man has to learn to plan and use his energies purposefully—the level achieved by Berne's Adult. The eighth stage is the experimental level, when man uses his intelligence in creative experiment, learning from trial and error. Finally there comes the 'progressive level', the level at which he thinks for the fun of it; Maslow called this level 'self-actualisation', the conscious striving to evolve.

Some readers may be tempted to dismiss this list as another of those academic exercises in classification, but it is far more. It is a fairly accurate picture of a *hierarchy of levels* in man. Each one, Janet was convinced, is as distinct as a step in a flight of steps.

What actually *happens* when a man develops from one level to another—say from the level of purposeful action to the level of learning by trial and error—is that he develops a new set of responses, you could almost say of nervous circuits. I have elsewhere described this process as 'promotion'. In the RAF, I saw a number of ordinary aircraftmen who were promoted to take charge of the billet. At first they felt awkward and embarrassed to give orders. But within a few days, they *became* leading aircraftmen, giving orders as if they had been doing it all their lives. The inherent capacity had already been there; they had only to develop the responses, the 'nerve circuitry'.

It is true that I develop a new set of 'nerve circuits' every time I learn something new. But all learning does not involve 'promotion'. If I change my car for a different model with all the switches in different places, no 'promotion' is involved. Promotion always involves circuits on *a higher level of complexity*.

The vital point to grasp is that these 'circuits' are the *servants* of the impulse that brings them into being. A simple parallel would be an opera singer, a ballet dancer, a writer. Each has to spend years developing a *technique* of self-expression. But unless he has something to express, all the technique in the world will be useless. Technique is the servant of the creative impulse. Neither is of much use without the other; but a man with creative impulse and no technique is in a better position than a man with technique and no creative impulse; he can still make a start.

The philosopher and scientist, Michael Polanyi, makes this recognition a vital part of his argument against 'nothing-but-ness' (man is 'nothing but' a machine, etc.). The reductionist biologists argue that life has built up its higher levels of organisation (or 'circuits') automatically, by the mere struggle to stay in existence. Man's 'higher activities' are simply the result of these 'higher circuits'. If a baby was born with a 'circuit' capable of creating great symphonies, it would create great symphonies, just as an apple tree produces apples.

Polanyi points out that this is a crude fallacy, like saying that a man who thoroughly understands the rules of chess will be a great chess player. Of course, rules (or techniques) are the basic condition for any kind of creation; but what matters is how the creator *uses* those rules. His *choice* is a higher principle. In the same way, a shoemaking machine is governed by the laws of mechanics; but its higher principle is making shoes. This writing is governed by the laws of grammar; its higher principle is to convey my ideas. 'Smash up a machine, utter words at random, or make chess moves without a purpose, and the . . . higher principles . . . will all vanish.'[11] 'Living beings', says Polanyi, 'consist in a hierarchy of levels, each level having its own

structural and organismic principle.' The reductionists make the fatal
mistake of mixing up the lower and the higher.

All of which may seem to have taken us a long way from the
problems of Doris Fischer, Christine Beauchamp and Sybil Dorsett.
In fact, it has brought us back to them. Think of Janet's 'hierarchy of
consciousness' as a flight of stairs. You and I and practically everyone
we know has had to climb that flight from the time we emerged from
the womb; we have all gone through a compressed version of human
evolution. What was wrong with Jung's cousin and Doris and Achille
and Christine and Sybil was that they had become arrested; they had
ceased to climb.

Why? Because various problems and catastrophes had convinced
them that *it was not worth while*. This state of 'unexpectant passivity' is
common to every case of multiple personality so far recorded. (For
example, Thigpen and Cleckley's *Three Faces of Eve*[12] begins: 'This
neat, colourless young woman . . . seemed too retiring and inert to
utilise, or even to be very clearly aware of, her good features and her
potential attractiveness.')

Why should 'passivity' produce such alarming consequences? This
is a problem whose nature was first fully recognised by Viktor Frankl.
A Jew, Frankl spent much of the Second World War in Nazi concentration camps, and he observed that the prisoners without any sense of
purpose or hope succumbed most readily to the appalling conditions.
Abraham Maslow had made a similar observation. Man is the only
animal whose basic instinct seems to be to *evolve*. His mind is intended
to flow forward, like a stream. If forced to stand still, it becomes
stagnant, and various illnesses develop. One could use another simile
and say that man is like an automobile whose battery becomes flat if he
is left in storage for too long. It is the use of his *will* that keeps his vital
batteries recharged.

All this is comprehensible enough. What is incomprehensible is
why 'flat batteries'—or a sudden loss of nervous energy through
shock—should lead to the extraordinary phenomenon of multiple
personality. One is almost tempted to assume that our bodies contain a
multitude of different persons—like a boarding house—but that only
the ground-floor-front tenant (who occupies the best room) can *operate* the body. But all the other tenants are anxious to move in, and may
take advantage of periods of illness. The following notes—supplied by
Major George Sully–illustrate the point:

Around the end of 1950 I had completed all but the last eighth of a novel, and the conviction had been growing on me that it was pretty terrible—well-written, but stagy and fundamentally incompetent. As I had decided to be a writer, this did not bode well; I became understandably depressed.

I awoke one morning—or someone did—using my eyes and a complement of my consciousness. Or maybe two people awoke, using the same body—mine. They were arguing volubly with each other, and there was a feeling that the body had become awake without their noticing. I, at all events, as the 'I' with whom one daily lives, was apparently not directly concerned, as all I now recall is that they were discussing 'him'. There existed a state of consciousness which would normally have been single and 'mine', but either suppressed or suspended. The state was acutely horrifying and nightmarish. In a nightmare one often longs to bring the self to wakefulness. In this state connection with the self was cut off. For some minutes at least, the body lay inertly possessed by the arguers, unable to summon up the dominating self to its rescue.

Ultimately 'I' gradually took over, but it seems that for the space of time the argument—the details at once forgotten on the emergence of self—went on, two 'alternative' personalities had taken priority over it. They have, luckily, not once appeared since. One of them might indeed be 'me'—but I have a feeling that they were distinct from me. Are they, one wonders, voicelessly arguing still?

It is interesting that Major Sully starts to refer to 'the body' rather than 'my body', as if the experience has awakened doubts about ownership.

The same hypothesis could explain a curious experience recorded by William James in his essay 'A Suggestion about Mysticism'. He described it as 'the most intensely peculiar experience of my whole life.' On February 12, 1906, James awoke in his bed at Stanford University from a peaceful dream and then seemed to recall a dream of a quite different nature—about lions. He concluded, not unreasonably, that this must have been an earlier dream. But the following night he had the same experience, this time with *two* other dreams 'that shuffled themselves abruptly in between the parts of the first dream. Each had a wholly distinct emotional atmosphere . . . and yet, in a moment, as these three dreams alternately telescoped in and out of each other, and I seemed to myself to have been their common dreamer, they seemed quite distinctly *not* to have been dreamed in succession, in that one sleep. *When*, then, and *which* was the one out of which I had just awakened? *I could no longer tell*: one was as close to me as the others, and yet they entirely repelled each other, and I seemed thus to belong to three different dream-systems at once . . .'

Read in the context of the essay about mysticism, this experience seems to make no sense at all, and it is difficult to see why James thought it so significant—surely most of us have awakened from a deep sleep feeling rather confused. But if we think of it as a variation on George Sully's experience, his alarm becomes comprehensible. It was as if *three people* were all dreaming inside the same head. Worse still, he was not certain which of the three dreams belonged to him and which to the other two. We take it so completely for granted that we are masters of our bodies that it is a frightening thought that the 'me' who looks out of my eyes may not be the *owner* but some temporary occupant. James goes on to describe poignantly the awful mental distress into which this threw him and adds that he suddenly found himself filled with deep sympathy for people suffering from mental illness or multiple personality. 'We ought to assure them and reassure them that we will stand by them and recognise the true self in them to the end . . .'

But *is* there a true self? Could there be some other explanation of this frightening phenomenon?

When Janet was hypnotising a neurasthenic girl called Lucie, he plunged her into such a profound sleep that it was impossible to make her react in any way. She had reach 'zero consciousness', the 'hypnotic syncope'. After half an hour, she began to breathe more deeply, opened her eyes—and became another personality.

Lucie had been suffering from hysteria—an artificially narrow state of consciousness—for fifteen years. Janet had reached down into her depths and awakened a sleeping personality, which had lain there like a seed in the earth, waiting for spring. The baffling inference would seem to be that this other Lucie *was* a kind of seed, a separate stage which ought to have appeared normally—fifteen years earlier—and integrated with 'Lucie 1'.

That is just comprehensible—the notion that we have earlier stages of our being lying dormant inside us. But how in that case, do we explain 'higher' personalities, like Ariel and B-4 and Vicky, and the 'Ivenes' personality of Jung's cousin? Are they explainable on the same hypothesis—that they were waiting there to be awakened and to integrate with the rest of the personality? And that *because* Doris and Christine and Sybil and Jung's cousin succumbed to hysteria—and non-development—they remained 'unrealised' until some accident or shock allowed them to emerge?

However unorthodox, this hypothesis fits the facts as we know them. We can think of a human being as a small garden containing a number of seeds at various depths. If all goes well, and the human being strives for self-actualisation, for the realisation of his or her potentialities, then the 'seeds' awaken one by one, and quietly integrate with those that have already started to germinate. But if the human being becomes severely discouraged and refuses to climb Janet's 'staircase', the whole personality becomes static. The seeds start to germinate, put out a few buds, then 'freeze'.

If I open our family photograph album, I see a picture of me at the age of eighteen months, sitting on my grandfather's shoulders. A later one shows me as an awkward looking ten-year-old, with his head on one side and a hesitant smile. If I try hard, I can remember what *that* Colin Wilson was like, because he had just been given a chemistry set and had started to read science fiction. A few pages later I see myself in an RAF uniform. I can remember *him* all right. I still have a lot of the stuff he wrote. And I can remember how awkward he felt with pretty girls. By reading his work and recalling some of his embarrassments (which still make me wince), I can just about put myself inside his skin. Was he 'me'? No, he certainly wasn't. Am I him? That is harder to get into mental focus; but when I succeed I see that the answer is a qualified yes. He is a bit of me. Not too badly integrated, I hope. . . .

I find myself looking at the people around me, and wondering how far their various 'selves' have managed to get integrated. I can think of a lot of rather colourless, timid people who are quite obviously fragmentary personalities. And even in a few people who seem fairly well integrated, I can suddenly catch a glimpse of a more sophisticated, confident personality that has never succeeded in emerging.

The great personality-inhibitor, it seems, is caution—or, in its commoner form, fear. I think of the number of people I have met who told me they thought they could have been a writer or musician or painter but decided to settle for a secure job with a pension. And I think of the number of talented men I have met who dissipated their capacity for self-expression in drinking or seduction. This hardly sounds like caution; yet caution *is* a desire for quick returns, a decision to

> take the cash in hand and leave the rest,
> Nor heed the music of a distant drum.

Even criminality is a form of caution, the desire for immediate and tangible returns, based upon the feeling that the universe has no intention of giving you anything you are not prepared to take by force. In fact, the study of murder leaves one with an impression of weak and crippled personalities who left half their potentialities to stagnate.

But if our personality is a hierarchy of 'possible beings', where has nature drawn the line? How far *could* we develop, given the courage and opportunity? This question takes us beyond the area of abnormal psychology, into the psychology of creation. Did Dante realise his potentialities? Or Michelangelo? Or Leonardo? Or Shakespeare? Or Beethoven? Or Balzac? Or Shaw? The answer, of course, ought to be yes; that would satisfy our sense of rightness and justice. But is it? Dante was a melancholic, according to his friend Boccaccio. Michelangelo was irritable, suspicious and touchy. Leonardo died lamenting that he had 'failed to practise his art as he should have done' and reproaching himself for squandering his life. Shakespeare was litigious and seems to have had an odd streak of meanness. Beethoven's bad temper and dishonesty are legendary. Balzac's vanity and conceit were the joke of Paris. Shaw ceased to develop when he became the slave of a self-created monster called GBS. All seven men were geniuses by normal standards, yet it seems clear that none could be regarded as completely fulfilled men. (And the above list was chosen at random; it would be far more difficult to make a list of seven great men who *were* fulfilled and happy.)

Does this mean that all were 'fragmented personalities' in the sense that Doris and Christine were? Clearly not. But then, man is an evolutionary animal. He is never satisfied to have achieved a certain level of integration. The prospect of higher levels drives him to further effort.

It would seem, then, that 'Janet's staircase' does not come to an end after the ninth step. In fact, it continues upward. Which means that not only are past 'personalities' already present inside us, but future ones too. This was the suspicion that Jung entertained about his cousin—that she was unconsciously aware that she was destined to die young, and was trying to 'reach into the future'. Moreover, she succeeded; apart from creating the trance personality Ivenes, this colourless, dull teenager became a highly-efficient dress designer and manager in her early twenties.

So the study of multiple personality seems to confirm not only that we contain a 'hierarchy of selves', but that the hierarchy continues beyond the 'fully developed' human being. In a sense, this is what we might expect. After all, if someone dies at an early age, then presumably a number of 'higher selves' remain in embryo. And what reason have we for believing that this ever ceases to be true? In fact, the notion of a continuing hierarchy is embodied in the very notion of self-consciousness. All intelligent people are characterised by a tendency to 'duality'. No matter how involved they become in an emotion or enthusiasm, a part of the ego remains detached, uninvolved. (When people experience arrested development, this sense of duality becomes painful.) But all human beings, no matter how lacking in self-awareness, are self-conscious—conscious that they are conscious. We are all 'divided' from the moment of birth; it is a condition of our evolution.

These recognitions are not a discovery of modern 'depth psychology'. They are part of an esoteric tradition that is older than civilisation. Oddly enough, its name is magic.

3

In Search of Faculty X

'Magick,' said Aleister Crowley, its most notorious modern exponent, 'is the Science and Art of causing Change to occur in conformity with the Will.' He was echoing the thought of his nineteenth-century predecessor Eliphaz Levi (of whom he believed himself to be a reincarnation): 'Would you learn to reign over yourself and others? Learn how to will. How can one learn to will? This is the first arcanum of magical initiation . . .' He added that the force of will is 'as real as steam or the galvanic current'. Yet Crowley's biographer John Symonds once remarked: 'The only trouble with magic is that it doesn't work'—an attitude that reflects the view of the majority of people. It is common sense *not* to believe in magic.

But it is worth pausing to ask: *why* is it common sense? The answer is: because our everyday experience offers no support for the claims of people like Crowley. But then, everyday experience offers little support for the claims of will either. In order to call upon the uninhibited force of the will, you must *want* something intensely. And few of us experience really powerful desires—except, perhaps, in a state of sexual excitement.

Modern civilisation induces an attitude of *passivity*. When a Stone-

Age hunter set out to trap wild animals, he was aware of his will as a living force. When the prehistoric farmer scored the surface of the earth with a crude plough, he knew that his family's survival through the winter depended on his effort, and his will responded to the challenge. When a modern city dweller walks down a crowded thoroughfare, he feels no sense of challenge or involvement. This city was built by other people; all these shops and offices are owned by other people. He can get through an ordinary day's work in a state approximating to sleep. Most of his routine tasks are carried out by the 'robot'. There is neither the opportunity nor the need to use the will.

There is a simple experiment that anyone can carry out to demonstrate the role of the will; it was described once by Dr C. E. M. Joad on a BBC Brains Trust programme. In a Gloucester pub, Joad overheard someone asserting that any four people could lift a seated person with their index fingers alone. He then saw this demonstrated on the landlord—an enormous man, who was lifted easily by four fingers placed under his armpits and knees. (One of the lifters was the landlord's small daughter.)

The procedure is for the chosen subject to sit in a chair, while the other four attempt to lift him by placing index fingers under his knees and arms. It is, of course, impossible. Then the four persons place their hands on top of his head in a 'pile', taking care that no person's hands should be next to one another. They should concentrate hard for about a quarter of a minute, then, at a signal, remove their hands, place fingers under the subject's knees and arms, and try again. This time, the seated person rises effortlessly into the air. Joad mentioned that he had tried it many times and watched fat men sailing towards the ceiling.

There is some controversy about why this works, as it undoubtedly does. In *The Mysterious Unknown*, Robert Charroux asserts darkly that 'it cannot be explained by physicists any more than by metaphysicians'. He seems to believe that it is some accumulation of will-force during the period of concentration. Others assert that no concentration is necessary. Joad says that the experiment should begin with each of the four laying their hands *separately* on the subject's head. The likeliest explanation is that the sudden concerted effort produces intense concentration, which supplies the necessary strength for the few split seconds during which it has to be exerted. We arouse ourselves momentarily from our 'robotic' state.

But it is worth keeping our minds open to alternative explanations. A dowser friend showed me a similar experiment, which he claimed depended on 'earth forces'. He held out his right arm parallel to his body, and told me to try to pull it down, using both hands; I succeeded without too much difficulty. He then began to shake his arm to remove all its muscular tensions, beginning by shaking the hand until it moved loosely on the wrist, then the forearm, then the whole arm. Again he raised the arm, and told me to try to pull it down. This time, it was impossible; the arm seemed to be made of rock. He explained that as he stretched the arm, pointing at the horizon, he tried to imagine that earth forces were moving up through the soles of his feet, and out along the arm, like a ray of light. Whatever the explanation, it produced an extraordinary rigidity.

It is worth describing one more experiment to illustrate the power of willed concentration. Again, it requires the presence of four or five people. This time the subject stands with his eyes closed, with the others forming a circle round him. They place their fingers lightly on his shoulders, back and chest. The aim of the experiment is to cause him to sway in whatever direction they predetermine. The four simply concentrate, making sure not to push. It usually takes only a few seconds for the subject to sway in the desired direction.

The first time I tried this, I stood in the centre and allowed my mind to become a blank. Suddenly there was a strong sensation of being pulled forward, as if by a magnetic current, and I had to be caught as I swayed.

The friend who introduced me to the experiment said that it worked even if the subject resisted, but that if he resisted too hard, it would produce dizziness. A few days later, I described the experiment at a business meeting, and someone suggested that we try it. I was dubious—convinced that the atmosphere of a board room would be unpropitious. The man who stood at the centre warned us that he intended to resist. We tried hard for a minute; nothing happened. It was more or less what I had expected; nevertheless, I suggested we have one more try. This time, to my surprise, he suddenly swayed backwards—the direction we had decided on. He admitted that his efforts to resist had made him feel dizzy.

This experiment has not always proved successful; it seems to work best in the evening, when everyone is relaxed and receptive. The only occasion when it was a total failure was in front of television cameras, in a museum of witchcraft; we were using the continuity girl as a subject. But it was an icy cold midwinter day, and our discomfort —and the girl's heavy fur coat—may have had something to do with it. On another occasion, when Uri Geller was one of the group, the subject swayed backwards instead of to the right—whereupon Geller admitted that he had been willing her to move in the opposite direction to the one we had decided.

My own original suspicion was that it worked by means of suggestion, transmitted by the scarcely perceptible pressure of the fingers. This was disproved when we tried it without the fingertips actually touching the person in the middle; it seemed to work just as well, although the reaction time may have been slightly longer. I found myself inclined to accept the explanation of the friend who first told me of the experiment: that the operative principle was telepathy, that it was simply a matter of 'thought pressure'—four wills overruling the will of the subject in the centre.

The matter of 'telepathic commands' has been studied extensively in the laboratory. In the 1890s, Dr P. Joire conducted experiments at the University of Lille in which blindfolded subjects were telepathically ordered to perform certain simple actions—bend their arms and legs or walk in a certain direction. The results were positive. Joire discovered that the experimenter had to concentrate very hard throughout the tests. It usually took between ten and twenty seconds for the subject to start to obey the suggestion, then he did so very slowly—which suggests that the 'force' being applied was very weak. In 1926, the Russian scientist L. L. Vasiliev repeated these experiments in Leningrad with a woman suffering from hysterical paralysis of the left side. She was placed under hypnosis and mentally 'ordered' by Vasiliev and two colleagues—to make various movements, including moving her 'paralysed' arm. She not only made the movements but was usually able to identify the 'sender' of the order.[1]

It may be objected that this demonstrates only telepathy, not the power of the will. But Joire's subjects declared that they experienced a feeling of tingling in the muscles, after which they 'succumbed to this influence almost unconsciously'. Joire never tried to find out what would happen if they resisted. J. B. Priestley has a story of an occasion when he practised 'telepathic suggestion'.[2] At a dinner of a poetry society in New York, Priestley told his neighbour: 'I propose to make one of these poets wink at me.' He chose a sombre-looking woman, 'obviously no winker'; after he had concentrated on her for a minute or two, she winked. Priestley's companion was inclined to doubt whether it had really happened, but after the dinner, Priestley was approached by the poet, who apologised for winking and added: 'It was just a silly sudden impulse.' Priestley thought that the general feeling of boredom at the dinner, 'when everybody's mind is empty-ing', aided his mental suggestion.

Can this force operate directly on matter? The effect is known as psychokinesis, and although it is still a matter of controversy, there seems to be little doubt that it has been frequently observed, both in the laboratory and under less rigorous conditions. In her book *The Decline and Fall of Science*, the psychical researcher Celia Green cites a case that sounds oddly like the experiment I have already described:

> My only experience of levitation occurred during a lunch-time break at school when I was seventeen . . . Each girl took her turn lying on a long wooden table at the front of the classroom, with the others gathered *tightly* around her, so that were no gaps. . . As one lay there, the girls chanted a rhyme—the actual words of which I have forgotten, but which referred to the person on the table as looking white, ill and then dead. It was spoken quite slowly and in unison so that its drone-like tone had great depth and was very penetrating.
>
> Several girls took part before me without much success. Some . . . were quite disillusioned. Others however did admit to feeling a strange sensation . . . and it was this plus the declaration of a friend that she had experienced slight levitation that encouraged me to try it.
>
> I have absolutely no explanation why I was able to rise approximately three feet from the table surface. I was perfectly conscious that I was rising and might even have uttered an exclamation of surprise. . . The rapidity of the rise and indeed the fact that I had risen at all caused me to jerk my body out of the lying position, and with much commotion the girls cushioned my fall.

Can this 'psi' power operate on inanimate matter? As a matter of fact, the modern scientific study of 'psi' began as an attempt to answer this question. One day in 1934, a gambler walked into the office of Dr J. B. Rhine, and told him that he was convinced he could influence the fall of the dice. 'Show me', said the sceptical Rhine. So the two crouched on the floor—the traditional gambler's pose—and the visitor proceeded to demonstrate. As he did so, it occurred to Rhine that this might provide the solution to a problem that had been bothering him for years. The Parapsychological Laboratory had been set up in 1927, under the guidance of Dr William McDougall, one of the foremost psychologists of his time (and, like Driesch, a convinced vitalist). McDougall wanted to investigate telepathy and survival after death. The only obvious way to do this was to test mediums and clairvoyants; and the sceptics never lost an opportunity to point out that a skilful fraudulent medium could fool anybody. Moreover, Rhine had recently been in correspondence with Jung, who had told him the odd story about the exploding table and bread knife. Rhine agreed this was probably psychokinesis; but how could one test it in the laboratory? It was impossible to make bread knives explode at will. And now a gambler was providing the answer—how to test 'mind over matter' in the laboratory. Moreover, the tests did not have to be restricted to professional psychics; most students were expert at throwing dice.

Rhine tried it, and his results revolutionised parapsychology. For they showed beyond all possible doubt that when someone first made a determined effort to influence the dice, the results were significantly above expectation. What was equally interesting was that if students went straight on to perform a second test, the results dropped steeply. For a third test, they became lower still. In other words, students could exert PK powers when they were fresh and really put their minds to it. Then their attention began to waver, and the results fell off.

Since Rhine's experiments, there has been a steady and impressive accumulation of evidence for psychokinesis. A Russian housewife, Nina Kulagina, discovered her powers accidentally when she was trying to find out whether she could 'sense' different colours with her fingertips alone. With her eyes blindfolded, she held her fingers above small bits of coloured paper. Someone noticed that one of the pieces was making slight movements. Kulagina practised hard and soon discovered that she was able to move matchsticks, fountain pens and compass needles. Tests in both Russian and American laboratories have detected no sign of fraud. A New York artist, Ingo Swann, was able to deflect the needle of a magnetometer when it was buried in concrete. Another New Yorker, Felicia Parise, was inspired to try psychokinesis after she had watched films of Madame Kulagina and was soon demonstrating her power to move small objects in the laboratories of the Maimonides Institute. Both Nina Kulagina and

Felicia Parise have said that they find their efforts exhausting and often lose pounds in weight during the course of experiments.

In 1973, the feats of the Israeli Uri Geller suddenly made psychokinesis front-page news. Geller was able to bend spoons by rubbing them with his finger and alter the time on watches by clenching his fist above them. Sceptics labelled him a fraud, and professional conjurors offered to duplicate any of his 'tricks' on the stage. Even Geller's admirers had to admit that his best performances were on television, not in the laboratory. Yet his laboratory performances were impressive enough; at Stanford, he demonstrated remarkable powers of telepathy, extrasensory perception, and the power to deflect a compass needle by concentrating on it. Many scientists who have tested him have concluded that his powers are genuine—or, to put this controversial topic at its lowest: no sceptical opponent has been able to prove that he is *not* genuine.

Geller's feats raise a fundamental question. All laboratory tests so far have indicated that our PK powers are very slight. To test them, scientists have had to devise apparatus that will measure fractions of a milligram; even the highest estimate so far has been a mere ten per cent of the force of gravity exerted on a dice (i.e. one tenth of the weight of the dice). Kulagina and Felicia Parise perspire heavily as they move very light objects. Why should Geller's powers be apparently so much greater than theirs?

The answer takes us to the heart of this strange problem. There is no obvious direct relation between these powers and ordinary will-power. When Felicia Parise first tried moving small objects, she failed, although she made overwhelming efforts of concentration. One day, she received a phone call saying that her grandmother was dying; it was a severe emotional shock. As she reached out for a small plastic bottle, it moved away from her hand. After the funeral, she tried moving the bottle again by 'thought pressure' and was this time successful. The emotional shock had somehow released her latent PK powers. When students were tested by Dr Helmut Schmidt at the Parapsychological Laboratory at Durham, North Carolina, they somehow achieved the *opposite* effects from the ones they were trying for. They were supposed to make a delicate light meter move clockwise; instead, it moved anti-clockwise. Their attempts to 'will' were apparently putting their powers in reverse.[3]

We know that the conscious will is connected to the narrow, conscious part of the personality. One of the paradoxes observed by Janet is that as the hysteric becomes increasingly obsessed with anxiety—and the need to exert his will—he also becomes increasingly ineffective. The narrower and more obsessive the consciousness, the weaker the will. Every one of us is familiar with the phenomenon. The more we become racked with anxiety to do something well, the more we are likely to botch it. It is Frankl's 'law of reversed effort'. If you want to do something really well, you have to get into the 'right mood'. And the right mood involves a sense of relaxation, of feeling 'wide open' instead of narrow and enclosed. And in the case of Janet's hysterics, we can see what goes wrong. The hysteric literally became two people, one of whom could answer questions while the other talked to someone else. That is to say, the hysteric divided himself in half. And, as you would expect, divided his powers in half too. Janet cured such patients by persuading them to relax into the 'full self', so to speak.

As William James remarked, we *all* have a lifelong habit of 'inferiority to our full self'. We are all hysterics; it is the endemic disease of the human race, which clearly implies that, outside our 'everyday personality', there is a wider 'self' that possesses greater powers than the everyday self. And this is *not* the Freudian subconscious. Like the 'wider self' of Janet's patients, it is as conscious as the 'contracted self'. We are, in fact, partially aware of this 'other self'. When a man 'unwinds' by pouring himself a drink and kicking off his shoes, he is adopting an elementary method of relaxing into the other self. When an overworked housewife decides to buy herself a new hat, she is doing the same thing. But we seldom relax far enough; habit—and anxiety—are too strong. As Felicia Parise strained her will to move the plastic bottle, she was calling on the depleted powers of the 'contracted self'. And the very intensity of her effort frustrated its own purpose, for it made her narrower still. This always happens when something goes wrong, and we become increasingly frantic and obsessive. The shock of the telephone call cut the knot, released her from the vicious circle. It made her aware that there were bigger and more important issues, and released her into the 'wider self', which lost no time in moving the bottle.

When the will is hindered by too much self-consciousness it often produces the opposite effect from the one intended. (Poe called it 'the imp of the perverse.') The 'wider self' would be happy to oblige, but the 'contracted ego' is somehow opposing itself, like someone trying to open a door by pushing it instead of pulling it. So it does the next best thing. In the case of Dr Schmidt's students, it made the meter revolve the other way.

But both cases make the same point: when the ego contracts into a state of anxiety, it cuts itself off from its source of power. It is as if we had placed a tourniquet around an arm or leg, and caused it to go 'dead'. The problem then is to relax, untie the tourniquet and get the blood flowing back into the nerveless area. The simile is inaccurate in only one particular. When your arm or leg has gone 'dead', it is incapable of movement. But when the ego applies a torniquet of anxiety to a part of itself, the excluded area remains very much alive and capable of independent functioning.

These observations bring us back to the definitions of magic quoted at the beginning of this chapter. Magic is the art and science of using the will. Not the ordinary will of the contracted ego but the 'true will' that seems to spring from some deeper area of the being.

This notion of the 'true will' plays an important part in the magical tradition. It also seems to be the key to many—if not all—paranormal phenomena, from poltergeists to psychokinesis. It enables us to explain why the antics of the poltergeist, or Geller's ability to bend spoons, cannot be correctly described as 'magic'. With a few rare exceptions, poltergeists seem to have been beyond the control of the people who caused them. Geller admits that he is never certain whether his powers will work, or whether some piece of metal that he handles casually—like the fork with which he eats his dinner—will bend in his fingers. But the aim of traditional magic has always been the control of the 'hidden self', sometimes called the 'daemon' or 'guardian angel', as well as of the forces of nature.

At this point, it is necessary to look more closely at the ideas of the Western magical tradition.

In their book *Techniques of High Magic*, Francis King and Stephen Skinner speak of four basic assumptions of magic:

1. That the [physical] universe is only a part of total reality.

2. That human will-power is a real force, capable of being trained and concentrated, and that the disciplined will is capable of changing its environment and producing paranormal effects.

3. That this will-power must be directed by the imagination.

4. That the universe is not a mixture of chance factors and influences but an ordered system of correspondences, and that the understanding of the pattern of correspondences enables the occultist to use them for his own purposes, good or evil.

These principles can be found, in various forms, in all the major magical texts, from the writings attributed to Hermes Trismegistos and the medieval grimoires to the works of Levi, Crowley and Dion Fortune. The Jesuit scholar Martin Del Rio defined magic, in his famous *Disquisitionum Magicarum* (1599) as 'an art or skill which, by means of a non-supernatural force, produces certain strange and unusual phenomena whose rationale eludes common sense'. Since Del Rio believed in angels and demons, his insistence that magic is a 'non-supernatural force' is of special interest here. Lewis Spence, the historian of occultism, defines magic as 'a power, latent in human beings, of controlling cosmic matter by their will and faith'. Dion Fortune introduced an interesting variation: 'Magic is the art of causing changes in consciousness at will.' But all these definitions involve the underlying assumption that the 'will' is of a special kind.

The third principle is equally important: that the will must be directed by the imagination. MacGregor Mathers, one of the founders of the magical Order of the Golden Dawn, stated in a lecture: 'To practise magic, both the Imagination and the Will must be called into action, they are co-equal in the work. . . The Will unaided can send forth a current . . . yet its effect is vague and indefinite. . . The Imagination unaided can create an image . . . yet it can do nothing of importance, unless vitalised and directed by the Will.'[4] And Mathers goes on to give several examples of his own magical practices, each involving clear visualisation. After conversations with a certain fidgety old gentleman, Mathers observed that he was listless and exhausted and concluded that the old gentleman was somehow 'vampirising' his energy. To counteract this, he imagined himself surrounded by a 'force field' that insulated him from the outside world. On another occasion, when he suspected that a man was using magical techniques to try to seduce a girl, he imagined himself holding a sword and severing a kind of psychic 'web' between them. In these and other cases, Mathers claimed, he was totally successful.

Mathers had recognised a basic principle of human perception: that it is 'intentional'. When you look at something, it is as if your eyes reached out and grasped it. And the 'grasp' can be powerful or weak.

This can easily be tested by means of a simple exercise. In looking at a drawing of a 'transparent cube', we can see it either as if looking at it from above or from below:

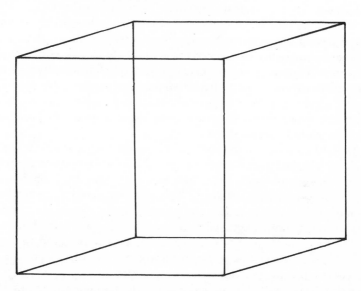

As the cube 'changes' from one to the other, we can become aware of the mental act of turning it over, exactly like flipping a coin from one side to the other. With a little effort, it is possible to 'turn' the cube as easily as flipping the coin. The effort that changes the cube from one side to the other is what the philosopher Husserl calls intentionality, and what Mathers means by imagination.

One of the most balanced and sensible of modern textbooks of magic by David Conway,[5] devotes a whole chapter to the practice of 'visualisation'. The student is advised to look at diagrams or pictures, then close his eyes and envisage them clearly. When he has accomplished this, he should try to visualise solid objects and to imagine them from various angles. The exercise can be extended to include the senses of smell and touch. Finally, it should be possible to visualise with the eyes open, so that the images are 'projected' into the real world. 'This "projection",' says the author, 'is a knack which, like learning to swim, will be acquired all of a sudden.'

But he goes on to point out that this faculty must be controlled;

'involuntary hallucinations belong to the realm of mental illness, not magic'. He is making a point that is of fundamental importance in all such studies and disciplines. All highly developed faculties are a potential danger. Everyone knows how irritating it can be to have some silly tune or jingle running in one's head. But this can happen to us only because we possess highly developed powers of memory; dogs and cats never experience such annoyances. Similarly, people with intense powers of concentration are prone to nervous breakdown because they subject themselves to greater strains than people with butterfly minds. Goethe's *Sorcerer's Apprentice* and other such cautionary tales have their foundation in common sense. It is easier to develop unusual powers than to control them.

Mathers sees the imagination as an essential adjunct of the will, analogous to the range-finder on a gun. Its purpose is to direct the will clearly and unambiguously towards its object. And this is obviously true of all our willed activities. The effect of wanting something strongly is not only to arouse one's desires, but to arouse the *energies* that will enable one to pursue it. If we only half want something, or feel ambiguous about it, our energies will be sluggish, and we will probably fail to achieve it. So even where everyday purposes are concerned, the imagination is of central importance. But the magical tradition insists that the will has a power that is independent of the physical world. It can be transmitted directly, as it were, like radio waves. So for Mathers, there would be nothing unusual in the idea of a man using 'magic' to seduce a girl. It would simply be a part of what is known as 'natural magic' (to distinguish it from spiritual magic, or a magic that uses the 'higher forces' of the universe). In *The Occult*, I quoted the poet Robert Graves, who told me that many young men use a form of unconscious sorcery to seduce girls. When a man wants a woman badly, he fixes his desire on her and broods on it until it permeates his being. He spends much of his time daydreaming about possessing her and enacting his desires in imagination. Mathers would say that the 'true will' is awakened by the intensity of the desire and proceeds to use its strength to dominate the will of the girl. Graves's point was that many seducers use this method naturally without even being conscious that it is a simple form of sorcery. He would probably add that all self-confident people use the same kind of unconscious magic to achieve their ends.

This notion of the magical power of the imagination is not confined to the Western tradition; it can be found all over the world. In her book *Magic and Mystery in Tibet*, Alexandra David-Nell tells the classic story of the 'hat that walked'. The hat was blown off the head of some traveller, and settled in a valley below the road. From a distance it looked like some strange creature, and the villagers who passed the spot were too frightened to investigate. Eventually, their fears and imaginings imbued the hat with a life of its own, and it began to move around like an animal. This story is typical of the type of magic practised in Tibet. She also explains how a knife can be 'bewitched' so that it can lead someone to commit suicide. The sorcerer has to spend months in intense concentration on the knife, envisaging the death of his enemy and performing magic rituals. When the knife is sufficiently charged with malevolent energy, it is placed in the house of the intended victim, and if he is incautious enough to pick it up, he will experience a sudden overpowering impulse to kill himself.

Max Freedom Long's book *The Huna Code in Religions* deals with the magical and religious system of the Polynesians and relates this natural magic of the will to the complex operations of the superconscious or higher self. According to Long, the Kahuna priesthood recognise three levels in man, the subconscious, the 'everyday' self or middle self, and the superconscious self. Each level makes use of its own type of 'mana' or force. The 'mana' of the middle self is will or hypnotic force. But the 'mana' of the higher self actually creates the future of the individual, 'this future gradually becoming materialised as actual events or conditions'. So the Kahuna go farther than most Western exponents of the magical tradition in believing that man actually dictates his own future through his deepest desires. It would seem to justify Goethe's comment: 'Beware of what you wish for in youth, for you will get it in middle age.' Long relates the Huna code to the religion of the Gnostics, and to the beliefs of the Egyptian priesthood.

By comparison with these non-European traditions, the 'will-magic' of the West often seems two-dimensional and crude. A typical example can be found in Joseph Glanvill's *Saducismus Triumphatus* (1681), concerning the famous Scholar Gypsy—familiar to every schoolboy from Matthew Arnold's poem. The 'gypsy' was an Oxford student who left university because of poverty and joined a band of gypsies. Some time later he met two of his former fellow students and told them that the gypsies could 'do wonders by the power of imagination'. To demonstrate the art, he left the room and went to another part of the inn. When he returned, he was able to give them a detailed account of their conversation after he left the room. Astounded at his accuracy, they asked him how he did it. 'In which he gave them satisfaction, by telling them that what he did was by the power of imagination, his phantasy leading theirs; and that himself had dictated to them the discourse they had held together while he was from them. . .' The Scholar Gypsy added that 'there were warrantable ways of heightening the imagination to that pitch [so as to be able to] bend another's'.

Clearly, the sense in which we are now speaking of imagination differs fundamentally from its normal usage. If I try to imagine Notting Hill Gate as it used to be in my early days in London, the image that comes into my mind is like a blurred photograph. It is 'like' the original in outline, but that is all—rather, say, like whistling the opening bars of Beethoven's Ninth Symphony; no amount of brooding can 'orchestrate' my image. Yet Glanvill is speaking of the imagination not as a poor imitation of the original, but as an independent force. Mathers even makes the assertion: 'When a man imagines, he actually creates a form on the Astral or even on some higher plane; and this form is as real and objective to intelligent beings on that plane, as our earthly surroundings are to us.' If, for 'Astral plane', we substitute Lethbridge's 'next whorl of the spiral', or perhaps some higher level of human consciousness, then Mathers is asserting that the imagination can act as a messenger between different levels of existence.

It is civilisation that has debased—or at least enfeebled—our idea of imagination. When Stone-Age hunters relaxed around the fire in the evenings and listened to stories of the chase or of battles with neighbouring tribes, they *re-lived* the events, yet in a completely different form from the original experience. (Children still have this capacity to become 'totally lost' in a story.) When the modern city dweller relaxes in front of his television, he cannot, by any stretch of the imagination, be said to 're-live' the events he watches. He consumes them as casually as he smokes his hundredth cigarette. So he comes to think of imagination as a counterfeit reality. When he accuses someone of being 'imaginative', he simply means that he is a liar. He has blurred the distinction between imagination and reality.

Our remote ancestors never made that mistake. Life was hard, and their mental powers were part of their survival kit. Some thirty-five thousand years ago, our Cro-magnon ancestors embarked on a career of genocide. The victim was their ape-like half-brother, Neanderthal man. And, in a surprisingly short time, there were no more Neanderthals. It was not that Cro-magnon man was stronger or more numerous than Neanderthal man; only that he had more brain power and imagination. And during the next twenty-five thousand years, he laid the foundations of civilisation by inventing art, religion and technology. Yet he had no way of storing knowledge except inside his own head. When a man died, his knowledge died with him, except for the little that was stored in the memory of other members of the tribe. The power of his mind was his only ally against the encroaching darkness.

We now know that Cro-magnon man came surprisingly close to inventing writing. In the early sixties, Alexander Marshack became fascinated by the complex markings on hundreds of pieces of bone and other Stone-Age artifacts. By microscopic examination, he established that they were not simply decoration—they were made with too many different tools—but some form of notation, probably of the phases of the moon. Our Stone-Age ancestors had stumbled on the basic principle of writing as long ago as thirty-four thousand years, but had failed to develop it. That failure was probably one of the best pieces of luck that ever befell the human race. It meant that Cro-magnon man had to rely on brain power to preserve his essential knowledge—on memory aided by a few simple devices (the equivalent of tying knots in a handkerchief). He had to learn the difficult art of using the brain as a storehouse, and enlarging its capacity for storage. His descendants benefited from that long training when they came to live together in cities around 5000 BC. Däniken and his followers cite that sudden flowering of civilisation as evidence that space men must have had a hand in it. They forget that, space men or no space men, Cro-magnon man had been preparing to take the leap for thirty thousand years.

Finally, around 3500 BC, the Sumerians invented pictorial writing, and the principle was developed in Egypt, China and the land of the Hittites; at last, certain forms of knowledge—mostly religious rituals—could be preserved. More than two thousand years later, the Phoenicians and the Greeks developed the phonetic alphabet, and it became possible to capture the actual flavour and texture of everyday speech. It should have revolutionised civilisation as completely as the invention of the motor car or radio. In fact, the effects were at first almost imperceptible. Man had been relying on his memory too long to change his ways overnight. Plato expresses this curious distrust in the *Phaedrus*, when he tells how the Egyptian god Thoth invented the art of writing. Thoth boasts to King Thamus that he has invented the 'elixir of wisdom and memory'; the king replies that he has done nothing of the sort—he has only discouraged the people from relying on their own mental efforts. Plato, like most ancient philosophers, felt that man's chief distinction lay in his powers of memory and imagination, and that he ought to develop these in the way that an athlete develops his muscles.

In fact, the ancients developed an incredibly complex 'art of memory', which survived down to the age of Shakespeare. The astonishing story of this now-forgotten art has been told by the historian Francis Yates.[6] But perhaps the most remarkable thing about it is that the art of memory was regarded as magical and was developed by such celebrated cabbalists as Raymond Lull, Marsilio Ficino (who translated *Thrice Great Hermes*) and Giordano Bruno. Why magical? What was magical about an 'art' that merely trained you to commit whole books to memory?

The answer was self-evident to the ancient Greeks. Aristotle states it in his treatise *On the Soul*: 'Memory belongs to the same part of the soul as imagination.' Think of a scholar surrounded by a library of books. He may be merely a dull pedant who knows how to find information. But if he had the contents of all the books *inside his head*, that would be a different matter. He would *know* the books, be able to compare Plato's views on the soul with those of St Augustine, or Alexander the Great's military strategy with Julius Caesar's. Such a man would possess wisdom rather than knowledge; he would be a genius, a kind of god.

The argument will strike some readers as a sophistry. Surely a man is none the wiser for having his head crammed with information? But that, again, is a typical modern misconception. The basic problem of human consciousness is its narrowness. From the moment I get up in the morning, my chief occupation is observing what goes on at the end of my nose. That is not really consciousness. A dog could say the same. My real glimpses of consciousness—of the potentialities of consciousness—occur in these moments of sudden intensity, or deep relaxation, when these limitations are suddenly transcended.

It is difficult to describe what happens in such moments, except to say that the world seems to become a deeper and a richer place. If you read poetry in such a mood, it is a sensual pleasure, as if it caused vibrations in the senses of smell and touch. If you listen to music, it seems to reach into every corner of your being. If you read a travel book, the places described seem to become real.

Clearly, what we are talking about is 'Faculty X', the strange ability suddenly to grasp the reality of other times and places. But here I must make a point of central importance. There is no good reason why a baby should not experience flashes of Faculty X. But they would mean far less to a baby than to an adult. All children experience Faculty X, particularly at holiday times and at Christmas; there is a sense of excitement and multiplicity, of endless horizons. But the child's actual horizons are limited by inexperience; so the insight is also limited. On the other hand, a scientist who experienced Faculty X might glimpse the immense complexity of the universe. A historian who experienced Faculty X might grasp the reality of remote epochs of time. You could compare Faculty X to the power of distant vision. Obviously, it will mean more to a person standing on a hilltop than to someone in the valley.

It should be obvious, then, that the meaning–content of such an experience depends on the amount we *know*. For an ignoramus, Faculty X would be merely a pleasant sense that 'all is well', that the world is a marvellous and complex place. For a philosopher, it could be an insight into the meaning of human existence.

The ancient 'art of memory' was not simply an attempt to turn the human brain into a library. It was a deliberate attempt to create Faculty X, a wider and deeper form of consciousness. Hence the magical significance of memory. We can see the connection if we think of Proust's description of his feeling as he tastes the cake dipped in tea and is transported back to his childhood. Or the description in Hesse's *Steppenwolf* of the hero's mystical intensity: 'For moments together my heart stood still between delight and sorrow to find how rich was the gallery of my life, and how thronged the soul of the wretched Steppenwolf with high eternal stars and constellations.' In both cases, memory ceases to be a 'carbon copy' and becomes a reality. This is the true significance of the art of memory. And it is no linguistic accident that we use the word 'magic' to describe these enriched states of consciousness: 'the magic of childhood', 'the magic of the distance', 'the magic of the senses'. The powers that the ancients called magic—and that we prefer to speak of as paranormal—spring from those hidden realms of consciousness that lie beyond our usual limited horizons.

That this was, in fact, the fundamental aim of the 'art of memory' becomes clear from the words of some of its chief practitioners. The Venetian Giulio Camillo (1480–1544) actually built a 'memory theatre', which scholars of his own time classed with the seven wonders of the world. The spectator stood on a stage at the centre of the 'auditorium', and looked out on the whole sum of human knowledge arranged in seven blocks of 'seats', each in seven tiers with seven aisles in between—the number refers to the seven planets and Solomon's seven pillars of wisdom. We would probably prefer to call it an 'Exhibition', but the word was unknown in Camillo's time. The individual 'exhibits' consisted of 'images'—probably paintings, statues, painted symbols—and underneath these, drawers containing speeches based on Cicero, the most celebrated of Roman orators. The whole intention was to awaken the mind to a wider sense of reality. Camillo said that it would enable the spectator to 'perceive with his eyes everything that is otherwise hidden in the depths of the human mind'. (In Latin, 'hidden' is *occultus*.) It would give him a kind of bird's-eye view of the universe. Camillo further explained his intention by using the illustration of a man standing in a forest who can see only the trees that surround him. But if there is a hill nearby, and he climbs to the top, he can see the whole forest. In short, man is trapped in the present, unable to see the wood for the trees. But once he has learned the shape of the wood (in a simplified form), he can hope to ascend to a state of consciousness in which the whole thing becomes comprehensible.

This was why Camillo was one of the most famous men of his time—even though the 'memory theatre' was never finished and disappeared after his death. He had touched on one of the deepest aspirations of his age. To modern ears the theatre sounds absurd; but that is only if we fail to grasp its basic aim. Even today, a good exhibition can be a kind of revelation. Anyone who saw Richard Buckle's Diaghilev Exhibition in London in 1954 will recall its almost magical effect; the use of décor and lighting—and even scent—was so cunning that it was like stepping backward in time to the St Petersburg of 1910 or the Paris of 1920. A decade later, Buckle created the same effect in his Shakespeare Exhibition, so there was a sense of double-exposure as you stepped out of the age of the first Queen Elizabeth into the traffic of modern Stratford.

This was the effect Camillo intended—and apparently partly succeeded in creating. His contemporaries immediately recognised the grandeur of the conception. They were living in an age of intellectual revolution. Columbus's voyage to America had demonstrated conclusively that the earth was a sphere. Cortes and Pizarro brought back from the New World incredible tales of alien civilisations and savage customs. In Cracow, Nicholas Copernicus had reached the astonishing conclusion that the earth was a satellite of the sun. In Basel, Theophrastus Bombastus von Hohenheim, better known as Paracelsus, one of the greatest doctors—and magicians—of the age, never tired of telling his students that the imagination constitutes the stars or firmament in man, and that this 'inner firmament' is the foundation of all magical powers. And now Camillo was suggesting that man could become master of both the inner and the outer firmament by entering a kind of magic theatre. It was more than an exciting idea; it was a new vision of the power and dignity of man.

Yet Camillo himself was a modest man who stuttered badly; perhaps that was the secret of his survival. Fifty years later, Giordano Bruno had the courage—and intemperance—to state in plain terms the idea that was only hinted at in Camillo and implied in Paracelsus: that if man is the 'great miracle' mentioned by Hermes Trismegistos, then the discovery of his own inner powers will turn him into a god. This is the vision at the heart of his major work, *The Art of Memory*.[7] The mind of man is divine, and contains within itself the starry heavens. If man can grasp this universal plan—by means of a magical art of memory—then he will be able to tap the power of the cosmos. The magic power emanates from the 'seals', the images of the stars. He who understands the 'seals' will become a magus and possess the power to open the 'black diamond doors' in the psyche. Bruno also hints that such a man will burn with a kind of 'heroic frenzy' (*eroici furori*) and will bring salvation to the human race.

Such ideas were highly dangerous—to Bruno himself as well as to orthodox Christians who might be led astray by them. The flat truth is that Bruno was basically hostile to Christianity. His attitude was not unlike that of Swinburne three centuries later. But while Swinburne rejected the 'pale Galilean' in favour of Greek paganism, Bruno's ideal was Egyptian hermeticism, with its worship of the sun. In fact, Bruno seems to have harboured Messianic delusions in which he *was* the sun. He makes an English admirer say of him: 'Although I cannot see your soul, from the ray that it diffuses I perceive that within you is the sun or perhaps some even greater luminary.' Bruno begins *The Art of Memory* by claiming that the work is divinely inspired, like the Holy Scriptures. He told Mocigeno—who betrayed him to the Inquisition—that he hoped to found his own religious sect in Germany. In Padua, shortly before his arrest, he prepared himself for his clash with the Church by performing magical operations to give himself charismatic powers, 'working at hermetic seals and links with demons'. This was the man who would 'stop at nothing, who would use every magical procedure, however forbidden and dangerous'.

Bruno was going through the typical martyrdom of the Right Man, obsessed by his divine mission, subject to 'pathological accesses of rage in which he said terrible things which frightened people'. All the signs are that he was headed for the kind of nervous breakdown that often overtakes Right Men. But before he could take that final step towards the 'black diamond doors', the Inquisition pounced and consigned him to a dungeon. Two centuries later, Bonaparte's police would do the same thing to the Marquis de Sade, and for precisely the same reason: they found his ideas blasphemous and terrifying. The human race has never cared for moralists who tell man that he ought to be a god.

Paranoid or not, Giordano Bruno was the last great magician of the Renaissance to understand the magical significance of imagination. His learned contemporary John Dee—Queen Elizabeth's astrologer—was more concerned with 'natural magic', telepathy, crystal-gazing, and what would now be called trance-mediumship. Robert Fludd, one of the greatest cabbalists of his age, was a doctor by profession (like Paracelsus), and even his magical works are basically scientific in spirit. Besides, the old magical art of memory, which depended heavily on images and symbols, was being swept aside by a new logical variety, invented by the Frenchman Pierre de la Ramée. Peter Ramus (to use the name by which he was better known) was a Protestant who died in the massacre of St Bartholomew; his martyrdom increased the popularity of his system in Protestant countries. 'Ramism' was basically a kind of learning by rote, and it appealed to the seventeenth century more than the classical system with its 'occult' overtones.

Not that magical ideas were unpopular in the 'age of reason'. Even Sir Isaac Newton was an enthusiastic alchemist who devoted much of his life to the quest for the philosopher's stone. But the new 'magicians' thought of themselves as scientists and rationalists; they felt they were simply trying to uncover the laws of nature. Such laws were independent of the human mind; so there was no more talk of imagination of the inner firmament. Franz Mesmer thought that he had discovered that the 'hidden forces' inside human beings are a form of energy called 'animal magnetism', which can be moved around the body by means of magnets. In a treatise on the divining rod entitled *Occult Physics* (1693), the Abbé Lorrain de Vallemont explained that dowsing works through perspiration from the hands; he also offered an interesting formula for causing the spectre of a rose to appear in a bottle when it is exposed to sunlight. (His theory that all living things leave behind an 'occult image' is surprisingly close to Lethbridge's idea that ghosts are a kind of 'tape recording'.) The only 'magician' whose fame was comparable to that of Paracelsus or Bruno was the Count de Cagliostro, half imposter, half genuine psychic. He possessed a remarkable imagination, but of the wrong kind; his 'Egyptian freemasonry' was largely of his own invention, designed to coax money out of the pockets of gullible admirers. Dr Johnson summarised the eighteenth-century mistrust of imagination when he declared: 'All power of fancy over reason is a degree of insanity.'[8]

At this point one of the most remarkable events in human cultural history occurred. It was nothing less than a universal revolt on behalf of the imagination. The surprising thing was that it was not confined to a few occultists or philosophers, but occurred simultaneously from one end of Europe to the other. The man who was the innocent cause of this tidal wave of romantic feeling was a middle-aged printer named Samuel Richardson. Richardson had been commissioned to write a Teach-Yourself book on the art of correspondence; he got carried away and turned it into a detailed account of the attempted seduction of a servant girl by her master. When it appeared in 1740, *Pamela* instantly became the first best-selling novel. In fact, it was the first novel of any kind in the sense that we understand the word today.

The popularity of *Pamela* was undoubtedly due to its sexual theme. But that fails to explain the magical, almost mystical effect it had on so many readers—particularly of the female sex. The seduction theme provided *Pamela* with its thread of interest; but what was important was that the reader could *lose* herself in it, plunge into it as into deep water, leave her own life behind and become wholly identified with the life of the heroine. *Pamela* penetrated to remote country areas where the only exciting event of the week was the Sunday sermon. (And in those days before the advent of the novel, volumes of sermons were read avidly—not out of piety, but because they were a re-creation of the only imaginative experience of the week.) For thousands of bored housewives—and even more unmarried women—*Pamela* provided a more intense emotional experience than anything in their own lives.

Novel-writing became the fastest-growing industry in Europe. Richardson had taught the middle classes the use of the imagination, and the appetite grew with feeding. Rousseau's *New Heloise*—another novel about seduction—was so popular that libraries found they could lend it out *by the hour*. Goethe's *Werther*, in which the hero kills himself for love, caused an epidemic of suicides. Within half a century of the publication of *Pamela*, the free use of imagination had transformed the European mind. It was largely responsible for the French Revolution, many of whose leaders were rebels who had learned their dissatisfaction from Rousseau and Schiller. And it was responsible for that extraordinary revolution of the human spirit that we call romanticism: the revolt of the dreamers against the boredom of the material world.

The irony of romanticism is that it was rendered impotent by its own premises. Giordano Bruno had taught that the magus can become a kind of god if he dares to pursue the magical art to its ultimate limits. The romantics felt that man is *already* a kind of god—but a god in exile. Trapped in the dreariness of everyday life, he is like a fish out of water. And it cannot be long before he suffocates.

Imagination is man's salvation and his downfall. The hero of Balzac's mystical novel *Louis Lambert* possesses an imagination so intense that when he reads a book, he is transported to the scenes it portrays: 'When I read the story of the battle of Austerlitz, I saw every incident. The roar of the cannon, the cries of the fighting men rang in my ears and made my inmost being quiver. . .' But this intensity of imagination leads to brain-fever and he dies more-or-less insane.

One of the most remarkable figures of that remarkable movement was the novelist E. T. A. Hoffman. And since there is no space here for a longer account of romanticism, he can serve as the representative of the whole movement.[9]

Hoffmann was a musician and an alcoholic, whose world of strange characters influenced almost every major writer of the nineteenth century. It was in his novel *The Serapion Brothers* that Hoffmann created the supreme symbol of the romantic imagination. The Serapion Brotherhood is a group of poets and musicians who take their name from an insane nobleman who believes that he was martyred in the reign of the Emperor Decius. It is useless to argue with 'the monk Serapion', for nothing will convince him that he is living in nineteenth-century Germany. When the narrator tells him he is mad, he replies calmly that it is the narrator who is suffering from delusions. The world 'out there' is actually inside our own brains. So how can anyone prove that what is inside his own brain is 'truer' than what is inside someone else's?

Now the 'monk Serapion' had once been a very good poet, noted for the power of his imagination. All that has happened is that his imagination has triumphed over 'real' life. It was a triumph that the romantics dreamed about. Yet Hoffmann himself was unwilling to state frankly that this was what he had in mind. Instead, the Brotherhood admires the sheer intensity of Serapion's imagination, which can defy the whole world.

> It is useless for a poet to try to make us believe in a thing that he does not believe in himself—*cannot* believe in because he has never really seen it. If a poet is not a genuine seer, what can his characters be except deceptive puppets, glued together from bits and pieces? But your hermit Serapion was a true poet. He had actually seen what he described, and that was why he affected people's hearts and souls.

This 'secret' of poetic greatness that Hoffmann speaks about is the 'magical' imagination of the hermeticists. And Hoffmann, like Bruno, has a strong intuition that it is the key to greatness of another kind: that it is in short, the basic secret of human evolution. Yet he finds it difficult to reconcile this conclusion with the facts of the material world in which we are forced to live.

Poor Serapion! What did your madness consist in, except that some hostile star had taken away your faculty for grasping the duality which is the essential condition of our earthly existence? There is an inner world, and a spiritual faculty for discerning it with absolute clearness—yes, with the most minute and brilliant distinctness. But it is part of our earthly lot that it is the *outer* world, in which we are entrapped, that triggers this spiritual faculty. . . But you, happy hermit, lost sight of the outward world, and did not notice this trigger that set your inward faculty in motion; and when, with that gruesome acumen of yours, you declared that it is only the mind that sees and hears and notices events, . . . you forget that it is the outer world that causes the spirit to use its powers of perception.[10]

'There is an inner world, and a spiritual faculty for discerning it with absolute clearness.' This is the essence of the vision of Paracelsus and Bruno, and the name of the faculty is imagination. The poet Blake echoed Paracelsus when he wrote: 'All animals and vegetations, the earth and heaven [are] contained in the all-glorious Imagination.' But unlike Hoffmann, Blake was writing in a spirit of optimism and defiance; he was not afraid to assert that 'imagination is the real and eternal world, of which this vegetable universe is but a shadow, in which we shall live in our eternal or imaginative bodies when these vegetable mortal bodies are no more'. Blake actually believed that imagination is a genuine principle of immortality. Hoffmann was convinced that imagination is a magical power, but not that it can somehow outlast the reality of the physical world.

The fact remains that Blake, Hoffmann and their colleagues were instrumental in bringing about one of the greatest advances in the history of the human race. To say they re-discovered imagination is misleading; they rediscovered something even deeper. Richardson had invented a magic carpet, and it differed as much from earlier forms of imagination—as practised by Homer and Malory and Chaucer—as an aeroplane differs from a motor car. Imagination ceased to be a way of escaping reality, and became a way of creating reality. The romantics had re-discovered one of the basic principles of magic.

The claim sounds excessive. But was it coincidence that the nineteenth century produced a greater advance in Western civilisation than the past three thousand years? We may object that these advances were brought about by science, not magic or imagination; but Newton's *Principia*, the foundation of modern science, was published as long ago as 1687. It was not science or technology that transformed nineteenth-century Europe, but a new spirit; and it was the spirit that had made the Inquisition burn Bruno at the stake. The old spirit had been based on authority; the common people bowed their knees to the lord of the manor; the lord of the manor to his lord; and his lord, eventually, to God. Changes happened with infinitesimal slowness because no one believed in change. Above all, no one thought he was capable of *causing* change. Everyone was part of a system, which was greater than any of its individuals.

But at the beginning of the French Revolution, the Marquis de Sade declared that God was abolished. Byron's Manfred shook his fist at God. Men executed the king in the name of freedom. It was the age of heroes and the age of imagination, in which men threw steel bridges across estuaries and railways across continents. The artistic schemes were grandiose: Beethoven's symphonies, Balzac's novels, Wagner's Ring cycle; so were the engineering schemes: Brunel, the builder of the world's largest steamship, posed for a photograph against a chain whose links were larger than a man's head. Some historians have blamed romanticism on the Industrial Revolution and the need to escape from the 'dark satanic mills'. This is to put the cart before the horse; it was romanticism that *caused* the Industrial Revolution. It was romanticism that created the great colonial empires of the European powers. And it could be argued that it was romanticism that caused the great wars of the twentieth century.

But what concerns us here is not the historical consequences of the 'magical revival', but its effect on the spirit of certain individuals.

Shortly after the turn of the nineteenth century, a Polish nobleman named Joseph Maria Hoene-Wronski came to the Observatory of Marseilles to pursue his studies in science. And in 1810, when he was thirty-four, Wronski announced that he had made a tremendous discovery: a method of achieving nothing less than 'the Absolute', the knowledge of ultimate truth. Wronski claimed that he had stumbled upon the basic Law of Creation by which a man could use the sense-impressions of a lifetime to create the ultimate reality inside his own head. Wronski actually claimed to have done so. His system is obscure, since he claims to derive it from the philosophy of Kant by means of mathematics. But it seems fairly clear that he had actually rediscovered the 'magical memory' of the hermeticists, possibly through study of the Cabbala.

Perhaps because the man himself was as bombastic and intolerable as any of his magical predecessors, Wronski's ideas achieved little influence, though he succeeded in persuading a businessman named Arson to finance publication of his Messianic works. He died in poverty in Paris in 1853; his wife continued to believe she had been married to a god.

Wronski's cousin, the Marquis de Montferrier, was the proprietor of various radical journals, and one of his contributors was a young left-wing journalist named Alphonse-Louis Constant. Constant had abandoned the priesthood when he realised that he could not renounce sex. He seduced both the assistant mistress of a girls' school at Evereux and one of her sixteen-year-old pupils, a girl named Noémi. Threatened by Noémi's father, Constant made her his wife.

Montferrier met the wife of his radical contributor and was fascinated by her youth and beauty. Possibly as a means of getting to know her better, he invited her to become a contributor to one of his newspapers. Soon Noémi became his mistress, and deserted the shattered Constant, who had not even noticed that his wife was having an affair.

But Constant derived one minor bonus from his meeting with the Marquis; in 1852, he was introduced to Wronski and fell under the spell of his Messianism. Wronski confided to Constant that he was secretly a student of the Jewish Cabbala, the mystical system of 'levels of creation', derived from the Gnostics. Constant had read a few magical works—Cornelius Agrippa and Jacob Boehme—without being convinced. Now Wronski initiated him into his own secret system for achieving the Absolute, and Constant was delighted to discover that it was possible to be a scientist *and* a magician. When Wronski died in the following year, Constant helped his widow to catalogue his manuscripts, plunged into the study of hermetic magic, and changed his name to Eliphaz Levi. Under that name he wrote several influential books on magic, which exerted a powerful influence on MacGregor Mathers, W. B. Yeats, Aleister Crowley, and other founder members of the Order of the Golden Dawn.

And so the 'magical memory' system somehow filtered down to the poets and occultists of the nineteenth century via Wronski and Eliphaz Levi, and the magical concept of the imagination as a living force mingled with the romantic concept of the imagination as the creator of visionary worlds. And in the case of Yeats, it may be said to have accomplished a certain amount of good. Yeats was a typical romantic, convinced that poets are not of 'this world', and that the 'land of heart's desire' can be reached by mortal men only through death. Yet unlike most of his contemporaries of the 'tragic generation'— Verlaine, Dowson, Wilde, Beardsley—Yeats succeeded in living into old age and producing a poetry of human affirmation.

The 'magical' heirs of Levi's legacy were altogether less successful, at least from the historical point of view; it would not be unfair to say that the Golden Dawn and its various offshoots simply 'fizzled out'. Mathers died in the influenza epidemic of 1918, having been deposed by his fellow members many years previously. Crowley became a drug addict and spent the last decades of his life borrowing from friends. Dion Fortune, who founded another breakaway movement, died of leukemia at the age of fifty-four; someone who knew her in her last year described her as 'a burnt-out shell'.

Yet what is clear from the bulky volumes of rituals and ceremonies that have been published is that the members of the Golden Dawn were not dilettantes; they took the art of magic as seriously as Paracelsus or Bruno. They believed in the will and the imagination and in the 'magical correspondences' (which will be discussed in the following chapter). So what went wrong?

Looking through the four volumes of Golden Dawn rituals, published by Israel Regardie, it is difficult not to feel that they may have the made the same mistake as Bruno, and perhaps Wronski—that of complicating something that is essentially simple. After all, 'magic' is basically the art of tapping man's 'hidden powers', whether we mean the power to influence dice by psychokinesis, or to achieve a vision of the 'Absolute' by mystical disciplines.

This notion of a 'direct' solution has persisted throughout the history of magic and mysticism, and it explains the emphasis that has always been placed on memory and imagination. Marcel Proust achieved his own mystical vision of *'temps perdu'* in the simplest manner—by eating a cake dipped in herb tea. He spent the remainder of his life pursuing this vision with the same directness—by locking himself in a soundproof room, and attempting to re-create his own past in minute detail. He was pursuing the same ideal as Wronski, utilising the sense impressions of a lifetime to create the ultimate reality inside his own head. If he failed to discover Wronski's 'Law of Creation', he discovered his own inner laws of creation and produced

a masterpiece. His 'direct method' failed, since he never learned the art
of re-creating the past inside his own head at will. Yet as we read him,
we have a sense of excitement, a feeling that he was on the right track,
and that a complicated magical ritual would not have brought him any
closer to his goal, any more than it brought Mathers or Crowley or
Dion Fortune to theirs.

The annals of crime produce another curious example of a man who
tried to use 'the direct method' to achieve 'magical memory.' In
October 1932, the psychiatrist Dr Frederick Wertham was called to a
New York hospital to see a twenty-four-year-old youth named
Robert Irwin, who had attempted to cut off his penis after winding a
tight rubber band around the base. The wound was sewed up—it took
seven stitches—and Irwin eventually left the hospital. He explained
that he had tried to persuade doctors to amputate his penis on three
occasions, and that he finally decided to do it himself. 'But why?'
asked Wertham. 'You should ask me first where I got the visualising
idea,' said Irwin. And he proceeded to explain the notion that had
obsessed him since his teens: the development of imagination until
anything that had been seen or heard could be reconstructed in the
head.

> To develop this mental sight, you must simply exercise it, just as you
> would exercise a muscle to develop it. In other words, you just sit down
> every day and practice *visualizing*, and the more you practice, the sooner
> you'll get there. But this practice is extremely difficult, as anyone who
> tries it will find out. It is easy at least for me to visualize an object in my
> mind. But to keep at this visualizing consistently, and especially to hold
> one particular image in my mind for any time, that is another matter.
>
> I hope some day not only to be able to visualize and hold an object in
> my mind's eye as long as I want to . . . but to be able to project such an
> object into space, to fix such an object in physical visibility: a projected
> living reality . . .

Irwin described in detail the 'magical' exercises described by David
Conway earlier in this chapter. Irwin went on:

> We have all read Shakespeare, the Bible, the dictionary. How much do
> we remember? Very little. Yet it is all there, right in our very heads.
> Every word, every line, every syllable. The time will come, given
> enough development in this direction, when a man could lie in his bed at

night and be able to actually open up the book of Shakespeare there in the dark. In his mind. And read it—yes, read it, with his eyes closed. . . And what's more, you'll be able to see those plays enacted in your mind. Those characters will step forth in living, projected reality. . .[11]

This, said Irwin, was why he had tried to amputate his penis; he felt that his sexual desires were robbing him of the energy that he needed to achieve 'visualisation'.

He had not arrived at these ideas by reading magical texts but through his natural talent as an artist. The desire to re-capture living forms was so strong that at the age of fourteen he was modelling figures in butter and soap. He collected pictures and reproductions of Greek statues and spent hours staring at them. And one day, as he was working as an errand boy, it suddenly struck him—like a revelation—that before a sculptor can make a statue, he has to visualise it, to make a mental statue in his brain. He began to train himself to visualise pictures in his collection, staring at them for minutes, then staring at the wall and trying to re-create them in detail. He made a metronome to see how long he could concentrate. He was also struck by the fact that masturbation involves 'visualising', and that it is one of the few departments in which man has developed visualisation with a high degree of success.

He fell in love with a girl called Alice, and asked her to marry him and help him in his development of 'visualisation'. She agreed. Irwin began to read philosophy, for he was now convinced that if he could learn to journey into his own mind, he could eventually contact the 'universal mind', the 'central radio station'. At this point, he discovered Will Durant's book *The Story of Philosophy*, and read about Schopenhauer. This was the worst thing that could have happened to him. Schopenhauer's central theme is that life is a continual violent striving of the will, which always leads to misery, since existence is meaningless. The most powerful urge of most human adults is reproduction, which prolongs the misery. Man's only hope of salvation lies in liberating himself from desire and attempting to live a life of detached contemplation. And art is one of the most powerful means that man has yet discovered to achieve this state of contemplation. . .

Irwin was shattered; it verified his worst fears. He instantly broke his engagement with Alice. And he decided to defeat the blind urge to reproduction by amputating his penis. It was at this juncture that Dr

Wertham met him for the first time, and listened to his plans to achieve total 'visualisation'. Wertham's view—which emerges clearly in his account of the case—was that Irwin was a nut.

The Depression years were a bad time for would-be artists. Irwin had to take a series of jobs that bored him. When jobs became impossible to find he slept in parks and begged food at the back doors of restaurants. After the attempt to amputate his penis, he was in and out of mental hospitals for several years. He took lodgings with a Hungarian family named Gedeon and fell in love with the eldest daughter, Ethel. For a while she helped him with his 'visualisation', then got bored. Ethel's attractive younger sister Veronica also liked Irwin; she was an artist's model and posed for him naked. In fact, she suggested that he should sleep with her; but Irwin was determined to conserve his sexual energy.

In 1937, Irwin succeeded in obtaining a place at a theological college; but after a fight with a fellow student, he was expelled. In deep despair he decided to commit suicide, and also to kill Ethel Gedeon. He called at the Gedeon home and found his ex-landlady in alone. Towards midnight, she became irritated at his determination to stay and tried to push him to the door. Irwin strangled her. When Veronica came home, he dragged her into the bedroom in the dark and forced her to lie still for hours; when he realised that she had recognised him, he strangled her, then went and killed the lodger, a bar-tender, with an ice pick. He gave himself up shortly afterwards. He was tried in November 1938 and sentenced to life imprisonment. Wertham's insanity plea was rejected. Irwin's last words before he was sentenced were: 'Nobody understands me. Nobody wants to understand me.'

There seems to be little doubt that Irwin was mentally unbalanced in the last years of his freedom; the strains of a lifetime of hardship and frustration had undermined his sense of reality. There can also be little doubt that it was the arch-pessimist Schopenhauer—who was particularly fond of good living—who drove Irwin to the point of violence, first against himself, then against other people. What is curious and also rather disquieting, is that in none of the many accounts of the case has his 'visualising' ever been taken seriously. Wertham himself had no doubt that it was simply another symptom of his insanity. Irwin was an 'Outsider' in the fullest sense of the word. If he had achieved success as a sculptor, his idea of visualising might have been taken as seriously as Proust's '*recherche du temps perdu*'. As it was, it led him to a lifetime in Dannemora Penitentiary.

We can take the Irwin case as a convenient symbol of the problem of the Outsider in the twentieth century, a problem defined by the hero of Henri Barbusse's novel *Hell*, who explains his own unhappiness by saying: 'I see too deep and too much.' He is the creative individual whose instinct is to bring order out of chaos, to question the foundations of society. In all ages, such a man is likely to be misunderstood, since human beings have a powerful instinct of conservatism, and regard innovators with mistrust. But since the Outsider's impulse is fundamentally religious—the desire to be more 'serious' than other people is the essence of religion—he tends to be less of a misfit in ages of faith than in ages of materialism and scepticism.

The Outsider is a 'non-acceptor'. And his non-acceptance is based on a sense that human beings underestimate their own powers. The 'unknown philosopher', Saint-Martin, expressed it most clearly when he stated that man is always having flashes of god-like faculties: 'Man possesses innumerable vestiges of the faculties resident in the Agent which produced him.' This is why so many Outsiders of the past have been students of magic, and why the figure of the magician—Faust or Cornelius Agrippa—has always exercised such popular appeal.

Let us try to summarise the concept of imagination that has begun to emerge in the past few chapters:

Human beings seem to have an incorrigible tendency to constrict their everyday consciousness. They do this out of anxiety, out of the need to focus clearly on immediate problems. But the paradoxical effect is to strangle their vitality.

This 'constriction' or narrowing of consciousness is like looking at an object through a magnifying glass. Its basic features are enlarged, but at the same time you can see less of it. If you place it under a microscope, even greater magnification is obtained, but the visual field is made smaller than ever. As we constrict consciousness, we lose our over-all sense of meaning.

But this sense of meaning is our strength. When we can see meaning clearly, we know exactly what we are supposed to do, and our energies respond. When we cannot perceive meaning, we yawn with boredom, and our energies fail.

This explains one of the chief problems of everyday life. We can be perfectly comfortable, in an enviable situation, and yet thoroughly bored. We can be uncomfortable, in a highly dangerous situation, and yet feel intensely alive. Danger forces us to make a mental effort. We 'stand back' from life, like a painter standing back from his canvas, and see over-all meanings. The result is a flood of vitality.

It begins to look as if civilisation is man's downfall, since it subjects him to increasing comfort. Healthy spirits usually dislike it and may actually go out and seek discomfort. This explains the apparently 'paradoxical' actions of so many 'Outsiders' like Gauguin, Van Gogh and T. E. Lawrence, who turned their backs on comfort. But man possesses an instrument for adjusting the balance. It is called imagination.

The romantics failed to plumb the powers of the imagination because they failed to recognise clearly that what is wrong with human beings is *that we keep losing our sense of reality*. We are the victims of 'closeupness'. A man may still be deeply in love with his wife after twenty years of marriage and not 'realise' it until she has to go home to nurse her mother for a fortnight. He may love his home, yet take it for granted until he comes back to it from his holiday abroad. But if a friend asks him how he met his wife and urges him to tell the story of their courtship and marriage, this has precisely the same effect as losing her for two weeks. He takes the trouble to *focus* past events. Suddenly he is re-living them and realising how much he loves his wife.

The key word here is 'focus'. Human beings are mentally lazy. We look at things with only half an eye, listen to music with only half an ear. We are always trying to economise on *attention*. It is rather like gulping food down too fast; it produces a kind of permanent mild indigestion. Sometimes, if life gets too hectic, and we lose the habit of paying careful attention to *anything*, this indigestion becomes acute, and the result is what Sartre calls 'nausea', a sense of total meaninglessness. By contrast, if we can somehow summon *all* our attention and focus it on a single object or idea, the result is a curious build-up of inner power, analogous to the way a laser beam builds up power by being reflected from one mirror to another. When this power has been generated, we focus on things that normally leave us indifferent and grasp their inner meaning. In such a state, a man would not need to talk about his wife for half an hour to realise that he loves her. He would think about her, and instantly grasp her total reality.

In short, imagination is the power to *get back to reality*, to re-focus our true values, to combat the curious erosion of our vitality that James calls 'inferiority to our full selves.'

We might use another image, and say that 'attention' has a mechanism like a bow, or the spring of an air rifle. If we feel that something deserves our total attention, we pull back the bowstring—or spring —to its limit. On the other hand, if you shot an arrow by pulling back the string only a couple of inches, you would expect the arrow to fall on the ground a few feet away. And this sickly, half-hearted way of paying attention is typical of our everyday lives.

Now the bowstring—or air rifle—analogy is only another way of saying that consciousness is 'intentional'. But Paracelsus and Bruno and Levi would draw a further conclusion. The purpose of the bow or rifle is to fire a projectile, and the projectile is intended to exert a certain 'action at a distance'—let us say, to bring down a running stag. Paracelsus and Bruno would assert that the imagination, when correctly used, also has power of 'action at a distance'. This power they called magic.

Yet it would be a total misrepresentation to say that imagination is the essence of magic. It *is* the driving force, but that is another matter. Petrol is the driving force of a car; yet there is a great deal more to a car than its petrol tank. According to the hermeticists, magic will not work unless it also utilises a certain law of nature. This is known as the Law of Correspondences.

4

The Rediscovery of Magic

In the year 1909, Freud and Jung set out together from Bremen for the United States. They took the opportunity to psychoanalyse one another, and every morning for seven weeks, told one another their dreams. Freud found one of Jung's dreams particularly baffling:

> I was in a house that I did not know', [Jung relates], which had two storeys. It was 'my house'. I found myself in the upper storey, where there was a kind of salon furnished with fine old pieces in rococo style. On the walls hung a number of precious old paintings. . . But then it occurred to me that I did not know what the lower floor looked like. Descending the stairs, I reached the ground floor. There everything was much older, and I realised that this part of the house must date from about the fifteenth or sixteenth century. The furnishings were medieval; the floors were of red brick . . . I came upon a heavy door and opened it. Beyond it, I discovered a stone stairway that led down into the cellar. Descending again, I found myself in a beautifully vaulted room which looked exceedingly ancient. Examining the walls I discovered layers of brick among the ordinary stone blocks, and chips of brick in the mortar. As soon as I saw this, I knew the walls dated from Roman times. My interest by now was intense. I looked more closely at the floor. It was of

stone slabs, and in one of these I discovered a ring. When I pulled it, the stone slab lifted, and again I saw a stairway of narrow stone steps leading down into the depths. These, too, I descended, and entered a low cave cut into the rock. Thick dust lay on the floor, and in the dust were scattered bones and broken pottery, like remains of a primitive culture. I discovered two human skulls, obviously very old and half disintegrated. Then I awoke.

Freud's conclusion was that the two skulls indicated death. 'Is there anyone you'd like to see dead?' asked Freud. Jung said no. But as Freud pressed the point, Jung admitted—to please him—that the skulls could be those of his wife and sister-in-law. 'That's it,' said Freud with satisfaction. 'You want to get rid of your wife and bury her under two cellars.'

Jung disliked this kind of arbitrary interpretation. To him it seemed more likely that the dream was about a descent into the past. But the idea of a descent had another significance for a psychoanalyst—the descent into the depths of the mind, in which case, the 'house' must represent the dreamer himself, and the different periods of history, different levels of his own being. That seemed to imply that the individual psyche was *not* all that individual but was built upon the foundation of past generations. It was then, says Jung, that he first conceived the idea of the 'collective unconscious', the notion that all human beings might share the same subconscious mind, or at least, certain basic feelings and ideas.

In the following year, two events provided confirmation of the theory. Jung came across the translation of a Greek magical papyrus, believed to be a liturgy of the Mithraic cult, and was struck by a description of a tube hanging down from the sun, which was described as the origin of the wind. Four years before, in 1906, an insane Greek patient had taken Jung to the window, pointed at the sun, and asked him if he could see the sun's phallus, which was the origin of the wind. Jung also found evidence of the same notion in medieval myths. It looked as if the unconscious mind of the patient had some-how produced one of the basic magical symbols.

In the same year, Jung read an account of the discovery of a cache of 'soul stones' near Arlesheim. No details were given about the stones, but Jung suddenly knew that they were oblong, blackish, and had the upper and lower halves painted different shades. At the same time, he recalled a forgotten event of his childhood: he had carved a small wooden figure from the end of a ruler and made a cloak for it. This figure was kept in a pencil box, together with an oblong stone which Jung had painted in two colours, and the box was carefully hidden on a beam in the attic. During school hours, Jung wrote coded messages on tiny pieces of paper and periodically stole up to the attic to place these 'scrolls' in the pencil case. It now struck Jung that his little wooden man was like the cloaked figure of Telesphoros, the guardian spirit of convalescence, who is often seen on Greek monuments reading a scroll to Ascelepius, the god of healing, and that he had been instinctively performing some primitive rite connected with the release of the creative impulse. (Years later, he saw a similar ritual performed in Africa by natives.) Describing the event later in his autobiography, Jung tells how 'there came to me, for the first time, the conviction that there are archaic psychic components which have entered the individual psyche without any direct line of tradition'. He called these 'archaic components' archetypes.

(It is worth mentioning in this connection a story reported by Charles Fort in *The Book of the Damned*;[1] Fort took it from the *Proceedings of the Society of Antiquarians of Scotland*. In July 1836, some boys searching for rabbit holes on the slopes of Arthur's Seat near Edinburgh came upon a small cave concealed by sheets of slate; it held seventeen tiny coffins, three or four inches long. The coffins were arranged in three rows, the bottom two consisting of eight coffins each, the third row of only one. They proved to contain small wooden figures wrapped in graveclothes. In the bottom row, the coffins were decayed, and the wrappings were mouldering. The second row was less decayed, while the single coffin in the top row was relatively new. Whatever strange ceremony was involved, it had been taking place for a long time—perhaps centuries—and was still taking place. In ancient Egypt, small wooden carvings known as Shabti figures were buried with the dead; their purpose was to act as servants in the underworld. Is it possible that, in some Scottish family, an actual burial of a member of the family was accompanied by this ritual entombment of a kind of Shabti figure?)

Another wooden figure played a central role in one of Jung's dreams in 1913, the year after his break with Freud. Jung dreamed he was walking down a lane with rows of tombs, and as he passed the figures on the tombs, they stirred and came to life. The last was a wooden figure of a crusader in chain mail, which at first seemed quite dead; then a finger stirred, showing signs of life. Again, Jung had a feeling that the dream was more than a personal fantasy; that it was expressing an objective meaning by means of symbols.

In October 1913, on a journey, Jung had a kind of waking vision of floods covering the land, and thousands of drowned bodies. Then the sea turned to blood. Similar visions and dreams kept recurring. When war broke out in August 1914, Jung concluded that his dreams had been premonitions of the European disaster, not merely the expression of personal problems. He had even dreamed of shooting the legendary hero Siegfried with a rifle—a clear indication of the identity of the 'enemy'.

But it was not until 1918 that Jung finally overcame his lingering doubts—and his Freudian training—and became convinced of the reality of archetypes and the collective unconscious. An increasing number of his patients, deeply disturbed by the war, produced dream images that Jung recognised as symbols out of myths or fairy tales.[2] 'The archetypes I had observed expressed primitivity, violence, cruelty.' One woman dreamed that, as she was singing a hymn about redemption, she looked out of the window and saw a bull running wild. Suddenly it fell, broke its leg, and lay writhing in agony on the ground. Jung had no doubt that the bull symbolised the war and was somehow connected with Christian sacrifice. But in Christianity, the saviour is symbolised by a lamb; it is in the parallel religion of Mithraism that the sacrifice is a bull. Jung was not suggesting that his patient's subconscious mind was somehow aware of the cult of Mithras; only that the bull in her dream and the bull in Mithraism are archetypal symbols representing animal instinct.

Many Jungians have insisted that the 'collective unconscious' should not be understood as a kind of 'group mind'. But Jung himself contradicts this in *Memories, Dreams, Reflections*. He tells the story of a patient who went through a period of depression, from which Jung was able to rescue him. The patient then made an unsatisfactory marriage; his wife became jealous of Jung and his influence over her husband. The patient's 'transference'—identification with the doctor—had created a particularly powerful link between them. One evening, Jung returned from a lecture and went to bed in his hotel room. Suddenly he woke with a start, convinced that someone had opened the door and come into the room; he switched on the light, but there was no one there. At this point he recollected that he had been awakened by a dull pain, as if something had struck his forehead, then the back of his skull. The next day he received a telegram telling him that his patient had shot himself. He learned later that the bullet had entered the forehead and come to rest at the back of the skull. Jung's explanation is that the phenomenon took place 'by means of the relativisation of time and space in the unconscious', and goes on: 'The collective unconscious is common to us all; it is the foundation of what the ancients called "the sympathy of all things". In this case, the unconscious had knowledge of my patient's condition. All that evening, in fact, I had felt curiously restive and nervous.'[3] We may question Jung's explanation about the cause of the experience and prefer to ascribe it to telepathy; but the story leaves no doubt that Jung saw the collective unconscious as somehow common to all human beings. Oddly enough, Freud himself, who began by totally rejecting the idea, came to accept it in his later works; in *Moses and Monotheism* he speaks of 'the archaic heritage of mankind' which includes 'memory traces of former generations'.

The outline of Jung's analytical psychology, as it began to emerge around 1920, could be summarised as follows. The human psyche consists of three parts: the conscious, the 'personal unconscious', and the collective unconscious. The personal unconscious lies near the surface; one of its chief components is known as 'the Shadow', the primitive, uncivilised part of ourselves. (Jung felt that the Second World War was a case of a whole nation becoming possessed by its Shadow.) When it appears in dreams, the Shadow is usually symbolised by a person of the same sex as the dreamer. Below the fairly shallow waters of the personal unconscious lie the immense depths of the collective unconscious, some so deep that they can never, under any circumstances, come to consciousness. According to Jung—and here he differed fundamentally from Freud—the collective unconscious contains man's religious aspirations. (For Freud, these were merely sublimated sex drives.) He insisted that one of man's fundamental needs is to find the meaning of existence, and that neurosis is often the result of trying to live 'within too narrow a spiritual horizon'. 'Their life has not sufficient content, sufficient meaning. If they are enabled to develop into more spacious personalities, the neurosis generally disappears.' When these deeper aspirations from the collective unconscious appear in dreams, they usually manifest themselves as a person of the opposite sex from the dreamer. This manifestation of the dreamer's 'soul' Jung called the *anima*, Latin for soul. (In the case of women, this soul-being is male, and is called the *animus*.)

The collective unconscious contains dreams and symbols from the whole history of mankind. Jung would see nothing surprising in an untutored peasant, with no knowledge of ancient history, dreaming of prehistoric animals; memories of them are floating somewhere down there, in the depths of the sea. Moreover, they are not dead memories; they possess a life of their own. And on occasions, like the Loch Ness monster, they may decide to surface.

Perhaps the simplest way of demonstrating the actual use of these concepts is to describe a case in which they played a central part, like the one described in *The Lady of the Hare* by the Jungian psychiatrist John Layard.[4]

In 1940, Layard was asked if he could help a sixteen-year-old girl, who was so subnormal that she seldom spoke. When Layard interviewed the girl, Margaret Wright, he was unable to persuade her to say anything but yes and no as she stared in front of her with expressionless eyes. Unwilling to concede defeat, Layard decided to see if he could reach her through the medium of her mother.

Mrs Wright was the wife of a labourer, with whom she was obviously very much in love. She was a midwife, an Irishwoman of only moderate intelligence but calm and placid. She was deeply, though not demonstratively, religious. The only negative force in the household seemed to be Mrs Wright's sister, an embittered woman who was disliked by everyone. Mrs Wright allowed her to live with them because no one else would put up with her.

Mrs Wright was apparently psychic—at least, on occasions. At the age of nineteen she had seen a vision of a shining angel, pointing upwards; shortly afterwards, she had narrowly escaped death by being run over. She also saw strange yellow lights when someone was going to die.

The 'therapy' consisted almost entirely of analysis of Mrs Wright's dreams. Layard was inclined to treat her problem—and ultimately her daughter's problem—as 'trying to live within too narrow a spiritual horizon', and to regard the symbolism of her dreams as basically religious rather than sexual: an attempt by her animus to make her understand what was going wrong. In one dream, she was standing by a lake of deep and muddy water with a steep mountainside behind her and a beautiful pasture on the other side. She wanted to get to the pasture but for some reason, thought she had to do it by climbing the mountain. However, the loose earth kept slipping, making it impossible to climb.

The symbolism here was fairly clear. The deep and muddy water was Mrs Wright's situation. She wanted to get to the green meadow but for some reason thought she had to reach it by climbing the mountain. Layard linked this with the vision of the angel pointing upward, and asked her what she thought the angel was pointing to. 'Heaven!' 'But heaven was the green pasture, so you were going the wrong way.' Mrs Wright said she had always been taught that heaven was above; Layard replied that perhaps this was a misconception: perhaps heaven was to be found inside her.

Layard continued to interpret her dreams in terms of religious symbolism—an approach she found immensely reassuring. But the climactic dream of the series, at least, as far as the psychiatrist was concerned, was the dream of the hare from which the book takes its title. The dreamer walked from the snow—in which she had left no footprints—into a kitchen that was full of white light. The hare lay in a bowl of water on the table, and Mrs Wright was ordered to sacrifice it. As she was about to plunge the knife into its back, the hare looked round at her with an expression of extreme satisfaction and trust. As she cut it down the centre of its back, her hand trembled, but she observed that the hare did not seem to mind the operation.

This was how Layard interpreted the dream: 'The bowl is the [Communion] cup. The whole dream is a preparation for the Communion Rite, in which Christ sheds His blood for the redemption of your sin. *Your* sin has been being too 'good', in a mistakenly idealistic way, so God sends his blood to correct the too great whiteness of the snow.' Mrs Wright was deeply impressed by this interpretation—so much so that Layard goes on to comment: 'The analytical process is itself like the Mass, and like all true ritual as well as great works of dramatic art, in that it leads to peaks of emotion from which the participant has to be led back from scenes of glory very gently into the realms of everyday life.'

From the point of view of both the patient and the doctor, the analytical process was highly successful. Mrs Wright was steadily gaining self-confidence. After one session she remarked, 'I had thought it was only in olden times that men had had dreams to show them how to live. I never dreamt we had it in us now.' The thought that her dreams—and perhaps God himself—were trying to *tell* her something, improved her self-esteem and made her less passive and fatalistic. The daughter, who reflected her mother's attitudes, also became less passive and began to speak normally.

But for Layard, this was only the beginning of the investigation. He was intrigued by the symbolism of various dreams, but particularly by the hare. He asked the same question that Jung had asked in the case of the lady who dreamed of a bull: why had the 'lamb' been transmuted into another animal? Like Jung, Layard interpreted the sacrifice as the transformation of animal instinct into spiritual power. But why had Mrs Wright's subconscious mind chosen this symbol? What was the significance of the hare archetype?

Layard spent more than two years studying the symbolism of the hare in world mythologies: the results of his investigation occupy more than half his book. Predictably, the hare is one of the major symbols of the moon; many cultures have a 'hare in the moon' instead of a man in the moon. It also seems to be widely known as a symbol of sacrifice, and in Christian mythology is associated with Easter. Layard quotes a legend that if a hare-breeder wishes to kill the hare, he has only to tell it so, and the hare will kill itself—another example of the notion that the hare is capable of self-sacrifice. Another legend states that the hare will sacrifice itself by leaping into a fire. (This may have arisen from the behaviour of hares when farmers are burning stubble. Instead of running away long before the flames reach them, as rabbits do, the hare will often wait until its fur catches fire and then burns to death.) Layard also discovered that the hare is constantly associated with snow and with the colour white.

Layard's final interpretation of the case of Mrs Wright was as follows: Mrs Wright had been brought up in a strict Presbyterian tradition. When her daughter was born, she stifled her maternal feelings and refused to have the child in bed with her. The girl's later illness was basically the result of this early starvation of love. But after the dream of the hare, Mrs Wright had another dream in which a man told her; 'Margaret and her mother may sleep together.' The symbolic sacrifice of the hare meant that Christian love had overcome her dogmatic religious notions, and that from now on 'her own improvement would convey itself automatically to her daughter through the channel of the Collective Unconscious'. And this seems to have happened.

There are obvious objections to this kind of interpretation. It could be argued that the daughter's illness stemmed from her mother's emotional passivity. Mrs Wright's religious upbringing tended to strengthen this attitude by encouraging her to accept the general unsatisfactoriness of her life fatalistically. Layard's role was less that of a psychiatrist than a spiritual adviser, re-awakening her sense of religious realities. As to the symbolism of the hare, it may simply have originated in Mrs Wright's country childhood.

Obviously, no one can prove that Mrs Wright's hare was a symbolic archetype rather than a real hare. Yet this hardly invalidates Layard's book. What is surprising is that the hare proves to be a universal religious symbol, and that its meaning is so remarkably constant. Lethbridge noted the symbolism of the hare when he dug up the tile associating the hare with the moon.[5] It was Lethbridge who pointed out that 'the hare is the commonest type of animal into which a witch is supposed to be able to change and in which form she could only be killed by a silver bullet'. Lethbridge would have regarded the universality of hare symbolism as a proof of Margaret Murray's theory about *wicca*, the ancient religion. Layard never once mentions Margaret Murray, although he notes the association of hares with witches. But he demonstrates beyond all doubt that the hare symbol is to be found in most primitive cultures, from the Ancient Greeks and Egyptians to American Indians, and that it is almost invariably associated with the moon. (Layard also points out that in the oldest cultures, it is also associated with the sun, although in these cultures, the sun was regarded as feminine.)

My own attitude towards Layard's theory was at first intensely sceptical. I knew Layard slightly and heard a great deal about him from friends who knew him well; everything I heard inclined me to believe that he was a silly old man who was obsessed by sexual symbolism. (Contrary to the general view, Jung never rejected Freud's notion of the importance of the sex-drive.) I read *The Lady of the Hare* only after his death, and it re-awakened my feeling that he was inclined to assign his own wildly arbitrary interpretations to dream symbolism. Yet the long section on the mythology of the hare is, by any standard, a remarkable piece of scholarship, designed to convince the most irritable sceptic that the recurrence of the hare symbol in world mythology cannot be explained in terms of coincidence. The hare is not a common animal; it can never have been as common as the rabbit, which seems to have no particular mythological meaning. (For example, it is not even mentioned in J. E. Cirlot's *Dictionary of Symbols*.) In short, Layard proves, as far as anyone can prove, that the hare is a 'universal archetype'.

Once this is granted, his cure of Mrs Wright and her daughter becomes altogether more acceptable. It is quite clear, from its context alone, that Mrs Wright's dream is full of symbolism, and that this symbolism has to do with religious redemption. Which raises the question of why a hare should be associated with sacrifice and redemption. It could still be argued that there is no necessary connection between Mrs Wright's dream hare and the hare as a symbolic archetype; but then, I doubt whether there *is* any logical method of establishing such a connection. On the whole, I have to admit that Layard has me fairly convinced.

It remains to wonder whether Layard missed the ultimate significance of the hare symbol. It is probably pointless to ask how the hare became associated with the moon originally (although one possibility is that hares in northern latitudes become white in the winter, grey in summer—both 'moon colours'). The association is obviously of the greatest antiquity. But is it possible that the hare was the moon-sacrifice of our remote ancestors, and that this is the reason it remains associated with sacrifice, witches and the moon? (Even the legend that it can be killed only with a silver bullet suggests that it is the property of the moon goddess.) In which case, it would seem conceivable that the 'ancient religion' of the mother goddess is one of the major sources of the Jungian archetypes. The association of the hare with fertility religions is suggested by the fact that the animal was reverenced in ancient Europe as the spirit of the corn; cutting the last of the corn was known as 'cutting the hare' or 'cutting off the hare's tail'. In Hallaton, in Leicestershire, a large hare pie is baked every Easter Monday, and the locals 'scramble' for it; the ceremony has the overtones of a ritual sacrifice. Layard points out that 'Hallaton' is said to be a corruption of 'Holy town', that its piece of 'holy land' was known as 'hare-cropleys.'

In an essay on 'The Nature of the Psyche',[6] Jung quotes an opponent of the whole idea of depth psychology: 'Once [the unconscious] is admitted, one finds oneself at the mercy of all manner of hypotheses concerning this unconscious life, hypotheses which cannot be controlled by any observation.' Jung accuses the critic of fear of encountering difficulties. Yet it cannot be denied that the objection is perfectly fair. Science is an attempt to become *conscious* of the laws of nature; and how can we become conscious of the unconscious? Freud declared that we can explore the subconscious through dreams; but we have no guarantee that his interpretation of dreams is not the wildest kind of arbitrary nonsense.

It was in 1913, in the period when he was experiencing visions of the coming war, that Jung stumbled up on an answer to this problem. He had been attempting to translate his highly-disturbed emotions into images. As a result, he began to feel as if he were becoming the victim of fantasies. He decided upon a dangerous solution: 'In order to grasp the fantasies which were stirring in me "underground", I knew that I had to let myself plummet down into them.' On December 12, 1913, he decided to try the experiment. 'I was sitting at my desk . . . thinking over my fears. Then I let myself drop. Suddenly it was as though the ground literally gave way beneath my feet, and I plunged down into dark depths.' His experience sounds rather like Alice falling down the rabbit hole. 'But then, abruptly, at not too great a depth, I landed on my feet in a soft, sticky mess.'

What followed was a *waking* dream, in which Jung found himself in a cave, guarded by a mummified dwarf. In an underground stream he saw the floating body of a blond youth with a head wound; this was followed by a gigantic black beetle, then a rising sun. Again the dream ended with a vision of water turning to blood.

Jung was once more convinced that the images welled up from the collective unconscious. (The dead youth seems to have been another vision of Siegfried.) What was even more important was that he seemed to have discovered a more-or-less conscious method of investigating the unconscious. Most of wish that we could descend into our own dreams and control them; the trouble is that once we fall asleep, the controlling ego vanishes. Because Jung was in an intensely disturbed state, he was able to 'dream' while still fully awake. Later still, there were equally 'real' fantasies of Elijah, Salome, and an old man who called himself Philemon. Jung noted that in his conversations with Philemon, 'he said things which I had not consciously thought. For I observed clearly that it was he who spoke, not I'. It led him to recognise that 'there are things in the psyche which I do not produce'.[7]

Jung developed this 'conscious dreaming' into a technique, which he called 'active imagination'. He regarded it as one of his most important discoveries and taught it to some of his patients. Yet oddly enough, there is very little about it in the sixteen volumes of his collected works, and his major paper on the subject is disappointingly cagey.[8] One of his few clear statements of the principle appears in his book on alchemy, *Mysterium Conjunctionis* (1955–6):

> Take the unconscious in one of its handiest forms, say a spontaneous fantasy, a dream, an irrational mood, . . . or something of the kind, and operate with it. Give it your special attention, concentrate on it, and observe its alterations objectively. Spare no effort to devote yourself to this task, follow the subsequent transformations of the spontaneous fantasy attentively and carefully. Above all, don't let anything from outside, that does not belong, get into it, for the fantasy-image has 'everything that it needs'.[9]

One of his few actual descriptions of 'active imagination' in action occurs in some lectures he gave at the Tavistock Clinic in 1935. Jung described the case of a young artist who at first had the utmost difficulty in grasping what he meant by active imagination. 'The difficulty with him was that he could not think. Musicians, painters, artists of all kinds, often can't think at all, because they never intentionally use their brains.'

On his way to see Jung, the artist often looked at a poster advertising the Bernese Alps on the wall of a railway station. One day, he decided to try 'active imagination' on the poster. 'I might for instance imagine that I am myself in the poster, that the scenery is real, and that I could walk up the hill among the cows and then look down on the other side. . .' He sat in front of the poster, stared at it and imagined himself walking up the hill. On the other side, there was a hedge with a stile. The path ran around a ravine and a rock, and on the other side of the rock was a small chapel with its door standing ajar. He pushed open the door and saw an altar decorated with flowers and an image of the Virgin. As he looked at her face, something with pointed ears disappeared behind the altar. At this point the fantasy dissolved, and the artist left the station.

The artist found himself wondering whether the chapel really existed, in some odd sense. So he tried imagining the poster, and himself walking up the hill. Everything was exactly as it was before—the stile, the ravine, the rock, the chapel. As he went into the chapel he again saw the image of the Virgin Mary, and again saw the figure with pointed ears vanishing behind the altar.[10]

Unfortunately, Jung tells us no more about the history of his patient. But he adds the interesting warning that 'active imagination' demands the use of 'true imagination', not the 'fantastical one'. He is distinguishing between imagination as a faculty for creating false images and as an instrument for grasping reality, that is, as a form of Faculty X.

In recognising the archetypes of the collective unconscious, Jung had re-discovered the basic principle of magic. The simplest form of magic is based upon the saying attributed to Hermes Trismegistos: 'As above, so below.' This meant that the laws of the heavens—the macrocosm—were reflected in man himself, the microcosm. A modern practitioner might well interpret this to mean that man contains an inner universe (or 'firmament'), with its own equivalents of stars and planets; William Blake said as much when he stated that eternity opens from the centre of an atom. But for the ordinary student of magic in the Middle Ages, the saying had a more concrete meaning.

The ancients knew of seven planets: Mercury, Venus, Mars, Jupiter, Saturn, and the sun and moon, which they also classified as planets. Each planet had a cosmic principle associated with it (i.e. Jupiter was the ruler, Venus the planet of love, Saturn of wisdom, and so on.) And each planet had various colours, metals, flowers, animals, birds, numbers, even perfumes, associated with it. So Venus was associated with the number seven, the colour green, the metal copper, with emeralds and turquoises, with myrtles, roses and clover, with sparrows, doves and swans, with sandalwood and other 'voluptuous' odours, and with the symbol of the girdle. Mars was associated with the number five, the colour red, the metal iron, with horses, bears and wolves, rubies, absinthe and rue, and its symbol was the sword. Jupiter was associated with the number four, the colour violet or blue (both regal colours), the eagle, the oak, the amethyst and lapis-lazuli, and his symbol was the sceptre. This system was known as 'the magical correspondences'.

It is perfectly natural to feel that a list of this sort is an absurdity, a purely arbitrary system invented by primitive people who knew no better. But before jumping to this conclusion, it may be worth recalling Lethbridge's tables of 'rates' for the pendulum. We may, of course, totally reject the idea that various objects and substances have 'rates'; but we must at least acknowledge that Lethbridge was a careful and serious investigator, and that he believed that there was a sound reason for classifying together under the number ten such a heterogeneous collection as: east, fire, sun, light youth, graphite, milk, red, Bulgaria and Italy; or under thirty: west, water, hydrogen, green, sound, moon and age.

In his chapter on 'Correspondences' in *The Black Arts*, Richard Cavendish points out that people's reactions to colours match their 'occult significance' fairly closely. Green, the colour of love and harmony, *does* exert a peaceful and tranquilising influence; red has an exciting influence, and so on. We could take this observation further, and study the psychological significance of colours in the well-known Lüscher colour test, devised by the German psychologist Max Lüscher, and widely used by psychologists in character analysis and the detection of hidden stresses. In the simplified version of the test, subjects are asked to look at eight cards of different colours and place them in order of preference. They consist of four primary colours—green, blue, red and yellow, and four 'mixed' colours, violet, brown, grey and black. Normal, balanced people show a preference for the primary colours and usually place these in the first four places; to choose one of the 'mixed' colours in the first three places indicates the presence of anxieties. These tests were arrived at, not by considering the 'occult significance' of the colours, but simply by thousands of trials and errors. Lüscher points out that the colour blue is associated with sweetness, which is why sugar manufacturers use it on their packages. Green is the colour of astringency (associated with green apples, etc.), and sugar in green packs would stay on the grocer's shelves.

Dark blue—the colour of one of the eight cards—is a colour of peace and passivity probably because primitive man associated it with the coming of night, a time when he was compelled to cease his activities. In the magical correspondences, blue is associated with Jupiter, the king of the gods and the peace-bringer. According to Lüscher, the colour green is associated with defence and preservation; it is the colour of firmness of purpose and resistance to change; in the correspondences, it is the colour of Venus, the female component in human existence, who possesses all these qualities. Red, the colour of Mars, is, according to Lüscher, associated with attack; it is the colour of energy, the will to success and change. (Hence its association with revolutionary movements.) Psychological tests have shown that when subjects are exposed to bright red, blood pressure increases and the heartbeat speeds up. (Exposure to green causes a drop in blood pressure; the same is true of dark blue.) Yellow, the sun colour, is obviously associated with brightness, cheerfulness, outgoingness and relaxation: here the Lüscher characteristics correspond exactly to the magical ones. The same is true of the colour grey. According to Lüscher it is the colour of detachment, of non-involvement, of the man who tries to stand aside from—and above—the problems and involvements of normal human beings. Such people are, in actuality, either philosophers, priests or magicians (three vocations that obviously have much in common). In the magical correspondences, grey is the colour of Hermes, the god of magic. It is also the traditional colour of magicians (as in Tolkien's Gandalf the Grey).

So, for whatever reason, the colours *do* correspond remarkably with their 'magical' significance. This is largely explainable in perfectly ordinary terms. Green soothes us because it is the colour of nature; brown strikes us as dull and drab because it is the colour of autumn leaves and the bare winter earth. (Market researchers discovered —according to Lüscher—that brown packaging caused beauty preparations to become a drug on the market.) Red excites because it is the colour of blood and therefore of violence. Blue has a subduing effect because it is the colour of nightfall. This has always been so, since animals first developed colour vision. (Oddly enough, experiments have shown that the Lüscher tests work just as well for colour-blind people, which seems to suggest that colours can somehow produce effects even when not recognised.) So, in effect, colours are Jungian archetypes, a part of the collective unconscious.

In traditional magic, the various planets and their corresponding substances or qualities were converted to symbols, and these symbols were used for magical purposes. For example, one of the most widespread uses of natural magic was in the manufacture of talismans or amulets, worn for protection and luck. This again involves the notion that the symbols have a precise and objective meaning. Jung was by no means the first to stumble upon this notion; it runs throughout the history of Western magic and formed the basis of the 'magic' practised by the Order of the Golden Dawn at the turn of the century. This was one of the things that startled W. B. Yeats when he first came into contact with MacGregor Mathers, the weird and unbalanced magician who helped to found the Order. In his *Autobiography*, Yeats tells how the actress Florence Farr visited Mathers and was told to hold a piece of cardboard with a symbol on it against her forehead; she immediately 'saw' herself walking on a clifftop with screaming seagulls overhead. She also told Yeats that Mathers had said: 'I am going to imagine myself a ram', and that the sheep in the field had run after him.

When Yeats called on Mathers, he was also given a piece of coloured cardboard to press against his forehead. After a few moments he began to experience mental images that he could not control: a desert, with a black Titan rising up among ancient ruins. 'Mathers explained that I had seen a being of the order of Salamanders [spirits of fire] because he had shown me their symbol, but it was not necessary even to show the symbol, it would have been sufficient if he had imagined it.'

It seems likely that the symbol shown to Yeats was one of a set known as tattwa symbols—tattwa is a system of Hindu philosophy—which are described by Israel Regardie in the fourth volume of his *Golden Dawn*. These consist of the earth symbol (a yellow square), the air symbol (a blue disc), the fire symbol (a red triangle), the water symbol (a silver crescent moon lying on its back) and the spirit of ether symbol (a black or indigo egg). Regardie goes on to explain the use of these symbols, and it is startlingly close to Jung's active imagination. The student is advised to stare hard at the symbol for twenty seconds, then to transfer his gaze to the ceiling, or any other white surface; its 'after image' will be seen in its complementary colour: yellow will become mauve, and red will become green. He must then close his eyes and try to imagine the symbol in its new colour and at the same time to enlarge it to the size of a door. When this is done, he must imagine himself passing through it. When the 'door' is behind him, he should try to see objects or landscapes. 'Most always these take the form of pale stilled pictures . . . hillocks, meadows, rocks, vast brown boulders.' Slow repetition of the name of the deity concerned will cause this landscape to become vivid and dynamic, and a 'being' may appear, like Yeats's salamander. If the student is willing, he may then allow himself to be guided through this realm by the spirit. When the tour is over, he must thank the spirit and return through the door, and conclude the experiment by making the sign of Silence, raising the left forefinger to the lips and stamping the right foot. All this strange procedure sounds a great deal less absurd after one has read Jung on 'active imagination'. In fact, the two are obviously identical.

Yeats goes on to say; 'I had soon mastered Mathers' symbolic system, and discovered that for a considerable minority—whom I could select by certain unanalysable characteristics—the visible world would completely vanish, and that world summoned by the symbol would take its place.' At first Yeats was inclined to believe that the effect might be due to imagination or telepathy. What convinced him was that when he accidentally gave someone the wrong symbol, the person saw a scene appropriate to the symbol, not to what Yeats was imagining. If Yeats clearly imagined another symbol, the person would see a mixed vision, appropriate to the two symbols. When he tried imagining a mixed symbol of air and water (a crescent moon on a blue circle), the other person had a 'vision' of a pigeon with a lobster in its beak. When he tried a star symbol on a female subject (probably Florence Farr), she saw a rough stone house with the skull of a horse in it. When he tried it with a male 'seer', he saw a rough stone house with a gold skeleton in it.

At this time—the early 1890s—Yeats was working with Edwin Ellis on an edition of the poems of William Blake. He was fascinated to discover that certain symbols evoked strange personages who corresponded to the mythical beings in Blake's prophetic books, 'Though differing a little, as Blake himself said visions differ with the eye of the visionary'.[11] Orc, Blake's spirit of revolution, was seen by one person as black instead of fiery red, and by another as a wolf in armour. Yeats was convinced that Blake's prophetic books were some form of automatic writing whose source was beyond his conscious mind.

In a footnote to the essay on Magic, added in 1924, Yeats comments on the possibility that these 'visions' emerged from the subconscious, and adds: 'I am certain that [they] draw upon associations which are beyond the reach of the individual "subconscious".' Certainly, it is clear that Yeats and Jung are talking about the same thing. 'The collective unconscious,' says Jung, 'seems to be . . . not a person, but something like an unceasing stream or perhaps ocean of images and figures which drift into consciousness in our dreams or in abnormal states of mind.' Yeats states one of the basic principles of magic: 'That the borders of our memory are [ever] shifting, and that our memories are a part of one great memory, the memory of Nature herself, [and] that this . . . great memory can be evoked by symbols.'[12] Elsewhere, he observes 'that our little memories are but a part of some great Memory that renews the world and men's thoughts age after age, and that our thoughts are not, as we suppose, the deep, but a little foam upon the deep.'[13] Here, in an essay written in 1900, Yeats is already making Jung's distinction between the personal and the collective unconscious.

Yeats' essay on magic contains a detailed account of a 'magical operation' conducted by MacGregor Mathers and his wife, the sister of the philosopher Bergson, and it enables us to see the interaction of the world of imagination and the underlying world of 'correspondences' or magical realities. Yeats tells how he and an acquaintance—a man who was interested in magic but not deeply convinced—went to call on Mathers and his wife, who were then living at a house in Forest Hill, South London; Mathers was curator of a small private museum. The 'magical chamber' was a long room with a dais at one end; Yeats and his friend sat in the middle, Mathers on the dais, and Mrs Mathers between them. Mathers held a wooden mace in one hand and turned to a tablet covered with coloured squares, each square bearing a number (or symbol?), repeating some form of incantation.

> Almost at once my imagination began to move of itself and to bring before me vivid images that, though never too vivid to be imagination, . . . had yet a motion of their own, a life I could not change or shape. I remember seeing a number of white figures, and wondering whether their mitred heads had been suggested by the mitred head of the mace, and then, of a sudden, the image of my acquaintance in the midst of them. I told what I had seen, and [Mathers] cried in a deep voice, 'Let him be blotted out,' and as he said it the image of my acquaintance vanished . . .

In his place was a man dressed in black, in the style of the sixteenth century. Mrs Mathers thought he looked like a Fleming and declared that this figure was Yeats's acquaintance, as he had been in a previous existence. She then 'saw' a detailed scene, which Yeats was able to see in glimpses—often seeing what she described *before* he heard her description. The man walked along a narrow street and went into a building. At this point, Yeats 'saw' a dead body on a table near the door, but said nothing, wondering whether Mrs Mathers saw it too. She went on to say that the man in black was a doctor, lecturing to his students. Yeats asked if she saw anything near the door, and she replied: 'Yes, I see a subject for dissection.' After this, she de-scribed—and Yeats saw in flashes—the man enter a laboratory and out of a vessel over a fire take a model of a human figure. Mathers —who also seems to have shared this vision—said that the man had been trying to make living flesh and had drawn down evil spirits. Yeats thought he heard squeals but said nothing; a moment later, Mrs Mathers said she heard squeals. Mathers also heard them and explained that they were sounds made by pouring some red liquid over the mouth of the clay image. In the vision, they saw the man become seriously ill, then make a partial recovery. But his reputation as a magician had spread through the town, so that he lost all his students.

Yeats's friend, whom all this concerned, was the only one who saw nothing. (Yeats says this is because he was 'forbidden' to see his own life; in the same way, people with powers of precognition are usually unable to foresee their own futures.) Yet he was thoroughly shaken by the description, and admitted that ever since childhood he had had a recurrent dream of trying to animate a figure like the one in the vision. (Yeats does not mention—perhaps he was unaware—that the anima-tion of magical statues is among the oldest of all magical ceremonies.) He added that perhaps his ill health was due to this dangerous experi-ment in a previous existence. By the time Yeats wrote the essay on magic ten years later (1901) his acquaintance was dead.

In answer to Yeats's request to reveal some scene of his own past lives, Mathers made another invocation, and this time the three of them experienced another lengthy 'hallucination'—so long that they broke off in the middle for supper—about a medieval knight who built a great stone cross and spent his days standing against it with his arms outstretched, apparently in penance for some past sin. (Yeats seems to think it was connected with two lovers and the cutting off of the man's hands.)

Yeats expressed doubt as to whether he was really seeing a vision of his own past life; he seemed inclined to believe that it was some kind of dream created by three minds. If this view were correct, it would be a powerful argument in favour of Jung's collective unconscious. Tele-pathy involves simply transmission—usually of a single idea or impression—from one mind to another. If a kind of dream could be shared by three of those present (although not by the fourth; Yeats remarks of his friend that 'his imagination had no will of its own'), it would seem to imply that men are not separate island universes, each with its own subconscious, but that some part of the mind is 'shared'.

This view is supported by a certain amount of evidence. P. D. Ouspensky once described how he walked down a thoroughfare in Petrograd in such a state of mystical intensity that he seemed to see people surrounded by their dreams, which hovered like clouds in front of their faces. He experienced the conviction that if he could stare at anyone long enough, he would be able to see the actual content of his dreams.[14] A Philadelphia explorer, Harry B. Wright, has described witnessing the Leopard Dance of Dahomey, West Africa; as a naked girl performed the dance to the beating of a drum and the incantations of a priest, Wright's native companion asked; 'Look, do you see the two leopards walking beside her?' Wright saw nothing, but the other natives appeared to be following the leopards with their eyes. And then, in the midst of the ceremony, three leopards walked out of the jungle and across the clearing; Wright was convinced that these were real leopards—perhaps summoned by the 'imaginary' leopards in the same way that the sheep were summoned by Mathers' imaginary ram.[15]

Perhaps the most striking example of such a collective 'vision' is one that occurs in Bruce Lamb's *Wizard of the Upper Amazon*, which describes the experiences of Manuel Cordova, a Peruvian youth captured by the Amahuaca Indians of Brazil. After drinking *hini xuma*, the 'vision extract', the natives—including Cordova—experienced shared visions of snakes, birds and animals that continued all night. On a later occasion, after a 'shared vision' of jungle cats, Cordova suddenly remembered a black jaguar he had once encountered, and the jaguar immediately appeared, stalking through the middle of the group, causing a terrified shudder. Realising that Cordova was responsible for the vision, the natives nicknamed him 'black jaguar'.[16]

What is perhaps most difficult for the Western mind to grasp is the notion that magic could be a purely *natural* phenomenon, like botany or the game of chess. We tend to think of a 'magician' as a man with some strange spiritual power, based on slowly acquired wisdom. This is far from the truth; in *The Occult* I pointed out that most of the 'great magicians' have been highly unsatisfactory human beings, and that it would hardly be unfair to say that most of them were fools. Most of them were certainly 'Right Men'; and nearly all were unlucky. Mathers is an interesting case in point. Born in West Hackney, London, the son of a commercial clerk, he was already, by the age of twenty-three, signing himself 'Comte de Glenstrae'. His Christian names were Samuel Liddell; the MacGregor was assumed later when he decided he was of Highland descent. (He was convinced that he was the Young Pretender in a previous incarnation.) Even Yeats, who liked him, conceded that he lived almost entirely in a world of fantasy. Apart from magic, his other major interest was military strategy; he believed he was a great commander and once had a photograph of himself taken in an artillery lieutenant's uniform—to which he had no right. Yeats once met him in the street in Highland regalia, with knives stuck in his stocking; Mathers told him: 'When I am dressed like this I feel like a walking flame.' His overbearing manners and demand for total obedience finally led the other members of the Golden Dawn to rebel and throw him out. This kind of character-disorientation goes beyond eccentricity and verges on madness. It would therefore be a perfectly fair assumption that his magic was entirely fraudulent or illusory. Yeats's autobiographical writings—and the accounts of other members of the Golden Dawn—make it clear this was not so. He undoubtedly possessed genuine 'magical' powers. And the anomaly vanishes if we can once reconcile ourselves to the idea that magic is not a branch of 'the supernatural' but an acquired skill, like repairing cars or performing on a trapeze.

It is worth bearing in mind that Mathers' peculiar psychological make-up endowed him with an abundance of the two qualities most necessary to a 'magician'—will and imagination. A frantic desire to 'be' somebody, a craving for self-esteem, produced an abnormally powerful will-drive, and a Walter-Mitty-ish inclination to fantasise developed his imagination. Fantasy is not the same as imagination, but it provides its foundation. All Mathers had to acquire was a knowledge of the correspondences, the symbolic foundation of magic. By comparison, Yeats, who also practised magic, lacked the fanatical will-drive and single-mindedness. This comes out in a story told by the mystic George Russell (AE) of how he watched Yeats walking up and down the room holding a magical sword and repeating incantations; every time he passed a bowl of plums, Yeats took one. 'Really Yeats,' said Russell, 'you can't evoke great spirits and eat plums at the same time.'[17] The humourless and ascetic Mathers would never have been diverted from a magical operation by a desire for food. And this is what made him a competent magician.

Having said all this, it is necessary to admit that the modern scepticism about magic and magicians is by no means unfounded. It is only necessary to glance into Cornelius Agrippa's *Occult Philosophy* or Francis Barrett's *The Magus* to see that no amount of 'symbolic interpretation' could make sense of most of it. And this is because, in spite of the three hundred years between them, Agrippa and Barrett both accept that the world is full of sinister and maleficent powers, from basilisks (which can 'kill with their gaze') to demons and vampires, as well as all kinds of angels and benevolent spirits, and that magic consists to a large extent of invoking the aid of these spirits.

There are plenty of modern students of the 'paranormal' who might be willing to concede that there are such things as disembodied forces of good and evil; but there is a world of difference between their attitude and that of the medieval churchman, who felt that demons were always looking over his shoulder. One of the best known works on magic ever written, Dom Augustine Calmet's *Treatise on Apparitions* (first published in 1751, and still immensely popular a century later) devotes its first six chapters to proving the existence of good and bad angels by means of the Scriptures, then goes on to argue that magic is usually the result of intercourse with demons. The 'examples in proof of magic' that he offers are so preposterous that it is impossible to take them seriously: for example, Apollonius of Tyana (a famous magician of the ancient world) rid Ephesus of a plague by persuading the citizens to stone an old man to death; the old man promptly turned into a dog, proving that he was the demon who had caused the plague. Yet Calmet concludes the same chapter with a remarkably accurate description of a Lapland *shaman* going into a trance to the beating of a drum and returning from the spirit world with messages for the living. We have plenty of modern eye-witness accounts of the supernatural power of *shamans*, for example, Arthur Grimble's description of the *shaman* of the Gilbert Islands, who was able to sink into a trance and 'summon' porpoises from far out at sea. Grimble was actually present as the porpoises, in a semi-hypnotised state, swam ashore and allowed themselves to be clubbed to death by natives.[18]

No one would expect a scientific textbook of the seventeeth century to be wholly valid today; we might expect to dismiss as much as fifty per cent of it. This would not prevent us from accepting the other fifty per cent. And it would be logical and sensible to take the same attitude towards works on 'magic', particularly in view of the fact that the magic of earlier centuries *included* science. Modern chemistry grew out of alchemy; modern astronomy grew out of astrology. Isaac Newton practised both magic *and* science without feeling there was any contradiction. The tremendous advance of science in the century after Newton seemed to make most of the old grimoires and magical works obsolete. The spirit of reason made their obsession with angels and demons seem laughable. The result was that for more than a century, the magical books of the Middle Ages were virtually forgotten. Francis Barret's attempt to revive the forgotten art in *The Magus* (1801) was treated by most cultured people as a joke. (Yet Barrett himself knew that magic was not entirely medieval superstition; he wrote: 'I have, in the country, by only speaking a few words and using some other things, caused terrible rains and claps of thunder.')

It is significant that the next major work on magic—Eliphaz Levi's *Dogme de la Haute Magie* (1855)—pays little attention to demons or other spirits and concentrates almost entirely on magical symbolism. Levi's approach to magic was basically Jungian. And MacGregor Mathers, who picked up most of his basic ideas from Levi, also remained obsessed with symbolism and 'correspondences'. There was, in effect, a total break between the magic of earlier centuries, and this new, streamlined tradition of 'psychological' magic. But the break was not as drastic as it looks. Mathers translated traditional grimoires like *The Key of Solomon* and *The Sacred Magic of Abrahamelin the Mage*, and included elements from them in the Golden Dawn rituals (which he devised). He was a dedicated cabalist and translated Knorr von Rosenroth's *The Kabbalah Unveiled*. He simply discarded the obsolete parts of medieval magic and concentrated on its underlying reality, or what he was able to discern of that reality.

It so happened that W. B. Yeats was the ideal person for transmitting these ideas to the twentieth century, although Mathers was inclined to dismiss him as an aesthete. In Dublin, Yeats and George Russell had founded a group for the study of paranormal phenomena which they called the Hermetic Society, and at the first meeting Yeats suggested as a basic principle the notion that 'whatever the great poets had affirmed in their finest moments was the nearest we could come to an authoritative religion, and that their mythology, their spirits of water and wind, were but literal truth'. Paracelsus would have dismissed such an idea as a contradiction of the objective reality of magic, but he would not have been entirely correct. As a romantic poet, Yeats knew something that Paracelsus and Bruno glimpsed only in flashes: that the efficacy of magic is basically a matter of *inner pressure*. Yeats knew that the poet's problem is that he feels dwarfed, negated, by the drabness of the 'real world'. His problem is analogous to that of a jet aircraft: to maintain a certain inner pressure in spite of the low pressure of the surrounding atmosphere. Most human beings are like punctured tyres; they take low-pressure consciousness for granted. Yeats also spent much of his time in a state of nervous exhaustion; partly because of a habit of auto-eroticism with its attendant guilt feelings but largely because of his distaste for the ugliness and triviality of everyday existence. He records that 'the toil of getting up in the morning exhausted me'. Like his fellow poets Ernest Dowson and Lionel Johnson, he made a kind of virtue out of his permanent fatigue by creating a poetry of world rejection. Unlike Dowson and Johnson, he never got into the habit of maintaining his inner pressure by means of brandy and absinthe. Instead, he mastered the first principle of magic: *focusing* his dream world and holding it clearly in his mind's eye as he transferred it to paper. His early poems are full of dream images: fading meteors, and mournful lovers who renounce one another as they stand in the twilight. Yet it is always convincing; there is nothing ineffectual about it. The pressure is never high, but it is consistent. And it was this ability to focus his mental world that endowed Yeats with the strength to meet the world on its own terms instead of being destroyed by it, as Dowson and Johnson were.

All of this is simply to say that Yeats recognised the connection between magic and Magic: that is, between moods of deep and intense delight and the ability to summon 'paranormal' powers. And he remained a lifelong student—and practitioner—of magic. Long after the occult revival of the 1890s had run out of steam, Yeats continued to act as the propagandist for magic and the principles of hermeticism. He was not notably successful; most of his admirers tended to regard his magical interests as an amiable eccentricity, the price he paid for his poetry. A later generation has come to understand that the two were interdependent: the poetry sprang out of the magic and the magic out of the poetry.

Yeats married in 1917, at the age of fifty-two. A few days later, at a hotel in the Ashdown Forest, his wife decided to try automatic writing. The sentences that came were so exciting that he persuaded her to continue. Yeats spent the next eight years studying and arranging the results; they appeared at the end of 1925 in a book called *A Vision*. It was dedicated to Mrs Mathers (Mathers had died at the end of the First World War) and is arguably the most important hermetic book since Bruno's *Art of Memory*.

A Vision is hermetic in the most precise sense of the word; it is based upon the fundamental proposition of Hermes Trismegistos: 'As above, so below', which means, as we have seen, that the world inside man—and down here on earth—corresponds to the world up there in the heavens.

At this point we must pause to examine this highly controversial proposition, which is, of course, the cornerstone of astrology. How is it possible to take seriously a theory that is based on a fundamental error: the notion that there are only seven planets, and that these include the sun and moon?

Most astrologers have a simple answer to this: they don't know why, but it *does* work. Astrology is remarkably successful in describing the types of character who are born under various signs of the zodiac.[19] The underlying assumption is that the bodies in the solar system exert various forces on one another, and that all living things are influenced by the interaction of these forces. We know, for example, that the moon controls the tides; most people will also agree that the moon affects some people's mental balance. (Townspeople may find this hard to accept, but most country areas have their list of people who become a little 'queer' at the time of the full moon.) The planets are to be sure much farther away than the moon. But we have no idea of what forces we are discussing, and what element in living things could be affected by them.

The picture of the solar system developed by 'ley hunters' like John Michell is consistent with the view of astrology. Michell, as we have already seen, believes that human beings are sensitive to earth forces—indeed, that animals navigate by their aid. These earth forces are in turn influenced by the other bodies in the solar system.

According to this view, ancient man would have become aware of these forces, not by studying the heavens and making arbitrary guesses about the planets (i.e. Mars is red and therefore the planet of war), but by the same kind of direct intuition that he uses in dowsing. Presumably the most sensitive dowsers were also the best astrologers, since what they would be 'sensing' would be the magnetic influence of the planets on the earth under their feet. It would obviously not make the slightest difference whether or not they thought the sun was a planet or the earth the centre of the universe. Neither would it matter that they were unaware of the existence of Neptune and Pluto and even (until Herschel discovered it in 1781) Uranus; these are too far away to exercise much magnetic influence.

It may, of course, be a mistake to think in terms of simple 'forces'. Animals and birds can be influenced by sounds that are too high for the human ear to detect; they are not influenced by the 'force' of the sound, but by the *meaning* it has for them. Dowsing also suggests that man can be influenced by 'meanings' as well as by mere forces; what forces are involved when a map dowser detects a sunken wreck on the other side of the world? So it is at least conceivable that planets might exert an influence out of all proportion to the actual gravitational force they represent.

This, at all events, enables us to grasp what the hermeticists meant by 'As above, so below'. The solar system becomes a great complex web of forces and significances, instead of the scientist's mere physical system, which can be described in terms of vectors and the law of angular momentum. This is the view not only of astrologers but also of poets and mystics. In Dostoevsky's *Brothers Karamazov*, Alyosha Karamazov experiences a moment of intense relief and ecstasy when he stares at the stars and feels that 'there seemed to be threads from all those innumerable worlds of God, linking his soul to theirs. . .' This vision of meaning follows a crisis of belief in which he comes close to losing his faith; the body of a saintly monk has shown no sign of being incorruptible, like St Teresa's, and Alyosha is suddenly struck by the suspicion that the world might, after all, be a mere physical system, on which men try to impose their dreams. His vision of universal meaning is not unlike that of the hermeticists.

By comparison with the intricacies of astrology, the system that Yeats outlines in *A Vision* is relatively simple. Like all hermeticists, Yeats is inclined to see human existence as a kind of 'test', a struggle for power and knowledge. Like Jung, he discerns two basic types of human being, introvert and extravert; Yeats distinguishes them by saying that one gains power through his struggle with himself, the other through his struggle with the world.

Astrology claims that a man's 'type'—his personality—depends basically on his birth sign, Leo or Cancer or whatever. In other words, human personality is like a plastic entity, moulded in a logical manner and in a logical order by the forces of the heavens. This is also the basis of *A Vision*, except that instead of *all* the heavens, Yeats is concerned only with the moon. He posits twenty-eight types of human personality—corresponding to the twenty-eight phases of the moon—ranging between total extravert and total introvert. (These latter are, of course, Jung's terms, not Yeats's.) The phases from one to fourteen show man expanding outwards, from negative to positive; from sixteen to twenty-eight, he contracts again. The difference seems to be that the men of the first fourteen phases are 'acted upon', while those of the sixteenth to the twenty-eighth phase are 'actors'. (Yeats remarks at the end of Phase 16: 'From this phase on we meet with those who do violence instead of suffering it.')

Yeats sees man as being a balance of four basic forces or aspects. Here, again, we are startlingly close to Jung, who sees man in terms of four basic faculties: thinking, feeling, sensation and intuition. Everyone belongs to one of these four 'psychological types'—some people are primarily thinkers, some primarily feelers, etc.,—but we all need a certain balance of the four 'faculties' if we are to be healthy human beings. Jung saw great significance in this idea of a 'quaternio', which occurs again and again in religious and mythical systems. Yeats's quaternio is of a different sort; for he is trying to classify men in terms of their purpose, their 'fate', their creative drives. So each of his phases is divided into four subheadings: Will, Mask, Creative Mind and Body of Fate. These mean, respectively, (1) a man's purpose or basic aim, (2) the way he appears to the world, (3) his mode of self-expression, (4) his fate, what the 'stars' intend for him.

These are four interacting factors (Yeats has a drawing of two cones fitting into one another), continually altering their balance as the moon goes through its twenty-eight phases. Phase 1 is a dark and formless chaos, from which anything can emerge. Phase 2 is a type of person who is basically animal, a kind of crude energy symbolised by the nature god Pan. And the remaining phases up to fourteen might

be regarded as a symbolic picture of the evolution of the human personality—the awakening of ambition, assertion of individuality, self-
assertion and so on. (Here we have something very like Janet's
psychological hierarchy, developing through nine levels).[20] As
examples of Phase 14, 'The Obsessive Man', he mentions Keats,
Gorgione and 'many beautiful women'. In other words, it is a kind of
apotheosis of sensuality. And the kind of men who are given as
examples of other earlier phases—Whitman, Dumas, Parnell,
Baudelaire, Dowson—tend to be 'primitives'. (This is not to say that
there are no intellectuals—Yeats mentions Carlyle, Nietzsche and
Spinoza; but he sees them, too, as primitives.) The remaining
phases—from sixteen to twenty-eight—show what might be called
the development of civilisation or spirit, and, as one might expect, we
now find Shelley, Napoleon, Swedenborg and Luther among the
examples.

As explained here, the system may sound rather arbitrary, but it is
not so. Yeats is fascinated by the gradual change of balance between
the four faculties, so that reading the book is like looking at a beautiful,
complicated mobile with four colours that shade into one another in
various ways as it turns in the air. Moreover, each of the 'types' has
several possibilities. A man has no real choice over his destiny ('Body
of Fate') or over his basic aim (his 'Will'); but he *does* have a choice over
his 'Mask'—the face he presents to the world—and over his creative
self-expression. So, for example, in Phase 7 we have a man whose
basic drive is 'Assertion of Individuality'. He cannot help this; it is a
kind of itch, and if it were suppressed, he would become a vegetable.
His 'destiny' or fate is adventure, the kind of adventure that turns you
into a 'somebody'. As examples of this type, Yeats mentions four
writers: George Borrow, Alexandre Dumas, Thomas Carlyle and
James Macpherson. Borrow is the highly assertive, controversial
character who became famous with books like *The Bible in Spain* and
The Romany Rye, representing himself as a swashbuckling character,
most at home among gypsies and sporting bloods. Macpherson was
the folklore collector who forged the work of an imaginary Scottish
bard called Ossian and was finally denounced as a fraud. The only one
of this four who achieved a balance of his natural powers was Dumas,
that enormous, joyous, heroic character who liked to eat all day and
make love all night. Yeats says that when such a man's creative mind is
true to itself, it expresses itself naturally in terms of heroic sentiments,

like those we find in *The Three Musketeers*. When it is untrue to itself, it tends to lapse into dogmatic sentimentality, such as we find in Carlyle's paean of praise to the Middle Ages, *Past and Present*. When the Mask (what Jung calls the Persona) is true to itself, it expresses itself in the form of altruism or generosity; when he is untrue to himself, such a man likes to present to the world a face of efficiency and practicality, and his admiration for the heroic becomes an admiration of power and ruthlessness. (Some critics have seen Carlyle's philosophy as a fore-runner of Nazism.)

Whether or not we find Yeats's 'phases' convincing, we cannot deny their fascination. We seem to be watching complex changes in a balance of forces, and there is a feeling of revelation as Yeats points out that a particular balance is identical in Shakespeare, Balzac and Napoleon, or in Flaubert, Swedenborg and Darwin. The system appeals to the intuition rather than the intellect and is, in this sense, typical of the hermetic tradition. This probably explains the embarrassment of critics who were asked to review the original edition in 1925, an embarrassment that had not diminished notably when a new edition appeared in 1938. Even now, more than half a century after the first edition, *A Vision* remains one of the major unexplored works of our time.

I have devoted so much space to Yeats's system of 'psychological types' because it is the only modern representative of the old hermetic tradition. His contemporaries were inclined to regard it as a perverse intellectual game; and Aleister Crowley, one of the few who were qualified to understand it, was too jealous of Yeats's success to make the effort to understand it. (He was convinced that he was a far greater poet than Yeats.)

The one thing no one seems to have thought of asking is why Yeats called it *A Vision*. It was dictated to his wife over many dreary months and then painstakingly sifted and rearranged by Yeats. What was visionary about that?

The answer is that Yeats was expressing not his own 'vision', but the hermetic vision: the vision of a coherent, connected, meaningful universe, based on a mysterious yet demonstrable sense of order. In the *Autobiography*, he speaks of a conviction he developed at the age of twenty that 'the world was now but a bundle of fragments' and he blamed the scientists for this new chaotic universe. They had reduced the stars to lumps of dead matter and man to a collection of appetites. *A Vision* was more than an astrological system; it was a defiant assertion of the coherence of the universe.

It is important to remember that this was not merely a matter of poetic conviction, which might have been no more than wishful thinking. Yeats felt that his paranormal studies provided a certain basic evidence for the first principle of magic—'that the universe of the physical scientist is only a part, and by no means the most important part, of total reality'.[21] In his autobiography G. K. Chesterton says of Yeats:

> He staggered the materialists by attacking their abstract materialism with a completely concrete mysticism; 'Imagination!' he would say with withering contempt; 'There wasn't much imagination when Farmer Hogan was dragged out of bed and thrashed like a sack of potatoes—that they did, they had 'um out and thumped 'um; and that's not the sort of thing a man wants to imagine.' But the concrete examples were not only a comedy; he used one argument which was sound, and I have never forgotten it. It is the fact that it is not abnormal men like artists, but normal men like peasants, who have borne witness a thousand times to such things; it is the farmers who see the fairies. It is the agricultural labourer who calls a spade a spade, who also calls a spirit a spirit; it is the woodcutter . . . who will say he saw a man hang on the gallows and afterwards hang around it as a ghost.[22]

It is unfortunate that Yeats's 'concrete mysticism' convinced few people apart from Chesterton. A sceptic might believe him when he said that a farmer had seen a fairy, but not when he said that a farmer had been dragged out of bed and thumped by fairies. The irony is that we can now give Yeats the benefit of the doubt, since we know a little more about poltergeists and the odd forces that seem to hang around dragon paths (or 'fairy tracks', as they are called in Ireland). We know that these forces are more likely to hurl a man flat on his face or throw him out of bed than serenade him with the horns of elfland. Lethbridge would certainly have found nothing improbable in the idea that 'ghouls' might hang around a gallows; if gallows still existed on lonely hilltops, that would be the very place you might expect to find a ghoul.

From the biography of Yeats by Joseph Hone, we discover that Yeats was also aware of the mystery of the 'hierarchy of selves'. When

Maud Gonne—the woman with whom Yeats was in love—joined the Golden Dawn, she told Yeats of the apparition of a woman in grey that she used to see in her childhood. Yeats had occasionally speculated whether she might be under the influence of some spirit; 'possession' seemed a possible explanation for her sudden changes of mood. He spoke to Mathers about the apparition, and Mathers gave his opinion that the spirit could be made visible by means of the appropriate symbol. Mrs Mathers made the symbol 'according to the rules of the order'. Presumably it was some kind of talisman, since Yeats himself could have made an ordinary tattwa symbol without troubling Mrs Mathers. The spirit then became visible—Hone does not specify to whom—and Maude Gonne discovered that it was a part of her own personality, seeking for reunion. The spirit provided the information that Miss Gonne had been a priestess of Tyre in a previous existence and had allowed a priest to persuade her to utter a false oracle. As a result, the personality of that life had split off and remained a half-living shadow. It seemed to confirm the evidence of a recurring dream that she had since childhood, in which she went into the desert to die alone.

Perhaps the most interesting part of this story is in its postscript. Before he joined the Golden Dawn, Yeats had been a member of the Theosophical Society, founded by the extraordinary Helena Petrovna Blavatsky. Yeats told Hone that a number of 'secret doctrines' had been imparted to him during his initiation, and that one of these was that the soul is made up of many 'personalities'; it was possible for these to become dissociated, whereupon each 'must seek for a reunion that must always be refused'. No such idea is to be found in either of Madame Blavatsky's major works, *Isis Unveiled* or *The Secret Doctrine*, although she states that crime can snap the thread 'which links the spirit to the soul', producing a state of alienation of the soul.[23] So the doctrine of the multiplicity of personalities seems to have been regarded by Madame Blavatsky as one of the 'secret doctrines' that should never be expressed to non-initiates. It was his recollection of this doctrine that persuaded Yeats that Maude Gonne's vision of her past life might be literally true, not merely the symbolic expression of some emotional problem.

Although it is never stated explicitly, the same idea forms the foundation of *A Vision*. The soul passes through many incarnations. In each life, it is subject to certain cosmic factors that determine its destiny. Yet the ultimate choice lies within itself. A man can choose whether his mask or creative drives are true or false, which means that he can also choose whether to stagnate or to evolve. It was not until he was near the end of his life that Yeats stated this doctrine fairly explicitly, in the long poem *Under Ben Bulben*: 'many times man lives and dies', and the ultimate aim of the process is 'profane perfection of mankind'.

The same poem contains another phrase that is vital to the understanding of Yeats's doctrine:

> You that Mitchel's prayer have heard,
> 'Send war in our time, O Lord!'
> Know that when all words are said
> And a man is fighting mad,
> Something drops from eyes long blind,
> *He completes his partial mind*,
> For an instant stands at ease
> Laughs aloud, his heart at peace. . .

Yeats also clearly recognised that our everyday consciousness is 'partial'. (The italics are mine.) And the phrase must be linked with his image of the moon, which is also 'partial' for most of the month. Yeats is making the point that Nietzsche often made: in sudden moments of ecstatic intensity, man suddenly seems to become complete, to relax and breathe more deeply. It is as if the larger part of his being was in a kind of permanent eclipse, except for these rare moments. Like Christine Beauchamp and Doris Fischer, we are all 'partial' personalities. But how can we learn to establish contact with the occluded areas? This is the question that lies at the heart of all 'occultism.' It is also the question that lies at the heart of this investigation.

5

Descent into the Unconscious

———

'There exists a reciprocal influence between the heavenly bodies, the earth, and the bodies of living creatures.' So said Dr Charles D'Eslon, physician to the Comte D'Artois, in an appearance before the Royal Society of Medicine in Paris on September 18, 1780. This influence, claimed the speaker, was due to an unknown 'fluid' which pervades all space. The health of human beings was governed by the movement of this mysterious influence, which, because of its similarity to magnetic attraction, might be called animal magnetism. (To a later generation of occultists it became known as the 'astral light', and to a still later generation of scientists as the luminiferous ether.)

D'Eslon was not expounding his own doctrine, but that of his admired master, Dr Franz Anton Mesmer, who had come to Paris two years previously. Mesmer believed literally in the curative power of large magnets, an idea he may have picked up from Paracelsus, who had stumbled on the discovery more than two centuries earlier. When patients were 'magnetised'—stroked with large magnets—their aches and pains vanished. Moreover, if a tree was 'magnetised', and patients leaned against it, the effect seemed to be just as powerful.

Inevitably, the doctors and scientists were opposed to Mesmer's ideas, perhaps with some reason. Mesmer's 'magnetic' sessions were crowded with half-naked men and women who increased the flow of magnetic fluid with mutual caresses; doctors suspected that the invigorating effects were not entirely the result of the cosmic ether. Mesmer never achieved professional recognition, and Dr D'Eslon's attempt to convince his colleagues of the Royal Society of Medicine was a total failure; they voted to disqualify any doctor who advocated or practised animal magnetism. Mesmer died, forgotten and embittered, in 1815.

In the same year that the Royal Society rejected Mesmer's claims, one of his pupils made a discovery that was to revolutionise the future of medicine. Armand Marie-Jacques, Marquis de Chastenet de Puységur, was an aristocrat who lived on an estate near Soissons with his younger brothers, Viscount Jacques Maxime and Count Antoine-Hyacinthe. They had paid Mesmer four hundred louis for instruction in the art of magnetism, which they then proceeded to practise on the local peasantry. In accordance with Mesmer's instructions they magnetised a lime tree in the park and made their patients lean against it to absorb its influence. One day in 1780, the Marquis was treating a twenty-year-old shepherd named Victor Race. He had tied him loosely to the tree and was making passes with a magnet over his head and body, to induce a flow in the magnetic fluid. To Puységur's surprise, Victor closed his eyes and fell asleep. The Marquis ordered him to wake up and untie himself; with eyes still closed, Victor did as he was told. Then, walking like a somnambulist, he wandered off across the park. Puységur knew enough about medicine to know that he had induced some kind of trance, but he had no idea of its nature.

Two centuries later, we are still in ignorance. We know that most people can be hypnotised if they fix their eyes on some monotonous movement, like the swinging of a pendulum. Contrary to general belief, this has nothing to do with weakness of will. Weak-minded people are more difficult to hypnotise than intelligent, normal people, and it is impossible to hypnotise idiots.

The puzzling thing about hypnosis is that it appears to work by making the patient fall asleep—the monotonous movement of a train has the same effect. But in hypnotic sleep, some part of the mind remains fully awake, so the subject can answer questions or obey suggestions. Most books on the subject contain a chapter called 'What is Hypnosis?' The answer could be summarised in three words: 'We don't know.'

Yet Janet's observation of his hysterical patients[1] offers a clue. When patients were in a state of nervous hypertension, Janet found that he could hold whispered conversations with them without the patient's *conscious* self being aware of what was going on. Part of the personality had gone into 'eclipse', leaving only a contracted and anxiety-ridden ego; yet the eclipsed part of the mind could still answer questions and respond to suggestions.

It seems clear that we are dealing with a closely related phenomenon in hypnosis. Ordinary sleep seems to have a chemical basis; poisons accumulate in the brain, and the order to sleep is transmitted to various centres by a chemical called acetylcholine. In hypnosis, the chemical system seems to be by-passed; there is nothing to prevent a person being hypnotised immediately after a good night's sleep. Hypnosis seems to cause the same kind of 'narrowing' of consciousness as hysteria, but the contracted part of consciousness falls asleep, while the eclipsed part remains awake, capable of responding to stimuli. Moreover, the hypnotised person becomes capable of feats that would be impossible while awake; everyone has heard of the stage-hypnotist's trick of making someone lie rigid across two chairs with a heavy weight on the stomach.

What happens in hypnosis? The phenomenon appears to be clearly associated with *passivity*, that is, the 'robotic' part of the mind. For centuries before the Puységurs made their discovery, farmers knew that if you held a chicken's head against the floor and drew a chalk line extending from the tip of its beak, the bird would lie still, apparently fascinated by the line. Placing blinkers over a horse's eyes seems to have a similar 'tranquilising' effect, not only preventing it from seeing oncoming traffic, but reducing its level of nervous excitability. And in human beings, hypnosis causes a similar 'switching off' of the active part of the consciousness.

From our point of view, one of the most interesting things about hypnosis is that seems to be capable of activating Jung's 'creative imagination'. In the winter of 1976, I was present at an experiment in the BBC television studios in Bristol, to determine whether a hypnotised person could be made to 'see' a ghost. A volunteer—a housewife who was known to be a good hypnotic subject—was placed under hypnosis by a doctor. She was told that when she awakened, she would be taken to another place, where I would approach her (followed by a television camera). As I spoke to her, she would 'see' the sinister figure of a seventeenth-century clergyman standing nearby; the man's appearance was described in detail. She was awakened and taken to the Bristol docks, where I was waiting. As I walked towards her, she smiled at me, then her eyes strayed across the water to an abandoned wharf. Her smile vanished, and she asked me with amazement; 'Where did he go?' 'Who?' 'That man . . .' She pointed to the dock and described the unpleasant, sallow-looking man dressed in old-fashioned clothes, who had been standing on the wharf, then vanished. Even when the hypnotist explained that she had been responding to a suggestion made under hypnosis, she was obviously only half-convinced. Several times during the rest of the afternoon, she tried to persuade us to admit that it had been a joke and she had seen a real man. She said there was nothing 'ghostly' about him; he looked quite solid and normal.[2]

Hypnotism appears to be one method of reaching the 'wider' areas of the self, beyond the narrow little wedge of ego-consciousness that most of us think as 'me'. This was why hypnosis was the logical way of re-integrating the dissociated personalities of Doris Fischer and Sybil Dorsett—and also why it released the mischievous fragment of Christine Beauchamp like a genie from a bottle. This fragment —Sally—had been floating around in the 'eclipsed' area, what we would normally call the unconscious, without being able to struggle into conscious existence because Christine guarded the door to consciousness. When Christine fell asleep under hypnosis, Sally was able to emerge from the true 'unconscious' into that subliminal or twilight area that lies on either side of it. (For the sake of simplicity, I shall refer to this twilight area as 'penumbral consciousness'.) Prince's mistake was in trying to suppress her again instead of trying to integrate her with Christine.

What is the mechanism of 'expansion'? What happens when the *opposite* takes place—when a man 'completes his partial mind' and 'laughs aloud, his heart at peace?'

This is a question that took on an urgently personal note during my 'panic attacks', and some of the observations that I made during that period may provide a convenient starting point. To begin with, there was that basic recognition that *I* was causing the panic. A part of me was gripping my own windpipe, cutting off the air. Obviously, I didn't *want* to go through this particularly unpleasant experience. So how did I manage to split into these two warring factions?

The answer, I realised, lay in the personality I have been forced to acquire since I reached the 'age of responsibility'. When I now look at my face in the mirror—battered and lined with its forty-five years—I realise that the person most of my friends know as Colin Wilson has come into existence over the past quarter of a century. He hardly existed in my teens. This 'me' is conscientious, hard-working, a passable husband and father. Most people regard him as fairly tolerant and good-natured, and he enjoys a glass of wine with friends. The only characteristic he shares with his ancestor of thirty years ago is a certain tendency to obsessiveness; once he gets his teeth into a task, he finds it difficult to let go.

That earlier Colin Wilson was not much liked. He detested the dreariness of everyday living and its tedious responsibilities. Ever since childhood he had regarded most adults as fools, and now he still found most people irritating and stupid. He hated modern civilisation because he felt it was designed to encourage mediocrity. He had no idea of what he wanted to do with his life, except for some vague idea of becoming a scientist or a writer. All he knew was that he wanted as little as possible to do with the world around him.

I say all this without any implied condemnation. I think that my instinct was basically sound. But it certainly made life difficult. When I left school at the age of sixteen and took a job in a warehouse (having no qualification for any other kind of work), I found it all exhausting and depressing. Yet it was through this exhaustion that I made a discovery that I still regard as one of the most interesting and important of my life. It was the trick I call 'gliding'.

When I came home from work, I would feel physically tired and mentally depressed; it seemed that I was trapped in a system that made no allowances for 'outsiders'. I would go to my bedroom, where I kept my books, and spend a whole evening reading poetry. I would start by reading poems that reflected my pessimism: Eliot's *Waste Land* and *Hollow Men*, Thomson's *City of Dreadful Night*. This would produce a catharsis of the loathing, and a gradual sense of relaxation and expansion. Suddenly, I would notice that my mental energies had returned, although I was still physically tired. The result was an astonishing state of susceptibility. I could turn to any poet and totally immerse myself in his mood. There was an identification so complete that it was like *becoming* the person I was reading. And this power of identification could be applied to poets who had nothing in common. I could turn straight from Milton to Lorca, from Whitman to Verlaine, from Poe to G. K. Chesterton, without any loss of sympathy or any feeling of disparity. In each case, there was a feeling of entering the poet's world and momentarily living a part of his life. What I was experiencing—although I did not know it then—was a form of Faculty X.

The analogy that best seemed to describe the process was that of gliding. There was the initial period when the glider had to be towed gently up into the air. It was important not to release it too low, or it would bump straight back to earth. But once the mood of relaxation had been induced, I was safe. Then I could float gently in any direction I liked, taking advantage of the air currents. There was an amazing sense of freedom; I could dive or climb or turn somersaults. No negative emotions could interfere with this mood of exaltation, and if I thought back on some event that had made me miserable or embarrassed at the time, it seemed laughably trivial. Moreover, it seemed self-evident to me that this mood of relaxed detachment should be normal for all human beings.

The main problem, of course, is getting *up* there, where the winds will allow you to float freely. Here, my exhaustion obviously played an interesting part. It prevented the practical part of me from interfering. The everyday self sat there passively, allowing this other self slowly and carefully to induce a mood of relaxation and freedom. If I tried to induce this mood on a Sunday, when I had all day to do it, it might take me until evening. The problem was that I felt *too* free to begin with; my energies ran around like a flock of sheep and declined to be herded into one single act of attention. And I might be distracted by a noise or a sudden impulse to rearrange my books. It was better when exhaustion gave my mind a certain unity.

The result of these moods of freedom was an instinctive loathing of the everyday world which I later called 'the Bombard effect', after the Frenchman Alain Bombard, who sailed across the Atlantic in a rubber dinghy, to prove that shipwrecked mariners did not have to die of thirst and starvation. He lived on plankton, the juices of squashed fish, and small quantities of sea water, until one day he made the mistake of accepting the invitation of a passing ship to go on board for a meal. This was disastrous, for when he returned to his dinghy, his stomach rejected the squashed fish and sea water, and he vomited for days before it readjusted. I felt that these states in 'gliding' were normal, and I found my everyday diet of experience revolting after such glimpses of freedom. Like Yeats, I found the act of getting up in the morning unspeakably tedious. As an employee I was thoroughly unsatisfactory—bored, inefficient and resentful.

And yet as my teens drew to a close, I found that I was learning to make the adjustment to physical reality. I had to if I wanted to escape the treadmill of frustrating jobs. After a brief stint in the RAF, I became a kind of tramp, taking any labouring job that was offered, and giving it up the moment I grew tired of it. Basically, I remained what I had always been—one of Isaiah Berlin's 'hedgehogs',[3] preferring to ignore the practical side of existence and unwilling to spare a thought for anything except ideas. But I found that I had to develop another personality, a beast of burden, capable of dealing with the boring problems of keeping me alive and able, like the camel, to go for days without water—that is, without relaxation or moments of intensity.

When, at twenty-four, my first book brought me sudden notoriety, it looked as if the hedgehog were going to have things all his own way. I soon found out my mistake. The camel proved to be more necessary than ever. There were deadlines to meet, letters to be answered, trains to catch. And eventually, like everybody else, I found myself paying off a mortgage, driving the kids to school and mowing the lawn. What was even stranger was that I, who had once agreed with Villiers de L'Isle Adam's Axel that our living ought to be done for us by servants, now found myself deriving pleasure from repairing a broken window or sawing logs for the fire.

That alliance of hedgehog and camel has never been entirely amicable. The hedgehog remains preoccupied with the mystery of human existence and the paradox of human freedom; the camel has to make sure that articles are delivered on time and that the bills get paid. They usually regard one another with wry tolerance; but when things get difficult, they tend to quarrel. That is what happened in the autumn of 1973, when the camel decided to meet his obligation to the encyclopedia of crime, and the hedgehog turned away in disgust and curled up into a ball.

In less metaphorical terms, I pushed myself too hard, ventured too far from the subconscious 'source of power, meaning and purpose'. The camel ran out of water. I found myself reduced to the state of one of Janet's hysterics, and it tended to be self-perpetuating. Anxiety about my work pushed me into 'contracted consciousness', and anxiety to escape kept me there. Every time I tried to relax, a new challenge would cause me to flinch back into a state of hypertension.

But I knew, intellectually speaking, that the problem was to relax, to expand out of the hysteria. It was a question of de-conditioning myself, and the old experience of gliding now proved invaluable. Admittedly, this time I was trying to 'glide' under totally different conditions, in something more like a storm. A dozen times in the course of an evening (it tended to happen mostly when I was tired), the glider went into a sudden dive, and a dozen times I managed to get the nose up again. It was frightening to realise how easy it would be to plunge into total depression and destroy all my inner resources. When you let yourself 'crash', the world looks self-evidently meaningless and dangerous, and your energies are poisoned at their source. Yet after half a dozen nose-dives and recoveries, I began to realise that the situation wasn't half as bad as I thought; that was the first step towards recovery.

What was so fascinating about it all was to realise how much our lives and our sanity depend on the winds that blow from the subconscious. The actual mechanism of gliding, the rudder, is one's attention. When one is earth-bound—as most of us are most of the time—it seems to be a purely practical device for steering one through the working day; one's attention merely switches from one object to another. Some things raise the spirits; others depress them, but because one is on the solid earth, one doesn't move far in one direction or another. It takes a fairly powerful stimulus, like falling in love, to make one feel one is 'walking on air'. But when one has succeeded in getting off the ground, the same slight changes of attention can hurl one a hundred yards one way or the other. Ramakrishna spent so much time 'in the air' that the mere thought of God was enough to make him unconscious with ecstasy. Nietzsche's ecstasy brought him a vision of the superman and an equally mystical vision of a giant stable universe in which everything recurs eternally, but his depressions hurled him into insanity. Van Gogh's ecstasies revealed nature as a living flame; his depressions convinced him that 'misery will never end', and drove him to suicide.

At least the habitual glider is aware of a fundamental truth about the universe: that it is his own will, his own moods, his own attention, that determines ecstasy or misery. Everyone else remains trapped in the delusion that happiness and misery are a logical response to external circumstances. So they waste their lives struggling with the circumstances and feel cheated when they realise that an improvement for the better often leaves them as unfulfilled as before. If they are intelligent enough to express themselves in general terms, they probably explain that human beings are 'creatures of circumstance' and that all our effort is 'vanity of vanities'.

This tendency to hold things upside down, to put the cart before the horse, matters a great deal more than we realise. Even 'on the ground', our moods and reactions permanently colour the world we see around us. We are always declaring that things 'are' good or bad, when we merely mean that we are wearing rose-tinted or dark-coloured spectacles. We think we are reacting to the outside world when we are merely reacting to our involuntary inner feelings. We are like bats who mistake shadows for solid objects. Because our moods change so quickly, we change direction from moment to moment, imagining that we are steering to avoid obstacles. It takes a sudden crisis, or a surge of deep purpose, to make us see things as they really are; otherwise, the shadow-play of our own mental states keeps us in a condition analogous to trance.

'Gliding' rescues us from the dream by permitting a bird's-eye-view. Once we are off the ground, we realise that most of our strength is wasted in dealing with trivial or negative emotions; we are like wrestlers who tie themselves in knots. These emotions keep us confined to the ground. This in turn explains the observation made in an earlier chapter: that we all spend most of our lives in a state analogous to Janet's 'hysteria', and that we regard this as *normal* consciousness. In fact, it is so contracted that we can hardly breathe. A narrow, anxiety-ridden consciousness is inevitable when we spend our lives in such a state of psychological confusion. So is a great deal of violence and over-reaction; gliding makes us aware that we over-react to almost everything.

The mind has a series of internal barriers, like lock-gates on a canal. Once you have got inside a certain barrier, it is difficult to get out, as I discovered when I became trapped within the panic barrier. Our 'normal' consciousness is another such barrier. And each barrier represents a further separation from the 'source of power, meaning and purpose', the spring of vitality whose origin is in the subconscious mind. Many philosophers of the nineteenth century—including Schopenhauer and Nietzsche—believed that man fell into 'sin' when he learned to think. It enabled him to grasp the world more clearly, but it separated him from his subconscious mind. There is more than an element of truth in this view. If you wake up in the middle of the night and begin to think about money, or try to work out a mathematical puzzle, you will find it difficult to get back to sleep. The use of reasoning faculty has dragged you away from the warm depths of the subconscious. If you can fill your mind with *images*—velvet curtains, drifting clouds, immense buildings—you sink gently back into the world of the unconscious.

As you pass into unconsciousness, you linger briefly in a twilight realm that has been labelled the hypnogogic state.

Everyone has experienced these states, if only for a few seconds. And anyone who takes the trouble to reflect on them will observe the most astonishing thing about them: that these images seem totally independent of 'you'; it is like watching a surrealistic film on television or in the cinema. It is almost as if you had another person inside you, hurling these images up into your brain like a child throwing coloured balls over the roof. This might be an alarming thought if we were not fairly certain that the child is also 'you'. In his important book about the mystic Swedenborg,[4] Wilson Van Dusen, a professional psychologist, writes: . . . Whatever is true of the individual at that moment tends to be spontaneously represented or symbolised. For instance, I was meditating on the richness of the hypnogogic state and heard someone say "my liberal arts course." The liberal arts course is a representation of my feeling that the inner is varied and informative. I did not have the idea of liberal arts course in mind at that moment. . .'

He also notes that the subconscious seems to have a sense of humour. As Swedenborg, on the edge of sleep, was reflecting, that desire for position and wealth is vanity, 'I seemed to hear a hen cackling, as takes place at once after she has laid an egg.' Van Dusen cites his own experience as well: 'One morning while awakening, someone said, "Here is a mondo for you," and I opened my eyes to see the world. A "mondo" is a Japanese Zen term for a problem given by a master to plague the student in a productive way. My higher self was playing with me, saying: "You want a problem from your master? Here is a little one. Existence itself!". . .' Van Dusen has no doubt that these messages come from the 'higher self', not from some Freudian subconscious, and he speaks of his everyday personality as his 'little self'. His contention is that this higher self can contact us when we are on the edge of sleep—and perhaps in dreams—in a symbolic way, and that what it tells us is usually the truth about our own lives.

The same view has been developed by an English psychologist, Dr Rachel Pinney, who writes: 'When I have a problem that has touched me acutely and at depth I need to consult my unconscious about the problem; I also need to consult my God, the cosmos, the universal unconscious . . . I need to consult on the *total* human well-being which will emerge from the problem, not just my own.' She goes on to describe two methods of doing this: to be wakened shortly before her normal time, and to have a 'sleep-satiated dream'.

The example she cites concerns a prison officer with whom she clashed during a period she spent in prison for defying a court order. The female officer was widely disliked for her unpleasantness, which was directed particularly against lesbian inmates. Finally, Dr Pinney herself clashed with the warder, and her prison liberties were severely curtailed. 'I hated her for what she had done, but at some level I couldn't totally hate her because one of my good friends liked her.' She decided to consult her 'dreams'. She asked the officer on night duty to wake her up earlier than usual by merely repeating her name. The dream she was having as she woke up concerned the hated warder.

> In the dream, the officer was driving a car. It was something like a station wagon, with plenty of room behind. I noticed she was dropping off to sleep. I went up to her and very gently got near enough for body contact . . . and asked her if I could take over. She shook herself awake, denied being asleep, and went on driving. I stayed with her and saw that she again fell asleep. I took the wheel from her with concern and gentleness and successfully steered the car off the road.'

Her dream-self had realised that the woman was not evil, but only 'asleep at the wheel', slave of some automatic function. The insight enabled her to treat the warder with a certain sympathy and often to help some of her intended victims. In her paper describing the experience, she even speculates on whether it might not have been possible to do the same for Eichmann.

Van Dusen is convinced that Swedenborg's 'visions', in which he conversed with angels and brought back messages from the dead, were a kind of controlled hypnogogic state. It was basically the technique that Jung discovered in 1913: confrontation with the unconscious, and the ability to explore it through active imagination. 'One doesn't explore 'these things for long', says Van Dusen, 'without beginning to feel there is a greater wisdom in the inner processes than there is in ordinary consciousness.' And he concludes that the 'individual's sphere, in which he rules within his mind, is relatively small', the conclusion reached by every major psychologist of the past century.

How can this technique of 'dream study' be developed? Everyone who has written about it seems to agree that it is simply a matter of being sufficiently interested to make the effort. I accidentally discovered an interesting technique almost twenty years ago. I was sitting in an armchair in the cottage where we were then living, while a friend was playing a recording of Strauss's *Salome*. I was exceptionally tired and drifted off to sleep; but *Salome* is a fairly noisy opera, and it kept waking me up. Whenever I woke up, I listened to the music in a trance-like state, with intense enjoyment, and would feel myself slowly drifting towards sleep again. The music kept me hovering in the borderland between sleep and waking, and I was surprised that the sensation was so delightful. There was a languid feeling of total relaxation and also an 'expanded' sensation; it was like lying on the grass on a sunny afternoon with eyes half-closed, listening to birds and the sound of the sea. I have practised this technique many times in the intervening years. If I feel pleasantly tired in the evening, I put on a record of music I enjoy—something with climaxes is a good idea, otherwise you tend to drift into sleep—and make a gentle effort to stay awake as I listen. The only effort required is to avoid plunging into ordinary sleep, and this is aided by the music. The condition achieved is a variant on 'gliding', and it is easy to observe the strange images and ideas that float through the mind. Van Dusen remarks:

> Those who have explored these states come to feel like a vessel into which life is poured. Moreover, after much watching of thoughts coming forth on their own, one can detect the same process in normal waking consciousness. The little fringe thought that pops into one's head in the daytime is no longer seen as one's own creation. . . Some will be frightened by the idea that there is little that we actually rule in our mind. But this is the normal, common state. We are some kind of

coming and going, flowing life process. The main effect of watching this coming and going is a greater humility about how much one is master of.

This, says Van Dusen, is why Swedenborg, the proud author of many scientific works, felt that he had no right to put his name on his theological works.

For the modern psychologist, perhaps the most fascinating thing about Swedenborg is that his great religious 'conversion' was preceded by all kinds of strange dreams, of which he kept a record in a volume that has survived. Swedenborg was born in 1688, the son of a bishop, and became an engineer and geologist. Scientific works poured out of him in a flood until his fifty-sixth year, when he began to experience increasing distress and dissatisfaction. His dreams all involved images of anxiety and mistrust. He was standing by a machine and was caught up in a great wheel, which carried him into the air (this sounds like a symbolic warning against science); he was in a garden thinking of purchasing a fine bed when he noticed someone picking out bed bugs; he was lying beside a woman and felt between her thighs to discover her vagina had a set of teeth. The strains and dissatisfactions of his subconscious were forcing their way into consciousness; finally, he spent a whole night—eleven hours—in a semi-trance-like state, between sleeping and waking, observing hypnogogic images. Fortunately, Swedenborg was exceptionally good at interpreting his dream symbols; like Jung, he learned to come to terms with his unconscious. The culminating dream was unambiguous; after a great wind had flung him on his face, he held a conversation with Jesus, who urged him to do something about his life. It was then that he began to study the Bible, to experience ecstatic trances, and to see the 'visions' that have made his works a matter of controversy ever since.

Swedenborg claimed that he visited heaven and hell and conversed with spirits; he also gave accounts of travel to the moon and the planets. He described the inhabitants of the moon as being like children with thunderous voices, while those of Mars were piebald and lived entirely on fruit and vegetable seeds. But then, when the widow of the Dutch ambassador wanted to know the whereabouts of a receipt for a silver tea service—the silversmith was demanding a second payment—Swedenborg contacted her husband in 'heaven' and told her that the receipt would be found in a secret drawer in the bureau, and the information proved to be accurate. He was able to give the Queen of Sweden an equally accurate message from her dead brother, the Prince Royal of Prussia. How can we reconcile the contradiction? The answer becomes clear if we turn to his accounts of his visits to the spirit world. The following is taken at random from *The True Christian Religion* (para 332):

> I once heard loud shouts which sounded as if they were bubbling up through water from lower regions; from the left came the shout: 'Oh, how just!', from the right: 'Oh, how learned!', and from behind: 'Oh, how wise!' And as I wondered whether there could be any just, learned or wise persons in hell, I strongly desired to see the truth of the matter. A voice from heaven then said to me: 'You shall see and hear.' So I departed in the spirit and saw before me an opening, which I approached and examined; and behold!, there was a ladder, and by this I descended. When I had got down, I saw a plain covered with shrubs intermixed with thorns and nettles. I inquired whether this was hell, and was told that it was the lower earth which is immediately above hell. . .

He goes on to tell how he saw a group of corrupt judges who were crying, 'Oh, how just.' The description of the building they were in is extraordinarily precise, as are all Swedenborg's descriptions of places. A man who is merely writing in parables does not bother with this kind of accuracy: 'an amphitheatre built of brick and roofed with black tiles. In the midst of the amphitheatre appeared a fireplace, into which the stokers were casting pine-pitch dipped in sulphur and bitumen, the light of which, by its flickerings and plastered walls, formed representations of birds of the twilight and night.' We feel that Swedenborg is describing something he has seen; not with his physical eyes but in a hypnogogic trance. A few pages later he confirms this: 'Once, when I awoke at daybreak, I saw . . . diversely shaped apparitions floating before my eyes; and when it was morning I saw a various display of false lights.' These, he says, were like rising and falling meteors. And then: 'Presently, my spiritual sight was opened'; and there followed a typical vision involving angels and spirits.

Apparently some kind of spontaneous hypnogogic vision, encountered on waking, could be turned into a kind of waking dream. So we might expect that his visions of the moon and planets would possess all the weird—if precise—features of a dream. However, the trance state is not unlike that of mediums. Swedenborg could have obtained his information about the secret drawer from the same source that map dowsers obtain information about mineral deposits or underground springs. That is to say, in the hypnogogic state, Swedenborg had escaped from the 'normal' state of contracted consciousness; he had 'completed his partial mind', or at least expanded it well beyond the normal limits, as far as the next set of 'lock gates'.

It was Armand Marie-Jacques de Chastenet, the Marquis de Puységur, who discovered that hypnosis had the power of releasing the subject's telepathic abilities. A girl called Madeleine was so susceptible to 'mental suggestion' that Puységur was able to use her for public demonstrations. Madeleine was hypnotised and stood with her eyes firmly closed. Then Puységur would point at some object in the room, or simply stare at it. With tightly closed eyes, Madeleine would walk over to it and touch it.

In itself, this experiment is hardly conclusive; Madeleine might have been peeping through half-closed eyelids; or she and the Marquis might have arranged the whole thing in advance. The Marquis would allay these suspicions by offering to allow anyone in the audience to direct Madeleine. All that was necessary, he said, was to concentrate unwaveringly on the object she was to find. The results were highly convincing. If someone fixed her firmly with his eyes, she would make her way to some object and touch it with her hand; if the person were timid or uncertain, Madeleine would waver and hesitate as she made her way towards it. One sceptic, whom Puységur calls 'the Baron de B.', suggested changing the locale of the experiments from Puységur's house to that of another sceptic, M. Mitonard. Mitonard was told to 'control' Madeleine, and for several minutes he made her walk around the room, sit down and take up various objects. Then Mitonard stood in front of her and simply stared hard at her. After a few moments, Madeleine reached into his pocket, took out three small screws, and handed them to him. Both Mitonard and Baron de B. were convinced.[5] As we have already seen,[6] the same phenomenon was demonstrated under laboratory conditions by Dr Paul Joire in the 1890s.

Telepathy was not the only unusual ability manifested by hypnotic subjects. In the 1820s, a certain M. Didier was hypnotised so frequently that he developed a curious habit of falling into spontaneous trances. He occasionally did this at the breakfast table, while reading the morning paper. His two young sons, Alexis and Adolphe, would watch fascinated as their father continued to read aloud from the newspaper, unaware that he had dropped it on the table. Sometimes the boys would remove the paper to another room, but their father would continue reading aloud as if he still held it.

In the early 1840s, Alexis took a job as a clerk in the office of an ex-cavalry officer, J. B. Marcillet, whose business was transport. One day at the theatre, Alexis answered a stage hypnotist's call for volunteers and proved to be an excellent subject, so good that Marcillet decided to become his manager. Alexis became one of the most celebrated 'somnambulists' in Europe. His brother Adolphe showed similar powers and was almost as famous. A typical Didier séance is described in the English journal *The Zoist*—which was largely concerned with hypnotism—for July 1844. Alexis was hypnotised by Marcillet, who simply made a few passes over him. Then Marcillet had Alexis stretch out his legs in front of him (he was seated in an armchair), and a man stood on his thighs without causing them to move. Alexis' eyes were bandaged with wadding and handkerchiefs and he was given a pack of cards which he opened and proceeded to run through, discarding the smaller cards at a great speed. Still blindfolded he played a game of ecarté with a certain Captain Daniell. When the narrator—E. S. Symes—played cards with him, he noticed that Alexis often left the cards lying face downward on the table and played without making mistakes. Finally, a large book was placed upright on the table, making a screen between the two players. Unable to see the cards that his opponent threw down, Alexis still played impeccably. It was evident that he was able to see the cards in his opponent's hands, as well as his own cards, lying face downward on the table.

Later, Captain Daniell held Alexis' hand and suggested that he travel with him mentally to his father's house. Didier was able to describe correctly the positions of doors and windows, pictures, ornaments and furniture. Daniell said that he made one mistake—about the colour of the curtains. But, on returning home, Daniell discovered that Alexis had been right.

The power Alexis displayed is known as 'travelling clairvoyance'. As described here, it sounds more like telepathy—except that he was correct about the colour of the curtains. E. J. Dingwall's account of Didier[7] cites dozens of other examples; in one case, he 'projected' himself from Cambridge to Fontainebleau, went into a house, located a bureau in a certain room and described (with an expression of disgust) a skull standing on it. What is even more curious is that Alexis was unable to *see* the skull but was able to describe it when ordered to 'touch' it.

Like many clairvoyants, Alexis felt his powers were diminished by the presence of sceptics. He was usually able to describe correctly the contents of sealed packages or envelopes; but if a sceptic handled the package first, his mind became a blank. The explanation seems to be provided by the classic 'sheep and goats' experiment, described on page 198; sceptics seem capable of generating a subconscious will *not* to make the experiment work.

We have so far discussed four methods of establishing contact with the unconscious: active imagination, hypnogogic experience, hypnotism and 'gliding'. Of the four, 'gliding' is probably the simplest and most accessible to the ordinary person, and there are few people unlucky enough never to have experienced it. It happens frequently when you relax in front of the fire and pour yourself a drink, or when you're having a pleasant conversation with someone you like and trust. It happens to children at Christmas time, when a whole range of reinforced stimuli—presents, Christmas carols, attractive decorations, smells of turkey and Christmas pudding, paper hats and crackers —build up a mood of intensity and delight. (When I was a child, I seem to recall that those bright silver ornaments on the Christmas tree exercised a kind of hypnotic effect; and if I stare at the blue-silver strip at the end of my typewriter ribbon, I experience a momentary flash of the same distinctive joy.)

In all these cases, it is easy to see how the effect operates. The mind relaxes into a state of *trust*, and what might be called 'pleasant expectancy'. Among the normal anxieties and tensions of modern life, we grow accustomed to a fairly constant flow of negative stimuli, and we finally slip into a state of negative expectation, as if flinching away from a blow. If we try to relax, this negative element may shatter the mood in a split second, as easily as you can destroy half-formed crystals by shaking the liquid. When 'pleasant expectancy' is slightly higher than usual, we can gradually de-condition ourselves out of the negative responses. And as we persuade the robot to cease its negative interference, our capacity for positive response steadily increases and *redoubles* with each positive stimulus. A person who has unusually strong reasons for feeling happiness or relief may quickly reach the normal 'ceiling' for positive response and pass straight through it into a 'floating' state of ecstasy. Such states are, in fact, fairly 'normal'; there is nothing ineffable or mystical about them. Yet because they make us realise that our everyday self is a mere fragment of 'us', they can produce an effect of stunning paradox and overwhelming joy that can produce floods of tears or an ecstatic sense of the goodness of the universe.

The state of 'gliding' also brings the feeling of 'absurd good news'; this is based on the astonished recognition of *how easy* it is to leave behind normal anxieties. There is also the realisation that most people fail to make the effort to get beyond their emotional debris because they fail to realise how little effort it takes. Most people spend their lives among scum and floating seaweed because they have no conception of the purity of the open sea. They fail to learn from their brief glimpses of a more relaxed consciousness, because what it tells them is so paradoxical and fails to fit in with their preconceptions about the world. Moreover, they are inclined to accept these glimpses as their 'due', as some kind of reward for past discomforts. So instead of trying to grasp and analyse them, they go to the opposite extreme and abandon all their critical faculties, relaxing into a kind of vapid ecstasy.

Gurdjieff was one of the few 'mystical' philosophers to recognise this truth and state it in so many words. By providing us with certain drives and instincts, nature has guaranteed our evolution up to a certain point. The basic need for sex, security and self-respect drives most of us to a certain level of achievement. But nature is totally uninterested as to whether we go beyond this point; we serve its purposes well enough if we produce healthy children. If we choose to take experience just as it comes, without thinking about it, nature has no objection, because healthy fools reproduce themselves just as efficiently as philosophers and saints, more so, in fact. So the man or woman who attempts to generate an intenser form of consciousness will get no help from nature, none of the pleasant ecstasies of sexual intercourse or the exhilaration of fighting. He will have to go it alone. And this is as it should be. For the peculiar, lonely exhilaration of the 'search for truth' is far more rewarding because it is 'unsubsidised'. Moreover, the sense of having done it solely by one's own effort brings a sudden recognition of *freedom*, a knowledge of the possibilities of the will. The process could be compared to the experience of a teenager who lives away from home for the first time and discovers that he or she is capable of cooking his own meals and making his own bed. This freedom can be bewildering, and offers possibilities of mistakes and disasters; yet it is also the beginning of adulthood.

Oddly enough, there *are* human beings for whom 'gliding' is a purely instinctive skill. Ramakrishna is an example. Even as a child, his natural response to beauty was so intense that he once fainted at the sight of a flock of white cranes flying across a black thunder cloud. Ramakrishna never tired of teaching his disciples to ignore negative emotions, to avoid saying: 'I am a fool, I am a weakling, I am a sinner.' Such notions, he said, prevented a man's spiritual progress; if he had been a sinner, he had better forget about it and concentrate on union with God. William Blake was another 'natural' mystic; at the age of eight, he looked up into a tree and saw that it was full of angels; on another occasion, he saw angels walking among the hay-makers. But eighteenth-century London was a less propitious place for a mystic than nineteenth-century India; Blake spent most of his life in poverty whereas Ramakrishna lived in the security of the temple of Kali.

Perhaps the most important natural mystic of the twentieth century was Yeats's friend George Russell; and his neglected writings are full of the insights of a man for whom 'gliding' was almost as natural as breathing.

Three years Yeats's junior, Russell was born in Lurgan, Northern Ireland, in 1867, the son of a clerk. Unlike Blake, he had no visions in childhood; but like Ramakrishna, he was intensely sensitive to beauty from an early age. In *Song and Its Fountains*,[8] he records how, at the age of four or five, he wandered into a park, and was so overwhelmed by 'some enchantment flickering about a clump of daffodils' that he had to lie down on the grass. When he read a story about a sword with a silver hilt and a steel-blue blade, he was enchanted by the words 'blue and silver' and later by the colours of lilacs and primroses. He notes: 'This love of colour seemed instinctive . . . and it was only in that retrospective meditation I could see that the harmonies which delighted me had been chosen by a deeper being and were symbolic of its nature.' That sentence must have been incomprehensible to most of

Russell's contemporaries, who were unfamiliar with the doctrine of magical correspondences as applied to colours.

When Russell was eleven, his family moved to Dublin, which he found a delightful change after the sectarian bitterness of Lurgan. He proved to be a good scholar with unusual aptitude for literature and art. When he left school in Rathmines, he attended art classes in the evening, but the family was too poor to send him to art school. At the Metropolitan School of Art in Kildare Street he met Yeats in 1884. Russell had just begun to write verse, and the two were to exert a powerful influence on one another. The meeting with Yeats came at exactly the right moment; about a week before, Russell had begun to experience visions and waking dreams. Significantly, he mentions[9] that at this time, his life was 'already made dark by those desires of body and heart with which we soon learn to taint our youth'. Russell's father—a Protestant—was deeply religious, with strong leanings towards Primitive Methodism; so these intense stirrings of sexual desire must have had a disturbing effect on the seventeen-year-old boy. The result was a build-up of psychological pressure such as we have already encountered in the cases of Jung and Swedenborg. Russell found that the pressures of the unconscious could invade the waking mind: 'walking along country roads, intense and passionate imaginations of another world, of an interior nature began to over-power me.'

A similar effect occurs if someone is kept awake for days on end; dreams begin to force their way into the conscious mind. 'They were like strangers who suddenly enter a house, who brush aside the doorkeeper, and who will not be denied.' This led to the realisation that 'they were the rightful owners and heirs of the house of the body, and the doorkeeper was only one who was for a time in charge, who had neglected his duty, and who had pretended to ownership. The boy who had existed before was an alien. . . Yet whenever the true owner was absent, the sly creature reappeared and boasted himself as master once more.' This was an astonishing insight for a teenager: that his body was not his own, that his ego was a mere fragment of some larger being. Even more astonishing, he began to conclude that his 'inner being [is] not one but many', a whole host of personalities, who might be brought into some kind of unity by an immense inner effort.

Perhaps the sexual conflict simply acted as a kind of depth charge to fling fragments of these inner selves into consciousness. Whatever the reason, the disturbance was followed by a reconciliation of the inner forces. And, like Ramakrishna after his suicide attempt with the sword,[10] Russell discovered that these states of intensity had become accessible at will. There was a continuous sense of being close to hidden forces of nature, and a feeling that nature itself was only a veil over some deeper reality:

> As I walked in the evening down the lanes scented by the honeysuckle my senses were expectant of some unveiling about to take place, I felt that beings were looking in upon me out of the true home of man. . . The tinted air glowed before me with intelligent significance like a face, a voice.[11]

A climactic 'vision' occurred as he lay on the hill of Kilmasheogue:

> . . . one warm summer day lying idly on the hillside, not then thinking of anything but the sunlight, and how sweet it was to drowse there, when suddenly I felt a fiery heart throb, and knew it was personal and intimate, and started with every sense dilated and intent . . . and then the heart of the hills was opened to me, and I knew there was no hill for those who were there, and they were unconscious of the ponderous mountains piled above the palaces of light, and the winds were sparkling and diamond clear, yet full of colour as an opal, as they glittered through the valley, and I knew the Golden Age was all about me, and it was we who had been blind to it but that it had never passed away from the world.[12]

In order to make a living, Russell worked in various offices where his experiences do not seem to have been too unpleasant, as he acknowledges gratefully in *Candle of Vision*. He also continued the attempt to capture some of his visions on canvas. Like Blake, Russell is an important but not a great painter. One of his early paintings was conceived in a state of intense excitement; he was trying to capture the idea of God creating man. As he lay awake, wondering what to call the picture, he experienced a sense of expectancy, and when his attention was almost overstrained with anticipation, a voice seemed to say: 'Call it the birth of Aeon.' The word Aeon excited him although he had no idea of what it meant. In the library a couple of weeks later he was waiting for an art magazine when his eye fell on a book on the table and caught the word 'Aeon'. It was a dictionary of religions, and Russell discovered that it was not his own invention but had been used by the Gnostics 'to designate the first created beings'.[13] This was not in fact correct. The Gnostics, as we have already noted, believed that the universe was not created by God but by some inferior god or demiurge, who falsely believes himself to be the ultimate godhead. This false god created six more demiurges, or archons, to help him with creation. The universe in which man finds himself is a vast prison, like those endless dungeons in Piranesi's engravings, and the earth is its bottommost dungeon. Above us are a number of heavens or 'spheres', which are emanations of the original godhead; in most Gnostic systems there are seven, although in some there are as many as 365. These 'heavens' are, in fact, the Aeons. Man's problem is to struggle upward through the Aeons to achieve reunion with God. In other Gnostic systems, the Aeons become vast epochs of time (which, say the Gnostics, is an illusion) which lie between the soul and its ultimate goal. This is how the word 'aeon' came to be used of epochs of time.

So Russell was mistaken in believing that Aeons is a name for the first created beings; however, the mistake is not important. What excited him was to discover that his 'own' word was part of one of the most ancient of all religious systems. Moreover, in the two weeks between 'hearing' the word and seeing it in the library, he had experienced waking dreams in which a being called Aeon was a kind of Miltonic rebel against God. Now he looked up the Gnostics in Neander's *Church History* and found a story to the effect that the original demiurge who created the universe was called Aeon. The legend was part of the theology of the Sabians or Mandaeans, a small breakaway Christian sect of Lower Mesopotamia, whose religion combines Christian, Jewish and Gnostic elements. Again, it seemed a startling confirmation of his notion that there are things in the mind that have been there since remote ages. In fact, George Russell had formulated the idea of the collective unconscious at least a quarter of a century before Jung. He wrote: 'I believed then, and still believe, that the immortal in us has memory of all its wisdom, or, as Keats puts it in one of his letters, there is an ancestral wisdom in man and we can if we wish drink of that old wine of heaven.'

Russell was so deeply impressed by the Gnostic religion, and by the concept of the rebel Aeon, that he decided to adopt the first two letters of Aeon as his pseudonym; hence the name under which he eventually became famous: AE.

From these early Gnostic studies came one of Russell's most interesting ideas: that there might be some primeval language that sprang directly from man's unconscious. At about this time Russell and Yeats founded the group called the Hermetic Students, and the notion of a primeval language is clearly influenced by the theory of the magical correspondences. In a strange vision, he had seen a book with magic symbols on each page; the symbols had vanished to be replaced by parts of the human body; he saw a series of fiery colours mounting the spinal column to a ball of white fire in the brain, then becoming wing-like pulses on either side of the head. As the vision closed, he saw only the symbol of the caduceus of Mercury—the rod with intertwined serpents—on the last page. It was some time before Russell learned of the Hindu doctrine of the force of *kundalini*, the vital force that rises from the base of the spine, vitalising the *chakras* or spiritual centres, until it reaches the 'third eye' in the brain. But if symbols and planets and colours and flowers and precious stones can be interconnected, why not individual sounds and syllables? (Joyce's *Finnegan's Wake* seems to be based on a similar theory.) Russell worked for years trying to reconstruct this '*ur*-language', although he never completed the task.

All these events convinced Russell that the external world somehow responds to the laws of man's inner being. This is perhaps the most central and important of all 'magical' doctrines. Russell discovered that he encountered people—and ideas—as he needed them, so that 'I could prophesy from the uprising of new moods in myself that I, without search, would soon meet people of a certain character, and so I met them.' One of them was Yeats. But there were many others, even 'people [met] seemingly by accident on country roads' turned out to be 'intimates of the spirit'.

> I remember one day how that clerk with wrinkled face, blinking eyes and grizzly beard, who never seemed, apart from his work, to have interests other than his pipe and paper, surprised me by telling me that the previous midnight he waked in his sleep, and some self of him was striding to and fro in the moonlight in an avenue mighty with gigantic images; and that dream self he had surprised had seemed to himself unearthly in wisdom and power.

There were also the coincidences, like the library book open at the right page.

I have glanced in passing at a book left open by some one in a library, and the words first seen thrilled me, for they confirmed a knowledge lately attained in vision. At another time a book taken down idly from a shelf opened at a sentence quoted from a Upanishad, scriptures then to me unknown, and this sent my heart flying eastwards because it was the answer to a spiritual problem I had been brooding over an hour before.

All this brought a deep conviction that in the flux of life 'there was meaning and law; that I could not lose what was my own; I need not seek, for my own would come to me; if any passed it was because they were no longer mine.' He also came to believe that everyone with whom we come into contact has some affinity for us, and that we get as much out of their companionship as we deserve—or, perhaps, are able to understand.

Russell now discovered a new use for his power of active imagination. Most of us cannot clearly recall what happened the day before yesterday, and certainly not this time last month. Russell commenced a system of meditation which started with the present moment, then tried to recall his own past. At first he found it difficult, but practice brought increasing proficiency. No doubt his power to surrender to hypnogogic vision was helpful. He already had a certain ability to touch subconscious springs of feeling; what he was now trying to do was to tap those hidden 'tape recordings' of memory that Wilder Penfield was able to stimulate with an electric probe in the brain. The detailed childhood recollections of his autobiographical books were one result. But he also found that he had sudden intuitions of other existences, previous lives. He told his friend Carrie Rea in a letter that he was convinced that he had been a friend of William Blake in one of his previous lives, and had lived in ancient Assyria. He was also convinced that he had lived in Chaldea, ancient Egypt, pre-Columbian America, Gaelic Ireland, and had been a soldier in a Spanish army of the ninth century fighting the Moors.

He discovered that ancient ruins conjured up definite pictures in his mind. His biographer, Henry Summerfield, relates: 'Visiting the remains of a chapel in Ulster, he saw the worshippers who had once prayed there, and noticed how the fervour of a kneeling red-robed woman contrasted with the pompous vanity of the altar boy and the proud detachment of an onlooker. At prehistoric mounds, he was able by a deliberate effort to conjure up visions of the Gaelic past, and

to see clearly the material details of its crude civilisation.' He even
seems to have seen something that sounds like a UFO: 'It was probably
soon after [this] . . . that he first saw a fleet of majestic airships bearing beautifully robed passengers over the mountains; five or six years
later one of the mysterious vessels reappeared and passed so close to
him that it was within arm's reach.'

Russell developed remarkable powers of telepathy. Yeats tells a
story of how a young lady told Russell: 'I am so unhappy', and was
embarrassed when Russell replied: 'You will be perfectly happy this
evening at seven o'clock'—in fact, the time she was supposed to meet
her boyfriend. On another occasion, as he sat beside an office colleague, he had a sudden vision of an old man in a small dark shop and a
red-haired girl behind him; his companion verified that Russell had
seen his father and sister. He was sitting there with his mind momentarily emptied of thought when the 'vision' came. Henry Summerfield spoke to Russell's son, who testified that his father often
knew facts about people that he could not have learned by normal
means.

In 1889, when he was twenty-two, Russell gave up art—he told
Yeats it would weaken his will—and joined the Theosophical Society,
apparently uninfluenced by the widespread belief that Madame
Blavatsky was a fake. Five years earlier, a housekeeper with a grudge
had 'exposed' her employer in a Bombay magazine, asserting that
various 'psychic' effects were achieved by trickery; not long before, it
had been discovered that parts of the famous 'Mahatma Letters',
supposedly dedicated by a supernatural being called Koot Hoomi,
were lifted from the work of an American spiritualist, Henry Kiddle.
But, in spite of the scandal, Russell and Yeats became Theosophists.
An article on Russell's 'primeval language' had been published in *The
Theosophist* two years before. Now Russell began to practise the
Hindu system of meditation, deliberately attempting to arouse the
spirit-force, *kundalini*. He describes how 'once at the apex of intensest
meditation I awoke that fire in myself of which the ancients have
written, and it ran like lightning up my spinal cord, and my body
rocked with the power of it, and I seemed to myself to be standing in a
fountain of flame, and there were fiery pulsations as of wings about
my head, and a musical sound not unlike the clashing of cymbals with
every pulsation.'[14] He suddenly recalled the danger involved in the

awakening of this power—that in one who was not completely purified, it could 'turn downward and vitalise his darker passions and awaken strange frenzies and inextinguishable desires'—and deliberately refrained from attempting to open the 'third eye'. His friend H. W. Nevinson asserted that he had twice seen Russell deliver a speech when possessed by this power, and could see lights and hear voices; afterwards Russell could no longer remember what he said.[15] Eventually, he ceased to attempt to arouse the *kundalini* power; his natural powers of vision were enough.

Yeats and Russell drew apart after 1890. Yeats had become a member of the Golden Dawn, and Russell distrusted ritual magic. Although he accepted all the basic principles of magic—as his work reveals—Russell remained basically a mystic, absorbed in his vision of the fundamental oneness of the universe and his certainty that individual consciousness is only a tributary of the collective consciousness of humanity.

But the difference between Yeats and Russell was more fundamental than this. Russell's mystical and religious insights were deeper than anything Yeats ever experienced. Yeats remained hard-headed, consumed by intellectual curiosity, intent upon creating a bridge between the universe of the mystic and the universe of the ordinary man. The result is that Yeats is a great poet while Russell is a minor poet. Russell wrote at least as much poetry as Yeats, much of it delicate and beautiful:

> Its edges foamed with amethyst and rose,
> Withers once more the old blue flower of day;
> There where the ether like a diamond glows
> Its petals fade away.

Judged simply as poetry, there is something soft about this. The language is careless; you get the feeling that he never spent more than a few moments over any line. This is true of most of AE's poetry and, to a lesser extent, of his prose. His two 'mystical' books, *Candle of Vision* and *Song and Its Fountains*, from which I have quoted so extensively, are certainly among the most important of their kind; but you never cease to be aware that he was influenced by Emerson and Thomas Traherne's *Centuries of Meditation*. There is a certain lack of concreteness that finally becomes cloying. Typically, Russell disliked Yeats's later poetry with its more down-to-earth flavour and was distressed at Yeats's later alterations to the early poems.

As a result of his naturally mystical temperament, Russell never realised his potential as a writer—and, possibly, even as a human being. While Yeats was struggling to conquer literary London, Russell was working as a book-keeper at a large Dublin drapery store, Pim's, and spending his evening with fellow Theosophists and mystics, among whom was an English girl, Violet North, who became his wife. In 1891, he moved into a house in Upper Ely Place, together with a number of other 'disciples', and in this semi-monastic community he lived for seven years. Since he was so late in maturing, this existence suited him ideally. He saw many visions involving celestial beings from other levels of reality (he identified them with the Hindu *devas* or angels) and came to recognise that human beings 'live like frogs at the bottom of a marsh knowing nothing of that Many-Coloured Earth which is superior to this we know, yet related to it as soul to body'. At the same time, he was deeply involved with the rising Irish literary movement and became convinced that Ireland could become a spiritual centre for modern civilisation. He was as fervent an Irish patriot as Yeats. So when, in 1897, Yeats suggested that he should work for Horace Plunkett, founder of the Irish Agricultural Organisation Society, Russell was able to abandon other-worldly mysticism for practical patriotism without any sense of betraying his ideals. In fact, Russell had reached the age—thirty—when he needed contact with the real world. His task was to promote the cooperative movement among backward Irish farmers. It determined his direction for the remainder of his life. For the next eight years he travelled around Ireland, making speeches and organising loans and then, from 1905 until 1914, was the editor of the cooperative movement's newspaper, *The Irish Homestead*. The years of 'the troubles' were a difficult time for Russell, since he was an ardent pacifist, and he was often plunged into depression. In 1923, after the British had granted independence to Eire, Russell became the editor of *The Irish Statesman*, a 'non-political' newspaper, also financed by Plunkett. In this capacity he became, as Henry Summerfield calls him, 'the conscience of a nation', a voice of reason and sanity in a country that is inclined to allow emotion to overrule logic. His books had brought him fame in his own country and a certain amount of celebrity abroad, perhaps because of the association of his name with those of Yeats and Joyce. Yet after his death—from a cancer, in 1935—his work was largely forgotten, and there have been few reprints. The first full-length biography appeared forty years after his death.

Russell's closest friends and associates would have argued that he was perfectly fulfilled, within his own terms. He was a mystic and a visionary, and he succeeded in living out his life without compromise. Yet when he gave up his semi-monastic existence for the work of spreading the Irish cooperative movement, he was inspired by the example of the Buddha, who renounced Nirvana to bring spiritual enlightenment to other men. Russell never believed that his only business in life was to reach mystical self-fulfillment; like the Buddha, he wanted to bring it to others. And in a sense he succeeded; his kindness, his detachment, his idealism, influenced a whole generation of Irishmen who could never have been persuaded to read the Upanishads. His real influence should have been through literature; he was as great a spirit as Shaw or Yeats and deserved to become known to as many people. Yet for all his spiritual insight, for all his brilliance as a talker and his natural talent as a writer, he remains the author of only two small volumes of 'spiritual autobiography', one bad novel,[16] one volume of assorted essays and reviews,[17] and a few volumes of beautiful but essentially minor poetry. And the reason seems to be that he never achieved the kind of self-discipline necessary to make the best use of his talents. He was *too* close to his subconscious, and its warm security prevented him from making the kind of effort that produces great literature.

This raises a point of crucial importance to the main argument of this book. Security is essential to human existence; it is also one of our worst enemies. To begin with, it slows down the learning process. Everyone who has been in a strange town knows that the easiest way to get to know it is to walk around it *alone*. If you are driven around by friends who live there, it takes ten times as much effort to get to know the place. A subconscious sense of security causes your attention to go to sleep. When you walk around alone, navigating with the aid of a street map, you notice everything. Your robot is also located in the subconscious, and it is he who goes to sleep when you feel secure.

Security can even destroy life itself. This is interestingly illustrated in the story of an experiment conducted in 1958 by two zoologists, Jay Boyd Best and Irvin Rubinstein.[18] Rubinstein and Best were investigating the learning powers of a primitive creature known as the flatworm or planarion worm. Planaria have no stomachs, rectums or digestive systems, and their brains and nervous systems are so primordial as to be almost non-existent. Yet planaria showed a remarkable aptitude for learning, demonstrated by means of a simple experiment. The worms were placed in a Y-shaped plastic tube with water in it. (Planaria, being aquatic creatures, need water to live.) At a certain point, the water was drained away, and the alarmed worms started out in search of more. They soon reached the parting of the ways. One branch of the Y was lighted, the other was dark. The lighted branch led to water, the other didn't. In no time at all, the worms had learned to choose the fork that led to water.

Then a strange thing happened. The worms began choosing wrongly. After still more trials, they simply lay still and refused to move when the water was drained out, as if they were saying: 'Oh God, not again!' They actually preferred to die rather than move.

The scientists considered every possible explanation for this perverse conduct and rejected them all. Finally, one of them made the apparently absurd suggestion: Suppose the worms got *bored*? This seemed unlikely for creatures with hardly any brains, but it was the only answer left. They devised an experiment to find out. This time they made the task far more difficult. They used *two* tubes, one with smooth plastic inside, the other with rough plastic, so the worms could feel the difference with their bellies. In one of them the water was down the dark alleyway; in the other, down the lighted one. Starting with a new set of worms, they transferred them from one tube to the other between each trial. This time, only one third of the worms succeeded in mastering the problem and finding the water. But this third *never regressed*. They never chose the wrong alleyway, or lay down and died. So the problem *had* been boredom. The first lot of worms had learned too easily.

When we learn to do something 'automatically', it is transferred from the conscious to the subconscious mind. And, depending upon how much *effort* it has cost us to learn, it carries with it a small label which says 'Important' or 'Unimportant'. Whenever we do an 'Important' thing, our subconscious robot sends up the appropriate amount of energy. For 'Unimportant' things, it sends up a very small amount. So if an 'Unimportant' thing goes wrong, or has to be repeated over and over again, we soon run out of energy and patience and become careless or discouraged. As we all know, repetition of some boring task leaves us exhausted and enervated. This is not because we have no energy left; there is plenty in the reservoir of the subconscious. But the robot won't let us have it. Like planaria, human beings often die of boredom—not because they can't be bothered to find water, but because they can't be bothered to take some vital precaution, like remembering to turn off an oil stove before they go to bed. When the planaria had to put twice as much effort into learning, the skill was transferred to the subconscious mind with a 'Very Important' label, which ensured that they never became bored by it.

Russell's writing, like his mystical experience, came to him too easily; consequently he ceased to develop beyond the age of about thirty. When he was dying in London, someone told him that Yeats was also in town; Russell said he didn't want to meet him, because they had known one another so long they had nothing to say to one another; the sad confession of a man who had long since ceased to make new discoveries. It was Yeats, for whom writing was always a painful effort, who taught himself to use his intellect, who got 'second wind', and continued to develop to the end of his life. If Russell had been forced to put as much effort into achieving mystical illumination as the 'double ambiguity' planaria put into learning to find water, he could have become the greatest spiritual force of his age.

6

Revelations

—◆—

The work of AE raises the fundamental problem of 'revelation'. Like all the mystics, he assures us that the world we see and touch is somehow an illusion, and that the real world is quite different. He says he knows this to be true because he has *seen* it.

We are willing to consider what he has to say with an open mind, but it is not easy. We find ourselves in a solid world of familiar objects. We have learned to find our way around in this 'real' world. It certainly looks logical and consistent enough—except, perhaps, in certain moments when we are touched with doubt like a twinge of toothache. (When did the universe begin, and what was there *before* that? What ceases to exist when someone dies?) If we are mistaken, we want to know precisely *where* we went wrong. Galileo didn't simply tell us we were wrong about the sun going round the earth; he explained precisely why, and how the error came about. We feel that Russell and the mystics owe us the same kind of explanation. Above all, we want to know why this universe looks so convincing if it is unreal.

To do the mystics and visionaries justice, they have often done their best to explain themselves clearly. But the results have seldom been particularly enlightening. What seems to be required at this point is an attempt to find some kind of cumulative logic in their explanations and descriptions.

We can conveniently begin with that master of straightforward exposition, William James, whose attitude to mysticism was somewhat ambivalent. In the early 1880s, James tried sniffing pure nitrous oxide, 'laughing gas'. He reported that 'the keynote of the experience is the tremendously exciting sense of an intense metaphysical illumination'. He went on: 'The mind sees all the logical relations of being with an apparent subtlety and instantaneity to which its normal consciousness offers no parallel.' Here again, the word 'instantaneity' emphasises that the experience was based on *seeing* rather than mere 'knowing'. Under nitrous oxide, James felt that opposites had ceased to exist—good and evil, mine and yours, subject and object. 'It is impossible to convey an idea of the torrential identification of opposites as it streams through the mind.' He made rambling, jumbled notes with sentences like: 'What's mistake but a kind of take? What's nausea but a kind of ausea?' He also notes that the rapture of viewing this endless blending of opposites would quite suddenly change into horror and futility or gloomy fatalism. When the experience was over there would be a sense of anticlimax; he compares it to watching a marvellous sunset on a snowy mountain peak, then seeing it fade into a black extinguished brand.[1]

In an essay called 'A Suggestion about Mysticism', James cites the example of a man called Frederick Hall, who experienced a similar revelation under ether:

> When one of the doctors made a remark to the other, he chuckled, for he realised that these friends 'believed they saw real things and causes, but they *didn't*, and I did . . . I was where the causes *were* and to see them required no more mental ability than to recognise a colour as blue. . . The knowledge of how little [the doctors] actually did see, coupled with their evident feeling that they saw all there was, was funny to the last degree.'

Again, there is the sense of actually *seeing* something we normally know merely as a concept, the bird's-eye view. James himself had experienced the same mystical sensation without ether or nitrous oxide; in the midst of a conversation, some memory of a past experience seemed to remind him of another experience, and this in turn of another 'and so on, until the process faded out, leaving me amazed at the sudden vision of increasing ranges of distant fact'. Again, the sense of being jerked into the air and seeing far horizons. James observed that all this happened so quickly 'that my intellectual processes could not keep up the pace. The content was thus entirely lost to retrospection'.[2]

Consequently, of course, he could neither remember much about it nor, above all, set out to *recapture* it.

This is the major problem of using drugs as a means of 'contact with the subsconscious'. They can achieve the desired effect of widening the bounds of the normal ego and helping to 'complete the partial mind'; but the sheer ease of the achievement brings the disadvantages of Rubinstein and Best's planaria: a tendency *unconsciously* to devalue what has been too easily achieved. The fact that the devaluation is unconscious makes it far more dangerous, and increases the risk of 'the Bombard effect', rejection of everyday consciousness. Thomas De Quincey, the 'English opium eater', describes how, under laudanum, he was able to bring together 'all creatures, birds, beasts, reptiles, all trees and plants, usages and appearances, that are found in all tropical regions. . . From kindred feelings, I soon brought Egypt and all her gods under the same law. I was stared at, hooted at, grinned at, chattered at, by monkeys, by parakeets, by cockatoos.' Opium endowed De Quincey with the magical power of 'active imagination'. But it also produced all the familiar after-effects: lassitude, spleen, boredom, inability to complete a task.

In 1953, Aldous Huxley took a dose of the drug mescalin, one of the hallucinogens, and described its effects so attractively and persuasively in *The Doors of Perception* that the 'psychedelic' craze swept across Europe and America. Mescalin made everything look far more vivid and real, as if reality had been lighted up from inside, and produced again the sense of being above petty emotions and trivial worries. Huxley was so impressed that he recommended that mescalin and other 'psychedelic' drugs be made as freely available as tobacco or alcohol. But he overlooked one of the chief disadvantages of the 'anaesthetic revelation', the 'bad trip', which can be many times worse than delirium tremens. I quote from an account of such an experience written at my request by the American composer, Jerry Neff:

I was already feeling tired and disoriented, and the classical 'bad trip' I then proceeded to undergo, with a partial dissolution of the ego and an unbearable terror, was very near the vastation experience as described by William James or the kind of thing given in a clinical account of paranoia. I knew that unutterable horror which lies just under the surface of life—the veneer of civilisation—and is bound up with existence itself. (I thought of an interesting metaphor: the sleepwalker who wakens and finds himself on a narrow wall with a thousand-foot drop on either side.) . . . I needed to be told who I was and reassured about the normalcy of everything.

The experience is obviously analogous to my own 'panic attacks'. The problem here is that when the mind is 'gliding', the slightest 'push' can send it in one direction or another; it could be compared to carrying a flat tray full of water; the slightest tilt will cause it to flood over.

Another extract from the same letter describes the classic mystical experience:

Good fortune procured for us some extraordinary acid: a type called 'windowpane'; it appears semi-transparent, each tab like a tiny fleck of mica. The purity, one assumes, is important to the effect produced—as in good whiskey. . .

It was one of those gorgeous California days: golden sunlight and a clear sky. In the little back garden, a charmingly enclosed spot like a room with greenery for walls, I remember seeing the dew still fresh on the grass and the exquisite garden-of-Eden look about everything. Behind it, however, one could still sense the teeming city. The day warmed and we relaxed in bathing suits in the half shade of the garden, reclining and looking up into the marvellous blue of the sky.

My thoughts began to wander and, out loud to Jill [his wife], I began to construct a concept of reality and man's place in it. I know I could not now do it the same way again. The primary sources were: Yeats's poetry and his idea of art, magic, reincarnation, as much as I could understand of *A Vision*; different kinds of time, i.e. the cyclical and historical concepts; ideas gleaned from Einstein and Arthur Clarke . . . John Cage's many stories concerning Ramakrishna and Zen. . . At one point, two jet fighter planes flew over. I felt I was able to *realise* what they were, to reach up and touch them with my mind. I simply *knew* all the technology and power as well as the uselessness and waste involved . . . I recalled Shelley's 'Life like a dome of many coloured glass/Stains the white radiance of eternity.' Curiously, I kept thinking that Eliot, great as he was, had not seen the 'truth' as Yeats had, and had misled himself and a whole generation. (I don't now think this.) The whole process became dizzying, like a juggler attempting to juggle several more balls than he is used to. I remembered Alan Watts's remark after you had told him how mescalin had opened up your thought channels but destroyed your ability to think or concentrate. He said that on acid it *was* possible to concentrate, to go 'in, in, in' as he put it, until a tremendous intensity had been achieved. This seemed to be happening to me. I felt as if I had scaled an incredible tower of a spidery structural steel up to a vast height, like a 'god's eye view', but without looking down. I had been reading from Auden's book of essays *The Dyer's Hand*, and recalled his remark: 'Time is not a road, it is not a river, it is a room where one notices different things.' This suddenly seemed to make the time problem clear. Then I did a mental act of 'looking down' from this enormous height, and at that moment something happened to my brain and nervous system.

The feeling was as if every brain cell had been simultaneously activated. I lost consciousness, but had no sense of that. In front of my eyes, as if in a dream, I could see only what seemed like a blazing pool of white or slightly golden light—what you might see if it were possible to look straight into the sun. But I did not see it so much as *feel* it, and that feeling was one of absolute ecstasy, involving every 'good' sensation and every 'rightness' imaginable, and in a moral sense as well. This bliss included benevolence, joy and reconciliation of opposites—literally *everything* all at once. . . The incredible thing is the absolute certainty that what one is seeing is the *real* reality—a timeless source of all that exists. . .

I have no idea how long I was 'there'. Afterward it seemed like three or four seconds perhaps. The intensity was so tremendous. In Fred Hoyle's story "The Black Cloud", a scientist is given information from an enormous galactic intelligence which, in attempting to explain itself, ends up killing him by overloading his brain circuitry. I now wonder if something like this could conceivably happen in a transcendent spiritual experience.

The next thing I recall was flashing back to the garden with a sense of being awakened roughly as if from a divine dream. It was like a taste of dishwater after two or three spoonfuls of superb soup. My first response was despair. 'I want to go back in.' I actually screamed and remember rolling on the grass tearing at it in frustration, literally weeping at the prospect of having to live 'here' when 'there' was obviously the place to be.

Perhaps the oddest part of his experience is that his wife had seen several flashes of brilliant white light' around his head at the time he was undergoing the experience.

When telling me this story—an account that so fascinated me that I asked him to write it down—he mentioned that the after-effects had been negative: after such an experience of intensity, everyday life seemed dull and futile—the 'Bombard effect'. He concludes his written account by saying: 'As for me, changes in outlook, life style, daily habits—hardly any. As the Zen story says: "Now that I'm enlightened, I'm as miserable as ever."'

Jerry Neff's account of the 'anaesthetic revelation' makes it clear that the subject *can* experience a far deeper state of reality than is accessible to ordinary consciousness. Yet he was unable to bring much of the inner content of the experience into everyday consciousness. Neither has he been able to use the experience to re-establish contact with the inner forces. There is still no bridge between this deeper reality and ordinary consciousness.

In his important book *The Centre of the Cyclone* (1972), Dr John Lilly has attempted to go one stage farther, and the results are remarkably consistent with what we have so far learned of 'the geography of consciousness'. The book is subtitled 'An Autobiography of Inner Space', and is basically an account of Lilly's experiences with LSD, hypnosis, and various forms of meditation.

Lilly explains how, after a bad trip on LSD, he accidentally injected himself with a small quantity of detergent foam, which produced headache, vomiting, and eventually resulted in coma. In this state, he says, he 'left his body'. 'I became a focused centre of consciousness and travelled into other spaces and met other beings, entities, or consciousnesses.' 'There is a golden light permeating the whole space everywhere in all directions, out to infinity.' Two beings, who seem to be some kind of guardian angels, overwhelm him with a sense of love and concern. (He mentions that he had encounted them earlier in life, when under anaesthetic.) 'They say that . . . they are with me always, but that I am not usually in a state to perceive them. I am in a state to perceive them when I am close to the death of the body. In this state there is no time. There is an immediate perception of the past, present and future as if in the present moment.' (The similarity to Lethbridge's 'second whorl of the spiral' is worth noting.) On recovering consciousness, Lilly found he was blind; but since the 'beings' had assured him that all would be well, he felt no fear. During the blindness he experienced hallucinations, or visions, that were like waking dreams.

The result of the experience was a determination to attempt a systematic exploration of 'inner space' using LSD and a sensory-deprivation chamber. During this first experience, he found himself in a totally black and silent space which he labelled 'the absolute zero point' or the centre of the cyclone. 'This became a reference point to which I could return in case things got too chaotic or too stimulating in other spaces.' A later 'trip', in which he increased the dose of LSD, seems to have brought an experience closely similar to Jerry Neff's: 'I became a bright luminous point of consciousness, radiating light, warmth, and knowledge. I moved into a space of astonishing brightness, a space filled with golden light, with warmth and with knowledge.' The two 'guardians' were again experienced; Lilly was told: 'You still have some evasions to explore before you can progress to the level at which you are existing at the moment. You can come and permanently be in this state. However, it is advisable that you achieve this through your own efforts while still in the body; so that you can exist both here and in the body simultaneously.' From this it seems clear that Lilly believes that he was, in some sense, no longer inhabiting his physical body during these experiences.

From the point of view of paranormal research, perhaps the most interesting thing about Lilly's account is his conviction that during two of his 'trips', he experienced telepathic contact with a girl on the other side of the United States. Lying in his own bed in a trance state, he seemed to be in her bedroom, when suddenly the bed cover caught fire. He rang her a few moments later to ask what had happened; she said that she had lost her temper looking for her glasses and hurled the bed cover on the floor together with several books—he had seen her rage symbolised as fire. Shortly after this, in a trance induced by a hypnotic repetition of words, he experienced a sense of looking at a beautiful chandelier. A telephone call to California established that at the same moment, the girl had been standing on the stairs, staring at a chandelier and admiring its beauty.

But perhaps the most challenging assertions of Lilly's book are contained in its eleventh chapter, where he speaks of levels of consciousness. These pages are of such importance that they deserve to be considered at some length.

Lilly likes to speak of 'natural man' as 'the human bio-computer' (the title of his first book). He emphasises that man is, on the physical level, an immense computer or robot. A man could, in theory, go through his whole life in a purely robotic state, simply responding to external stimuli and carrying out his basic 'programming'. This kind of automatic response can hardly be called living at all; it is what T. S. Eliot meant when he asked, 'Where is the life we have lost in living?' and when he spoke of 'partial observation of one's own automatism'. The fact remains that most of us spend the greater part of our waking lives merely staring at the outside world and responding to it—in other words, in purely robotic consciousness. This is not to say that this level is the equivalent of imbecility. Almost everything that goes on in schools and universities—all learning and teaching—takes place on this level. Gurdjieff would call it the 'sleeping level'.

According to Lilly, there are four positive levels, above everyday consciousness, and four negative ones, making nine levels in all. He claims to have experienced all nine levels, either in the course of everyday experience or through LSD.

Each of the positive levels is less 'mechanical' than the ones below it. So everyone, without exception, has experienced the first level above ordinary consciousness. This happens whenever you become deeply interested in something. Lilly says that he has experienced this level a great deal while doing research work in the laboratory. And everyone knows that when you become 'absorbed' in anything, you feel *freer*. (T. E. Lawrence said: 'Happiness is absorption.')

Level two is the 'blissful state', what you feel when you fall in love, what De Quincey experienced when he took opium. There is a feeling of 'belonging', of being a part of a living world. The state can also be achieved through absorption in poetry or music. In fact, we can 'glide' up to this state without too much difficulty.

Level three is of far greater intensity. This, says Lilly, is the level he achieved under LSD when he met his two 'guides'. More significantly, he claims that this is the level at which we can exercise 'paranormal' powers, telepathy, for example, and 'out of the body experiences'. (These will be considered at greater length in the next chapter.) Above this is the fourth positive level—Ramakrishna's '*samadhi*', union with God, a sense of deep bliss that springs from union with the universal mind.

The four negative levels are a kind of mirror image of the positive states. The first is one we have all experienced—pain, guilt and fear. Level two is equivalent to Sartre's 'nausea', a feeling of total isolation, of meaninglessness; of being trapped. This is basically the level of the bad trip.

Level three is the negative equivalent of plus three; Lilly describes it as a kind of purgatory. Consciousness has become a single point, but a point of misery and guilt.

The lowest level is a mirror image of the highest—universal union, but with forces of negation and evil. Lilly says it is 'the deepest hell one can conceive', and there is no hope of escape from it. On the other hand, since he describes an experience of this level in a chapter entitled 'A Guided Tour of Hell', this assertion is presumably not intended to be taken literally.

Lilly prefers to call his levels by a system of numbering borrowed from Gurdjieff. One of Gurdjieff's central doctrines was that the universe consists of a series of vibrations—as Lethbridge found. Gurdjieff distinghished seven distinct levels of vibrations.[3] The higher you are on the ladder (or 'ray') of creation, the freer you are. The lower you are, the more you are subject to 'mechanicalness' and various laws. Gurdjieff claimed that the lowest level, which he called the moon level, is subject to no less than ninety-six laws. Our earth is subject to forty-eight laws. The planets are subject to twenty-four; the sun to twelve, the stars to six, the 'worlds' (or galaxies) to three. The absolute, at the highest level, is subject only to its own single law. If Gurdjieff is speaking literally (and no one can ever be quite sure when he was doing that), we could become twice as 'free' by taking a space ship to the nearest habitable planet. On the other hand, if we lived on the moon, we would soon find ourselves twice as 'entangled' as on earth.

Gurdjieff also made the interesting assertion that man has four levels, or four different 'beings'—the carriage, the horse, the driver and the master. The carriage is our physical body. The horse is our feelings and desires, which, according to Gurdjieff, are another name for the astral body. The coachman is the mind or intellect and has a 'mental' or 'spiritual body'. The master, who owns the whole thing, is the 'I', the consciousness, the will, which Gurdjieff calls the divine or causal body. The 'carriage' (physical body) belongs to the earth level, the level of forty-eight laws. The horse (astral body) belongs to the planetary level of twenty-four laws. The driver (the mind) belongs to the sun level of twelve laws. The master belongs to the star level, the region of only six laws.

All this may sound unnecessarily abstract. But for the purposes of the present discussion, it is necessary to grasp only the central part of the scheme. Lethbridge, we recall, believed that the 'next whorl of the spiral' was on a different vibrational rate from earth, so that beings from that level might be present without our being aware of them. Above that, if we can believe the evidence of the pendulum, is a higher level still, and above that, an even higher level. Lethbridge and Gurdjieff would appear to be in agreement that the universe of 'matter' consists of various distinct levels of vibrations, with gaps in between them.

Gurdjieff goes on to say: 'In right knowledge, the study of man must proceed on parallel lines with the study of the world, and the study of the world must run parallel with the study of man. Laws are everywhere the same, in the world as well as in man. Having mastered the principles of any one law, we must look for its manifestation in the world and in man simultaneously.' In short, 'As above, so below.' He adds: 'This parallel study of the world and of man shows the student the fundamental unity of everything, and helps him to find analogies in phenomena of different orders.'[4]

It is logical to expect the human psyche to have various levels too, and for these levels to be quite distinct. John Lilly has taken over the vibrational rates so that ordinary consciousness (or 'the human bio-computer') is labelled with the number 48—Gurdjieff's 'earth level'—while the level above that ('absorption') is 24, and so on. It is worth noting that Gurdjieff's levels extend only as far as number 6 the master, or mind-body, while Lilly places *samadhi*, union with God, one stage higher than this, at number 3. Either Gurdjieff did not regard it necessary to speak of this higher state—since his chief concern was the evolution of man to a 'fully human' stature—or he and Lilly are not, after all, talking about precisely the same thing.

Gurdjieff and Lilly are clearly in agreement not only in positing higher states of consciousness but in recognising these states as 'higher selves'. Lilly has a story that makes this quite clear.

> At a certain point at the trip in Chile, I was doing an ego reduction with another man. . . I went up quite automatically into Satori +6 yet holding in at +24 and +12. This part of me in +6 took a look around and

saw that part of him was peaking into +6 *but that he didn't know it.* [My italics.] I came back down and reported this to him, including one sentence on having met him before in a previous life. He apparently wasn't aware of the part of himself that went into +6, nor the part in +12 and +24. 'He' was in 48. He became extremely angry, going into 96 immediately upon hearing me talk about previous lives in which his self-metaprogrammer does not believe; he broke off our contact.

That sentence: '"He" was in 48' makes the point unambiguously. The 'self' the man 'identified' with was on earth level, not even (according to Lilly) recognising part of his being in fairly 'ordinary' states of 'absorption' and 'bliss'. (It is an interesting point to note: that we can be happy and yet not *notice* we are happy. When Maslow, for example, talked to his students about 'peak experiences', many of them recalled such experiences in the past *which they had not recognised as peaks at the time.*)

A story like this could sound absurd if it were not for the purely clinical evidence examined in the chapter on multiple personality. The narrow personality is ignorant of what the wider one is doing. If it can *become* aware, the narrowness vanishes; the two fuse together like raindrops, and the person 'becomes' (or identifies with) the wider personality. And this wider person looks down on the 'self' of a few moments before with a mixture of surprise and amusement. 'How *could* I have thought that narrow-minded idiot was me?'

It should also be noted that Lilly describes himself as having reached level six, the 'point of consciousness' level in which telepathy and astral travel become possible; in this state he apparently 'recognised' the other man as someone he had known in a previous existence. This, again, seems to support the hypothesis advanced in the opening chapter of this book: that higher levels of the personality involve paranormal powers.

Gurdjieff seems to hint that these powers are somehow bound up with the mystery of reincarnation. In Ouspensky's record of his teaching, Gurdjieff is twice asked about reincarnation. His answer, predictably, is that most men hardly 'exist' at all; they merely respond to external circumstances; so how can we speak of reincarnation and life after death? Yet, he goes on to say, man *can* ultimately develop all four 'bodies'. 'According to an ancient teaching . . . a man who has attained the full development possible for man . . . consists of four bodies. These four bodies are composed of substances which gradually become finer and finer, mutually interpenetrate one another, and form four independent organisms, standing in a definite relationship to one another, but capable of independent action.' *Such* a person, Gurdjieff clearly implies, would be capable of survival after death and of reincarnation.[5]

Ouspensky said much the same thing in answer to a question.[6] He preferred the theory of 'eternal recurrence' to reincarnation, the Nietzschean idea that everything happens over and over again, like the swing of a pendulum. (This concept is embodied in Ouspensky's novel *The Strange Life of Ivan Osokin*.) He insists that human beings cannot possibly *know* whether reincarnation or recurrence are true, because even the best of us succeed in achieving only the first three 'bodies' (the carriage, the horse and the driver) and in order to *know*, we would need to rise to the master level.

This raises an obvious question. If paranormal powers like telepathy and precognition belong to a higher body—let us not concern ourselves for the moment with which one—and if human beings have to *create* their 'higher bodies' by sheer hard work, how is it that some people are born with psychic abilities? Ouspensky himself admits that the answer seems to point to reincarnation—that such individuals have 'carried over' their powers from a previous life. 'At the same time,' he says, 'the fact that one person has one kind of essence and another another kind is one of the strongest arguments for pre-existence, because essence cannot be born out of nothing—it is too definite. But the system [of Gurdjieff] takes man only from birth to death.'[7] By 'essence', Gurdjieff means some kind of essential self, distinguished from mere personality.

This enables us to pinpoint the most important question raised by John Lilly's book and by anaesthetic revelation in general. The effect of drugs is basically to enfeeble the will. So although they may bring insights into higher levels of being, they also block any effort to gain voluntary access to that level.

Lilly has a convincing answer to this objection. He insists that substances like LSD should be used purely for their heuristic value: as a means of *learning* about 'other states of consciousness'. When LSD became illegal in the mid-sixties, he ceased to use it and began experiments with hypnosis, meditation and other religious techniques. LSD served only to make him aware of the existence of the higher levels of consciousness. Perhaps the most important part of achieving an intenser state of consciousness is to be *certain* that it exists. Once it has been achieved several times, the 'bio-computer' has been pre-programmed to achieve it and can do so by other means, in much the same way that someone who is accustomed to alcohol can get 'high' on a glass of orange juice if they believe it contains alcohol. Lilly's experiments seen to confirm Aldous Huxley's view that 'psychedelics' can provide an important access to higher states of consciousness; at the same time, they emphasise the strictly *limited* value of such drugs, and flatly contradict Huxley's view that a general use of mescalin (or LSD) would be preferable to tobacco or alcohol.

Lilly's experiences help to throw light on one of the most baffling accounts of the anaesthetic revelation written in our century. In 1941, the French critic Jean Paulhan asked a number of writers to describe the most significant experience of their lives. One of the few to do so was a thirty-three-year-old essayist and reviewer, René Daumal, who would die three years later from tuberculosis.

In *A Fundamental Experience*, Daumal describes how, at the age of six, he began to experience an increasing terror of death, the thought of the absurdity of simply ceasing to exist. 'One night, relaxing my entire body, I calmed the terror and revulsion of my organism before the unknown, and a new feeling came alive in me of hope, a foretaste of the imperishable.' At sixteen, Daumal made a remarkable attempt to 'descend into the unconscious' by sniffing carbon tetrachloride, a substance he used to kill beetles for his collection. He held a handkerchief soaked with the chemical against his nostrils, knowing that as soon as he began to lose consciousness, the hand would drop, and he would again breathe pure air.

He describes choking and suffocating, and how his whole life flashed through his mind, as it is supposed to when someone is drowning. He describes William James's sensation of his mind travelling too rapidly for words to keep pace. Then, he says, words seemed to lose their meaning. Suddenly, there was a sensation of entering another world 'an instantaneous and intense world of eternity, a concentrated flame of reality'. All he can now salvage of that feeling of certainty, he says, is a conviction of the existence of 'something else, a beyond, another world, or another form of knowledge'.

It is important to repeat that in that new state I perceived and perfectly comprehended the ordinary state of being, the latter being contained within the former, as waking consciousness contains our unconscious dreams, and not the reverse. . . I told myself clearly: 'In a little while I shall return to the so-called "normal" state, and perhaps the memory of this fearful revelation will cloud over; but it is in this moment that I see the truth.' Another thought came: 'For all eternity I was trapped, hurled faster and faster towards ever-imminent annihilation through the terrible mechanism of the Law that rejected me. . .' Under the threat of something *worse* I had to follow the movement. It took a tremendous effort, which became more and more difficult, but I was *obliged* to make that effort, until the moment when, letting go, I doubtless fell into a brief spell of unconsciousness.

He then attempts to convey in words what it was that he saw under the anaesthetic, emphasising again that it was on a higher level of significance than our normal thoughts. First, there was a strange geometrical arrangement of circles and triangles.

A circle, half red and half black, inscribed itself in a triangle coloured in the same fashion, with the red/half-circle against the black segment of triangle, and vice versa. And all space was endlessly divided thus into circles and triangles inscribed one within another, combining and moving in harmony, and changing into one another in a geometrically inconceivable manner. . .

There was also a sound accompanying the movement

and I suddenly realised that it was I who was making it. In fact, I virtually *was* that sound; I sustained my existence by emitting it. The sound consisted of a chant or formula, which I had to repeat faster and faster in order to 'follow the movement'. That formula (I give the facts with no attempt to disguise their absurdity) ran something like this: 'Tem gwef tem gwef dr rr rr.

He speaks of a vision of circles continually expanding to infinity in a kind of curved non-Euclidean space, and also of time being somehow curved: 'It all vibrates simultaneously in an instant . . . everything re-commences in identical fashion in each instant, as if the total nullity of my particular existence within the unbroken substance of the Immobile were the cause of a cancerous proliferation of instants.' In the same way, all the circles and triangles dissolve in every instant back into a Unity, 'perfect *except for me*'. Cause and effect also blended into one another, separated, and blended again.

This greatly condensed account can hardly be more bewildering than the original. Yet a number of points emerge. The first—and most central—is Daumal's feeling that this experience was *more real* than everyday consciousness, in the way that everyday consciousness is realler than a dream. Next, this 'real' universe he saw was somehow timeless, and re-created itself from instant to instant.

But what of the red and black triangles and circles? What of the 'mantra' (tem gwef tem gwef . . .) that he seemed to be repeating to sustain his own existence? What of his feeling of being somehow rejected or diminished by this 'perfect' universe?

Lilly's chapter 'A Guided Tour of Hell' throws some light on Daumal's experience. He describes how a dose of LSD plunged him into the 'minus three' stage that he calls 'bottommost Hell'.

> Suddenly I was precipitated into what I later called 'the cosmic compu-ter'. I was merely a very small programme in someone else's huge computer. There were tremendous energies in this computer. There were fantastic energy flows and information flows going through me. None of it made any sense. I was in total terror and panic. . . The whole computer was the result of a senseless dance of certain kinds of atoms . . . stimulated and pushed by organised but meaningless energies. . . Everywhere I found entities like myself who were slave programmes in this huge cosmic conspiracy, this cosmic dance of energy and matter which had absolutely no meaning, no love, no human value.

Lilly says that this 'was the most punishing experience I had ever had in my whole life'. Yet he recognised later that what he had seen was created from his own 'scientific' assumptions about the universe: it was the meaningless, godless universe of nineteenth century science.

But Lilly himself is a computer expert, and the vision of the mind-less computer came from his own subconscious. The same may well be true of Daumal's strange vision of triangles and circles. It is equally possible that he was glimpsing some fundamental universal symbol. The circle divided into two halves—the Chinese yin and yang—seems to be such a symbol. The triangle and the circle are also two basic tattwa symbols, signifying respectively fire and air. Again, the 'man-tra' that sustained his own existence may have been a symbolic recognition that all life is sustained by a continuous act of will, or of 'intentionality'.

What seems fairly clear is that Daumal's experiment with carbon tetrachloride (hardly an ideal anaesthetic) produced a certain negativity. He himself compares his 'glimpse' to the vision that confronted Bluebeard's wife when she opened the locked room. There must also have been a certain element of bewilderment about his own identity. Which level of his consciousness witnessed this universal dance? It was the 'narrow self' that sniffed the tetrachloride. Was it this 'self' that felt rejected and diminished by what it saw?

Daumal's 'revelation' occurred about 1924. He subsequently threw himself into the Dadaist movement, becoming something of an *enfant terrible*. At the age of twenty-two he fell under the influence of Gurdjieff's disciple Alexandre de Salzmann—and, indirectly, of Gurdjieff. A period of renewed interest in Eastern philosophy—in Zen Buddhism and Hinduism—followed. He compared his 'revelation' with Arjuna's vision of God in the *Bhagavad Gita*—a vast, overwhelming display of universal power and meaning. Interestingly enough, the title of his first volume of poems was *Counter-Heaven*, a denial of the religious notion of heaven. Daumal's vision had imbued him with the belief that if man is to be 'saved', he must save himself.

At the time of his death, in 1944, Daumal was writing a symbolic novel called *Mount Analogue*, about an attempt to scale a mountain that symbolises wisdom or salvation. The central character is called Father Sogol (logos spelt backwards). Even as a fragment, it is not particularly successful; these symbolic voyages (like Hesse's *Journey to the East*) usually end in anti-climax. Yet it makes clear that Daumal saw spiritual achievement as an immense and painful effort. Perhaps the best commentary on the book, and on Daumal's life, is a remark Gurdjieff made to Ouspensky's group in Moscow:

The earth is a very bad place from the cosmic point of view—it is like the most remote part of northern Siberia, very far from everywhere; it is cold, life is very hard. Everything that in another place either comes by itself or is easily obtained is here acquired only by hard labour; everything must be fought for, both in life and in the work. In life it still happens sometimes that man gets a legacy and afterwards lives without doing anything. But such a thing does not happen in the work. All are equal, and all are equally beggars.

Daumal's vision, in spite of its negative overtones, seems to have created a similar conviction.

The more we consider the anaesthetic revelation, the more clear it seems that it is of strictly limited value. Gurdjieff seems to have taken a similar view. Although he never recommended the use of drugs, he invited his followers to meals at which vast quantitites of alcohol were consumed. When the English physician Kenneth Walker first visited Gurdjieff in Paris after the Second World War, he was obliged to drink toasts in vodka until he was in a highly intoxicated state, all in no more than ten minutes or so.

> Everything [was] getting bigger and bigger and then smaller and smaller. . . Mr Gurdjieff was behaving at this moment just as the gas jet in my old nursery used to behave whenever I was kept in bed with a temperature. He would recede to an immense distance away and then, a minute later, come rushing towards me, until he eventually became so big that he completely swamped the room.[8]

These Alice-in-Wonderland effects prepared Walker's mind for the knowledge that Gurdjieff was able to convey.

Nevertheless, the essence of the work was immense psychological effort. Gurdjieff's basic aim was to strengthen the will—not the mere physical will, but the 'true will'. And the main discipline towards this end was the practice Gurdjieff called 'self-remembering'. Ordinary consciousness, said Gurdjieff, is purely mechanical. It is not true to say 'I think'; it would be more accurate to say '*It* thinks'.

This point can be illustrated by an example from an article by Dr Milton Erickson describing some 'experiments in consciousness' that he conducted with Aldous Huxley.[9] Huxley was able to immerse himself in a state which he called 'deep reflection'. In this state, he was sufficiently conscious of the outside world to write down his ideas, or to perform other physical tasks. One day his wife returned from shopping and asked if he had written down a message she gave him over the telephone. Huxley had no memory of taking a phone call. Yet the message was recorded, on the pad by the telephone, in Huxley's writing. On another occasion she asked him about the time of delivery of a registered letter; he had no memory of any such letter. Yet it was clear that, in a state of deep reflection, he had gone to the door, signed for the letter, placed the letter where his wife would see it, then gone back to his chair.

This is only an extreme example of something we all do every day. ('Where *did* I put that hammer?') We *forget* an enormous number of things we do only a few seconds after we have done them. But where am 'I' when I carefully put something down, then forget where I've put it? On some occasions, I am 'elsewhere', thinking of more important things—of the end rather than the means. But there are many occasions on which I cannot make this excuse. Although I do something with only a small part of my attention, the 'rest of me' is nowhere in particular. You could say I am in a trance-like state. I have retreated into a mere narrow segment of my 'being' and closed the door behind me.

Gurdjieff insisted that this 'forgetfulness' had to be countered. He insisted that his followers should make a constant attempt to *remember themselves*. When I close my eyes, my attention points inward, towards myself. When I look at something external, my attention points outward, towards the object. If I make an immense effort, I can make my attention point in *and* out at the same time, like a double-headed arrow. In fact, this happens naturally when I am in a state of intense happiness. I am aware of my surroundings and of myself among them. A man who has just fallen in love experiences 'self-remembering'. So it clearly beongs to a higher level of consciousness—to John Lilly's 'plus twelve' state.

Ouspensky describes what happened when he walked around in a state of self-remembering. 'I used very much to like to wander through St Petersburg at night and to 'sense' the houses and the streets. St Petersburg is full of these strange sensations. Houses, especially old houses, were quite alive. I all but spoke to them. There was no 'imagination' in it. I did not think of anything. I simply walked along while trying to remember myself and looked about; the sensations came by themselves.'[10]

Our first reaction is to doubt Ouspensky's word when he says that it was nothing to do with imagination. After all, houses are dead objects; they cannot 'speak' to you. Unless, of course, he had become 'psychic', and was picking up 'tape recordings'. But neither of these is the true explanation. We are inclined to make a fundamental error about perception.

We believe that the process of seeing is like taking a photograph; the image enters our eyes and makes an impression on the retina which is in turn transmitted to the brain. So if Ouspensky 'sensed' something more than this photographic impression, he must have been putting it there himself.

We forget that a photograph can be in monochrome or colour; it can be dim and blurred or clear and sharp. And what makes a difference is not what *comes in* through our eyes so much as what *goes out*. The ancients believed that sight involves an 'eyebeam' which probes the world like a searchlight. Modern science has taught us better, yet the fact remains that the ancient notion of the eyebeam is, in a fundamental sense, a more accurate description of perception than the scientific picture. When I perceive something, I make an act of *grasping* it. If, for example, I am staring into the distance, looking for someone's arrival, I am conscious of firing my perception like a bullet. If I look casually, without this effort, I notice the scene without grasping its individual parts. And if I stare blankly, without any effort, I see nothing at all.

It is as if my eyebeams were jets of water, projected from hoses. When my inner pressure is low, the water droops mournfully to the ground just in front of my feet. When I am happy and excited, the pressure is high, and the water creates a kind of foam as it strikes objects. When my perception is in this state, everything I see is not only sharper and clearer but more *meaningful*. It is bound to be, because it has more detail.

My mechanised perception is inclined to simplify things. If I turn my head and look out of my window, I see winter trees against low clouds, with a blue sky overhead; I can 'take it in' in a moment. But if I stare out of the window, and take the trouble to look carefully, I see that it is far more complex. The clouds are fleecy white on top, with golden flecks, and blue-grey lower down. The trees are actually thousands of twigs outlined against this soft greyness. In the clear blue above, there are several smoky fragments of cloud. And even in the grey and white clouds, there are a dozen different shades of colour.

If I now decide that it is time to leave my typewriter and go for my afternoon walk, I may plod around quietly for half an hour or so without seeing anything particularly interesting—the country lanes and fishermen's cottages I have seen a thousand times. It is all totally familiar. Yet if I suddenly galvanise my perception, forcing myself to look as if my life depended on it, I discover, to my astonishment, that it is like waking up from sleep. I feel as if I am in a strange place, and I see things that I have never seen before. Moreover, everything I look at somehow *reminds* me of other things, as if interesting memory circuits have been activated inside my head.

This effort brings another recognition. As soon as I realise that things are more interesting and complex than I had supposed, I experience a surge of vitality and *curiosity*, a sudden recognition of the importance of keeping my perceptions alive. I realise that my boredom was self-perpetuating, that it was causing me to waste my life just as surely as if I spent the day fast asleep in bed. When I look at things without expecting anything, the water pressure behind the fire hose drops, and things actually *look* dull. I experience the 'seen it all before' feeling. In fact, this is a preposterous lie. *I haven't* seen it. I haven't seen anything. Most of us die without even glimpsing the richness and complexity of the incredible world in which we live.

How did this depressing situation come about? We do not live in the physical world. We live inside our heads. When a baby is born, his brain is virtually an empty house, with the plaster still drying on the walls. He immediately proceeds to furnish it with various items of knowledge. And eventually, it becomes a fairly comfortable residence, so that when he lies awake on a dark night, he can amuse himself for hours by wandering through its room. Still, a child's mental house has far less furniture than an adult's, which is why children are so much more easily bored, and so much more dependent on what goes on around them.

Throughout my life I gain experience and knowledge of the universe around me by means of 'attention'; by directing the jets of water at external objects. Having done that, I store the information on a kind of microfilm and put it in its appropriate place in my 'house'. So when I come to live in a new town, I have first of all to find my way around by means of a street map; but in no time at all, the map is inside my head. My library of microfilms also contains far more complicated maps with such labels as 'French', 'Counting', 'English language', 'English literature'—in fact, every subject you would find on a school curriculum, and hundreds more.

From the biological point of view, the aim of this system is simply to help us cope more efficiently with the external world. And for the first million or so years of his evolution, this is precisely what man used it for. Then, a mere four or five thousand years ago, he made an interesting discovery. Instead of merely using the maps to help him cope with the outside world, he began *comparing the maps with one another*. For example, there was a microfilm labelled 'Territory', containing his instinctive knowledge of what belonged to him and what belonged to his neighbours. There was another labelled 'Counting', which he had developed in order to keep a check on his animals. At some point, he realised that the two microfilms could be combined into a new subject called 'Measuring', which was of inestimable use in towns and villages. A mere thousand years or so later, man had developed Measuring into yet another new subject called Geometry, which proved to have practical uses far beyond those of the old counting and territorial instincts from which it sprang. A new breed of men called Philosophers devoted their whole lives to this strange game of comparing mental microfilms, and they paid so little attention to the practical world around them that their absent-mindedness soon became a subject of general hilarity.

To some extent, of course, the mockers were right. It *is* too easy for the thinker to 'lose touch with reality'. But it is not inevitable. In fact, the whole aim of these unusual mental powers is to place us more closely in touch with reality. A stupid man sees only what is at the end of his nose, and he quickly forgets what he learned last week. An intelligent man stores his knowledge in his microfilm library and brings it to bear on his everyday experience.

We must never forget that it is horribly easy to waste our lives in mere physical existence. Most of my experience is repetitive. And for most of my waking hours, my consciousness is quite passive, as if I were sitting in an armchair watching television. This is not living; it is vegetating. It explains why most people are as ignorant when they die as when they were born. This brain of ours, with its microfilm library, is evolution's device for trying to raise us above this vegetable existence.

But all new inventions have their drawbacks, and here we are coming to the heart of the matter: to what the Bible symbolises in the legend of Original Sin. The unfortunate tendency to absent-mindedness, to being not 'quite all there', is not confined to philosophers. Our special equipment makes us *all* philosophers to some extent; that is our peculiar human distinction. And most adults spend far too much of their time living 'inside their heads'.

The house inside our heads has an interesting structure; indeed, it is more like a medieval castle than a modern house. You can walk over the drawbridge and lower the portcullis; this is what happens when your 'attention wanders'. You may then retreat into the inner courtyard, which has another fortified gate; this may happen when you are thoroughly bored. It is important to realise that we have a whole series of inner courtyards, and that we can retreat into various 'depths' of ourselves. At the centre of the whole structure is the 'keep', the ultimate stronghold. We retreat there only when we are in the deepest depression; anyone who spends much time there is probably seriously mentally ill. (The illness of people who have locked themselves in the inner keep is called catatonia.)

Below the castle, as Jung observed in his dream referred to earlier, are cellars, leading to still deeper cellars. This is where we store our vital energies. But at the moment, this aspect of the castle is of no concern to us.

We are concerned here with the curious fact that one can spend most of one's time inside the castle and still lead an apparently fairly normal life. We have television monitors that show us what is going on outside, and years of experience have taught us how to deal with most everyday problems without much effort. This can soon become such a normal state of affairs that we do not even realise how far we have become invalids. We look at the world reflected in the television screen—or even out of the window—and there seems to be no point in actually going outside. We can see everything just as well from in here. What we forget is that we have other senses besides sight. When one actually goes outside, one realises with amazement that one had forgotten about the smell of grass and the sound of running water and the feel of the wind against one's face.

Human beings have a dual problem, whose root cause is laziness. Because they live too much 'inside themselves', they lose contact with the real world, and they fail to put enough energy into perception; their attention is a feeble trickle instead of a powerful jet. Their senses fall asleep and their vitality drops; they are at the mercy of trivial worries and negative emotions. The human computer is working at about one-tenth of its proper efficiency. This is why, as Gurdjieff says, man tends to perceive illusion as actuality. He lives in a kind of a dream world inside his own head.

The situation is not as bad as it sounds. We are always experiencing brief flashes of 'wakefulness'. When we find ourselves in some new and interesting situation, we quite unconsciously increase the power of the 'jets' and recognise for a moment how fascinating the 'real' world is. Our main problem is that we promptly misinterpret the information. For example, if we are on holiday, we assume that it is the holiday itself that is giving us pleasure. If we have fallen in love, we imagine that the lover is responsible for the feeling of 'newness' and delight. And when our habitual laziness leads to disappointment, we may even look for someone else to fall in love with, simply to renew the experience. If we are the sort of person whose love affairs are on the physical level, this can lead to the tendency called Casanovism, or satyriasis. In fact, most of man's more unpleasant characteristics can be explained in terms of this confusion of ends and means.

But if we are intelligent enough to understand the source of the feeling of 'newness', then we recognise that our chief problem is laziness: a laziness of the senses. Hence Gurdjieff's emphasis on self-remembering. The method taught by Ouspensky is discouragingly difficult. It involves trying to look at something and at the same time to remain aware of the 'you' who is looking at it: the double-headed arrow. If one attempts to do this—for example, by looking at one's wristwatch—one will discover that one can do it for only a second or so at a time; then one's attention flags, and one either 'forgets' the watch or forgets to observe oneself looking at it.

There are far easier methods than this kind of 'self-remembering', the simplest being suddenly to *look* at something as if one's life depended on it. Or imagine that, like Tolstoy's Pierre Bezukhov, you are standing in front of a firing squad, looking at the world for the last time. The aim is to recognise that things have an *independent existence*. They are not mere photographs inside one's head. Huxley found that mescalin can produce this effect; but it is just as easy to achieve it without mescalin if only for a brief glimpse.

To begin with, such glimpses are their own reward; there is no after-effect. But a little practice brings an important recognition: as you stare at things with a deliberate attempt to 'reach' them, you realise with a shock of delight that they are interesting in themselves. It is almost as if the tree or whatever is communicating back to you, acknowledging your presence. This is, of course, an illusion; but the *meaning* you are suddenly perceiving is not. It is as real as the meaning on this page. From now on, the realisation that the meaning is actually *there*, outside you, will lead to an automatic effort to 'reach out', so that you will experience a spontaneous shock of 'newness' as you glance casually at some object.

Why is it that a painting of a scene can capture your attention more than the scene itself? The answer is not simply that the painter has been more selective. It is because when you look at a painting, you know that it is *intended* to convey certain information, so your attention automatically 'sharpens' as you look.

Let us take a closer look at this mechanism of 'withdrawal from reality'. When some emergency arises, I am forced to come out of my 'inner castle'. As I prepare to face the problem, an order goes down to my subconscious mind to send up reinforcements in the form of energy. When I retreat across the drawbridge and relax my vigilance, the subconscious assumes that the emergency is over, and it also relaxes. This is why we so often feel a sense of anti-climax after some great effort.

If the effect of this sudden drop in pressure is to make me feel bored and discouraged, I may retreat into one of the inner courtyards. There the sounds of the outside world are even farther away, and the response of the subconscious mind is to send up even less energy. This is why it is so important to resist impulses of self-pity and gloom. William James points out that chronic invalids who have fallen into a state of depression and exhaustion can often be made to rally by 'bullying treatment'. The paradoxical truth is that *we* are in charge of our energy supply; when we groan with a sense of exhaustion and suffocation, it is because we are accidentally standing on the supply line.

Watch a child when he falls down and hurts himself; his face twists with self-pity and he prepares to identify with his misery. If you smile at him and say: 'What a brave boy you are!' he smiles back, and instantly rejects the 'lower self'. Or watch a man who has become very angry or upset. It is almost as if the emotion has created a kind of phantom self, with which he is tempted to identify. If he is strong enough, he will reject the temptation by sheer moral effort, and in a few seconds, the phantom will fade away.

In other words, when we retreat into an 'inner courtyard', we not only lose energy but are also faced with the choice of assuming or not assuming a new identity. The same thing happens if someone dislikes you and lets you see it; in effect, he is inviting you to see yourself as he sees you; to devalue yourself. You may allow his will to over-rule yours, or you may attempt to turn the tables by showing your dislike and trying to force *him* to devalue himself. Or you may simply tell yourself that he is a fool, and ignore him.

The most important thing to realise is that *our senses can show us only a fraction of reality*. If I pick up a book, my senses can give me information only about its colour, weight, and so on. My *mind* has to complete the book's reality through a knowledge of its contents. In the same way, if I speak to an old friend, my senses can show me only his superficial characteristics; it is my mind—my knowledge of his character—that must complete his reality.

Even slight fatigue will cause reality to lose its quality. The brain works on energy, and energy illuminates reality in the way that light illuminates a picture gallery. (Imagine the difference between a picture gallery with the sun streaming through the windows, and the same gallery by night, illuminated by half a dozen candles; the pictures would lose a whole dimension of meaning by candlelight.)

Think what happens in those moments of intensity, such as Alyosha Karamazov experienced under the stars. Everyone has experienced something of the sort, when the senses seem more awake. But this is less important than what happens to our inner being, which expands from the size of a small room to the size of a cathedral. There is a strange feeling of inner *connections*, as if the vibration of one part of your being could cause another to vibrate. In such moods you find yourself remembering forgotten episodes of childhood or the name of a former next-door neighbour you haven't seen for twenty years.

It is in moods like this that we suddenly realise that we grasp reality with the mind, not with the senses, and that our 'normal' perception of reality is as mediocre as a blurred photograph, because the mind is usually asleep.

Since our minds are numb most of the time, we assume that the blurred photograph is an accurate representation of reality and make no effort to achieve closer contact. Most people go through their lives totally unaware of the astounding potentialities of the computer. For, of course, it is the computer we are talking about. It is the computer whose communication system suddenly improves in moments of expanded consciousness.

This enables us to grasp what Ouspensky meant when he said he enjoyed walking around St Petersburg at night, 'sensing' the houses and the streets. There was no imagination involved. The effort of self-remembering simply galvanised his senses and restored the circulation to numb areas of his mind. He was *beginning* to see things 'as they really are'.

The same process enables us to establish closer contact with the subconscious. Daumal, with his absurd and dangerous experiments with carbon tetrachloride, was approaching the problem with a familiar misconception. The subconscious is not some remote and inaccessible Mount Analogue, waiting to be conquered by a team of daring explorers. This particular mountain is mobile and perfectly willing to come to Mahomet. All we have to do is deliberately increase the 'intentionality' of perception and to become accustomed to the higher level of effort; our deepened sense of reality will do the rest.

This recognition affords us a completely new insight into the whole problem of the 'supernatural' and paranormal. We find it difficult to accept because it is *beyond the range* of our everyday experience. But that is precisely what we might expect. The world is an immensely complex, three-dimensional continuum which our mechanisms of perception reduce to a distorted, two-dimensional monochrome blur. When we catch a brief glimpse of reality, we find it impossible to grasp, because it conflicts with the preconceptions we have carried around with us since childhood; we have no words, or even concepts, to fit it. One woman who had such an experience at the age of twelve—she was standing on the seashore watching a breaking wave—told me that she suddenly remembered that it had happened several times before, but that after each previous occasion, she had totally forgotten it. On the last occasion when it had happened—as she stood in a garden in Scotland, looking at the mountains—she had experienced a curious conviction that this was for the last time; when it happened again on the seashore, she felt that it was some kind of freak accident. Her own attempt to explain the nature of what she experienced was to say that it was a completely *simple* kind of consciousness, 'primal perception', as it might be experienced by an animal whose mind is undistorted by verbal concepts. But when I asked her if she thought it was the same kind of insight described by Aldous Huxley in *Doors of Perception* (with which she was familiar), she was emphatic that it was not.

Works like James's *Varieties of Religious Experience*, Bucke's *Cosmic*

Consciousness, Marghanita Laski's *Ecstasy*, contain dozens of records of similar glimpses of a wider reality. What we find far more difficult to accept is that this reality is not subject to the same laws as our own dull and constricted variety. After all, the altered states of consciousness described by poets and mystics *sound* like a more exciting version of the kind of consciousness we are all familiar with. Tennyson described how he used to repeat his own name over and over again 'till all at once, as it were out of the intensity of the consciousness of individuality, individuality itself seemed to dissolve and fade away into boundless being, and this not a confused state but the clearest, the surest of the surest, utterly beyond words—where death was almost a laughable impossibility . . .' This is again William James's 'bird's eye view' of reality; we can believe that it would show us *more of* reality, but not a different *kind of* reality.

What we are saying is that 'knowledge of reality' is limited by the senses. If I have very good sight, I may be able to see a ship when it is ten miles out at sea; but I still cannot see *through* a ship. With exceptional hearing I may be able to hear a thrush singing a mile away; but I cannot hear what it sang the day before yesterday.

But this kind of logic may be deceptive. Our senses are basically receivers of information. The universe is full of information that is beyond their range—sounds too high for me to hear, colours beyond the visible range of the spectrum. When I hold a dowsing rod above an underground stream, I receive information that is beyond the normal range of my senses. When a psychic sees a ghost (or a ghoul), he is receiving another kind of information. When a psychometrist like Gerard Croiset holds an article of clothing and can describe the person it belongs to, he is presumably using a sense that lies dormant in most of us; but his success rate leaves no doubt that such a sense exists. The psychic investigator Charles Richet liked to talk about 'the sixth sense'; but the astonishing range of psychic phenomena—precognition, mediumship, radiesthesia, second sight—suggests that there may be far more than six.

In a novel called *The Philosopher's Stone*, written in 1967, I suggested that the senses may be restricted by the narrowness of everyday consciousness rather than by any built-in limitations. This is easy to understand if we think of Janet's M. Achille, the hysteric subject who believed he was possessed by the devil. When Janet spoke to him in a whisper, Achille himself was unable to hear, but the 'devil' (his 'wider personality') heard and replied. Hysteria had limited the range of Achille's normal senses. But if—as we have established—we are *all* hysterics, does it not follow that our 'normal' senses are also limited?

Our 'contracted' state is caused by tension, which, in turn, is caused by mistrust. Life is difficult and dangerous; we have to keep on guard, like someone expecting a blow. Yet, as Maslow discovered, healthy people are subject to regular 'peak experiences', moments of over-flowing delight, which are also characterised by a feeling of trust. Maslow and Hoffer discovered that alcoholics could be cured by means of peak experiences induced by psychedelic drugs and music.[11] Alcoholism is a disease of contracted consciousness, rooted in a sense of mistrust. In *The Philosopher's Stone*, I invented an operation on the pre-frontal lobe of the brain (believed to be the source of poetic and mystical experience), able to induce a peak experience of such intensity that it could produce a permanent state of openness and trust. Sitting on the lawn of an Elizabethan house, the hero relaxes into a state of expanded consciousness and suddenly finds himself looking at the house as it was four centuries before.

Such cases are not unknown. By far the most famous case of such 'retrocognition of the past' is the one recorded by two maiden ladies, Charlotte Moberly and Eleanor Jourdain, successive principals of an Oxford college, in their book *An Adventure* (1911). On August 10, 1901, the two ladies visited the Trianon park at Versailles and were surprised to encounter a number of people in eighteenth-century dress. Two 'gardeners' gave them directions, and a man who hurried past them warned them not to take a certain path. They passed a woman in old-fashioned dress who was drawing, but only Miss Moberly saw her. Both ladies felt oddly depressed and experienced a dream-like sensation. They went into the Petit Trianon, followed a wedding party at a distance, then went back to their hotel for tea. A week later, when Miss Moberly was describing the visit in a letter, the two ladies compared notes and decided that there had been something odd about the afternoon. Miss Jourdain wrote her own detailed account. The following January, she returned alone to Versailles on a cold, rainy afternoon. Again she experienced 'the old eerie feeling'; 'it was as if I had crossed a line and was suddenly in a circle of influence'. She saw two labourers in bright tunics and hoods loading a cart; when she looked back a second later, they had vanished, although she could see a long way in all directions. She heard the rustling of silk dresses around her and heard voices, but she saw no one.

When the two ladies returned to the gardens three years later, they found everything totally changed. The trees had vanished; so had a rustic bridge, a ravine, a cascade and a 'kiosk'. Convinced now that they had seen the place as it was in the reign of Marie Antoinette and Louis XVI, they studied books on the period and concluded that they had actually seen historical personages of the period just before the Revolution, and that the woman seen by Charlotte Moberly could well have been Marie Antoinette. After publication of their book in 1911, three people who had lived in a house overlooking the park at Versailles told them that they had experienced the same kind of thing so often that they had ceased to pay any attention to it.

In 1938, a member of the Society for Psychical Research, J. E. Sturge-Whiting, strongly criticised the account of the two ladies. He had examined the grounds and concluded that they had simply followed paths that still exist on the first occasion and failed to locate them on their second visit. In 1965, Philippe Jullian published a biography of Count Robert de Montesquiou (the dandy on whom Proust based Baron de Charlus), which described how Montesquiou took a house near Versailles in the early 1890s and often spent whole days in the park. His friend Mme de Greffulhe organised a fancy-dress party in the Dairy. And this, remarks Jullian in an aside, could easily explain the 'adventure' of the two English ladies. 'Perhaps . . . the "ghosts" . . . were, quite simply, Mme Greffulhe, dressed as a shepherdess, rehearsing an entertainment with some friends. . .'

The explanation sounds plausible, and together with Sturge-Whiting's theory of the paths, it so convinced Dame Joan Evans, the literary executor of the two ladies, that she decided to allow *An Adventure* to go out of print.[12] Yet on closer examination, the two theories still leave nine-tenths of the incidents unexplained. Sturge-Whiting fails to explain away the topographical problem. Charlotte Moberly says quite clearly about her 1904 visit:

> From this point [the guard house] everything was changed . . . We came directly to the gardener's house, which was quite different in appearance from the cottage described by Miss Jourdain in 1901 . . . Beyond the gardener's house was a parterre with flower beds and a smooth lawn of many years' careful tendance. It did not seem to be the place where we

had met the garden officials. We spent a long time looking for the old paths. Not only was there no trace of them, but the distances were contracted . . . The kiosk was gone; so was the ravine and the little cascade which had fallen from a height above our heads, and the little bridge over the ravine . . .

And so on for several more detailed pages. Which suggests that either the ladies were exaggerating, or Sturge-Whiting must be wrong.

Philippe Jullian apparently failed to check the date of the Versailles adventure. Montesquiou moved to Versailles in the early 1890s and moved again—to Neuilly—in 1894, so the fancy-dress party took place at least seven years too early for the English ladies to have seen a rehearsal.[13]

Finally, Joan Evans makes no attempt to explain what happened on Miss Jourdain's 1902 visit, when she saw the disappearing carters. On this occasion, Miss Jourdain again saw the 'old' Versailles, as on her first visit. During the next two years, she returned many times and must have become fairly familiar with the geography of the park; on all these occasions she found the place completely changed and 'modernised'.

And so the Versailles adventure remains one of the most baffling and incongruous incidents in the history of modern psychical research. It is nevertheless worth pointing out that the experience is not inconsistent with the conclusions reached by Lethbridge and others. The Trianon was eminently suited to become the site of a 'tape recording' of powerful emotions. Their researches led the two ladies to conclude that they had glimpsed the park as it was in 1789. The Bastille had fallen on July 14; on August 4, the nobles agreed to surrender all feudal rights. On August 10, the Tuileries was sacked, the Swiss guards murdered and the king and queen arrested. In those last days at Versailles, where Marie Antoinette had once been so happy, the atmosphere must have been heavily charged with fear and anxiety. The ghoul hypothesis seems to be strengthened by Miss Jourdain's description: 'It was as if I had crossed a line and was suddenly in a circle of influence', an observation that agrees closely with Lethbridge's observation of such 'recordings'. Finally, we know that Miss Jourdain was psychic—Miss Moberly admits that her friend possessed powers of second sight but had left them 'deliberately undeveloped'. (Both ladies disapproved of 'occultism', regarding it as morbid and dangerous.) The two ladies were lifelong friends; they may even have been in physical contact—one holding the other's arm—as they walked in the park; so that Miss Moberly could have picked up her friend's 'sensitivity' as a dowser can transfer his power to another person by touching his hands.

When Professor Joad discussed the Versailles incident in his *Guide to Modern Thought*, he spoke about 'the undoubted queerness of time', and added: 'While admitting that the hypothesis of the present existence of the past is beset with difficulties of a metaphysical character. . . I think that it indicates the most fruitful basis for the investigation of these intriguing experiences.' But to admit 'the present existence of time' is only the beginning of an explanation. If precognition exists at all, it seems to prove that our human view of time, as a one-way stream, is somehow an illusion. But *how* can precognition take place? What causes flashes of 'retrocognition' like the one described by Miss Jourdain?

Here again, Janet's psychology offers at least a theoretical basis for understanding. The heart of his psychology lies in the notion of the 'reality function'—our ability to grasp reality. When we are acting automatically, says Janet, our 'coefficient of reality' is at its lowest, whereas when we are learning to ski—or to do something equally difficult and potentially dangerous—it is at its highest. Janet says that mental illness is always accompanied by a low coefficient of reality, and that if the psychiatrist can somehow raise this coefficient, he will cure the illness. When our reality function begins to fail us, we experience the 'narrowing of the field of consciousness' known as hysteria. Conversely, when our coefficient of reality increases, we experience a widening of consciousness accompanied by an increase in our powers and perceptions.

The 'widening' produced by hypnosis can activate certain powers beyond the range of 'normal' consciousness. (Janet's first patient, Léonie, could be hypnotised—telepathically—from several miles away and summoned to the doctor's house.) If Janet's theory is correct, then an increase in the coefficient of reality ought to have the same effect and widen our 'natural' powers. And *if*—the question is admittedly a crucial one—these wider powers should include precognition or second sight, these should also be activated by an increased coefficient of reality.

In the course of researching this volume, I heard about an interesting case of 'retrocognition' that seems to confirm Janet's view. In answer to my request, Mrs Jane O'Neill of Cambridge supplied me with a lengthy account of her experience, which I condense here:

> In October 1973 I was the first person to arrive at a serious accident; a car had driven head-on into a coach behind which I was travelling. I pulled the passengers from the wreck, waiting with them till the ambulances arrived. Afterwards, with my hands covered with blood, I drove to London Airport to pick up a friend. Driving home later that night I began to 'see' all over again the dreadful injuries of the passengers. They continued for days; I am usually a very sound sleeper, but I now found that I could not sleep at all. The doctor said I was suffering from shock, and I was away from school for five weeks [Mrs O'Neill is a schoolteacher]. A fellow teacher [Shirley] invited me for the half-term holiday to her cottage in Norfolk, where several inexplicable things happened. I would be sitting in her sitting room and would quite suddenly see very clearly before me a vivid picture. It would last a couple of seconds, during which my riveted attention was apparently obvious [and] Shirley would ask me what the matter was. I don't remember the sequence of these sights, but I remember them very clearly. After one I told Shirley: 'I have just seen you in the galleys.' As I hardly knew her, I was astonished when she replied: 'That's not surprising. My ancestors were Huguenots and were punished by being sent to the galleys.' While wide awake I also 'saw' two figures walking by trees beside a lake, and I knew, though I don't know why, that one of them was Margaret Roper [daughter of Sir Thomas More]. (My maiden name was Moore and I have wondered whether there is any connection with Thomas More.) I also 'saw' two strange animals facing each other, one a horse, the other resembling an armadillo, but tied in what looked like string . . . After each of these I felt quite exhausted.

What is clear so far is that the accident produced a severe psychological shock, whose first effect was a perhaps over-active imagination. Visions of the accident were succeeded by visions of the past, which may have been pure hallucination. But in the 'retrocognition' that followed, she was able to obtain a certain amount of corroboration.

On a visit to Fotheringhay church about two months after the accident, she spent some time in front of a picture of the crucifixion behind the altar, on the left side of the church. 'It had an arched top and within the arch was a dove, its wings following the curve of the arch.'

Hours later, in their hotel room, Shirley read aloud from an essay by Charles Williams that infinity was sometimes symbolised by a straight line meeting an arc. Mrs O'Neill commented that this was what she had seen in the picture in the church, 'the upright of the cross meeting the curve of the arch with the dove'. 'What picture?' asked Shirley, and when she was told, replied that *she* hadn't noticed it.

> She is very observant—much more so than I am—so I was bothered by her remark. Two days later I decided to phone the vicar and ask him about the picture. I got through to the post office and asked for his number, to be told they hadn't had a vicar for three years. I apologised and asked the postmistress if she knew the church. She said she knew it well because she arranged flowers there every Sunday. I asked her if she could tell me about the pictures. She said there weren't any.

Two days later, the postmistress confirmed this in a letter. There was no painting, although there was a board with a dove on it behind the altar.

A year later, the two women revisited the church. 'While the outside of the building was exactly as I remembered it, I had no recollection at all of having been inside that church. It was much smaller than the one I had been in and there was no crucifixion. The dove—to my amazement—was not the one I had seen; this one is in a cloud, and its wings are outstretched, not curved.'

In Joan Forman's book *Haunted East Anglia*, Mrs O'Neill discovered that people had reported hearing Plantagenet music issuing from Fotheringhay church. She wrote to Joan Forman, who put her in touch with Tom Litchfield, a Northamptonshire historian who had studied the history of the church. On December 13, 1974, Litchfield wrote her a long letter explaining that the present church was the surviving remnant of a former collegiate church. The adjacent college and the cloisters and chancel had been pulled down in 1553 by Dudley, Duke of Northumberland, leaving only the nave which became the present church. A print of 1821 shows 'arched' panels on the east wall, behind the altar; 'the two central ones have a larger arch to embrace both, in the spandrel of which is the painting of a dove with outspread wings . . .'

Mrs O'Neill was inclined to believe that she had known Fotheringhay church in a previous existence and her experience was some kind of 'far memory'. Then one night as she lay awake in hospital (where she was being treated for asthma)

> I suddenly became aware that Nana (a nurse we had as children, who died of leukemia twenty years ago) was there. I couldn't see her, but I knew she was there. And I found myself saying to her (not aloud): 'You are outside time. Tell me about Fotheringhay.' And she replied that the picture I saw was one of a pair; the other also had an arched top and was of a bright blue sky with gold stars and angels. Higher up on the wall in a niche, she said, was a statue of the Blessed Virgin (I can see it, very clearly) and on the corner of the wall, jutting out, a statue of the Archangel Michael with a sword. I asked her when this was and she replied, '1570'. I asked her, 'Was I there?' but she replied 'No.'

In 1976, Mrs O'Neill had been in Sallé church, in Norfolk, when she heard the tramp of feet over her head. She knew no one was there and wondered if it could have some connection with the Civil War, when the church had been despoiled. After asking about the Fotheringhay experience as she lay in hospital, Mrs O'Neill also asked about the sound of feet at Salle church and was told that what she had heard had taken place in 1680 and had been made by men storing grain.

Mrs O'Neill's experiences are open to certain criticisms. There is a discrepancy between her painting—of the crucifixion, surmounted by a dove—and Tom Litchfield's description of the dove in the *spandrel* of the arch (i.e., above it.) Litchfield's information seems to correspond more closely to that obtained from her nurse Nana, but by then she had read his letter, so the Nana episode could have been a waking dream, or hypnogogic experience, based on what she already knew. It is also possible that she had at some time read about Fotheringhay church as it used to be—perhaps as a child, reading about the birth of Richard III or the execution of Mary Queen of Scots at Fotheringhay—so that the whole experience was simply a hallucination based upon something she once knew and had forgotten.

When all these possibilities are taken into account, it still seems remarkable that she should have 'seen' a far larger church, with a painting including a dove, when Fotheringhay church *had* once been larger and had contained a painting of a dove on the east wall, behind the altar.

If we are willing to grant that Jane O'Neill's vision *could* have been a genuine case of retrocognition, it can be explained more easily than the

Trianon experience. The key was the shock of the accident. Human beings maintain their mental balance by a kind of selective blindness. Every day we read accounts of violent accidents or watch them on the television screen. Yet although we may be shocked by the death toll, we deliberately avoid making the mental effort that would raise it beyond the level of an abstraction. In most cases, this is just as well; to grasp the reality behind the statistics would only increase our own sense of vulnerability.

But most healthy people also make an effort to face the violence of the modern world; this is because they wish to strengthen their reality function, which increases their chance of survival in our chaotic society. Jane O'Neill's accident strengthened her reality function a little too abruptly and traumatically. The result was a forcible widening of the boundaries of ego-consciousness. A similar effect might have been produced by a psychedelic drug. It also produced, as a by-product, one of the effects a magician strives for: the intensifying of active imagination. In short, a form of Faculty X.

The episode in Fotheringhay church could be explained in terms of Lethbridge's 'tape recordings'. The walls of Fotheringhay have witnessed a great deal of violence and tragedy, including its partial destruction by the Duke of Northumberland (who was beheaded a year before his son, and his daughter-in-law, Lady Jane Grey) and the execution of Mary, Queen of Scots. Jane O'Neill's accident may simply have endowed her with sensitivity to the 'recordings'. Lady Jane Grey, who was tried at Fotheringhay, must have been familiar with the panel, and perhaps she stared at it during her ordeal.

On the other hand, if precognition is a direct knowledge of the future, there is no reason why retrocognition should not be a direct knowledge of the past, without the intermediary of tape recordings. If the 'second whorl of the spiral' is a timeless realm, from which past and future are equally visible, perhaps Jane O'Neill's accident sensitised her to a level of her being that exists in the timeless realm.

This view is supported by an account of retrocognition given by Rayner Garner, a psychic whose work has been concerned with the interaction between human beings and plants. Garner describes how he was practising a meditation technique which involved holding a matchbox, and preventing it from 'getting away'. The effect seems to have been similar to Ouspensky's ability to 'sense' the houses of St Petersburg. He writes:[14]

The effect that it had on me. . . was to notice that if I stared at an object for more than a fleeting glance, I would begin to see superimposed, or rather underimposed, another picture. On this occasion, I was staring at a light plug and saw a picture which appeared to be people in a factory, which I took to be the place where it was manufactured. If I continued to gaze, a further series of pictures, rather more hazy, would appear —scenes which appeared to be the places where the raw materials of the plug were mined or extracted. I found this to be true of just about everything that I looked at for any length of time.

I was aware that this could have been an illusion, but when I discovered that the phenomena still took place when I was out of doors, it was possible to subject this to some form of test. I visited my mother who had lived in Harrow for most of her life and knew the surrounding countryside before it had been built on. With her, I walked around Harrow and its surrounds, describing, to her astonishment, the landscape with its farms, streams and fairly small pockets of dwelling places in existence before I was born. According to her memory I was very accurate. I cannot, of course, discount the possibility that I had at some time heard her describe what it was like in the past. . . all I can say is that I cannot consciously remember anything of the sort.

I also noticed that, as with the light plug, if I continued to look at one area, earlier dwellings would appear, then scrub or forest only; finally, in one case, earlier types of primitive dwellings such as I imagine a Stone-Age settlement would look like.

As to myself, I noticed that I appeared to be somewhat insubstantial. As I walked, everything, including my own body, appeared to be shimmering—at first I thought that I would have difficulty negotiating stairs and kerbstones. . . The whole universe seemed to be unreal, shimmering with energy. The only real thing was 'I'. For the first time in my life, I felt myself to be totally real. The observer was really 'here', and observing; everything else was an illusion. I could *see* particles which, for some reason, were slowed down. What a change from my usual state in which 'I' felt insubstantial and the rest of the universe too horribly real.

This state lasted about three weeks, during which time I lived in a curiously placid emotional condition, rather like being in a mild state of shock, not unpleasant, but oddly unreal.

He mentions that after he returned to 'normal', he again practised the technique of holding objects and preventing them from 'getting away'. (He ascribes the exercise to L. Ron Hubbard.) He found that it now had the effect of enabling him to re-live certain traumatic incidents of his childhood.

Rayner Garner's attempt to explain what happened is that the unconscious mind is a mass of 'heavy energy', which includes traumas and neuroses, and that the exercise of controlling consciousness can somehow release this energy, 'in which case, you are going to become very euphoric, insubstantial and not particularly stable'. This suggests that the original exercise produced some kind of violently disruptive effect, not unlike Jane O'Neill's accident, acting as a kind of depth charge that disturbed the normal balance of the subconscious. (There is also a parallel with my own panic attack, which was precipitated by an attempt to suppress the rising anxiety by sheer brute will-power.) Garner mentions that Hubbard stopped recommending the technique after he discovered that it made people ill.

In *The Doors of Perception*, Aldous Huxley quotes a remark by C. D. Broad:

> that we should do well to consider . . . the type of theory which Bergson put forward in connection with memory and sense perception. The suggestion is that the function of the brain and nervous system and sense organs is in the main *eliminative* and not productive. Each person is at each moment capable of remembering all that has ever happened to him and of perceiving everything that is happening everywhere in the universe. The function of the brain and nervous system is to protect us from being overwhelmed and confused by this mass of largely useless and irrelevant knowledge, by shutting out most of what we should otherwise perceive or remember at any moment, and leaving only that very small and special selection which is likely to be practically useful.

In other words, perhaps our senses are intended to keep things out rather than let them in, and the nervous system is a filter to stop us from being flooded with information.

Note that Broad says we are 'capable of remembering all that has ever happened [to us] and perceiving everything that is happening everywhere in the universe'. Why did he not add: 'everything that *has happened*'? This is no more startling—or preposterous—than the notion of perceiving everything that *is* happening.

This theory conflicts with our common-sense, ingrained notions. Supposedly, our senses are designed to tell us things about the world around us, not to keep things out. They do this by reacting to energy, which 'strikes' them rather like a pea shot from a pea-shooter.

If I now look up from my typewriter and glance across my study (which is in its usual chaotic state of untidiness) my eyes light on a manuscript bound in purple covers; the purple is shiny and is reflecting the rather grey, rainy light that comes in through the window. Scientifically speaking, all that is happening is that white light is striking the cover, which absorbs everything but the purple particles, leaving these particles to bounce around the room. Some of them strike my eyes. The result ought to be very straightforward, like a pattering noise. Yet as I gaze at the rich purple, I realise I am receiving far more than a pattering noise. The colour gives me a curious shock of pleasure, and if I stare at it for a moment or so, it causes ripples in my consciousness, and strange, agreeable feelings begin to well up inside me. It is pointless to tell me that all that is happening is that 'peas' of purple light are bouncing off my ocular window panes. I am receiving *meaning*. And I am receiving it by staring at the purple covers for several moments. If I merely glance at them, I observe their colour but nothing else. By staring at them, I am admitting more of their meaning. So our senses *are* filters. When I relax, they open wider and admit still more meaning. It is almost as if I was a radio set, and the meaning is being 'broadcast' through the ether. Most of the time, I am simply too busy—or preoccupied—to 'tune in'.

Such a view could explain psychic powers in general and why animals and primitive human beings seem to be more 'psychic' than the average modern city dweller. In a modern city, psychic powers have lost the obvious survival value they have in a jungle. So our natural balance system suppresses the psychic faculty and develops our alertness.

In many cases, a gain in psychic awareness is accompanied by a loss of some more useful faculty. For example, Jane O'Neill reports that she now often wins raffles—something that never happened before her 'accident'. But her long-term memory has become unrealiable; only a month after seeing a new production of *A Streetcar Named Desire*, she absentmindedly bought tickets to see it a second time. Yet it would be a mistake to conclude that this 'law of compensation' is inevitable. It may apply when psychic faculties are released by a violent accident, or by drugs, or even (perhaps) by hypnosis. This is because these methods involve a decrease in our coefficient of reality. Other methods such as meditation, 'gliding', self-remembering, or merely concentration exercises, lead to an increase in the coefficient of reality, and are equally effective. The dowser Robert Leftwich has commented that when he allows his health to deteriorate, his psychic powers decrease.[15] We could say that the 'negative' methods merely increase our psychic powers; the 'positive' methods increase Faculty X.

If all this is true, there is a further interesting consequence. We would *expect* ancient man to know more about the universe than we do in ways that involve direct intuition of psychic powers and a great deal less in ways that involve logic and rational observation. Yet we must bear in mind that man is higher on the evolutionary scale than any animal and that since his earliest appearance on this planet, his superiority has been based on brain-power. This means that we would expect him to do his best to *organise* his intuitive knowledge into systems.

And this is precisely what we do find. Because we have forgotten the importance of intuition, we are inclined to regard magical systems—shamanism, astrology, alchemy, cabbalism, divination—with patronising contempt. But if man really possesses a wider self which is hidden behind the barriers set up by his ego, and if this wider self is capable of receiving a greater range of information than the partial self, then these systems are less nonsensical than they seem. They may, in fact, be precisely what occultists claim they are: systems of forgotten knowledge.

7

Worlds Beyond

Possibly the most interesting first impressions of my life came from the world of dreams. And from my earliest years the world of dreams attracted me, made me search for explanations of its incomprehensible phenomena and try to determine the inter-relation of the real and the unreal in dreams . . . When still a child, I woke on several occasions with the distinct feeling of having experienced something so interesting and enthralling that all that I had known before, all that I had come into contact with or seen in life, appeared to me afterwards to be unworthy of attention and devoid of any interest.

In these words, Ouspensky describes the starting point of his lifelong search for a meaning beyond the 'triviality of everydayness'. This chapter on dreams and hypnotism occurs in his *New Model of the Universe*, the book he wrote after becoming acquainted with the teachings of Gurdjieff. It is a curious hotch-potch of a book, a mixture of acute psychological observation and disjointed speculations on magic, the fourth dimension, the Tarot, the New Testament, the Superman and the pyramids. But the chapter on dreams describes Ouspensky's own attempts to 'experiment with consciousness', and has an air of precision that is lacking in his poetical effusions on the Tarot cards and the Sphinx.

Like René Daumal, Ouspensky was anxious to observe states of consciousness normally inaccessible to human beings, but the method he chose was rather less hazardous. Ouspensky merely tried to observe his dreams and remember them on waking. He soon made the observation that can be tested by anyone at any time: that if your mind remains active when you are asleep, dreaming begins to approximate thinking. In fact, you merely begin to sleep badly. Ouspensky found that his efforts produced a state that was half-dreaming, half-thinking, which he called the 'half-dream state'. He found it best to create these states when he woke up in the morning, closing his eyes and dozing off again. If he tried them at night they only made him sleep badly. By concentrating on some thought or idea to keep the will awake, he was able to drift into a semi-sleeping state in which dreams recurred as usual, and in which it was possible to understand the cause of certain dreams. (For example, a recurring dream of sinking up to his knees in mud turned out to be due to the entanglement of his legs in the sheets.)

This constitutes Ouspensky's most important discovery in the realm of dream psychology: that it is possible to 'dream' while remaining sufficiently conscious to observe them. This state is midway between true dreaming and Jung's 'active imagination'. Ouspensky describes allowing himself to drift into a half-dream state and seeing golden dots and sparks appearing and disappearing in front of his eyes, while he is also conscious of his heartbeat. The gold sparks turn into a golden net, which in turn becomes the helmets of a marching Roman legion in Constantinople; his heartbeat is transformed into their tread. He is looking down on all this from a high window; then he floats out of the window, towards the sea and the Golden Horn; as he smells the sea and wind, and feels the warmth of the sun, he experiences deep pleasure and opens his eyes.

In another waking dream, he is in a room with a black kitten, and tells himself: 'If I am dreaming, let me transform this kitten into a dog.' Instantly it becomes a large white dog; at the same time the wall disappears, revealing a mountain landscape. He tries hard to remember why the landscape is familiar but realises that if he tries too hard, he will forget that he is dreaming and fall into a true dream. At this moment he feels himself flying backwards and wakes up.

Dreams of this type, in which the dreamer knows he is dreaming, are known as 'lucid dreams'. Primitive tribes regard them as particularly important because they believe that they are a means of entry into the spirit world. A Caribou Eskimo *shaman* described to Knud Rasmussen how 'unknown beings came and spoke to him [in sleep], and when he awoke, he saw all the visions of his dream so distinctly that he could tell his fellows all about them. Soon it became evident to all that he was destined to become an *angakoq* [*shaman*].'[1]

He was taken by his instructor to a tiny snow-hut in the coldest season of the year and left there for months with scarcely any food or drink, ordered to 'think of the Great Spirit'. During such ordeals, *shamans* 'die a little', and this half-death qualifies them as intermediaries with the spirit world. In the initiatory period of intense suffering, the *shaman* has vivid dreams amounting to hallucinations; in such dreams he is frequently killed and dismembered, then restored to life. When fully initiated, the *shaman* lives simultaneously in two worlds and is able to converse with the dead. In such cases, there seems to be no clear distinction between lucid dreams and visions.

Charles Leland, the historian of witchcraft, makes a close connection between dreams and magical powers. 'The fact is indisputable that when our ordinary waking consciousness or *will* goes to sleep or rest, or even dozes, that instant an entirely different power takes command of the myriad forces of memory . . . This power . . . knows things hidden from Me, and can do what *I* cannot.'[2]

Primitive men, he says, believe that these powers come from beings outside us—spirits or gods; in fact, they spring from the hidden depths of the mind. And he goes on to recount an interesting example of a lucid dream, in which he woke up in bed in Hamburg, in Germany, and realised that he should not be there. He concluded that he was dreaming and asked a nurse to tell him whether he was asleep or awake; she assured him that he was awake. He went into the street, and asked several people to pinch him to see if he was awake; one of them said he recognised him as someone he had met before and obliged him by squeezing his arm. It had no effect. He now began to believe he was awake and returned to his room where he found a child speaking to the nurse. He asked her to shake his hand, and the feeling was so real that he was now quite convinced that he was awake. 'And the instant it came home to me that it was a reality, there seized me the thrill or feeling as of a coming nightmare—and I awoke.' Leland comments that the 'Dream Artist' has a sardonic sense of humour and moreover is 'a very different kind of person from me'. He seems to be hinting at the mystery of multiple personality as well as at the connection between dreams and magical powers. Yet Leland, who was never a logical thinker, failed to pursue this important clue to the foundations of magic.

In a short paper on dreaming,[3] the Dutchman Frederik Van Eeden made a number of important observations on lucid dreams. Like Charles Leland, he often found them highly deceptive. Floating over an April landscape, watching the perspective of the branches changing as he passed over them, he reflected that his sleeping fancy would never be able to invent anything so natural. One day when he dreamed he was lying on his stomach, looking through a window, it struck him that he was actually in bed, lying on his back.

> And then I resolved to wake up slowly and carefully and observe how my sensation of lying on my chest would change into the sensation of lying on my back. And so I did, slowly and deliberately, and the transition—which I have since undergone many times—is most wonderful. It is like the feeling of slipping from one body into another, and there is distinctly a *double* recollection of the two bodies . . . It is so indubitable that it leads almost unavoidably to the conception of *a dream body*.

Van Eeden quotes a sceptical remark by Havelock Ellis to the effect that only dabblers in the occult believe in 'the astral body', and comments that if Ellis had experienced lucid dreams, he would have recognised the existence of the dream body. Here Van Eeden is identifying his 'dream body' with the 'astral body', whose existence is a basic tenet of most forms of occultism; but he has nothing more to say about this interesting identification.

An Englishman named Oliver Fox[4] went a stage further. As a child, Fox had experienced almost continual illness, and became accustomed to vivid dreams and nightmares. In 1902, when he was sixteen, he dreamt he was standing on the pavement outside his house on a sunny morning when he suddenly observed something odd about the pavement. Instead of being at right angles to the kerb, the paving stones were parallel to it. It suddenly struck him that he must be asleep and dreaming. 'Instantly the vividness of the sky increased a hundredfold. Never had sea and sky and trees shone with such glamorous beauty . . . Never had I felt so absolutely well, so clear-brained, so divinely powerful, so inexpressibly *free*.'

He determined to try to repeat the experience, which he decided depended on noting incongruities in the dream. Before going to sleep at night he would concentrate on trying to observe such inconsistencies. It proved to be extremely difficult; but eventually he became better at it and learned to turn ordinary dreams into lucid dreams. In such dreams, he discovered he could fly or levitate or pass through brick walls. But the sense of freedom never lasted long; his physical body would demand his return; when he resisted, he would experience a pain in the forehead of his 'dream body'.

One day, as he was dreaming of walking on the seashore, he noticed some incongruity and passed into a lucid dream. When his body began to draw him back, he deliberately resisted. There was a kind of tug of war in which the dream landscape faded and his bedroom became real, then the bedroom faded and the seashore reappeared. As the pain in his forehead intensified, he fought against it. Suddenly, it disappeared with a click. 'I had won the battle. My body pulled no longer, and I was free.'

He continued his walk for a time, then began to worry about getting to college (he was studying engineering at Southampton at the time). He tried to will himself to wake up, but without effect. He tried to ask a passer-by the time, but the man walked on without seeing him. After more frantic effort, there was another 'click', and he was back in his body again, but totally unable to move. Eventually, by an immense effort of will, he moved his little finger, then the rest of the hand, then, eventually, his whole body. For the next three days he felt depressed and lethargic.

The experience raises the obvious question of whether he had really been walking on the seashore in his dream body and had somehow caused this body temporarily to separate from his physical body. Natural scepticism inclines us to believe that the whole thing was probably an elaborate 'dream within a dream'. This was Fox's own suspicion until he tried a practical experiment. On the night before an exam, he dreamed he was in the examination room and did his best to memorise the questions. He succeeded in remembering only two of them. Both questions were on the exam paper next day. The first was a likely question, but the second had not been asked for many years, as he discovered by looking up past exam papers.

Two friends who were also interested in dream projection agreed to try to meet Fox on Southampton Common in their dreams. Fox dreamed that he was on the common, but that only one of the two turned up; they commented on the absence of their friend Slade. The next morning, the two met at college and Fox asked his friend about his dreams. 'I met you on the common all right and knew I was dreaming, but old Slade didn't turn up.' Slade, it transpired, had not dreamt at all.

Like Robert Monroe, the American businessman whose experiences were described in an earlier chapter,[5] Oliver Fox discovered that he could 'leave his body' by inducing a semi-trance state. He would lie down, relax completely, close his eyes, and try to hurl himself against an imaginary trapdoor which he called 'the pineal door', referring to the 'third eye' of Hindu philosophy. The room would seem to fill with a golden light, and if he could prevent himself from falling asleep, he could then leave his body, 'as if climbing out of bed', and embark on one of his strange 'astral journeys' without having lost consciousness. But he found the 'pineal door' method somehow unpleasant and frightening and eventually lost the ability to achieve astral projection by this means. But he continued to be able to use the old technique of inducing a lucid dream, which would often pass into false awakening and a trance condition from which he could hurl himself into the astral world by means of what he called instantaneous projection. He apparently maintained this remarkable ability to the end of his life.

It may, at this point, be worth mentioning my own rather limited experience of lucid dreams. Since first reading of Oliver Fox's experiences, I have occasionally tried, in a rather half-hearted way, to make myself conscious that I am dreaming. I have tried to do this by fixing the notion firmly in my mind before I fell asleep. This had very little effect. On the other hand, I have been more successful when not trying so hard. The trick seems to be to think *about* the possibility of lucid dreams at intervals during the day, until the whole notion has become a part of one's mental furniture. This, I think, is what Oliver Fox did. During the writing of this book I have had two lucid dreams that had a definitely 'different' quality. In one, I dreamed of my father, who died a few years ago. As I was walking along with him, I suddenly had the suspicion that he was dead. I looked at him and thought: 'Of course he's dead.' At the same time, I placed my hand on his shoulder and verified that he was solid. Then I looked at him closely, observed that I could see him in detail, and thought: 'Well, even if he's dead, he's certainly here.' The dream faded away.

A few nights later, I had an even clearer dream. I was in bed in a strange town; I was experiencing some physical discomfort—in reality as well as in the dream—from a desire to urinate. I walked towards the town square, where there was a public lavatory, but somehow missed it. The town was high up, on a hilltop, and I found myself looking at a delightful prospect of grass and trees and thinking: 'This looks very beautiful, yet I am sure this is a dream.' As soon as this thought occurred to me, I looked at the scenery even more intently and was even more convinced of its reality. I thought: 'If this is a dream, I may as well fly', and held up my hands. I immediately floated off the ground and up into the air, feeling rather pleased that I had at last accomplished what Oliver Fox had described. But the clarity vanished as I floated upwards, as if my mind could no longer sustain the sense of reality, and the dream changed into a 'normal' dream, and I woke up.

I attach a different significance to 'vivid' dreams. These are dreams in which the scenery is exceptionally real. I dreamed once that I had landed in New York with my mother. I had been in New York, but this was quite different. I was looking over the river with a tremendous bridge arching overhead and the buildings looking immense and very beautiful. I was struck chiefly by the richness and variety of the colours, and a sense of wonder and excitement.

Closely related to these vivid dreams are dreams in which one's creative consciousness seems to work at top pressure. I recall a dream in which I was conducting a symphony, and can recall the beauty and complexity of the music, which seemed to go on for several minutes. In another dream I was reading aloud a poem I had composed (I never write poetry), and could still recall some of it when I woke up. It convinced me of the truth of Coleridge's account of how he dreamed *Kubla Khan*, which I had always been inclined to doubt.

Vivid dreams seem to me to convey a message from the subconscious—or superconscious—mind. Most people are more accustomed to anxiety dreams—dreams that seem to undermine our confidence; we find ourselves in a public square without any trousers, or hurtling at a hundred miles an hour over a road in a car without brakes. Vivid dreams have always given me a strong sense that the subconscious is trying to convey the opposite message: that ordinary experience is somehow debased and unreal and that this is related to our pessimism and lack of courage. And as if to prove its *bona fides*, the subconscious proceeds to compose a symphony or to create a scene of such startling beauty *and reality* that it is impossible to doubt that it is a message from some higher level of the mind.

All this substantiates Jung's feeling that characters like Philemon, whom he encountered in his 'descent into the unconscious', possessed a kind of reality of their own. It also suggests that Oliver Fox's dreams of astral travel, in spite of their vivid sense of reality, may have been no more than dreams.

It must be said that the evidence for out-of-the-body experiences is abundant and impressive. There are literally hundreds of records of such happenings. In *The Romeo Error*, the zoologist Lyall Watson describes how the vehicle he was driving in Kenya overturned and he suddenly found himself outside the bus, looking at the head and shoulders of a boy who had been hurled halfway through the canvas roof and who would be crushed if the bus rolled over any farther. Seconds later, Watson recovered consciousness in the front seat, clambered out of the bus, and rescued the boy, who was in exactly the same position that he had seen moments earlier.[6]

The American artist Ingo Swann describes how, at the age of two and a half, he had an operation for removal of his tonsils.[7] Under anaesthetic, he found himself watching the doctor removing the tonsils, and also saw the knife slip and cut the back of his tongue. The doctor swore as he removed the tonsils; then he dropped them into a bottle and placed it on a sideboard. When Swann woke up a few minutes later, he demanded his tonsils, pointing to the bottle (which was hidden behind two rolls of tissue), and commented that the doctor had said 'Shit' as he performed the operation. His mother was baffled by the accuracy of the description of what had taken place. In later years, his ability to leave his body—he prefers to call it 'distant viewing'—was tested at Stanford University by Targ and Puthoff (who also tested Uri Geller)—and the results seemed to prove beyond all doubt that he could somehow 'project' himself to a distant place and describe what he saw there. Perhaps his most spectacular success was in describing many features of the planet Mercury—including the precise shape of its magnetic field—before the space craft Mariner 10 arrived there and verified his observations. But his observations on Jupiter—also written down and notarised at the time—proved to be far less accurate.

The novelist William Gerhardie awoke from a feverish sleep one day to find himself floating in the air above his body, although attached to it by a kind of shining cord that seemed to extend from the forehead of his sleeping body to the back of his own neck. When he walked, he felt as if he was wading through water. He describes the experience in some detail in his novel *Resurrection*[8] and admits that it convinced him of the reality of survival after death. He also adds that his 'monitor, my unconscious will, who in the physical body was the silent and invisible engineer', had 'in these uncharted seas . . . come upon the bridge'. The implication is clearly that in his out-of-the-body state, Gerhardie felt a direct contact with his subconscious mind he had expanded beyond the usual narrow wedge of ego-consciousness.

Oliver Fox was in poor health when he began to explore the secrets of astral projection; Gerhardie was in a feverish sleep. Sylvan Muldoon, perhaps the best-known of all writers on the subject, also experienced poor health throughout childhood and early manhood.

Muldoon had his first experience of astral projection when he was twelve, and on a visit with his mother to the Mississippi Valley Spiritualists' Association in Clinton, Iowa. He woke up in the middle of the night with a feeling of paralysis and found himself floating in the air above his bed. Like Gerhardie, he observed a 'shining cord' attached to the base of the brain (medulla oblongata), where it joins the spinal cord. This was the first of many such experiences. A few years later, when he read a book by the psychical researcher Hereward Carrington, Muldoon wrote to him to describe his own experiences. The result was a book written in collaboration, *The Projection of the Astral Body* (1929), containing detailed accounts of Muldoon's experiences. A second volume, *The Phenomena of Astral Projection* (1951) is devoted largely to dozens of reports of similar experiences taken from the literature of psychic investigation and from correspondents. Muldoon is distinctly sceptical about astral travellers who claim to have visited other spiritual planes; his own experiences were all confined to the earth, and he comments: 'I wouldn't know where to look for the higher planes.' He was occasionally able to verify his experiences. He describes how he once found himself in a farmhouse, watching four strangers, including a girl of seventeen. Some weeks later he saw the girl in the street and accosted her, asking her where she lived. Understandably she told him to mind his own business. But when Muldoon described the room where he had seen her, she had to admit the accuracy of his description of her home and family. She later became a close friend, and collaborated in many of his experiments. Increasing celebrity and financial security had the paradoxical effect of making astral projection more difficult; in later life (he died in 1971) he lost the ability completely.

The Phenomena of Astral Projection was one of the first extended studies of the subject; since then, there have been many more, including Celia Green's *Out-of-the-Body Experiences* (1968), and many books by Dr Robert Crookall such as *The Mechanisms of Astral Projection* (1978.) Crookall's books, which contain well over a thousand cases, suggest that astral projection is either the commonest of psychic phenomena or the most universal form of hallucination. Once again, an enormous percentage of such experiences seem to be associated with crisis situations—illness, accidents, operations under anaesthetic, intense pain.

In his book, *The Twenty-Fifth Man*, Ed Morrell describes his experiences in the Arizona State Penitentiary, where he was often subjected to a form of torture. Refractory prisoners were tied into two strait jackets, which were then soaked with water. As they dried, they shrank, so the prisoner felt he was being crushed to death by a boa constrictor. The first time this happened, Morrell felt as if he were smothering, and sparks danced in front of his eyes. Then suddenly, he found himself walking around outside the prison, apparently free. Since Morrell was a difficult prisoner with strong anti-capitalist views (Jack London made him the hero of his last novel *The Star Rover*), he was often tortured in this manner; his guards found it baffling that his reaction to the pain was apparently to fall asleep. During this 'sleep', Morrell wandered freely and explored the streets of San Francisco. Like Muldoon, he was able to verify many of the things he saw in this condition, including a shipwreck in San Francisco Bay. The Governor of Arizona, George W. P. Hunt, was also able to verify that Morrell described accurately certain events that had taken place while his body was in a state of 'sleep' in his cell. When Morrell was no longer subjected to torture, he immediately lost his ability to leave his body.

A remarkable English psychic, Robert Cracknell, has described in his autobiography an experience that combines lucid dreaming and precognition. When he was in the RAF, Cracknell had not yet realised that he was psychic, although he experienced a curious fear of the dark. One night when he was the Guard Commander, he went to sleep on a bunk, arranging with one of the men that he should be awakened instantly if the Orderly Officer appeared.

> I remember lying in this bunk, fully dressed, and drifting into sleep. And it was as though I woke up. I could hear quite distinctly the voice of the Orderly Officer in the main guardroom asking where I was . . . And I tried to call out: 'Here I am, sir, just coming.' But not a sound came out. I struggled to get up and found, to my absolute horror, that I was completely paralysed. I knew in a strange way that I was not asleep. This was not a dream. And yet I could not move a muscle, and for what seemed at least three minutes I was calling out for help . . . And then, from somewhere at the back of my mind, came the impression that I should relax. The panic, however, was too strong. I recall hearing somebody walking down the corridor, and a voice saying: 'Quick, Corp, wake up.' This time I managed to struggle out of the peculiar paralysis . . .

But the room was empty. And a few moments later, one of the guards came in to warn him of the approach of the Orderly Officer. Cracknell had dreamed it in advance, yet he remains convinced that this was *not* a dream. His paralysis sounds like the state that so many have experienced before projection of the astral body. It was the beginning of the development of his remarkable psychic powers.

It is evident from such cases that there is no sharp dividing line between astral travel and lucid dreaming. Sceptics regard this as a good reason for rejecting both. But the 'ladder-of-selves' hypothesis suggests a less wholesale view. When a map dowser locates a sunken wreck on the other side of the world, he seems to be utilising some unknown power of the mind—as if he possessed a being like Shakespeare's Ariel that could move at the speed of light. It seems a reasonable supposition that 'Ariel' is a higher level of consciousness. Gerhardie seemed to feel himself more in touch with the 'subconscious engineer' when he was out of the body. So it is possible that a person in this state should be able to take a trip to see the sunken wreck.

In fact, there is a considerable body of evidence to connect the power of thought with astral projection or the phenomenon known as phantasms of the living. In the well-known Verity cases, cited by F. W. H. Myers in *Human Personality and Its Survival of Bodily Death*, a young man named S. H. Beard made a deliberate attempt to project himself to the house of his fiancée, Miss L. S. Verity, and was seen by her and her eleven-year-old sister. He did this by a deliberate effort of intense concentration. But in the majority of cases, the 'phantasm' seems to be projected accidentally when one person happens to be thinking intently about another, or about a certain place. There is a famous story of St Anthony of Padua that asserts that while he was preaching in a church at Limoges on Holy Thursday, 1226, he suddenly recollected that he was supposed to be in another church at the other end of town; the congregation in the other church saw him there at the same moment. In 1774, Alphonsus de' Liguori, imprisoned at Arezzo, woke up at the end of a five-day fast and announced that he had been present at the deathbed of Pope Clement XIV; his description proved to be accurate, and he was seen at the bedside of the dying pope.

Goethe tells how, as he was walking home one day after a heavy shower, he was surprised to see a friend named Friedrich walking in front of him wearing his—Goethe's—dressing gown. He arrived home to find Friedrich in front of the fire in his dressing gown; Friedrich had been on his way to visit Goethe when he was caught in the rain. No doubt he was thinking of Goethe as he put on the dressing gown and somehow managed to make Goethe see an apparently solid image of himself some distance away.

On another occasion, also described in his autobiography, Goethe was riding along a road in Alsace, having just said goodbye to a sweetheart, when he saw 'with the eyes of the spirit' his own apparition coming towards him dressed in a grey and gold suit. (The phenomenon is known as a doppelgänger.) Eight years later, on his way to visit the same girl, he passed the spot and suddenly realised that he was now dressed in the grey and gold suit. He had 'seen' his future self. In this case, he was aware that it was a mental image rather than a real person; but if a phantasm is, in fact, a thought-projection, the difference may be less important than it seems.

Perhaps the most striking case in the whole literature of phantasms of the living is that of Emilie Sagée, an attractive French schoolmistress who lost eighteen jobs in sixteen years because of her strange—and involuntary—ability to be in two places at once. Many authorities, including Professor Charles Richet, have expressed disbelief on the grounds that the evidence is insufficient. On the other hand, the case was reported by Robert Dale Owen, an American of Welsh descent, who was regarded in his own time as an honest and reliable psychical researcher. Owen had it direct from the Baroness von Güldenstubbe, a pupil and friend of Mlle Sagée, who supplied an impressive abundance of names and dates.

Emilie Sagée was born in Dijon on January 3, 1813 and was educated in the convent school next to the Hotel de Ville. She seems to have been an orphan. In 1829, at the age of sixteen, she left Dijon and took her first job as a teacher. Sixteen years—and seventeen jobs —later she obtained a post at a school for aristocratic young ladies at Neuwelcke, near Wolmar, on the shores of the Baltic. There were forty-two pupils.

The pupils often argued about precisely where Mlle Sagée had been at certain times, since she seemed to have a curious ability to be in two places at once. One day, as she was writing on the blackboard, her pupils were astonished to see two Emilie Sagées standing side by side, both apparently writing with chalk. As Emilie turned, startled at the sudden noise, the 'double' vanished. On another occasion, as Emilie was helping to fix the dress of a Mlle Antoinette de Wrangel, the girl looked into the mirror and saw two Emilies; she fainted.

One warm summer day, as Emilie was picking flowers in the garden, the girls asked the teacher if they might do their lessons there. The teacher went off to consult the headmistress. Suddenly, the form of Mlle Sagée was seen sitting in the teacher's chair in the schoolroom. Two of the bolder pupils tried to touch her and said that the apparition felt like muslin. One of them even walked through her. Then the image vanished. When Baroness von Güldenstubbe asked Emilie about the occurence, she said that she had looked into the room through the window, seen that the teacher had left, and felt concerned that the class would waste their time. One of the girls had noticed that the 'real Emilie', in the garden, became pale and looked ill when her double suddenly appeared.

Some of the pupils found these events alarming, and when a number of them had been removed from the school, the directors decided that they had to ask Emilie to leave, although she was an excellent teacher. Baroness von Güldenstubbe later visited her at the house of her sister-in-law and found that everyone there was quite accustomed to Emilie's curious ability to be in two places at once. But when Robert Dale Owen met Baroness von Güldenstubbe in London eight years later—in 1853—the Baroness had lost sight of Emilie Sagée, who had left her sister-in-law's home and vanished.

The story bears so many resemblances to dozens of other cases recorded in *Phantasms of the Living* that there seem to be no reasonable grounds for dismissing it as an invention. The appearance in the schoolroom while Emilie was in the garden suggests that it was basically some form of thought transference. The doppelgänger effect occurred most often when Emilie was tired or absent-minded, and not when she was healthy and absorbed in her work. Apparently her 'control' over her astral body—or whatever it was—became weaker when her mind was 'elsewhere'.

This again raises the problem of what we mean when we say that the mind is 'elsewhere', or that somebody 'isn't all there'. Where precisely is my mind when my attention wanders? Sometimes, of course, I am simply thinking of something else or free-associating. But if I am tired or bored, I may stare blankly out of the window and think of nothing in particular. In this state, I am not far from the basic condition of hypnosis, or even sleep. And if Lethbridge and Monroe are right in believing that the astral body leaves the physical body during sleep, then we can easily see that it might also wander off during moments of abstraction.

Emilie Sagée was plainly one of those rather neurasthenic young women who lack the vitality to cope with the problems of everyday life. Her mind was always wandering. And, for some unknown physical or psychological reason, her double wandered off too. Sometimes it merely drifted a few feet away. Sometimes she projected it to some place she was thinking about. And in this case, she became obviously 'devitalised'. Antoinette de Wrangel was in Emilie's bedroom one day when Emilie was suffering from some minor ailment and saw her suddenly become as pale as death. Antoinette looked round to find the 'other Emilie' standing at the end of the bed. In moments like this, Emilie Sagée looked blank, as if she had been hypnotised.

Scotland and Norway have their own peculiar version of the doppelgänger, known as the forerunner or vardøger. In the many recorded cases, the phantasm of the living *precedes* the person concerned on a journey and may be seen getting off a train or walking into a hotel where his physical body is not expected for days or weeks. The obvious explanation is that the 'thought form' of the person is projected to a place he intends to visit, exactly as in the majority of cases of phantasms of the living. But there is room for doubt. The Reverend W. Mountford of Boston, Massachusetts describes how when he was visiting friends he observed their brother and sister-in-law driving up to the house in a horse-drawn buggy. To everyone's surprise, the buggy went straight on past the house. A daughter of the expected visitors, who was outside the house at the time, saw her father and mother drive by without glancing at her. And while everyone was discussing this strange occurrence, the buggy actually arrived with the real brother and sister-in-law. If the projection theory is to be accepted, we must assume that someone's mind projected a threefold apparition.

Stranger still is the case of Erkson Gorique, a New York importer who went to Norway for the first time in 1955 to set up business connections. The clerk of the Oslo hotel remarked politely that it was nice to see him again, and obviously disbelieved Gorique's assurance that this was his first visit to Norway. A wholesale dealer named Olsen reacted in the same way when Gorique called on him the next day, and assured him they had met two months before. Olsen finally reassured the bewildered Gorique that no one had been impersonating him by explaining about the vardøger. But it seems that in this case, Gorique's phantasm had not merely preceded him, but had presumably spoken to a number of people.

On February 23, 1883, Dr Charles Féré, of the Asylum Bicêtre in Paris, was attending a twenty-eight-year-old hysteric. At the height of a particularly painful attack, Féré was surprised to see an orange colour appearing on the white skin of her head and hands. A few seconds later, both head and hands began to emit an orange coloured light. This strange glow persisted for about four hours; then the woman vomited, and it vanished as her skin returned to normal. Féré mentioned the case in an article in the *Annales des Sciences Psychiques* in July 1905, together with another example which he had observed in a patient who suffered from violent headaches at the menstrual period. He referred to the phenomenon as a 'neuropathic halo' and had no doubt that it was some kind of electrical emanation of the nervous system.

Fifty years earlier, Féré's observations would have excited a certain amount of scientific curiosity. In 1845 an eminent German scientist, Baron Karl von Reichenbach, who, among other things discovered paraffin, had announced that crystals and magnets emit a curious radiation that can be seen by 'sensitives'. For example, the previous

May, Reichenbach had taken a large piece of mountain crystal to the home of a sick girl named Angelica Sturman and placed it in a completely dark room. The girl was brought into the room, and within seconds was able to tell Reichenbach where he had placed the crystal. Reichenbach and a doctor who was present could see nothing in the pitch blackness, but the girl said that the crystal was glowing with blue light and a tulip-shaped blue light sprayed like a fountain out of one point of the crystal, emitting tiny sparks. When Reichenbach groped his way to the crystal and turned it upside down, she said she now saw a smoky yellow light coming from the other end. With German thoroughness Reichenbach conducted thousands of experiments to make sure this was not all imagination. When magnets were used, the blue light came from the north pole and the yellow from the south. When the sensitive placed her hand in the blue glow, she felt a pleasant, cooling current, like air; the yellow glow produced an unpleasant, warm sensation. Experiments with precious stones revealed the curious fact that the colours associated with them were the same colours found in a table of 'magical correspondences'.

Further experiment revealed that a person did not need to be a sick sensitive to see the emanation; many healthy people could see it if they made the effort (it sometimes took several hours). Moreover, human beings themselves emitted the same kind of coloured radiation—for example, it could be seen as light streaming from the fingertips. Reichenbach·called this radiation 'od'; English disciples preferred to call it the odic force. Reichenbach made the interesting observation that the aura of a sick person was duller than that of a healthy person; this could explain why sick people were more sensitive to the odic force; they presumably attracted it.

Before this important observation could be properly investigated, science abruptly changed its mind about the odic force. Hypnotists were beginning to realise that many of Mesmer's cures could be explained by suggestion, and Dr James Braid, one of the founding figures of the science of hypnosis, believed the same might be true of Reichenbach's observations. The experiments with magnets sounded ominously like Mesmer's own original discovery that patients could be cured by massaging them with magnets. Was 'odic force' in fact anything more than Mesmer's discredited animal magnetism?

To some extent, Braid was obviously correct. If you spend four hours in the dark, striving to see emanations from a crystal, you will almost certainly influence yourself into seeing *something*. On the other hand, the majority of Reichenbach's experiments left no room for the power of suggestion. Sensitives with absolutely no knowledge of his theories made identical observations about crystals and magnets. Nevertheless, the scientific establishment again demonstrated its own peculiar form of religious intolerance and declined to pay any further attention to Reichenbach's theories. One eminent scientist dismissed his major work, *Researches on Magnetism, Electricity, Heat and Light in their Relation to Vital Forces* (1845) as an absurd romance. Reichenbach died at the age of eighty, in 1869, 'his reputation having predeceased him'.

At the same time in America, Professor James Rhodes Buchanan was discovering the odic force under another name. Buchanan was Dean of the Faculty at the Eclectic Medical Institute in Covington, Kentucky, and he was intrigued when Bishop Leonidas Polk told him that he could detect brass in the dark because its touch produced an unpleasant metallic taste in his mouth. Polk was also highly sensitive to atmospheric conditions. Buchanan was unable to explain how the sense of touch could affect the organs of taste. Yet his experiments convinced him that it could. He tried wrapping various medicines in parcels and seeing whether his students could detect the nature of the medicine by holding the parcel in their hands; again, the success rate astonished him. His conclusion was that the nerves produce some kind of current or force—he called it the nerve-aura—which operates like an extra sense. He also invented a word for the ability to discover information by the sense of touch alone: psychometry.

He tried further experiments. He asked a friend to write his name on a sheet of paper and handed it, folded, to a woman who had shown a remarkable talent for psychometry. She was able to describe the character of the man with astonishing accuracy. When psychometrists held objects belonging to a certain person, they were often able to describe the person and even produce intimate details of his life. Buchanan concluded that all substances give off 'emanations', which are affected by human emotions. (Lethbridge was later to make the same discovery when he tested sling stones that had been thrown in anger in battle.) He reached the astonishing conclusion that the history of the world lies all around us, recorded upon objects, and that anyone who developed the power of psychometry could read that history as the geologist reads the record of the rocks. But he dismissed the notion that there is anything supernatural about such a faculty. It is no more miraculous than our powers of sight and hearing. According to Buchanan, everyone possesses to a greater or lesser extent, the power of retrocognition. The experiences of Jane O'Neill and Rayner Garner described in the last chapter would not have surprised him in the least. In his *Manual of Psychometry* (1889) he asserted that 'the mental telescope is now discovered which may pierce the depths of the past and bring us in full view of the grand and tragic passages of ancient history'.

But, as in the case of Reichenbach, his careful experiments failed to impress other scientists, for Buchanan made no secret of the fact that he was a spiritualist. When the Fox sisters inaugurated the turbulent history of spiritualism by producing their mysterious rappings at Hydesville, Buchanan was one of the few scientists who did not believe that they were frauds. So his observations on psychometry were open to the suspicion of being influenced by wishful thinking. Yet, as in the case of Reichenbach, the design of his experiments was usually above reproach. To preclude the possibility of telepathy, many objects were wrapped in parcels which were shuffled so that Buchanan himself had no idea of what was in each parcel until it was finally unwrapped.

His friend and colleague William Denton, a professor of geology, began to conduct a similar series of experiments in 1849 and published the results of hundreds of them in several books, beginning with *Nature's Secrets* in 1863. Understandably, Denton's 'objects' were usually geological samples, and many of the results were spectacular: a fragment of lava from a Hawaiian island gave the psychometrist a picture of an ocean of fire pouring over a precipice; a pebble of glacial limestone produced a picture of being deep under the sea and frozen into ice. Like Buchanan, Denton became convinced that the whole history of the earth is imprinted in the objects that surround us and can be read by anyone who takes the trouble to develop the faculty. He concluded that one man in ten, and one woman in four is able to read the past in this manner.

Why do we not all possess such a faculty as a matter of course? Again, the answer is because it is not particularly important to our survival, which demands constant attention to the present. Where everyday living is concerned, an over-developed psychic faculty is little more than a nuisance to its possessor.

Although the theories of Reichenbach, Buchanan and Denton had fallen into general disrepute by the turn of the century, Dr Walter J. Kilner of St Thomas's Hospital in London felt there was still some advantage to be gained from assuming the existence of the nervous aura. Born in 1847, Kilner could recall the time when Reichenbach was still taken seriously in England. Unlike Denton and Buchanan, he had no psychic interests; he simply felt that *if* the aura exists, and if it changes according to the health of the patient, it could be an important aid to diagnosis. The problem he set himself was to discover how the aura could be seen by a medical practitioner without psychic faculties.

He approached the problem scientifically. If the aura is a form of radiant energy, then it ought to be possible to sensitise the eyes to see it, just as we can sensitise them to see in the twilight. He placed his subjects against a black background and tried viewing them through various dicyanin dyes sealed hermetically between two glass plates. To sensitise his eyes he looked at daylight through a dark screen, which would act like an artificial twilight, and then looked at the human body through a much lighter screen. Under these conditions, it was easy to see that the human body was surrounded by a kind of envelope of energy, which seemed to have three distinct layers. At least, so Kilner claimed in his book *The Human Atmosphere* (1911). He even included one of his special screens with every copy of the book.

The innermost layer, which he concluded was made of some form of fine matter, Kilner labelled 'the etheric double'. The other two layers he called the inner and outer auras; altogether these extend for well over a foot from the human body. The entire aura was sensitive to magnets and when subjected to the negative current from a Wilmshurst machine—a device for producing an electric charge—it vanished completely, then reappeared with an increased intensity. Kilner made many observations of the change in size and colour of the aura during illness; he also noted that it becomes duller under hypnosis. He reasoned that it seems to be a function of human vitality and is probably produced by the higher brain centres.

Kilner failed to realise his basic aim: to enable any person to study the aura. Once again, critics could explain his results by suggestion. Kilner asserted that once the eyes had become accustomed to the use of the screens, they became sensitised and were able to perceive the aura without apparatus. Critics replied that there is no known medical reason why the eyes should become sensitised to a new kind of energy.

Yet anyone who has ever listened intently for a telephone call will know that the ears continue to pick up non-existent telephone bells for hours afterwards. The same 'expectation' phenomenon could apply to the aura. Kilner died in 1920, but he still has many followers, and one of them, H. Boddington, claims to have discovered a kind of glass manufactured in Czechosolvakia that renders the screens unnecessary. But the majority of the medical profession classifies Kilner screens as crank aberrations.

Yet in spite of the lack of organised research, new discoveries continue to be made. In the mid-1930s, two Yale physicists, Harold Saxton Burr and F. S. C. Northrop, published a paper called 'The Electrodynamic Theory of Life', which suggested, in essence, that living creatures are held together by a kind of magnetic—or electrical—field. We have all seen iron filings pulled into a certain shape by a magnet; Burr and Northrop were suggesting, in effect, that the electrons of living creatures are given their shape by a similar field. The chief problem in attempting to test such an idea was to devise a voltmeter delicate enough to measure fields of a thousandth of a microvolt. Once this had been developed, the rest was straightforward. When the voltmeter was attached to a tree, it not only registered the tree's electrical field but showed that this varied with thunderstorms, sunspots and changes of season. These fields appeared to be the 'matrix', or mould, for the shapes poured into them. A frog's egg showed varous lines of electrical force; as the egg turned into a tadpole, these were found to be the frog's nervous system, already drawn, as it were, by a kind of electrical pencil.

Burr later called these fields of force 'L-fields', the L standing for life. Burr and Northrop discovered that the L-field rises sharply when animals ovulate; one of Burr's female patients used this discovery to conceive a child. L-field measurements could also reveal the presence of cancer and other latent illnesses and predict when mental patients would have 'attacks'. In short, Burr verified most of the things that Kilner had said thirty years earlier. Admittedly, his machine did not photograph the aura; but it revealed the presence of electric fields associated with life.

No one has ever questioned the validity of Burr's methods of measurement. This is not true of the discovery made by the Russian Professor Semyon Kirlian in 1939. When Kirlian was visiting a hospital in Krasnodar in the USSR, he stopped to watch a patient receiving treatment from a new high-frequency generator. As glass electrodes were brought close to the patient's skin, there was a tiny flash, not unlike the flash in a neon tube when you turn on the light. In a neon tube, the flash comes from the presence of a gas, which is charged by the electric spark. What was being 'charged' by the high-frequency electrode? The obvious way to find out was to try to photograph it. Kirlian and his wife Valentina set up two metal plates to act as electrodes and placed a photographic film on one of them. The he put his hand between the plates and turned on the current. The result was painful—if the plates had been closer together, a high voltage spark would have leapt between them—but when the photograph was developed, it showed Kirlian's hand surrounded by a strange glowing corona.

When a leaf was photographed between the plates, it showed hundreds of dots of energy and small flares of energy exploding around its edges. When the stem of a newly-cut flower was used, the photograph showed sparks flowing from the stem. Strangest of all, when a torn leaf was placed in the machine, the photograph seemed to show the piece that had been torn away. A dead leaf showed no sparks or flares.

It took another forty years for these interesting discoveries to reach the West; they were first popularised in Schroeder and Ostrander's *Psychic Discoveries Behind the Iron Curtain*. But anyone who thought that the reality of the human aura had finally been established was in for a disappointment. Scientists lost no time in pointing out that similar effects had been recognised since the early years of the century. Electrical engineers have made use of them to pinpoint sudden changes in voltage; a roll of film is connected to electric transmission lines driven by a clock; when voltage is regular, nothing is registered, but if there is a sudden change of voltage due to lightning or a short circuit, the film shows a distinctive photograph with a tree-like pattern, due to ionisation. These are known as 'Lichtenburg figures', after their discoverer Jiri Lichtenburg. Moreover, it is known that the flow of a high-frequency current in a condenser is not constant, so a photograph taken by such means might well show strange spots and blurs.

This, say the sceptics, explains Kirlian photography. But the case of Reichenbach suggests a certain reserve before one accepts this as conclusive. Suggestion explained only part of Reichenbach's results; the same seems to be true of Kirlian photography. The Lichtenburg effect cannot explain how the Kirlian machine can photograph the part of a leaf that has been torn away. But if Harold Burr is correct, the machine *could* photograph the L-field that still exists. The 'surge' in Maxwell currents cannot explain why a living leaf is covered with bright spots and flares, while a dead one shows a constant and unchanging pattern. One attempted explanation is that a living body fills the air with tiny particles which become ionised (charged with current), producing an effect like an aurora borealis; Kilner would have argued that this is another point in favour of the existence of the etheric body, which he believed was made of material particles.

At the Neuropsychiatric Institute at UCLA, California, Thelma Moss and Ken Johnson have constructed their own type of Kirlian apparatus. In her book *The Probability of the Impossible*, Dr Moss freely acknowledges that all kinds of spectacular effects can be obtained by quite ordinary means, such as increasing the current or the pressure of the finger on the photographic plate. But even when these are eliminated, the results remain extraordinary. Healers are able to produce flare-like effects from their fingertips when they are exerting their healing powers. When a man was photographed before taking a drink of alcohol, his fingertip was black; after the drink, the tip was literally 'lit up'.

Like the Chinese, the Russians are deeply interested in the science of acupuncture, the assumption that the body is crossed by lines of force, and that their junctions—acupuncture points—control the health of the body. Cures are effected by inserting a needle at these points and vibrating it. The same technique can be used to produce anaesthesia, and Western television teams have photographed serious operations being carried out while the patient was fully conscious and smiling at the camera. An associate of the Kirlians, Viktor Adamenko, has constructed a device for locating the acupuncture points by measuring their L-fields. In effect, the device measures skin resistance—the same principle as a lie detector—but does so by moving an electrode on the surface of the skin. At acupuncture points, the resistance suddenly drops, whereupon a bulb lights up.

Perhaps the most startling implications of the theory of human electrical fields were suggested by Dr Max Toth of the Backster Research Foundation, at the first Western Conference on Kirlian Photography in New York in 1972.[9] Toth presented a brief historical survey of electrical phenomena relating to Kirlian photography, and discussed such natural curiosities as 'fireballs' and St Elmo's Fire, which are, in effect, balls of ionised air. He went on to speak of many cases in which human beings had become living storage batteries; a girl in Missouri whose charge was powerful enough to knock a grown man unconscious; a boy who was virtually a walking magnet and could suspend thick steel rods from his finger-ends. (Reichenbach had observed that magnets sometimes stuck to his subjects, as if their flesh was made of iron.) These seem to be cases in which the normal human electrical charge has got completely out of hand. It also seems likely that this could explain the hundreds of recorded cases of spontaneous combustion,[10] in which people have suddenly burst into flame, or been found charred to a cinder in fireless rooms. Cases like these seem to suggest that, under certain circumstances, human beings may produce a freakishly powerful electrical field.

These observations on electricity and magnetism may seem to have taken us a long way from the problems of astral travel, but at least they enable us to separate the physical and the psychical—or psychological—aspects of the problem. When D. H. Lawrence was dying in a sanatorium in Vence, he seemed to be floating above his own body, looking down at it from the ceiling.[11] If this is a genuine out-of-the-body experience and not mere hallucination, it differs from the projection of Emilie Sagée or Goethe's friend Friedrich. Lawrence's astral self apparently had its own separate consciousness, able to look down on himself and Maria Huxley from above. But in the majority of cases of phantasms of the living the person responsible has had no idea that his apparition appeared to someone else. Many occultists are of the opinion that phantasms of the living are spontaneous projections of the etheric body, the innermost ring of Kilner's aura.

This useful distinction still leaves many basic questions unanswered. If it was really Emilie Sagée's etheric double that appeared beside her, why was it fully clothed instead of naked? The same goes for the apparition of Goethe's friend Friedrich. The obvious alternative theory is that these apparitions have no existence outside of the mind, which was the theory put forward by Frank Podmore, one of the authors of *Phantasms of the Living*, and also by G. N. M. Tyrell in his classic work *Apparitions*. To explain cases in which more than one person saw the apparition (for example, the case of the Verity sisters), Podmore's co-author Edmund Gurney suggested that telepathic impressions spread from one mind to another. But there are the cases—admittedly rare—in which a phantasm has been seen by a total stranger who had no telepathic link with the sender. The ghost hunter Andrew Green cites such a case in *Phantom Ladies*. In September 1975, a young priest, Keith Boland, was standing outside a telephone booth in Station Road, Erdington, Birmingham, waiting to use the phone. The box was occupied by a youngish woman in a dark-blue costume and reddish jumper. Just as he was beginning to feel irritated at the length of time she was taking, she vanished. It would have been impossible for her to leave the box and walk away without his seeing her. Green points out that there are no records of apparitions of the dead being seen for more than a few seconds, and that since this woman was in the box for more than a quarter of an hour, it seems probable that this was a case of a phantasm of the living, perhaps someone deeply anxious to make a phone call and for some reason unable to leave the house.

The difficulty here lies in our assumption that a phantasm is either physical or mental—that is to say, either public or private. Emilie Sagée's phantasm was public; Goethe's doppelgänger was private; he specifies that it was purely 'in his mind's eye'.

But suppose the mind is not the private place we always assumed? 'My mind to me a kingdom is', said Sir Philip Sidney. But a kingdom is a public place, inhabited by many people. Moreover, it looks the same to all of them. Is it conceivable that such a description could be applied to the mind?

The idea sounds startlingly modern, but it is as old as magic. Magic, as we have seen, rests upon the notion that human beings are capable of influencing the external world through the imagination. If the magician can conceive an event clearly enough in his imagination, he will influence the forces of the spirit world, and the event will take place in the real world. This implies that the mind is already part of the spirit world. In almost every known religion, the spirit world is conceived as a realm, a kingdom, with its own hierarchy of levels.

The earliest extant magical traditions, if we except the strange cave drawings of Cro-Magnon man, are Jewish. The word 'magic' derives from Magi, the priests of the Persian Zoroaster, who probably lived in the fifth century BC; but according to Jewish tradition, Moses was among the first of the great magicians, and he predates Zoroaster by at least six centuries. Maria the Jewess—also known as Maria Prophetissa and Mary, Sister of Moses—is the legendary founder of alchemy. The most famous magical work is the *Key of Solomon*, and Solomon predates Zoroaster by three or four centuries. These attributions are, of course, legendary; but there can be little doubt that the Jews are the founders of the mystical tradition in the sense that we understand the word today.

In *The Neanderthal Question*, the anthropologist Stan Gooch suggests that the Jews are direct descendants of Neanderthal man, and that this explains their innate mysticism and artistic achievement. Man possesses two brains, the 'old brain', or cerebellum, inherited from our animal forebears, and the 'new brain', the cerebrum, the reasoning brain. The old brain is intuitive, the new brain, logical. Our Neanderthal ancestors had a greater proportion of old brain than new; the Cro-Magnon men who exterminated them sometime between 35,000 and 25,000 years ago had a larger proportion of new brain. But Cro-Magnon man mated with Neanderthal woman, so that we, his descendants, are a combination of both, with Cro-Magnon predominating. However, on Mount Carmel, in Israel, archaeologists have uncovered skeletons showing a more equal mixture of Cro-Magnon and Neanderthal characteristics, dating from about 35,000 years ago. Similar remains date from as much as ten thousand years later, suggesting that the half-Neanderthal, half-Cro-Magnon race kept its stock pure, the descendants, Gooch believes, are the Jews.

If he is correct, it would explain why the Jews are sometimes known as the magic people, and why magical and mystical traditions owe so much to them. Gooch also points out that Swedenborg equates the cerebrum with intelligence, the cerebellum with wisdom—that is, with a deeper, intuitive kind of knowledge—and this again seems to be a recognition of the importance of the cerebellum in mystical experience.

The essence of Jewish mystical and magical tradition is found in the body of esoteric doctrine known as Cabbala (the word means tradition or reception), which achieved its definitive form in Spain and Southern France in the twelfth and thirteenth centuries AD but traces its roots back to Gnosticism and the inspired prophetic mysticism of the Old Testament, in which man is able to speak directly to God.

Around the year 1280 AD, the Spanish Cabbalist Moses ben Shemtob de Leon began to circulate the vast commentary on the first five books of Moses that became known as the *Zohar*, or Book of Splendour. It claimed to be the work of the Rabbi Simeon bar Yohai, who died in an ecstatic trance and left his disciples to write down the wisdom he had gained from his visions. This might be regarded as the final and definitive form of the Cabbala, which exercised such an immense influence on the magicians and occultists of the Middle Ages.

According to the *Zohar*, the ultimate godhead is the Macroprosopus or Ain Soph, who remains forever hidden. However, this *deus absconditus*, known simply as 'I am' (yah), somehow gave birth to a lesser God, the Yahweh of the Hebrews, also known as the Tetragrammaton because his name has four letters (JHVA). In the Cabbala, this Creator is also known as Kether, the Crown, which split into its nine attributes—wisdom, understanding, love, power, beauty, endurance, majesty, foundation and kingdom (the earth).

The Cabbalists arrange these ten holy names—or Sephiroth—into a form which they call the Tree of Life, although the diagram makes it look rather more like a chemical molecule. God (the Crown) is at the top; earth (kingdom) is at the bottom. Man finds himself trapped in the lowest realm; with a great spiritual effort, he can climb the tree and once again become united with God. But this ascent is not simply a matter of climbing. The tree passes through ten different realms and wanders from side to side.

The Jewish Cabbalists who studied the *Zohar* regarded it as a mystical treatise that would enable them to invoke the holy powers of the universe and combat demons. And this was the aspect of the Cabbala that interested most of the medieval magicians. Others, like Paracelsus, recognised that the Cabbala was actually a map of man's inner worlds, a 'geography of consciousness', and that it could yield the magical secrets of the universe.

Modern Caballists like MacGeggor Mathers, Aleister Crowley and Dion Fortune are inclined to regard the Cabbala as the foundation of all occult science and a chart of the astral worlds, and the Sephiroth as a series of states of inner being that have the same objective existence as the planets in our solar system. The Cabbalist is a space traveller who flies from one to the other. Each planet has its own individual life system, totally unlike all the others. But the twenty-two 'paths' between the 'planets' (a glance at the diagram of the tree of life on p. 496 will show why there are twenty-two) are the subjective states of mind along which the traveller must go to achieve the different worlds.

There are various methods for travelling in this spiritual realm. One would be the method of active imagination recommended by the Golden Dawn. Another would involve projection of the astral body, which could be dangerous—at least, to the uninitiated. The method suggested by Dion Fortune in *The Mystical Qabalah* begins with meditation on the symbols of the various realms; Yeats's method of drawing the symbol on a card and pressing it to the forehead could be employed. She writes: 'The formulation of the image and the vibration of the name is designed to put the student in touch with the forces behind each Sphere of the Tree, and when he comes into touch in this way his consciousness is illuminated and his nature energised by the force thus contacted, and he obtains remarkable illuminations from his contemplation of the symbols.' She goes on: 'These illuminations are not a generalised flooding of light, as in the case of the Christian mystic, but a specific energising and illumination according to the Sphere opened up: Hod [Majesty] gives understanding of the sciences, Yesod [Foundation] understanding of the life force and its tidal modes of functioning . . .'

Moreover, each Sephiroth and each of the twenty-two paths has a whole system of correspondences: a magical symbol, colour, planet, precious stone, and so on. Eliphaz Levi related the twenty-two paths to the twenty-two cards of the Major Arcana of the Tarot pack; Aleister Crowley went farther and related them to the hexagrams of the *I Ching* and the signs of the zodiac. This is why, in his letters to a magical neophyte,[12] Crowley referred to the Cabbala as the 'alphabet of magick', and declared: 'You must take it on trust, as a child does his own alphabet . . . The Tree of Life has got to be learnt by heart; you must know it backwards, sideways and upside down; it must become the automatic background of all your thinking . . .' Dion Fortune reinforces the point when she says: 'Approached in this way, we shall find the association–chains far richer in symbolism than we have ever believed to be possible, for the subconscious mind has been stirred and one of its many chambers of imagery thrown open . . .'

Since Fortune refers to Jung elsewhere in *The Mystical Qabalah*, one might suspect that the reference to the subconscious is simply an attempt to link the Cabbala with modern psychology. This is not so; Paracelsus wrote in the early sixteenth century:

If we would know the inner nature of man by his outer nature; if we would understand his inner heaven by his outward aspect; if we would know the inner nature of trees, herbs, roots, stones by their outward aspect, we must pursue our exploration of nature on the foundation of the Cabbala. For the Cabbala opens up access to the occult, to the mysteries; it enables us to read sealed epistles and books and likewise the inner nature of man.

And elsewhere he writes: 'All of you, whose faith leads you to divine man's future, past and present . . . remember that you must take unto yourselves the teachings of the Cabbala if you want to accomplish all this. For the Cabbala builds on a true foundation.'[13] Paracelsus had no doubt that the Cabbala is an accurate map of man's 'inner firmament'.

The Cabbala's real importance however, is as a philosophical system whose basic assertion, like Plato's, is that the physical world is a reflection of a deeper reality. According to the Cabbala, there are three 'spiritual worlds' underlying physical reality, and, our earthly realm is only the most solid and visible part of a fourth world, Assiah, the world of matter and action. The Tree of Life itself is divided into four 'boxes' by the three horizontal paths. These boxes are the four different worlds or levels of reality: Atziluth, the world of emanations; Briah, the world of creation; Yetzirah, the world of formation; and Assiah. The four worlds increase in density until in our world we find ourselves trapped in appearances and surfaces. Immediately above us is Yesod, the 'astral' realm, which gives our world its shape and direction. If Harold Burr is right in believing that life is organised by some basic blueprint, that blueprint exists in Yesod. And if—*pace* Professor John Taylor—Kirlian photography can really show the missing portion of a torn leaf, this also exists in Yesod. If Lethbridge's pendulum gave accurate results, it is Yesod to which the pendulum responded beyond forty inches. (There are, of course, two more Sephira in the world of Assiah, Hod [Majesty] and Netshah [Endurance], but these are shared with the 'next' world, Yetzirah; our physical universe and the astral realm are the only two that belong wholly to the world of Assiah.) And presumably the pendulum responds to the world of Yetzirah when it is extended beyond eighty inches—to Briah at one hundred and twenty, and to Atziluth at one hundred and sixty.

Lethbridge himself would probably have declined to follow the speculation this far, pointing out that there is no evidence whatever that the worlds of the Cabbala have anything to do with 'the second whorl of the spiral' and the realms that seem to lie beyond it. Occultists like Crowley and Dion Fortune claim to have had direct experience of the realm of the Sephira; but there is no reason why we should take their word for it. In fact, as every occultist would agree, untested belief is not only unnecessary but undesirable.

Yet anyone who is interested in 'occultism'—if only as a historical phenomenon—should gain a basic acquaintance with the Cabbala, for the Cabbala is to magic what Newton's *Principia* is to science: an attempt at a comprehensive system. If magic is based on correspondences, the Cabbala is the ultimate system of correspondences. Anyone who takes the trouble to glance at the lengthy tables of correspondences in Dion Fortune's book on Cabbala (or Gareth Knight's even more comprehensive *Practical Guide to Qabalistic Symbolism*) will agree that they appear to make a good deal of sense in both magical and psychological terms. Clearly, Yesod is what would generally be called the realm of the occult, the realm of Graves's White Goddess and her intuititive knowledge system, of Lethbridge's Magog. Yet according to the Cabbala, it is only one step beyond our physical universe, and belongs to the same 'world'. Beyond it are eight distinct levels, each with its own system of correspondences. And just as the above remarks on the sphere of Yesod would sound totally meaningless to a thoroughgoing rationalist (i.e., someone whose intelligence is limited by the physical world), so the characteristics and correspondences of the next sphere (Hod—Glory or Majesty) seem meaningless to the ordinary 'occultist'. The meaning of the higher Sephiroths can be squeezed out only little by little, by a long process of meditation.[14]

As a philosophical system, the Cabbala can provide more plausible answers to the mysteries of the human psyche than any modern system of philosophy or psychology, including that of Jung. Its fundamental principle is a recognition of the 'hierarchy of selves', the ladder of consciousness. The chief practical problem in grasping this notion is that we are limited by our sense of time. I can quite see that the 'me' who is writing this book already existed 'in embryo' in the 'me' who was born forty-five years ago; he just had to wait a long time to *come into existence*. Yet if the hierarchy of selves is to make any sense, those higher selves must be in existence *already*.

The Cabbala is built upon this paradox. It asserts that the Sephiroth exist objectively, as powers in the universe, and also inside us. And just as the totality of the Sephiroths add up to the ultimate godhead, so the totality of the inner selves add up to the ultimate self. In the physical sense, we exist at the bottom of the tree, in the physical universe. (Typically, its physical symbol is the anus.) And in the psychic sense, although our higher levels already exist, we are trapped in the level of being that corresponds to this universe. It is as if we were trapped in a dream that must be dreamed through to the end though the 'real' self is lying comfortably in bed. (The cabbalist would say that you have nine other selves in nine beds.) And these theoretical statements are born out in practice. Janet's Achille existed in a mental hell while his body lay in bed; he was tormented by a devil who was a part of his own mind. Janet cured him by injecting him with enough courage and optimism to persuade him to clamber out of this mental pit to a higher level, which already existed while Achille was 'in hell'.

Our reality function (Faculty X) is more than the ability to adjust to physical reality. When Beethoven wrote the Ninth Symphony, his problem was to focus on the *meaning* conveyed by the music; this meaning had to be translated into notes on music paper. He had to ignore the physical reality around him—his untidy room, the pile of bills, the soup-stained piano—and tread the path from Malkuth to Yesod. When he was suddenly carried away by the joy of creation, he found it easy to ignore the physical world and focus on the world of meaning. He climbed to the next rung of the ladder of selves and, until his creative force began to run out, and felt no temptation to surrender to distraction.

Even Janet's creative tension can be interpreted in cabbalistic terms. Yesod is the energy of organisation and integration, the underlying blueprint of meaning. When we are exhausted, our sense of meaning diminishes; the world appears to be a meaningless procession of matter. A sudden sexual stimulus can cause sudden concentration.

Janet sees creative tension as something that we have to build up by sheer mental effort. In fact, what usually happens is that some sudden glimpse of meaning galvanises us into mental effort; the tension is the result. We sustain this tension by *focusing* the meaning. If we feel tired or a sense of wellbeing causes us to relax, the meaning vanishes. This is why, creatively speaking, misery is usually so much more productive than happiness.

.   .   .

Our Western philosophy asserts that meaning is something created by the human mind. If I look at a sunset when I am tired, it means nothing to me. If I look at it in a mood of happiness and relaxation, it strikes me as 'beautiful'; I have converted my surplus energy into feeling. Similarly, a man sitting alone in a dark room conjures up the image of a naked girl; he is *creating* her meaning out of his own mind. This is the view held by most Western philosophers from Descartes to Bertrand Russell. Plato, on the other hand, believed that meaning exists independently, in a world of ideas. He would say: a man may conjure up the image of a naked girl, but he doesn't conjure up her meaning; that already exists independently.

The Cabbala agrees with Plato. The difference is that Plato recognised only one realm of meaning or ideas, a world of 'universals'. The Cabbala recognises many such worlds and places them in an order of existence. Most of them are completely beyond the realm of human comprehension, almost as if they existed in other dimensions. Nevertheless, because all the worlds are linked together, all can produce an effect on the physical universe, and on human consciousness.

Janet liked to talk about mental health as a matter of 'psychological economy'. When someone becomes severely neurotic, it is because he has mishandled his psychological energies and become a bankrupt. This notion works admirably when we are describing negative states. It is less enlightening when we think in terms of creativity. Dickens' Mr Pickwick was psychologically healthy; was he also psychologically wealthy? And if so, how would we distinguish between his type of 'wealth' and that of a Leonardo or Einstein? It is not so much a question of energy as of what the energy is *transformed into*.

8

Ancient Mysteries

There is a remarkable, now almost forgotten Anglo-Irish novelist named Thomas Amory whose *Life of John Buncle* (1756) is one of my favourite bedside books. In this highly eccentric narrative, the hero is always wandering into remote country houses or garden pavilions and becoming acquainted with beautiful and accomplished young ladies who engage him in abstruse philosophical arguments. If one can believe Amory, the country houses of Britain in the eighteenth century were almost entirely populated by such young ladies and their widowed fathers. John Buncle marries several dozen of them at one time or another. His creator has the distinction of being the only noteworthy British novelist who was totally insane.

If John Buncle had been around a century later, he would have felt perfectly at home in the company of Mary Anne South, the daughter of Thomas South, a scholar and gentleman of private means who lived in Bury House, Gosport, in Hampshire. He is described as 'the possessor of an exceptionally fine specialised library of classical, philosophical and metaphysical works, many of them old, rare and foreign editions.' Thomas South and his daughter seem to have stepped straight out of the pages of *John Buncle*.

South had been a young man at the time when Mesmer's theories were being discussed all over Europe, and he was fascinated by hypnotism. He was also excited by the phenomena of 'Spiritism'. It would be a mistake to assume that this was unknown until 1848, when the Fox sisters produced their rapping sounds at Hydesville, New York. The great Elizabethan magician John Dee had communicated with spirits through his medium (or 'scryer') Edward Kelly. In Paris in the 1780s, the celebrated Cagliostro had talked to spirits through the medium of children who gazed into a bowl of water. And in the 1830s, every educated man had read Justinus Kerner's book *The Seeress of Prevorst* about Frederica Hauffe, the 'sick sensitive' who specialised in astral travel and reading the future by gazing into soap bubbles.

South was convinced that the nineteenth century was on the threshold of immense spiritual discoveries, and he was determined to be among the first in the field. He was a member of a circle that performed experiments in hypnosis and spirit communication. And the conviction grew upon him that modern students of the paranormal were simply re-discovering secrets known to the ancients.

With his private income and his classical scholarship, he was in an ideal position to investigate this theory. He communicated his enthusiasm to Mary Anne, whose Greek and Latin were as good as his own. Their biographer W. L. Wilmhurst remarks that 'she grew up in his library and from being his pupil became his secretary and intellectual comrade, possessing his entire confidence both in respect of range of information and intellectual grip of the recondite subject to which they were devoted'.[1]

Like many classical scholars, South preferred the Greek and Roman poets to those of the modern world. Inevitably, he was also fascinated by their mythology. Since, like his daughter, he was of a mystical disposition, he attached particular importance to the Mysteries of Orpheus and Eleusis. These were secret rites of purification and initiation, often involving days of 'ordeal'. Solemn secrets were imparted to the initiate, and he swore never to divulge them on pain of death. The Eleusian mysteries were a celebration of the forces of the earth and of Demeter, the corn goddess, whose daughter Persephone was stolen by the Lord of the Underworld and finally allowed to return part-time to her mother, after Demeter went on strike and allowed the earth to become barren.

This legend is obviously an attempt to explain why the earth blossoms in spring and becomes barren in winter. (Because she ate a few pomegranate seeds, Persephone had to return to the Underworld every winter, and the earth goes into mourning.) So most classical scholars of the nineteenth century took the predictable view that the Mysteries of Eleusis were a harmless religious rite whose basis was ignorance of the laws of nature. Not so Thomas South. He believed that the priests of ancient Egypt and Rome understood mysteries of the spirit that were only just being re-discovered by men like Mesmer and Reichenbach, and that myths themselves were probably symbolic expressions of this forgotten knowledge.

South and his daughter-secretary moved on from the myths of Greece and Rome to the works of the Magi, particularly the legendary Hermes Trismegistos, founder of magic, to whom both mystical and magical works are attributed. The mystical works—like the *Pimander* and *Asclepius*—owe a heavy debt to Gnosticism, but the magical works include the famous Emerald Tablet and one of the earliest treatises on alchemy, which Mary Anne proceeded to translate into English.

The revelation that came to Thomas South and his daughter was that this ancient science of alchemy was not, as is generally assumed, a crude form of chemistry, based on misconceptions about the elements, but a coded form of the Mystery religion of the ancients.

Even in 1845, this idea was not entirely original. More than two centuries earlier, a German cobbler named Jacob Boehme who had been staring at the sunlight reflected in a pewter dish fell into a mystical trance and had a vision of the divine love and wisdom. Walking in the fields immediately afterwards, he seemed to be able to look into the heart of the trees and plants and see their vital life principle. He called this their 'signature'. Now alchemists had always taught that trees and plants—and even minerals—possess such a secret essence, and that it can be extracted by certain mysterious processes. This may be why Boehme chose to use the complicated jargon of the alchemists in such famous works as *Morning Redness* and *The Signature of All Things*, written around the time that Shakespeare was writing his last plays. Because of their almost impenetrable obscurity they were half-forgotten in the century following Boehme's death. But in the eighteenth century they were re-discovered in England by another mystic, William Law, who translated many of them and wrote commentaries on others. South may have become acquainted with Boehme through Law. But he and his daughter refused to believe that Boehme was using alchemy as a complicated form of analogy—or perhaps simply out of a desire to sound erudite. Here, they felt, was more evidence that alchemy enshrined the ancient Mysteries in symbolic form.

At some point, Mary Anne herself seems to have received some kind of mystical illumination—or so she hints in her first published work, a little book called *Early Magnetism*, written in her late twenties and published in 1846 when she was twenty-nine. It deals with the phenomena of hypnotism, which she relates to mystical trance and religious illuminations. Her father apparently felt that her book came close to revealing the essence of their startling discoveries—that the ancient Mysteries made use of some form of hypnotic trance state—and that it was time to state this in a more accessible form. Accordingly, he began to write a long epic poem about the ancient wisdom, while Mary Anne crystallised her own discoveries in a massive prose work entitled *A Suggestive Inquiry into the Hermetic Mystery With a Dissertation on the More Celebrated of the Alchemical Philosophers*, which was brought out by a London publisher, Trelawney Saunders, who printed it at South's expense. South himself was too absorbed in his vast poem to do more than glance at the manuscript and nod approvingly. The book appeared in 1850, and about a hundred copies were sent to libraries and reviewers.

Then a strange thing happened. Thomas South took the trouble to read the book. His reaction was instantaneous. He went to enormous trouble to call in the copies that had been sent out, made a pile of all available copies on the lawn of Bury House, and burnt them. A very few managed to survive, and the book was finally reprinted in Belfast in 1918, a decade after Mary Anne had died in her ninety-second year.

Why this violent reaction? According to Wilmhurst, 'they had upon their consciences the responsibility of publicly displaying a subject of extraordinary and . . . sacred moment'. He also suggests that Thomas South was touched by the religious revival led by John Henry Newman and his 'Oxford apostles' and may have felt that he was doing Christianity an injustice by equating it with pagan religions. Neither of these reasons holds water. Mary Anne knew perfectly well what she was writing from the moment she set pen to paper; so did her father. The notion that South suddenly became 'evangelical' can be neither proved nor disproved (and Wilmhurst admits it is only a guess), but Newman exercised his most powerful influence in the 1830s, a good ten years before Mary Anne began her *Suggestive Inquiry*; he had left the Church of England and become a Roman Catholic by the time the book was published.

Whatever the reason, South felt strongly that the book must not be read. He even seems to have destroyed his own long poem. Mary Anne apparently agreed with his verdict. When her father died, not long after, she made no effort to have the book reprinted, although she admitted that its destruction had been a 'crushing sorrow' and had permanently destroyed her literary ambitions. In 1859, she married a clergyman named Alban Atwood, and spent the remaining half-century of her life at a house in Yorkshire. Her husband died in 1883. Mary Anne subsequently became known in theosophical and mystical circles in England and presented one of the few remaining copies of her book to the mystic Anna Kingsford.

In the 1920s, A. E. Waite, one of the original members of the Golden Dawn and the author of numerous works on the Cabbala, the Holy Grail and ritual magic, wrote *The Secret Tradition in Alchemy*, which dealt rather severely with Mary Anne Atwood. He points out that there is no evidence whatever that the Greek Mysteries contained elements of secret teaching about trance states—in fact, the Lesser Mysteries (which took place every February) were attended by vast crowds and were probably rather like a modern football match. He summarises her central thesis—or what he declares to be her central thesis—in the sentence, 'The alchemical process is thus a secret method of self-knowledge which the soul follows far through its realm of being.' This, he observes, is nothing more than a repetition of Boehme's idea that the Philosopher's Stone is Jesus himself and the Elixir of Life only another name for salvation.

Waite's view has persisted. The few people who know about Mary Anne's book assume that she was a forerunner of Jung. Even in 1893, this 'psychological' view was taken for granted by members of the Golden Dawn. Wynn Wescott, another of its original members, wrote a pamphlet[2] called *The Science of Alchymy—Spiritual and Material* in which he says: 'The doctrine that Alchymy was religion only, and that its chemical references were all blinds, is equally untenable in the face of history, which shows that many of its most noted professors were men who had made important discoveries in the domain of common chemistry, and were in no way notable as teachers either of ethics or religion.'

But *was* that what Mary Anne had said? There is only one way to come to grips with this question, and that is to go to the book itself. And there, at the very beginning, is a flat contradiction of the view put forward by Waite. Her long 'Preliminary Account' is a history of alchemy showing that there is plenty of evidence to prove that alchemists really *could* transmute base metals into gold.

This notion is obviously a major stumbling block to modern readers. Everyone knows that the individual elements take their identity from the number of protons and electrons inside the atom. No purely chemical process can get inside the atom, so it is impossible to transmute one element into another by chemistry alone. The alchemists were apparently working from a totally false premise. Even Mary Anne must have known this, for although electrons were not discovered until the 1890s, the world had accepted Dalton's atomic theory since the first decade of the nineteenth century, and Dalton had shown that atoms are the 'ultimate units' of the elements.

No doubt most of the stories of transmutation *are* invention or myth. But a few tales sound so circumstantial that they demand, at the very least, a better explanation. On March 22, 1417, a Parisian named Nicholas Flamel, known for his good works and his generous endowment of chapels and hospitals, died in his house in the rue des Ecrivains. He had been a scrivener by profession, but was widely suspected of being a successful alchemist, and after his death, his house was often ransacked by people who thought they might find the secret of the Philosopher's Stone. Two centuries later, in 1612, one of his alchemical works was printed, describing in some detail how he had actually become rich by transmuting base metals into gold. It is a detailed and convincing account, printed in full in many books on alchemy.[3] Flamel accidentally came upon a magical manuscript by Abrahamelin the Jew. He and his wife Pernella studied this manuscript for twenty-one years, trying out its alchemical formulae, and Flamel made a pilgrimage to Spain, where he met a Jewish doctor who was able to offer him further enlightenment. In 1383, he succeeded in making the 'red stone' (the Philosopher's Stone) and transmuted mercury into gold. He did this three times, obtaining enough money to live comfortably for the remainder of his life. The manuscript could, of course, be a forgery; but we know that Flamel existed, that he was an alchemist, and that he became a rich man and gave away large sums of money.

In the early seventeenth century, the Belgian chemist Van Helmont, who invented the word 'gas' and has an important place in the history of chemistry, described how he had converted four ounces of mercury into gold by means of a powder obtained from a stranger. Van Helmont seems to have been an honest and thoroughly scientific investigator; his account of the Stone was published by his son, who was a disbeliever in alchemy, so the chance of forgery seems minimal.

The Dutch physician Helvetius (whose real name was Johann Friedrich Schweitzer) also left a long and circumstantial account of how he obtained a tiny quantity of Philosopher's Stone from a man who came to call on him, and used it to convert half an ounce of lead into gold.[4] E. J. Holmyard comments in his book on alchemy: 'In most accounts of "transmutations" it is not difficult to perceive where trickery could have entered, but in the case of Helvetius, no one has yet discovered the loophole.'

John Dee's 'scryer', Edward Kelly, who was something of a confidence trickster, wrote two interesting works on alchemy in which he claimed to have demonstrated the transmutation of metals by means of a powder he discovered in Glastonbury Abbey. The Elizabethan writer Elias Ashmole claims that Kelly cut a piece of metal out of a warming pan and transmuted it into gold, then sent the gold and the pan as proof to Queen Elizabeth. Unfortunately, Kelly's reputation as a villain makes it difficult to take these stories seriously. But this does not apply to the career of the Scotsman Alexander Seton, who became friendly with a Dutch pilot, Jacob Haussen, when he was wrecked off the coast near Edinburgh. Seton later visited Haussen in Holland and demonstrated the transmutation of lead into gold—Haussen left an account—then travelled around Europe, repeating the demonstration in front of many 'doctors', who wrote their own accounts. In 1603 he was tortured by the Elector of Saxony, Christian II, in an attempt to force him to reveal his secret; he escaped with the aid of a young student named Michael Sendivogius, but died as a result of his sufferings on New Year's Day, 1604. He presented Sendivogius with the remainder of his 'powder', together with the secret of how to use it, and Sendivogius in turn became a famous alchemist and the author of a number of noted works on the subject, although he never succeeded in manufacturing the powder itself. Again, the story of Seton has a wealth of circumstantial detail and was attested by a number of independent witnesses.

One of the saddest—and most puzzling—stories in the history of alchemy is that of James Price, a wealthy young scientist who was a Fellow of the Royal Society. In 1782, when he was thirty, Price set up a laboratory in a house in Surrey and soon announced that he had succeeded in transmuting mercury into gold. In May 1782 he invited a distinguished gathering of men to witness the transmutation. They saw him add a white powder to mercury together with nitre and borax, heat them in a crucible and produce an ingot of silver. When he used a red powder, the result was gold. The specimens were submitted to a goldsmith, who found them to be genuine. Price published a pamphlet about his discovery, which caused great excitement; but he declined to say how the powders were prepared. He added that the cost to his health had been so great that he felt unable to prepare more. The scientists moved in to the attack, and the controversy became bitter. The Royal Society demanded another demonstration. Under enormous pressure, Price agreed; but when the three delegates from the Society arrived at his laboratory, Price drank prussic acid and died before their eyes.

This is the kind of evidence that Mary Anne presents. She then goes on to offer a clear and undistorted view of the basic aim of the alchemist to discover the *materia prima*, the basic pure substance, which can be converted, by various chemical processes, into some form of 'perfect matter'—gold, for example. There follows her translation of the *Tractatus Aureus* of Hermes Trismegistos.

The opening chapter of the second part of the book is significantly entitled: 'Of the True Subject of the Hermetic Art, and Its Concealed Root.' And within the first two pages we have this curious statement: 'No modern art of chemistry . . . has anything in common with Alchemy . . . For though aqua fortis and aqua regia seem to dissolve metals, and many salts be found useful in analysis . . . yet nothing vitally alternative is achieved, unless the vital force be present and in action . . .' Having said which, she makes the statement that all subsequent writers have taken to be her dismissal of the possibility of physical alchemy: 'The pseudo-Alchemists dreamed of gold, and impossible transformations, and worked with sulphur, mercury and salt of the mines . . .'

We read on, waiting for her to explain what she means by a true alchemist. Instead, she quotes the book of Tobit to the effect that it is honourable to reveal the works of the Lord but good to keep silent about the secrets of the king. The old adepts, she says, makes no mention of the king at all, and many worthy intellects have been starved of important knowledge. Therefore, she says she will 'feel emboldened to hazard evidence of the forbidden truth; and without, we trust, transgressing the spirit of the prophet's advice, it may be allowed to lay open the [king's] regalia . . .'

If this forbidden knowledge is merely the conviction that alchemy is a purely 'spiritual' affair, and that the secret vessel in which it takes place is man himself, she is certainly making a great deal of fuss about nothing. A page later, she is still intent on convincing us that she is withholding tremendous secrets:

> Thus it appears to have been a religious principle with the ancients, to withhold the means of proving their philosophy from an incapable and reckless world; and if any by hazard, less prudent or envious than the rest, alluded openly in his writings either to the concealed vessel or art of vital ministration, his revealment was instantly annulled by false or weakening commentaries.

And she cites as an example a treatise of Michael Sendivogius in which the alchemist tells a king: 'This matter, o king, is extracted from thee'—and then instantly covers up his tracks by talking about gold teeth, as if this were what he was referring to. 'Such instances are not rare,' she remarks sorrowfully, 'and it has been found easy by such similar equivocations, without absolute denial, to protect from foolish and profane intrusion that living temple wherein alone the wise of all ages have been securely able to raise their rejected Corner Stone and Ens of Light.' She adds that when the writings of Jacob Boehme first appeared, the alchemists of the time were quite convinced that their deepest secret was about to be revealed.

It is easy to see why Mary Anne South's few readers concluded that she considered alchemy to be some kind of spiritual discipline, perhaps allied to yoga. Again and again, she remarks that the basic secret has to do with 'concentrating the vitality'. Waite believes she was hinting that the ultimate secret was somehow connected with projection of the astral body. But she goes to the trouble of denying this, admittedly, in rather obscure language: 'It is not . . . that the Spirit is free from material bondage, or able to range the universe of her own sphere, that guarantees the truth of her revealments, or helps the consciousness on to subjective experience; for this a concentrative energy is needed, and an intellect penetrating into other spheres.' Again, 'concentrative energy'. Yet why the obscure language? Why doesn't she say: 'I agree that the spirit is capable of astral travel, but that is not what we are talking about; we aren't talking about leaving the body, but about concentrating the mind'? Waite thinks it is because she is an amateur writer. However, she is doing what all alchemists have done: she is hinting as heavily as she dares, then covering up her traces.

But at what is she hinting? Waite comes close to giving the game away in a final exasperated paragraph, where he says: 'She leaves her tales of veridic transmutation at a loose end, serving no manifest purpose', and writes 'as if she had forgotten the concern with which her "dissertation" opened. It is . . . as if an important section had been torn out of the work, or a final chapter omitted.'

In fact, she leaves us in no possible doubt that she believes that certain alchemists *have* succeeded in turning lead into gold and manufacturing the Philosopher's Stone. And, quite simply, she does not believe this is a purely chemical process. She believes—she is actually pretty certain—that at a certain point in the operation, the alchemist has to put something of *himself* into it. There is a point at which his *mind* must enter the crucible and effect certain basic changes in the metal. Most of the great alchemical treatises contain mysterious references to an element called 'the double mercury', but this is never defined. Is half of the 'double' something that comes from the alchemist himself at a certain vital point in the process?

Why did the alchemists take such trouble to cover their tracks and to impose solemn oaths of secrecy on those who penetrated the basic mystery? There were two reasons, and the first of them is touched on by a modern adept, Bernard Husson:

> Beginning from the seventeenth century . . . it was believed that the 'secret of alchemy' consisted in knowing what were the mineral substances to be manipulated, and in understanding how to carry out the manipulations. But of course, a 'secret' of this description was bound sooner or later to be found out. So why has silence, or at any rate, extreme discretion, been enjoined right up to the present day? It was not, let it be emphasised, due to mere childishness; but, as far as traditional alchemists are concerned, it was a point of honour, as it was among the ancients, who swore never to betray the 'secret' of the Eleusian mysteries—which could not properly be called a secret at all, because almost everyone in the higher walks of life underwent initiation.[5]

But having said this, Husson takes care not to give any further hint about the 'secret'. He has, however, made an important observation. Anyone who has ever been through even the simplest initiation ceremony knows how impressive it can be. All magical and religious societies know the importance of initiation. Gurdjieff made constant use of it. Many of his pupils have written of the conspiratorial atmosphere of his groups; members were ordered to disperse the moment they left the meeting place, so as not to attract attention by hanging about in groups; they were solemnly bound not to speak about 'the work' when they were not at meetings. This was not mere play-acting. Gurdjieff's central aim was to make his students build up a certain inner pressure to prepare them to make enormous mental efforts; the secrecy was one more discipline, like 'self-remembering' or his elaborate 'movements', to push them in the right direction. The psychological basis of the method can be recognised in the 'double ambiguity' experiment with planarion worms described in Chapter Five.[6] When we learn something too easily, we 'devalue' it; when we are forced to put twice as much effort into the learning process, it becomes a kind of instinct, and can never be forgotten or lost.

But there is another, more practical reason for secrecy about the alchemical process. In the wrong hands, it could be dangerous. The alchemists of the Middle Ages rightly felt that all kinds of unqualified people would try to dabble in the sacred art if it became too accessible. They also believed that such people could achieve a certain degree of success if they understood the secret. And this obviously runs counter to Mary Anne Atwood's assumed view that alchemy was essentially a spiritual discipline. It was not, and she knew it was not.

The reason that she and her father decided to suppress the book is, almost certainly, that they had absorbed themselves in the whole idea of 'the hermetic mystery' until they felt identified with the long line of adepts from Geber to Thomas Vaughan. They believed they had stumbled on the basic secret which no alchemist had ever stated in so many words, and that they had no right to break the silence of more than a thousand years. Mary Anne did her best to be as discreet as any of her predecessors. Yet she was writing the first *general* treatise on alchemy in the whole of its long history. All previous works had been written for practising alchemists or students of the occult; no one had ever written a book aimed at the general public. Its very obscurity might stimulate readers to search for hidden meanings. In later life, however, she realised that the secret was safe; even though her book—in its few surviving copies—had become a kind of cult and was studied by theosophists and hermeticists, no one seemed to guess what she was talking about.

Yet even now, we have not penetrated the whole secret of Mary Anne South and her remarkable book. To do that, we must make a mental journey back to the year 1850. To a serious student of 'the occult', it must have seemed that the world was on the verge of a new age of discovery. In the past, 'magicians' had been hardly distinguishable from charlatans. Paracelsus and Cornelius Agrippa were contemporaries of the buffoon Johannes Faust, whose grotesque pranks are described in Johann Spies's *Faustbuch*.[7] Even Cagliostro, one of the most remarkable 'magicians' of the late eighteenth century, was half charlatan and half genuine psychic. But Mesmer and his successors were an entirely different breed; they had created a new foundation for psychical research, or 'occult science' as it would have been called in those days. John Elliotson's journal *The Zoist* was devoted to the study of hypnotic phenomena. In the early 1840s James Buchanan discovered the 'unknown psychic faculty' which he called psychometry. Reichenbach published his discovery of the 'odic force' in 1846. The Fox sisters achieved their sudden fame, and launched the modern spiritualist movement, in 1848. The Souths had every reason to believe that the world was on the threshold of a psychic revolution and that, in another decade or so, clairvoyance and astral travel would be accepted as casually as railway engines and paddle steamers.

The Souths were themselves practising occultists, members of a secret society called the Zojese, founded by the platonist Thomas Taylor; they practised a carefully-guarded technique of mesmeric healing which had been taught to them by Taylor himself. And they were aware that psychic powers are, unfortunately, not confined to the virtuous. George Du Maurier later dramatised one unpleasant possibility in *Trilby*, where the wicked hypnotist uses his powers to seduce and dominate a young girl. Criminals could conceivably use 'travelling clairvoyance' to aid them in planning burglaries. (Aleister Crowley later claimed to use astral projection to commit a kind of psychic rape on women he wanted to possess.) The evilly-disposed might discover that they could harm their enemies merely by directing a beam of psychic malevolence. So it was understandable that the Souths should feel misgivings about revealing the secrets of alchemy—the epitome of the psychic sciences. They had no way of knowing that the 'psychic revolution' would never take place, and that another century would pass without the slightest dent in the universal scepticism about telepathy, clairvoyance, astral travel and spirits.

We shall return to the problem posed by the destruction of the *Suggestive Inquiry* in a moment. Meanwhile, if we are to understand why the Souths were so obsessed by alchemy, we must look more closely into the tangled history of 'the spagyric art'.

The oldest form of alchemy derives from China, or possibly India. In *Science and Civilisation in China* (Vol. V:2), Joseph Needham points out that the word 'elixir' is probably of Chinese origin, and that the earliest alchemy in China—dating from the fourth or fifth centuries BC—was centrally concerned with the science of 'macrobiotics', the preparation of semi-magical drugs and elixirs for prolonging life. It was profoundly influenced by the Taoist doctrine that man and nature are intermingled and that man can discover his true powers by merging into harmony with nature. At about the same time, metalsmiths were absorbed in the problem of gold-making and gold-faking, that is, attempting to make metals that looked like gold. Because gold has always been regarded as a sacred metal, these attempts blended with macrobiotics as part of alchemy.

But it is important to remember that macrobiotics was the older science; men were concerned with curing their illnesses and prolonging their lives by natural remedies long before they learned the use of metals. And macrobiotics rested upon the belief that each plant and herb had its individual essence or tincture—what Boehme would have called its 'signature'—and that this essence could be extracted by means of certain chemical processes and used in medicine. In later alchemy, this became known as the lesser work. The greater work was the manufacture of the Philosopher's Stone.

Alchemy first appeared in Greece in the second century BC in a treatise called *Physika and Mystika*, by Bolos of Mendes, also known as the pseudo-Democritus. It has sections on gold-making and also on plants, particularly their reputed magical powers. Bolos speaks of one plant (possibly the peony) used by magicians for calling up the gods and another that, taken in drink, caused menacing visions (possibly some form of psychedelic herb).

Democritus, whose name Bolos often used, was known as the laughing philosopher and pre-dated Bolos by about two centuries. Democritus was the first to express the notion of atoms, and later generations regarded him as the father of alchemy. Stories about him make it clear that he was also interested in the occult, although he was firmly convinced that there is no life after death. According to Plutarch, Democritus believed that all substances emit a radiation called *eidola*, which sounds oddly like Reichenbach's odic force. Living creatures also emit *eidola*, and this carries images of their thoughts and feelings. Human beings are particularly susceptible to *eidola* in sleep, and the result is dreams. Democritus never actually advanced the view that *eidola* can produce telepathy—perhaps he was unacquainted with the phenomenon—but declared that, when directed in a maleficent beam, they can cause psychic damage. In other words, according to Democritus, thoughts are living things that can exercise a direct influence on people.

Democritus's disciple Bolos made it clear that he belonged to a mystical school whose greatest secrets he had promised not to reveal: 'The pledge has been imposed on us to expose nothing clearly to anyone.' This determination to remain obscure is so typical of the alchemists that the word 'gibberish' is derived from the name of the great Arabian adept Geber.

If a modern occultist made this sort of claim, we might suspect that he was a charlatan in quest of gullible disciples. But, as Waite points out, the early alchemists had no motive for this kind of exaggeration; many of the early alchemical manuscripts were not even written for publication.

These considerations lead us back to the obvious basic question: wasn't the whole thing nonsense anyway? It could be argued that all Western alchemy is based on a passage in Aristotle's *Metrologica*, which declares that all mineral substances are produced by two kinds of vapour 'exhaled' from the depths of the earth, one moist and one dry. All things that can be melted, like copper and gold, are formed from the moist vapour, and all things that cannot be melted, like stones and fossils, from the dry one. How can there be anything serious in a science based on this kind of muddled guesswork?

There are two possible lines of defence. The first asserts that alchemy is basically a spiritual, not a chemical doctrine. The second states that alchemy really works—or can be made to work. Let us spend the rest of this chapter looking a little more closely at the first argument, whose chief modern exponent is C. G. Jung. The second requires a chapter to itself.

In 1928 Jung's friend Richard Wilhelm, the sinologist, sent him the translation of a Chinese alchemical treatise called *The Secret of the Golden Flower*. Jung began to read, and was immediately struck by its use of the Mandala symbol—the 'magic circle' or wheel of life—which had intrigued him for years. He had first encountered it in the strange cosmology of his female cousin who had stimulated his interest in occult phenomena. Ever since then, Jung had observed the symbol recurring in the drawings of patients. He had even found it in his own drawings and paintings at the time of his traumatic 'confrontation with the unconscious'.

In *The Secret of the Golden Flower*, the soul is symbolised as both a masculine cloud demon and an earth-bound white ghost; Jung suspected that these were the animus and the anima, the spirit father and earth mother. The aim of alchemy, according to this treatise, was to produce an etheric body known as the 'diamond body'. This was accomplished by transferring one's aims and drives away from the ego into the realm of pure impersonality. One section, entitled The Book of Consciousness, was introduced by the words:

> If thou wouldst complete the diamond body with no outflowing,
> Diligently heat the roots of consciousness and life.
> Kindle light in the blessed country close at hand,
> And there hidden, let thy true self always dwell.

In this Taoist text, alchemy was obviously being used as a metaphor for spiritual integration. The 'roots of consciousness and life' and 'the blessed country close at hand' could be interpreted as references to the subconscious, the blessed country into which we sink in sleep. This, it seemed to Jung, was a hint of the archetypal psychology he had been looking for.

He commissioned a Munich bookseller to find him Western works on alchemy, mostly in Latin. But when they arrived, he pushed them aside and forgot about them for two years. When he finally made an attempt to come to grips with them, around 1930, he experienced all the frustration and irritation that comes to everyone who tries to approach an original alchemical text. From Bolos of Mendes onward, most alchemists make a virtue of being obscure, boring and exasperating. But when it dawned on Jung that they were talking in symbols, he found the challenge irresistible and applied himself to their decipherment, a task that was to occupy him for the remainder of his life. His interest in alchemy found its fullest expression in his last major work, *Mysterium Coniunctionis*.

Perhaps the clearest expression of his view of alchemy is in his introduction to *Psychology and Alchemy* (1944). Here he states one of his basic principles: 'that the soul possesses by nature a religious function.' Western man has fallen into a state of impotence because his civilisation is rational and superficial. And the Christian Church is to some extent to blame for this predicament. Christianity with its increasingly dogmatic content has 'alienated consciousness from its natural roots in the unconscious'. And so alchemy has become a mystical, underground form of Christianity, full of strange, repressed images. The Mandala is a symbol of man's desire for wholeness, for what Maslow called 'self actualisation' and Jung 'individuation'. The soul of Western man lies in bits and pieces, and the alchemical processes, the search for the Philosopher's Stone, are a symbol of the process of integration.

It is worth noting at this point that Jung's approach to the problem was conditioned by his patients. They tended to be solid, well-integrated citizens—typical phlegmatic Swiss—whose intelligence was often above average. 'About a third of my cases are not suffering from any clinically definable neurosis, but from the senselessness and aimlessness of their lives.' Freud's patients tended to be overwhelmed by their subconscious minds; many of Jung's were not sufficiently in contact with theirs. The result was that Jung recognised the inadequacy of the concept of mere social integration and saw the need for some deeper process of unification.

Although the major writers on alchemy differ on a thousand minor points, they agree on the basic steps in the process. The alchemist begins by selecting a substance, *prima materia*, the basic material. Some say this is earth, others that it is water, or salt, or mercury, or any number of other substances. Most alchemists agree it is 'lowly', an extremely common substance, which seems to rule out gold or mercury. Jung explains that it differs from person to person because 'it carries the projection of the autonomous psychic content'. It is not quite clear whether he thinks of it as a mental state—perhaps as a neurosis—or as some actual substance, which somehow carries the 'psychic content'.

The Work is best begun in spring, under the sign of Aries (although Taurus and Gemini are also acceptable). The first step is to purify the *materia prima*, pulverise it, mix it with a 'secret fire' and place it in a sealed vessel, where it is heated. Again, there is much controversy about the nature of the secret fire. One authority says that it is simply a catalyst prepared from cream of tartar (potassium tartrate). But the seventeenth century alchemist Eirenaeus Philalethes—an unknown Englishman who claimed to have completed the Work at the age of twenty-two—states in his *Principles* that 'the secret, hidden fire is the instrument of God' and 'we often refer to this fire in a way that might make it appear that we are speaking of external heat . . .' It is, therefore, just conceivable that this may be the point in the operation where the alchemist himself somehow pours his own concentrated vitality into his *prima materia*.

The *prima materia* contains two elements, one male and one female, and these are referred to as sol and luna or sulphur and mercury. Pictorial representations of the Work—like the ones contained in the famous *Mutus Liber*, an alchemical treatise consisting entirely of pictures—show a king and queen lying down together in a bath. They are dissolved and 'married', presumably by the fire which is applied to the sealed vessel. They blacken and putrefy. This part of the process is known as the nigredo. There seems to be general agreement that at this point the crucible ought to be filled with a pulsating black mess; if it is, the alchemist can congratulate himself on having achieved the first major transformation. The heat drives off all the vapours—the soul of the king and queen (who are now symbolically united in the form of a hermaphrodite). The black mess should begin to show white flecks, like a night sky full of stars, and then slowly turn white—the process known as the albedo. The whole mass becomes volatile, then re-crystallises as 'the white stone'. This has powers of healing and of transforming mercury into silver. The alchemist has now successfully completed the first part of the work.

In Jung's interpretation, the *prima materia* is some form of psychic energy, which contains the two opposites, the sun and moon or the conscious and the subconscious. These must be united, perhaps in the fire of experience and suffering, perhaps by the intervention of the analyst himself. Jung would probably have described his own painful 'confrontation with the subconscious' as the fire that brought about a new 'marriage' or '*coniunctionis*'. The strain produces exhaustion, a dark night of the soul, which is slowly succeeded by a resurrection. The end product of this phase, the white stone, is a moon symbol, sometimes represented as a white tree with silver apples. The conscious mind has become 'lunarised', imbued with intuition.

Yet this is not the end of the process. The white stone is used as the basis of the second stage; it is added to mercury, in which gold has been dissolved. (Other authorities say that this 'albedo' *is* 'the philosopher's mercury', which needs merely to be added to gold.) At this point, most of the authorities become more than usually obscure or simply hurry over the next process; this is known as 'exaltation'—one of twelve stages—and consists of some form of purification, with the continuous addition of more mercury. At some point, the substance is dissolved in acid and turns green, a stage known as the green lion. Finally, after still more purification, it turns red. This is the Philosopher's Stone, which can turn base metals into gold and prolong human life indefinitely.

The significant point here is that the process ends with the sun symbol, the Red King. Consciousness is again supreme, but this time it unites with unconsciousness. Jung regards this point in the process as individuation or self-actualisation.

Jung's writings on alchemy occupy three bulky volumes of the *Collected Works*; they show his extraordinary grasp of the subject and the degree to which it acted as a stimulant to his creative thinking. Yet in the most important of the volumes, *Mysterium Coniunctionis*, it becomes increasingly clear that he regards the actual chemical side of the operation as merely a ritual that parallels the psychic processes. Detailing a process by which the alchemist Gerhard Dorn claims to be able to produce essential spirit of wine; the *caelum*, he depicts the *caelum* as man's deepest inner truth—a form of the Philosopher's Stone—and dismisses the alchemical description as 'a hair-raising chemical fantasy'. He declares that the extraordinary experiment described is 'a representation of the individuation process by means of chemical substances and procedures, or what we today call active imagination', and gives one of his clearest accounts of the operation of this 'active imagination'. As a starting point, you can choose a dream or fantasy image, or even a bad mood, and concentrate on it. 'Usually it will alter, as the mere fact of contemplating it animates it.' 'A chain of fantasy ideas develops and gradually takes on a dramatic character: the passive process becomes an action. At first it consists of projected figures, and these images are observed like scenes in the theatre. In other words, you dream with open eyes.' A few pages earlier he remarks that Gerhard Dorn was 'unable to recognise the—for us—blatant projection of psychic contents into chemical substances. . .' Active imagination is a more efficient way of carrying out the same processes.

Jung seems to be unaware that he is demolishing his own position. He started from the belief that alchemy is something more than a misunderstanding based on ignorance; that it is, in fact, a true science whose premises differ from our own. After all, there has never been the slightest doubt that alchemy is a transcendental, mystical art *as well as* a physical science. The thirteen propositions of the famous Emerald Tablet of Hermes, reputed to be the earliest of all alchemical documents (although in actuality it probably post-dates Bolos of Mendes)[8] makes this quite clear: 'You shall separate the earth from the fire, the subtle from the gross. . . It ascends from the earth into the heaven, and again descends into the earth and receives the power of the superiors and inferiors. So thus you will have the glory of the whole world . . . Thus was the earth created.'

Hermes is claiming that his alchemical processes are the processes of *all* creation. It follows that one of the basic tasks of the alchemist is to strive to become godlike, so that he can imitate the work of creation. But if all the alchemist's laboratory work is confusion and nonsense, then the whole enterprise becomes an absurdity. A modern parallel might be the search for the Loch Ness monster. If the monster does not exist, then the men who sit at the side of Loch Ness with cameras are wasting their time. And if the aim of the alchemist was really 'individuation' or self-actualisation, and he spent his life seeking a red chemical called the Philosopher's Stone, then the enterprise was basically futile.

Jung himself may not have been unduly disturbed by this recognition. He justified his own psychological insights by asserting that the four elements, the four stages of the Great Work and the four arms of the mystical cross are all symbolic recognitions of his four psychological types. (Jung was also fond of quoting the axiom of Maria the Prophetess: 'One becomes two, two becomes three, and out of the third comes the one as the fourth.') Yet he failed to justify alchemy as a hidden knowledge *system*. And his leading follower and commentator, Aniela Jaffé, practically admitted as much when she wrote: 'There was no particular book that he valued above all others. He would single out one or another according to its applicability to the theme he was interested in . . . at the moment.' This is, we must agree, a rather unsatisfactory scientific procedure. Is there a viable logical alternative?

There is at least one interesting possibility that Jung overlooked. *The Secret of the Golden Flower* speaks about 'the diamond body'. Jung's explanation of this term in his *Commentary* on the book is both ingenious and impressive. He points out that we tend to 'identify' too much with our feelings and problems, like savages who fail to distinguish between subject and object; they say, for example: 'My soul *is* that tree.' In the same way, we are always getting so involved with our problems and miseries that we *become* them. But if we can once recognise the real existence of the unconscious mind, we can shift the centre of gravity of the soul from everyday consciousness to the true self. In so doing, we become detached and rise above our problems, recognising that we are more durable than they. This 'superior personality', Jung wrote, is the 'diamond body'.

But is that what the author of *The Golden Flower* meant? Why should a change in the centre of gravity of consciousness be described as the *creation* of a separate body?

Clearly, the use of the word 'diamond' implies that this body is indestructible, or at least, less destructible than the physical body. And the text implies that it is to be created by spiritual effort. Gurdjieff often spoke to his students of a similar kind of body. For example, when someone asked him about life after death, he explained: 'Many things are possible. But it is necessary to understand that man's being, both in life and after death . . . may be very different in quality. The "man–machine" with whom everything depends on external influences . . . has no future of any kind; he is buried, and that is all. Dust returns to dust . . . In order to speak of any kind of future life, there must be a certain crystallisation, a certain fusion of man's inner qualities.'[9] This sounds more like the idea of a 'diamond body'.

Gurdjieff went on: 'Fusion, inner-reality, is obtained by means of "friction", by the struggle between "yes" and "no" in man. If a man lives without inner struggle, if everything happens in him without opposition . . . he will remain such as he is.' He also makes clear that the 'essential body' that emerges from the struggle is what is usually called the astral body. 'What may be called the "astral body" is obtained by means of fusion, that is, by means of inner hard work and struggle.' In short, this essential body is what he elsewhere calls 'essence', and it is developed by suffering, or rather, by resisting suffering through a concentration of the will. He asks: 'What is there to withstand physical death in a man who faints . . . when he cuts his finger?' He told Ouspensky that he had only once met a man who possessed natural 'essence': a brigand who had achieved it by standing in the hot sun all day, peering down the sights of a rifle as he waited for unsuspecting travellers.

So it seems that essence is created by will-power, not by a mere change in the centre of gravity of personality. According to Gurdjieff, personality is the opposite of essence; it is the mere shell of our being, the mask we have developed to come to terms with other people.

The concentration required to develop 'essence' sounds remarkably like the 'concentrative energy' that Mary Anne South describes as the heart of the alchemical process. And this point seems to be confirmed by a Gurdjieff disciple, J. H. Reyner, in a book called *The Diary of a Modern Alchemist*.[10] He writes that when man is in his normal state of 'sleep'—what we like to call waking consciousness—'essence cannot receive the nourishment it requires and so does not grow'. He goes on: 'It needs a certain transformation of the available energies, analogous to the cooking or preparation of the physical foods which the body eats. This is the alchemy, to achieve which a "second education" is required'. By way of emphasising that he is not using the word alchemy in a merely figurative sense, he goes on to mention the famous *Mutus Liber* and even reprints its first picture, showing two angels on a ladder that stretches from heaven to earth, trying to awaken a sleeping man by blowing their trumpets. (Jung also attached importance to the ladder symbol, which appears so frequently in alchemy, and associated it with the link between the lower and upper storeys of the personality.) 'Fortunately,' says Reyner, 'there are influences continually available from higher levels, from which assistance can be derived once a man has wakened from his sleep.' Which, to anyone who has been reading Mary Anne South, again raises the question of whether such 'higher influences' could somehow be channelled into the alchemical process itself—not 'soul alchemy', but the kind that takes place in the laboratory.

The complexities of this question demand a chapter to themselves.

9

The Great Secret

In the winter of 1936, a young student of magic named Israel Regardie was confined to his bed by bronchitis; he spent his convalescence making a determined effort to plod through Mary Anne South's *Suggestive Inquiry into the Hermetic Mystery*, a work he had attempted on many previous occasions without success.

Regardie was a Londoner who had emigrated to the United States at the age of thirteen and later became an art student in Philadelphia. In the middle of 1926, when he was nineteen, Regardie attended a reading in Washington of a book on yoga by Crowley and wrote Crowley an admiring letter. The result was an invitation to go join Crowley in Paris as his secretary. He arrived in October 1928, and the association lasted for three stormy years. In those days, the 'Beast' was frequently evicted from hotels for not paying his bills. But at least Regardie learned the fundamentals of magic from one of its greatest modern exponents. On his return to London, he wrote *The Tree of Life*, a book that many regard as the finest modern introduction to magic and cabbalism.

In 1934, Regardie joined the Order of the Golden Dawn, then known as the Stella Matutina. He soon came to the conclusion that, as magicians, some of the Chiefs were thoroughly inept. He resigned from the Order and decided to publish all the ritual and magical practices that had been a closely-guarded secret since the Order was founded in 1888. Deprived of its secrets, the moribund Stella Matutina collapsed.

The *Rituals of the Golden Dawn* occupy more than fifteen hundred pages; of these, a mere half dozen are devoted to alchemy.[1] Regardie admitted in his introductory note: '. . . the section on Alchemy remains quite obscure since the subject does not interest me'. The *Rituals* were still awaiting publication in the winter of 1936 as Regardie lay in bed and struggled through Mary Anne South's *Suggestive Inquiry*, conscientiously doing his best to make sense of her luminous obscurities.

And then, as he made notes and underlined key passages, he began to experience a glimmer of understanding. 'Suddenly, and to my utter amazement, the whole enigma became crystal clear and alive. The formerly mysterious *Golden Tractate of Hermes* and *The Six Keys of Eudoxus* [both included in Miss South] seemed all at once to open up to unfold their meaning. Feverishly I wrote . . .' What he wrote was influenced by Jung's commentary on *The Secret of the Golden Flower* as much as by Miss South. *The Philosopher's Stone* draws upon both in about equal proportions. Regardie also knew about Miss South's first book, *Early Magnetism and Its Higher Relations to Humanity*, which had made him aware of the importance she attached to the ideas of Mesmer, who, it may be recalled, believed that all space is pervaded by a kind of psychic ether in which the heavenly bodies cause 'tides'. These tides of etheric current wash through the human body, keeping it healthy; blockages make us unhealthy. That is why Mesmer began his career using magnets to move the currents around the body. (In Scotland even today magnets are placed under pillows to cure muscular cramps.)[2]

Mesmer also believed that all bodies emit certain dynamic forces that act upon other bodies, a view that sounds oddly similar to Democritus's notion of *eidola*. Later mesmerists dismissed the 'psychic ether' theory; but Miss South felt that it held more truth than the notion that 'suggestion' accounts for all hypnotic cures. She believed that when someone is placed in a trance, the mind becomes unusually concentrated, and 'related to the Universal, becomes . . . one with the great magnetic Will of Nature.' That is to say, she had the curious idea that an ordinary state of mesmeric trance can lead to some kind of heightening of consciousness, some mystical insight, 'until', as she states, 'the divinised microcosmic epitome moves with demiurgic power and grace'. In plainer language, she believed that the psyche of the mesmerised subject can take on the actual *creative* power of the demiurge (who, in the Cabbala, is God the Creator).

Regardie, in spite of his Jungian affiliations, went straight to the heart of Mary Anne South's theory of alchemy. She believed that the spirit of the alchemist could take on 'demiurgic powers' in a trance state, and directly affect the matter in the crucible. This is the great secret she was terrified to divulge, and which she believed to have been the essential secret of the alchemist through the ages. And Regardie himself recognised that she is speaking of something more than a purely 'spiritual' operation, for he writes: 'The first way of approach and the closed entrance to these manual operations [i.e., the transmutation of metals] remained a mystery, and its secret . . . had not yet been unfolded. Yet the process itself, as a technical method . . . is said to have been in itself a very simple one. For it is called by some of them a play of children and is represented as very trivial.'

Regardie recognised that the chemical part of alchemy really took place in the laboratory, but he believed that the essential part was psychic *or magical*. In fact, the alchemical passage in his own book on the Golden Dawn should have given him the clue even without Miss South, for it speaks continually about the invocation of magical forces. (One passage states: 'Certain of the processes may take weeks, or even months to obtain the necessary force, *and this will depend on the Alchemist rather than the matter.*' [My italics.] This is to say that the important part of the process is what the alchemist puts into it, either psychically or magically.)

Yet basically Regardie's *Philosopher's Stone* is a Jungian interpretation of alchemy. He throws in the 'magnetic forces' for good measure but his approach is psychological. Mercury becomes consciousness, sulphur is emotion ('the *anima* principle of the psyche'), salt is intellect, and the dissolution of mercury and sulphur into the nigredo is the dissolution of the conscious personality into the unconscious by means of the hypnotic trance.

Still it would be a mistake to dismiss *The Philosopher's Stone* as just another orthodox Jungian interpretation of alchemy. Regardie was too steeped in the magical tradition to allow himself to be blinkered by any single theory. His book remains one of the best and most stimulating of all works on alchemy, and certainly one of the clearest.

This makes it all the more surprising to discover him, in the 1968 edition, making a public confession of error: or, as he puts it, 'eating crow and enjoying it'. What has happened, it seems, is that he has met a real laboratory alchemist:

> Through a friend of mine, I was introduced to Mr Albert Riedel of Salt Lake City, Utah, while he was visiting Los Angeles. At the time I was domiciled there, enjoying the sunny climate and occasionally ruminating over the inclement weather of London, where I was born. It took only a few minutes to realise that I was talking to the first person I had *ever* met who *knew* what he was talking about on the subject of Alchemy. We promised to keep in touch—and we did.
>
> This promise later eventuated in an invitation to attend a seminar on Alchemy that he was conducting at the newly instituted Paracelsus Research Society in Salt Lake City. Most of the material presented in the seminar concerned Alchemy, Qabalah, Astrology, etc.—with which I was already theoretically familiar—though even there some radically new and stimulating viewpoints were obtained. But the *piece de resistance* was the laboratory work. Here I was wholly dumbfounded.
>
> It took no more than a few minutes to help me realise how presumptuous I had been to assert dogmatically that all alchemy was psychospiritual. What I witnessed there, and have since repeated, has sufficed to enable me to state categorically that, in insisting solely on a mystical interpretation of alchemy, I had done a grave disservice to the ancient sages and philosophers.

And he goes on to say that when Basil Valentinus tells the alchemist to take some antimony, pulverise it and place it in a dish over a fire, he means exactly what he says. There is no spiritual symbolism involved.

Unfortunately, Regardie fails to describe the experience that caused this astonishing change of heart; we gather only that Riedel actually demonstrated some of the basic transmutations in his laboratory. In his preface to *The Alchemist's Handbook* by 'Frater Albertus' Regardie is still less forthcoming; he even withholds the true name of Frater Albertus. Yet the book itself gives us a clear idea of at least some of the things Regardie witnessed in Riedel's laboratory. Frater Albertus explains frankly that he has no intention of giving away the secret of the Great Work, the transmutation of metals. But he offers a clear and detailed account of the 'lesser work'—the extraction of the essence of plants or the vegetable stone.

Albertus explains that all plants and vegetables contain an essence or a life principle. (This sounds rather like Boehme's 'signature'.) The essence can be extracted by placing the herb, either fresh or dried, in pure alcohol or ether, or, better still, using a Soxhlet extraction apparatus. In this apparatus, alcohol vapour is passed through a 'thimble' of filter paper which contains the herb. The alcohol vapour then enters a condenser above the apparatus and runs back down into the flask. Eventually the filter paper will contain only the dead residue of the plant, which may be burned and reduced to 'salt'. The essence of the plant, including a delicate oil ('sulphur'), will run back into the alcohol in the flask. The salt (burnt ashes) should be placed in the flask and some of the extract poured over it—as much as it can absorb. Then the process is started all over again until the flask contains an oily substance, which becomes solid when cold. This, says Albertus, is 'the alchemical elixir in its first state'. It can be burned again (calcined), and the whole process repeated. Each time, says Albertus, the strength is increased. And if the elixir is placed in a hermetically sealed flask and subjected to moderate heat, the result is 'the stone of the vegetable kingdom'—i.e., the equivalent of the Philosopher's Stone on a lower level.[3] (This last process is obviously parallel to the first stage of the Great Work, where the sulphur and mercury are converted to the albedo.)

What is the point of this peculiar operation? The alchemist must begin with a knowledge of the medicinal properties of plants (i.e., the greater celandine is good for liver trouble; honeysuckle for kidney stones and whooping cough; rosemary for gout and general health). Most books on plants[4] contain instructions for extracting the medicinal properties by infusion, maceration, decoction, and so on. Albertus asserts that his method will produce the same kind of thing, but many times more powerful.

On the scientific, or medicinal level, the whole thing sounds preposterous. To begin with, science denies that plants have an 'essence'. When a plant is dead, after it has been dried (which Albertus recommends), it is merely a compound of various organic chemicals. Alcohol may well extract certain of these chemicals or oils, as it extracts the oil of orange peel to make the liqueur called Cointreau. But the result will be merely a mixture of chemicals, like dissolving sugar in water. Burning the residue produces only ordinary carbon, and mixing this carbon with the extract should do no more good than using ashes from the fire.

Albertus declares that this view is short-sighted. The vegetable essence is its active force; the salt contains its individual qualities; the mixture of these produces a concentrated elixir with powerful medicinal properties. If science fails to recognise this, it is because science has not yet come to grips with certain essential facts about living matter or dead matter, if we can consider minerals 'dead'. What is essential is a certain order or structure—a 'blueprint'. This blueprint comes from 'above', not in any mystical or religious sense, but in the sense used by a scientist like Michael Polanyi, when he says that living hierarchies cannot be reduced to purely physical energies. And the blueprint, says Riedel, can somehow be extracted by ordinary chemical processes. Moreover, according to Regardie and to *Parachemy*, the magazine of the Paracelsus Research Society, it has been extracted many times, by Brother Albertus himself and by his pupils. (Edward Campbell, a journalist in contact with the school, reports: 'My correspondents . . . tell me that a dozen people have now made the vegetable stone and can, by using it, extract in moments the 'soul' of any vegetable material.' He adds: 'The *materia medica* of such vegetable souls is only just beginning to be studied. I suspect that homoeopathy by its laborious process of succussion extracts a pennyworth of vegetable soul. The vegetable stone extracts the soul of whatever plant it is applied to, and produces in a few moments megawatts of vegetable soul (as it were!).[5]

This notion of 'vegetable soul' cannot be dismissed as unscientific. It is thoroughly consistent with the discoveries about the 'blueprint of life' made by Harold Burr, and supported by Kirlian photography. So if Riedel's strange processes produce genuine results, it is possible that he has stumbled on some principle of living organisation that has not yet been recognised by our crude laboratory science. It is also worth bearing in mind that these principles were first formulated by the Chinese more than two thousand years ago in the science they called macrobiotics, which in turn became alchemy.

But what about the Great Work, the manufacture of the Philosopher's Stone? Albertus declines to speak of this in his book, and he gives his reasons. The precise details of the magnum opus have never been stated plainly in print. 'Those who wait for a complete description . . . of the Grand Arcanum will wait in vain. It cannot be given. It is not permissible. But—and this is of the utmost significance—he who can accomplish in his laboratory what the following pages present by way of instruction can surely accomplish the Grand Arcanum, *if he is ready.*'

If Albertus is trying to fob us off with the usual alchemists' excuse, he at least takes some trouble to explain what the Great Work is all about. In the opening paragraph of the book, he answers the question, What is Alchemy: 'It is "the raising of vibrations".' And he repeats the definition at intervals throughout the book. This immediately brings to mind Lethbridge's insight that the pendulum is responding to vibrations, and that 'higher worlds' consist of higher rates of vibration. Moreover, Gurdjieff told Ouspensky: 'It is necessary to regard the universe as consisting of vibrations. These vibrations proceed in all kinds, aspects and densities of the matter which constitutes the universe, from the finest to the coarsest; they issue from various sources and proceed in various directions, crossing one another, colliding, strengthening, weakening, arresting one another, and so on.'[6]

Albertus explains that the vital essence of any animal, vegetable or mineral is what the alchemists mean by its mercury, and then goes on: 'Yet . . . although the mercury is of the same origin, it is of a certain vibration in the vegetable kingdom, of a higher vibratory rate in the animal kingdom, and of a higher rate still in the mineral realm.' If Albertus is speaking of sheer electrical frequencies, it is easy to see his point. The finest astronomical clocks are driven by a quartz crystal, because of its high vibratory rate; the thought of using a piece of animal or vegetable matter in its place is obviously absurd. Organic structure may be more complex; but the forces locked up in it are far less powerful than those in minerals. Rocks remain unchanged for millions of years, because the forces holding them together are so enormous; organic matter decays in a matter of days when the life force evaporates. As to the notion that minerals are 'dead', it was disputed by the philosopher Whitehead, who held that the whole universe is a single organism, and that all its parts are permeated with life. This same view was held by the alchemists, who believed that metals and minerals grow inside the earth. They are 'dead' only in the same sense as our fingernails or hair. 'Man is holding the balance of the three kingdoms,' says Albertus, 'and can partake of any one according to his liking.'

All substances in the vegetable, animal and mineral kingdoms, Albertus goes on to explain, are made up of three elements, which alchemists call salt, mercury and sulphur. The mercury is positive, the salt negative, and the sulphur a neutral or binding force. The vibrations of each realm can be obtained through the alchemical process. The 'lesser work' of separating the plant or vegetable into its three elements, then re-combining them, can be carried out by any competent chemist, but the Greater Work is a different matter; ordinary men cannot do· it, for it requires some special power in the alchemist himself. 'No one can accomplish anything alchemically in the laboratory without the Philosopher's Mercury, so-called. But this is not common metallic mercury or quicksilver.'

This seems to be as far as Albertus is willing to take us. But he offers one interesting hint. He speaks of the way individual organs of the body act as if they had a will of their own, producing their own special substances. One of the riddles of modern biology is that our bodies have various sub-systems, which in some animals behave like intelligent sub-communities. The nineteenth century philosopher Edouard von Hartmann believed that the answer lay in the unconscious, which he saw as the basic driving force of all creation—in other words, its vital essence. Albertus declares that vegetables, animals and minerals each have their own vital essence, and that the essence of minerals is higher than that of human beings, while that of vegetables is lower. Could this be why it is fairly easy to extract the essence of plants, but incredibly difficult to extract the essence of minerals or metals? Could it be that the alchemist needs to be able, at a certain point, to supply a higher level of vibrations from inside himself?

Albertus claims to have extracted the essence (or oil) of copper, lead and gold. His reply to the objection that this flies in the face of all science is that modern science still knows nothing of the secrets of matter, and that the ancient alchemists, for all their absurd jargon, knew something essential. And Regardie is convinced that Albertus is telling the truth.

Again, it is Gurdjieff who hints at a possible solution. The basic law in his system is the Law of Three, according to which all phenomena are produced by three forces, the active, the passive and the neutral.

'The first two forces are comprehensible to man,' says Gurdjieff, 'and the third may sometimes be discovered either at the point of application of the forces, or in the "medium", or in the "result". But generally speaking, the third force is not easily accessible to direct observation and understanding.' Similarly, Albertus begins by explaining that all substances contain two elements: mercury (the positive force) and salt (the negative). He later explains that there is a third component, sulphur, which is difficult to separate from the mercury. According to Gurdjieff, the Law of Three is 'at the root of all ancient systems'. So it is conceivable that the ancient alchemists were simply applying the Law of Three of matter.

Gurdjieff and Albertus also seem to agree on a more practical level. According to Albertus, the alchemist's purpose is to distill the vibrations—the vital essence—of a plant or mineral, so they can be used medicinally on human beings. In his discussions with the Moscow group, Gurdjieff explained that there are four possible ways to achieve heightened consciousness. The way of the fakir involves physical discipline and self-torture; his purpose is to create 'a certain substance' in his own body. The way of the monk involves prayer and meditation; his chemistry is emotional, and it takes him only a week to create the substance that costs the fakir a month of torment. The way of the yogi involves concentration; he can create the substance in a single day. But, says Gurdjieff, there is a fourth way: the way of the 'sly man'. The sly man knows that the 'substance' 'can be introduced into the organism from without if it is known how to do it'. And so he 'simply prepares and swallows a little pill that contains all the substances he wants'.[7]

What could be the nature of such a pill? I have suggested elsewhere[8] that intelligence and the power of concentration may be connected with a chemical called serotonin, which is used by the pineal gland of the brain to produce the hormone melatonin; but it is doubtful whether serotonin, swallowed in the form of a pill, would reach the pineal gland. It also seems unlikely that Gurdjieff was speaking of a drug or stimulant. There is still the interesting possibility that the 'little pill' could be one of the 'essences' mentioned by Albertus —particularly the mineral essences, whose rate of vibration is higher than that of the animal kingdom.

Albertus is not the only modern alchemist to insist that the Great

Work requires a thoroughly pragmatic approach. Perhaps the most fascinating of all modern works on the subject is the curious little volume called *Gold of a Thousand Mornings* by a French adept, Armand Barbault.[9]

Like Albertus, Barbault claims to have manufactured 'oil of gold'. In fact, he prints letters from scientists who have tested it, including one that describes how it cured a woman of multiple sclerosis.

Like Albertus, Barbault begins from the belief that it is possible to capture the life essence of plants, and his description of the apparatus he constructed for this purpose sounds oddly similar to Albertus's Soxhlet Extractor. In order to capture this essence, says Barbault, the ancient alchemists picked the plants at dawn and kept them in containers filled with fresh dew. Barbault attempted to produce the elixir according to this formula, but found that it was unstable. And then, 'thanks to inspiration and the guides which accompanied me on all these spiritual labours', he realised what was wrong. The elixir needed to be stabilised with a third element—a mineral. And the mineral was the most commonplace of all the alchemical elements—earth. This, Barbault asserts, is the *prima materia* of the alchemists. But the earth, like the plants and the dew, has to be collected under special conditions. For the earth is also a living substance, permeated by living forces.

Barbault's assumptions are consistent not only with those of Albertus, but with those of the 'ley hunters'. The earth is a living entity, as our remote ancestors realised. And its forces wax and wane according to those of the heavenly bodies. Human beings are quite unconsciously conditioned by these forces from the moment of birth, as are all living things. There is nothing 'unscientific' about the notion of living creatures being influenced by planetary forces, as Harold Burr discovered when he connected his voltmeter up to trees, and observed that their life field was affected by sunspots. The earth under our feet is full of living organisms, so it seems reasonable to assume that they also might be affected.

Seen in this light, there is nothing unreasonable in Barbault's assertion that alchemy is closely related to astrology—that, in fact, the two are inseparable. Oddly enough, this is a fact that Mary Anne South was inclined to overlook, although all the major alchemical texts bear witness to it. (We have already noted that it is best to begin the Great Work under the sign of Aries, Taurus or Gemini, the spring and early summer signs.) As a typical daughter of the Victorian age, she prob-ably felt that this was a little more than sensible people could be expected to swallow. According to Barbault, she was wrong. Astrol-ogy is the most pragmatic of the 'occult sciences', and, from the scientific point of view, the easiest to investigate. Any open-minded person who spends half an hour with a textbook of astrology will acknowledge that, for some strange reason, it actually works. Astrol-ogy asserts that the character of a baby is determined at the moment of its birth by the positions of the heavenly bodies; and in a remarkable number of cases, the character of individuals *does* seem to correspond to their astrological sign.

Ley hunters find nothing strange in this. The earth is a magnet; so are the planets. The earth's forces are continually affected by its position in the solar system, and they in turn affect all living creatures. This is why it makes no difference that the ancients thought there were only seven planets and that these included the sun and moon. They were concerned only with the forces themselves, and their *shamans* were probably as directly aware of these forces as we are of the change of seasons.

Barbault disagrees that the Great Work *has* to begin in the spring. He says that the alchemical process is a *continual interaction* between the alchemist and his 'matter', and that therefore he should choose the time to begin according to his astrological chart. He writes:

> Not only are there times when nature's life forces are at their most intense, there are also privileged areas where these forces are concen-trated. [Again, no ley hunter would disagree.] This has caused numerous adepts to declare that the First Matter should be taken from black earth where, they say, it is distinguishable by its pellet-like appearance at the moment when it should be gathered. Some even go as far as to consider searching with a hazel rod, an implement well-known to the ancients . . . In my case, I relied mostly on astrology.

On August 3, 1947, Barbault and his wife went to the spot which he had fixed, 'in order to inspect the ground . . . in which . . . intensifica-tion of certain currents should take place'. He explains in detail his reasons for choosing this particular moment. 'The following week saw intensification of the currents while the sun passed successively through conjunction with Saturn and Pluto. Saturday February 15,

1948, night of the new moon in Aquarius, was fixed as the date of acquisition; the time was to be soon after midnight, at the moment when the sun passed to the depths of the sky under the feet of the seeker.' So the First Matter was obtained, from about ten centimetres below the earth and taken back to the laboratory. He emphasises that his wife's psychic faculties played an important part in the whole operation: 'My companion. . . existed for long periods in a trance-like condition and carried out her functions as a guide in the fullest possible manner. It was she who chose the location for the acquisition.' (John Dee would have called her a 'scryer'.)

The 'sacred earth' was sifted for stones, washed in dew (collected by dragging large canvas sheets over the grass at dawn, and wringing them out into a bucket, as shown in the *Mutus Liber*), dried and pulverised. Young plants, collected at dawn, were added daily. The mass was heated to a temperature of 40°C. Periodically, it was moistened with dew.

This process was continued for *three years*, during which the whole mass turned black, as one would expect from rotting vegetable matter. When it was covered with dew, the dew itself became black. Barbault drew it off, and left it to stand; the black deposit settled to the bottom. Six more years brought the 'second degree of corruption', and then, an unspecified time later, the third degree. Now the matter was at last ready to be incinerated and ground into ash. This, says Barbault, is called the Philosopher's Peat. (Albertus calls it the salt.) Presumably the dew containing the vital essence has also been subjected to some kind of distillation.

The next step is again one we have already encountered in Albertus; the ash is placed in a sealed tube and mixed with dew. Barbault also adds powdered gold. The tube is then placed into an oven and boiled for four-hour periods. The result is vegetable oil of gold. This can be re-distilled, with the addition of more sap and dew, to produce a more concentrated version. The resulting liquor, says Barbault, has powerful medicinal properties, although spectrum analysis shows no trace of gold. Paracelsus referred to this essence as 'vegetable gold', and wrote: 'The solvent of metallic gold is vegetable matter.' According to Barbault, a similar method can produce oil of antimony and oil of silver.

There is another view of alchemy which regards the 'forbidden secret' as being essentially sexual in nature. It is expressed by the poet

Kenneth Rexroth in his introduction to the works of the seventeenth-century alchemist Thomas Vaughan.[10] Vaughan was the twin brother of the mystical poet Henry Vaughan, and he wrote a number of alchemical works under the pseudonym of Eugenius Philalethes (not to be confused with his contemporary Eirenaeus Philalethes, author of the famous treatise called *The Open Door*). Vaughan died tragically in a laboratory explosion in 1665, at the age of forty-two.

Rexroth indulges in a certain amount of tongue-in-cheek mystification, but his basic theory emerges clearly enough. He points out that the illustrations used by Jung in his edition of *Secret of the Golden Flower* are taken from an alchemical treatise by the great Chinese alchemist Ko Hung, and that Jung failed to include the most significant of these illustrations. It shows a naked man in meditation, and in place of the plexuses of the nervous system there are drawings of the instruments of alchemy—retorts, furnaces and so on. Chinese alchemy, says Rexroth, involved yogic practices and techniques of sexual yoga. The Hindu religious philosophy known as Tantrism makes deliberate use of the sexual energies in an attempt to raise the level of consciousness; it is regarded as a form of alchemy, and is based on the notion that the two basic forces of the universe are male and female (Shiva and Shakti). The Tantrist attempts to arouse his sexual energies, and to cause them to rise up the spine, through the vital centres (known as *chakras*), to the brain, where it will produce illumination. The practice can be attended by much danger, for unless properly controlled, these energies can produce madness and serious illness. Chinese alchemy, says Rexroth, makes use of the same techniques.

So does Western alchemy, and this could be one of its most closely-guarded secrets. But Vaughan, according to Rexroth, comes close to 'giving the whole show away'. He fails to specify which passage he is referring to, but it could well be the postscript of Vaughan's *Aula Lucis*, or House of Light. Here Vaughan hints that he is going to come as close as he dares to stating the great secret in so many words, although he has been vowed to silence. What he goes on to say is that the 'Vessel of Nature', the vessel in which the alchemical operation takes place, is a 'menstruous substance'. 'It is the matrix of Nature, wherein you must place the universal sperm as soon as it appears beyond its body. The heat of this matrix is sulphureous, and it is that which coagulates the sperm. . . This matrix is the life of the sperm, for it preserves and quickens it.' And he ends his postscript by stating that he is convinced that this basic secret of alchemy was originally 'revealed' to man, 'for it is the secret of Nature, even that which the philosophers call "the first copulation". . .' Such sexual symbolism is not rare in alchemy. It looks as though either Vaughan is hinting that the 'vessel' is the female vagina, or the alchemical operation closely parallels sexual intercourse.

Vaughan married in 1651, and the union was apparently exceptionally happy. When his wife died in 1658, Vaughan was shattered, and his notebooks are full of expressions of his longing to be reunited with her in heaven. He believed that her spirit continued to visit him in dreams, and, on one occasion, she correctly foretold the death of his father. One entry declares that on the day his wife fell ill, he suddenly remembered how to extract the 'oil of Halcali', which Waite is inclined to think refers to the First Matter (*prima materia*) of alchemy. He had previously succeeded in making it—almost by accident—when he and his wife were living at an inn called The Pinner of Wakefield; but he had forgotten exactly how he did it. On the day his wife died, he once again succeeded, 'so that on the same day, which proved the most sorrowful to me . . . God was pleased to confer on me the greatest joy I can ever have in this world after her death'.

Vaughan obviously believed that he was a sinful man. He had several dreams of a dark-skinned man, 'and I believe it is the evil genius'. But his dreams of this demon became less terrifying, 'my life, I bless God, being much amended'. Nevertheless, he prays for death, 'for I desire to be dissolved and to be with Christ, which is far better for me, than to live, and sin in this sinful body'.

Rexroth leaves little doubt about his own conclusion:

> Thomas Vaughan and his wife, his *soror mystica*, wrapped in entranced embrace at the Pinner of Wakefield were, it is true, blundering into a region of revelation which they little understood and which, it would seem, eventually destroyed both of them. They were doing what the Chinese adepts had done at least four hundred years before Christ and what others may have done in the Indus Valley three thousand years before. But they were also, and concomitantly, performing a chemical experiment, and they believed that neither could be successful without the other.

This is Rexroth's view of the nature of 'the double mercury'. The success of the experiment somehow involved the channelling of magical sexual energies into the operation. There is only one objection: if the preparation of oil of Halcali required a parallel sexual ritual, how did Vaughan succeed on the day of his wife's death? Moreover, if the preparation of the oil was Vaughan's greatest joy, why should he feel—as Rexroth implies—guilty about it for the rest of his life?

For readers who are inclined to believe that alchemy is a compound of mystification and ignorance, this chapter will have produced no proof to the contrary. Indeed, after days of hopeless struggle with the obscurities of *The Hermetic Museum* or *The New Pearl of Great Price*— or Jung's *Mysterium Coniunctionis*, for that matter—I have often been tempted to dismiss the whole thing as a total waste of time. Yet, like Jung, I find myself possessed of a basic conviction that something of immense importance is being said.

Indeed, the whole history of parapsychology is the story of people who have demonstrated powers that, according to science, 'ought not' to exist.

Alchemy is puzzling because it seems to stand in a different category from other branches of the paranormal, such as psychometry, radiesthesia, telepathy and so on. Most paranormal faculties are passive; they work best when the mind is tranquil, and they take place without any conscious effort. Alchemy is active, an attempt to produce transformations in the composition of matter. And alchemists maintain that it is not a purely chemical process, it involves a parallel transformation in the mind of the alchemist. But how can a change inside the alchemist make any difference to what is going on in his retort or athanor?

Mary Anne South knew something about the theory and practice of mesmerism, and that hypnosis can actually widen the inner being. Rexroth put his finger on it when he wrote: 'It is only in recent years when neurological research has turned its attention to yoga that we have come to realise that, although these practices include autohypnosis, they are primarily concerned with the production of states which, although entranced, are psychologically, and even neurologically speaking, *exactly the opposite of the hypnotic state*.' [My italics.] States like these are active rather than passive. The same applies to astral projection which, Miss South hints, plays an important part in alchemy.

But it is the sexual alchemy of the Tantrists that offers what is perhaps the most important clue. The more closely we look into it, the more we realise that sex itself is a form of alchemy, and that its secret points to the secret of the Great Work itself.

Sex is a physical act, and we think of it in physical terms. For example, we speak of 'sexual hunger' as if it could be compared to physical hunger. But no one ever died of sex starvation. Moreover, sex differs from most physical processes in having no predictable effect. We can respond to the same stimuli with ecstasy, boredom, or even alarm.

This is perhaps the most interesting thing about the sexual process: its physical results are almost entirely dependent on its psychological component. Generally speaking, habit tends to erode the intensity of the experience; the 'hunger' abates. All sexual abnormalities, from rape to sadism and necrophilia are an attempt to add spice to an experience that has become bland and tasteless.

But if we think of a Romeo and Juliet making love for the first time, we can see that it is not simply a matter of spice. They are *intensely awake*—in the state Gurdjieff calls self-remembering. They are deeply aware of themselves and of one another. If they had been able to marry and 'live happily ever after', they would have allowed an element of sleep to enter the relationship. This is not to say that they would not have continued to be in love; but they would have ceased to be aware of one another *as realities*.

Gurdjieff often remarked that we habitually misuse our sexual energy. He insisted that this energy is of a completely different kind from emotional energy, instinctive energy or physical energy. 'It is a very big thing when the sex centre works with its own energy, but it happens very seldom.' People often use sexual energy for what ought to be intellectual or emotional activities (for example, when a puritan preaches vehemently against 'impurities'). They are also prone to use emotional energy in their sexual activities, particularly negative emotional energy. (The Marquis de Sade is an extreme illustration.) Gurdjieff remarked that anyone who wanted to engage in 'the Work' must be sexually completely normal, or deliberately make himself so; any perversions would act as obstacles. Sexual perversions are basically a form of fantasy, of unreality. They arise because of our tendency to become enmeshed in habit.

It is important to understand why habit can be so disastrous for human beings. The factory that manufactures our vital energy is controlled by the subconscious mind. When I prepare to undertake some dangerous or difficult task, my subconscious makes sure I am well supplied with energy; consequently I feel 'fully alive'. When, on the other hand, I do something as a matter of habit, the subconscious sends me far less energy—reasoning that there is no emergency—and I feel dull and half-alive. Consciousness takes on an unreal, dreamlike quality.

In this case, I may try to deceive my subconscious mind through the use of my imagination. If I imagine some sudden emergency, or some intense sexual stimulus, I am immediately flooded with energy. But if I try it too often, it ceases to work; I need to increase the strength of the stimulus and imagine something even more violent and shocking. This was the fate of de Sade.

On the other hand, there is no reason why habit should be a synonym for boredom. The 'double ambiguity' experiment with the planaria demonstrates that everything depends on the amount of energy we put into the learning process. *I* decide at precisely what point I begin to take something for granted. There is no law of nature that says that Romeo must get tired of Juliet if their love life runs too smoothly. It is true that he will *tend* to take her for granted if there are no obstacles. But if he is conscious of this tendency, it becomes a matter of his free choice. He can make a deliberate effort *not* to take her for granted; he can continually galvanise himself into re-focusing her reality—perhaps by a deliberate mental exercise of recalling how they fell in love. The act of love-making can be transformed from a mechanical habit into an experience of intensity. In which case, it is fair to say that he is performing a kind of alchemy—remembering Albertus's definition: 'Alchemy is the raising of vibrations.' Janet would say that he is deliberately increasing his 'coefficient of reality'; but this amounts to the same thing. What he is actually doing is inducing a state of 'creative tension', and thereby transmuting mere force into creative energy.

All this is simply another way of saying that the essential component in 'sexual alchemy' – transforming a 'mere' sexual experience into a an experience of reality – is Faculty X.

Gurdjieff's remarks on alchemy, as reported by Ouspensky, are complicated and obscure; they contain, nevertheless, some intriguing clues. He explained to the Moscow group that, according to the esoteric tradition of alchemy, various substances in the universe are referred to under the name of Hydrogen.[11] It seems a pity that this tradition should make use of the name of the chemical element, for it soon becomes clear that this is really a generic term meaning 'substance'.

According to Gurdjieff, there are twelve different types of Hydrogen, and to these, he gives numbers which are multiples of 6; so there is Hydrogen 6, Hydrogen 12, and so on to Hydrogen 6144.

All the Hydrogens from 6144 to 96 are various types of matter, 6144 being the densest and coarsest. But the interesting Hydrogens are the four at the top end of the scale—48, 24, 12 and 6. These are the energies required to work our various 'centres'. Hydrogen 6, the highest of all, is the fuel used by the higher thinking centre, a centre which already exists in us, *but of which we are unaware*. The same is true of our higher emotional centre, which runs on Hydrogen 12. If man could actually learn to manufacture these higher energies, and use them to drive the appropriate centres, he would become a kind of god—or, at any rate, experience a kind of mystical insight that is almost unknown to human beings.

In fact, says Gurdjieff, the body *is* an alchemical machine, for transforming food (Hydrogen 748) into the Hydrogens we need to work our lower centres (48 and 24). You could say, then, that the problem of evolution is for man to learn to transform these lower Hydrogens into the higher type. It is interesting to note that, in Gurdjieff's view, we already possess the necessary 'higher centres', but that they exist outside the range of our everyday consciousness; this seems to be Gurdjieff's equivalent of the 'superconscious mind', the higher rungs of the ladder of selves.

When speaking about sex at a later meeting, Gurdjieff added another piece of information which is immensely obscure, but obviously of central importance. It is to the effect that Hydrogen 12, which we are capable of manufacturing in very small quantities, can be transformed into Hydrogen 6 by a certain kind of 'shock'. But this 'shock' can take place both *inside* and *outside* the organism.

In other words, alchemy is not simply a transformation that takes place inside the alchemist; it is also a chemical (or physical) process that takes place in the world of matter. Gurdjieff seems to provide a bridge between the transcendental alchemy of Jung, and the physical variety of the ancient alchemists. Moreover, he asserts that the two are closely linked; physical and spiritual alchemy are simply two aspects of the same process.

In short, what Gurdjieff is saying is that alchemy is a process by which lower energy is transformed into higher, and the actual process is much the same whether it takes place inside us or in the world of matter. He offers no clues to the actual process, but a certain amount can be inferred from his remarks on the 'law of octaves'. For example, man's chief problem is that he is subject to the law of the *slowing of vibrations*. He starts out on some important task with a great surge of determination and vital energy; then, after a short time, this energy drops quietly to a lower level, then to a lower level still, until all his drive has leaked away. This can be avoided, says Gurdjieff, if we apply a 'shock'—or sudden vital effort—at exactly the right moment. The story of Fritz Peters shows that Gurdjieff could not only apply this shock to himself, but also to other people. He seems to have applied it to Bennett at Fontainebleau. Could it not, therefore, be applied also to some purely chemical process which is governed by the same law of octaves?

Gurdjieff, it seems, may have known the answer to the secret that is only hinted at in the *Suggestive Enquiry* of Mary Anne South.

If this—or something like it—was the alchemists' great secret, why did they go to so much trouble to preserve it? Surely it would be virtually useless to anyone but the spiritually qualified?

The answer to this question takes us to the heart of the mystery of alchemy. It also enables us to understand why alchemy was regarded as the epitome of the occult sciences.

'As above, so below' is more than a formula about 'correspondences'. Mystics have always taken it to mean that the world 'below' is a kind of debased reflection of what is above. Goethe expressed the same thing in the last lines of *Faust: 'Alles Vergängliche/Ist nur ein Gleichnis.'* 'All things destructible/Are but reflection.' Or, more accurately, are images or symbols of reality. The alchemist attempts to transmute this lower reality to the higher level. The criminally-inclined attempt to reverse the process.

Here again, the sexual analogy makes the point clearer. The basic ingredients of the sex act, like those of the alchemical process, are lowly—two human bodies. Every day, in brothels all over the world, millions of sex acts take place that are in no sense alchemical; the female might as well be a lifesize rubber doll. On the other hand, when

Paris and Helen, or Romeo and Juliet, or Tristan and Isolde, come together, the result is a raising of vibrations. The lovers experience a form of intensified consciousness, freedom from the 'robot'—Wagner expressed it in the love music of *Tristan*—and their vision of the world is alchemically transformed.

When sex is taken for granted, it is largely mechanical, and no magic is involved. After twenty years of marriage, the average couple have ceased to experience the 'magic'; they cannot be accused of 'reductionism' because they have forgotten that sex *can* be a form of alchemy.

The Marquis de Sade, by contrast, was as susceptible to the 'magic' as Shakespeare or Wagner; sex remained an obsession to his dying day. But his response to the magic was an attempt to drag it down to his own *personal* level. It is as if he resents beauty and innocence and their implied demand that he should raise his own 'vibrations'. He wants to deflower them as quickly as possible, using them as a crude physical 'shock' to enhance his sense of personal power. He could be compared to an alcoholic for whom the finest wine is only a means of getting drunk. He makes use of 'sexual alchemy', but only in the sense that the Black Mass makes use of the sacred wafer.

It may seem that I am now using 'alchemy' in some purely metaphorical sense which has nothing to do with the down-to-earth labours of the traditional alchemist. This is not so. If alchemy is the raising of vibrations, it is also, on the personal level, the act of *gaining freedom from the robot*.

It is almost impossible to over-estimate the importance of this recognition. Nothing is more difficult than for human beings to grasp the extent to which their powers are *held in captivity* by the robot. It is as if we had been injected with some drug that keeps us in a state of paralysis. And just as a man who had spent his whole life in an iron lung could have no conception of what it feels like to be a champion athlete, so we chronic invalids have no idea of what it means to be free and healthy. Or of the powers possessed by a healthy person.

A simple experiment will underline the point. Put down this book for a moment and stare at the opposite wall, allowing your mind to go blank. In this state, 'the real you' has abdicated. Your body ticks on like an enormous clock, your brain continues to register images—perhaps there is even a tune running in your head—yet all this is purely mechanical. You have ceased to be a person, and become little more than a mirror reflecting the reality around you. Yet as far as other people are concerned, you are still there, sitting in the chair, looking solid and real. If some accident to your brain caused you to live out your life in this state, you would still be able to function perfectly adequately, and few people would notice the difference. They would not notice that 'you' had disappeared.

If someone asks you a question while your mind is blank, note how little effort it costs you to respond. Your robot does most of the work for you. And so it is with almost everything you do during your waking hours. You inhabit a machine which does most of your 'living' for you.

But observe what happens in moments of happiness—when some obstacle suddenly vanishes, or you have something delightful to anticipate. The 'real you' begins to emerge, like a snail from its shell, and there is an increasing feeling of happiness and wonderment. In these moments we catch a glimpse of a completely new way of apprehending the world. It is a revelation, as unlike 'ordinary consciousness' as being awake is from being asleep. Yet nothing very startling has happened. We have merely become *minimally* free of the stranglehold of the robot. And that extra small degree of freedom—perhaps one per cent—is enough to transform the whole world and make life seem *totally different*.

Gurdjieff taught that man is permanently asleep and has little chance of awakening, except through some immense and painful effort. I am inclined to feel that this is an exaggeration. It is relatively easy to 'glide' into freedom—or some small degree of freedom—in moments of relaxation. And a little optimism—the knowledge that it *can* be done—can make a world of difference. The problem is that it is just as easy to glide out again. We need to develop a technique for 'fixing' the insights.

The most interesting thing about these moments of 'freedom' is the feeling of *expanded powers*. I have already made this observation when speaking about 'gliding'—how easy it becomes to 'identify' with the music of Mozart or the poetry of Ronsard (Faculty X), or to remember the name of some distant relative you haven't thought about in years. In such moments I can recall the actual smell of the printing ink used on comics when I was a child, or the taste of the lollipop with artificial flavouring they sold during the Second World War. In other words, the 'real me' seems to have far greater access to my memory archives than my everyday self. He also has greater access to energy supplies.

We often use the phrase 'under the weather' to indicate a general sense of debility; it would be more accurate to say 'under the robot'. In this state of 'mechanicalness', every effort costs me twice as much energy. By contrast, in moments of 'freedom', I am astonished at how much can be accomplished by so little effort.

Is there any evidence that 'freedom from the robot' involves a real extension of our powers? There is, in fact, a great deal. If we think of the robot as a kind of prison—like a straitjacket of a suit of armour—there are two ways of escaping his constriction. The first is the method taught by Gurdjieff: to flex the muscles until there is more room inside the straitjacket. The other could be called the way of Houdini. The great escape artist used to flex his muscles while the straitjacket was being tied on; then, when he was locked in his cabinet, he *relaxed*, creating more room inside the straitjacket, which allowed him to wriggle free. Human beings seldom achieve freedom from the robot by Gurdjieff's method, because we are so little accustomed to effort. But we often achieve it by relaxation, which is just as effective. This is why we drink alcohol, smoke cigarettes, take holidays.

Most writers on the paranormal are agreed that relaxation is often an essential component in 'psychic experience'. In *The Occult* I tell the story of a musician friend who was returning home late one night from a concert in a state of relaxed fatigue; as his taxi drove along the Bayswater Road, he suddenly *knew*, with total certainty, that at the Queensway traffic light another taxi would shoot across the road and hit them. He felt embarrassed about telling the driver; but at the Queensway lights, a taxi shot across the road and hit them.

Relaxation also facilitates powers of telepathy. The painter Kokoschka tells in his autobiography how his mother was one day visiting her sister in Vienna. In the midst of a casual chat, she suddenly cried: 'A cab, quickly. I must go home. The boy is in the garden, bleeding.' Her sister tried to dissuade her but she insisted on rushing home—and found that her son had cut his leg badly with a hatchet; he would have bled to death if she had not arrived.

The same principle explains why certain natural powers can be strengthened under hypnosis so that a man can keep his arm raised in the air for hours without fatigue, or a man with poor eyesight can see into the distance. Total relaxation frees our latent powers. (The Taoists lay central emphasis on the same principle.) This probably explains the otherwise puzzling fact that sick people so often display a high degree of psychic sensitivity. Healthy people make full use of their robots to meet the problems of everyday living; sick people are exempted from this effort, so the robots do not achieve the same stranglehold. (This also explains why primitive peoples often possess highly developed psychic powers.) Accident or sudden shock can also release psychic faculties, as we have seen in the case of Peter Hurkos (who fell off a ladder and fractured his skull) and Jane O'Neill. In the latter case, it seems clear that it was not the initial shock of the accident that activated her psychic powers so much as the nervous strain and sense of vulnerability that came later.

Compared to the Gurdjieff method, the Houdini method has distinct disadvantages. It achieves its effect by weakening the robot, whereas the Gurdjieff method depends on strengthening the real self by arousing the vital energies. Ramakrishna was making involuntary use of this method when he seized a sword and prepared to run himself through; the shock released his latent vital powers. A story told by the poet Ronald Duncan in his autobiography makes the same point. In India, Duncan was suffering from an exceptionally bad cold, and Gandhi advised him to see a certain Hindu doctor. The doctor strapped Duncan to an upright cast-iron bed frame, then pulled a lever so that it fell backwards with a crash. Duncan stood up feeling that every bone in his body had been jarred—but totally free of the cold. (It is interesting to speculate whether it would have worked as well if he had been forewarned, giving the robot time to prepare.)

It is because most psychics belong to the Houdini type and have achieved their powers by some freak of nature that we tend to think of psychic powers as essentially passive in nature. But there are certain ones, like Gurdjieff's powers of telepathy, or psychokinesis, the power to move objects by the mind alone, that are active in nature. Poltergeist activity is now believed to be an unconscious form of psychokinesis, which the 'focus' (or cause) of the activity can seldom control—is, in fact, usually unaware of having anything to do with. The few exceptions only serve to emphasise the point. The young psychic Matthew Manning, for example, began to cause poltergeist activity at the age of eleven. At his boarding school, the flying objects and moving furniture caused such chaos that he was twice almost expelled. At the age of sixteen, he discovered that he had the faculty of automatic writing and drawing. When left to itself, his hand would produce writing in languages unknown to him—for example, Greek and Arabic—and drawings in the manner of Dürer, Goya, Beardsley and Picasso. The poltergeist activity ceased; apparently learning to channel his powers, enabled the robot to take a hand—and to dilute them. After watching Uri Geller bending spoons on television, in January 1974, Manning tried the same thing and immediately succeeded; one scientist, Graham Hodgetts of Cambridge University, was present with other witnesses at a session on 8th March 1974 when a spoon curled up on the table when no one was touching it. Nevertheless, Manning is now unable to make a heavy piece of furniture move across the room.

In 1976, I had the opportunity to spend some time with Matthew Manning and Uri Geller; it confirmed my feeling that their powers are basically a kind of controlled poltergeist activity. I was also interested to note that both Manning and Geller seem to possess only a limited control over their 'powers'. Both seem to exercise a maleficent influence on electronic equipment. I spent a morning trying to record Matthew, but my cassette recorder—which had worked perfectly up till then, and has worked perfectly ever since—developed a whole series of baffling faults; tapes that should have contained conversation were blank. With Geller, the tape recorder worked, but objects like electric light bulbs and broken spoons fell out of the air, apparently as much to his surprise as mine. When Uri was invited to dinner by some friends of mine—the screen writer Jesse Lasky and his wife Pat—a silver button suddenly flew into the kitchen like an angry wasp. Uri was standing at the sink with a bottle of milk in one hand and a tin of cocoa in the other. Pat identified the button as one that had been on a card in her bedroom drawer (which proved to be closed); to reach the kitchen it would have had to penetrate three walls. Later, it was discovered that a large metal dragon on the front door had become twisted while Geller was in the flat; he apologised, but explained that such things happened without his volition.

In studying Matthew Manning's EEG chart (i.e., his 'brain waves'), Dr George Owen discovered that, when attempting to bend a key paranormally, Manning's brain showed an unusual amount of theta activity. Theta rhythms are associated with certain deep stages of sleep and meditation, but also with aggression and frustration.[12] Dr Grey Walter writes in *The Living Brain*: 'In bad-tempered adults, especially in those with an unusual tendency to aggressive behaviour, the theta rhythms are often prominent.' What was even more unusual in Manning's chart was the 'linear relationship between the peaks in the Theta, Alpha and Beta ranges.' Alpha rhythms are typical of relaxation, beta rhythms of attention or concentration; when beta increases, alpha diminishes or stops altogether. Yet Manning's chart not only showed the rare theta rhythms typical of aggression, but showed them somehow marching in step with alpha *and* beta, almost as if his brain were maintaining a balance between violence, concentration and relaxation.

Theta rhythms are typical of frustration—and *poltergeist activity is usually associated with a frustrated adolescent*. This reinforces my suspicion that powers of psychokinesis are basically a form of controlled poltergeist activity.

Now it may be difficult to see any obvious relationship between the spoon-bending of Geller and Manning and the highly complex operations of the alchemists. But a demonstration by Geller at the U.S. Naval Ordnance Laboratory in November 1965 offers a clue. Geller was asked to try out his powers on a piece of wire made of an alloy called Nitinol. Nitinol has a 'molecular memory'; like those paper flowers that unfold in water, Nitinol can be squashed into a ball, then made to resume its former shape by immersion in boiling water. As Dr E. Byrd held the Nitinol wire stretched between two fingers, Geller gently stroked it. When Byrd looked again, the wire had a kink in it. It was dropped into boiling water, which should have caused it to straighten immediately; instead, the kink remained. Even heating the wire to melting point failed to remove it. Geller had somehow affected its 'inner blueprint'.

Now such a change is, of course, purely on the molecular level; transmutation of metals would, presumably, require a change on the electronic level, and involve far greater energies. All the same, the Nitinol experiment seems to reveal the possibility of the direct action of 'mental' energies on the structure of matter. And this was demonstrated even more impressively by Geller at London University on September 10, 1974, in an experiment supervised by John Hasted, David Bohm and Ted Bastin. A small circular piece of vanadium foil from an electron microscope was sealed in a plastic capsule, which one of the scientists covered loosely with his hand. When Geller placed his own hand on top of the scientist's, the capsule was seen to leap like a jumping bean. When examined, it was discovered that half the foil was now missing. It had not broken off; it had simply vanished. Geller had apparently disintegrated its molecular structure.

This raises the obvious question: where does Geller obtain the *energy* for these demonstrations of power over matter? Professor John Taylor, who has also subjected Geller to exhaustive tests, is on record as believing that it is basically muscular in origin. He points out that a frantic mother has been known to lift a heavy car from off her child, who lay trapped under the wheel. Our reserves are obviously immense. He also points out that metals can be heated to the point of melting by radio waves, but then admits that there is no evidence that Geller is emitting such waves.

Yet these scientists could be overlooking the most interesting clue to Geller's powers: the fact that they appear to operate *only on metal*. Geller says he gains power from metal. I have often seen him placing an object he wishes to bend on a radiator, or simply placing his foot against the radiator while he holds the spoon up in the air, gently stroking it with his other hand.

This reliance on metal suggests that the powers may be in some way 'magnetic'. In that case, where do they come from? A possible explanation came to me as I watched him bend a spoon with his foot against a radiator. Electricians use radiators and water-pipes for earthing because they often vanish into the ground. Could Geller be using the magnetic force of the earth itself—the 'telluric currents'—or ley power? He explained to me that his powers are often greatest in dry areas; they work better in California than in New York. They work best of all in Mexico, especially in ancient pyramids. And if, as Michell believes, such pyramids were erected on 'nodal points' of ley power, than this might certainly help to explain why Geller feels himself 'recharged' in such places.

Geller claims that he first noticed his 'psychic' powers at about the age of five. When I questioned him closely about this period, he recalled an incident that he had never bothered to mention to any other interviewer because he thought it unimportant. He had been fascinated by a blue spark that showed inside a hole in his mother's sewing machine. One day he reached in and tried to touch it. The shock knocked him on to his back.

Many psychics have dated the development of their powers from electric shocks received in childhood, which may point us towards a theory that could bind together the many strange phenomena we have considered in the past two chapters.

We know that man is susceptible to 'earth forces' or telluric currents because the phenomenon of dowsing is so well attested. Alchemists like Armand Barbault insist that the vegetable kingdom is fed by the earth not merely with food, but with some form of vitality. When a plant is torn carelessly out of the ground, this vital essence returns instantly to the earth. Barbault's aim is to preserve this vital essence and somehow to 'extract' it. Alchemists also assert that stones and minerals 'grow' in the earth.

The essence of human-ness is our separation from the earth—the fact that we can move around. In human beings, this separation is far greater than in other animals. We have seen that the powers of many psychics may have come from sickness or serious accidents, which seems to imply that some internal mechanism may have been damaged, some kind of valve, not possessed by the lower animals, the purpose of which is to *exclude* unnecessary information. The possibility that psychic powers are triggered by an electric shock immediately suggests the idea of 'blowing a fuse'. If we think of the valve as a fuse, designed to stop us from being too susceptible to the forces of the earth, it is logical to suppose that damage to the fuse would either make us totally non-psychic, or possibly far *too* psychic.

It is conceivable that a scientist like John Taylor—who would like to 'explain' Geller's power in terms of laboratory physics—might ask impatiently what 'psychic' faculties have to do with the forces of the earth. Most dowsers will instantly reply: A great deal. Dowsing has traditionally been involved with 'second sight'. In a long essay on the divining rod in *Curious Myths of the Middle Ages*, S. Baring-Gould writes: 'The fourteenth law of the Frisons [i.e., Frisians] ordered that the discovery of murders should be made by means of divining rods used in Church.' And he goes on to relate in detail the story of the dowser Jacques Aymar, who, in July 1692, solved the murder of a Lyon wine seller and his wife by tracking down the three murderers with his dowsing rod. The rod enabled him to follow the trail for more than twenty miles—including a journey down the river by boat. But then, if Taylor insists on explaining Geller's powers in terms of some muscular energy, how does he explain Geller's own 'second sight'? When tested by Targ and Puthoff at Stanford, Geller's most remarkable successes were with ESP. For example, a small object was placed inside an aluminium can—one of a row of eight—and Geller was then brought into the room and asked to indicate the can. The experiment was repeated fourteen times, and Geller was correct twelve times.

We have also noted how often supernatural or abnormal phenomena—such as ghosts and UFOs—seem to be associated with ley lines, a subject to which we shall return later.

Altogether, then, there seems to be at least an a priori possibility that psychic powers somehow derive from the earth. This is consistent with our speculation that alchemy may involve the same forces. We have noted Barbault's insistence that alchemy cannot be understood without astrology. For most scientists, astrology is as thoroughly discredited as alchemy. But open minded scientists, like Professor H. J. Eysenck, are willing to concede that for some incomprehensible reason, astrology seems to *work*. Eysenck has been deeply impressed by the researches of the Gauquelins[13] into the relation between human personality and the position of the 'planets' at birth; he has now publicly conceded, on several occasions, that for some reason, there *is* such a correlation. In an astonishing number of cases, eminent doctors are born under Mars and Saturn, athletes and soldiers under Jupiter, politicians and writers under the moon. (It happens, for example, to be true in my own case.) But it seems absurd to suppose that the tiny gravitational force experted by the planets of our solar system could possibly affect our biological make-up. On the other hand, we know that the moon exerts forces on the earth itself—and not merely on the tides. Any doctor or psychiatrist will tell you that the mental state of his patients is affected by the full moon. (For example, Dr Arthur Guirdham has written of a patient who invariably became a sleep-walker at the time of the full moon.) And scientists have now come to recognise that alignments of the planets can have the same powerful effects on the surface of the earth. John Gribbin and Stephen Plageman, two scientists who set out to investigate the cause of earth-quakes,[14] concluded that these are related to the position of the planets. They write:

> Now, to the surprise of many scientists, there has come evidence that in one limited respect the astrologers were not so wrong after all; it seems that the alignments of the planets can, for sound scientific reasons, affect the behaviour of the earth. The gravity of the planets can affect the sun, through tidal interactions, and disturbances on the sun can influence the

earth through changes in the magnetic field which links all the planets in the solar system.

And they add, rather alarmingly: 'Only on very rare occasions can these small effects add up to produce any dramatic results on earth. But one of these occasions—an alignment of the planets which occurs once every 179 years—is due in 1982.'

If it is these *earth* forces—some form of magnetic current—that can influence our biological and psychological make-up, then astrology can no longer be dismissed as an early and muddled form of astronomy. Ancient man was probably *directly* sensible of the effects of the 'planets' on the earth, and, of course, it made no practical difference that he thought the moon and sun were planets. He was only concerned with their observable effects.

And now alchemy itself begins to fall into place as an occult science. The essence of John Michell's theory of the ancient use of leys is that there was some kind of *interaction* between the mind of the 'priest' and the forces of the earth. Somehow man can tune in to these forces, *at the right time of the year*, and use them. And the secret of the alchemists also seems to be concerned with such an interaction between the mind of the alchemist and the forces in the crucible. And this, at last, allows us to offer an explanation for the riddle posed by Mary Anne South and her father.

If alchemy is a purely 'mystical' science, as Jung believed, there would have been no need for secrecy, on the part of either the ancient alchemists or Mary Anne herself. The same is true if it is a purely mental or spiritual discipline, as Gurdjieff seems to imply. For only 'qualified' people would be in a position to make use of it.

But if alchemy somehow involves 'natural' forces—of the earth and the human mind—then there is good reason for secrecy. Such powers may be developed accidentally, or men may be simply born with them. In a book on Rasputin, *Rasputin and the Fall of the Romanovs*, I pointed to the parallel situation that exists with men of great 'charisma'—power over other people. Ramakrishna once said that when a man becomes a saint, he attracts followers as honey attracts wasps. The fact that he has had to become 'holy' in order to acquire the power guarantees that he will not misuse it. But certain men, like Rasputin and Hitler, may be born with this power. And the danger here lies in the fact that they are entirely dominated by ego-drives. So, instead of using these powers for their proper purpose—human evolution—they degrade them to their own purposes.

Of all the occult sciences', alchemy is the one that demands the most concentrated and directed effort of the will. A man who mastered this secret would possess considerable powers for good and evil. Prince Yussupov, who murdered Rasputin, insisted that when Rasputin stared at him intently, he became paralysed. Several people have insisted that Crowley possessed the power to produce a kind of temporary insanity.[15] The writer Rom Landau insisted that Gurdjieff somehow hypnotised him on their first meeting,[16] producing a sensation of weakness. And after reading Fritz Peters' account of how Gurdjieff revitalised him, it is easy to imagine how Gurdjieff might have misused these powers if he had been as egotistical and vengeful as Crowley.

These comments apply to ritual magic as well as to alchemy. But the magician is concerned with the use of his 'true will'. If our reasoning has been correct, the alchemist makes use of far greater forces. He uses these forces in the Great Work as a blacksmith uses his hammer to mould red-hot iron. And it is obvious that a man can do far more damage with a sledge hammer than with his bare hands.

10

Powers of Evil?

———

One evening in the early 1950s, a young drama student named Bill Slater, later to become head of BBC Television drama, attended a party that turned into an impromptu séance. Most of the guests sat around a circular table, with an inverted glass in the middle and the letters of the alphabet arranged around it. A few people laid their index fingers gently on the glass, and it proceeded to move quickly from letter to letter, spelling out the answers to questions. Bill Slater found it fascinating but was unwilling to accept it as anything more than a party game. He made some facetious remarks which the glass seemed to resent. When it was asked if there was anyone present it would prefer to have leave, it shot unambiguously towards Slater. He had no objection—he was getting bored anyway—and went off to flirt with a pretty girl.

In the early hours of the morning, he returned to the room where he was staying with a fellow drama student; they talked for a while, then retired to bed. Slater explained to me in a letter describing the incident that two hours later:

> I found myself half-awake, knowing there was some kind of presence

massing itself on my chest; it was, to my certain knowledge, making every effort to take over my mind and body. It cost me considerable will-power to concentrate all my faculties to push the thing away, and for what seemed like twenty minutes this spiritual tussle went on between this awful presence and myself. Needless to say, although before going to bed I had felt perfectly happy and at ease with a very good friend, in a flat I knew well, I was now absolutely terrified—I have never known such fear since. I was finally able to call my friend's name; he woke up, put on the light, and was astonished to find me well-nigh a gibbering idiot.

I have never since had any psychic experience.

I cite this incident, not because it happens to be one of the more startling tales of possession (or attempted possession), but simply because I know Slater well and regard him as totally honest. Oddly enough, he seems to regard his friend Bob—a mystical Celt who later became abbot of a monastery—as somehow responsible for causing the alarming visitation. 'I am sure, to this day, that Bob had somehow brought that force into the room.' One would have thought that a more obvious assumption was that the offended spirit from the party had come to teach him a lesson.

We have seen how cunningly the subconscious mind can simulate possession by an 'evil spirit'. But Bill Slater strikes me as sturdily normal. It is possible, of course, that he dreamed the whole thing; but he is certain that he lay there, trying to prevent the spirit from taking him over, for a good twenty minutes.

There is another possibility: that some *person* at the party was infuriated by his flippancy and directed a beam of ill-will at him. No one with any acquaintance with witchcraft would deny that this could happen. I quote from a letter from a correspondent at St Leonards on Sea:

> Some years ago my husband was treated very badly by the man he worked for. We had been to his house, and I knew the room where he slept. This night I was feeling a lot of anger and hate, and felt myself concentrating very hard on the side of the bed which I thought he would be sleeping on; I was sticking pins into his stomach slowly, one by one. I heard the next morning that his wife had been taken to hospital during the early hours of that morning in terrible pain. They thought it was gall-stones, but the tests showed nothing wrong. Did I do that, do you think? I know I felt drained the next morning because I had concentrated so much . . .

.   .   .

The Reverend Donald Omand, author of *Experiences of a Present Day Exorcist*, has no doubt that concentrated ill-will can have a malefi-cent effect and also states his belief that when a worker is 'sent to Coventry'[1] by his colleagues, the concentrated dislike of so many minds can actually cause psychological damage. But it is hard to square this with Bill Slater's experience, which involved a sense of an *active entity*, not some vaguely defined feeling of ill-will.

Mankind has always been inclined to believe in the existence of objective forces of evil. This may indeed be the main reason for our modern scepticism about the occult. Almost every important work on magic contains endless lists of demons, with details of how each might be invoked or dismissed. Even a work as late as Barrett's *The Magus* (1801) explains that there are nine different varieties of demons, rang-ing from Vessels of Iniquity, who invented cards and dice, to the Ensnarers who dwell in every man. Nowadays we know that 'devils' tend to be the gods of overthrown religions. Baal, the god of the Canaanites, became the Christian demon Beelzebub. Even the word devil is derived from the Hindu deva, a shining one or angel. We also recognise that the 'devils' that possessed the nuns of Loudun and Aix-en-Provence were merely the expression of the violent desires aroused by their unfortunate Father Confessors, Urbain Grandier and Louis Gaufridi, who paid for their sexual magnetism at the stake.[2] Understandably, therefore, we are sceptical about the objective exis-tence of powers of evil.

But the determination to reduce all problems to their psychological components may have caused us to swing too far in the opposite direction. The easiest way of illustrating this may be to cite a personal experience. In 1966, I picked up a copy of the selected works of the Marquis de Sade at the airport of a small American town where I was due to lecture; I read a few pages in my hotel room that night before falling asleep. I was already familiar with de Sade's work and inclined to regard him as a boring fool who made a mess of his life. He seems to have been a nasty, spoilt little man, but as far as we know, his worst cruelties were confined to his imagination. In the early hours of the morning, I woke up from an appalling nightmare about de Sade; he had committed some horrible atrocity in the hotel, then come into my room holding a bloodstained knife. As I woke up, I had a strong sense that this was not entirely a dream. The feeling of menace in the room was so powerful that I got out of bed and looked in the bathroom, then out into the corridor, which was empty. When I got back into bed, the feeling of evil had disappeared. My subconscious mind obviously took a more serious view of de Sade than my waking intellect.

The point is an important one. De Sade's works are cruel to the point of insanity, but the intellect can place them in perspective, regarding him as sick rather than wicked. We achieve this detachment by seeing them, as it were, through de Sade's eyes. But cruelty takes place in the real world and involves terrified victims. And even imaginary cruelty has an unpleasant power to propagate itself. Two centuries after de Sade, the so-called 'Moors murderers', Ian Brady and Myra Hindley, were inspired by his works to torture and murder children. There are few viruses that are infectious at the end of two hundred years.

Rationalists are inclined to argue that it is the crime itself that is evil—or socially undesirable—not the person who commits it. If a tree falls down in a storm and kills a passing pedestrian, nobody 'blames' the tree. In the same way, many murderers seem only partially responsible for their crimes. In a recent case in Germany, the killer not only murdered and raped more than a dozen children, but also carried away parts of their bodies, presumably to eat. In the public imagination, he became a figure of pure evil. When finally arrested, Joachim Kroll—a public toilet attendant—proved to be something of an anticlimax; he was a mild, absent-minded little man who was unable to recall most of his victims. He was convinced that, after medical treatment, he would be allowed to return home. When the police burst into his room, a hand of his latest victim, a five-year-old girl, was being boiled in a stew with carrots; Kroll regarded his taste for eating small girls as unusual but not reprehensible.

The Middle Ages also recognised this frequent disparity between the crime and the criminal, but they regarded it as a proof of the objective existence of evil. If the crime is more evil than the individual who committed it, then it seems to follow that evil has an independent existence. In the mid 1920s, the 'Reverend' Montague Summers acquired a certain notoriety by setting himself up as an advocate of the same view and using it as the basis for his books on witches, vampires and werewolves. But he based his argument on an observation that was later confirmed by Lethbridge: tragic events seem to be able to 'imprint' themselves on physical objects.

He cites the case[3] of a Devon craftsman, who married at the age of twenty-five and moved into a coastal cottage. Two weeks after the honeymoon, the husband returned home completely drunk; his wife was horrified, since he had a reputation as a sober and reliable workman. The next day he was miserable and penitent, swearing never to drink another drop. A month later it happened again. When he came home drunk a third time, the wife consulted a 'wise woman', who came to the house, pointed to a wooden armchair, and advised the girl to burn it. It had been given to them as a wedding present. When the chair was burned, the trouble stopped immediately. Investigation of the chair's history revealed that it belonged to a drunken butcher who had committed suicide while sitting in it.

Another case is reported by Dr Robert Morris, a psychologist affiliated with the Psychical Research Foundation of Durham, North Carolina. A rat, a cat, a dog and a rattlesnake were taken to a haunted house in Kentucky; the two reputedly haunted rooms were ones in which violent deaths had occurred. The dog was taken into one of the rooms, snarled, and backed out; no cajoling could persuade it to re-enter. The cat was carried in its owner's arms; it leapt onto his shoulders, digging in its claws, and spat at the empty chair in the corner. The rat showed no reaction at all, sniffing around the room. But the rattlesnake instantly assumed an attack posture in the direction of the empty chair. None of the creatures showed any reaction when taken into rooms where no tragedy had occurred.[4]

In his book *Design for Destiny*, Edward Russell calls these imprints or recordings 'T-fields' (or thought-fields). He writes: 'One of the commonest forms of the [phenomenon] are the thoughts of horror or despair imprinted on the structure of a building in which some murder or tragedy has taken place. These powerful thoughts seem to saturate the building materials and to last indefinitely.' He mentions an observation made by the psychic Geraldine Cummins: if two letters are kept together for a time, the psychic field from the letter from the stronger personality will tend to imprint itself on the other in the same way that a magnetic tape can 'print through' and cause pre-echo effects. Russell also adds the interesting observation that this is the basis of the ancient custom of blessing material objects or putting curses on them.

There is a great deal of documentation on 'curses', and on objects that carry bad luck. One of the most striking cases is the subject of a chapter in *Together We Wandered*, by C. J. Lambert, who, with his wife Marie, was actually involved. In 1928, the Lamberts saw the statuette of Ho-tei, the Japanese god of Good Luck, in a junk shop in Kobe, Japan. It was made of ivory, yet the owner of the shop charged them less than five shillings for it. En route to Manilla the next day, Mrs Lambert began to suffer agonies of toothache which lasted until they arrived two weeks later. On the next lap of the sea voyage to Australia, Ho-tei was somehow transferred to Mr Lambert's luggage; he now suffered the toothache all the way to Brisbane. In Sydney, when the luggage was in bond, the toothache stopped; back in their cabin, it started again. When the luggage was transferred to the hold, it stopped. In America, they gave the statuette to Lambert's mother; when her teeth began to ache a few hours later, she gave it back. And now, for the first time, the Lamberts thought about their months of intermittent agony, and realised that the statuette might be to blame. It was made of the base of an elephant's tusk, and there was a tiny hole in the bottom where its nerve had ended. So in London, the Lamberts took Ho-tei to a Japanese art shop and described their problems. An art expert explained that it had probably come from a temple, and that such gods are sometimes given 'souls', in the form of small medallions hidden inside them. An ivory plug in the base of the figure suggested that this was so in this case. Ho-tei was placed in a tiny shrine in the shop, and the Lamberts saw the last of it.

If we can accept this story—and it is difficult to see why a middle-aged couple would invent it, and insert it in the middle of a book about their travels around the world—it raises some interesting questions. The most obvious is that the explanation about the 'soul' inside the statuette seems superfluous. If it was originally an elephant's tusk and still had the nerve-hole in the base, is it not conceivable that the Lamberts were experiencing some kind of reflection of the elephant's death agony? Perhaps the tusk was removed while it was still alive? Perhaps the 'T-field' of its pain and terror clung around the tusk, and the *suggestions* of pain conveyed itself via the subconscious mind of its owners, manifesting itself as toothache.

But this fails to explain the oddest part of the story: the pain affected *only* the 'owner'. When it was in Mrs Lambert's luggage, she had the pain; when transferred to her husband's bags, he felt it; when given to his mother, she suffered. And when its owner was not in the immediate vicinity, the toothache ceased, as though there were some limitation on distance. It is almost impossible to account for this apparent ability to 'choose' its victim except by assuming some kind of intelligent entity. We can try other ways around the difficulty—for example, supposing that the negative T-field 'tuned in' through the possession it was in contact with, so that when it was in Mrs Lambert's baggage it 'fixed' on her. But how did it know when its ownership was transferred to his mother, unless she put it in a drawer full of her clothes. (But surely the logical place would be the mantelpiece—a fairly neutral situation.) And why did the mother's toothache cease as soon as she gave it back?

The 'soul' hypothesis at least offers a semblance of explanation. Tibetans believe that an object can be 'animated' by the thoughts of living people. If the figure was originally worshipped in a shrine, it might well acquire something like a living aura. But even this hypothesis involves some highly 'unscientific' assumptions: either that life can be transferred to material objects, or that disembodied 'spirits' can enter them.

How do we explain the notion that certain ships are unlucky, which every experienced sailor takes for granted? Conrad's story *The Brute* dramatises the belief, but there have been innumerable real-life examples. A whole book has been devoted to the astonishing story of the *Great Eastern*, the most ambitious project of the great nineteenth-century engineer Brunel.[5] At 19,000 tons, it was the world's largest ship. Misfortunes began when a riveter and his boy apprentice disappeared during its construction. In June 1859, as it was about to be launched, Brunel realised that the splash might drown spectators and ordered a halt; the ship became stuck in the runway and took three months to free. When it was finally launched, Brunel collapsed on the deck with a stroke and died a week later.

From then on, the career of the *Great Eastern* was one long disaster. A funnel expoded when someone accidentally closed a safety valve; five firemen died; another was crushed in the paddle wheel. In port for repairs, the ship was damaged in a storm. The captain was drowned in a boat with a young boy. In America, another sailor was crushed in the wheel, and a man fell overboard and drowned. A two-day excursion was a non-stop catastrophe, climaxed when the ship drifted a hundred miles out to sea; many passengers got off at the first opportunity and went home by train. Now the ship had acquired such a bad reputation that she seldom carried enough passengers to pay the wages of the crew (over 400). And the disasters continued: wrecked paddle wheels, wrecked funnels, storm damage. When the ship was hired to lay the trans-Atlantic cable, she lost it halfway across and had to return empty-handed. A mere fifteen years after its launching it was left to rust in Milford Haven. And when it was finally broken up for scrap in 1889, the skeletons of the missing riveter and his boy apprentice were found trapped in the double hull.

Lethbridge would have said the ship was haunted by a ghoul. But ghouls are supposed to be mere tape recordings. It might depress the crew and cause a certain amount of carelessness; but how could it cause storms and similar disasters?

The *Hinemoa*, launched three years after the *Great Eastern* was destroyed, had a similar history of disasters, which the crew attributed to the fact that its first ballast had been gravel from a London grave-yard. There was a different captain for each of its first five voyages; one went insane, another ended in prison, another drank himself into DTs, another died in his cabin, and the fifth committed suicide. On its sixth voyage the ship overturned; on the seventh two sailors were washed overboard. In 1908 she became a write-off after drifting in a storm.

The troubles of the German battle cruiser *Scharnhorst* began when she rolled over while only half-completed, crushing sixty men to death. If jinxes are caused by ghouls, this must be when it acquired its aura of nastiness. When Hitler and Goering arrived for the launching in October 1936, the ship had already launched itself in the night, destroying several barges. Three years later, in the ship's first major engagement—the bombardment of Danzig—a gun exploded, killing nine men, and the air-supply system broke down and suffocated twelve more. A year later, bombarding Oslo, it was struck by so many shells that it had to be towed away. Entering the River Elbe by night, it collided with the passenger liner *SS Bremen*, which sank into the mud and was destroyed by British bombers. Returning to sea again after repairs, the *Scharnhorst* passed a disabled British patrol boat in the dark; the boat radioed the alarm, and British warships closed in. It looked as if the *Scharnhorst* might be saved by falling darkness, but one of the warships fired a chance broadside at 16,000 yards; inevitably, the *Scharnhorst* was directly in the line of fire and burst into flame. Hours later, she sank. Even now the bad luck was not over. Two crew members reached shore on a raft, but died when their oil heater exploded.

There are just as many stories of jinxed houses, jinxed planes and jinxed cars. And again, many of them seem to start from a tragedy. Misfortune began for the Lockheed Constellation aircraft AHEM-4 from the moment a mechanic walked into a propeller in July 1945 and was cut to pieces; from then on there were endless disasters until it crashed near Chicago in July 1949, killing everyone on board. The car in which Archduke Ferdinand and his wife were assassinated at Sarajevo—thus precipitating the First World War—went on to bring disaster or death to its owners. General Potiorek of the Austrian army died insane after a catastrophic defeat at Valjevo; an Austrian captain who took over the car broke his neck after owning it for only nine days; the Governor of Jugoslavia lost his arm in it; a doctor who bought it was crushed to death when it overturned; a Swiss racing driver was killed when thrown over a wall; a Serbian farmer was killed while starting it; a garage owner died in a crash when overtaking dangerously as he returned from a wedding; so did four passengers. The car was placed in a Vienna museum, where it has been ever since.

The Porsche racing car in which the film star James Dean was killed in 1955 seemed to have the power to cause accidents even when dismantled. Bought by a garage owner, George Barris, it slipped as it was being unloaded from the breakdown truck and broke both a mechanic's legs. The engine was sold to a doctor, who was killed when the car in which it was placed went out of control during a race. Oddly enough, another car in the race contained the drive shaft from the Porsche; its driver was injured when the car turned over. The battered shell of Dean's car was used in a display on Highway Safety; in Sacramento it fell off its mounting and broke a teenager's hip. Weeks later, en route to another display, the truck carrying it was involved in an accident; the driver was thrown out and killed by Dean's car as it rolled off the back. A racing driver who bought the heavy-duty tyres from the car was almost killed when both tyres exploded simultaneously, causing the car to swerve off the road; George Barris was unable to find anything wrong with either tyre. In Oregon, the truck carrying the car slipped its handbrake and crashed into a store. In New Orleans in 1959, it broke into eleven pieces while on stationary supports. Finally, in 1960, it vanished when being sent by train back to Los Angeles. In their book *Cars of the Stars*, which contains many similar tales of jinxes, George Barris and Jack Scagnetti mention that Dean's mechanic Rolf Weutherich, who suffered a broken arm and leg in the original crash, was convicted of murdering his wife in 1968; but it seems to be stretching a point to lay the blame for this on the car.

Where houses are concerned, it is perhaps easier to understand how a ghoul can cause mental depression and therefore bring tragedy to a succession of owners. Dr Arthur Guirdham has described a house in Bath where a whole series of tenants have committed suicide or become mentally ill. In this case, the first suicide could have caused the ghoul, which then continued to cause mental illness.

The notion of some actively malevolent spirit seems unacceptable, from the commonsense point of view, until we remember Bill Slater's battle. Alan Vaughan's story of the wife of the Nantucket sea captain who 'got inside his head' seems to point in the same direction. The ghost encountered in Torquay by Beverley Nichols and Lord St Audries[6] sounds like an active force rather than a tape recording of some tragedy. The same applies to a ghost encountered by Jung in England in 1920.[7] He spent several weekends in a rented country house, and there were knockings, sounds of rustling and dripping and unpleasant smells. One night he opened his eyes and found himself looking at *half* a woman's head facing him on the pillow, its single eye wide open and staring at him. He lit a candle and it vanished; Jung spent the rest of the night in an armchair. He learned later that the house was haunted and that all other tenants had been driven away. The house was demolished soon after.

In cases like this, the tape recording theory begins to wear thin, or at least, to show its limitations. Why do we try so hard to find a theory that rules out living forces? It is as if a doctor tried to find a theory of disease that made no use of the concept of germs. Why do we experience a certain unwillingness to entertain this hypothesis of 'discarnate entities'? It is not simply a matter of 'evidence'—most people have read about dozens of ghosts and met people who have seen them, so we at least have plenty of second-hand evidence. But there is an unwillingness to introduce a frightening unknown factor into our picture of the universe. We can remember unpleasant experiences of childhood: the terror of empty houses and dark rooms, made all the more disturbing by the vulnerability of the unformed personality. As we grow up, the personality solidifies, and the night terrors are left behind. We want to believe in the secure universe we have created. Why should we introduce a new fear of the unknown?

And, of course, there is the common-sense objection to the idea of 'evil spirits'. As embodied in human beings, evil is usually a mixture of spoiltness and stupidity. Evil men are usually 'Right Men' who are trying to convince themselves that they are natural rulers and leaders; it is the Haroun Al-Raschid syndrome. To assume that 'spirits' can be evil seems rather like assuming that they have a taste for beer and cigarettes.

Yet the study of multiple personality shows that we are mistaken in thinking of ourselves as unified personalities. We are bundles of psychic and biological impulses loosely held together by habit. These disconnected parts of the personality can sometimes behave like independent entities. Moreover, under certain circumstances, they seem able to make use of unknown forms of energy to manifest their dissatisfaction: in which case they are known as poltergeists. And poltergeists behave remarkably like evil—or at least, mischievous—spirits. The study of the poltergeist throws an interesting light on the problem of 'discarnate entities'.

Until the mid-nineteenth century it was generally assumed that poltergeist disturbances were the result of witchcraft, or evil spirits, or both. One of the best documented of the early cases occurred in the house of the Reverend Samuel Wesley; in December 1716, his family were puzzled but not unduly alarmed by a 'banging ghost' that usually announced its presence after dark in the rectory at Epworth, Lincolnshire. There were loud crashing noises, as if a 'vast stone' had been hurled among several bottles, and thumps, raps and dismal groans. At first the family were afraid that these disturbances portended the death of their son Samuel, also a clergyman and living in London. (He was the father of the founder of Methodism, John Wesley, who was born in the rectory ten years before the disturbances began.) The phenomena continued for two months, then stopped. The modern view is that a nineteen-year-old girl, Hetty Wesley, was the 'focus'—she would often tremble violently in her sleep before the knockings began. The scientist Joseph Priestley, who took an interest in the case, was convinced that it was basically a hoax.

This was also the conclusion arrived at by Dr Samuel Johnson when he investigated the famous Cock Lane ghost. The knocking noises began in the house of Richard Parsons, clerk of St Sepulchre's church in Smithfield, London, in November 1759; a certain Mr William Kent was lodging there at the time with his common-law wife, Fanny Lynes. The unfortunate Fanny died shortly thereafter of smallpox, and Kent moved out. The knockings continued in the following year, and seem to have been connected with Parsons' eleven-year-old daughter Elizabeth, who was subject to convulsive fits. The 'ghost' became increasingly famous, and witnesses tried putting questions to it, using the usual code—one knock for yes, two for no. In this way, the 'ghost' identified itself as Fanny Lynes, who asserted that she had been poisoned by William Kent. Poor Kent was understandably frantic. A committee of eminent gentlemen, including Dr Johnson, was asked to investigate; but, like most poltergeists, it declined to perform on request. Johnson concluded that 'the child has some art of making or counterfeiting particular noises'. Now Elizabeth's father was in a serious position. If his daughter had deliberately manufactured 'evidence' of Kent's guilt, it must have been because Richard Parsons would gain by it. There had been some unpleasantness with Kent over a debt; the general opinion was that Parsons was trying to blackmail his former lodger. Elizabeth was taken to a house in Covent Garden to be examined. The knocks went with her; her examiners had to agree that they continued even when Elizabeth lay motionless in the middle of the room. Nevertheless they told her that unless the ghost proved its existence the following night, she and her family would be sent to Newgate prison. She was carefully watched by servants; understandably, she climbed out of bed when she thought no one was looking and knocked on a piece of board. When this became known, there was universal ridicule. William Kent brought a case against Parsons and various other supporters of the Cock Lane ghost. Two of the five accused were dismissed when they paid nearly £600 to Kent. Parsons was sentenced to two years in prison and to stand in the pillory three times; his wife was sentenced to a year, and a woman named Mary Frazer, who had taken part in the séances, to six months. Parsons protested vigorously that many other people beside himself had heard the rappings, and that he had no reason for malice against Kent. The poor of London evidently believed him, for he was treated with sympathy when he stood in the pillory.

The case bears some startling resemblances to that of the Fox sisters ninety years later. The Hydesville rappings which inaugurated the history of modern spiritualism were almost certainly poltergeist phenomena; the Hydesville 'ghost' also claimed to be the victim of an undetected murder.

Perhaps the most interesting thing about the Cock Lane case, from our point of view, is that so many 'unprejudiced witnesses' chose to ignore the evidence that Elizabeth could not have counterfeited all the rappings. The public swung from extreme credulity to total scepticism, and seemed relieved to be able to dismiss the ghost as a fraud. The only full-length book to be published about the case[8]—as late as 1965—still takes it for granted that Parsons and his wife were guilty.

In the second half of the nineteenth century, it began to dawn on trained investigators that a frustrated adolescent was often the focus of poltergeist phenomena. Moreover, such children were unaware of causing it. Understandably, this view was too subtle for the public at large, who preferred to think in terms of frauds or malevolent spirits. And the pendulum often swung from one assumption to the other. This is again what happened in the remarkable case that became known as the Amherst Mystery, one of the most important of all poltergeist cases.

The shoemaker Daniel Teed lived in a small house in Amherst, Nova Scotia, with his family, which included his wife and two sons and his wife's two unmarried sisters, Jennie and Esther Cox. Jennie was pretty and popular; Esther was plain and inclined to sullenness. There were also two other adult males in the house, brothers respectively of Mr and Mrs Teed.

In the year 1878, Esther was eighteen, and had acquired a boyfriend, a good looking young man named Bob McNeal, who had a reputation for instability. The trouble appears to have begun with what seems to have been the attempted rape of Esther by Bob. On August 28, he took her for a buggy ride and asked her to go for a walk in the woods. She refused. He lost his temper and pointed a gun at her, ordering her to get out. At that moment the sound of another vehicle was heard; Bob climbed back into the buggy and drove her home. Although it rained heavily, he refused to raise the hood. That night, he left town. Esther kept her secret for a month but went around red-eyed and obviously upset.

On September 4, lying in the bed she shared with Jennie, Esther started crying and admitted that she was thinking about Bob. Soon after they blew out the light, she screamed and declared that there was a mouse in the bed. A search revealed nothing. The same thing happened the next night. The rustling noise seemed to come from a box that stood under the bed. They placed it in the centre of the room and prepared to surprise the mouse, when the box rose a foot in the air. Their screams brought Daniel Teed, who told them they were dreaming and went back to bed.

The next night, Esther leapt out of bed shouting: 'Janie, I'm dying.' Her face was bright red. The other adults came into the room and Esther was helped back to bed. She began screaming and grinding her teeth. Her whole body seemed to be swelling. There was a loud bang, like a thunderclap, and Esther ceased to swell. There were two more loud bangs that seemed to come from under the bed. By this time, Esther was peacefully asleep.

Three days later, Esther again felt herself swelling. The bedclothes flew off the bed of their own accord and floated across the room. Again there were loud bangs, and Esther deflated and fell asleep.

The next night, the local doctor was called in. He felt Esther's pulse and declared she was suffering from shock. At that moment, the pillow inflated like a balloon, there were rapping noises, and the bedclothes flew off. They all heard a scratching noise on the wall above the bed. An invisible hand or claw traced the letters: 'Esther Cox, you are mine to kill.' The letters were scratched deep into the wall. A large piece of plaster fell off the wall, and the room resounded with raps. Esther lay there, wide awake, as terrified as everyone else.

Soon after, Esther began to complain of electrical sensations in her body. When she was given morphia, loud bangs began. When the doctor left, they sounded as if someone was pounding on the roof with a sledgehammer.

Three weeks later, Esther suddenly went rigid and fell into a trance. In this state, she told the story of the 'attempted rape' for the first time. On recovering consciousness, she admitted it was true.

In December, the manifestations ceased when Esther became ill. But in January 1879, she told Jennie that a voice had warned her that the house would be set on fire by a ghost. The next morning, as the members of the family laughed about the idea, a lighted match fell out of the air and onto the bed. More lighted matches rained out of the air for the next ten minutes, but were all extinguished. That evening, a dress belonging to Esther was found burning under the bed. Three days later, a barrel of wood shavings in the cellar burst into flame and was extinguished with difficulty.

Daniel Teed was deeply worried. When a neighbour offered to take Esther in, he agreed. For two weeks nothing happened; then a scrubbing brush flew through the air. It signalled another outbreak of poltergeist activity. At work in the neighbour's restaurant, Esther was attacked by a flying jacknife that stabbed her in the back and drew blood. Some iron spokes placed in her lap became too hot to touch. A heavy box was moved across the floor. Rappings resounded along the main street of Amherst. The neighbour sent her back home. For the next three months, she lived out of Amherst as the guest of two sets of kind-hearted neighbours. During this time, no manifestations occurred, although Esther claimed that she saw ghosts who threatened her. One was called 'Bob Nickle'.

When she returned to the Teed cottage, a professional magician named Walter Hubbell had moved in to observe her. In 1888, he published a book called *The Great Amherst Mystery*, in which he described all the poltergeist phenomena he witnessed: flying knives and umbrella moving furniture, loud bangs and raps. Questioned by means of the raps, the 'spirits' correctly named the serial number of his watch and the dates of coins in his pockets. Hubbell was so impressed that he persuaded Esther to make a public appearance in a rented hall; every seat was taken, but nothing happened.

Esther spent another peaceful holiday with the kindly neighbours, then went to work on a nearby farm. There she was accused of theft when some missing clothes turned up in a barn. Before further action could be taken, the barn burned down. Suspected of arson, Esther was put in the town jail for four months. And the manifestations ceased as abruptly as they began.

The ending of the story certainly suggests that Esther was somehow responsible for the phenomena, and that when the penalties became too serious, her subconscious mind was cowed into good behaviour. It is interesting that the manifestations ceased when she stayed with people she liked. The 'spirit' hypothesis is, however, just as plausible as the 'over-active subconscious' theory. We can believe that Esther was a bored and frustrated young woman who longed for attention. But she was as worried and frightened by the phenomena as everyone else. It is hard to believe that she would—even subconsciously—cause so much damage to her sister's home, which was virtually a wreck when she left. Furthermore, Hubbell describes Esther as a pleasant, honest-looking girl with well-shaped features and pretty teeth, who

loved housework, and was in constant demand with the neighbour-
hood children 'who were always ready to have a romp and a game of
tag', which does not sound like a house-wrecker.

Esther herself asserted repeatedly that she heard and saw ghosts.
When she called on the minister to ask him to pray for her, one of the
spirits attacked her with a bone, which cut her head open, and jabbed a
fork in her face. When she and the doctor went down to the cellar to
investigate, they were met by a hail of potatoes. There seems to be no
doubt that whatever was causing the disturbances enjoyed attacking
Esther. We also have to explain how the spirit knew the dates of the
coins in Hubbell's pocket, which presumably he himself did not
know. It is, admittedly, an easy to endow Esther with second sight as
with powers of psychokinesis. But it is just as easy to see that whatever
wrote 'Esther Cox, you are mine to kill' could have been a real spirit.

The Rosenheim case has some curious similarities to the Amherst
mystery. Here again, the focus of the outbreaks, Anne-Marie
Schaberl, was a bored and dissatisfied girl in her late teens. She started
to work for the lawyer, Sigmund Adam, as soon as she left school in
October 1965. His office was in the Königstrasse, in the small town of
Rosenheim, south-west of Munich. Two years later, in November
1967, Adam's lighting system began to go wrong. Strip lights kept
failing, and a specially installed meter revealed that there were sudden
inexplicable surges of current. The Stadtwerke—the local lighting
company—investigated and decided that there must be something
wrong with the power lines. But when they tried running a cable
direct from the office to the generator, the lights continued to explode.
Adam decided to install his own generator out in the yard and changed
all the strip lights to ordinary bulbs; it made no difference. Moreover,
when an ordinary voltmeter was tested by connecting it to a 1.5 volt
battery, it registered three volts. That was a physical—or electrical
—impossibility. When Adam received his telephone bill, it was many
times bigger than usual. The telephone company installed a device to
register every number that was dialled, and in this way they discovered that someone was dialling the speaking clock for hours on
end. This also failed to make sense; it took at least seventeen seconds to
get through to the speaking clock, and the monitoring device revealed
that it was being dialled four, five, even six times a minute. Someone—or something—must be getting straight through to the relays.

The affair was talked about all over the town, and a reporter came to investigate. As he was leaving the office, a bulb fell out of its socket and almost hit him on the head. His story about 'the Rosenheim spook' was taken up by the national press. It came to the ears of Professor Hans Bender, in his Institute of Paranormal Research at Freiburg.

It was Bender's young assistant who realised that Anne-Marie was probably behind the disturbances. He noticed that as she walked along the corridor, the overhead lights began to swing back and forth. Further investigation soon showed that the surges of current occurred only when she was in the office.

Now, the poltergeist began to manifest itself in a more normal manner. Pictures turned on the wall, lights swung—sometimes changing direction in mid-course—and a heavy filing cabinet was moved away from a wall.

Anne-Marie was given leave of absence to go to Bender's Institute. Bender found her in many ways typical of the personality that causes poltergeist phenomena. She was tense, mistrustful, aggressive and unhappy. She had been brought up in the country, and she hated the town. Her family background had been difficult; her parents were Catholics and her father was a rigid disciplinarian. And now, although she was engaged, her emotional life was thoroughly unsatisfactory.

Yet at first, the tests revealed no kind of psychic ability. It was not until Bender began to question her about a painful illness—a year spent in plaster with a tubercular hip—that she became deeply disturbed. Bender switched to ESP tests and was amazed by her scores. She showed remarkable telepathic abilities.

As soon as Anne-Marie walked back into Adam's office, the equipment began to go wrong. Understandably, he decided to dispense with her services. She got another office job and the same thing happened there. At about this time, her engagement was broken off. Her fiancé was fond of bowling and used to take her to a Catholic youth club where the scoring, pin-setting and return of the balls were all controlled electronically. As soon as Anne-Marie walked in, the board began to register random scores and the pin-setting equipment went mad. Her fiancé was not amused and ended the engagement. She took a job in a mill; but when a man was killed in an accident with the machinery, people began to avoid her. She decided to leave. Eventually she married someone else, moved to a house on the outskirts of Rosenheim, and had three children. The poltergeist activity ceased.

Hans Bender has no doubt that this was a case of spontaneous psychokinesis. But that explains very little. What is so baffling is the disparity between Anne-Marie's own personality—and education—and the behaviour of her poltergeist. For months, the disturbances seemed fairly natural; it was not until Bender's assistant noticed the swinging lights that the spook decided to show its hand and behave like a conventional poltergeist. Again, it seems to have known a certain amount about electricity—enough to interfere directly with the relays. Anne-Marie didn't even know what a relay was.

But perhaps the most interesting thing is that the battery registered 3 volts instead of 1.5. This strongly suggests that the poltergeist was able to generate an electric current. It caused the lights to fuse by the same means. In the Amherst case, a Baptist clergyman, the Reverend Edwin Clay, studied Esther Cox and became convinced that the answer to the riddle lay in electricity. Esther frequently complained that she felt as if an electric current was running through her body. Clay came to believe that Esther was a kind of human battery. He observed that she seemed to have a particular attraction for metals, like the knife that jumped from a small boy's hand and stabbed her in the back. He thought that she emitted some form of lightning, and that the loud noises were claps of thunder.

At the New York seminar on Kirlian photography, Max Toth described a number of well-attested cases of 'human batteries'.[9] In 1877, Caroline Clare, of Bondon, Ontario, began to waste away, although there was nothing obviously wrong with her; from 130 pounds she dwindled to less than ninety. Then she began to have seizures when her body became rigid. As she slowly recovered, she turned into a human battery, capable of giving shocks to anyone who touched her. Pieces of iron stuck to her and had to be pulled off by force. She was seventeen when she became ill; the electric charge vanished when she grew out of her teens.

In 1895, fourteen-year-old Jennie Morgan of Sedalia, Missouri, generated enough electricity to knock a grown man flat on his back. When she reached out to touch a pump handle, sparks flew from her fingertips. Her charge also faded as she reached maturity.

Another Missouri teenager, Frank McKinistry, developed an electric charge during the night and lost it slowly as the day wore on.

Perhaps the most interesting thing about McKinistry is that when highly charged, *his feet stuck to the ground*, so that walking became immensely difficult.

Most doctors who have worked in mental homes will testify to the prevalence of 'electrical cases', patients who suspect that someone is trying to electrocute them by unknown means. The Swedish playwright Strindberg became convinced, during a period of mental illness, that someone in the next room was trying to suffocate him with a current of electricity. 'Then I feel, at first only faintly, something like an inrush of electric fluid . . . the tension increases; my heart beats violently; I offer resistance, but as if by a flash of lightning is charged with a fluid which chokes me and depletes my blood . . . A new discharge of electricity strikes me like a cyclone and forces me to rise from my bed.'[10]

Now if the Reverend Edwin Clay was right and Esther's poltergeist made use of some kind of electrical energy, it would explain a great deal more than the thunderclaps that took place in her vicinity. It could also explain how Anne-Marie could fuse electric lights and cause electronic equipment to go haywire, and how an electric light can change direction in mid-swing. When a light is switched on, its wire is surrounded by an electrical field, which could, in turn, be attracted or repelled by another field.

Many of these cases seem to begin with a severe shock, either an electric shock, as in the case of Uri Geller, or a psychological shock of the kind Esther received when Bob McNeal pointed a gun in her face. Anne-Marie was having severe emotional trouble when the disturbances in Adam's office began. Caroline Clare became an electric battery after an unexplained severe illness—probably psychosomatic—had reduced her from an overweight teenager to a walking skeleton. Elizabeth Parsons, the focus of the Cock Lane disturbances, suffered from violent convulsions before the 1762 phenomena.

We may recall that a large number of cases of multiple personality have also begun with a shock. Doris Fischer became Margaret after her father hurled her on the ground. Christine Beauchamp's illness began when William Jones tried to climb in the window from a ladder. Sybil Dorsett became Peggy Lou to escape her mother's sexual assaults. Shock can cause the fragmentation of the personality into several selves, and the evidence strongly suggests that poltergeist phenomena are a special form of split personality. It is worth recalling that Christine Beauchamp's alter-ego Sally emerged only under hypnosis. Before this, Christine had suffered from tiredness and depression but not from multiple personality. Apparently the shock of William Jones's wild behaviour caused a fragmentation of her personality, but the 'new' Christine remained concealed, in the unconscious. It seems likely that something of the sort happened to Esther Cox when Bob McNeal tried to rape her; the 'new' Esther was invisible. Yet two weeks later she began to manifest herself as a mischievous spirit.

This raises the obvious possibility that *all* 'spirits' are manifestations of the unconscious mind. But the Doris Fischer case makes us aware of an alternative hypothesis. One of Doris's alter-egos, Ariel, claimed to be a spirit who had appeared in response to the prayers of Doris's mother; Dr Walter Prince was actually inclined to believe her. *If* we can admit the possibility of disembodied spirits, then it is difficult to rule them out as an explanation of some of the cases we have been considering.

And what of the energies used by the poltergeist? The Anne-Marie case suggests that they could be electrical. But when Strindberg held a compass close to his body as he was convulsed with shocks, the needle showed no response. Besides which, Anne-Marie's poltergeist later began moving heavy objects and making pictures turn on the wall, which suggests that it could exert ordinary physical force. The likeliest explanation seems to be that the poltergeist can convert energy into any form it prefers.

Then there is the closely related question of why all kinds of psychic phenomena—from banshees to phantom black dogs—are associated with ley lines? This question has been examined at length by a dedicated ley hunter named Stephen Jenkins in his book *The Undiscovered Country*. Jenkins is a schoolmaster who enjoys wandering around the English countryside with an ordnance survey map and a camera. He has observed repeatedly that various kinds of psychic phenomena seem to be associated with the 'nodes'—or crossing points—of leys. His first experience occurred at the age of sixteen, on a track near Mounts Bay in Cornwall.

> The clumps and bushes were very still in the windless evening light when suddenly I experienced what I took to be a startlingly vivid optical illusion. Scattered among them, motionless but frighteningly distinct, was a crowd, a host of armed men. For a moment I stood stock still,

unable to believe my eyes, then I began to run towards them. At once something like a curtain of heated air wavered in front of them briefly—and there were only bushes and stones.

Years later, when he became aware of the existence of leys, Jenkins examined an ordnance survey map and realised he had been walking along a ley and approaching a nodal point. In 1974, he returned to the spot with his wife. 'And again, as in the deepening light of that August afternoon thirty-eight years before, the illusion of armed men! And again the vanishing as one took a few paces forward.'

This tale is one of many stories of similar hauntings. Near Wroxham, in the Norfolk Broads, a phantom Roman army has been reported by many witnesses, and placed on record. In *Archives of the Northfolk* for 1603 a Mr Benjamin Curtiss describes swimming across the lake known as the Great Broad of Wroxham, and suddenly glimpsing around him a Roman amphitheatre; a companion who was swimming beside him saw it too. It vanished as they swam on a few yards. In 1709, the Reverend Thomas Josiah Penston recorded seeing a procession of Roman soldiers there. In 1829, Lord Percival Durand described in a private letter how he suddenly found himself in a Roman amphitheatre and watched a Roman procession.[11] At Edgehill, in Warwickshire, where one of the great battles of the Civil War was fought, the battle was 'repeated', complete with noises of cannons, within a year. A pamphlet about it included accounts by a justice of the peace and several army officers, who had recognised old companions among the ghostly combatants. King Charles I was so intrigued by the story that he sent a group of officers to investigate; these officers, led by Colonel Lewis Krike, witnessed the phantom battle themselves and testified to it on oath before the king. A twentieth-century clergyman, the Reverend John Dening, collected accounts of many witnesses who had heard the sounds of the battle.

Stephen Jenkins has experienced many supernatural occurrences on ley lines, although perhaps none as remarkable as his vision of the phantom army in Cornwall. But his most significant story concerns a spot near Acrise in Kent. Following a ley line running past Eastry church, he paused to consult his map and to take his bearings. To his surprise, he was unable to measure the necessary angle. There was a feeling of light-headedness and a sense of disorientation. It vanished when he walked on a few yards, and he had no difficulty taking the bearing. Whenever he went back to the spot, the dizziness returned. Two years later, he took three of his students to the same spot without telling them anything about his sensations, and asked them to take their bearings on the map. All three experienced the same disorientation and were unable to do it; when they moved on, the problem vanished. The point at which the dizziness occurred was a nodal point—a crossing of two ley lines.

Near a stone which he calls the Merlin Stone, on Dartmoor—again, a crossing point of leys—he set out to take a photograph of the stone from the north and discovered that he had moved south-east. He tried a second time and this time went to the west. Even when the mist cleared enough to show a camp to the north, he found it impossible to orientate himself.

I can testify to this curious experience of totally losing one's bearings in a place where there should be no difficulty. In 1975, I took some friends to look at the ancient stone circle at Boscawen-un, in Cornwall, one of the oldest in the British Isles. About a quarter of a mile away, on a hilltop, there is a landmark known as the Giant's Footprint, a rock with a hollow in the centre; my wife had been there, and told me that the view was spectacular. I had half an hour before we had to leave to get my friends to a train and I decided this was plenty of time to go there and back. So I left my friends and cut across the heather towards the hilltop. The bracken proved to be more of an obstacle than I had expected; finally, I looked at my watch and decided that I had better go back. The stone circle was no longer visible, but the countryside is open, and I could see the direction I had come from. I plodded on downhill. Soon, to my astonishment, I realised I was lost. I decided that I had been bearing too far to the right, so I went left, which should have brought me to the path at the bottom of the hill. I climbed over a wall and found myself in a strange field. It took me half an hour to find my way back to the circle, and when I arrived there, I found it completely impossible to work out how I had succeeded in losing myself. To end up at the main road, as I had done, I must have gone in the *opposite* direction to the one intended. Since then, I have walked from the standing stones to the Giant's Footprint many times, and never succeeded in finding out how I managed to become so totally confused in such a short distance.

Stephen Jenkins has no simple explanation as to why so many strange things should happen on ley lines, or why nodal points should produce disorientation. He seems to agree with Lethbridge that some kind of powerful field can operate in certain spots, and that in such places, the interaction between the human mind and the forces of the earth is particularly powerful. And he cites a statement made by Air Marshal Sir Victor Goddard, when discussing UFOs at a meeting of the British Interplanetary Society in May 1969; Goddard commented that there was no need to assume that UFOs were visitors from other planetary systems; they might come *from an invisible world that coincides with the space of our own.* (This was also Lethbridge's suggestion.) Jenkins, who spent some time in Tibet, goes on to cite the teaching of his Tibetan masters to the effect that there are six 'realms of being', of which only two are perceptible to our physical senses. They also taught that the 'heavens' listed in the teaching of Mahayana Buddhism are *planets*, three-quarters of which are metaphysical or paraphysical in nature.

And so the explanation that begins to emerge is very clear. There are other realms of being that run parallel with our own, and the nodal points of ley lines can create some kind of bridge between the realms. Jenkins' teacher added the astonishing piece of information that Shambhala, the legendary island of bliss of Eastern mythology, is not—as is generally believed—situated in the Gobi Desert, but in the Island of Britain, at Glastonbury. Glastonbury is, of course, the nodal point of a record number of leys.

Stephen Jenkins was also able to throw interesting light on a case of haunting I presented on BBC television. This took place at Ardachie Lodge, near Loch Ness. In 1952, Mr and Mrs Peter McEwan moved into the Lodge, which had been built in the nineteenth century, with the intention of turning it into a pig farm. They advertised for a housekeeper, and engaged a Mr and Mrs McDonald; McDonald had been a London postman who gave up his job and his pension for the chance of moving back to Scotland. On the night of their arrival, the McDonalds had been in bed only half an hour when they were awakened by footsteps that came up the stairs and into the room opposite. When the footsteps were repeated a few minutes later, they were curious enough to go and peep into the room; it was empty. They went downstairs to the McEwans, who were still awake, and asked if the house was haunted; the McEwans said that, as far as they knew, it wasn't. They in turn asked if Mrs McDonald was psychic; she said she wasn't. But back in her bedroom, Mrs McDonald was petrified to see an old woman beckoning to her; neither her husband nor the McEwans saw it. They moved to another room, and this time were kept awake by loud rapping noises on the wall. They wakened the McEwans; then, in the corridor outside their bedroom, Mrs McDonald saw an old woman, crawling on all fours, with a lighted candle in one hand.

This convinced the McEwans that their housekeeper was not simply a hysteric. For Mrs Brewin, the wife of the previous owner of the house, had suffered from severe arthritis in her last years and had crawled around on all fours. She had also been convinced that the servants stole various items and hid them, so she used to crawl around at night with a candle in one hand. But the McDonalds had never been in Fort Augustus before, and had not spoken to anyone about Mrs Brewin; there was no way in which Mrs McDonald could have known about her habits.

The Society for Psychical Research sent two investigators, who were impressed. Mrs McDonald 'knew' that the arthritic old lady had spent hours in the rose garden, tending a particular tree; the 'spirit' was apparently upset that her tree had been allowed to die. The gardener confirmed that he had dug up the tree and moved it to the greenhouse, where it died.

Mrs McEwan found the whole situation so nerve-racking that she left the house with the children. The McDonalds returned to London. And the house remained empty until, in 1968, it was blasted and bulldozed to the ground by the army.

The curious feature of the case is that the housekeeper had had no previous 'psychic' experience. She was a rather tense, highly-strung woman, but otherwise apparently normal. Why was she the only one to see the Ardachie ghost?

Stephen Jenkins saw my presentation of the case on television and took the trouble to get an Ordnance Survey map of the area. Just as he had suspected, Ardachie Lodge had stood on the crossing point of four major leys.[12]

This could explain another curious episode. When the two investigators were present, Mrs McDonald rose to her feet and stared, white-faced, at the door; she was obviously seeing something. But what she saw, she claimed, was Mrs McEwan, her employer, who was in bed at the time. If the house was haunted by the unquiet shade of Mrs Brewin, this seems all wrong. But if some quality in the house itself—or the land it stood on—was capable of 'boosting' psychical phenomena, then anything is possible; Mrs McDonald simply saw her employer's doppelgänger.

Yet clearly, Mrs McDonald herself was a 'trigger' for the whole situation. No one had even suspected the house was haunted before she arrived. But her first comment when she stepped into the house was that there was 'something wrong with the place'. Presumably Mrs McDonald *was* psychic, but so minimally that her powers had to be boosted by some force in the house. Possibly because of her nervous constitution, she was open to the force.

This again raises the tantalising question we have touched on so often in the course of this book. *Was* the ghost a mere tape recording? Mrs McDonald certainly thought not. On that first night, she was convinced that it beckoned to her, and that the crawling old lady actually saw her. (It is not quite clear whether both apparitions were of the same person.) Moreover, if the ghost was a tape recording, how did it know that its favourite rose tree had been destroyed?

It is by no means rare for people who have seen a ghost to be convinced that it has also seen them. In 1975, I interviewed a couple in Mevagissey who had lived for a time in a haunted cottage; the ghost had apparently been the previous tenant, an old man who had died there. The husband saw the old man several times on the upstairs landing; he said nothing about it to his wife, for fear of alarming her. But his wife herself encountered the old man in the bedroom. When I questioned her about it, she insisted that he had actually looked *at* her. Both of them said they felt no fear, because he was obviously a gentle and friendly character. Nevertheless, they moved when the opportunity arose.

All this is not to suggest that Lethbridge was mistaken about his tape-recording theory. What he recognised instinctively was that there is some intimate, and at present unexplained, connection between the forces of the earth and the forces of man's mind. He realised that this strange interaction could produce all kinds of so-called psychic phenomena. His central recognition was that, through this interaction, man can *know* all kinds of things that are normally inaccessible to consciousness. Richet spoke of the sixth sense, as if it were a one-sided affair; as a dowser, Lethbridge knew that it is a two-way involvement. It was natural that he should apply this important new insight to one of the oldest mysteries known to man: ghosts. Yet, although he was inclined to believe that ghosts are tape recordings, he also believed that there *is* a realm beyond death that is, to some extent, accessible to living creatures. Which suggests that our world should also, under certain conditions, be accessible to the dead. Lethbridge was an empiricist; he had never encountered a ghost that behaved like a conscious individual. If he had done so, he would have made room for it in his theory.

Let us now look at some of the evidence that Lethbridge might have considered valid.

Robert Monroe's description of the astral realm is, as we have noted, remarkably close to Lethbridge's own deductions from the pendulum. A whole chapter of his *Journeys Out of the Body* is devoted to his experiences with various alarming non-physical entities. He begins: 'Throughout man's history, the reports have been consistent. There are demons, spirits, goblins, gremlins and assorted sub-human entities always hanging around humanity to make life miserable. Are these myths? Hallucinations?' His first experience was not particularly frightening: a ten-year-old boy came and clambered on to his back as he lay on a couch, inducing an out-of-the-body experience. Monroe felt that this creature was more animal than human. 'He seemed confident that he would not be detected, perhaps through long association with humans to whom he was invisible.' Monroe avoided an encounter by re-entering his body. Ten days later, two curious rubbery entities made of flesh kept trying to climb on to him when he was out of the body. He became panic-stricken and fought frantically. They turned momentarily into his two daughters—some attempt to deceive him, he thought—then resumed their former shape when they saw he was still hostile. Eventually, a man in a monk's robe came and pulled the two creatures off.

The 'rubbery entities' became a constant hazard of his astral journeys; in May 1960, he succeeded in driving one away by imagining that he had stuck two electric wires into it. 'Immediately the mass deflated, went limp, and seemed to die. As it did, a bat-like thing squeaked past my head and went out of the window.' In July 1960, Monroe was suddenly attacked as he was about to fall asleep. He was unable to see what he was fighting, but it bit and scratched. Eventually, he threw it out of the window—and then realised, for the first time, that his body lay asleep in bed, and that he was on the astral plane. Three days later, he again had a long and exhausting battle with some unseen entity that seemed to go on for hours. 'This struggle was not like fending off an animal. It was a no-holds-barred affair, silent, terrifyingly fast, and with the other seeking out any weakness on my part.' Feeling that he would finally lose the battle, Monroe succeeded in dropping back into his physical body. His struggle sounds remarkably like Bill Slater's.

In *Beyond the Body*, Benjamin Walker suggests that some of the entities described by astral travellers are nature spirits or elementals, 'who depend for their existence on the substance provided by the exhalations of the material elements, hence their name'. And he makes the startling suggestion that the fairies and elves of mythology are basically such nature spirits.

Oliver Fox also has an account of an alarming encounter with some kind of elemental.

> As I opened my astral eyes, I turned right round within my physical body so that I faced the other direction. Great forces seemed to be straining the atmosphere, and bluish-green flashes of light came from all parts of the room. I then caught sight of a hideous monster—a vague, white, filmy, formless thing, spreading out in queer patches and snake-like protuberances. It had two enormous round eyes, like globes filled with pale blue fire, each about six or seven inches in diameter.

When he looked again, the monster had vanished. He comments: 'The "monster" may have been some form of elemental or non-human entity.'

It is interesting to compare this passage with a description by Henry James senior—father of William James—of how he came to the verge of a mental breakdown:

> One day . . . towards the close of May [1884], having eaten a comfortable dinner, I remained sitting at the table after the family had dispersed, idly gazing at the embers in the grate, thinking of nothing, and feeling only the exhilaration incident to a good digestion, when suddenly—in a lightning flash as it were—'fear came upon me, and trembling, which made all my bones to shake'. To all appearances it was a perfectly insane and abject terror, without ostensible cause, and only to be accounted for, to my perplexed imagination, by some damnéd shape squatting invisible to me within the precincts of the room, and raying out from his fetid personality influences fatal to life. The thing had not lasted ten seconds

before I felt myself reduced to a wreck; that is, reduced from a state of firm, vigorous, joyful manhood to one of almost helpless infancy. The only self-control I was capable of exerting was to keep my seat. I felt the greatest desire to run incontinently to the foot of the stairs and shout for help to my wife—to run to the roadside even and appeal to the public to protect me; but by an immense effort I controlled these frenzied impulses, and determined not to budge from my chair till I had recovered my lost self-possession. This purpose I held to for a good long half hour, as I reckoned time, beat upon meanwhile by an ever-growing tempest of doubt, anxiety and despair, with absolutely no relief from any truth I had ever encountered.[13]

After two years in a condition of despair, it was recommended to James that he read the works of Swedenborg, whereupon he decided that he had undergone the spiritual experience Swedenborg called 'devastation' or simply 'vastation'. Doctors assured him that he had simply 'overworked his brain', and it would certainly be convenient to accept some similar explanation. But James makes it quite clear that he was not overworked or tense at the time. It is easy to understand how this kind of experience can happen in a state of fatigue and worry; in fact, William James experienced precisely such a breakdown when he was depressed about his future prospects. It is important to understand that such attacks come from a *collapse* of vital energies, like the ice on a pond suddenly giving way; then the situation is made worse by fear, a generalised distrust of life. On the other hand, James says nothing about exhaustion and worry; in fact, he states that he was relaxed and cheerful, thinking about nothing in particular.

It was this last comment that led me to undertake an interesting piece of research. James's description of the evil presence makes it sound not unlike the 'blanket of depression and fear' that almost suffocated Lethbridge on Ladram beach. Which suggests that James may have encountered a ghoul or elemental.

When this suspicion occurred to me, it struck me as a pity that we know nothing about the house, presumably in America, where James's experience occurred; whether, for example, it was situated on a ley line, or had been the scene of some violence or tragedy. At this point, I re-read the passage as it occurs in James's *Society, the Redeemed Form of Man*, and was startled to realise that James was in England at the time, near Windsor. The whole Windsor area is famous for its hauntings—particularly the castle—while the park has the interesting legend of Herne the Hunter, who is clearly a Celtic fertility god. It struck me that it might be worthwhile to try to discover precisely where James had been living.

Leon Edel's four-volume biography of Henry James offered slightly more information: the cottage was 'near Windsor Great Park', and the 'vastation' took place in 1844. I turned to Ralph Barton Perry's two-volume biography of William James and opened it casually. The first thing I saw was a date: 'H.J. to his mother, May 1, 1844.' And, in fact, the letter it refers to is dated from Frogmore Cottage, Windsor. James describes the cottage that he has just rented at the exorbitant price of £4.10s a week. 'It is a little cottage standing between the Great and the Little Parks, next to the residence of the Duchess of Kent, and fronting the entrance to the Little Park.' He speaks of the 'beautiful avenues of the Little Park [now known as the Home Park] sweeping over hill and dale until they reach the Thames'. If he was opposite the entrance to the park and could see an avenue stretching into the distance, he must have been in the direct line of an avenue; and such avenues, as we know, often follow the routes of old roads, which in turn follow ley lines.

I turned to Peter Underwood's *Gazetteer of British Ghosts*. This has two entries for Windsor, one for the Great Park, the other for the castle. The latter has many ghosts, apparently, including those of Charles I and George III. There is also a story of a young Grenadier guardsman who committed suicide in the Long Walk, and whose ghost was seen subsequently by two sentries at the same spot. In his chapter on Windsor,[14] Elliott O'Donnell—writing long before any-one associated ley lines with ghosts—makes the perceptive comment: 'Of all the famous historic buildings of the Thames Valley none are reputed to harbour more ghosts than Windsor Castle, an argument in favour of the theory that hauntings do not necessarily originate in tragedies, for, as far as is known, few if any tragedies have occurred in the Castle itself, and none in connection with the best known of its ghosts.'

Underwood states that the original Herne the Hunter was probably a huntsman of Richard II who hanged himself on an oak tree. When it was blown down in 1863, Queen Victoria had it replanted. The ghost of Herne, complete with stag's antlers, is supposed to appear in times of national crisis: it was reported in 1931, before the Depression, and again before the Second World War. In 1926, Mrs Walter Legge, a JP, heard the baying of hounds coming from Smith's Lawn and retreating towards the Castle. She and her daughter heard the sounds again two weeks later.

Folklore, Myths and Legends of Great Britain declares that Herne's last appearance was in 1962 when some youths found a horn and blew it in the forest; Herne appeared, riding on a black horse, followed by hounds. It adds that the horns 'almost certainly identify him with Cernunnos, Celtic god of the Underworld'. In *The Undiscovered Country*, Stephen Jenkins refers to the Celtic god of the Underworld as Arawn, which is even closer to Herne, and is obviously a Welsh version of Cernunnos. Margaret Murray identifies Herne the Hunter with the Celtic god of the witches, and mentions that he was 'seen in Windsor Forest by the Earl of Surrey in the reign of Henry VIII' —complete with horns.

But where was Frogmore Cottage? My rather inadequate three-inch-to-the-mile road atlas showed it on the main avenue from Old Windsor to the castle. A biography of Queen Victoria revealed that this was, in fact, the residence of her mother, the Duchess of Kent. The avenue certainly looks as if it could be a ley line. But as I looked more closely at the map, I saw an altogether more likely candidate: an avenue called the Long Walk, which runs due south from Windsor Castle and continues in a ruler-straight line for about three miles into the middle of the Great Park. The Long Walk was the place where the sentries saw the ghost of their colleague who had committed suicide.

I tried ringing the Windsor Tourist Board; there a helpful lady named Mrs Yeomans was able to give me some interesting information. She knew very little of Herne the Hunter, but there were several other ghosts associated with the area: a headless poacher who haunts the Great Park and a grey lady who is seen at the Royal Adelaide Hotel. She also mentioned a recent incident that I had not heard of, but which had been reported in the local paper: a young soldier had seen something when he was on guard duty, and had received such a shock that he had collapsed and had to be taken to hospital. It had occurred—as I might have guessed—on the Long Walk.

When I mentioned Smith's Lawn, Mrs Yeomans told me that this was also near the Long Walk. Smith's Lawn was the place from which Mrs Legge had heard the baying of hounds, retreating towards the castle. They could, then, have been retreating along the Long Walk.

But Mrs Yeomans was unable to tell me where Herne's Oak was situated. She thought it was between Frogmore and the Long Walk. *Man, Myth and Magic* added the interesting information that Herne's Oak stood on the edge of a hollow called Fairy Dell. 'Fairy' occurs in many place names on ley lines.

Now convinced that I had found one major ley, I wrote to Stephen Jenkins to ask him if he knew anything about ley lines in Windsor Great Park. His reply showed that my guess about the Long Walk had been correct: 'The ley line starts at the Round Tower [of the Castle] and coincides with the north end of the Long Walk'—that is to say, with the part close to Smith's Lawn. 'The ley line runs almost due south, touching the west edge of the circular earthwork at Albury Bottom, through the church at Chobham, across the west face of Loseley House, through Farncombe church, the spot height 586 at Hydon's Ball, to the site of the Roman building north east of Chiddingfold.'

And what of my other guess—that the other ley ran from the castle down the main avenue, out to Runnymede? This proved to be very nearly correct. In fact, the ley runs *parallel* with this, about a hundred feet to the north. It runs 'south-east from the Round Tower of Windsor Castle, parallel with but about a hundred feet from Frogmore House, across the west end of the old mansion Great Fosters, through the earthwork on St Ann's Hill, east of Virginia Water, along the west edge of a tumulus on Ockham Common, through the church of Westcott, and south-west of Dorking to the church at Rusper'.

This still left unsolved the mystery of Herne's Oak and its location. I decided to try ringing the Royal Library at Windsor. The librarian—Sir Robin Mackworth-Young—was courteous and helpful. No, he said, Herne's Oak was not situated on the Long Walk. It was not situated anywhere any more, since it had blown down in a storm. Its traditional site was in the Home Park.

I asked if he could describe exactly where it had been—for example, in relation to the main avenue running diagonally across the park. 'Yes, there's a road running off the avenue to the north, and it's about fifty feet along it.' He verified that there is a hollow called Fairy Dell next to the site.

His description of the site places it, of course, right on the ley line described by Stephen Jenkins, give or take a few feet—the ley that runs parallel to Frogmore.

And what of the experience of Henry James senior? Frogmore Cottage is not *on* a ley, but it is only a hundred feet away. There seems to be no common agreement among ley hunters about how far the influence of a ley can extend—or rather, the general view is that it depends on the force of the telluric current and on the time of year. Stephen Jenkins describes a vigil at the nodal point of two leys near Saltwood in Kent, when the whole group saw a ghostly figure about *sixty yards* away, which moved over a considerable distance before it turned grey and vanished. Lethbridge's description of his experience on Skellig Michael makes it clear that the 'sinister influence' extended not only over the whole area of the ruined monastery, but also down the cliff to the sea. It was halfway down the cliff that he felt that something wanted to push him over, and the unpleasant sensation increased for another fifteen feet, before he decided to turn and go back. The poltergeist knocked him on his face in the middle of the chapel area.

Lethbridge's experience is relevant to James's vastation at Frogmore because it seems highly likely that the whole Windsor Park area is a site of the ancient religion associated with the horned god of the witches and with Diana. Since the area is associated with the kings of England, it is even conceivable that the park was *the* centre of the old religion. Lethbridge felt that there was a hostile force on Skellig Michael that resented his presence. Henry James senior was a healthy Victorian rationalist when he moved into Frogmore; before the end of that month, some hostile presence had reduced him to a nervous wreck, a man who believed in the reality of forces of evil. It may or may not be significant that the letter to his mother, written immediately after moving into the cottage—perhaps on the same day—is dated the first of May, the festival of Bel, when the forces of the earth are traditionally at their most powerful.

The picture that begins to emerge is foreign to our Western modes of thought; yet it can be found everywhere among primitive people who live close to the earth. It is the notion that nature is alive, that certain places are holy, and that the spirits that inhabit such sites need to be treated with respect if their displeasure is to be avoided.

A relevant example can be found in Laurens Van Der Post's book *The Lost World of the Kalahari*. Van Der Post was seeking the vanished bushmen of South Africa, and his guide Samutchoso offered to take him to a place where they might be found—the Slippery Hills. His one condition was that there must be no killing as they approached the hills, otherwise the gods would be angry. Van Der Post forgot to tell the advance party, who shot a warthog. From then on, they were a prey to endless misfortunes. They were attacked by bees; the new camera jammed continually; when Samutchoso tried to pray in a sacred place, something pulled him over backwards. He asked: 'Did you see, master, I was not even allowed to pray.' The camera and tape recorder continued to jam and there was another invasion of bees. The steel swivel on the camera failed, a part so reliable that no spare was ever carried.

At this point, Samutchoso offered to consult the spirits. He threaded a needle and placed it along the lifeline of his left hand, then stared into it. After ten minutes, he began to speak to invisible presences—there seemed to be a crowd—and then listened intently. Finally he told Van Der Post that the spirits *were* angry because they had approached with blood on their hands and failed to observe the proper ceremonies. 'If they had not known your intention in coming here was pure they would long since have killed you.' The spirits told Samutchoso that they would have killed *him* if he had tried to pray again.

Van Der Post had an idea. Suppose he wrote a message of apology and everybody signed it, then they buried it in a bottle at the foot of a sacred rock painting? Samutchoso thought it was worth trying. The next morning, they buried a lime-juice bottle with their message. Again, Samutchoso consulted the spirits. This time they told him that all was well. But they warned Van Der Post that when he reached the next place he was going to, he would find bad news.

From that moment, the jinx went away. They left the hills, and he said goodbye to Samutchoso, who remarked regretfully: 'The spirits of the hills are not what they were . . . Ten years ago they would have killed you all for coming to them in such a manner.' When they arrived at the next stopping place, Van Der Post's assistant found a letter saying that his father had died and asking him to return home immediately.

Van Der Post's comment on all this is interesting. 'From the moment of burying the letter at the foot of the painting, I had a feeling of having broken through one dimension of life that was full of accident and frustration, into a more positive one.' And he says of the Slippery Hills, with their natural temples: 'We seemed to be in the presence of a single system of spirit dedicated to the translation of flesh and blood into a greater idiom of the world beyond.'

Let us pause to review the argument so far.

The occult, like any other subject, deserves to be approached in a rational and logical frame of mind. Certain phenomena, like curses and poltergeists, give the impression that disembodied spirits exist. On the other hand, the tape-recording theories of Buchanan and Denton—that objects somehow store up everything that has ever happened to them—makes it possible to explain curses as negative vibrations without recourse to the spirit theory. As to poltergeists, we are now fairly certain that they are connected with the frustrations of adolescents and the phenomenon of multiple personality. Yet this leaves just as many unanswered problems. Where does the 'disconnected' part of the personality get its energy? And how does it succeed in using it at a distance? The 'earth' theory provides, on the whole, a more convincing explanation than Professor John Taylor's notion that some form of muscular electromagnetism is involved (if only because he has so far found no evidence to support his theory). It offers us a convincingly simple explanation of all kinds of psychical phenomena in terms of the interaction of two factors: the human mind and the forces of the earth. Yet even this is not as convincing as it might be. For it seems that all kinds of strange psychical phenomena tend to occur on ley lines, and that not all these can be explained in terms of the mischievous forces of the subconscious mind. The Ardachie ghost does not seem to have been either a tape recording or a projection of living human beings.

So we find ourselves giving serious consideration to the notion that our material world may be only one realm of being, and that others might exist parallel to our own. This could include the realm of the dead or of disembodied spirits. It could even involve a realm of evil—or, at least, badly-disposed—spirits.

The trouble with the parallel universe theory is that it leaves us out on a limb. Our remote ancestors believed in ghosts and evil spirits, which led them to burn witches and cross themselves when there was a clap of thunder. When science began to reveal that thunder and eclipses are natural phenomena, Western man went to the other extreme and declared that belief in the supernatural is pure superstition and ignorance. We have attempted to show that this view was too simplistic; there are all kinds of phenomena, from telepathy to poltergeists, that seem to lie outside the paradigms of modern science. But if we are going to accept parallel universes, and the possibility of evil spirits—or any kind of spirit for that matter—then we are coming alarmingly close to the world-view of our ancestors, a completely irrational world in which anything can happen.

But is this entirely true? In fact, the analytical approach has enabled us to make some useful distinctions. We have seen, how, in the case of Janet's patient Achille, split personality can look incredibly like 'possession'; yet it seems it was not possession. On the other hand, Alan Vaughan's story of his 'possession' by the wife of the Nantucket sea captain sounds like the real thing. So does Bill Slater's story of his battle with the 'spirit'. The ancients believed that there is a universal interaction of the dead with the living, and you were likely to meet your grandfather's ghost any time you went out to the coal hole. Our researches suggest that this is highly unlikely. On the whole, our world obeys ordinary material laws, and can be expected to go on doing so. These laws may be broken at certain places, under certain conditions, but not otherwise.

This means that we must preserve an open mind. In 1975, a married man named Michael Taylor joined a revivalist religious group in Barnsley, Yorkshire, and became convinced that a girl in the group had gained some psychic influence over him. He asked his local vicar, the Reverend Peter Vincent, to help him, and the vicar decided that exorcism was called for; Taylor, he declared, was possessed of forty devils. The exorcism ceremony lasted all night and left Taylor violently disturbed; he rushed home and murdered his wife in a particularly gruesome manner, tearing her to pieces with his bare hands. He was found lying naked and unconscious in the street a few hours later. But the 'spirit' that possessed him had apparently left him; during his trial—which ended in a sentence of detention in a mental home—he seemed balanced and normal. The judge declared that the vicar should have sent for a psychiatrist instead of attempting exorcism, and it is difficult not to agree with him. But the facts make it impossible to state dogmatically that Taylor was suffering only from mental illness. When people begin to dabble in witchcraft and the 'psychic'—as Taylor apparently had before the exorcism—anything must be regarded as possible.

There is an even more fundamental difference between the ancient world-view and the view based on modern paranormal research. Ancient man believed in all kinds of spirits and demons; but he was, for the most part, unaware of his own psychic potentialities. Other people's psychic powers frightened him; those who had them he regarded as witches or magicians. But ever since Dr Rhodes Buchanan began testing the students of the Cincinnati medical school for psychometric powers in the 1840s, modern researchers have realised that such powers are far commoner than we think. Nine out of ten people can dowse, and probably the tenth could develop the ability if he made the effort. Poltergeist disturbances occur every day of the week; investigators like Hans Bender and William Roll have examined hundreds. And even the least psychic people can tell remarkable stories of coincidence or synchronicity. We are surrounded by the psychic all the time, but we seldom notice it unless we look for it.

When speaking of psychic forces, like the entity that caused Bill Slater so much alarm, it is also important to realise that most human beings possess greater powers than they are aware of. My correspondent from St Leonards on Sea, who caused the boss's wife severe stomach pains, was not a witch; she was simply very angry. The novelist John Cowper Powys records that people he hated met with unpleasant accidents with such frequency that he was finally reduced to a state of 'neurotic benevolence', terrified of unleashing his irritation.

A French criminal case of the nineteenth century provides a well-documented illustration of the use of such powers.[15] On March 31, 1865, a club-footed beggar knocked on the door of a farm labourer, M. H., in the village of Solliés-Farliéde (Var) and asked for food and shelter; the kindly labourer gave him supper and allowed him to sleep in the haystack. The beggar was a hairy, repulsive-looking man of about twenty-five, who seemed to be a deaf-mute (although later evidence suggests he was shamming). By means of a pencil and paper he explained that his name was Thimotheus Castellan, an out-of-work cork cutter who had become an itinerant healer and dowser. The daughter of the house, twenty-six-year-old Josephine H., found him terrifying. The next morning, the father and his fifteen-year-old son went to work; Castellan soon joined Josephine in the cottage. During the morning, crowds of curious neighbours wandered in and out; one of them claimed that he saw Castellan making strange signs in the air behind Josephine's back. Later, as they were eating the midday meal, Castellan suddenly reached out and made a movement with his fingers, as if dropping something into her food; she felt her senses leaving her. Castellan carried her into the next room and raped her. The girl remained conscious, but unable to resist. She was also unable to move when a neighbour came and knocked on the door.

Later that day, Josephine was seen to leave the house with Castellan; she seemed upset and made incoherent noises. For the next three days she remained with Castellan. At a farmhouse at La Cappelude, she seemed to experience extremes of tenderness and violent revulsion towards her companion. She asked a girl to allow her to go home with her for the night, but Castellan ordered her to stay. He made signs with his hands, and she seemed to become paralysed. He asked if they would like to see her laugh, and she immediately burst into peals of hysterical laughter. When he slapped her face, she suddenly recovered and seemed perfectly normal. She accompanied Castellan to bed without protest. The next morning, Castellan again demonstrated his power over her by making her crawl around like an animal. The farmer was so outraged that he threw Castellan out. The girl now seemed to become partly paralysed, so Castellan had to be called back; he slapped her face, and she recovered.

The following day, the girl managed to run away while Castellan was engaged in conversation with some hunters. She remained violently disturbed for the next six weeks, but slowly recovered. Castellan was sentenced to twelve years in prison for rape.

What precisely happened? We get the impression that, as soon as Castellan saw her, he recognised her as a potential victim, while the girl herself felt that she had been somehow marked down. She described at the trial how she lay awake, fully dressed, on her bed throughout most of the night when Castellan arrived. And if the neighbour was not mistaken about the strange gestures he made behind her back, it sounds as if he was able to exert some kind of pressure on her even when her back was turned. When they were finally alone—over the midday meal—he was able to paralyse her will merely by making a movement with two fingers. It sounds as if he was exercising some direct form of thought pressure on her.

A notorious case that took place in Heidelberg in 1934 suggests the same curious powers. A woman travelling on a train, on her way to consult a doctor about stomach pains, fell into conversation with a man who introduced himself as a healer and homoeopath. She felt nervous and insecure with him, but accepted when he invited her to join him for coffee. The man—whose name was Franz Walter—suddenly took hold of her hand, and she felt weak and dizzy, with no will of her own. Later, he took her to a room in Heidelberg, placed her in a trance by touching her forehead, and had intercourse with her. His power over her was absolute. He made her prostitute herself and give him the money. She also gave him 3,000 marks of her savings. Finally, he ordered her to murder her husband, either by poison or by shooting him; he added a hypnotic suggestion that she should not, under any circumstances, reveal his own part in the affair, or even his identity. But the husband became suspicious after her sixth attempt at murder (she had cut the brake cable of his motor bike, causing a serious crash), and he reported his increasing misgivings to the police. The police psychiatrist, Dr Ludwig Mayer, who described the case in *Crime Under Hypnosis*, had the interesting task of somehow by-passing Walter's complex system of commands and inhibitions. He succeeded so well that Walter was sentenced to ten years in gaol.

Perhaps the most interesting part of the woman's evidence was her insistence that she fought hard against Walter's powers but found them too much for her. As she felt him raping her, she tried to push him away but was unable to move. She experienced the same reluctance to give herself to the various clients he selected for her but was unable to help herself when they uttered a certain word of hypnotic command.

What was the nature of this peculiar power exercised by Walter and Castellan? The common-sense view is that it was simply the ordinary power of suggestion exercised by a dominant man over a neurotic, weak-willed woman. But this view ignores too many problems. Even ordinary hypnosis takes a certain amount of time and requires the co-operation of the subject; Castellan and Walter apparently exercised their power in a more *direct* manner, somehow dominating the will.

It is worth bearing in mind that this same power was attributed to Rasputin, Gurdjieff and Crowley. Prince Yussupov tells how 'the holy devil' hypnotised him into a state of total paralysis at their first meeting: 'His hypnotic power was immense. I felt it subduing me and diffusing warmth throughout the whole of my being . . . I lay motionless, unable to call out or stir.'[16] In *God is My Adventure*, Rom Landau has a similar account of the peculiar power exercised by Gurdjieff at their first meeting: 'the feeling of physical weakness pervaded me more and more . . . I was sure that if I tried to get up my legs would sag under me and I would fall to the floor.' Landau makes the interesting suggestion that 'it may have been a form of electric emanation such as Rasputin is said to have possessed in a high degree'. Landau has an even more significant story of a lady novelist who sat in a restaurant near Gurdjieff.

> Gurdjieff caught her eye, and we saw distinctly that he suddenly began to inhale and exhale in a particular way. I [realised] Gurdjieff was employing one of the methods he must have learned in the East. A few moments later I noticed that my friend was turning pale; she seemed on the verge of fainting . . . 'That man is uncanny,' she whispered. 'Something awful happened . . . He looked at me in such a peculiar way that within a second or two I suddenly felt as though I had been struck right through my sexual centre. It was beastly . . .'

Crowley's hypnotic powers have been described many times; but most writers assume that they emanated from his peculiar, basilisk-like stare. An account given by Oliver Marlow Wilkinson, son of Crowley's literary executor Louis Wilkinson, makes it fairly apparent, however, that Crowley's powers had much in common with those of Rasputin and Gurdjieff.[17] Wilkinson was speaking to a scene-designer in a Gloucestershire mansion where Crowley had spent a great deal of time.

> When I, in discussing Crowley, doubted his magical powers, the scene-designer said: 'You would not have thought that if you had been with us when Crowley was here. After dinner, we came down to a room on the first floor . . . Crowley sat on his haunches, there by the fire . . . Two others beside myself were in the room. As Crowley talked, the man on the other side of the fireplace from Crowley fell sideways, his head a few inches from the flames, and stayed there. Another got up, dropped on all fours, sniffed round the chairs, begged, barked and whined, scratched at the door . . .' At this point I remembered Frances [his mother] describing how a man who had called at the same time as Crowley . . . had begun to act like a dog, and how Crowley had continued to talk, watching with mild interest, till the man recovered, passing the obscene exhibition off as a joke . . . 'Like a dog,' the man continued, 'and the man over there got up, without a word, rushed through the window, and didn't come back till noon next day, his

clothes torn and his face bleeding. I couldn't move for a while, and when I did, Crowley had gone to bed.' 'Crowley might have used drugs,' I suggested. 'And hypnotism . . . But he used something else too . . .' 'What?' I asked. 'Magic,' said the young man.

We have, in fact, already touched on this question in discussing the basis of magic: the power of the will. J. B. Priestley was able to induce a woman to wink at him by sending a 'mental order' across a dining room. Joire could make hypnotised and blindfolded subjects perform certain actions purely by telepathy. But sexual magic seems to involve even stronger forces. I have elsewhere quoted Robert Graves's remark that many young men use a form of unconscious sorcery to seduce women. Not, one should note, the other way round. The 'unconscious sorcery' of woman tends to be passive, a kind of invitation. (We can see this in sex goddesses like Marilyn Monroe and Brigitte Bardot, who possess a quality of innocence and vulnerability. Actresses whose seductiveness is more self-conscious never achieve this almost mythological status.) Masculine seduction, by contrast, is basically an attempt at domination. This can be clearly seen in the writings of professional seducers like Casanova or 'Walter' (the anonymous author of *My Secret Life*); they mark down the woman as prey; their aim is to convince her that she is destined to submit, that she has no choice. In order to do this, they induce in themselves an attitude of dominance, in which the result is a foregone conclusion, then attempt to transmit this to the woman. It seems to require a total commitment of the will and absolute single-minded determination to achieve possession. And this in turn seems to involve an unconscious belief in the power of the will to achieve its object by sheer intensity of desire, not unlike the belief of a devout Christian in the power of prayer. All this certainly adds up to magic, either in Sartre's negative definition ('wishful thinking') or Crowley's ('magick is the science and art of causing change to occur in conformity with the will').

However, the most important common denominator in the cases cited above, is that Castellan, the German Franz Walter, Rasputin and Gurdjieff *were all healers*. And healing often seems to involve an actual transfer of some form of energy from one person to another. Rasputin saved Anna Vyrubova's life by taking her hands and staring into her eyes—draining himself of energy in the process. The same is true of Gurdjieff, after he had revitalised Fritz Peters simply by staring at him.

Peters said that it was 'as if a violent electric blue light emanated from him and entered into me'. Castellan influenced Josephine by making movements with his hands *behind her back*. And Franz Walter's victim described how, at their first meeting: 'Suddenly he took hold of my hand, and it seemed I no longer had a will of my own. I felt strange and giddy . . .'

Let us, at this point, try to summarise some of the findings of the present chapter, and of the second part of this book.

While it would be a pity to return to the old, simplistic belief in evil spirits, it would be short-sighted not to admit the likelihood of the existence of intelligent non-human powers and entities. Such entities are not necessarily *more* intelligent than human beings; many of them seem to be a great deal less so. Whether they could be considered 'evil' is another matter. It should be borne in mind that, from the point of view of cows and sheep, human beings are evil. We slaughter and eat them; we even tear their unborn children from their wombs as a special delicacy. But this does not mean that human beings are 'evil' *per se*. The phrase is probably meaningless; evil *per se* does not exist.

No honest evaluation of the known universe can exclude this possibility of other intelligences and of disembodied spirits. But this second part of the book has been concerned mainly with a more interesting and immediate problem: the hidden potentialities of the human spirit. And this phrase in itself makes us aware of the inadequacy of our paradigms. We naturally see ourselves as a certain type of body and a certain type of consciousness that we call 'human'. Freud and Jung showed us that this level may be only a single floor of the building; below there can be endless basements and catacombs. On the other hand, we have seen that various strange phenomena—from multiple personality to second sight and precognition—seem to be most easily explainable by assuming that there are also a great many levels *above* this everyday consciousness. The picture that emerges is of a kind of skyscraper which continues below the ground. Should we think of the whole skyscraper as the human being? This seems to involve a kind of conceit, as if a tobacconist's kiosk on the ground floor of a skyscraper regarded the rest of the building as an extension of itself.

Besides, the study of multiple personality suggests a more startling possibility. It seems that this body of mine is not really 'mine' at all; it can be taken over by squatters. This is a flat contradiction of the materialist view—expounded in our own time by Wittgenstein and Ryle—that 'I' am the sum of my bodily and mental states. Doris Fischer's body and brain remained the same, yet her personality varied according to whether she was 'occupied' by herself, Margaret or Ariel. This in turn suggests another possibility: that 'I' am not a genuinely self-complete being, in spite of my sense of selfhood, but am merely the tobacconist on the ground floor of the Empire State Building.

It is worth adding, in passing, that this image enables me to explain the development of my own field of interest from 'outsiderism' to the paranormal. The 'outsider' is aware of being trapped in his own narrow personality, and he suffers from a sense of suffocation. 'We each think of the key, each in his prison.' But the outsider suffers so much because he has had moments in which he experienced an intoxicating sense of freedom, in which his consciousness seemed somehow enlarged. He has, in effect, managed to escape from the kiosk and explore some of the rest of the ground floor. The great romantics, from Rousseau to T. E. Lawrence, were all driven by this desire to escape from 'themselves' and explore the realms of freedom.

But there are also other floors, both above and below. And although it seems to involve considerable effort, there seems to be no 'law' forbidding the owner of the kiosk from exploring the rest of the building. The problems are purely practical. It is not easy to go downstairs, because we tend to fall asleep when we try to descend into ourselves. As to exploring the higher floors, it is a problem that has preoccupied philosophers and mystics ever since Plato. Direct attempts to climb the stairs are usually defeated by the sheer effort involved; it is as if the force of gravity increased with every step.

But at least there seem to be telephone lines to other floors, and these lines are habitually used by dowsers, clairvoyants and psychics. Mystics and philosophers agree that this is a far less satisfactory method than direct exploration. Psychics usually seem to pay for their unusual abilities with a kind of lop-sidedness, as if clairvoyance were due to some kind of deficiency. And much of their evidence is confused and ambiguous—as if they were not certain whether the telephone line led to the upper floors or the sub-basement. All the same, many of them *have* presented convincing evidence of the existence of the other floors.

One of the most interesting clues to the mystery is the existence of the poltergeist. Although no one realised it at the time, the recognition that poltergeists are of human origin was one of the greatest intellectual landmarks in human history. It was the first convincing proof that we possess other floors. The materialist philosophers of the nineteenth century could dismiss psychics like Frederika Hauffe, the Seeress of Prevorst, as puzzling exceptions to the laws of nature. But if dozens —or hundreds—of disturbed teenagers can produce the same curious manifestations, then it seems unlikely that Frederika was merely an exception to the general rule. It is altogether more logical to suppose that we are *all* like that. We are all multi-storied.

As we have already noted, the most baffling thing about the poltergeist is the source of its energy. It could be, as John Taylor suspects, electromagnetic; it could be electrical; it could be from the earth itself; it could come from other people. But if we think of the poltergeist in the light of our observations on multiple personality, an even more interesting problem emerges. It is easy enough to understand—in theory, at least,—how our higher levels can make use of these unknown energies. But as far as we can see, the poltergeist is not a higher level. It usually seems to be a kind of mischievous child. Why should *it* have powers that are not accessible to our conscious, everyday self?

The study of multiple personality suggests an answer. Janet noted that when people become neurotic and obsessed by anxiety, their energies diminish; they find everything an immense effort. By contrast, the best way for a human being to increase his energy is to *widen* his personality, to expand his sympathies, to throw himself open to new and interesting experiences. This is the most reliable way to contact our 'vital reserves'—or perhaps that great lake of energy that Gurdjieff spoke to Bennett about in the forest at Fontainebleau. The whole mind is like a full moon; everyday consciousness is like a mere shaving of it. We find it easy enough to imagine that if a human being could expand his consciousness to the full moon, he would become godlike and his energy would be boundless. Somehow, the hidden part of the moon is connected with the lake of energy.

Independent 'personalities' like Sally Beauchamp and Margaret Fischer have something in common with poltergeists: they are mischievous sprites, often destructive but seldom malicious. And if they exist anywhere, then it is in that hidden part of the mind. Some confine themselves to playing tricks on the current occupant of the body.

Some, like Anne-Marie Schaberl's alter-ego, play tricks on other people with the use of an unknown form of energy.

The evidence seems to suggest that these energies are available in another part of our consciousness. Why should that be? Here again, Janet's observations suggest an answer. Why do people suffering from acute anxiety also suffer from exhaustion? Because the more anxious and tense we become, the more we fall into the hands of the robot, our mechanical part. People who plod through habit-ridden, automatic lives seldom call upon their vital reserves, so their energies become constricted by habit. But everyday life is bound to be governed largely by the robot, merely because it involves so much repetition. So my conscious being, no matter how busy and creative, is also largely in the hands of the robot. And its energies are therefore seriously restricted. This is not true of the unconscious (or superconscious) part of my mind. Like the open countryside, these areas of my being are largely unmechanised, and their forces are immense.

But are there any limits to what can be achieved? If so, no one has discovered them. Bennett experienced a far wider area of his being at Fontainebleau; but he never suggested that was all there was to be explored.

The full significance of this insight takes a great deal of grasping. But an anecdote about Colonel Olcott, Madame Blavatsky's friend and disciple, may point the way. In Ceylon, a local Buddhist priest told Olcott that the Roman Catholics were hoping to turn a nearby village into another Lourdes, complete with miracles. Olcott replied that the priest had better learn to perform miracles; the priest replied sadly that he had no powers. Olcott decided to apply his knowledge of hypnotic suggestion; when he met a partially paralysed man, he made a few mysterious passes in the air and told him that he should improve. Later the same day the man came back saying he was already feeling better and asking for more treatment. Olcott made more mysterious movements. The man continued to improve. Suddenly, Olcott found that he had a reputation as a miracle worker; sick people appeared in hordes. And, to his own astonishment, he found that he was gradually learning to cure them; something flowed from him into his patients, and he felt drained, while the patient went away much improved. Olcott had developed healing powers simply by trying.

In the same way, when Abraham Maslow began to talk to his students about 'peak experiences'—experiences of sudden overwhelming happiness—many of them recalled peak experiences they had half-forgotten, or hardly noticed at the time. And the more they discussed peak experiences, the more they began to have. Merely thinking about them, talking about them, was enough to make them happen.

In both these cases, the crucial element was an *attitude of optimism*. The Buddhist priest told Olcott that he had no miraculous powers. *That* was why he was unable to perform miracles. Olcott began by thinking he had no miraculous powers, but he made the effort, and discovered he was mistaken. The conscious knowledge that such powers exist is the most important step towards developing them.

All human beings share a desire to expand their powers, to experience greater freedom and vitality, to 'have life more abundantly'. What deters them from making an effort is a lack of any idea of where to begin. If our reasoning has been correct, we have solved that problem. All that is necessary is to *know* that these powers are associated with the hidden part of the mind, and that they can be called upon by conscious effort. We simply need to be convinced that they exist. And this conviction can be gained by studying the evidence until dawning understanding turns into insight. No 'belief' is required, and no mystical disciplines are necessary: only the kind of straightforward effort that is needed to verify that the angles of a triangle really add up to a hundred and eighty degrees, or that the square on the hypotenuse is really equal to the square on the other two sides. Study the problem of multiple personality with an open mind, the phenomena of poltergeist activity, the curious powers of men like Rasputin and Gurdjieff, the observations of Lethbridge and Underwood on dowsing, and it is almost impossible to avoid the conclusion that the human mind is a vaster and stranger realm than we ever supposed. Moreover, the greatest step towards exploring its latent powers is simply to recognise clearly that they exist.

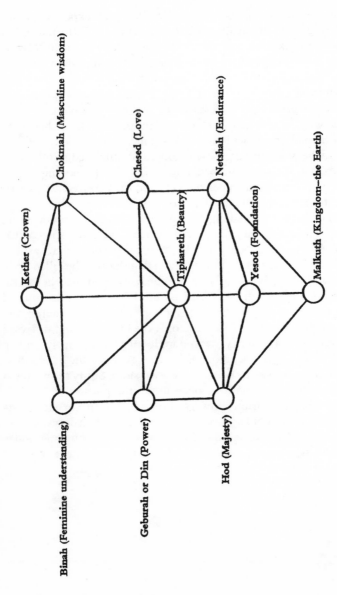

The Tree of Life

PART

THREE

1

Evolution

———◆———

Seen in retrospect, human life has a curious quality of unreality.

A child would find this idea almost impossible to grasp. To him the world seems, if anything, too solid and real. It strikes him as incredible that adults can handle so much complexity—and even stranger that they can spend so much time immersed in practical affairs without dying of boredom. Every child has an urgent need to retreat into a world of imagination for a few hours every day, through fairy tales or dolls or soldiers, or just television. By comparison, the real world seems singularly uneventful and dreary. He hopes that his own life is going to be exciting and romantic; but it never enters his head that it might seem unreal.

The rest of us grow up, find a job, get married, produce children, struggle to create a home. It all seems interesting and exciting enough at the time. But a point arrives when we realise that our most important years are behind us, and we contemplate the passage of time with a kind of bewilderment. Was that *all*? No matter how we may have succeeded in our chosen aims and objectives, there is still a sense of anti-climax. It is like arriving at the end of a book much sooner than you expected and wondering if you somehow missed out a hundred pages in the middle.

No animal has this trouble, because animals lack our remarkable capacity for *mental experience*. If I read a book or see a film that absorbs me, I feel as if the experience has lasted for months; then I look at the clock and realise that it has taken only a few hours. I have a similar feeling if I wake up from a nightmare and find myself in the familiar bedroom. Mental experience happens so much faster than physical experience that the world around us seems to be as permanent as the mountains. And my actual life seems to share this quality of permanence; it moves forward with reassuring slowness.

It is this permanence that provides human beings with their basic sense of security, the security without which it would be impossible to live. People whose sense of security is continually undermined by accidents or difficulties, soon become nervous wrecks and can easily go insane. If I look into myself with honesty, I have to recognise that I seem to live and act upon a basic *assumption* of permanence, as if I had a certain guaranteed 'security of tenure' on this earth. In fact, as Hazlitt pointed out in a well-known essay, the young proceed on the assumption that they are immortal.

Because of its serenely unconscious nature, this sense of security can easily be shaken. I have elsewhere[1] cited the experience of the novelist Margaret Lane, who, in a state of extreme sensitivity after having a baby, read John Hersey's account of the dropping of the atom bomb on Hiroshima and went into a state of shock in which she ceased to be capable of any sort of feeling or response. Again, I can recall the description of a woman friend, the wife of a poet, of how she plunged into nervous breakdown; it was shortly after the Second World War, when the Allies had entered concentration camps like Buchenwald and Belsen, and the newspapers were full of photographs of enormous piles of emaciated corpses. She described waking up in the middle of the night, and brooding on them, and suddenly realising that living people *like herself* were gassed or thrown alive into furnaces. It struck her that the millions of people who had seen those photographs of corpses had failed to grasp their meaning; had erected a kind of mental defence, as if it were all a kind of make-believe. And now she suddenly grasped what it would be like for a mother to stand in the queue in front of a gas chamber, holding her child, and something seemed to collapse inside her; she began to tremble uncontrollably and sob. It was the beginning of a long period of deep depression and total inability to cope with life.

We are now entering the territory of the existentialist philosophers. There is one minor difference in approach. Existentialists like Kierkegaard and Sartre are concerned less with problems of good and evil than with the apparent *meaninglessness* of human existence. They want to know why we are in the world and what we are supposed to do now we are here. They find human life and experience similar to waking up in a strange place with no memory of one's identity. This image occurs frequently in existentialist literature. The hero of Tolstoy's *Memoirs of a Madman* wakes up in the middle of the night in a distant province with the feeling: What am I doing here? Who am I? Roquentin, the narrator of Sartre's *Nausea*, recalls a time in Indo-China, 'when suddenly I woke from a six-year slumber . . . What was I doing in Indo-China?'

The existentialists imply that we take our narrow, everyday values for granted, like a man walking along with his eyes fixed on the ground, concerned only with avoiding puddles; then suddenly, he looks up and realises with a shock that he has no idea where he is.

One of the best examples of this kind of 'change of focus' occurs in an autobiographical essay by the French 'common sense' philosopher Theodore Simon Jouffroy.[2]

> I shall never forget that night in December in which the veil that concealed from me my own incredulity was torn. I hear again my steps in that narrow naked chamber where long after the hour of sleep had come I had the habit of walking up and down. I see again that moon, half-veiled by clouds, which now and again illuminated the frigid window panes. The hours of the night flowed on, and I did not note their passage. Anxiously I followed my thoughts, as from layer to layer they descended towards the foundation of my consciousness, and, scattering one by one all the illusions which until then had screened its windings from my view, made them every moment more clearly visible.

What Jouffroy was doing was questioning the emotional certainties by which he had so far lived:

> Vainly I clung to these last beliefs as a shipwrecked sailor clings to the fragments of his vessel; vainly, frightened at the unknown void into which I was about to float, I turned with them towards my childhood, my family, my country, all that was clear and sacred to me: the inflexible current of my thought was too strong; parents, family, memory, beliefs;

it forced me to let go of everything. The investigation went on more obstinate and more severe as it drew near its term and did not stop until the end was reached. I knew then that in the depth of my mind nothing was left that stood erect.

That moment was a frightful one; and when towards morning I threw myself exhausted on my bed, I seemed to feel my earlier life, so smiling and full, go out like a fire, and another life opened, sombre and un-peopled, where in future I must live alone; alone with my fatal thought which had exiled me thither, and which I was tempted to curse. The days which followed this discovery were the saddest of my life.

Jouffroy's motive in this exercise in ruthless self-analysis was to discover whether the use of the mind, the power of reason, can provide human beings with a solid foundation of certainty. His conclusion, like that of so many other philosophers, was negative. His 'fatal thought' led him to conclude that life is a tissue of illusions, and that without self-deception human beings would find it intolerable. Sartre's nausea is a physical revelation of the same disturbing truth.

But *is* it a truth? When we look more closely at the nausea experience, we detect an element of fallacy, especially if we compare it, for example, to Bennett's experience in the forest of Fontainebleau.

As I recalled [Ouspensky's] words I said to myself: 'I will be astonished.' Instantly, I was overwhelmed with amazement, not only at my own state, but at everything I looked at or thought of. Each tree was so uniquely itself that I felt I could walk in the forest forever and never cease from wonderment. Then the thought of 'fear' came to me. At once I was shaking with terror . . . I thought of 'joy', and I felt that my heart would burst from rapture.

Bennett was careful to point out that these were not mere 'feelings'. His heightened state of consciousness enabled him to see what was *already there*. Consciousness is a beam of light; in this case, the beam had suddenly become far more powerful than usual; consequently, it illuminated more.

By comparison, the state of mind described by Jouffroy, Tolstoy and Sartre is essentially *passive*. They merely contemplate the world and wait for meaning to reveal itself. This is like sitting in a car and waiting for it to drive itself. Consciousness is basically directional; it must be fired at its target like an arrow or a grappling hook. Meaning does not 'reveal itself'; it cannot be grasped by staring blankly and formulating questions.

Most of us believe that consciousness is already fully awake and that what we see around us is the world 'as it is'. In fact, every experience is a kind of engineering feat. It needs to be 'constructed'. Every act of grasping reality demands a highly complicated response of the senses, which must act in unison. The 'I' is like the conductor of an orchestra. Suppose, for example, I am walking in a garden on a sunny day. My eyes see many colours, my nostrils smell various scents, my ears hear the sounds of birds and bees, my skin feels the movement of the air. There is a noisy confusion of sensual impressions, like an orchestra tuning up. If I am feeling tired or depressed, I can concentrate on only one or two impressions at a time; I may actually increase my enjoyment by closing my eyes and excluding visual impressions. On the other hand, on those days when I feel fully alive, over-flowing with vitality, the garden somehow becomes *real*, a complex and harmonious pattern that I can grasp all at once, without effort.

Why do these moments of 'reality' occur so seldom? Because passivity is so deeply ingrained, especially in civilised man. As babies, we rest passively in our mothers' arms. As children, we are made to attend school, where we listen passively to teachers. And the modern educational system means that any person of average intelligence can go on to secondary school, then a university, after which there is always the possibility of a job in some large corporation. The modern world as a whole creates a habit of conformity, of obedience to pressures. We become unaccustomed to the exercise of freedom.

Passivity is also induced by all forms of *waiting*. If I stand waiting for a bus, something inside my brain 'switches off'; I enter into a state of suspended animation until the bus arrives. As I sit on the bus, waiting to get to work or to get home, consciousness again 'switches off', and I stare blankly at the passing scenery. If the bus is late or delayed in traffic jams, waiting becomes tinged with impatience or anxiety, and all possibility of creative use of consciousness vanishes. I am like a man who is slightly off-balance; the slightest push can send me backwards into a negative and irritable state of mind.

Consciousness doesn't wake up until I experience some positive drive, some sense of purpose. Yet the pattern of human existence is that we spend ninety per cent of our time in a passive state, wondering what to do next. It is hardly surprising that we habitually waste most of our potentialities.

It may seem that these 'philosophical' questions have no place in a volume on the paranormal. Yet the paranormal often leads directly to questions of philosophy. For example, common sense tells us that 'life is a one-way street'. Yet Lethbridge reached the conclusion that the future has, in some sense, already taken place. There is obviously something wrong with the common-sense view of the nature of time.

Jane O'Neill's accident near London Airport undermined her sense of security, making her feel that life is continually at the mercy of chance. This might have been expected to lead to depression or a general sense of meaninglessness; instead, it led to strange flashes of second sight and to a 'time slip' into the past. This experience throws an entirely new light on the existential problem of nausea. What Jouffroy, Roquentin and Tolstoy's 'madman' have in common is a sudden realisation that life is not what it seems to be. Our senses confine us in a kind of prison; we are like blinkered horses, unable to see beyond the present moment. Most human beings are so preoccupied with their everday concerns that they are unaware of this lack of freedom. But they suddenly *awakened* to their lack of freedom, and their immediate reaction was like that of a person who awakes to find himself bound hand and foot—they felt a frantic desire to escape. Gurdjieff used the same basic fear to galvanise his pupils when he compared human beings to a flock of sheep who have been hypnotised by a magician to keep them quiet until they are ready for the slaughter house.

Experiences like Jane O'Neill's point to a less frightening possibility. When her blinkers are removed she is confronted by a profusion of bewildering and useless 'paranormal' experience. What good did it do her to know what Fotheringhay church looked like four or five hundred years ago? From the point of view of her everyday life and her personal development, it was a totally useless piece of information. Which seems to suggest that the purpose of the blinkers may not be to keep us quiet until the butcher arrives but to provide the basic condition for self-control and self-development.

Bennett's experience at Fontainebleau supports this view. He says: 'I wanted to be free from this power to feel whatever I chose, and instantly it left me.' This sounds paradoxical. If he had achieved a higher degree of freedom than most human beings glimpse in a lifetime, why should he want to get rid of it? He explains: 'I felt that if I plunged any more deeply into the mystery of love, I would cease to exist.' He felt that the experience was undermining the foundations of his *personality*. And the personality is the basis of our control over our experience; weak personalities find life overwhelming. Ramakrishna once compared the personality to the peel of an orange, which prevents the juice from evaporating. It may be 'false', but it is indispensable. Bennett recognised instinctively that he was not yet *ready* for this degree of freedom; he had not reached it through *a genuine process of personal evolution*. He had to return to an earlier stage to continue the slow process of internal development. He still needed the 'skin'.

An experience like Bennett's leaves no doubt that the blinkers are not protecting us from a vision of meaninglessness, but from too much meaning. Gurdjieff went to the heart of the problem when he said: 'Life is real only when "I am".' Our total being is far larger than we can grasp with our daylight-consciousness. The problem is to expand into the darkened areas.

The real importance of these insights is that they establish evolution—mental evolution—as a basic law of the universe. Scientists continue to insist that evolution is a purely mechanical process, driven 'from below' by the need to survive. Experiences like Bennett's suggest that our mental evolution is drawn upward, from above. It is as if a higher level of consciousness was trying to persuade us to bring it into actuality. All of which suggests that mind is not an accidental product of the material world, a mere spectator of a process it did nothing to inaugurate. In a deeper sense, the material world is its plaything, its instrument. Nature's meanings remain incomplete without the activity of mind, as the nausea experience demonstrates. And this again points to the conclusion that the ecstasies of the romantics and mystics were a glimpse of the possibility of the true relation between mind and nature.

How far does all this help us towards answering the fundamental question: Who are we? What are we doing here?

Bennett's experience at Fontainebleau has something in common with the experience of all mystics in all ages; it was a glimpse of some ultimate reality. The glimpse convinces the mystic that his normal feeling of limitation is false. Man is like a gramophone record that has got stuck in a groove, so it repeats the same phrase over and over again, instead of going on to play the whole symphony. Or, differently put, man is a god who has forgotten his identity.

Again, there is remarkable unanimity in the solutions proposed by various religions. Man is in a fallen state. Some religions, like Gnosticism and Christianity, attribute the fall to sin. Others, like Hinduism, prefer what might be called the 'Game theory'—the notion that God descended voluntarily into matter as a kind of game.

Science, of course, rejects the whole notion of a 'fall'. It insists that man is merely the result of two hundred million years of evolution. But this raises questions even for scientists themselves. If man has developed purely through 'survival of the fittest', then his intelligence ought to be strictly proportional to the challenges he has so far had to overcome. But this is not so. His brain has a complexity out of all proportion to the problems of survival. Calculation, for example, is a fairly recent art, in the evolutionary sense; our ancestors of a few thousand years ago could not count beyond the number of their fingers and toes. Yet certain children—known as calculating prodigies—are able to work out sums involving enormous numbers inside their heads in a matter of seconds.

One five-year-old boy, Benjamin Blyth, out walking with his father one morning, asked at precisely what hour he had been born. A few minutes later he announced the exact number of seconds he had been alive, taking into account two extra days for Leap Years. The Canadian 'lightning calculator' boy, Zerah Colburn, was asked whether the sixth number of a Fermat series was a prime (not divisible by any other number). The number was over four thousand million. After a brief calculation, Colburn replied, 'No, it can be divided by 641.' Yet there is no known method of finding out whether a number is a prime except by painstakingly dividing every possible smaller number into it. Ten-year-old Vito Mangiamele, son of a Sicilian peasant, was asked to calculate the tenth root of 282,475,249 (i.e., a number that, multiplied by itself ten times, gives the above figures). It took him only a few moments to give the correct answer: seven.

Calculating prodigies tend to lose their powers as they grow up, but in a few rare cases they actually increase them. The electrical genius Nikolai Tesla had such an incredible capacity for visualisation that he never had to write mathematical problems down on paper; he merely closed his eyes and wrote them down on a blackboard inside his head. This power also extended to physical objects; he had only to close his eyes to be able to conjure up a solid object and to maintain the image for any length of time. One day he decided to create new thought-forms. He wrote: 'I saw new scenes. These were at first blurred and indistinct and would flit away when I tried to concentrate my attention on them. They gained strength and distinctness and finally assumed the concreteness of real things . . . Every night, and sometimes during the day . . . I would start on my journeys, see new places, cities and countries. . .' In Budapest park, walking with a companion, he suddenly had a clear vision of how to construct an alternating-current motor. (At that time, the only form of electricity known was direct current.) He actually saw, as if with his eyes, every detail of the motor. He made no attempt to set this down on paper for another six years, when he simply transformed his mental blueprint into actuality, creating the first alternating-current generator.

A hard-line evolutionist could argue that nature has created the brain on the principle of a computer and that, like any computer, its capacities exceed the demands usually made upon it. But Tesla's power to focus a mental object was a form of Faculty X; there is no obvious 'demand' for it in nature. It makes more sense to think of Tesla as a freakish breakthrough to unknown areas of the human mind, a kind of short-circuit to a higher level that, paradoxically, *already exists*.

All animals show this same curious tendency to a higher level of intelligence than is strictly necessary according to Darwinian principles. The naturalist Birute Galdikas-Brindamour, for example, discovered this in her study of orang-outans. Even the shark possesses 'unnecessary' intelligence. For 300 million years, it has remained unchanged, with senses that guide it automatically to its food. With no choices to make, and no natural predators, it has no need of intelligence. Yet when tested in laboratory mazes, it proves to have an intelligence equal to that of a rabbit, a creature far higher on the evolutionary scale, and with far more need for intelligence. It would seem as though nature has a simple bias in favour of intelligence—or rather, as if intelligence itself experienced some compulsion to develop beyond the demands of nature.

This seems to suggest that there is something unsatisfactory about the Darwinian theory of evolution. It might be compared to the theory, generally accepted in the nineteenth century, that the pyramids were built by slaves who were forced to work by overseers with whips. But when this theory was examined more closely, a number of questions arose. Why did the overseers drive the slaves? Because they were ordered to by their masters, the pharaohs. Why did the pharaohs want pyramids? To serve them as tombs or monuments. So thousands of people were forced to work to serve the vanity of a few individuals.

But in the 1960s, a German physicist, Kurt Mendelssohn, became intrigued by the mystery of the strangely shaped pyramid of Meidun, in which a giant, step-like structure rises from a heap of debris. He reached the conclusion that, about 3000 BC, there had been an immense disaster during the final stages of building, a collapse that may have cost thousands of lives. The pyramid was abandoned. But the lesson of the disaster was, Mendelssohn believes, taken into account in the building of the 'Bent Pyramid' at Dahshur, where the angle of the sides suddenly becomes less steep halfway up, to lessen the danger of a similar collapse. This, and other evidence, suggests that the two pyramids were being built *at the same time*; in fact, it has been suggested that the king who was responsible—Snofru—had three pyramids under construction at the same time. Obviously he could not be buried in all three. Mendelssohn therefore advances the highly reasonable theory that the real purpose of the pyramids was to unite many tribes and villages into a nation state by giving them a common task.[3]

If he could be *proved* correct, it would mean that while the pharaohs may have been autocratic, they were not necessarily vain or cruel. And instead of a 'Darwinian' society based on ruthless compulsion, we would have something closer to the modern idea of a benevolent despotism, whose basic approach could be described as idealistic.

Is there a similar alternative to the Darwinian theory of evolution? We have already seen what happened when Driesch and Lysenko tried to revive Lamarck's theory about the inheritance of acquired characteristics. Since then, many scientists have expressed their misgivings about the claims of strict neo-Darwinism. In 1968, a group of them met at Alpbach, in the Austrian Tyrol, to voice their dissatisfaction with 'the totalitarian claims of neo-Darwinian orthodoxy' (Arthur Koestler's phrase). Yet none of them attempted to formulate an alternative theory. Only Koestler himself, who, after all, has no scientific reputation to lose, continued to attack the notion that the inheritance of acquired characteristics has been disproved. In *The Case of the*

Midwife Toad (1971), Koestler defended the reputation of the Austrian biologist Paul Kammerer, who committed suicide in 1926 after being accused of faking certain crucial results. Kammerer had claimed that male toads, raised entirely in water so they had no chance of copulating on land, developed on their thumbs the same kind of horny pads possessed by ordinary frogs to hold on to their mates in the water, and that they passed these on to the next generation. One of Kammerer's critics discovered that the pads of one specimen were injections of Indian ink beneath the skin. The scandal destroyed Kammerer's reputation and also the last vestiges of support for Lamarckian vitalism in Vienna. Koestler points out that even though these specimens were undoubtedly tampered with (probably by an over-enthusiastic assistant), there is also plenty of evidence that other specimens were genuine, and that the horny pads really existed.

A less direct approach to the problem has been adopted by the psychologist Stan Gooch, whose views on 'the Neanderthal question' have been discussed in an earlier chapter.[4] In *Total Man* (1972), Gooch argued that man is a dual being, consisting of the rational Ego, and a darker, more instinctive being that he calls the Self. The Ego, which most of us think of as 'the real me', is the daylight consciousness of the 'cerebrum', the new brain, which has evolved at an explosive speed over the past half million years. The Self inhabits the 'old brain' which man inherited from the mammals, the cerebellum. (In fact, man also possesses a third brain—the brain stem and medulla—inherited from our reptile ancestors, but this seems to be mainly concerned with reflex actions and with controlling our sleep mechanisms.) Gooch believes that all the legends of dark, sinister creatures—the devil, vampires, dwarves, troglodytes, doppelgängers—come from the depths of the cerebellum, which is the seat of the unconscious. When we experience hypnogogic visions on the edge of sleep, these have come from the cerebellum. When we have a strange feeling that a thought has been thrust into our minds, as if someone whispered it aloud, this is the doing of the cerebellum. When Carl Jung made his 'descent into the Unconscious' and conversed with dream creatures, it was the Ego conversing with the Self.

To see how this notion helps us to understand evolution, we have merely to cast our minds back to the violent inner conflicts of adolescence. There is the clash between thought and feeling, the drive of instinct—particularly sexual instinct—and the social need for self-control. All this adds up to a continual and painful inner battle between what Fulke Greville called 'passion and reason, self-division's cause'. A youth meets a pretty girl, and his rational part wants to talk to her, to establish a contact of ideas and sympathies; behind this façade, a cave man clamours for him to tear off her clothes. The stronger the two antagonists, the more likely he is to be reduced to a nervous wreck. On the other hand, if he has the strength to stand firm and to reconcile the two antagonists, he will learn something of the secret of creativeness; he may become a Beethoven or Dostoevsky or Nietzsche. The conflict presents him with the possibility of evolution.

Regrettably, it also presents him with the possibility of various kinds of surrender, or various kinds of short-cuts. Robert Irwin is an example;[5] the attempt to emasculate himself amounted to an effort to subdue the 'lower self' by violence. When that failed, he went to the opposite extreme and committed a double murder, thus effectively surrendering to the lower self. Arther Koestler has argued[6] that the sudden development of the 'new brain' constitutes the greatest danger to human survival, since it has led to the outbreaks of mass insanity that have punctuated human history. This is surely true; but it is also true that the very possibility of evolution implies the possibilities of evolutionary failures like Robert Irwin—or Adolf Hitler. Without the conflict, we would be a stagnant species, like the shark or the skylark.

The incredibly fast evolution of the new brain raises another question. Why has it developed so fast when there was no biological need for it? It is the problem of the calculating prodigies all over again. Cro-Magnon man possessed a brain that is, in all essentials, the equal of Einstein's; yet he used it only for hunting. Koestler illustrates the point with an amusing parable of an Arab shopkeeper who is poor at arithmetic and prays to Allah to send him an abacus—a simple counting frame. The prayer somehow goes to the wrong department, and he finds himself presented with a modern computer with thousands of knobs and dials. Baffled by its complexity, he gives it a kick, and a dial lights up with a figure 1. He kicks it twice, and the figure changes to two. So he uses his giant computer as an abacus, administering kicks instead of sliding beads.

Which again raises the question: how did we develop the computer? It is possible to see how man has gradually learnt to use it, through the conflict between the old and new brain. But where did it come from in the first place?

In his second book, *Personality and Evolution* (1973), Stan Gooch has a tentative explanation. As far as he is concerned, the main objection to Darwin is the theory of random mutations. The climate gets colder, and it is the polar bear with the thickest coat who survives and propagates the species. But an ice age can arrive with such catastrophic suddenness that natural selection would not have time to do its work; *all* the bears would freeze to death. Darwin makes the assumption that mutations occur more or less exactly when required.

Gooch explains this in terms of ethologist Niko Tinbergen's discovery of certain stimuli which he called 'releasers'. The sight of a baby releases a mother's maternal instinct; the sight of a girl undressing releases a man's sexual instinct; and so on. But Tinbergen discovered that some animals and birds respond to releasers that are *not* found in nature. The ringed plover responds more strongly to white eggs with black spots than to its normal light brown eggs with darker brown spots. Oyster catchers prefer a clutch of five eggs to their normal three and respond more strongly to an enormous egg than to their own natural-sized one. Grayling butterflies can be deceived by plastic models, but they prefer *larger* models; they also prefer black to the natural colours. Gooch likens this behaviour to the preferences shown by men for women in girly magazines—exaggerated breasts and hips, black underwear, and so on.

He goes on to suggest that Darwin may be wrong in believing that animals do not evolve a response to a natural challenge *until* that challenge appears. 'Super-normal releasers' suggest a certain inner freedom to develop responses to situations that have not yet arisen. In which case, perhaps they have an inner selection of responses to cope with new situations.

It is not difficult to carry Gooch's logic one stage further. Among human beings, the 'bigger and better' response is usually produced by a combination of frustration and imagination. For example, an imaginative and sexually frustrated male usually develops some sexual abnormality—a preference for enormous breasts, large behinds, pink silk underwear, black leather boots, or whatever. He has learned to trigger the sexual response with a simple 'releaser' that can be easily obtained in pornographic bookshops or off clothes lines. We find it easy to understand how imagination combines with frustration to produce this response. But we cannot credit oyster catchers and grayling butterflies with imagination in the ordinary sense. We can suppose only that some impulse inside them strives naturally to a kind of 'ideal'. And plainly, this ideal will influence evolution, if some bird or butterfly displaying the 'super-normal releaser' comes along. Again, we seem to be positing some kind of evolution 'from above' rather than from below.

One of the most interesting clues to the development of Gooch's ideas occurs towards the end of *Total Man*, when he mentions casually that he himself has experienced the 'mediumistic trance', which he seems to associate with the cerebellum. The point is expanded in his book *The Paranormal*. [7] There he tells how, at the age of twenty-six, he attended a seance in Coventry with a friend. Quite suddenly, he felt light-headed. 'And then suddenly it seemed to me that a great wind was rushing through the room. In my ears was the deafening sound of roaring waters . . . As I felt myself swept away I became unconscious.' (The resemblances to Ramakrishna's experience of *samadhi* are obvious.) When he regained consciousness, he discovered that several 'spirits' had spoken through him. It was, he writes, like being possessed, or as if another being had arisen or materialised within one's body—a sensation like someone else putting on yourself as he might a suit of clothes.

Gooch's views on life after death will be discussed in the last chapter. All that need be noted at this point is his conviction that paranormal experience arises from the cerebellum, the seat of the unconscious. But this raises as many questions as it answers. It is easy to believe that the sixth sense of danger arises from the cerebellum; our animal ancestors needed it to survive. The same is probably true of the ability to dowse both for water and for earth forces. Telepathy and the ability to see ghosts also seem to belong to the old brain. But what of experiences of super consciousness like Bennett's at Fontainebleau? Or glimpses of the future, like the one Alan Vaughan experienced when the spirit of the Nantucket captain's wife was driven out of his head? At first it is difficult to see how such experiences could be associated with a more primitive part of the brain, until we recollect that the cerebellum is the source of sexual excitement and of orgasm. And that Gooch's experience of mediumship resembled Ramakrishna's *samadhi*. If man's evolution is the result of a conflict between the old and new brain, *resulting in a degree of reconciliation*, then is it not conceivable that glimpses of higher consciousness are the result of a *momentary integration* of the old and new brains? At the moment, our three brains—reptile, mammal and human—are virtually independent systems, each with its own identity.

The psychologist Robert Ornstein has suggested that the left and the right sides of the brain are also separate entities, joined by an intercommunications system. Man seems to be a colony rather than an individual. At the moment, his independent parts are at war as often as not; particularly the old brain and the new. In *Steppenwolf*, Hermann Hesse symbolised these as a wolf and a human being and wrote a novel about their long-drawn-out conflict. But at certain moments, the man and the wolf seem to be at peace with one another, and that when this happens, Steppenwolf feels *akin to the gods*. Hesse recognised that the higher states of consciousness come from a *new* relation between the old antagonists.

This view is supported by research conducted into the brain patterns of creativity by Elmer and Alyce Green of the Menninger Foundation.[8] They discovered that hypnogogic images are accompanied by strong theta rhythms, which, if our speculation is correct, suggests that the cerebellum is the source of theta rhythms. Their research into biofeedback also showed that, while relaxation states are accompanied by alpha rhythms, deeper states of reverie produced long trains of theta rhythms. This led them to speculate that states of creativity might be accompanied by theta rhythms, since so many poets and scientists have received sudden bursts of inspiration when they were in states between sleeping and waking. Elmer Green himself developed an ability to slip into a meditative reverie when he had a problem to solve. The EEG machine showed that these states were accompanied by theta rhythms. Whether these would appear in more controlled forms of creativity—such as writing a novel or a symphony—is doubtful, because the 'inspiration' has to be monitored by the critical consciousness (which produces beta waves). On the other hand, most creators have observed certain moments when the novel or play or symphony seems to be 'writing itself' moments when ideas well up into consciousness with the spontaneity of hypnogogic images; it is a reasonable, though so far untested, supposition that such states are accompanied by theta rhythms.

But, as Grey Walter comments, theta rhythms are also associated with outbursts of rage and with violence; they are often found in pathological criminals. Outbursts of rage are governed—if that is the right word—by the cerebellum. So it seems that the part of the brain associated with creativity and deep meditation is also associated with crime and violence. And if we reflect on a man like Robert Irwin, who was capable of both, we can begin to see the relation between them. Violence arises from the conflict between the old and new brain, or rather, when the Ego fails to control the conflict. Creativity and the godlike moments arise from a close co-operation between the two and can be sustained only by a higher type of control. Again, crime can be seen as a failure to reconcile the old and the new, while higher states of consciousness result from a normally unprecedented degree of collaboration.

This history of science and philosophy shows that few important ideas occur to only one thinker at a time. Gooch's theory of evolution through inner conflict is no exception. In the mid-1960s, when he was still brooding on the role of the cerebellum in paranormal experience, a Hungarian refugee named Charlotte Bach had begun to consider the problem from a totally different angle.

Charlotte Bach came to England with her husband in 1948, after the Communist takeover; they had both lectured in philosophy at the University of Budapest, where she had taken her degree in philosophy and psychology. In 1965, she experienced a double tragedy when her husband died and her only son was killed in a car crash two weeks later. For nine months she felt numb, unable to think or work. Finally, the need to make a living forced her out of her apathy. Unable to sustain long bouts of concentration, she decided to compile a popular dictionary of psychological terms, which she hoped might open the way to a university appointment.

It was when she came to the definition of various sexual perversions that she began to experience bafflement. Sexual perversion itself seemed to defy definition. Where precisely does one draw the line between 'normal' and 'perverted' sex? Freud, Kinsey and the rest struck her as curiously abstract and theoretical. She began questioning homosexual acquaintances and discovered that most of them were perfectly willing to talk; in fact, they began to bring friends along. Soon she had compiled a large dossier on male and female homosexuals, sadists, masochists, fetishists and transvestites. And it struck her at an early stage that the usual definitions of these peculiarities are too simplistic. For example, homosexuality is defined as the attraction of like to like—a man to another man, a woman to another woman. But some homosexuals are really females in male bodies, so their attraction to a masculine male should actually qualify as heterosexuality. Similarly, some married couples may be attracted by the 'likeness' in the partner—a masculine man to a masculine woman; their heterosexual relationship obviously has a strong homosexual element.

The problem of fetishism has similar complications. The 'normal' male fetishist is attracted by some symbol of the female—a kind of distillation of the ideal: female underwear, shoes, hair. It struck Charlotte Bach that some males feel a compulsion to wear excessively male clothes—leather jackets, chains and so on. Conversely, some females go in for ultra-feminine clothes and perfumes. These also struck Charlotte Bach as varieties of fetishism.

She was struck by another observation that had never, apparently, occurred to psychologists. Transvestites seem to be in some way quite different from other kinds of 'inverts'. She went to interview a transvestite university professor, who asked her if she would mind if he behaved normally. When she said no, he removed his trousers, put on black stockings, high heeled shoes and a wide leather belt, then lit up his pipe and proceeded to talk with as little embarrassment as if he had been wearing old tweeds. He obviously felt no guilt whatever about his 'perversion'. And she discovered that this seemed to be typical of transvestites.

Light began to break when she came across a paper by Desmond Morris on the behaviour of the zebra finch and the ten-spiked stickleback. If sexually excited female sticklebacks are placed in a tank without males, one of them may begin to perform the male courting dance and the others to respond in the appropriate female fashion. Odder still, if the male zebra finch is rejected by the female while intent on sex, he may suddenly begin to do the *female* courting dance.

Plato observes in the *Symposium* that men and women were originally halves of a single creature, which was divided into two by the gods; now we all wander around searching for the other half. As a man holds a woman in his arms, he experiences a desire to *blend* with her, and the actual penetration of her body is only a token union. If we assume that sexual attraction is based on a desire of the male to *become* female, and vice versa, then various perversions suddenly begin to fit into a neatly symmetrical pattern.

Men and women can react to this pull towards the opposite sex in two ways, either by resisting it or affirming it. Charlotte Bach labelled the resisters 'denialists', and the affirmers 'asseverationists'. This means that we have four basic types. But then, a man can be anatomically male while psychologically female, and he can react to this situation in two possible ways. He might want to deny the pull towards becoming the opposite sex (which in this case is male—for he is *psychologically* a woman, and that is what counts) by dressing up in female clothes or generally behaving in a female manner. He might be a 'drag queen', or the femininity might emerge in subtler ways: in being obsessively tidy, a stickler for etiquette, etc. On the other hand, he might decide to affirm the desire to become the opposite sex by dressing up in excessively masculine clothes and behaving with exaggerated aggressiveness, like the leather-jacketed rowdy. Charlotte Bach labelled the drag queen a 'male negative denialist' (read: physically male, psychologically the opposite, denying maleness), while the leather-jacketed type is a male negative asseverationist (physically male, psychologically the opposite, asserting maleness.)

It can easily be seen that there are eight possible types: male and female negative asseverationists and denialists. Obviously the normal male is a male positive denialist, physically and psychologically male, and denying the tendency to become feminine. A normal female is a female positive denialist, physically and psychologically female, denying the pull to become male. The counterpart of the leather-jacket type is the excessively feminine female. She is, of course, basically lesbian (femme, not butch), just as the leather-jacket type is basically homosexual. She is a female negative asseverationist. Oddly enough, the butch lesbian is psychologically female as well as physically, but she asserts the desire to become a member of the opposite sex, dressing in tweeds, wearing riding boots.

And what of *her* opposite—the man who is also psychologically male, yet affirms the need to become a female? This is the professor who pulled on silk stockings and high-heeled shoes. He, like the butch lesbian, seems to feel no guilt about it; he is relatively placid and stable.

Bach's classification of human beings into eight types produced a satisfying sense of symmetry and provided a basis for explaining her multifold observations of various 'perverts'. Clearly, the usual distinction between a 'normal' person and a 'pervert' is superficial. One variation of the drag-queen type (male negative denialist) *looks* perfectly normal; the charming Casanova who finds every woman irresistible. If he finally settles down, it may be with his logical opposite (female negative denialist), who may also look perfectly 'normal', although slightly masculine or 'bossy'. Male negative asseverationists—the leather-jacket types—may look 'normal', and in fact, *be* normal as far as they themselves are concerned. Transvestites are 'normal', which is why they feel no guilt.

Bach also observed that none of these types is permanent; all tend to change. The femme lesbian may change slowly into a 'normal' housewife, or perhaps into the slightly masculine female negative denialist. The leather-jacket type may stop denying his femininity and become a pouf. Only the transvestite and the butch lesbian seem to be too stable to change much. What is equally important is that the various non-normal types may resolve—or at least minimise—their problems by becoming creative; the drag queen may become a poet or a novelist or painter; the leather-jacket may become a scientist or politician. The non-normals are natural pioneers.

At this point, we can see that Charlotte Bach was coming closer to Stan Gooch's theory of evolution through inner conflict; but for her, the conflict was not between old brain and new, but between various aspects of sexual behaviour, all stemming from that fundamental 'platonic' pull, the desire of each sex to become its opposite, or rather, to blend into unity. But at this stage, she was still not thinking in terms of evolution; she was still searching for clues in the world of animal ethology, and she discovered more in the writing of Niko Tinbergen. The concept of 'displacement activity' seemed particularly important to her. Two herring gulls, glaring at one another at the boundaries of their two territories, will suddenly begin tearing up the grass. Cocks who look as if they are prepared to tear one another apart suddenly begin to peck furiously at the ground. Two male sticklebacks, after making threatening motions at one another, suddenly dive head downward into the sand and stare at one another while waving their tails. It looks as if they have suddenly thought better of it and somehow have to get rid of the energy of aggression. In human beings, we can see 'displacement activity' when impatient drivers honk their horns, or a bored man begins to drum his fingers on the table or whistle tunelessly. A puzzled man scratches his head or his chin. A woman who is unsure of herself may dab at her nose or run her hand over her hair.

Tinbergen recognised that displacement activities sometimes become 'ritualised' into what he called 'social releasers'. When people are unsure of themselves, they smile, and a smile is a social releaser. So is talking about the weather, another response to embarrassment. It struck Charlotte Bach that sexual deviations can also be seen as displacement activities. They certainly have the same illogical quality: a fetishist caressing a crutch, or becoming excited at the sight of a black rubber apron. She preferred to call them 'spillover activities', because that implied an actual *overflow* of excess energy into some apparently irrelevant action. But then, there is something oddly pointless and comic in a man being spanked by a prostitute in a nurse's uniform. Sexual deviations all seem oddly self-defeating.

Two more sources finally showed her the answer she was looking for. She found in the zoologists the concept of neotony. This means, quite simply, that some species remain half developed: a Peter Pan species. Imagine what would happen, if some strange genetic mutation caused human beings to achieve sexual maturity at the age of two. They would begin to have babies at the age of two and might well die at the age of ten, worn out by child-rearing. In a few generations, older people might disappear, never to be replaced, and we would become a race of children. This astonishing situation *has* occurred in the case of certain species—the axolotl lizard, for example, which is really a baby land-salamander that never grows up.

In the 1920s, a Dutch anatomist named Ludwig Bolk proposed the theory that man is also a neotonous species. The embryo of an ape is not unlike a fully developed human being without the brow-ridges, body hair and specialised teeth that the ape goes on to develop. Bolk argued that man is an immature ape. This conclusion is less insulting than it sounds. Neotonous species have far greater possibilities of development than non-neotonous ones. The simplest way to understand this is by borrowing an analogy of Alec Nisbett from his biography of Konrad Lorenz. Nisbett compares the evolutionary characteristics of a species to a vast, rambling home, occupied by a succession of individuals in each generation. Whenever some new need arises, they build on new rooms or add chimneys, until the place becomes a nightmare of passageways and inconvenient rooms. But they can never move out and re-design the whole place; they have to go on living in it, until one day there is no room for further development. Then the species either becomes stagnant—like the shark—or dies out through failure to make further adaptations.

Bolk was not concerned simply with man's physical resemblance to an immature ape. He also observed what Shaw had noted in *Back to Methuselah*: that although we are sexually mature while still teenagers, we remain emotionally immature all our lives. The most obvious thing about human beings is that they are permanent adolescents; it is as if they needed a far longer life span to grow to full intellectual and emotional maturity (Shaw suggested three hundred years).

This was one piece of information that started Charlotte Bach thinking along new lines. Another came from a young man who was in the grip of religious obsessions. He told her that he had experienced an orgasm *lasting eight hours*. Understandably, she dismissed this as fantasy. Then one day, thinking about neotony, and about Mircea Eliade's observations on *shamanism*, and the ecstasies of the great religious mystics, she had a dazzling insight. It was so great that she leapt up from her desk and said aloud: '*That's* what it's about—evolution!' She describes it as one of the most exciting moments of her life.

The revelation that came to her was this. All sexual deviations seem to be self-defeating, yet stolidly normal people also strike one as somehow incomplete. There is something oddly immature about sexual deviates . . . Immaturity. Neotony . . . Could that be it? The 'normal' person has acquired a rather dull kind of equilibrium. In the *shaman*, who is 'assexual', the opposing forces have built up a strength that creates a glowing discharge of nervous energy that can go on for hours. These same opposing forces, on a far lower level—and in people who have not succeeded in balancing them—produce sexual deviation. The transvestite and the butch lesbian *have* balanced them, but on the lower level, so that they have, in effect, blocked the possibility of further evolution. Evolution springs from imbalance.

An analogy may help. Many major poets and artists have been 'unbalanced' and subject to severe inner conflicts. The travel writer Negley Farson once consulted a doctor in an attempt to cure his alcoholism; the doctor told him: 'I could cure your alcoholism, but I'd probably "cure" your talent for writing at the same time.' Yet it is not true that in order to be a great artist, you *have* to be unbalanced. The greatest creators—Rembrandt, Beethoven, Tolstoy—have resolved this purely neurotic type of unbalance, but they still experience inner conflict, on a higher level. Perhaps only the saint and the mystic have come close to a true 'resolution' of the inner conflicts; and this resolution produces inner ecstasies. As Nietzsche said, a man must have chaos within him to give birth to a dancing star. The task of the individual is not to try to escape the chaos, as the transvestite does, but to harness its energies, so that it becomes a kind of controlled atomic explosion.

This, in simplified form, is Charlotte Bach's conception of the mechanism of the evolutionary process. We are an immature species, and we are continually torn by a deep psychological urge to blend with the opposite sex. The frequent frustration of this urge produces the 'displacement activity' we call sexual aberration. And sexual aberration, according to Charlotte Bach, is the mother of invention, and therefore of evolution. She makes the curious statement that a foot fetishist invented shoes, a hair fetishist invented hats. . . Be that as it may, we can see the way that the conflict that has produced sexual aberrations can also, when ordered and controlled, produce human culture. Her immense work, *Concerning the Invention and Evolution of Writing*, argues that the letters A and B are symbols of the male and female and that all other letters—particularly in Chinese ideogrammatic writing—can be interpreted as symbolic expressions of the basic sexual conflict. She also claims that alchemy is a 'knowledge system' that evolved in the same way, and whose inner content has now been largely forgotten. Because of these inner conflicts, man continually changes his behaviour patterns, and this is the basis of the evolutionary process. It is driven not from without but within, although, of course, it is limited by the problems of the external environment.

It is this inner stress, Charlotte Bach believes, which has transformed our instincts into intellect, and which accounts for the extraordinary development of the human brain in the past half million years. The whole notion could be compared to Newton's theory of gravitation. Newton had to account for certain movements of the heavenly bodies. He did this by assuming one basic powerful force, gravitation. The earth and the planets are attracted towards the sun; yet they do not fall into the sun because there are counter forces; the result of these two opposing forces is their elliptical orbit. In Charlotte Bach's evolutionary theory, the force of gravity is the basic urge of the male to become female, and vice versa. But since, unlike the planets, we are living beings, the result is not a pattern simply of equilibrium but of evolution.

In the late 1960s, Charlotte Bach began to set down her theories in a book called *Homo Mutans, Homo Luminens*. Various friends who were interested in her work arranged to have it duplicated. She submitted it to various biologists and zoologists for their opinion but the whole theory was too strange and new to have an immediate appeal. The sheer size of the book was disconcerting—over three thousand pages—and the style was bare and abstract, devoid of the kind of analogies and illustrations that might have made her meaning clearer. (For example, she never gives a concrete illustration of what she means by saying that displacement activites become ritualised into social releasers, although it seems to be one of her basic propositions.) Nevertheless, her ideas slowly gained ground. Now she has acquired a considerable following and become something of a cult figure.

Critics of her theory have objected that she is a kind of disguised Freudian, reducing all human behaviour to sex. This is a misunderstanding. Freud *was* a reductionist, in the sense that he was capable of explaining art or religion in terms of sexual conflicts or taboos. Charlotte Bach recognises the basic 'trans-sexual' conflict in art and religion but never asserts that they can be *reduced* to these terms. She is like a scientist who points out that stones and trees and human beings are all made of atoms, but who never denies that organic molecules are more complex than inorganic ones. It would be more accurate to call her a sexual mystic, who sees sex as the mysterious force that drives creation. Goethe said that 'the eternal feminine draws us upward and on'; if he had been a woman, he might have said 'the eternal masculine draws us upward and on'. Charlotte Bach has simply taken both points of view into account.

From the point of view of existential philosophy, Charlotte Bach's theory has a great deal more to say than Stan Gooch's. The basic problem of existentialism is the feeling of the total meaninglessness of human existence. Kierkegaard objected to Hegel's philosophy of the evolution of spirit because it failed to tell *him* what he ought to do. But, according to Charlotte Bach, man is an emergent process, whose evolution depends upon the continual exercise of his freedom. The reward is an increased sense of freedom, perhaps even the ecstasy of the mystic or *shaman*. Like Sartre, she never tires of asserting that man is free; unlike Sartre, she has never contradicted herself by declaring that 'man is a useless passion'.

By comparison, Stan Gooch's account of human evolution is altogether more down-to-earth. At a certain point in the evolutionary chain, man's remote ancestors developed the central nervous system, with its control of consciousness and will and voluntary movement. So far, man had made do with the autonomic nervous system, which controls involuntary functions like digestion and breathing. The new brain came into existence as the controller of the central nervous system. (The autonomic nervous system is controlled by the old brain.) Sooner or later, random mutation produced a creature with a slightly more developed cerebrum, and with more intelligence. But this early ancestor must have found his intelligence a burden. While his fellows ate and slept and copulated, he found himself possessed of too much self-awareness to live so naturally. But this gave him no natural advantage in hunting or fighting, for these depend on sensitivity to a deep, instinctive response, and intelligence tends to separate us from this contact with the subconscious. He may have lived as a kind of outcast, never discovering a use for his unwelcome gift. Or he may, if he was aggressive and determined, have persuaded his fellows to accept him on his own terms and then have demonstrated to them that it was easier to capture a wild boar through cunning than brute force. We can assume that his intelligence was propagated through his children, and that some of his male and female descendants mated and produced children who were even more intelligent.

Each new increment of intelligence would be a burden to its possessor, raising the same conflict all over again. For men, it might well be a disadvantage, making them less quick in battle, less brave when confronting a charging animal. At every stage of evolution it has been a disadvantage to be slightly more intelligent and analytical than one's fellows; intelligence makes for change, and men are naturally conservative. If their hostility is to be defused, it must be done by beating them on their own ground, *by efficiency and dominance*. Which means that the intelligent man has to make twice as much effort as the less intelligent to become a well-adjusted human being. Yet such an effort would be the condition of his evolution.

There may appear to be a basic contradiction between this view of evolution and that of Charlotte Bach, but closer examination proves this to be untrue. Charlotte Bach asserts that the force of evolution operates through a type of sexual conflict, and that when a human being succeeds in resolving this conflict through an effort of will, the result is an increment of intelligence. Stan Gooch's theory concerns the way that man adjusts to this additional intelligence; it takes over, so to speak, where Charlotte Bach's leaves off. This does not necessarily imply that they would agree with one another's theories—only that there is no fundamental contradiction.

Stan Gooch's notion of man's three brains provides a basis for explaining the strange phenomenon of multiple personality. It is also worth taking into account Robert Ornstein's view that the left and right sides of the brain are also separate entities,[9] the left hemisphere controlling logical thinking, the right being responsible for what he calls 'holistic mentation'—recognising faces, painting pictures and so on. In other words, the left analyses, the right synthesises. The two sides remain in close intercommunication, like two friendly countries whose governments keep one another closely informed. But if they broke off diplomatic relations, their total independence would soon become apparent. This is not to suggest that the multiple personalities of Doris or Sybil were situated in different parts of the brain, only that brain physiology gives us additional reason for recognising that we are not 'individuals'. We are very *dividual* indeed.

Stan Gooch's theory has the additional advantage of suggesting the actual location of the seat of paranormal experience—the cerebellum. But what about the 'superconscious'? Is this also located in the cerebellum? It seems fairly logical to assume that it is the cerebellum that tells the dowser where to locate water. In that case, it is presumably also the cerebellum that told the Abbé Mermet where to locate sunken ships on the other side of the globe, and *this* sounds more like an attribute of the superconscious than of the subconscious. Or are we merely quibbling about words? Is the cerebellum connected to a part of our being that 'knows' all kinds of things that never get into the cerebrum?

When we raise the question of Faculty X, the problem becomes altogether more complex. Faculty X can be connected with the faculty that philosophers call 'insight', and with the Buddhist concept of realisation.

What actually happens when we get this flash of 'insight'? Suppose, for example, I am trying to work out a geometrical problem, and I suddenly 'see' the answer? What happens is that I suddenly become aware of *relations* that had previously escaped me. It is almost like taking off in an aeroplane and seeing the place where you live from above. You see it in a new, wider perspective. We may recall the story Arthur Koestler tells about his own flash of revelation when he was in

a Spanish prison during the Civil War, expecting to be shot.[10] To pass
the time, he tried to recall Euclid's proof that there is no 'largest prime
number'; as he succeeded, he was suddenly swept into a kind of
mystical ecstasy, feeling that he had transcended the world of contingency and was contemplating an absolute truth. Here realisation is
connected with a purely abstract insight.

The experience is analogous to that described by the jazz musician
Mezz Mezzrow in *Really the Blues*, where he speaks of opium eating:
'That fiery little pill was . . . lighting up a million bulbs in my body
that I never knew were there—I didn't even know there were any
sockets for them.' Realisation seems to be a similar experience, but it
takes place *in the brain*. It is as if a part of the brain that was normally
sleeping was suddenly awakened. We have already touched on the
problem of 'sleep'. It is caused by our automatic component, the
robot. When I am tired, I begin to economise on energy and perception; but I can still recite the twelve times table, or drive my car,
because these functions have been passed on to the robot. However, if
I drink a glass of wine in front of a pleasant fire on a winter evening,
I may find myself glowing with energy and optimism; things are
suddenly seen to exist in their own right. The energy induced by
relaxation has allowed the real me to take over. And this is also true of
my glimpses of Faculty X.

The concept of the robot can also be used to explain evolution.
Evolution *is* the development of the robot. Our hearts beat automatically. Our hair and nails grow automatically. Our stomachs digest
food automatically. These functions have already been automatised by
the evolutionary process, so that consciousness is free to deal with
other problems. If I had to *think* about my breathing. I would have no
attention to spare for anything else. At a certain point in evolution,
living creatures wished to become more mobile. Since movements
like walking and swimming depend on muscles that are controlled by
the central nervous system, the earliest amphibians had to *learn* to
walk. But they soon learned to make this function automatic, and in
due course, the voluntary muscles submitted to the same process of
automatisation as the muscles of the heart and stomach. To handle this
complexity, the cerebrum had to be enlarged. Man developed the
ability to think analytically and then to speak. Speech depended on
intellectual memory, and man also proceeded to automatise this function. Each new step in automatisation was also a step forward in

freedom. If I had to think about how to type, it would be far more difficult to write this page. As it is, my fingers do the typing for me, leaving my brain free to think about meanings. These are translated into words by my automatic speech functions, and then into letters on paper by my fingers.

For convenience, we can think of automatisation as a servant of will or spirit. (This view was first elaborated by Edouard von Hartmann in *Psychology of the Unconscious*, a book that has fallen into undeserved neglect in the twentieth century.) The aim is always to give will (and eventually consciousness) more freedom. But at a certain point in the process, something began to go wrong. The problem is that conscious awareness separates us from our instincts. We began to lose the sense of *why* we were doing all this, and so gave a free hand to the greatest enemy of evolution: laziness. If I am free, then I can choose whether to use my freedom to conquer new ground, or merely to lie in the sun and yawn. If I have lost all sense of urgency, and my conscious mind can perceive no particular purpose, then I am just as likely to choose inactivity. My robot, the perfect valet, now becomes the chief support of my laziness.

This brings us to one of the most controversial parts of the theory. Robotic functions require far less energy than willed functions. And we have all noticed how prolonged laziness causes loss of energy. When laziness becomes habitual, whole areas of consciousness go to sleep, like a limb whose circulation has been cut off by a tourniquet. *And this is the state in which man finds himself today*. The odd things is that the brain circuits that produce wider consciousness are not waiting to evolve; they are already there, like wings of a country house that have been closed down. The strange implication seems to be that there *was* a time when we made fuller use of them, and that our capacities have atrophied since those days. In fact, it looks rather as if something like the Fall in Genesis actually occurred.

In short, man's success in achieving 'self-automation' has now become the chief obstacle to his evolution. Gurdjieff once said that if the human race is to be saved, man must develop an organ that would enable him to foresee the precise hour and moment of his own death. *That* would stir him out of his laziness. Auden was pointing to the same defect when he said: 'Even war cannot frighten us enough.'

All this, of course, brings us no closer to an answer to the basic problem of why there is existence rather than non-existence. But it *does* throw a great deal of light on the problem of why human existence has a dream-like quality. The feeling of absurdity or nausea is a sense of being trapped in the present moment, without meaning or direction. And since man is an evolutionary animal, he feels oddly disconnected when he has no sense of purpose.

When consciousness is wide awake, it possesses a strong sense of meaning. If we can *grasp* this fact, we can see exactly what normal consciousness ought to be like. There is nothing 'mystical' about it, no sense of achieving some higher plane of existence. It is essentially *ordinary* consciousness, operating at its proper efficiency. And when we are in this state, we have a normal and proper sense of the potentialities of life. Wells's Mr Polly said: 'If you don't like your life you can change it', but most people have no idea of what they'd like to change it *to*. In wide-awake consciousness we can see all kinds of things we'd like to do; the world seems to be nothing but fascinating possibilities.

All this implies that everday consciousness has something *missing* from it, so that if fails to work with maximum efficiency, like a car that has a spark plug missing, or a clock with only one hand. And this has happened because man has allowed himself, by imperceptible degrees, to become too dependent on the robot, until low-pressure consciousness has become a part of our human heritage.

Like the Original Sin of Genesis, our low-pressure consciousness can be held responsible for most of our major defects. It produces a kind of nagging hunger for excitement that leads to all kinds of irrational behaviour. This is why gamblers gamble, sex maniacs commit rape, sadists inflict pain and masochists enjoy having it inflicted, and why men become alcoholics and drug addicts. It also explains why we are so prone to outbreaks of criminality and mass destruction. Violence and pain are preferable to boredom and frustration.

Yet the situation is by no means as disastrous as it appears. It is important to bear in mind that man is an immature species; he has not yet committed himself to an evolutionary cul de sac. So before we write the epitaph of the human race, let us examine its problems more closely.

Throughout his history, man has shown the same depressing tendency to escape his boredom through violence and destruction, and there is no reason to believe that the invention of nuclear weapons will improve his record. There is an element of absurdity in seeking out forms of crisis that will catapult him into 'wide-awake consciousness'; it is like persuading yourself to go out for a walk by setting the house on fire. On the other hand, man has also shown a long-standing tendency to recognise the futility of mere excitement, and to attempt to get to the root of the problem. This tendency is called religion. When religious ascetics wore hair shirts and slept on bare planks, it was because they recognised instinctively that the problem was to *de-condition* themselves from over-reliance on the robot. They were trying to shake the mind awake through pain and discomfort. But even this remedy contains traces of the old 'original sin', the reliance on external pressures. Discomfort *can* shake the mind awake; but a sense of purpose can do it more positively and effectively.

But what purpose? If we reject the various ways of galvanising the mind by indirect means—danger, gambling, love-making—what is left?

We can begin to see an answer if we consider what happens inside us in states of intense excitement or happiness. In addition to the sense of inner freedom, as if some bond that held us had been loosened or lengthened, there is a curious sense of *control*, an odd feeling as if we have *always* held the key to our freedom. Great art and literature can induce this strange sense of freedom. Music can actually sweep us away, into a milder version of Ramakrishna's '*samadhi*'. And we observe the same thing in sexual ecstasy: the same paradoxical insight that we are *freer* than we realised.

It is as if a muscle in the brain—what might be called a concentrative mechanism—suddenly convulsed, producing a momentary but overwhelming sense of meaning. In sexual ecstasy, we receive the impression that this mechanism is situated somewhere at the front of the brain. The feeling of insight seems to be based on a recognition that the mechanism has *an independent existence*.

This is a point of central importance. Ordinarily, we vaguely assume that a crisis or emergency makes us concentrate, rather as an electric current can make a frog's leg contract. In which case, we have no direct control over the ecstasy or excitement. But then, think what happens if I find that I am drifting into a situation fraught with danger or inconvenience. I 'pull myself together' and call upon vital reserves, and I do this quite *voluntarily*. There is nothing to stop me ignoring the danger or allowing myself to become bored and discouraged. I *activate* my concentrative mechanism to meet the emergency.

And now we come to an even more important insight. The concentrative mechanism *is* a mechanism, a kind of computer, rather than a mere 'muscle'. If I contract a muscle and allow it to relax again, there are no after-effects. Sexual ecstasy lasts for only a few moments, therefore we conclude that it is a kind of muscular convulsion that cannot be maintained. And we tend to make the same assumption about all flashes of inner freedom. But anyone who has ever practised the simplest meditation techniques knows that this is untrue. With a little practice, meditation can induce a mood of inner freedom that can last for hours. So can the technique I have called gliding. Ouspensky learned to wander around St Petersburg in an almost continuous state of self-remembering. And Bennett's intense efforts raised him to a completely new level of inner freedom at Fontainebleau. In both these cases the robot was made to move out of the driving seat—or at least, to relinquish some of his hold on freedom.

Again, Bennett's account provides an important clue. He speaks of the pain of continuing the Gurdjieff 'movements': 'A deadly lassitude took possession of me, so that every movement became a supreme effort of will . . . Soon I ceased to be aware of anything but the music and my own weakness . . . Time lost the quality of before and after. There was no past and no future, only the present agony of making my body move . . .' In such a state of exhaustion and discomfort, a man's movements become almost entirely automatic; the mind tries to withdraw from the suffering body. Yet sheer fatigue, the need to stop the body from collapsing altogether forces the mind to make continual efforts of concentration—sudden momentary *convulsions*. And, at a certain point, Bennett found that he 'was filled with the influx of an immense power.' The computer, the 'concentrative mechanism', had finally done its work and released immense supplies of 'vital reserves'.

The point to note here is that all that was required were sudden convulsions of effort; a number of convulsions continued over a certain time period. But the convulsions seem to have a *cumulative* effect on the computer until, at a certain point, it releases the vital reserves. It is like an inefficient business firm that needs to receive a dozen letters of complaint before it pays any attention; but when it finally does, it goes to enormous lengths to satisfy the customer.

This analogy also makes clear why the muscle comparison is unsatisfactory. A muscle can be strengthened if it is used enough; but this may take days or weeks. On the other hand, anyone who spends five minutes making sudden convulsive efforts of concentration—as if responding to extreme danger—and relaxing between each one, will discover that it is not difficult to induce flashes of freedom.

To recognise that we can induce states of heightened awareness through a fairly simple technique is to understand what Charlotte Bach meant when she said that human freedom is *continuous*, from moment to moment. It also enables us to see clearly how man differs from most other animals on this planet. Animal behaviour is almost entirely 'programmed'. This means, for example, that if two dogs are fighting, and one of them wishes to surrender, it only has to roll over and show its belly; no matter how angry the other dog might feel, it will stop fighting. Man is, by comparison, a de-programmed species; if the enemy raises his arms in a gesture of surrender, there is nothing to stop the winner from battering him to death. In a world with sophisticated weapons of war, this obviously has serious consequences for human survival. But the de-programming also means that man has far greater control over his inner freedom than any animal. And this freedom depends on intelligence—that is, on insight and knowledge. The technique of inducing inner freedom by reinforced efforts of concentration will not work for a very stupid person, because he has no clear idea of what he is trying to achieve. The more we can achieve *insight* into what we are trying to do, the easier it becomes.

This recognition has an interesting corollary. When we are in our usual semi-automatic state, we tend to be preoccupied with fairly trivial concerns—our *immediate* aims. In states of inner freedom, we become aware of wider horizons of values; matters that had previously caused us anxiety or tension now seem absurdly unimportant. But the process can be made to work the other way. We can achieve a degree of inner freedom by deliberately contemplating our wider values, the things we love and care about most. (These wider values can even be purely impersonal: philosophy, history, mountains; they work just as effectively.)

Moods of inner freedom can also induce a release from our normal physical limitations. William James noted that 'women excel men in their power of keeping up sustained moral excitement', and by way of evidence points to mothers who have gone without sleep for days while nursing sick children. He also cites the case of Colonel Baird-Smith, who sustained himself throughout the six-week siege of Delhi in 1857 almost entirely on brandy, yet never felt even slightly drunk; again, the sense of wider values—the town was full of women and children who would be massacred in the event of a surrender —released a capacity for endless physical effort, in spite of the pain of various wounds, sores and ulcers. The same principles can be seen in operation in Zen in the art of archery, as described by Herrigel; the archer achieves an incredible degree of accuracy simply by striving for inner freedom; the powers of the 'real self' are far greater than those of the robot. And to speak of Zen brings us to the dividing line between the physical and spiritual, and points to the interesting notion familiar to Hindu ascetics, that an increase in inner freedom involves a natural increase in psychic powers.

The robot is essential to all life, yet it is also a jailer. A man who has nothing to do but sit in an armchair all day or weed the garden is apparently free by all normal definitions; yet if his consciousness is largely controlled by the robot, then he is really tied hand and foot.

Darwin believed that life is basically a struggle for survival; and on the purely physical level, he is obviously right. But it is also a struggle for inner freedom. All creatures seek out stimuli that will excite them; that is why lambs gambol and kittens chase balls of wool and puppies indulge in mock battles. When a species—or an individual—has solved the immediate problems of survival, it faces the next and far more difficult problem: of preventing the robot from robbing it of its freedom. When monkeys are taken out of the wild and placed in a zoo, their sexual activity increases dramatically; it becomes a way of defeating the robot. This also explains why man's sexual activity continues all the year round, instead of being a periodic urge, as in most animals; he uses sex as a source of excitement, to make him feel more alive. He has utilised aggression in the same way. The conquests of Alexander the Great, Attila the Hun, Genghis Khan, cannot be explained in terms of any biological or territorial urge; they were absurd expressions of the urge to inner freedom—absurd because they were found to fail. The excitement of physical conquest causes a temporary increase in freedom, but it is like stretching a piece of elastic, which snaps back as soon as the end is released. When the Persians first swept on to the world scene, they were hardy nomads who could fight like demons and who quickly subdued the world from India to Egypt; yet within a generation or two, success had made them effete and lazy. When Alexander conquered the Persians, his empire was so vast that it took him five years to wander around it; when he returned home, he could think of nothing to do but set out to conquer Africa.

It may have been man's obsessive interest in sex that led to the first major step in his inner evolution. Creatures whose main problem is survival seek only one quality in a mate: strength, the ability to be a good provider and protector. But when species has achieved a degree of leisure, other qualities become desirable: grace, elegance, charm, intelligence. Men may be chiefly interested in a girl's sexual allure, but they rate intelligence among the desirable sexual qualities. (Even in the *Arabian Nights*, where women seem to be regarded chiefly as objects of male pleasure, it is the intelligence of Scheherezade that places her above the others.) So man began breeding for intelligence. And intelligence began to reveal the correct solution to the problem of the robot. War only 'tightens the sinews' for as long as it happens to last. Man possesses a strange ally capable of tightening the sinews while he sits in a chair. It is called imagination. And it is basically a form of inner purpose. Philosophers and artists and saints have discovered that their methods—involving imagination and disciplines of the mind—are more effective than those of the conquerors. They can produce a strange sense of widening horizons, of inner breathing-space.

In some men, this need for inner breathing-space has become so urgent that it takes precedence over all their other needs; it leads them to perform apparently masochistic acts of self-discipline. These men, whom I have labelled 'Outsiders', are driven by an obscure craving for wider horizons, for deeper knowledge, for greater control of their freedom. They feel an instinctive loathing of the people who are absorbed in the trivial values of everday life, and are impatient of the stupid, whose inner freedom is almost non-existent.

For the past two or three millennia, the history of civilisation could be written almost entirely in terms of these men whose major concern has been inner freedom: Socrates, Pythagoras, Confucius, Buddha, Jesus, Aquinas, Dante, Leonardo, Spinoza, Goethe, Nietzsche . . . Scientists should also be included, for, as Einstein pointed out, 'one of the strongest motives that lead men to art and science is to escape from everyday life, with its painful crudity and hopeless dreariness, from the fetters of one's own ever-shifting desires . . . This may be compared with the townsman's irresistible longing to escape from his noisy, cramped surroundings into the silence of high mountains.'

The past two centuries have seen an interesting development: the widespread reappearance of the Outsider as a social (and literary) phenomenon. Cultural historians have pointed out that this is a sign of a disintegrating society. But the phenomenon may be viewed less pessimistically. If we think again of that early human ancestor who felt out of place because he was more intelligent than his fellows, we can see that his solution of the problem depended entirely on his own effort. If others regarded him as an awkward misfit, he would probably not survive. If he was to be accepted as an equal, he had to prove that he could hunt and fight as well as the others. So a combination of intelligence and toughness came to be favoured by natural selection. Then came a point in the history of the human race when the Outsider found an easier way of adjusting. Man had discovered religion, and religion requires priests and *shamans*. The Outsider became a member of the priestly caste and made a virtue out of being a misfit. Religion offered him a natural haven, and allowed him to side-step the need for inner conflict.

The past few centuries have seen the steady decline of religion, so that the Church has ceased to be the natural refuge of the Outsiders. They have been forced to stand on their own feet and try to solve their own problems. Consequently, the casualty rate has been high. But from the evolutionary point of view, this can be only an advantage. And if the inner conflict theory of evolution is correct, man is now in a better position than he has been for the past two thousand years.

2

Messages from Space and Time

———◆———

In late August, 1976, I attended a Parascience Conference organised by Peter Maddock at London's City University. There were reports by Dr Ted Bastin on his experiments with Uri Geller, by Professor Douglas Dean on his experiments in precognition and psychic healing, and by Professor John Taylor on his lack of success with Kirlian photography. There was also a great deal of highly technical talk about electromagnetic fields, thermal radio frequencies, and organisationally closed biological systems.

The weather was oppressively hot that weekend; for the past few months, England had been suffering from its worst drought in two centuries. Stifled yawns suggested that some of the audience would have been grateful for less abstruse entertainment. It came in the middle of the afternoon from a big, broad-shouldered American who looked as if he were dressed for a camping holiday. His name was Ted Owens, and he was introduced as the 'the PK man'. He spoke in a booming voice that carried easily to every part of the room without the use of a microphone, and within minutes he had us all wide awake.

What he claimed, briefly, was that he was in touch with flying saucers, and that through them, he was able to control the weather and cause storms.

As a child, he explained, he had noticed that he often had the ability to read people's minds; but, in the manner of children, he had taken this faculty for granted. As an adult, he had been through fifty or so professions, including jazz drummer, boxer, private eye, lifeguard, knife-thrower and magician. He was now inclined, he said, to believe that he had been somehow prompted to take all these jobs, to prepare him for his future work.

One night in 1965, when he was forty-five, he had been driving along a road near Fort Worth, Texas; suddenly, he and his daughter saw a great cigar-shaped object approaching over the next field, flashing coloured lights. Then, as it came close to the car, it vanished, as if all the lights had suddenly been turned off. He suspected that what he had seen was a UFO.

From that day on, his life began to change. Not long after, there was a violent thunderstorm, and he proceeded to amuse his daughter by pretending that he could make the lightning strike wherever he liked. This was not entirely a joke; he believed—in theory at least—that it ought to be possible to control the weather by psychokinesis. To his mild surprise, it *seemed* to work. During the following weeks, there were several thunderstorms, and he had the opportunity to repeat the experiment. And he soon became convinced that the lightning really *did* seem to obey his suggestions.

When the family moved to Phoenix, Arizona, and found the place in the middle of a drought, it suddenly struck him that his curious abilities might be of some practical use. He told his family that he intended to make it rain, then tried willing it to happen. The storm that followed alarmed everyone with its violence. It also finally convinced him that this was not a case of wishful thinking or self-deception. Like H. G. Wells's Man Who Could Work Miracles, Ted Owens apparently possessed some strange latent powers. The next step was to make a public demonstration. So he wrote to the local newspapers, and explained that he intended to cause storms over the next week or so. And he did—eight of them.

Since he had copies of his original letters to the newspapers and the news items describing the storms, he felt it should be fairly easy to convince government agencies of his powers and persuade them to make use of him for the public good. But all his approaches were ignored. It gradually dawned on him that there is no place in the world-view of civil servants for men who can work miracles.

His own view of his powers was that they were some sort of interaction between his own mind and 'the intelligence behind Nature'. One day, a telepathic message seemed to float into his head, telling him that remarkable magnetic phenomena would appear over the North and South Poles. Shortly afterwards—on January 8, 1965—a huge, disc-shaped craft was seen over the South Pole and was reported in many newspapers. It suddenly dawned on Ted Owens that the intelligence he had contacted was not that of mother nature, but of beings from outer space.

By this point in his narrative, the audience didn't really care whether Owens was insane or not. His manner, of course, lacked the kind of nervous modesty that British audiences take to be a guarantee of honesty; but the newspaper reports, which he passed around the audience, looked authentic enough. Unless they were elaborate forgeries, produced on a number of different printing presses, they showed conclusively that he *had* frequently written to newspapers, predicting heavy storms, and that the storms had occurred on schedule. At the end of his lecture, he received loud cheers. He concluded by adding, as an afterthought, that he was going to demonstrate his powers by ending our British drought.

My wife and I wandered out into the stifling air of late afternoon, our minds now occupied with the question of what time the pubs would open. The sky had clouded over. Ten minutes later, as we walked in the direction of Holborn, the first large drop of rain splashed on the hot pavement.

Ted Owens proved to be right. Not only was the drought over; it proved to be the beginning of one of the wettest winters on record.

What is any rational person to make of all this? The obvious explanation, I suppose, is coincidence. But if you keep on applying it to case after case in the Ted Owens dossier, it begins to look a little thin. In May, 1971, Mount Etna erupted, and a river of lava half a mile wide and eighteen feet deep destroyed vineyards and orchards. By May 20, it was heading directly for the little town of Sant'Alfio. Ted Owens proceeded to exert his powers, through the agency of his 'space intelligences' (or SI's, as he calls them); the lava missed Sant'Alfio, turning aside shortly before it arrived at the town. On October 23, 1973, Owens notified Dr Max Fogel, director of Mensa in New York, that he would ask a UFO to appear within a hundred miles of Cape Charles, Virginia, and show itself to the police; on October 25, a UFO appeared over the head of a policeman in Chase City, within the specified hundred miles, and hovered for fifteen minutes; an affidavit by Dr Fogel attests this. In October 1970, Owens approached a post office employee named W. Ramos at Norfolk, Virginia, and told him that he had learned telepathically that someone intended to bomb the post office. One week later, a bomb was thrown at the West 20th Street post office, fortunately causing little damage. On August 10, 1972, Owens told a friend in the State Liquor Store at Cape Charles that robbers were planning to rob either a bank or liquor store in the area and to be on his guard. Later the same day, four men held up a bank at the nearby town of Keller, taking $52,000. Ted Owens' file includes press cuttings about the bombing and bank robbery and signed affidavits from the two people concerned, confirming that he predicted these events in advance.

All this, admittedly, suggests another hypothesis: that Owens may simply have highly developed powers of precognition. In that case, his space intelligences would be what another psychic, Susanne Padfield (Mrs Ted Bastin) calls 'psychic support figures'. She argues that the majority of people who claim psychic powers believe that some outside agency or force is behind their manifestation. When she herself discovered that she possessed powers of psychokinesis—which have been tested in the laboratory—she found it necessary to believe that she was obtaining the power from some kind of cosmic entity or space intelligence. She had to *imagine* that she was invoking these intelligences in order to make her powers work; other psychics, she discovered, had to imagine they were directing a laser beam of atomic power, or a vortex of rushing water. She decided to see if her powers still worked if she abandoned her belief in cosmic entities and tried to 'do it herself'. They worked as well as ever. She concluded, naturally, that the cosmic entities were basically a means of focusing her imagination, and counter-acting her negative expectations.

All this could certainly apply to Ted Owens. He explains that when he wishes to contact his space intelligences, he summons up an image of a small chamber, with two tiny, grasshopper-like creatures, who are looking down into some kind of oval machine with a television screen. They can see him on the screen, and the machine translates his words into high frequency sound waves. But psychic support figures or no, he can sometimes be wrong. Among the papers he sent me, I find a prediction of 'worldwide demonstrations of UFO power' during the summer of 1970 and an unprecedented number of UFO sightings—'the greatest show ever put on'. As far as I know, this did not occur. Neither did the widespread wars that he prophesised for 1974 and 1975, 'loss of life and bloodshed that will be incredible in modern times'. There were, admittedly, plenty of localised conflicts, like the one that reduced Beirut to a pile of rubble; but hardly anything 'incredible in modern times'. (Owens is honest enough to leave this prediction in his file.)

Ted Owens is a good example of the problems that arise when we venture into the field of space intelligences and cosmic entities. Anyone who has ever taken the trouble to look into the matter will agree that *something* seems to be going on. Of course, a large number of the reported sightings are either imagination or downright lies. Regrettably, it is probably necessary to rule out every case of a sighting in which there were no independent witnesses, since we have no means of knowing what motives might prompt an individual to invent a story. But that still leaves a large residue of cases that have been witnessed by many people.

One of the first of these occurred long before the Second World War and was witnessed by a party that included the Russian painter Nicholas Roerich, who designed Stravinsky's *Rite of Spring* ballet. From 1925 to 1927, Roerich and his party travelled from Mongolia to India, and in his book *Altai-Himalaya*[1] he describes how, on August 5, 1926, the whole party observed a big and shiny disc moving at great speed across the sky; like so many modern UFOs, this one abruptly changed direction above their camp. There was an even earlier outbreak of UFO sightings in Thanksgiving week of 1896 in the San Francisco area, with witnesses reporting multi-coloured lights and egg-shaped airships.

But what is the purpose of UFOs? The theories extend from Professor Fred Hoyle's belief that they have been around 'since the beginning of time' and that alien intelligences have 'probably controlled our complete evolution'[2] to the altogether more alarmist view (expressed in books with titles like *The Flying Saucer Menace*) that UFOs are the advance guard of an armada of alien space crafts that will take over the earth. The dean of modern ufologists, Brinsley Le Poer Trench, takes a midway view in *Operation Earth*, in which he suggests that there are *two* lots of space people, 'the real Sky People, who have been around since time immemorial', and some more sinister aliens, who live somewhere near (or inside?) this planet; these two factions, he suggests, are engaged in a war to control the minds of men.

Most of the writers on UFOs direct a certain amount of indignation—or sad reproach—at the millions of sceptics who persist in believing that the whole phenomenon can be explained in terms of hysteria or hallucination. But this attitude is in itself unrealistic. Before anyone can be justly blamed for refusing to 'face facts', it must be shown that the facts are there to be faced. And the most baffling and frustrating thing about the UFO phenomenon is that the 'facts' point in a dozen different directions. If, as ufologists believe, these craft are controlled by extra-terrestrial intelligences, then it seems to be their deliberate policy to provide evidence that will confuse even the believers.

Perhaps the easiest way to illustrate this point is to speak of the remarkable career of Dr Andrija Puharich, one of the most single-minded psychical investigators since the late Harry Price.

Puharich's first major case is described in his book *The Sacred Mushroom*, which so impressed Aldous Huxley that he described Puharich as 'one of the most brilliant minds in parapsychology'. It concerned a young Dutch sculptor named Harry Stone who, when examining an ancient Egyptian pendant, fell into a trance and began drawing hieroglyphics on a sheet of paper; he also began to speak about the upbringing in ancient Egypt. An expert verified that the hieroglyphics were genuine, and belonged to the period of the pharaoh Snofru. They appeared to identify the writer as Ra Ho Tep, a high priest of Snofru, and also mentioned his wife Nefert (or Nofret); both identifications proved to be historically correct. In a number of subsequent trances—supervised by Puharich—Stone wrote out many more messages in ancient Egyptian, and also spoke of a forgotten cult of a 'sacred mushroom', of which historians had never heard.

One day when Puharich was hypnotising Harry Stone, another acquaintance, Alice Bouverie, also fell into a trance, and identified herself as someone who had been born in Syria. She stated that the sacred mushroom was the type now known as *amanita muscaria*, and told Puharich that a specimen could be found not far from the house in

Maine where the séance was taking place. Against all expectation, she proved to be correct.

Puharich became convinced that Harry Stone had no knowledge of ancient Egyptian language, and that one of the main purposes of the communication was to reveal the long-lost knowledge of the sacred cult of the mushroom. Stone asserted that the mushroom could 'take a man out of his body'—i.e., cause out-of-the-body experiences; coincidentally, Puharich had his one and only such experience during this investigation. In one of his trances, 'Ra Ho Tep' demanded a mushroom, and then, in the presence of Puharich and Aldous Huxley, applied it ritualistically to his tongue and the top of his head. When Stone woke up five minutes later, he was able to perform an ESP test with a hundred per cent score and describe accurately what lay in the other side of a brick wall.

This story has no ending. Stone got bored and left; Puharich was never able to check his historical data satisfactorily because so little is known about the period. It is worth mentioning, though, that his assertions about the cult of the mushroom are supported by a piece of research published in 1970, *The Sacred Mushroom and the Cross* by John M. Allegro. Allegro, who appears to be unaware of Puharich's work, also argues that there was a universal fertility cult based on sacred mushrooms in the Middle East in Biblical times; he claims that the mushroom was regarded as sacred to the god of fertility because of its phallic shape, and because it could thrust itself out of the ground so quickly. He goes on to make the controversial assertion that original Christianity was a mystery religion based on the sacred mushroom. Though his arguments came under severe attack (and not only from Christians) his examination of Greek, Sumerian and Egyptian sources certainly seems to offer surprisingly detailed support for the words of Ra Ho Tep as relayed through Harry Stone.

Puharich's chief contribution to parapsychology can be found in his next book *Beyond Telepathy* (1962), a balanced account of experiments in telepathy conducted with well-known psychics like Peter Hurkos and Eileen Garrett. It is also an attempt to create a 'physics' of paranormal experience based upon a concept of 'psi plasma', a kind of mental substance that sounds like Kilner's 'human aura'. Puharich suggests that we become good telepathic senders when we are in states of anger, fear and aggression, and good receivers when we are in states of relaxation and serenity. The first state is called adrenergia because it

occurs when the inappropriately-named sympathetic nervous system
is activated by adrenalin. When the para-sympathetic nervous system,
which is concerned with sleep, relaxation and digestion, is activated by
acetylcholine, the state is known as cholinergia. Puharich argues that
in cholinergic states the psi-plasma expands, while in adrenergic
states, it contracts. The sender doesn't really transmit telepathic messages to the receiver; he somehow *sucks* or attracts the expanded
psi-plasma of the receiver by reason of his superior force of concentration, rather as a high-density comet, passing too close to the earth,
might suck away part of its atmosphere. The theory aroused considerable discussion, and *Beyond Telepathy* quickly became a classic in its
field.

If *Beyond Telepathy* buttressed Puharich's reputation, his next book
came close to destroying it. It was called *Uri: A Journal of the Mystery of
Uri Geller* (1974). This is a straightforward narrative of Puharich's
three-year investigation of Geller; yet it ends by producing total
confusion and bewilderment.

The book begins in 1952, long before the two men met; it tells how,
when Puharich was studying a Hindu psychic named Dr Vinod, the
latter began to speak in a strange voice with a perfect English accent.
The voice explained that it was a member of the 'Nine Principles and
Forces', superhuman intelligences whose purpose is to aid human
evolution.

Three years later, travelling in Mexico, Puharich met an American
doctor and his wife, who also passed on lengthy messages from 'space
intelligences'; the remarkable thing was that these messages were a
continuation of the communications that had come through Dr
Vinod. It began to look as if 'the Nine' might really exist.

In 1963, Puharich made the acquaintance of the Brazilian 'psychic
surgeon' Arigó, who performed his operations with a kitchen knife
which he wiped on his shirt after dealing with each case. Arigó
believed he was possessed by a the spirit of a dead German surgeon;
according to his biographer, he had an unbroken record of successes
over many years.[3] Puharich was informed of Arigó's death in a car
crash, in January 1971; he afterwards became convinced that he must
have received the telephone message a quarter of an hour *before* Arigó
died.

All this is a prelude to Puharich's meeting with Geller, which
occurred in a Jaffa discotheque in August 1971. Geller's feats of tele-

pathy and precognition impressed Puharich; and if the book was restricted to describing these feats, it would undoubtedly impress most open-minded readers. But at this point, the 'extra-terrestrials' re-enter the story, and it turns into a chronicle of marvels and improbabilities. Placed in a trance, Geller described how, at the age of three, he had fallen asleep in a garden opposite his home, and awakened to see a huge, shining figure standing over him and a bright, bowl-shaped object floating in the sky overhead. And while Geller was still hypnotised, a mechanical voice began to speak from the air above his head, explaining that 'they' (the 'space intelligences') had found Geller in the garden, and had been 'programming' him ever since. Puharich, the voice said, had been selected to take care of Uri. The world was in danger of plunging into war, because Egypt was planning to attack Israel, and somehow Geller and Puharich had been given the task of averting the conflict.

When Geller recovered from the trance, he grabbed the cassette on which Puharich had been recording the proceedings, and Puharich swears he saw it vanish in Geller's hand. It was never recovered. This was to be a recurring pattern whenever 'the Nine' communicated; they would either cause the tape to vanish, or wipe the recordings from it.

It would serve no purpose to detail the marvels that fill the rest of the book. Objects are always disappearing and then reappearing. UFOs are sighted. The car engine stops and starts again for no reason. Puharich's camera bag is miraculously 'teleported' three thousand miles from New York to Tel Aviv. The war between Egypt and Israel is somehow averted, although without Puharich's intervention. This relentless succession of miracles leaves the reader bewildered and exhausted and curiosity finally turns to a kind of punch-drunk indifference.

Understandably, the book did Geller no good at all with the general public. Instead of making converts, it turned believers into sceptics. There was something comic in the assertion that Geller was the ambassador of superhuman intelligences, and that the proof lay in his ability to bend spoons. Puharich was simply pitching Geller's claim too high, and his obvious sincerity did nothing to improve the situation. The opposition could be divided into two factions: those who believed Puharich had been hoodwinked by Geller, and those who believed that Geller and Puharich were trying to hoodwink the rest of the world. Not long after the book's publication, Geller and Puharich decided to go their separate ways.

At this point, one might be forgiven for assuming that the more extreme phenomena would cease. In fact—as Stuart Holroyd reveals in a book called *Prelude to the Landing on Planet Earth*—'the Nine' have continued to manifest themselves as bewilderingly as ever. His story begins in 1974, when Puharich went to Florida to investigate a half-Indian psychic healer, Bobby Horne (this is not his real name). In a hypnotic trance, Horne began to speak in a strange voice, and introduced himself as an extra-terrestrial intelligence named Ancore. His purpose, he said, was to inform the human race that the space intelligences would be arriving on earth *en masse* during the next year or so, and to try to prepare mankind for that traumatic event. Since the voices that had spoken through Geller had made the same claim, Puharich was understandably impressed.

Further tests took place at Ossining. Others present were the author Lyall Watson, an Englishman named Sir John Whitmore, and Phyllis Schlemmer, a 'psychic' who had introduced Puharich to Bobby Horne. They were told, through 'Ancore', that Bobby Horne had been specially prepared for his healing tasks by having invisible wires inserted into his neck by the space intelligences. Equally startling information came through an 'extra-terrestrial' called Tom, who spoke through Phyllis Schlemmer, and who offered a potted history of the human race. The first civilisation was founded 32,000 years ago, in the Tarim Basin of China, by beings from space. At this time, according to 'Tom', there were 'three cultures, three divisions, from three areas of the universe'. A more advanced civilisation was begun, then destroyed through a massacre.

This was to be the pattern of the communications for some time to come. 'Ancore' spoke (through Bobby Horne) about the projected landing of UFOs, and how the space intelligences were trying to devise methods of interfering with television transmissions, so as to be able to speak directly to mankind. And Tom, speaking through Phyllis Schlemmer, went into considerable detail about earlier civilisations, and the purpose of man on earth. The earth, says Tom, is unique in the universe; every soul must pass through it sooner or later. 'It is the love of this planet that generates the energy that becomes God.' The earth is a kind of school, designed to teach the balance between the spiritual and the physical. But mankind has become too negative, and has created a force of active evil. It has become a kind of bottleneck in the universe, blocking its evolution. Unless man evolves a new type of consciousness, or unless he receives help from outside, the earth will enter a new ice age within two centuries, due to pollution of the atmosphere.

Eventually, Bobby Horne began to find all this talk about space intelligences too oppressive, and went back to his wife in Florida. Lyall Watson also declined to become a permanent part of the team, on the grounds that he had to get back to writing books. This left Puharich, Phyllis Schlemmer and Sir John Whitmore, whose fortune was to finance some of the hectic activity of the next two years.

The remainder of Holroyd's long book is too confusing for me to attempt a detailed summary. What happened, basically, was that Puharich, Whitmore and Phyllis Schlemmer spent a great deal of time rushing around the world—often suspected of being spies—and sitting in hotel rooms listening to instructions from 'Tom' and praying for world peace. Periodically, Tom congratulates them, and explains that they have just averted some international catastrophe, such as the assassination of the Palestinian leader Yasser Arafat. The book ends, as all good books should, with a dramatic climax in which the three musketeers avert a Middle Eastern war by driving around Israel holding meditation sessions and otherwise 'diffusing a vapour trail of love and peace'. At the end of this agitated pilgrimage, 'Tom' assures them that their efforts have been successful and that the Middle East will cease to be a flashpoint for some time to come. With a sound sense of literary structure, he even advises Puharich to use these events as the climax of the book he intends to write. (In fact, Puharich passed on the job to Stuart Holroyd.) We are told in a postscript that equally weird things have been taking place since the successful peace mission in March 1975, but that these must wait for a future instalment.

In the bibliography of *Prelude to the Landing on Planet Earth*, Holroyd cites a nineteenth-century classic of psychical investigation, *From India to the Planet Mars*, by Theodore Flournoy, and readers of Holroyd may find the parallel instructive. In 1894, Flournoy, a well-known psychologist, investigated the mediumship of an attractive girl named Catherine Muller (whom he called Hélène Smith). He was soon convinced of the genuineness of her powers; she was able to tell him about events that occurred in his family before he was born. In later séances, Catherine went into deeper trances, and began to describe her 'past incarnations'—as the wife of a Hindu prince of the fifteenth century, as Marie Antoinette, and as an observer of life on Mars. Flournoy remains sceptical. The Hindu incarnation is often convincing; she seemed to have considerable knowledge of the language and customs of fifteenth-century India, and even named a prince, Sivrouka Näkaya, who was later found to have been a historical personage. By contrast, the descriptions of Mars are absurd, with yellow sky, red hills, bug-eyed monsters, and buildings that look like Arab mosques. The people, according to Catherine, look just like human beings; their language, as transcribed by her, is suspiciously like French.

If any charitable spiritualists felt inclined to give Catherine the benefit of the doubt, their justification for doing so vanished in September 1976, when the Viking landing on Mars revealed the planet to be an arid desert with no sign of life—even minute organisms.

Yet Catherine Muller cannot be dismissed as a fraud, even of the unconscious variety. Her knowledge of Flournoy's past showed that she possessed genuine powers of telepathy. While she was in trance, Flournoy witnessed 'apports' of Chinese shells and coins, and even roses and violets in midwinter. Paranormal forces undoubtedly *were* at work, but Flournoy declined to allow this to persuade him that Catherine had really been a Hindu princess or had visited Mars.

Flournoy would certainly have been equally sceptical about the narrative in *Prelude to a Landing on Planet Earth*. He would see no reason for rejecting the explanation that he applied to the mediumship of 'Hélène Smith': that the answers should be sought in the unconscious minds of the participants. And it must be admitted that Hélène's identification of herself with a Hindu princess and Marie Antionette is, if anything, rather more believable than 'Tom's' revelation that Puharich had once been the god Horus (and later, Pythagoras), while Whitmore had been Thoth and Phyllis Schlemmer Isis . . .

Still, in all fairness, one has to admit that anyone who experienced the events described in *The Sacred Mushroom*, *Uri* and *Prelude to the Landing on Planet Earth* would end up convinced of the existence of space intelligences. If the whole thing is some kind of trick of the unconscious, how does it work? And *whose* unconscious? My own conviction, formed at the time when I was studying Geller at close quarters, was that Puharich himself is the key to the enigma. Uri's powers of telepathy and metal bending struck me as remarkable, and almost certainly genuine; but I never witnessed anything as spectacular as the events that occur on every other page of Puharich's book. My suspicion, quite simply, was that Puharich is himself a gifted 'psychic', and that when he and Geller met, the combination of their subconscious powers, a kind of mutual interaction and prompting, was explosive. Since Puharich was already convinced of the existence of the Nine, it was logical—and almost inevitable—that Geller's trance messages should come from these non-human intelligences. In short, Geller and Puharich somehow united to form a kind of firework display of poltergeist effects. The main question in my mind was simply whether Puharich aided and abetted these effects through wishful thinking and general dottiness.

When I finally met Puharich, and his friend Mrs Joyce Petschek, in June 1976, it was almost an anti-climax. Throughout the whole of a long evening, he neither did nor said anything to suggest mental unbalance, or even the slightest eccentricity. He is a short, grey-haired man with a bushy moustache and rather vague manner. Although in his mid-fifties, he has the kind of innocence and enthusiasm that I associate with American students. He is casual, good-natured and unpretentious. When I explained my theory that he was himself a psychic, and had been partly responsible for the Geller effects, he brooded in it for a few seconds, then said: 'You could be right, but I'm inclined to doubt it.'

It soon became clear that Puharich has had so many strange experiences that he has come almost to take them for granted. He would spend ten minutes describing with great precision a laboratory experiment in which he had tested Peter Hurkos, then tell me of some utterly weird event involving Geller that sounded like science fiction. He told me, for example, of the teleportation of a unique chunk of stone from Ossining to the hotel bedroom of a couple who were making love more than a hundred miles away. A figure identical with Geller knocked on their door and handed them the stone; and afterwards, the stone was there to prove it. But at the time, Geller was in Ossining with Puharich, and knew nothing about it. Puharich told me he had deliberately left many such stories out of his book because it was already overloaded with incredible material.

Mrs Petschek told me an equally strange story. She had been driving from Oxford to London in an attempt to catch a plane, but realised that her chances were minimal; she should have set out at least half an hour earlier. Then, quite suddenly, she found herself close to London, with plenty of time to spare. What had happened, she thinks, is that the car dematerialised at a certain point and simply reappeared fifty miles further on. Both she and a friend who was in the car thought they knew just where it had happened, and where they had 'reappeared'. I should add that Mrs Petschek struck me as being as sane and normal as Puharich, and I had no suspicion that I was witnessing a *folie à deux*. Marvels like this occasionally dropped into the conversation, but always in a rather casual way; clearly, they both accepted them in the way that I have come to accept dowsing.

Puharich obviously found my theorising about subconscious poltergeist activity unnecessary. He had long ago reached the conclusion that the Nine are a reality, and that our earth has been observed by space men for thousands of years. He believes that the earth has reached a point in its history where the Nine feel that slightly more intervention is necessary. But public miracles, like a mass landing of UFOs, are probably undesirable. Human beings have to evolve and learn to use their freedom. Too much 'help' from outside would be disastrous because it would make us lazy and dependent, like some primitive tribe suddenly invaded by twentieth-century technology. Instead, Puharich believes, the extra-terrestrials are concentrating on individuals, particularly children, so that the race is changed from within, so to speak. He claims he has studied a large number of children of astonishing psychic gifts, not simply the ability to bend spoons, like the protegés of Professor John Taylor, but telepathy and other unusual powers. The great mathematical prodigies of the past, he thinks, are a foreshadowing of what is to come.

I found all this convincing, up to a point. Nothing is more obvious than that Puharich and Mrs Petschek are totally sincere in everything that they say. Does this mean that I am convinced by the existence of the Nine? Obviously not. It is not simply a question of whether I can accept Puharich, Sir John Whitmore and Phyllis Schlemmer as honest, but whether there is now sufficient evidence to convince *any* logical person of the real existence of space beings. In matters of the paranormal, it is facts not faith that are relevant. There is a certain area within which even the most reasonable people might differ. I would personally argue that there is now an abundance of evidence for the existence of telepathy and poltergeists, but I would not quarrel unduly with scientists who felt that it was still insufficient. I would be willing to admit that there is rather less evidence for the existence of ley lines;

nevertheless I am inclined to be convinced by what there is because I am influenced by my personal experience of dowsing. For the same reason, President Jimmy Carter believes in the existence of UFOs. But there are certain matters on which there is not sufficient evidence to convince anybody; for example, whether there is life on Venus, or whether the Virgin Mary ascended to heaven in her physical body. Anybody is entitled to his belief in these matters, provided he will admit that it is a matter of personal conviction (i.e., religion) rather than of science. In the same perfectly objective sense, there is no solid evidence for any kind of extra-terrestrial beings. UFO sightings may persuade us that *something* is going on, but there is no reason to suppose that this something comes from beyond the earth. The Nine may have convinced Puharich and his associates of their existence; but on the present showing, they have no reason to complain if the rest of us decline to commit ourselves.

The Catherine Muller case reminds us that there is one more basic similarity between Puharich's experiences and some of the famous cases of psychical research: the boring inconclusiveness of the whole thing. Anyone who has heard of psychical research only at second hand might be forgiven for expecting tremendous revelations from 'adventures with the dead'. Actual study of 'spirit communications' is always a disappointment, because the dead—or whoever is responsible—seem so staggeringly trivial minded. Even the spirits of the great composers, who communicate through the London housewife Rosemary Brown, seem capable of nothing but feeble echoes of the music they wrote when alive.

Which brings me to a phenomenon which I have observed ever since I began to take an interest in 'the occult', and which might be labelled 'ambiguity'. Again and again in cases of the paranormal there is a strange insufficiency of evidence. To which a believer in UFOs or ghosts might reply: 'Does that matter when there are so many hundreds of reported instances?' The answer is: Yes, if all the instances are inconclusive. Because when you put a hundred such instances end to end, the result is not to command conviction, but to leave the reader a hundred times more baffled. If any conclusion begins to emerge at the end, it is that the answer lies in a completely different direction from what we had supposed.

A case in point is described by a leading American investigator of UFOs, John Keel, in his book *The Mothman Prophesies*. Keel differs from Puharich in believing that the UFOs are basically malevolent. He describes his own investigations into various UFO sightings in West Virginia in 1966–67, usually accompanied by another journalist, Mrs Mary Hyre. He reports numerous sightings of a huge figure—about seven feet tall—with red eyes and gigantic wings folded on its back. It was able to keep up with fast cars without even flapping its wings. It was seen by two young couples near an old ammunition dump on November 15, 1966, and again by Mary Hyre's niece, Connie Carpenter, twelve days later. Connie Carpenter's eyes became red and swollen, as if from some kind of radiation, after she had seen the creature's red eyes at close quarters. In the spring of the following year, a young couple, making love naked in the back of a car, saw a large ball of bluish fire hovering near the car; the next morning, both were heavily 'sunburned' and had red, swollen eyes. Keel's book is full of the same electronic oddities as Puharich's. Calls come through on disconnected telephones; police messages are picked up on switched-off radios; films and tape recordings turn out to be blank; cameras refuse to work when pointed at UFOs. Olive-skinned men dressed in black make a habit of calling on UFO witnesses, warning them to say nothing about what they have seen. Cows and sheep are found with their throats neatly slit and their bodies drained of blood. Pet dogs and cats disappéar in large numbers. Keel finds that his movements are actually anticipated by the opposition; for example, when he casually chooses a motel to stay at, he finds a sheaf of incomprehensible messages waiting for him at the desk.

Perhaps the real point of the parallel between Keel's experiences and Puharich's is how easy it is to be drawn into some weird sequence of events and to become totally convinced that they have an enormous, universal significance. According to himself, Keel was finally subjected to a kind of non-stop persecution by the space men, with mysterious phone calls, people impersonating him or claiming to be his secretary, and strange warning messages. He was convinced that the space men were genuine because they were able to make accurate predictions of the future. When he hypnotised a contractee in 1967, a space man named Apol began to speak through her and made exact predictions about a number of plane crashes. He aslo predicted that the Pope would be knifed to death in the Middle East, and that this would be preceded by a great earthquake. He mentioned that Robert Kennedy was in great danger. Kennedy was, of course, assassinated in the following year. The plane crashes, says Keel, occurred exactly as predicted. In July 1967, the Vatican announced that the Pope would be visiting Turkey, and an earthquake killed a thousand people there. But the Pope was not knifed to death at Istanbul airport. It was three years later, when he landed at Manila airport, that a madman tried to kill him with a long knife; fortunately, the man was overpowered by guards. Keel believes that the entities simply misread the future or got the date wrong. Similarly, he was told that Martin Luther King would be shot in the throat while standing on his balcony in Memphis; the date given was February 4, 1968. That day passed without incident; but the assassination took place, exactly as described, two months later.

In long telephone conversations with Keel, 'Apol' made another prophecy: there would be a massive power failure that would affect a large part of the United States on December 15. It would happen when President Johnson turned on the lights of the Christmas tree on the White House lawn. Keel watched the event on television; there was no power failure. But immediately after the President had thrown the switch, the programme was interrupted for an announcement—a bridge on the Ohio River had collapsed, with great loss of life. Keel knew that the only bridge along the stretch mentioned was the Silver Bridge at Point Pleasant, the town near which all the strange occurrences noted by Keel and Mary Hyre had been taking place. The space men had even warned him that a major disaster would take place along the Ohio River, but implied that it would be a factory that would blow up. Keel believes that they told him the blackout story, rather than the truth, so that he would have no opportunity to warn people.

As with Puharich, it is difficult to take Keel's story seriously. No doubt most of the phenomena occurred more or less as he described them. But it is hard to believe that large numbers of hostile creatures from other worlds are trying to infiltrate the human race. To begin with, they seem curiously incompetent. One of the men in black tries to drag a girl into his car, but she succeeds in escaping. Another one actually persuades a female contactee to get into his car and go for a drive; you would expect her to be whisked off in a space ship to Mars (or Lanulos, as their world seems to be called). Instead, she is driven to a remote spot, interrogated, taken back to the place where she was picked up, and allowed to go.

In the face of all so much exasperating ambiguity, it is tempting to blame Keel himself for his muddle-headedness and gullibility. His answer is to point to all the other UFO experts who have had the same experiences and the same problems. Practically every serious book in support of UFOs gives the same over-all impression of confusion, and many of them mention the attempts by mysterious strangers to silence witnesses. There are even a number of well-authenticated cases in which witnesses have lost all memory of what happened, as if the UFOs themselves had a device for inducing amnesia. The best known is that of Mr and Mrs Barney Hill, who were driving home from Canada in September 1961, when they saw a UFO; two hours later, they 'woke up' in their car several miles away, with no memory of the time after they saw the UFO. Under hypnosis, they were able to recall being abducted by aliens and taken aboard the UFO, where they were cross-examined, then released. Hypnosis also restored the memory of police patrolman Herb Schirmer, who was (he claimed) taken aboard a UFO in December 1967 and questioned. Schirmer said that the aliens were wearing some type of overall with an emblem of a winged serpent.

This seems to suggest that UFOs are controlled by beings from other worlds who, for reasons best known to themselves, wish to keep humanity as ignorant as possible. Yet writers who have made an extensive study of the subject admit that this hypothesis fails to fit the facts. For example, in the cases cited above, why did the aliens not realise that human memory can be restored under hypnosis? Dr Jacques Vallee, one of the leading UFO experts, writes: 'In every instance of the UFO phenomenon I have been able to study in depth, I have found as many rational elements as I have absurd ones, and many that I could interpret as friendly and many that seemed hostile. No matter what approach I take, I can never explain more than half of the facts.'[4]

As we read through Keel's book *The Mothman Prophecies*, certain interesting points emerge. There is, for example, the curious episode of the 'fear zone'. In December 1966, Keel accompanied Connie Carpenter to the place where she had seen the huge winged man. They entered a ruined building on the old ammunition dump, when suddenly she saw its red eyes watching her. *The others saw nothing*, but Keel was convinced that Connie's hysterics were real. Later that evening, Keel drove around on his own for several hours, hoping for more UFO sightings. He saw nothing, but he came across an area (in the woods) 'where I was suddenly engulfed in fear'. 'I stepped on the gas, and after a few yards, my fear vanished as quickly as it came.' He got out of the car and walked back towards the 'zone of fear'. 'I was perfectly calm until I took one step too many, and was back in the zone. I almost panicked and ran . . . After I had gone about fifteen feet I stepped outside the zone and everything was normal again.'

Keel's guess is that he was walking through a zone of 'ultrasonic waves', presumably sprayed out by a UFO. Tom Lethbridge would have had a different suggestion to make. He would have instantly recognised the 'zone of fear' as what he called a ghoul, like the one he encountered on Ladram beach. Lethbridge had also noted that such zones begin and end abruptly, as if surrounded by an invisible wall.

The interesting thing is that Keel himself has a strong suspicion that he is dealing with something closer to the paranormal than to UFO phenomena. But, unlike Lethbridge, he has no general frame of reference, no basic theory of the supernatural. So his occasional comments on such matters only make confusion worse confounded. He speaks of a house in Greenwich Village that was reported to be haunted by a figure who wore a black cape and a wide-brimmed slouch hat. No person of that description had lived—or died—in the house; but a writer named Walter Gibson had lived there in the thirties; and his best known creation was a character called The Shadow, who wore a black cape and wide-brimmed slouch hat. 'Could this,' asks Keel, 'be some kind of residue from Walter Gibson's very powerful mind?' Could it be what the Tibetans call a *tulpa*, a mind-creature, brought into being by a magical act of imagination? He goes on to ask why so much UFO activity is concentrated around old archaeological sites in the Mississippi valley and around the Indian snake mounds of Ohio. He points out that these mounds are 'laid out and constructed with the same kind of mathematical precision found in the pyramids of Egypt', and that 'to plan and build such mountains of shaped earth required technical skills beyond the simple nomadic wood Indians'. And he completes the reader's bewilderment by asking whether UFOs could be *tulpas* 'created by a long forgotten people and doomed forever to senseless manoeuvres in the night skies'.

Considering that Keel knows nothing of Lethbridge's theory of tape recordings and has apparently never heard of leys, this is little short of inspiration. We are able to supply the missing links in the chain of his argument: that the mind of man can, under certain conditions, create phantoms, and that these phantoms can continue to exist indefinitely at certain places on the earth's surface, places that were chosen by ancient man as his 'sacred sites'. (It is also worth noting that these Indians were nomadic; like the Australian aborigines described by Charles Mountford, they probably moved from sacred site to sacred site at different times of the year.)

But is it remotely likely that UFOs themselves could be phantoms? Oddly enough, the idea had occurred independently to an English naturalist named F. W. Holiday, who arrived at the notion in a peculiarly roundabout manner. In August 1962, as he was standing beside Loch Ness at six o'clock in the morning, he suddenly sighted the famous monster, a black, glistening object looking like a vast overturned boat. He spend the next five years studying the phenomenon and marshalled all his evidence in a book called *The Great Orm of Loch Ness* (1968). He came to the conclusion that the monster was some kind of giant slug and even suggested the precise species: a Carboniferous creature called *Tullimonstrum gregarium*, an odd-looking thing like a submarine with a broad tail and long neck. He also noted the enormous number of 'worm' legends in British mythology, and how often the monster seemed to be associated with evil.

In the second half of the 1960s, there were many sightings of monsters in smaller lakes, not only in Scotland, but also in Wales and Ireland. Holiday went to investigate a particularly circumstantial report from Lough Fadda in Connemara; the monster had been seen at close quarters by the local librarian and three other witnesses. What puzzled Holiday was that Lough Fadda seemed too small to house a 'monster'; a creature of the size described would soon eat all the fish and die of starvation. The same was true of nearby Lough Nahooin, where Holiday and his team tried to trap the resident 'peiste' with nets. Something disturbed their nets, but there was no evidence that it was a monster.

Holiday's extensive reading in worm mythology led him to conclude that worms were ancient religious symbols, probably associated with evil. He also noticed that there seemed to be another symbol, often found in association with the worm or serpent: a disc. And the disc seemed to be a symbol of goodness. Bronze-Age tombs are full of disc artifacts, which archaeologists have always assumed to be images of the sun. Bronze-Age burial mounds are often shaped like discs and are known as disc barrows or saucer barrows. Sir James Frazer in *The Golden Bough* has gone on record as doubting whether the disc artifacts are objects of sun worship so much as symbols of purification, or protection against evil: the ancient equivalent of the Christian cross. (In fact, the post-Christian Celts combined the two symbols into the 'Celtic cross', which can still be found in hedgerows all over Cornwall.) Holiday made another interesting observation. From the air, disc barrows look exactly look UFOs, with their raised mound in the middle and an 'eye' in the centre of the mound. And the other type of Bronze-Age barrow, the long barrow, looks very like the cigar-shaped UFO from which smaller ones have often been seen emerging.[5] Many of the disc artifacts look more like UFOs than sun discs.

It was his totally frustrating experiences with many Irish loughs that finally led Holiday to the conclusion that the monsters are not solid creatures of flesh and blood but some kind of ghost. At least, they had two of the main characteristics of ghosts; they struck witnesses as perfectly real and solid, yet could vanish without leaving a trace. Moreover, the closest examination of the loughs failed to reveal the slightest ecological trace of their existence.

When he also noted the frequency of UFO sightings above lakes where there are reports of monsters, he came to the conclusion that he was not dealing with real dragons and discs, but with some kind of archetypal symbol of good and evil.. He argues this theory with considerable skill and conviction in his book *The Dragon and the Disc*. One of his main arguments is one that has also been advanced by Keel: the frequency with which UFOs and ghosts have been associated. Holiday mentions the case of a girl called Annabelle Randall who, on October 7, 1965, was approaching a bridge near Warminster in her car when she and her fiancé saw a figure sprawled in the road; when they looked again, it had vanished. Many fatal accidents had occurred near the bridge. On the way home near the same spot, she saw a UFO-like object soaring away into the sky and two strange-looking men in 'space suits' approaching the bridge; she drove off at top speed. A month later, a retired group captain and his wife saw a blood-soaked figure stagger out of the hedge near the bridge, and another 'space man'. By the time the group captain had stopped the car and reversed, both had vanished.

Unlike Keel, Holiday knows something about the significance of ley lines. But he seems to be unaware that *all kinds* of strange phenomena have been observed over leys—particularly at the nodal points: ghosts, ghouls and poltergeists, as well as UFOs. (Loch Ness itself has a major ley line running down the middle.)[6] So he is not aware that the ghosts and the UFOs could be unconnected: in other words, that they could be totally different types of phenomenon. If, as Lethbridge was inclined to believe, UFOs come from another dimension, then ley intersections may be the ideal crossing points between the two worlds. If an accident black spot happened to be at a ley intersection, one might expect the tape recording phenomenon to occur there. (If Stephen Jenkins is right about the disorientation that can occur at nodal points, then the ley may be responsible for the high accident rate.) But there need be no more connection between the two sets of phenomena than between a car and a train that happen to use the same level crossing. Moreover, the evidence seems to suggest that the serpent symbol is associated with the earth force rather than with evil.

However, Holiday had a number of experiences during the investigations that convinced him that there *were* hostile forces at work. To begin with, he became convinced of the existence of a 'neuralgia syndrome'. At Lough Nahooin, he experienced toothache throughout the investigation, and his companion also suffered neuralgic pains. The toothache stopped as soon as the investigation was called off. Later, two marine biologists told him of a similar experience when they had been investigating a lake monster; one of the two was told by a local dentist that he had an impacted wisdom tooth that had triggered off St Vincent's disease, but the Glasgow Dental Hospital could find absolutely nothing wrong. Holiday thought he might have found a solution when he discovered a quotation in Sir Wallis Budge's book on *Babylonian Life and History* about a 'worm' that drinks among the teeth, destroying the strength of the gums.

Holiday went to Loch Ness to investigate a UFO sighting reported by Jan-Ove Sundberg, a Swedish journalist, who claimed to have seen the aliens and their craft in a clearing in the woods above Foyers, where he had become 'unaccountably lost'. After reporting the sighting, Sundberg said he had been persecuted by a man in black; he ended by having a nervous breakdown. Holiday located three other people who had seen UFOs in the same area at about the same time as Sundberg's experience. As he sat talking to Mrs Winifred Cary, wife of Wing Commander Basil Cary, about UFO sightings, he mentioned that he meant to go and examine the place where Sundberg had seen the UFO; Mrs Cary advised him against it. At that moment, there was a tremendous rushing sound like a tornado outside the window, followed by several loud thumps. Holiday heard the noises, which went on for about a quarter of a minute; oddly enough, Wing Commander Cary heard nothing. Mrs Cary not only heard the noises, but, as she testified in a signed account, also saw something: 'Looking over my shoulder I got an impression that there was something at the window although I couldn't see exactly what it was. And then, looking at Ted [Holiday], I saw a beam of white light that shot across the room from the window on my left. I saw a white circle of light on Ted Holiday's forehead . . .' Wing Commander Cary searched the garden, but found no sign of disturbance.

The next morning, as Holiday left his caravan, he saw a man in black, who stood with his back to the loch, staring fixedly at him. 'Simultaneously I felt a strong sensation of malevolence, very cold and quite passionless.' The man wore a helmet, mask and gloves. Holiday walked past the man, tempted to lurch against him to see if he was real. As he passed him, he heard a 'whispering or whistling sound', and turned to find that the man had vanished, although there was nowhere for him to vanish to. This episode made him decide to take Mrs Cary's advice and avoid the place where Sundberg had seen the UFO.

The following year, when Holiday returned to continue his investigations at the loch, he suffered a heart attack at precisely the place where he had seen the man in black.

Can these observations bring us any closer to an understanding of this bewildering subject? Let us briefly review the evidence presented in this chapter.

According to Ted Owens, UFOs are controlled by a race of superbeings from another galaxy, whose intentions towards the earth are, on the whole, benevolent. Sceptics will object that there is no objective proof of the existence of these benevolent super-beings; they could just as easily be some unexplored power of the human mind, if indeed they have any existence or reality at all.

Puharich shares Owens' view about the super-beings, whom he identifies as the Nine, but adds that there are also hostile forces, which emanate from the human mind, but which have somehow taken on an independent existence. Puharich's 'communicators' also allege that there are many human 'souls' who are trapped in a kind of limbo, unaware that they are dead, and capable of exercising negative influences. But Puharich's super-beings are, to put it mildly, less than convincing, and could well be no more than a product of his own mind—a kind of poltergeist effect, emanating from somewhere else on the ladder of selves.

For there seems little doubt that the human mind *can* create elaborate fantasies, which then defy all the laws of nature by coming to life. In recent years. Dr George Owen and his wife Iris have underlined the point by devising one of the most dazzling experiments in the history of psychical research. In the early 1970s, members of the Toronto Society for Psychical Research decided to attempt to *create* a ghost. Their method was to invent a historical personage, work out his life-story and background in some detail, then try to bring him into existence through séances. They invented a character called Philip, a contemporary of Oliver Cromwell, who fell in love with a beautiful gypsy named Margo and made her his mistress. Philip's wife Dorothea found out about the affair and had Margo accused of witchcraft. Margo was tried and burned at the stake; Philip committed suicide by throwing himself from the battlements of his house, Diddington Manor. (The house actually existed, and photographs of it were placed around the séance room.)

After several months of 'meditation' séances, the group had achieved no success and decided to try a new approach. They relaxed and talked about Philip and even sang songs. One evening, there was a rap on the table. This was not quite what they had expected; they had hoped to cause Philip to 'materialise'. However, they questioned the 'spirit' in the usual way (one rap for yes, two for no), and soon verified that this was 'Philip', who repeated the history they had invented for him. Eventually, Philip caused the table to dance all over the room. He even gave a public exhibition of his powers, making the table dance, unaided, up a flight of steps on to the platform.

Philip's account of his life was so circumstantial that some members of the group found themselves wondering if such a person had actually existed and by strange coincidence they had invented a true story. On one occasion, when Philip declared he had been in Bohemia, Dr Owen asked him whether he had known Elizabeth, the 'Winter Queen'; Philip said that he had. Owen reminded him that he had earlier denied knowing Prince Rupert, the Winter Queen's brother-in-law. (Rupert was commander of the Royal Cavalry during the Civil War, in which Philip had fought on the king's side). Philip denied Rupert was the Winter Queen's brother-in-law; and when Owen checked it in a history book, he found that Philip was right. On the other hand, when

Philip was asked about his religion, he denied that he was a Catholic or a Protestant, then admitted to being Anglo–Catholic, a label which did not exist in Cromwell's time.

Here, then, is an example of a group of people inventing a fantasy and endowing it with life, a process that sound analogous to the Tibetan method of creating a *tulpa*, as described by Alexandra David-Neel. In *Magic and Mystery in Tibet*, she tells how she succeeded in creating a phantom monk, who looked so solid that a herdsman once took him for a real lama. But eventually, her creation began to escape her control; he became vaguely hostile and malignant, and it took her six months of hard work to 'dematerialise' him. In *Psychic Self-Defence*, Dion Fortune has a similar story of how she involuntarily created an 'elemental' in the form of a wolf, which terrorised the household until she 're-absorbed' it. [7]

Oddly enough, both John Keel and Ted Holiday subscribe to some version of the *tulpa* theory. Both accept that there are two sets of paranormal forces at work, one benevolent and one hostile. Both seem willing to grant that the benevolent forces may possess a real, objective existence, but that the hostile forces are not real in the same sense. They feel that these forces are *tulpas* that have escaped the control of the minds that created them or involuntarily conjured them into existence. Holiday seems inclined to identify the 'good forces' with UFOs (or discs), and the evil ones with dragons or serpents, although his later observations of hostile forces connected with UFOs appears to contradict this view. Both Keel and Holiday suspect that various paranormal phenomena are connected with the forces of the earth. Their belief that they *are* dealing with paranormal phenomena seems to be supported by the observation that many of the phenomena are not noticed by everyone—only by those who are 'tuned in' to them.

Perhaps the most frighteningly pessimistic view of the whole problem is the one that has been propounded by the scientist and ufologist Thomas E. Bearden. [8] Bearden writes:

> The personal unconscious can sometimes directly affect the material world; the poltergeist phenomenon and psychokinesis are direct examples. The collective species unconscious is vastly more powerful than the personal unconscious, and under appropriate conditions, it can directly materialise a thought form, which may be of an object, or even of a living being. The emerging thought form (*tulpa*) starts as an

archetype in the collective . . . unconscious and is progressively altered, shaped and formed by the shallower layers of unconsciousness which it must traverse on its way to materialisation. UFOs, fairies, angels, sasquatches, Loch Ness monsters, etc., are thus *tulpa* materialisations from the unconscious—i.e., they are 'dreams' of the race.

Jung also suggested that UFOs are psychological projections. What Bearden goes on to propound is rather more alarming, if also more incredible. He points out that Arnold's first sighting of UFOs corresponded with the beginning of the Cold War and that subsequent waves of sightings have often preceded or accompanied serious tensions: the Cuban missile crisis, the Yom Kippur war, and so on. He seems to take the view that they are not merely projections of anxiety on the part of non-aggressors but may also reflect the hostile intentions of aggressors. He believes that Stalin had every intention of attacking the West before the discovery of the atomic bomb made it impracticable, and that since then, the Soviets have continued to develop secret weaponry and to finance a left-wing terrorist war against the West. The new weapons are 'psychotronic'—capable of influencing the mind by some form of radiation. (He claims that there is evidence that the Russians have been using weak microwave radiation against the American Embassy in Moscow since 1960.)

He goes on, 'Now if all this unbelievable scenario has any validity . . . one ought to see an increase in the tulpoid phenomena of a sharply symbolic nature which can be appropriately psychoanalysed.' And this manifestation, he believes, is cattle mutilation. ('The cow is the Western symbol par excellence; Western children nurse on cow's milk.') As the Russians prepare to attack NATO, we will be forewarned by a new shock, 'the tulpoid symbology . . . raised to the highest degree', and represented by a wave of mutilations of human females.

Most readers may feel, as I do, that Dr Bearden is seeking a paranormal explanation where a normal one would be more convincing. Sex murders involving mutilation have increased sharply in the United States during the past decade or so, but no one suggests that *tulpas* are responsible; the same probably applies to cattle mutilations. Overcrowding tends to incubate abnormal sexual impulses, particularly sadistic aggression towards the female. In the past, this expressed itself chiefly in the urban areas; nowadays, when most people own cars, the urban violence and frustration can express itself in remote country areas, where the most accessible victims are cattle.

But before we accuse Dr Bearden of over-reacting to the whole problem, it is important to become aware of the facts he has taken into account. The writer Ed Sanders has published a lengthy account of cattle mutilations,[9] and of his own investigations into them, which makes it clear that something very strange is going on. This is no casual slashing with a knife. 'Tongues, eyes, ears, tails, genitals and udders were removed—all perfectly snipped as with a tailor's shears. The rears of the animals were sometimes bored as if the perpetrator were using a razor-sharp geologist's core sampler.' Some appear to have been killed by chemicals that cause degeneration of the inner organs, and one mutilated heifer found in New Mexico was apparently killed by a nerve gas. Coyotes and buzzards will not touch the carcases, which decay within days. The numbers are large; in one small area around Sterling, Colorado, fifty cattle were mutilated in one year. Sadistic delinquents or the members of weird 'blood cults' could be responsible for many of the deaths, but others seem to defy such explanations. Sanders cites witnesses who claim to have observed UFOs in the areas where mutilations took place.

Towards the end of *The Mothman Prophecies*, Keel seems to reject the *tulpa* theory. Speaking of lengthy telephone conversations with the 'alien intelligence' Apol, he says:

> I felt sorry for him. It became apparent that he really did not know who or what he was. He was a prisoner in our time frame. He often confused the past with the future. I gathered that he and all his fellow entities found themselves transported backward and forward in time involuntarily, playing out their little games because they were programmed to do so, living—or existing—only so long as they could feed off the energy and minds of mediums and contactees.

Keel obviously does not realise it—he throws off the comment casually, then goes on—but he has made a suggestion whose implications are breathtaking. The first thing to note is the comment 'he did not know who or what he was. He was a prisoner of our time frame'. What is immediately striking about this is that it applies to all of us. Philosophers and scientists do their best to investigate the universe; but when we have formulated our theories, we have to come back to the basic recognition that we have no idea of who we are or what we are doing here. *We* are also trapped in our time frame, and it seems impossible to see beyond it. So these creatures of Keel's are like human beings, only more so. We also play little games that we are programmed to play.

What Keel has said here suggests that these creatures belong to Lethbridge's 'next whorl of the spiral', or to Monroe's curious limbo between two worlds. Many ghosts behave in the same irrational manner, as if caught in a kind of nightmare in which they repeat the same action over and over again. Mediums have always insisted that the world is full of bewildered spirits, unaware that they are dead, wandering around helplessly. All this reinforces the suspicion that Keel is not dealing with genuine space men, but with some kind of supernatural phenomenon.

But perhaps the most significant comment in Keel's description of Apol is the final one: 'living—or existing—only so long as they could feed off the energy and minds of mediums and contactees'. By mentioning mediums as well as UFO contactees, Keel clearly implies that Apol and his kind are spirits, existing in a kind of limbo; not only this, but that they can only escape their shadow life by vampirising energy from human beings.

This comment suggests a startling new interpretation, not just of UFO phenomena, but of the whole history of spiritualism. Something is certainly going on, but probably not what has so far been thought. Half the spirits contacted by mediums are not what they profess to be, but are merely the tramps, con-men and petty crooks of the spirit world, doing their best to swindle human beings out of a little vital energy. The suspicion is reinforced by Alan Vaughan's 'possession' by the wife of the Nantucket sea captain; the entity who 'rescued' him made him first write out the sentence: 'Each of us has a spirit while living; do not meddle with the spirits of the dead.' In view of the history of spiritualism, this seems a curious piece of advice to come from a spirit. Even the phrasing seems odd; should it not be 'Each of us *is* a spirit while living?' Or is he using 'spirit' in another sense, the sense in which we speak of the spirit of Beethoven or Goethe, meaning their fundamental creative drive? In that case, what 'Z' was saying was: 'Each of us has an inherent vital purpose while he is alive; do not waste time trying to contact the dead.' Such contact is likely to waste your time and land you in the hands of unscrupulous entities like the wife of the Nantucket sea captain or Mr Apol.

G. K. Chesterton entertained much the same suspicion, as a result of early experiments with an ouija board. He wrote in his autobiography:

I saw quite enough of the thing to be able to testify, with complete certainty, that something happens which is not in the ordinary sense natural, or produced by the normal and conscious human will. Whether it is produced by some subconscious but still human force, or by some powers, good, bad or indifferent, which are external to humanity, I would not attempt to decide. The only thing I will say with complete confidence, about that mystic and invisible power, is that it tells lies.

Similarly, the novelist Nathaniel Hawthorne, commenting on the amazing phenomena produced by the Victorian medium Daniel Dunglas Home, wrote in his *Notebooks*: 'They are absolutely proved to be sober facts by evidence that would satisfy us of any other alleged realities; and yet I cannot force my mind to take any interest in them.' Like Chesterton, Hawthorne seems to have felt an instinctive revulsion for 'spirit phenomena', as if they were basically a waste of his time.

This theory would also suggest an answer to one of the most puzzling questions to arise from Keel's book: why the phenomena were on such a scale. After all, ghosts are usually individualists; they content themselves with haunting one place at a time; Keel's book gives the impression that most of West Virginia and Ohio was haunted by winged monsters and mysterious lights. Similarly, when news of the Hydesville rappings spread across America, then to Europe, spirits were suddenly manifesting themselves all over the place, from New York to Vladivostock. Why? The answer presumably is: because thousands of people were suddenly holding séances and playing with ouija boards, actually offering the spirits their energy and attention. And in West Virginia, newspaper reports of the sightings sent thousands of people out every night looking for UFOs.

'Waves' of strange phenomena seem to occur when there is a wide expectation of them. The same thing happened in Europe between 1700 and 1740, when there were suddenly thousands of reports of vampires. The epidemic started in Central Europe, probably Transylvania (the word *vampir* is of Slovak origin), and within a few years had spread across Europe, from Greece to Scandinavia. Many of the reports sound too circumstantial to be dismissed as hysteria; and, as with UFO sightings, the sheer number is impressive. The answer could be that vast numbers of people, living in lonely villages, began to brood on the reports of vampires, and to look for vampires around every graveyard. Huge quantities of psychic energy suddenly became available to the flotsam and jetsam of the spirit world.

The same explanation could be applied to the Philip case. George and Iris Owen are inclined to assume that they somehow created a *tulpa* by brooding on Philip, but the phenomena could just as easily be interpreted as some stray spirit deliberately impersonating Philip—a psychic version of the story of the Tichbourne claimant.

All these speculations fail to suggest a definite answer to the problem of UFOs. The point is quite simply that we cannot draw a line between the latent powers of the human mind, and the invisible powers that may exist around us in the universe. All we can do is to point out that, while most of Puharich's phenomena seem to be genuine, they are as ambiguous as most of the phenomena of spiritualism. And this is, in fact, an important insight. It means that we have recognised an uncertainty principle in paranormal phenomena. They may be 'genuine', and yet still not what they seem. Many paranormal phenomena may be simply the antics of psychic exhibitionists and attention-seekers, who had far better be ignored.

Nevertheless there is an interesting body of opinion that holds that UFO phenomena may be of immense significance. This is the conclusion arrived at by Jacques Valleé, in his book *The Invisible College*. (His 'invisible college' is an 'open conspiracy' of scientists who recognise the reality of UFO phenomena.) Valleé explains that, after twenty-five years of studying UFO reports, he has come to reject the idea that mankind is being contacted by benevolent intelligences from outer space. He also recognises the psychic component in so much UFO phenomena. Like Lethbridge and Stephen Jenkins, he has become convinced that what we are dealing with is a 'different level of existence, a reality that seems to cut through our own at right angles'. He goes on: 'I believe that a powerful force has influenced the human race in the past, and is again influencing it now. Does this force originate entirely within human consciousness, or does it represent alien intervention?' He is finally unable to reach any definite conclusion, but states: 'I think we are close, very close, to understanding what UFOs are, and what they do'.

What his theory amounts to is this. The whole nature of the UFO phenomenon is ambiguous; we cannot even determine whether they exist, and if so whether they are friendly or hostile. But the steady build-up of UFO sightings is causing a shift in human consciousness, a new attitude towards the universe. Vallée speaks of what he calls a 'control system' like the thermostat that regulates the temperature of a house. The whole point of a thermostat is to keep temperature *within certain limits*, neither too high nor too low. And in the same way, the UFO phenomenon is a kind of control system. There are sudden rashes of UFO sightings, like the ones in West Virginia in 1966, that cause widespread interest. But before everybody begins to believe in them, the sightings diminish, until once again we feel that it was nonsense after all; and just as credulity has reached its lowest point, the sightings begin again.

Vallée goes on to speak about 'the reinforcement phenomenon'. When psychologists are trying to train pigeons or laboratory rats to behave in a certain way, they use 'reinforcement mechanisms' —certain pleasures or fears. If these pleasures or fears are too even and monotonous, development ceases; the animal can even slip back to a lower level. (Rubinstein and Best's planaria, which became bored with emergencies, are an example.) The best way, apparently, is to combine periodicity with *unpredictability*. In that way, learning is slow but quite continuous, and it is also irreversible.

It rather looks—Vallée is implying—as if UFO phenomena could be some sort of reinforcement mechanism to raise human beings to a new mental level. After all, the most fundamental characteristic of human consciousness is its narrowness, its tendency to mind its own business. Surrounded by a vast and inexplicable universe, we prefer to plod along in the old routine like blinkered horses. Life is infinitely strange, yet we spend a great deal of it yawning; and many people live in big cities as if they were in a tiny village; they hardly know the next door neighbours and have never bothered to wonder what lies on the other side of that railway embankment.

Our minds are essentially provincial when, ideally, they ought to be cosmopolitan. We are not merely earth-bound; we have our heads buried in the earth. The UFO phenomena, Vallée suggests, are forcing us to look up, to get used to the idea that we are citizens of the universe, not just of this earth.

But Vallée admits that he has no idea of who or what is controlling the learning curve. Could it be from 'out there', as the cybernetician David Foster suggests in his book *The Intelligent Universe?*

The present book, it is hoped, will at least have made the reader aware of the implications of the alternative hypothesis: that the 'control mechanism' may operate from 'in here'. For it has tried to show that man has many levels, many 'selves', and that, moreover, the level of everyday existence is, in some strange sense, untrue. The being who looks out of my eyes is not 'me' at all. He is an impostor. The real 'me' is up there, beyond my present consciousness. He knows things that 'I' do not know. Consequently he can plan things that are beyond my understanding.

This recognition could provide the basic hypothesis needed if we are to understand the nature and purpose of UFOs.

3

The Mechanisms of Enlightenment

———————————

The time has come to look more closely at the structure of the ladder of selves, and the actual mechanisms by which we move up or down.

In *The Varieties of Religious Experience*, William James cites an interesting case of a young man who suddenly fell *out* of love:

> For two years . . . I went through a very bad experience which almost drove me mad. I had fallen violently in love with a girl who, young as she was, had the spirit of coquetry like a cat . . . I fell into a regular fever, could think of nothing else . . . She was very pretty, good humoured, and jolly to the last degree, and intensely pleased with my admiration. Would give me no decided answer yes or no, and the queer thing about it was that whilst pursuing her for her hand, I secretly knew all along that she was unfit to be a wife for me . . . Our closer relations had to be largely on the sly, and this fact, together with my own jealousy of another one of her male admirers and my own conscience despising me for my uncontrollable weakness made me so nervous and sleepless that I really thought I should become insane.
>
> I was going to my work after breakfast one morning, thinking as usual of her and of my misery, when, just as if some outside power lay hold of me, I found myself turning round and almost running to my room,

where I immediately got out all the relics of her which I possessed, including some hair, all her notes and letters, and ambrotypes on glass. The former I made a fire of, the latter I actually crushed beneath my heel, in a sort of fierce joy of revenge and punishment. I now loathed and despised her altogether, and as for myself I felt as if a load of disease had suddenly been removed from me. That was the end. I never spoke to her or wrote to her again . . . From that happy morning onward, I regained possession of my own proper soul, and have never since fallen into any similar trap.

What had happened, quite clearly, is that the young man had got sick of being the victim of his own desires, and of regarding himself with contempt. His rational self told him that he was a fool to be in love with her; but its advice was ignored by his emotions and desires. The pain she caused led to increasing revulsion; one day, his mind rejected her as a healthy body rejects a splinter. He had moved up to the next rung of the ladder of selves. In doing so, he had not only left behind the young lady, but his 'old self' as well.

The case has one unusual feature. When people experience 'counter-conversion'—the sudden rejection of a previously held ideal—they usually descend to a *lower* rung of the ladder. A typical example occurs in Leonid Andreyev's story *Abyss*, in which a young couple walk in the forest as they talk about comradeship and idealism. Three ruffians set on them and knock the young man —Nemovetsky—unconscious; then they rape the girl. When he recovers, Nemovetsky at first tries to revive her, then is gradually swept away by his own desires. Andreyev clearly has some intuitive notion of the 'ladder of selves'; he writes: 'There was no Nemovetsky; Nemovetsky had been left somewhere behind, and the person who had replaced him was now mauling the submissive body . . .' And the story concludes: 'For an instant, flaming horror lighted up his mind, opening before him a black abyss. Then the black abyss swallowed him.'

The melodramatic wording produces a moment of puzzlement. Why 'flaming horror', why an 'abyss'? Surely this is slightly excessive, even for a rape? But Andreyev is not talking about the rape. He is saying that all their ideas were false, an illusion, and that the 'higher Nemovetsky' was an illusion too. He is implying that Nemovetsky has seen into the basic emptiness and meaninglessness of life, and he now has no future. His rape of the unconscious girl has shown him the truth about himself and about human beings in general. The ideals are window dressing. The underlying reality is 'the beast'.

Before condemning Andreyev as a facile pessimist (Tolstoy said: 'He keeps saying Boo, but he doesn't scare me'), it is important to recognise that he has caught the essence of the descent to a lower rung of the ladder: what might be called 'the negative revelation'. The mystic Thomas Traherne had a vision in which he saw that all men are angels. Nemovetsky's vision is that all men are swine. The German sex criminal Peter Kürten once described how he had been struck by a similar vision as he walked the streets of Düsseldorf, how it had suddenly seemed appropriate that he should commit as many murders as possible. The American mass murderer Carl Panzram liked to describe himself as 'the man who goes around doing people good', since he regarded human life as so vile that he felt that to murder someone was to do him a favour. The negative revelation always reduces life to its lowest terms, to the purely material. Hemingway's hero in *A Farewell to Arms* writes about: 'Nights in bed, drunk, when you knew that was all there was, and the strange excitement of waking and not knowing who it was with you, and the world all unreal in the dark . . .' They key phrase is 'when you knew *that was all there was*', the inability to conceive any other reality beyond or above the present.

It can be seen why the case cited by James is so unusual; the young man 'reduced' the girl to a lower level, while he himself succeeded in moving to a 'higher rung'. This was because his own innate sense of values had already made him aware that the girl 'was unfit to be a wife for me'. And in rising above the desire, he felt that he had 'regained possession of my own proper soul'.

But the most interesting phrase in his account is the one that describes how the sudden change came about. There is no description of increasing self-digust or sudden determination; instead, he writes: 'when, *just as if some outside power lay hold of me*, I found myself turning round and running to my room.' A psychologist would say that his disgust and rejection of the girl had built up 'subliminally', and that it suddenly overflowed; but he seems to deny this in speaking of 'some *outside* power'.

This can be found again and again in reports of mystical experience. In *Watcher on the Hills*, Raynor C. Johnson cites the case of a man who was out walking with his future wife.

We struggled on up the hill, and the next thing I noted was that the whole locality was illumined by an extraordinary bright light. It was a cloudy and dull day, and this extremely intense illumination did not appear to originate in any fixed centre, but was diffused equally throughout the entire terrain. Accompanying the light was the sense of the presence of an irresistible power wholly and utterly benevolent, and as far as I was concerned a feeling of complete happiness and well-being quite impossible to describe. The certainty of all-pervading and immutable love was so tremendous that I simply went on up the hill completely absorbed in this extraordinary experience and quite oblivious of the material surroundings. After an appreciable interval—I think a few minutes—the light gradually faded.[1]

Another case quoted by Johnson has this same emphasis on something *external* and unexpected:

I was a child of eight or nine playing by myself. . . I do remember that I was alone, when—Something . . . made me pause; Something . . . was happening . . . just out of sight; Something . . . was coming . . . nearer and nearer.

I looked hard. I could see the leafy trees and the golden glow of the gorse around me, but I could not see *what* was also present.

I listened hard, until I could almost hear the brook far below in the bottom. No call nor voice from *What* was coming . . . coming nearer and nearer to me, till *It* was breathing all around me, till the breath was coming through me—like the air itself—like the *Living One* . . .

It was all so strange and unexpected. I'd never dreamed of anything like this that was happening. I don't know how long it lasted, before I was left alone with the trees and the gorse . . .[2]

Taken at face value, both these experiences suggest that whatever happened came from outside. But it is clear that the external experience quickly led to an internal sense of illumination. Sometimes it can be the other way round. Richard Maurice Bucke, whose *Cosmic Consciousness* is a classic of mysticism, described his own experience after an evening of poetry and philosophy with friends. As he drove home in a hansom cab,

I was in a state of quiet, almost passive enjoyment, not actually thinking . . . All at once, without warning of any kind, I found myself wrapped in a flame-coloured cloud. For an instant I thought of fire, an immense conflagration somewhere close by . . .; the next, I knew that the fire was within myself. Directly afterward there came upon me a sense of exultation, of immense joyousness accompanied or immediately followed by an intellectual illumination impossible to describe. Among other things, I did not merely come to believe, but I saw that the universe is not composed of dead matter, but is, on the contrary, a living Presence; I became conscious in myself of eternal life. It was not a conviction that I would have eternal life, but a consciousness that I possessed eternal life then; I saw that all men are immortal . . . The vision lasted a few seconds, and was gone.[3]

Here Bucke for a moment *mistook* his 'inner fire' for a flame-coloured cloud caused by burning buildings. Then he ascended several rungs of the ladder, and found himself in a higher state of consciousness, not unlike Bennett's experience at Fontainebleau. An experience that comes from a higher state of consciousness seems to come from outside rather than within. But then there is an instantaneous 'transformation'; the 'self' that experiences the flame-coloured cloud is left behind, and Bucke *becomes* the self from which the cloud emanates.

There is an important lesson here. Suppose I am looking at myself in a full-length mirror while, on the other side of the room, another person watches me. I look at myself and say: 'That is me.' Then I experience a momentary dizziness, and suddenly find that I am now looking out from behind the eyes of the other person, while the former 'me' stands on the other side of the room, looking in a mirror. What would this experience teach me? Clearly, that I was mistaken to say: 'That is me.' For the 'real me' is something that is transferable from one body to another.

Now in the same way, Bucke drives home from his evening out with friends; he experiences a sense of 'This is me'. Then something happens, which he at first takes to be the reflection of burning houses. Suddenly, he realises that it is inside him. A moment later, he is another 'me', a higher 'me'. The lesson seems plain. His original sense of 'This is me' was mistaken; but so is the *higher* sense. Neither is 'me', although it is arguable that the higher of the two is closer to the 'real me' than the lower.

Bucke's next observation seems to support this view; he says that he became aware of himself as eternal life; not a conviction that he would *have* eternal life, but that he has it now. This is important. For if he had felt 'I will have eternal life', this instantly raises the question 'Which "me"?' He is momentarily aware of himself as something beyond 'me-ness' or selfhood, which does not age. When Alan Vaughan had a similar experience, he felt he could see into the future; *time in our sense had ceased to be a basic condition of his existence*.

Again, we confront the fundamental paradox. The 'me' who looks out of my eyes is not me at all. I am in error when I identify with him. Even my higher selves (if that is what they are) are not me either.

If all this is correct, it would seem to support the view that has always been held by saints and mystics: that a part of us is immortal, and survives bodily death. This is, of course, a view that any balanced, logical person will approach with caution; it looks a little too much like wishful thinking. Yet it is not necessary to take the word of an avowed mystic like Bucke. Even the case of the young man who fell out of love implies something of the sort. He was not wholly in love; a part of him remained detached, realising that the girl would make a bad wife. We may say, of course, that this was simply his power of reason, or his intuitive judgment. But that does not really contradict the ladder-of-selves theory. The down-to-earth view of man has been expressed with most clarity by the philosopher Gilbert Ryle, in *The Concept of Mind*. Ryle objects to the notion that man 'has' a body and a mind. This he calls the fallacy of the 'ghost in the machine'. Ryle says that man *is* a complex unity, which includes feelings, physical states, thoughts and desires. These all take place *in* the body, just as burning takes place *in* a fire. Mind is not separate from body, any more than the flames are separate from the wood and coal that constitute the fire. The whole concept of mind as something separate from the body is a misunderstanding.

But how can we explain the man who fell out of love in these terms? He was in love; he wanted the girl physically and emotionally. Ryle might reply: 'Ah, but his *reason* told him she was more trouble than she was worth.' But this is not consistent with the facts. He experienced a *whole level* of emotions and perceptions that rejected the girl; it wasn't simply a matter of reason. In fact, he behaved as if he were two people, one higher than the other.

Dr Julian Jaynes has outlined an interesting theory of mystical experience in his book, *The Origin of Consciousness in the Breakdown of the Bicameral Mind*.[4] He advances the startling theory that even as recently as 1000 BC, human beings *did not yet possess consciousness*. He is, admittedly, using 'consciousness' in a rather special sense, meaning man's inner life—what goes on behind his eyes. For example, I may be speaking to someone, apparently agreeing with everything he says, while I am thinking: 'The man's an idiot.' According to Dr Jaynes, primitive man did not possess this ability to withdraw inside himself; he reacted simply and directly to his experience of life. He claims, for example, that Homer's *Iliad* shows no sign that its characters were capable of self-reflection, awareness of their inner states. 'We cannot approach these heroes by inventing mind-spaces behind their fierce eyes . . . Iliadic man did not have subjectivity as we do.' And the odd result, says Jaynes, is that Homer's heroes do not have free will in the sense that we do. It is always *the gods* who keep intervening and making them do things. We would say that Paris caused the Trojan war by stealing Helen; but according to Homer, it was a goddess who prompted him to do it.

This leads Jaynes to the even more startling conclusion that instead of thinking things out for himself, ancient man experienced auditory hallucinations. This highly controversial notion occurred to him as a result of a personal experience. When he was wrestling with the ideas that led him to write the book, he lay down on a couch in a state of intellectual despair and heard a loud, distinct voice say from above his head: 'Include the knower in the known.' He leapt to his feet and looked around the room, convinced there was someone there, until it finally dawned on him that it was an auditory hallucination, *caused by stress*. Apparently hallucinations of various types, visual as well as auditory, are far commoner than we realise. A survey conducted in the 1890s revealed that seven point eight per cent of men and twelve per cent of women experience hallucinations at some time. Oddly enough, the rate was twice as high for Russians and Brazilians—both nations noted for psychic abilities. Jaynes goes on to reason that if ancient man had a 'lower stress threshold' he might experience hallucinations every day of his life.

These 'voices', he argues, originate in the right hemisphere of the brain, and make their way across to the left hemisphere, which, in human beings, controls speech. And by way of evidence, he cites some remarkable experiments on 'commissurotomised' patients (whose right and left hemispheres have been severed). If you stare at the white margin between the two pages of this book, the right-hand page is seen by your left hemisphere, and the left-hand page by your right.

But your right hemisphere is 'dumb', irrational, incapable of speech. So if the two halves of the brain are separated, the left-hand page would simply become blank. You would still see it, but you wouldn't *know* you saw it. If the left-hand page contained a dollar sign, and the right-hand page a question mark, you would 'see' only the question mark. If you were asked to draw what you saw, using your left hand, you would draw a dollar sign. If asked what you had just drawn —without being allowed to see it—you would insist that it was a question mark. It is, as Jaynes remarks, exactly like two people in the same head. If a dirty picture was placed on the left-hand page, you would find yourself blushing; but if asked, you would respond, *quite truthfully*, that you hadn't seen anything.

It looks, then, as if what you call 'you' is basically the part that can express itself in words. Also living inside your head is a non-verbal 'you'—who may, because he is more primitive, have closer links with your unconscious mind. He may 'know' a great deal more than 'verbal you' knows.

When seen in the light of this evidence, Jaynes's theory begins to seem altogether less far-fetched. What he is suggesting is basically a theory of evolution. In the days before he developed speech, man must have lived in an 'unconscious' way, altogether closer to nature, responding with his intuitions. The development of speech brought a kind of consciousness; but communication between the two levels was poor, so that non-verbal man literally had to 'put ideas' into the mind of his Siamese twin. (It could be a similar effect that makes very young children say 'Baby is hungry' instead of 'I am hungry'—their identity has not yet shifted to the left half of the brain.)

Jaynes's theory, then, throws a great deal of light on the problem of intuition, and perhaps of paranormal experience in general. 'I' am not really 'me'; I do not even have a right to the title 'everyday me', because even 'everyday me' includes that other, silent half. Moreover, my silent half often knows better than 'I' do. The more I allow myself to become possessed by ideas and concepts, the more I lose touch with this wiser self. One of man's chief problems is to remember that intellect is only telling him half the truth.

We may further speculate that if 'non-verbal you' is responsible for intuition, then he may also be responsible for flashes of precognition and second sight. The right side of the brain may be the gateway to the unconscious. Yet it would seen to be a mistake to think of him as an uneducated country cousin. Jaynes mentions experiments that show that the right hemisphere is able to understand complicated definitions and perform complex reasoning. It probably explains the prowess of mathematical prodigies. In which case, it is not merely a kind of gateway to the underworld, but also to the higher levels of consciousness. It seems conceivable that Jaynes's speculations about the bicameral mind contain an insight into the basic geography of our inner being.

Let us look at some more examples of mystical experience. Here is another from Johnson's *Watcher on the Hills*:

> I was travelling back to camp in early January 1948 in an empty railway carriage after a short leave . . . I pulled [Kenneth Walker's] *Diagnosis of Man* from my pack and began to read the chapter on Brahmanism. I was reading the words telling of the ever-present and all-pervading quality of Brahman, when suddenly my whole being was seized by an acute state of awareness, and immediately the words assumed a great significance. I knew somehow that they were true, that Brahman (at that time I suppose I translated it as God) *was* all about me, and through me, and in me. The knowledge did not come from without, unmistakably it came from within. The state was one of extraordinary joy; I realised happiness was within me. (I believe I also felt that I controlled great power, so that I could have stopped the train just by willing it.)

Again, as in the case of Bucke, the young soldier is suddenly aware of a knowledge he has always possessed, *yet was unaware that he possessed*. He has not, like Bucke, been translated to a higher level of being; he remains 'himself', but he suddenly catches a glimpse of a knowledge possessed by some higher level.

Even more fascinating is the comment: 'I believe I also felt that I controlled great power, so that I could have stopped the train just by willing it.' He may, of course, have meant this only 'in a manner of speaking'. But it would be in line with our speculations if he had experienced a genuine glimpse of a real power—the power that causes poltergeist effects. It would also be in line with the general theory of mysticism, which asserts that miraculous powers are one of the first—and least important—consequences of spiritual enlightenment (or, in our terms, of a movement up the ladder of selves').

There are innumerable well-authenticated stories of the miraculous powers of Hindu holy men. In the 1860s, an eminent French jurist named Louis Jacolliot was appointed Chief Justice of Chandernagore in India and devoted his spare time during a seven-year period to studying Hindu religion and the miracles of holy men. In *Occult Science in India and Among the Ancients*, he describes the extensive tests he conducted with fakirs. One of them was able to make a plant grow from its seed in two hours; another caused a small table to stick to the floor, and Jacolliot's most strenuous efforts to move it only caused one of its folding leaves to come off in his hand. Another conjured up spirits in a phosphorescent cloud and had one of them play a flute. The flute was left behind when the spirit vanished and proved to be one that Jacolliot had left in his locked house. In most cases, the fakir went into an ecstatic trance before producing these paranormal effects. Jacolliot was allowed to examine everything at close quarters, to assure himself there was no trickery.

Sai Baba, a contemporary Hindu saint, performs 'miracles' a dozen times a day; Lyall Watson describes him turning rocks into sweets, flowers into jewels, and producing showers of sacred ash from the air in quantities sufficient to fill large drums. His powers were studied by a Tasmanian journalist, Howard Murphet, whose book *Sai Baba: Man of Miracles* documents so many paranormal occurrences that if finally becomes almost as confusing as Puharich's book on Geller. And a great many of Baba's miracles are basically of the same nature as Geller's: 'apports', materialisation and de-materialisation of objects. The difference is that Sai Baba is totally in control of his powers. Murphet's book also makes it clear that Baba is a man of spiritual enlightenment and deep compassion. (Most of his miracles are of healing.) He clearly regards his powers as a by-product of higher consciousness. There can be no doubt that he would regard the powers of Uri Geller and Matthew Manning as some sort of freak short-circuit.

The theory of mysticism propounded by Raynor C. Johnson is based on the notion that man possesses not only a soul but also a higher soul or Oversoul, which Johnson calls Spirit. Mysticism, he says, 'is the union of the soul with its Spirit'.

An objection to this view is that it seems somehow unnecessary to suppose that we possess two different kinds of soul. But the problem vanishes if we think of the 'soul' as the 'everyday me', the 'I' who looks out from behind my eyes. This is the soul that can be corrupted by laziness and cruelty. This 'me' is not the 'real me'. But then, neither are the 'higher mes" that I experience in moments of intensity. The real me, the ultimate me, is the Spirit that Bucke became aware of in the hansom cab.

What then *are* these higher selves that I can experience? Obviously, they are states of being. But, apparently, they *already exist*, hidden from the view of my everyday self. How did they get there?

One possible answer can be found in another writer cited by Johnson: R. H. Ward, whose *Drug-Taker's Notes* is largely concerned with his experiences with lysergic acid and nitrous oxide. But he also cites a mystical experience described by a friend, who was on his way back from the station when he experienced mild indigestion. The thought occurred to him: 'It [the indigestion] belongs only to my body and is real only to the physical not-self. There is no need for the self to feel it . . . Even as I thought this the pain disappeared; that is, it was in some way left behind . . .' But he goes on: 'the sensation of "rising up within" began . . .', suggesting movement up the ladder. And he associates this with an actual physical sensation: 'First, there is the indescribable sensation in the spine, as of *something mounting up* . . . This was accompanied by an extraordinary feeling of *bodily lightness*, of well-being and effortlessness . . . It was also, somehow, a feeling of living more in the upper part of one's body than in the lower . . . Everything was becoming "more", everything was *going up to another level.*'

Anyone who has ever glanced into a book on yoga will recognise the similarity between this description and accounts of the rise of the '*kundalini*' serpent'. According to the Hindus, the *kundalini*, or spirit-power, lies coiled at the base of the spine. In conditions of spiritual enlightenment, it can rise upward via the Rod of Brahma (situated along the spine), passing through seven *chakras*, or spiritual centres, to the *chakra* in the crown of the head.

The *chakras*, it should be explained, are the points where man's physical body and his subtle body (or astral body) connect. There are, in fact, hundreds of such points, and they are basically the points stimulated in acupuncture. But there are seven major junctions situated along the spine; these are the *chakras*.

A modern yogi, Gopi Krishna, has described his own first experience of the *kundalini* serpent in a remarkable autobiography.[5] It took place during Christmas 1937, when he was thirty-four. He was sitting cross-legged in his room, practising meditation, his attention fixed on an imaginary lotus of light in the crown of his head (i.e. the topmost *chakra*).

> During one such spell of intense concentration I suddenly felt a strange sensation below the base of the spine, at the place touching the seat. The sensation was so extraordinary and so pleasing that my attention was forcibly drawn towards it. The moment my attention was thus unexpectedly withdrawn from the point at which it was focused, the sensation ceased . . . When completely immersed I again experienced the sensation, but this time, instead of allowing my mind to leave the point where I had fixed it, I maintained a rigidity of attention throughout. The sensation again extended upwards, growing in intensity, and I found myself wavering; but with a great effort I kept my attention centred round the lotus. Suddenly, with a roar like that of a waterfall, I felt a stream of liquid light entering my brain through the spinal cord.
>
> . . . The illumination grew brighter and brighter, the roaring louder, I experienced a rocking sensation and then I felt myself slipping out of my body, entirely enveloped in a halo of light . . . I felt the point of consciousness that was myself growing wider, surrounded by waves of light. It grew wider and wider, spreading outward while the body, normally the immediate object of its perception, appeared to have receded into the distance until I became entirely unconscious of it. I was now all consciousness, without any outline, immersed in a sea of light simultaneously conscious and aware of every point, spread out, as it were, in all directions without any barrier or material obstruction. I was no longer myself, or, to be more accurate, no longer as I knew myself to be, but instead was a vast circle of consciousness in which the body was but a point, bathed in light and in a state of exaltation and happiness impossible to describe.
>
> After some time, the duration of which I could not judge, the circle began to narrow down; I felt myself contracting, becoming smaller and smaller, until I again became dimly conscious of the outline of my body . . . and as I slipped back into my old condition, I became suddenly aware of the noises in the street.

It might be assumed that this was the beginning of a period of tremendous spiritual enlightenment; in fact, it heralded months of agony. He felt exhausted and drained, then sank into nervous depression. 'Whenever I closed my eyes I found myself looking into a weird circle of light, in which luminous currents swirled and eddied . . . Sometimes it seemed as if a jet of molten copper . . . dashed against my crown and fell in a scintillating shower.' He had apparently released a current over which he had no control, a result yogis continually warn against. Like a high-voltage electric current, *kundalini* can be dangerous; it can bring insanity and even death. 'Each morning heralded for me a new kind of terror, a fresh complication in the already disordered system.' He became exhausted, unable to work or eat, or sit still. His description tallies, in some respects, with my own experiences during my panic attacks. 'My consciousness was in such a state of unceasing flux that I was never certain how it would behave within the next few minutes. It rose and fell like a wave, raising me one moment out of the clutches of fear to dash me again the next into the depths of despair.'

According to Hindu mysticism, the Rod of Brahma has three channels: the central channel, the *sushumna*; the left hand (or female) channel, the *ida*; and the right hand (or male) channel, the *pingala*. For true *samadhi*, the energy has to rise up the central channel, which is normally blocked by the 'head' of the serpent. The *kundalini* energy is fiery in nature. Gopi Krishna suspected that it had somehow found its way into the *pingala*, the male channel, whose nature is already solar and fiery. One evening, when he was convulsed with pain, as if red hot needles were piercing his skin, he became convinced that he was on the point of death and made a convulsive effort to arouse the energy of the *ida*, the lunar channel: 'There was a sound like a nerve thread snapping and instantaneously a silvery streak passed zigzag through the spinal cord . . . pouring an effulgent, cascading shower of brilliant vital energy into my brain, filling my head with a blissful lustre in place of the flame that had been tormenting me . . .'

His troubles were still far from over. It took him another twelve years to achieve true *samadhi*, and the long, slow process is described in the remainder of his book. As the reader follows this strange spiritual odyssey, he finds himself asking the inevitable question: Is this all some kind of rare mental disease? It is impossible to believe that Gopi Krishna is inventing such highly circumstantial details. Yet if he is being strictly truthful, it sounds like no form of psychosis known to Western medicine. The most plausible explanation seems to be Krishna's own: that he accidentally released some strange form of energy *whose source does not lie in the physical body*. Gopi Krishna himself finds nothing unusual in the notion, although his basic habits of thought are Western rather than Eastern. His roots lie in Hindu philosophy, and this leads him to reject one basic tenet of Western scientific thinking: that life is a product of matter, like any other form of energy. He accepts the view that life comes from *beyond* the body; that, as James puts it, our life is fed at the breasts of a greater life, our individuality sustained by a greater individuality.

The essence of this view is that the body is a kind of *mirror*. It can reflect energy, but it has no energy of its own, apart from the rather low energies produced by the decomposition of food, which are necessary to support its physical organisation. Man gets his life by turning towards the source of greater life, as a sunflower turns towards the sun.

These images immediately suggest another used earlier in this book. The moon is also a mirror. It reflects sunlight according to how much of its face is turned towards the earth. Ordinary consciousness is 'partial', but in moments of intensity, man 'completes his partial mind', and the full moon appears for a moment. The image helps us to understand the riddle of multiple personality, which has claimed so much of our attention. At any given moment, the larger part of man's being is hidden in darkness. When he says 'I', he means a mere fragment of his total being. But all of his other fragments also say 'I' when the sunlight shines on them. All are liars, for the true 'I' is a union of all the fragments, the full moon. And even the full moon is only a fragment of a far greater individuality. We may find this view puzzling and difficult to grasp; but it must be acknowledged that it offers a better 'paradigm' than our Western psychology.

What precisely is meant by 'turning to the source of light'? The concept sounds Christian—rather drearily so. But Hindu philosophy gives it more precise meaning. Man is trapped in a kind of hall of mirrors, the maze of Maya. He is continually being tempted by false values; his problem is a problem of choice. The Western occult tradition is at one with Hinduism in believing that this choice has a direct effect upon the 'subtle body', causing it to become more or less radiant.

An astonishing document called *The Boy Who Saw True* offers some interesting examples. It is the anonymous diary of a late Victorian schoolboy, published after the author's death, with notes by the composer and occultist Cyril Scott. The schoolboy was a natural psychic and had no idea that this faculty was not shared by everyone else. Like many psychics, he was able to see the 'astral body' in the forms of 'lights' around people's heads. He judged their characters by whether their 'lights' were nice or not. Of a little girl called Marjorie whom he met on holiday, he notes: 'Her lights look like a sort of dirty blood and make me feel quite sick.' Marjorie seems to have been distinctly over-sexed; she asked the small boy to take down his trousers; when he declined, she removed her own knickers. The boy's mother thought that Marjorie had 'a face like an angel'; the boy's own judgment, based on her 'lights', was clearly more accurate.

We have seen that Baron Reichenbach's attempts to study these phenomena scientifically met with widespread ridicule. Kilner's 'human aura' made even less impression on his medical colleagues. But in our own time, as less orthodox approaches to medicine, like acupuncture, have gained ground in the West, the 'aura' has once again become a subject of serious study. One of its most impressive advocates is a Turkish-born doctor, Shafica Karagulla, who worked for several years with Wilder Penfield on brain physiology. Appointed Assistant Professor of Psychiatry at Downstabe Medical Center, Brooklyn, in 1957, she became intrigued by the achievements of the 'psychic diagnostician' Edgar Cayce, who could accurately diagnose illnesses while in a state of trance, even if the patient were hundreds of miles away. The phenomenon was so well attested that she found herself unable to dismiss it. She began to investigate psychometry, came across Kilner's book, and became convinced of the existence of what she called Higher Sense Perception (HSP). She soon came across doctors who possessed the same type of ability as Cayce, not faith healers, but ordinary general practitioners who could actually see the 'life-field' of the patient and tell what was wrong with it. One doctor could see a web of light interpenetrating the body and extending several inches beyond it. Dr Karagulla's investigations led her to the conclusion that beyond the physical–energy field there is an emotional field, extending about eighteen inches beyond the body, and a mental field extending two feet or more. The 'physical–energy field' contains eight major vortices of light, associated with the glands, and several minor vortices. Significantly, five of the major ones are situated along the spine in association with the endocrine glands, and correspond with the *chakras* of Hindu philosophy.

The results of Dr Karagulla's years of research are summarised in her book *Breakthrough to Creativity*.[6] Commenting on this book, Dr Edward Aubert has written:

> It seems that we live in a vast ocean of interlacing energies. These energies move in and out of our individual fields in a manner analogous to the process of breathing. Each person appears to have his own method of selecting energy; some do it predominantly through intellectual stimulation, others through emotional excitation. Depression and self-centredness greatly diminish the individual's access to the cosmic energy supply.[7]

This seems to confirm Gurdjieff's comment to Bennett about the 'Great Reservoir or Accumulator' of energy.

Let us consider the implications of this view. It states that our vital energy comes from beyond the body, from some kind of cosmic reservoir. The astral or subtle body is the link between the physical body and this lake of energy. (It is tempting to assume that Harold Burr's L-fields are another name for the subtle body, but this is probably not so; the electrical field detected by Burr's instruments is more likely something that happens to the energy *after* it has entered the physical body.) The major 'junctions' (or power-points) are the *chakras*, but there are also dozens of minor ones, the acupuncture points. Acupuncture, according to this view, works because it somehow stimulates the junction—perhaps clearing a blockage—enabling the energy to flow through. Significantly, the lowest of the *chakras* is situated between the genital and anal regions. And this suggests at least one tentative answer to the question of how we 'turn to' the source of energy. There are no obvious limits to sexual energy. If a man tries to make love to a woman who does not attract him, his energies may sink to the point at which he becomes impotent. If he is making love to a woman who touches his *sexual imagination*, he might make love to her a dozen times in one night. But sexual desire is not a physical appetite, like the need for food. It is far more like the desire a child feels for an attractive toy: an instinct to grab and possess. There is something more deliberate about it—an element of choice, of *will*. A man *decides* to fall in love; it requires the cooperation of his imagination. In the same way, he decides to *make* love; he can arouse his appetite for sex in a way that would be impossible with the desire for food. In short, drawing upon the sexual energies requires an act of intentionality and imagination. It is difficult to describe how we do it, but everyone knows perfectly well. It is a kind of 'reaching out'.

Ramakrishna used to say that anyone who longs for God with all his heart, who cries for God like a lost child for its mother, will find God. The reason most people never find God, he said, is because they don't want to. He also recognised that the basic act of 'turning to' God is an act of *reaching out*, of intentionality; in this case, it would obviously involve one of the higher *chakras*—in fact, the highest one, in the crown of the head.

It is also worth noting, parenthetically, that certain Eastern religious disciplines involve an attempt to control the sexual energy—not by suppressing it, as in Western monasticism, but by arousing it and then subjecting it to total conscious control. The American religious leader John Humphrey Noyes, who founded the Oneida Community, had the same interesting idea; he asserted that the Second Coming had taken place in the sky over Jerusalem in AD 70, and that therefore sex had ceased to be sinful. Marriage had also ceased to be necessary, according to Noyes; women should be shared communally. And childbirth could be avoided if sexual intercourse was conducted with no intention of reaching orgasm—a method known as *karezza*. Noyes affirmed that if sexual desire were controlled in this way, it could achieve far greater heights of intensity than normal intercourse—in fact, could reach almost mystical intensity and become a form of religious worship. The Tantrists would say that Noyes had learned to tap the source of sexual energy via the *Muladhara chakra*.

The correspondence noted by Shafica Karagulla between the endocrine glands and the *chakras* had already been pointed out by an Ouspensky disciple, Rodney Collin, in his book *The Theory of Celestial Influence*.[8] (This is, apart from Ouspensky's *In Search of the Miraculous*, perhaps the most important book to emerge from the Ouspensky group.) Collin seems to agree completely with Mesmer that man's body is permeated by a 'magnetic fluid' (which he identifies with Kilner's 'aura') and that the same is also true of the solar system. In fact, he sees close analogies between the body's various systems (nervous, arterial, lymphatic, and so on) and the 'magnetic tracks' of the planets. In a diagram labelled 'Man as Microcosm' he notes the vital position of the various glands, corresponding roughly to the *chakras*, and observes that if a regular spiral is drawn from the thymus, it passes neatly through all the other glands, as if their arrangement were deliberately symmetrical. Collin goes on to suggest that the glands are 'adaptors or transformers of the general energy created by the organism' (Gopi Krishna would say: the energy that comes from *beyond* the organism), and continues: 'Just as a galaxy appeared to be an expanding spiral of suns, and the solar system an expanding spiral of planets, so the human body now gives the impression of an expanding spiral of functions.'

What Collin then suggests is controversial, yet closely related to the basic theme of this book: that the endocrine glands are 'receiving sets' for planetary influences. Man stands at the centre of a web of magnetic influences—of the planet Earth and of the other bodies of the solar system. 'In other words, whether we like it or not, we find ourselves obliged to reconsider from a new and scientific point of view the general propositions of astrology.'

These propositions are, of course, that a man's character and temperament—and therefore, to some extent, his destiny—are influenced by the heavenly bodies, in particular, by the position of the sun during the month of his birth (his 'sun sign'), and, more especially, by the constellation that was rising at the moment of his birth. In *The Occult*, I commented on the work of the German astrologer Karl Ernst Krafft, who attempted to 'prove' astrology by statistical means, that is, by studying the horoscopes of thousands of professional men (he concentrated on musicians) and seeing whether these gave indications of their talent. Krafft studied 'sun signs' (Aries, Taurus, Gemini, etc.), and believed that he had proved his case. In 1950, the French statistician Michel Gauquelin put Krafft's figures through a computer and concluded that he had been deceiving himself. But Gauquelin then went on to test the other basic hypothesis of astrology, that the new-born baby is basically affected by the planet that is rising (just below the horizon) at the moment of his birth, and that doctors tend to be born under Mars, actors under Jupiter, scientists under Saturn, and so on; he was startled to discover that these new statistics were overwhelmingly in favour of the truth of astrology. His results were repeated in four European countries. In England (where the hour of birth is not recorded on birth certificates), Professor H. J. Eysenck, a tough-minded behavioural psychologist, was asked to check Gauquelin's results; he was equally astonished to find that they seemed to be accurate. Two of Eysenck's colleagues, J. Mayo and A. White, worked with him on two more well-known astrological theories: that people born under the three 'water signs' (Cancer, Scorpio, Pisces) tend to be very emotional; and that people born under the 'odd' signs of the zodiac (Aries, Gemini, Leo, Libra, Sagittarius, Aquarius) are extraverts, while those born under the even signs (Taurus, Cancer, Virgo, Scorpio, Capricorn, Pisces) are introverts. The study of two thousand people again produced results that were well above the laws of chance.

Largely as a consequence of this recent work, there is an increasing tendency among scientists and medical men to take astrology seriously or, at least, to regard it as a useful tool in psychotherapy. But the basic problem remains: how *can* the human temperament be influenced by the positions of the sun and planets? The theory of leys provides a partial answer: that human beings are deeply influenced by the earth's magnetic field, which is in turn influenced by the heavenly bodies. Rodney Collin knew nothing of leys, but he knew about magnetism—both planetary and animal—and he suggested a startlingly original answer to the question. 'Each endocrine gland or its associated nerve plexus is sensitive to the magnetism of a particular planet. If we imagine a set of seven photographic light-meters, each sensitive to the light of a different planet and made to register once and for all the reading recorded at the moment they are brought out of the dark room, we get some picture of this "setting" of the human machine at birth.'[9]

Collin has another suggestion that is relevant to our enquiry: that 'the functions controlled by the glands give . . . the strong impression of being graded from coarse to fine, from material towards immaterial'—each one using a finer type of energy than the one below. Lowest on the scale is the thymus, a mysterious gland whose function seems to be associated with physical growth, which gradually ceases to function after puberty; at the other end of the scale lies the gonads, which Collin associates with reproduction, creation and higher emotion, and the pineal gland, which he believes to be associated with man's future evolution. (Collin seems to be in disagreement with Hindu philosophy—he regards the sexual *chakra* as one of the highest; this is because he arranges the *chakras* in the form of a spiral—Lethbridge's favourite concept—rather than a ladder.)

What is so interesting about this notion is that it suggests that the 'hierarchy of selves' could be regarded as to some extent a physical concept. We have so far been thinking of the ladder of selves as a ladder of *consciousness*, with a series of rungs or distinct states. But consciousness is a bodily state—at least on the level with which human beings are familiar. The body is a mirror; consciousness is a reflection from the mirror. When I am tired, my consciousness is turned down like a light; when I am happy and excited, it becomes brighter.

Consider the following experience, recounted in Raymond A. Moody's book *Life after Life*. A college student tells how he fell asleep while driving a tractor, which went out of control:

> Now, during the period of time that the truck was skidding, I just thought of all the things I had done. I saw only certain things, the high points . . . The first thing I remembered was following my father as he walked along the beach; it was when I was two years old . . . I remembered breaking my new red wagon I had gotten for Christmas when I was five. I remember crying as I went to school in the first grade . . . Then I went to junior high, and got a paper route, and went to work in a grocery store, and it brought me up to right then, just before the beginning of my second year in college.
>
> All these things, and many others, just flashed across my mind, and it was very quick. It probably didn't last but a split second. And then it was all over and I was standing there looking at the truck . . . The truck was a total wreck, but I didn't receive a scratch.

This seems to confirm the notion that people 'see their whole lives' when drowning. Why? We know, from the work of Wilder Penfield, that the brain's playback mechanism holds every detail of our lives and can reproduce it. But Penfield stimulated the cortex with an electric current. What seems to have happened here is that the prospect of immediate death produced a similar effect, causing a whole series of memories to play back in a matter of seconds. And it is possible to see why: the urgency calls upon deeper levels of energy than are normally at the command of the conscious will.

I can recall only one similar experience. I was driving at eighty miles an hour along a broad double highway in North Devon. Far ahead of me, a lorry pulled out of a side turning. Assuming, naturally, that he would proceed along the road, I pulled over into the outside lane without slowing down. At that point, I realised that he intended pulling *across* the road into the opposite lane. As I hurtled towards him—at that speed the brakes seemed to have no effect—I remember feeling perfectly calm and concentrated, although it seemed inevitable that I would hit him. I drove towards the small space between the back of the lorry and a concrete wall, the car skidding and rocking wildly. A few seconds later, I came to a halt with the lorry behind me, and leaned out of the window to shout profanities at the driver, who had simply forgotten to use his indicators. I can still remember that sense of deep and total concentration, the kind that I might achieve once a year when I am writing particularly well. If I compare this with the constriction of the throat I experience before appearing on a television programme, it seems clear that some deeper—or higher—level of the mind will provide the necessary *control* when the importance of the occasion demands it. But not otherwise.

The student cited by Moody had no control over his vehicle. It was already turning over and skidding. The vital energies called upon by emergency had no opportunity for deployment; so we may infer that they turned inward, stimulating the memory cells like Penfield's electric probe.

The lesson is very clear. If we could call upon such a flood of 'emergency energy' at will, we could 'replay' the whole of our lives, as Robert Irwin suspected.

This, in turn, highlights the basic absurdity of human existence. A cybernetician once remarked that if we wanted to build a computer as complex as the human brain, it would have to be the size of the moon. Part of the human computer contains a vast library, containing records of everything that has ever happened to us, everything we have ever felt, everything we have ever seen or read or even dreamed. Every man is, in essence, a giant corporation. And it seems logical to suppose that he developed this immense organisation for some purpose. A Martian who had never actually seen a human being but only studied books about us might well conclude that we are a race of gods. And what do we actually do with these immense possibilities? Repeat the same banal experiences over and over again, like a gramophone record stuck in a groove. During the whole of his lifetime, the average human being never calls upon a thousandth of his tremendous capacity.

When it is expressed in this way, we can even begin to see the reason. There is simply not enough power to work most of the apparatus. You could compare the situation to an elaborate water mill driven by a thin, muddy trickle of water. Or to a complex electrical apparatus connected up to a two-volt battery. Or to a grandfather clock driven by a watch spring.

Why has this situation arisen? Theologians like to speak of original sin, but the answer is less sinister. The culprit is our ancient ally and enemy, the 'robot'.

In order to grasp fully what is at stake, we must also call upon another concept—Husserl's 'intentionality'. This means, quite simply, that before I can 'have an experience', even the simplest, I must *direct my consciousness towards it*. The concept is a familiar one. If I am hungry, it is not enough to place food in front of me. I have to eat the food. And if I go to a symphony concert or attend an art exhibition, I have to make a certain effort. If I allow my mind to wander, the symphony will mean nothing to me, the pictures will be meaningless splashes of colour. The same is true of reading a newspaper or watching television; unless I perform the equivalent of *eating*, of absorbing and digesting, I take in nothing at all.

On the other hand, this act of absorption need not involve much effort. I can eat a meal while carrying on conversation and not even notice what I am eating. f course, I don't enjoy the food, but at least I digest it. If I am trying to write a letter, and the children are playing Red Indians in the garden, I may find myself 'involuntarily' paying more attention to the war whoops than to my letter, and be unable to concentrate.

This explains how we fall into 'original sin'—the error of regarding experience as 'non-intentional'. If I can hear something *against my will*, then surely it cannot be true that hearing depends on an act of will?

The fallacy here lies in the word 'involuntary'. It is *not* 'involuntary' when I am distracted by the children's war whoops. The robot 'wills' it for me, and he uses my vital energy to do it. It is rather as if you give your accountant authority to pay your income tax for you by writing cheques on your bank account, and then assume you aren't paying any income tax because you didn't write the cheques yourself. The money still comes out of your account; you still have to earn it.

We have slipped into a habit of over-reliance on the robot and we have already seen how dangerous this can be. Reliance on the robot can become a habit—until we are bound hand and foot in a spider's web of habit, which strangles all our creativity. Creativity demands effort, and every time we try to work ourselves up into a state of creative tension, the robot says, 'Here, let me do that for you', and takes it out of our hands.

Think of what happens if I fall into the habit of paying no attention to my food, bolting it automatically as I read a newspaper. I begin to lose interest in eating, and probably to suffer from indigestion. Even if I *try* to take an interest in my food, I shall find it very difficult, once I have acquired bad habits, for as soon as I begin to eat, the habit takes over, and I slip into a kind of trance.

On the other hand, consider what happens in those rare moments when we 'live life to the full'. Every experience becomes a conscious transaction; we are so intent on not missing anything that we notice every single detail. The world offers us 'objects of interest', and we *pay for them in full* with avid attention.

Both Tolstoy and Dostoevsky have described the feelings of a man as he is about to be executed by firing squad—the sudden recognition that the world is an infinitely interesting place, the way that the eye lingers on every object, finding in it immense depths of meaning.

Even the common experience of lying in bed for a few minutes extra on a cold morning can reveal the same underlying truth. Because the warmth will last only for a few moments more, we pay for it with undivided attention, determined to savour the last drop. And the experience *repays us* by taking on a glowing intensity.

What is wrong with most of our experience is that, instead of paying an honest price, we are always trying to cheat. We try to have the experience with the minimum of attention; but we only get out of it exactly as much as we put in. When we have repeated any experience a few dozen times, the 'transaction' tends to become a habit, and we get even less out of it. Moreover, it becomes almost impossible to 'put more into it', even if we wanted to. (Try, as an experiment, deliberately putting more attention into any experience that has become a habit, and you will see how difficult it is.) We assume that the experience 'really is' like this, and the robot automatically doles out the customary minimum of attention. Life can easily become boring and flat and dull, and the spider-webs of habit wrap themselves around us more tightly. When life ceases to excite much response from us, we say we are 'disillusioned', the implication being that the moments of delight were a lie, and boredom is the underlying reality. And a point comes when the robot has finally bound us hand and foot; unless some external crisis intervenes to save us, to galvanise us back into effort, we might just as well be dead. It has even been suggested that states like this may be responsible for cancer.[10] This also explains why man has a paradoxical desire for disasters and wars; they can break the vicious circle of 'life failure'.

Let us abandon argument for a moment and indulge ourselves in the pleasures of myth-making. Let us pretend that there was a time, in the earth's remote past, when man was far more godlike than he is today. In that distant epoch, he was a magnificent and formidable creature who lived for several centuries. (His longevity was due to the fact that he never suffered from boredom.) Even at the moment of death he could still be fascinated by a sudden beam of sunlight or the smell of damp moss in the rain.

Of course, his civilisation was minimal. In that remote Golden Age, he didn't *need* much civilisation. We fail to realise how many of our modern amenities are the outcome of boredom. The basic rule of the affluent society is: when bored, go out and buy something; so our homes are full of gadgets we seldom use. Man of the Golden Age found everything so interesting that he felt no need to spice his life with variety. When he wanted to give himself a treat, he went and sat on a hilltop or looked at the stars.

He possessed a certain amount of skill in science and mathematics, for he was at least as intelligent as modern man; but he enjoyed them as we enjoy art and music, with no nervous compulsion to turn them to practical advantage. When catastrophes threatened, he used his knowledge to avert them; otherwise he had no use for 'progress'. For him, evolution was a purely inner process.

This evolution was interrupted by the advent of a new ice age. Suddenly, it was all he could do to stay alive and keep his children fed. Survival demanded qualities of cunning, ruthlessness, and, above all, sheer endurance. Vast numbers died of cold and starvation. Those who were left became machines geared to survival.

Oddly enough, the 'old consciousness'—the instinctive understanding of the mysteries of space and time—never vanished entirely. It only went into 'cold storage', waiting for the day when it could re-emerge. But that day never came. When the climate finally improved again, man had become a highly-mechanised creature. The robot had ceased to be a servant and was now an equal partner. Moreover, man had become accustomed to living on a half-ration of consciousness; he took this new reduced level of perception for granted, having forgotten that there was any other kind. If he had *wanted* to get rid of the robot, it might have been a different matter; but he wasn't even aware of what he was missing. All he knew was that when he went hunting, or made war on a neighbouring tribe and raped all the women, he felt 'more alive'. And from now on, this desire to feel 'more alive'—to win back a little of his old freedom from the robot—became the chief motivating force of his evolution. But since life had become so short and bloody, it was a losing battle; step by step, man has climbed down the ladder of consciousness. And now, after thousands of generations, his capacity for boredom and his capacity for self-destruction have both reached a new and far more dangerous level.

There remains one consolation. Freedom that has once been gained can never be entirely lost. Every new-born baby carries his godlike origin in his genes. We all experience sudden flashes of our former state, and in these flashes, we become aware of the ladder stretching up above us.

The parable is not intended to be taken literally; I do not believe that the Golden Age really existed. Nevertheless, I feel that it goes to the heart of the problem of modern man. In the past, his salvation has been the hardships he had to contend with; they kept him on his toes. Now his technology has created a civilisation that is becoming increasingly devoid of challenge. Vast numbers of men spend their weekdays performing some repetitive, mechanical job, and their weekends staring at the television. In such circumstances, more and more of our living is taken over by the robot. We feel vaguely, uncomfortably aware of the loss of freedom, but we have no idea what can be done about it. Buying a larger television set hardly seems to be the answer.

Ascetics and mystics have always understood that the answer lies in the mind itself. Evelyn Underhill expresses the simple basic discipline in her book *Mysticism*:

> All that is asked is that we shall look for a little time, in a special and undivided manner, at some simple, concrete, and external thing. This object of our contemplation may be almost anything we please: a picture, a statue, a tree, a distant hillside, a growing plant, running water, little living things. We need not, with Kant, go to the starry heavens . . . Look, then, at this thing which you have chosen. Wilfully yet tranquilly

refuse the messages which countless other aspects of the world are sending; and so concentrate your attention on this one act of loving sight [so] that all other objects are excluded from the conscious field. Do not think, but as it were pour out your personality towards it; let your soul be in your eyes. Almost at once, this new method of perception will reveal unsuspected qualities in the external world. First, you will perceive about you a strange and deepening quietness, a slowing down of our feverish mental time. Next, you will become aware of a heightened significance, an intensified existence in the thing at which you look. As you, with all your consciousness, lean out towards it, an answering current will meet yours. It seems as though the barrier between its life and your own, between subject and object, has melted away . . .[11]

This discipline actually works; and it works because one pours more *intentionality* into perception. The same result can be achieved rather more quickly simply by staring at some object and then concentrating all your attention, as if looking at it closely was a matter of life and death. The result, as Evelyn Underhill points out, is a sudden deepening of meaning. If, for example, you are staring at a book cover, its colour seems to deepen. If one could hold this concentration for a minute or two, the effects would be very like those of a psychedelic drug—for example, Aldous Huxley's description of the effects of mescalin.

John Humphrey Noyes had hit upon the same method. It may be difficult for a man to concentrate with any enthusiasm on a book or a statue for the requisite period of time; but if he happens to be engaged in the intensely pleasurable activity of love-making, he might, with sufficient control, remain in a state of concentration for minutes, or even hours. The result would be a strengthening of the 'muscle' with which we focus reality.

What we are speaking about, of course, is Faculty X. Faculty X is the ability to grasp the reality not simply of *other* times and places, but of the present moment as well. And this observation makes us aware of the basic problem. As we merely look around us at ordinary objects, we are not seeing 'reality'; only a kind of shadowy, symbolic reality. (It is typical of the inadequacy of language that I am forced to use the same word when I mean something different in each case.) It is necessary to grasp clearly that ordinary perception is little better than a fever, in which all objects are slightly unreal.

This realisation is the important first step in the right direction. The next is to recognise that Faculty X is not merely a matter of achieving brief glimpses of 'reality', which fade almost immediately, but is an entrance into a whole new world of meanings. C. S. Lewis gives some interesting examples in his autobiography *Surprised by Joy*. The first 'glimpse' makes very clear that he is speaking of the same thing that Proust experienced when he tasted the cake dipped in tea:

> As I stood beside a flowering currant bush on a summer day there suddenly arose in me without warning . . . the memory of that earlier morning at the Old House when my brother had brought his toy garden into the nursery . . . It was a sensation, of course, of desire; but of desire for what? Not, certainly, for a biscuit tin filled with moss, nor even (though that came into it) for my own past—and before I knew what I desired, the desire itself was gone, the whole glimpse withdrawn, the world turned commonplace again, or only stirred by a longing for the longing which had just ceased.

Here, as we can see, Lewis is talking about some specific 'other time, other place'. But not so in the other two examples he gives.

> The second glimpse came through *Squirrel Nutkin*, through it only, though I loved all the Beatrix Potter books. But the rest of them were merely entertaining; it administered the shock, it was a trouble. It troubled me with what I can only describe as the idea of Autumn. It sounds fantastic to say that one can be enamoured of a season, but that is something like what happened; and, as before, the experience was one of intense desire. And one went back to the book, not to gratify the desire (that was impossible—how can one *possess* Autumn?) but to reawake it. And in this experience also there was the same surprise and the same sense of incalculable importance. It was something quite different from ordinary life and even from ordinary pleasure; something, as they would say now, 'in another dimension'.

This last remark brings home the problem with a certain poignancy. Non-robotic perception, which ought to be the commonest thing in the world, is 'something quite different from ordinary life'. We have come to accept this dull, two-dimensional fake created by the robot for the real thing.

> The third glimpse [Lewis goes on] came through poetry. I had became fond of Longfellow's *Saga of King Olaf*: fond of it in a casual, shallow

way for its story and its vigorous rhythm. But then, and quite different from such pleasures, and like a voice from far more different regions, there came a moment when I idly turned the pages of the book and found the unrhymed translation of *Tegner's Drapa* and read

> I heard a voice that cried
> Balder the beautiful
> Is dead, is dead—

I knew nothing about Balder; but instantly I was uplifted into huge regions of northern sky, I desired with almost sickening intensity something never to be described (except that it is cold, spacious, severe, pale, and remote).

Lewis's sadness is due to a misunderstanding. He thinks that his 'glimpses' are of something unattainable—'How can one *possess* Autumn?' What he really wants to 'possess' is not Autumn, *but Faculty X*. Moreover, some of his later comments make it perfectly clear where he has gone wrong:

> You will remember how, as a schoolboy, I had destroyed my religious life by a vicious subjectivism which made 'realisations' the aim of prayer; turning away from God to seek states of mind . . . With unbelievable folly, I now proceeded to make exactly the same blunder in my imaginative life. . . I formulated the complaint that the 'old thrill' was becoming rarer and rarer. [And] by that complaint I smuggled in the assumption that what I wanted was a 'thrill', a state of my own mind. And there lies the deadly error. Only when your whole attention and desire are fixed on something else—whether a distant mountain, or the past, or the gods of Asgard—does the 'thrill' arise. It is a by-product. Its very existence presupposes that you desire not it but something other and outer.

Lewis is so pleased at seeing through his own 'vicious subjectivism' that he rushes into the arms of the opposite error. Of course meaning really exists 'out there'. It is not merely a creation of the mind, as Bishop Berkeley thought. But the mind has to go out and grab it. It is no accident that we use the phrase 'to *pay* attention'. The coinage is attention, concentration, intentionality.

Because he has failed to grasp that perception is intentional, he has lost the chance of arriving at an even more basic recognition—an insight that would have provided the key to his 'mystical' experiences. This is the recognition that consciousness is not only intentional; it is also *relational*. It is as if everything I look at has *invisible threads* running from it to all the surrounding objects. For example, a man may have an attractive wife; but when he sees her slaving over the kitchen stove, he fails to notice her attractiveness. When he sees her at a party, surrounded by admiring males, it becomes self-evident. You could compare the males to a battery of spotlights that had to be switched on before he could see that she was attractive.

When a hypnotist want to put someone into a trance, he gets them to concentrate on a *single object*. This cuts off the *relations* to other objects, and consciousness is quickly suffocated, just as when you fall asleep. Consciousness means grasping relationships. Without this sense of relations, a man will quickly sink up to his neck in 'reality' as a man without snowshoes will sink in a snowdrift. (This is what Sartre calls nausea.)

'Intentionality' suggests an arrow fired at a target; but when consciousness is doing its proper work, it is like a whole shower of arrows fired simultaneously. Unfortunately, human beings are lazy and passive; they are always trying to economise on energy, so that what ought to be a vast net of 'relations' shrinks to the size of a small spider's web. We call this dreary, half-suffocated state 'normal consciousness'. And when some sudden stimulus, like Lewis's 'toy garden' or Proust's cake dipped in tea, produces that delightful glimpse of other times and other places, we tend to regard it as a kind of mystical visitation, instead of recognising it as a glimpse of true normality. Even Bennett's experience in the forest at Fontainebleau was not 'mystical' consciousness; it was simply an example of 'wider relational consciousness' produced by his determined assault on his laziness.

The recognition that consciousness is 'relational' as well as intentional has an important corollary: *perception itself is a creative act*.

This at first sounds preposterous: the idea that what happens when you look out of the window could be compared to Michelangelo painting the ceiling of the Sistine Chapel, or Beethoven writing the Ninth Symphony. Nevertheless, it is true. And anyone who can grasp precisely why it is true holds the key to mystical experience—that is, to 'wider relational consciousness'.

If you are relaxing in a chair at the end of the day and a child kicks a ball through the window, this represents a challenge, to which you must respond. Your response can vary from the lazy to the highly energetic. You may tell your wife to telephone the odd-job-man, and go on reading your newspaper. You may decide to effect a temporary repair with a sheet of cardboard. Or you may—assuming you have glass and putty in the gardening shed—decide to repair the window immediately. This last decision would require a considerable effort of will, for the task is not a simple one. It requires you to *stretch* your consciousness, in order to co-ordinate a sequence of minor tasks. This stretching of consciousness is, in fact, the basic *creative act*. It differs from the 'inspiration' of a Beethoven or Michelangelo only in degree, not in kind.

In the case of the broken window, it is easy to see that I have a number of choices, involving more or less 'creative tension'. It is far more difficult to realise that I have just the same number of choices when I look out of the window. For what I do, quite habitually, is to make the choice that involves the least effort—the equivalent of telling my wife to telephone the odd-job-man. And this becomes easy to grasp if I imagine a man who is about to be hanged, looking out of the window for the last time. We can imagine him staring hungrily, as if his eyes could devour the scenery. Every object would take on a new significance, and every one would shed new meaning on other objects. Perception is creative; and like all other forms of creation, it yields results in proportion to the effort.

Once this is understood, the distinction between mysticism and common sense, between the normal and the paranormal, begins to dissolve.

The career of the half-forgotten German philosopher Fechner provides a remarkably apt illustration of the process. Nowadays, he is remembered chiefly as a psychologist who performed important experiments on the measurement of sensations. In his own day—in the mid-nineteenth century—he was known as a mystical philosopher who taught that plants have souls and that the earth is a living being.

Gustav Theodor Fechner was born in 1801, son of a pastor in a small Saxon village. After a poverty-stricken childhood—his father died when he was five—he became a medical student at Leipzig at the age of sixteen and proved to be a brilliant student. He supported himself by translating textbooks of physics and chemistry. Predictably, he lost his faith and became an atheist for a period. He performed a number of classic experiments in electricity, as a consequence of which he was appointed professor of physics at Leipzig University at the age of thirty. His interest switched to experimental psychology, and his work in this field led him to formulate Fechner's Law, which states that the intensity of a sensation is proportional to the logarithm of the stimulus.

So far, he seems to have been the model of the hard-working scientist. But in his late thirties, overwork and eye strain produced a peculiar illness that brought him close to death. His own lengthy account of the illness makes it sound oddly like the troubles that afflicted Gopi Krishna after he had accidentally awakened the *kundalini* serpent. Eye strain from looking at the sun during his experiments on after-images made it impossible for him to read, and this in turn produced deep depression and a feeling of mental confusion. Various 'cures' exhausted him still further, until he became a skeleton and went for weeks without food or drink. The most terrifying effect was that his thoughts seemed to be out of control; he felt they were 'boring and burrowing' into his brain, and that if he was not careful, they would exhaust the last of his strength. His description makes it clear that he suffered from months of panic attacks. 'I sometimes conceived of myself as a rider who was trying to subdue a runaway horse, or a monarch whose subjects had revolted . . .'

After three years of struggle, his health slowly improved. When he was again able to see, it was like a revelation.

> I still remember well what an impression it make upon me when, after suffering for some years from an ailment which affected my sight, I stepped out for the first time from my darkened chamber and into the garden with no bandage on my eyes. It seemed to me like a glimpse beyond the boundary of human experience. Every flower beamed upon me with a peculiar clarity, as though into the outer light it was casting its own. To me the whole garden seemed transfigured, as though it were not I but nature that had just risen up again. And I thought: So nothing is needed but to open the eyes afresh, and with that, old nature is made young again. Indeed, one will hardly believe how new and vivid is the nature which meets the man who comes to meet it with new eyes.[12]

The Fechner who finally returned to the University of Leipzig as a professor of philosophy was no longer deeply interested in physics or experimental psychology. The 'vision' in the garden had led him to recognise that the dull world of everyday experience is a kind of delusion; the world of reality is alive. In fact, it is *conscious*. His book

Nanna, or the Soul Life of Plants, is an attempt to express that vision in terms of the vegetable world.

We may speculate that his three years in darkness, and his extreme physical weakness, produced a state of sensitivity in which he became aware of the plants as living creatures, as if the garden were full of children. What he perceived directly was what Cleve Backster discovered accidentally in 1966 when he connected his rubber plant up to a lie detector and looked around for a box of matches to burn the leaf: plants are sensitive to the vibrations of other life-forms; or, to put it more crudely, that they can read our minds.

In his *Atomenlehre*, Fechner went on to argue that atoms are vortices of force or energy, and should be regarded as the simplest elements in a spiritual hierarchy. And in *Concerning Souls* (1861), he boldly states that the universe itself is alive, and that the earth and stars should be regarded as living beings. He suggests, the earth is an 'angel', 'so rich and fresh and blooming, and at the same time so stable and unified, moving in the heavens, turning wholly towards heaven its animated face'. His other work makes it clear that this is not a lyrical metaphor; he conceives the earth as part of a universal system of living beings, interconnected by a web of light, gravity and 'forces that are at present unknown'. He could have been voicing the doctrine of the fertility religion that man held for thousands of years before the coming of Christianity—or even of civilisation.

But Fechner's perhaps most interesting anticipation occurs in a book dating from before his breakdown, *A Little Book of Life After Death* (1836), written as a consolation for friends who had suffered a loss. In most ways it is less interesting than *Nanna* or *Zend-Avesta*, reading like any typical devotional tract of the nineteenth century. But its central idea is that life consists of three stages: continual sleep in the womb; a condition of semi-sleep; and life after death, or full consciousness. Fechner had the same central insight as Gurdjieff: that 'ordinary consciousness' is a form of sleep. In *Life After Death* he accepts the pietistic convention that death is the gateway to a higher world. His illness brought a deeper revelation: that what is wrong with ordinary consciousness could be altered by a change of vision; that reality overflows with meanings to which we are blinded by habit and laziness.

Gurdjieff also had an experience of near-breakdown, which brought certain fundamental insights. He describes it in his last book,

Life is Real Only Then When 'I Am'. [13] A few years before the First World War, Gurdjieff fell sick in Central Asia from a complication of fevers; he recovered in a small town on the edge of the Gobi Desert. He was well on the road to complete recovery when, one evening, he experienced a state of unprecedented mental clarity, and began to brood on the problems of how to achieve 'non-mechanical consciousness'. He became aware of all his blunders in his earlier searches and the shortcomings of the methods he had devised. He felt his strength waning as these thoughts took possession of him and found himself unable to stop them, in spite of an urgent desire to arouse himself. 'I don't know with what this would have ended if at the moment when instinctively I began to feel that I must lose consciousness, the three camels near me had not sat down. At this, I came to myself and got up.' Even after a cold bath in a nearby spring, he felt so physically exhausted that he had to lie down. Hours of self-examination finally led him to the conclusion that he had to develop some method of preventing himself from slipping back into 'mechanical living'—some kind of permanent reminder of the need for self-remembering. He concluded that this could be accomplished by making a vow to cease using his powers of hypnotism and telepathy from that time forward. He had become so accustomed to using these powers to gain his own ends that a decision not to use them any more would serve the same function as the saint's hair shirt or the yogi's bed of nails.

To read the Prologue of *Life is Real Then Only When 'I Am'*—describing a number of serious illnesses and accidents, including the almost fatal car crash of 1924—is to realise why Gurdjieff was so convinced that 'suffering' was the only true means to non-mechanical self-consciousness. Each new disaster threw him back on his own resources; each new recovery deepened his vitality.

But precisely what happened when his 'fatal thought', exhausted him almost to the point of losing consciousness? It sounds strikingly similar to Fechner's experience of losing control of his thoughts, until they threatened to kill him with exhaustion. And this, in turn, sounds sufficiently like my own experience during the period of panic attacks to suggest that we have here different versions of the mental 'black hole' phenomenon. Everyone knows what it is to have a 'sinking feeling', to suddenly feel drained of energy by some unpleasant thought. This loss of energy has no obvious physical cause; it is as if we had opened up some inner valve that caused a drop in vital pressure. I can recall, in my teens, feeling these 'shocks' for no particular reason—just experiencing the 'sinking feeling' about life in general, a kind of vague conviction that something or other would go wrong. (And it usually did.)

I once lived in a cottage where the electric lights worked off car batteries, which had to be recharged daily with a small generator. This generator had one unpleasant peculiarity. It would sometimes 'miss a beat', and stop charging. Then, if the automatic cut-out didn't work, its huge fly-wheel would begin revolving *backwards*, and proceed to drain the batteries of their charge. The same thing happens to human beings in states of over-anxiety. Normally, sleep acts as an automatic cut-out; but if we get too tense, it fails to operate, and the tension actually drains our vital batteries. Psychotic patients in mental homes can sink into 'exhaust status' and die of it.

This obviously describes what happened to both Fechner and Gurdjieff; tension pushed them into the state of inner crisis. Fortunately, both of them retained the power to fight back (although Gurdjieff seriously contemplated suicide in one of his later crises). The result was a strengthening of their vital powers, an increased control over the robot. In fact, as one reads Walter Lowrie's account of Fechner's life or Gurdjieff's own description of his various crises in his last book, one begins to feel more than a glimmer of a suspicion that their crises were not entirely accidental: that they were somehow subconsciously engineered to produce precisely this effect. This suspicion deepens when we read that Fechner's 'religious' tendency had been there since his early days, but was in conflict with his scientific temperament; some kind of radical rearrangement of his inner forces was necessary if his two aspects were to cease cancelling one another out. Gurdjieff's reactions to his own crises reveals that he regarded them as something more than accidents; he always took them as a signal for radical self-examination and re-alignment of direction.

In his autobiography, Yeats expresses the view that men of genius are deliberately brought to crisis by some inner destiny, 'spirits that we had best call Gates and Gate-keepers . . . They have but one purpose, to bring their chosen man to the greatest obstacle he can confront without despair. They contrived Dante's banishment, and snatched away his Beatrice, and thrust Villon into the arms of harlots, and sent him to gather cronies at the foot of the gallows, that Dante and Villon might through passion become conjoint to their buried selves . . .' Interestingly enough, Yeats recognises that the 'gate-keepers' are a part of man's own psyche. 'I know now that revelation is from the self, but from that age-long memoried self, that shapes the elaborate shell of the mollusc, and the child in the womb . . . and that genius is a crisis that joins that buried self at certain moments to our trivial daily mind.' Yeats conceives the 'buried self' as the puppet master who pulls the strings of the puppet called the everyday self.

Yeats believed, like Gurdjieff, that this 'conjoining of the buried self and the trivial daily self' can only be brought about by crisis. This is also the view we find in the saints and mystics: salvation comes through the death of the old self and the birth of the new.

Is this necessarily true? Where Gurdjieff is concerned, my own doubts began to crystalise in the spring of 1974, during a weekend I spent at the 'Gurdjieff school' opened by J. G. Bennett at Sherborne shortly before his death.

I knew enough of Bennett's activities in recent years—particularly his association with the Indonesian 'messiah' Pahk Subuh—to realise that he was no longer strictly in sympathy with Ouspensky's scientific approach to the problem of 'overcoming sleep'. But I was not prepared for the extent to which his approach had become oriented towards religion—he had recently become a Catholic convert—and Eastern mysticism. There was something anomalous in the sight of Gurdjieff's foremost living disciple listening intently to a lecture by an Anglican clergyman on the importance of prayer. And when a talk on mystical religion began with a quarter of an hour of sitar music, while the instructor—a bearded young man—sat with closed eyes in the lotus position, I felt my impatience begin to boil over.

In a discussion with Bennett that evening, I mentioned my misgivings, that all these vague generalities about love and 'tuning in' to the universe had little to do with Gurdjieff's 'fight against sleep'. Bennett replied that I was forgetting that Gurdjieff was himself a deeply religious man, who believed that Jesus was the son of God. (This seems to be confirmed by a passage in the Prologue of *Life is Real Then Only When 'I Am'*.) Bennett clearly felt that his work was still in the spirit of Gurdjieff. And since he knew a great deal more about Gurdjieff than I did (he told me he had read the whole of *All and Everything* a dozen times) I was inclined to give him the benefit of the doubt.

The next morning, as the dawn was breaking, we all sat cross-legged in a large bare room, while Bennett intoned some thoughts suitable for inducing meditation. Suddenly, I saw clearly the essence of my objection to this approach. Gurdjieff's 'method' has one simple aim: *to gain control over the robot*. To this end, he attempted to keep his pupils in a constant state of *alertness*. This is why he would often go into the dormitory in the middle of the night, and expect everyone to assume some complicated position at a snap of his fingers. Neither prayer nor meditation guarantee alertness; both can be comfortably taken over by the robot.

Yet I could also see why Bennett felt that his work was in the true Gurdjieff tradition. His pupils worked strenuously for ten hours a day, gardening and decorating the house (which needed extensive repairs). They meditated, attended lectures and practised 'Gurdjieff movements'. Gurdjieff and Ouspensky had insisted that effective 'work on oneself' can only be practised in a group, and this was the essence of Bennett's approach.

Yet if my analysis was correct and the aim of 'work on oneself' is to gain control over the robot, then the 'group' approach is not as important as Gurdjieff believed. The reason should be clear. The 'robot' is not basically an enemy; he was created to help us. I *need* a highly efficient robot. But the problem is a matter of balance. If we think of man as a limited company, then the 'real me' needs to hold a majority of the shares. Once let fifty-one per cent of the shares fall into the hands of the robot, and the 'real me' becomes the servant. But if a man is driven by a powerful sense of purpose, he can often capture as much as sixty per cent of the shares. Of course, the robot continues to expand, as we all continue to learn; in that case, it is important to bear in mind the lesson of Rubenstein and Best's planaria experiment (described on Page 327): to put *twice* as much energy into the learning process as seems to be strictly necessary.

My own panic attacks, which had continued almost up to the time I went to Sherborne House, confirmed this analysis. The turning point had arrived one day not long before Christmas, 1973, when I had driven to the post box to catch the evening post. The narrow drive that leads up to our house joins an almost equally narrow country lane, so that it is necessary to stop and look both ways. As I braked at the end of the drive, a car hurtled past, almost scraping my front bumper; if I had braked a second later, there would have been an accident. Yet I had braked automatically; I was feeling exhausted and bored. I found myself thinking of the enormous inconvenience of an accident and felt a flash of relief that it hadn't happened. And suddenly, I was forcibly struck by a recognition of the sheer *stupidity* of allowing myself to fall victim to exhaustion and boredom. For the truth is that *human beings determine their own energy levels. We* decide what is 'boring' and what is exciting. Tom Sawyer made that interesting discovery when he persuaded his friends to whitewash the fence by whistling and looking as if he were enjoying it. But he could have persuaded himself to enjoy it by telling himself that it was fascinating and deliberately setting out to generate that conviction. Conversely, when I contemplate some task or problem with the thought, 'How boring', my energies sink.

I agree that a man who had no energy and no hope would find it impossible to generate much enthusiasm. But most of us have plenty of reserve energy, and plenty of reason for being glad to be alive. We have simply allowed ourselves to *lose sight* of these things through an excessive preoccupation with the trivialities of our immediate purposes.

What struck me forcefully when I came close to losing my bumper, was that my tiredness was not really the result of overwork; it was the result of forgetfulness, laziness and spoiltness. Human beings are not *intended* to drag themselves around in this state. It reduces their efficiency, like walking around with their eyes closed. It is our *business* to keep our eyes open, if we want to avoid serious problems. And this can be done, quite easily, by forcing ourselves to pay attention, to redouble our sense of urgency.

That night, before I went to bed, I experienced a sudden sense of depression and fatigue, which brought a flash of fear. Then suddenly the fear turned to anger, and I thought: 'You stupid lazy bastard. If you have a panic attack it's your own bloody fault.' From that moment on, the panic attacks ceased.

Now, sitting in Bennett's meditation group, I saw that I had rescued myself from my fatigue through the 'planaria method'—that is, simply by *doubling* the energy and attention I put into living. I had galvanised myself into a state of alertness and gained an added degree of control over the robot. And that was precisely what Gurdjieff and Bennett had set out to teach their pupils. Ergo: Gurdjieff and Bennett were mistaken in their belief that group work was necessary. I had done it on my own. What was required was basically an intelligent understanding of the problem. Gurdjieff's fundamentally religious outlook had led him to think in terms of crisis and suffering, rather than of a logical and reasonable attempt at self-deconditioning.

There is another important lesson to be drawn from this problem of exhaustion and defeat. What happens when an attitude of pessimism produces physical and mental breakdown? It is as if some kind of inner valve has been opened, which allows all my vital energies to drain away. By contrast, when I am in a state of eager expectancy, possessed by a strong sense of purpose, I *instinctively* conserve my energies. My sheer concentration somehow closes the inner valve so tightly that nothing escapes. This is enough to make us aware that the state in which most of us live our lives is far from desirable. Could this, then, be the answer to the problem we have been considering throughout this book: that human beings are like 'grandfather clocks driven by watchsprings', or like water mills driven by a thin, muddy trickle? This is the basic message of Gurdjieff and Ouspensky. Man's being is like a vast mansion, yet he seems to prefer to live in a single room in the basement. And the reason for this curious waste of his potentialities is the permanent leakage of vital energy—a leakage of which he is totally unconscious. If he conserved his energy, kept this inner valve tightly closed when engaged in any form of purposive activity, there would be more than enough water to drive the mill wheel.

4

Other Dimensions

———◆———

And now, at last, we seem to be getting closer to a comprehensive theory of the paranormal. The human organism—this brain and body with which we are born—is an enormous computer, containing thousands, probably millions, of circuits that we never use. Absurd and paradoxical as it sounds, man actually *is* a god. His *capacities* are superhuman. What seems to have gone wrong is that he has allowed himself to become subject to some kind of law of diminishing returns that has reduced him to a mere fraction of his stature.

The chief problem, of course, is where the computer came from. In Arthur Koestler's parable about the Arab shopkeeper who prayed for an adding frame, and was given a modern computer, Allah was responsible for the mistake. Another notion is that man is some kind of fallen angel, a view that 'occultists' will find plausible enough, but scientific evolutionists will find difficult to swallow. Fortunately, we are not forced to choose between these two views; there is a third possibility. In *The Hunting Hypothesis*, Robert Andrey writes about a species of finch that has lived on the Galapagos Islands for hundreds of generations—long enough to sub-divide into fourteen species. On the Galapagos there are no predatory hawks as there are on the mainland, where the finch originated. Yet when a baby finch is taken from the Islands to California and sees a hawk for the first time, it instantly reacts with typical alarm. The instinct which meant life or death to its remote ancestors is still there, unimpaired after centuries of disuse.

According to the latest scientific estimates, man in his present form is about three million years old, and his various ancestors stretch back for half a billion years. His computer of a brain—all three of them—is perfectly adequate to store up every vital response he has learned during the whole of that period. Obviously, the majority are never needed—like the finch's response to hawks. Yet they are there, and can be activated under the right circumstances.

This provides an explanation for such powers as telepathy and second sight. If, as seems highly likely, animals and plants possess such powers, then we must possess them too. The same kind of explanation could even be stretched to fit such problems as psychokinesis and poltergeist activity. If we can accept the existence of unknown forms of energy capable of carrying thoughts from mind to mind, it is easy to imagine such energy being harnessed for other purposes. After all, radio waves can be used to cook a steak, or melt a piece of metal.

The real problem arises when we try to explain precognition. There is no way in which we can possibly grasp the notion that it is possible to see into the future. Our senses and our common sense tell us it is impossible. Yet hundreds of recorded cases of precognition assure us that our senses must be mistaken.

John Bennett believed he had found a solution in the theory of a fifth dimension. In his autobiography *Witness*,[1] he describes how he was fascinated by Einstein's hypothesis that the ether must be some kind of material substance with the apparently impossible property of travelling in all directions at once at the speed of light. He goes on:

> The following evening, at dusk, I was walking back to my office to finish some reports . . . when the solution struck me like an electric shock. In a moment of time, I saw a whole new world. The train of thought was too rapid for words, but it was something like this: 'If there is a fifth dimension not like space but like time, and if it is orthogonal [at right angles] to the space-time we know, then it would have the required property. Any matter existing in that direction would appear from our standpoint to be travelling at the speed of light. And moreover it would travel in all directions at once. This must be the solution of Einstein's riddle. If so, the fifth dimension must be as real as the space and time we

know. But the extra degree of freedom given by the fifth dimension opens all kinds of possibilities. It means that time itself is not unique, and that if there is more than one time, there is more than one future. If there are many times, there would be the possibility of choosing between them. In each line of time, there can be a strict causality, but by changing from one line to another we can be free. It is like a railway passenger; so long as he remains on one train his destination is decided in advance. But he can change the train at a junction and so decide his destination.

With these notions flashing through my mind, I saw that my own riddle of free will and determinism could be solved by the addition of a fifth dimension.

The reasoning here may seem obscure, but the conclusion is plain enough. As living creatures, we find ourselves confined in a world that appears to have four dimensions, three of space and one of time. Our science concerns itself with this world. But this 'real world', as grasped by reason, leaves no room for life, let alone for freedom. We *ought* to be totally trapped in cause and effect. Yet I can reach up and scratch my nose or decide not to scratch it; I can decide whether to think about philosophy, sex or my dinner. There is no *room* for freedom in the real world, yet it exists. Stare at your face in a mirror until you have lost all sense of identity; suddenly, you are seized with horror at this strange face looking at you. You were living in your own inner world of being and freedom and, suddenly, you are stranded in a world of objects in which freedom is an impossibility.

That is the problem Bennett is trying to solve by the addition of a fifth dimension; seen in this light, his solution is plain and sensible enough. If time is a fourth dimension, as Einstein asserts, then my inner freedom is a fifth dimension—a realm that declines to be 'placed' in the first four.

This odd idea suggests another interesting conclusion. Einstein said that time must be the fourth dimension because you need it to 'define' an event. I can say 'I'll meet you on the fifth floor of the building at the corner of Tenth Avenue and Twenty-Second Street', and I have defined the place in terms of three dimensions; but if I forget to mention the time of the meeting, it may well never take place. If we think of the fifth dimension as our inner freedom, we might say: 'No event can be entirely defined in terms of four dimensions. For I may decide not to go to the meeting—exercising my freedom—in which case, it will still not take place, even though you have specified the other four co-ordinates.' And from your point of view, this element *cannot* be defined or fixed, for I might make any one of a thousand different decisions. Think of a worm crawling across a cabbage leaf; it is virtually a creature of two dimensions; what lies over the next bump on the leaf does not yet exist. Yet as you look down on the leaf from above, you can say with confidence that the worm is shortly going to encounter a large caterpillar hole. Because the hole is *already there*, a definite place which can be defined in terms of certain co-ordinates.

If we can imagine a being that is able to look down on our freedom from above—from some sixth dimension, so to speak—we can see that whatever we choose to do is also 'fixed'; like the hole, it is already there.

But surely that destroys the whole idea of freedom? Not quite. Think again of the worm on the leaf. If it continues in a straight line, it will encounter the hole. But it may change its direction. It may decide to sit still. The only thing you can say with certainty is that it will not fly into the air, because it has no wings. So you can easily outline all the possibilities that are open to it. And if it is moving in a straight line, you can choose one of them as by far the likeliest. Yet the worm remains 'free'.

Such arguments may strike the reader as too abstract to be of value. But is is possible to arrive at similar conclusions from a strictly practical basis. An excellent example can be found in Charles Tart's book, *Psi: Scientific Studies of the Psychic Realm*. Tart describes how his colleague, Dr Lila Gatlin, a specialist in information theory, subjected the results of certain precognition tests to statistical analysis. Her studies convinced her that there was something wrong. When people tried to guess what the *next* target would be, they seemed to be getting results that were below chance. And that was absurd. Tart considered the problem and came up with an interesting theory. If I am asked to guess what number on a dice will turn up next, I will automatically take into account the *last* throw. For example, if the last throw was a six, then I probably won't guess six for the next throw, because I will feel that it is less likely than the other five numbers. (This is not true; it has exactly the same six-to-one chance of turning up.) We tend to avoid the past result. But if genuine precognition has taken place—so that the subject has an intuitive glimpse of the next target—is it not possible that he may react in the same way and avoid the future target in the same way that he avoids the past one? As Tart points out, many processes in physics are 'symmetrical'—if an atomic process creates a negatively charged particle, it will also create a positively charged one.

Tart ended by positing a second dimension of time (and, he adds, probably of space as well). 'This second dimension acts as a channel for psi information. I theorize that one property of this second dimension of time is that the experienced present of awareness is wider than the experienced present of ordinary consciousness.' What he is saying is that ordinary consciousness focuses on a very narrow 'band' of time, which we call the present. It lasts for a few tenths of a second, which is to say that we do not notice sensations that last for less than that. But we are aware of the 'second dimension of time' as a *wider* band, stretching a little further into past and future.

Tart makes use of another helpful analogy. If you take a sharp pencil and press it on your bare skin without looking at it you will at first feel as if you were being touched by a wide, blunt point. This is because the pencil stretches your skin, and affects more distant 'receptors'. But after a few moments, you will experience the pencil as a sharp point. This is a process called 'lateral inhibition'; the receptors have somehow cancelled one another out, to give you a sharper picture. The same technique can be used in space probes, so that a blurry photograph of a volcano on Mars can be sharpened to give more information.

Tart believes that our minds *naturally* have the ability to probe past and future, but that we also have a 'lateral inhibition' mechanism which gives us a sharper focus, so we concentrate on a hard, clear present moment. This enables us to function better. But we can deliberately develop an ability to 'blur' the present, so that we again become aware of the future, rather like looking through your eye lashes.

This is, of course, similar to the theory put forward by Bergson and Aldous Huxley (and discussed at the end of Chapter 6): that the nervous system is a filter, designed to keep things out rather than let them in, and that if the filter was removed, we would be flooded with all kinds of useless paranormal information. But Tart has arrived at his theory not through philosophical speculation, but through statistical analysis of laboratory experiments.

There is one obvious objection to Tart's theory of precognition: it fails to explain how psychics can sometimes foresee an event that may occur weeks or years in the future; his 'band of perception' of the second dimension of time is fairly narrow. And clearly, this problem is analogous to the question of how a dowser can accurately trace a stream on a map with the aid of a pendulum. Whatever faculty is at work, it is apparently not limited to narrow bands.

The problem may be that Tart, like Bennett, is still thinking in terms of scientific logic, while ultimately trying to deny the validity of such logic. The real task, of course, is to rebuild the whole philosophy of science on a new foundation. Bennett had the courage to make the attempt in his vast work *The Dramatic Universe*, whose title suggests its basic thesis: that the universe should be seen as an unfolding drama rather than as a machine; but the obscurity of the book makes it difficult to decide how far he succeeded.

One of the most remarkable and constructive attempts to 'rebuild science' in our own time is to be found in the work of Arthur Young, the author of *The Reflexive Universe* and *The Geometry of Meaning*. As early as 1927, Young, who later achieved fame as the inventor of the Bell helicopter, recognised that the problem is that logic, by its very nature, can make no allowance for freedom. This struck him when he was considering 'the Cretan paradox': that if a Cretan remarks that all Cretans are liars, then he must be telling a lie—in which case, he is telling the truth. But if he is telling the truth, then he is contradicting himself when he says all Cretans are liars. Young reasoned that the problem could be solved only by recognising that we have to take *time* into account. The Cretan has every right to say what he wants about the past; but his judgment cannot cover the statement he is now making. Judgments, says Young, cannot include themselves. But what he is really saying is that while a man is alive and free, he cannot be 'pinned down' as a liar, or anything else. In fact, Young anticipated Sartre, who declared that the human essence is freedom. A man may behave like a coward on a thousand occasions, but it is still untrue to *label* him a coward, because he may behave like a hero on the thousand and first.

Young's philosophy is too complex to be summarised here, but it is possible to describe at least its central idea. Young became convinced that the recurrence of the number seven in religious and mythological texts is no accident; that it corresponds to something fundamental in the structure of the universe. There are, he speculates, seven 'levels of existence'. In purely physical terms, there are sub-atomic particles (electrons, etc.), atoms, molecules, plants, and animals, each more complex than the last. Beyond these lies—potentially—the level we call the human; yet man is still ninety-nine per cent animal; true freedom is still no more than a potentiality. Even so, this is only six 'levels'. The seventh, he eventually concluded, is that of light, which is capable of creating particles. Light is the first step in the great process. And the evolution of matter—from light to molecules may be conceived as a kind of 'fall'. Light loses its freedom in creating sub-atomic particles; free electrons lose their freedom in condensing into atoms; atoms lose freedom by forming molecules.

But beyond these first four stages of the 'fall', a new ascent begins. Plants represent a new struggle for freedom, and animals a still higher level. The final level is still to come; this is the struggle we are still engaged in.

Like Charlotte Bach, Young believes that all evolution is purposive. He points out that light, in entering the earth's atmosphere, follows the path that will get it to its destination in the least time; Max Planck observed that in this respect, light behaves like an intelligent being. This tendency of energy to choose the path that will take the least time, Planck called 'action'; and he made the famous discovery that 'action' comes in discrete packets, which he called quanta. Young points out that 'wholeness' is also true of human action; we cannot perform any act one and a half times; if you jump out of a window, you either do it or you don't.

Readers without training in quantum physics may find all this bewildering; but Young's conclusion is clarity itself. 'The older concept of a universe made up of physical particles interacting according to fixed laws is no longer tenable. It is implicit in present findings that *action* rather than matter is basic, action being understood as something essentially undefinable and non-objective, analogous, I would add, to human decision.' And he takes the bull by the horns when he asserts that inventing the Bell helicopter taught him that evolution is essentially a purposive process.

In a sense, Young is trying to say the unsayable. Nothing is easier than to produce a philosophy that allows no room for freedom, that reduces the universe to material terms—as Hume does in the *Treatise of Human Nature* or as Professor Jacques Monod has more recently in *Chance and Necessity*. It has the alluring simplicity of a two-dimensional projection. Conversely, nothing is more difficult than to try to pin down freedom in terms of logic. A good example of the difficulty can be seen in Wittgenstein's *Zettel*, where he tries to define the meaning of the word 'intention'. 'Intention is neither an emotion, a mood, nor yet a sensation or image. It is not a state of consciousness. It does not have any genuine duration. "I have the intention of going away tomorrow." When have you that intention? The whole time; or intermittently?'[2] The truth is that an intention is a pure expression of my freedom. And although it takes time to carry out an intention, *the intention itself does not happen in time*. So when Arthur Young says that the basic unit of reality is 'action' and compares it to human decision (i.e., intentionality), he has carried the argument to a level where, in a sense, language cannot follow him.

When we look at the world through the spectacles of science, we are missing out a vitally important element: human freedom. This means that it is almost impossible to construct a 'scientific' theory of evolution, because the most essential element keeps getting left out. Yet the moment I approach the matter through intuition, the dilemma vanishes. Intentionality can be strong or weak. When a bored man lights his fiftieth cigarette of the day, it is weak; when Romeo climbs into Juliet's bedroom, it is strong. The effectiveness of an intention depends upon its strength. If I hold up my hand and waggle my fingers, my intention is instantly translated into action, because my muscles are obedient to even a weak intention. But if I try to control the pounding of my heart when I am feeling nervous, it may only make things worse. This is not because it is impossible; people can learn to control their heartbeat and even their blood pressure with the use of bio-feedback machines. It is because intentionality needs to be far stronger for such a difficult matter. On the other hand, heightened intentionality can bring an astonishing degree of control—as when Bennett told himself 'Be surprised', and was overwhelmed with astonishment.

This, as Charlotte Bach and Arthur Young have pointed out, is what evolution is really about: *using our freedom to increase our freedom*. And since the essence of freedom is 'mystical', then evolution is basically a mystical rather than a scientific concept.

It is now possible to see why science feels so embarrassed when faced with the concept of the paranormal. It finds it hard enough to come to terms with the basic tenet of existentialism: that man is free. It finds it almost impossible to cope with the main implication of occultism: that man possesses far more freedom than he realises. Yet this is, unmistakably, the message that comes from all fields of paranormal research. When Proust discovered that a cake dipped in tea could make the past as real as the present, he had discovered a new dimension of human freedom. (This is why he spoke of 'ceasing to feel mediocre, accidental, mortal'.) The same was true for Felicia Parise when she discovered that she could move a plastic bottle by concentrating on it. And for Jane O'Neill when she saw Fotheringhay church as it was five centuries ago. And for Tom Lethbridge when he used a pendulum to locate buried metal. And for Sylvan Muldoon and Robert Monroe when they found themselves hovering above their physical bodies. All paranormal experience carries the same message: man's everyday view of himself is somehow profoundly mistaken.

But even if we are prepared to acknowledge this much, we are still left with another major objection: the whole realm of the paranormal seems to be so mad and *disconnected*. It is as if someone took two hundred pages at random out of textbooks on physics, chemistry, biology, psychology and a dozen other sciences, bound them together in one volume, and called the result 'An Outline of Modern Scientific Knowledge'. It is tempting to regard the whole field of the paranormal as a realm of weird phenomena and peculiar people—Uri Geller, Daniel Dunglas Home, Madame Blavatsky, Aleister Crowley, Rasputin, Nostradamus, Cagliostro—all demonstrating utterly inconsequential powers like spoon-bending, levitation and automatic writing. Understandably, most scientists find it easier to condemn the whole thing as a kind of fantasy.

In this book I have attempted to show that one simple hypothesis can bring a certain amount of order into the confusion: the notion that the mind of man possesses many levels. We are familiar enough with the notion of unconscious levels, and the fact that such functions as digestion and body temperature operate on these levels. It is no more difficult to grasp the proposition that 'paranormal powers' could also operate on other levels of consciousness. The most controversial consequence of this assumption is that these powers are not *waiting* to evolve; they are already fully evolved, and are simply waiting for us to achieve a level at which we can make use of them. This is, admittedly, a paradoxical state of affairs; but when so much evidence points in this direction, it would be absurd to ignore it.

Which brings us once more to the question that human beings have always recognised as the greatest of all: the problem of death. It is all very well for Proust to say that he ceased to feel mediocre, accidental, mortal; the fact remained that he *was* mortal and met the same end as everybody else. Therefore, presumably, his 'insight' was untrue.

Spiritualism denies this and asserts that there is now abundant evidence to show that the spirit survives the death of the physical body. Paranormal research is less dogmatic; it agrees that the evidence seems to point in this direction, but denies that it is as conclusive as the spiritualists would like to believe.

Stan Gooch summarises the problem in his book *The Paranormal*. After describing his own experience of trance mediumship and even of 'memories of previous lives', he points out that most of the evidence seems to come from the most unreliable witness of all: the unconscious mind. For the unconscious mind has a remarkable ability to invent detailed and apparently factual stories—as demonstrated in our dreams. He goes on: 'I believe the strong tendency of the unconscious to produce stories is connected with a desire of the unconscious—the "female principle"—to divert and entertain.' As a human being, he admits to a desire to believe in life after death; as a scientist, he finds the case unproved.

The evidence for 'survival' falls into three main groups: so-called 'communication with the dead'; people who have experienced 'death' and returned to tell the tale; and doctors and nurses who have observed 'deathbed hallucinations'.

The ambiguity of the first kind of evidence can be seen in the case that started the spiritualist movement. The 'spirit' that made its presence known by rappings in the home of the Fox sisters identified itself as a murdered peddler named Charles B. Rosma, who had been buried in the basement. No person of that name could be traced, but digging in the basement uncovered fragments of hair and bone in quicklime. More than half a century later, in 1904, workmen repairing an old wall close to the cellar discovered an almost complete human skeleton and a peddler's tin box.

Against this evidence we must place the testimony of the second of the Fox sisters, Margaret, who in 1888 publicly 'confessed' that she and her two sisters had produced the knockings fraudulently. She said that the knockings were produced by dropping an apple or cracking their joints, and gave a demonstration in front of a theatre audience. But then, Margaret, and Kate, the youngest of the sisters, were on bad terms with their elder sister Leah by that time and had been embittered by poverty and illness after the death of their husbands. Leah was still a successful medium. The confession was clearly motivated by a desire to hurt and to earn money (their 'confession' made them one thousand five hundred dollars), and perhaps to regain some of the lost limelight. Above all, the knockings were often described as loud and distinct bangs and could not have been produced in the manner described by Margaret. So again we have to record another 'unproven' verdict.

This, as Stan Gooch points out, is the case in the great majority of instances of 'communication with the dead'. There are, he admits, a few that are slightly more convincing. After the death of F. W. H. Myers, one of the founders of the Society for Psychical Research, in 1901, his Cambridge neighbour Mrs Verrall began to receive 'communications' in automatic script that purported to come from Myers and his two collaborators, Sidgwick and Gurney. The most convincing part about these scripts is that similar messages were also received by other mediums in other countries as far apart as India and America; moreover, the various parts of the scripts fitted together like a jigsaw puzzle. (The case became known as the 'cross correspondences'.) But then, it must be admitted that many of the scripts were extremely obscure, being in Greek and Latin as well as English. It would take a very large volume to summarise all the evidence—the communications went on for decades—and few people would have the patience to arrive at an assessment. If Myers really wanted to prove that he was still alive, he chose a most unsatisfactory method.

Gooch also cites a more straightforward case described by Nils Jacobsen. In 1928, Jacobsen's uncle was run over by a lorry and died in hospital without recovering consciousness; the family naturally assumed that the death was due to concussion, since he sustained head injuries. Six years later, a 'spirit' purporting to be the dead uncle contacted his family through a medium and mentioned that he had not died of concussion but of some ailment originating in a lower bone. A check of the hospital records showed this to be true—a blood clot from the bone had caused a stoppage in the brain. If it could be established that *no one* knew this, then it would certainly be convincing proof that the information originated with the dead man. But, as Gooch points out, the surgeon who performed the post mortem knew, and a member of the family *could* have picked it up from him telepathically. So again, the evidence cannot be regarded as airtight.

The other two categories of proof are, by their hearsay nature, even less convincing. Raymond A. Moody's book *Life After Life* contains many remarkable accounts by people who have been pronounced dead, then recovered and described 'after death' experiences. The book is dedicated to Dr George Ritchie, a Virginian psychiatrist who is himself the author of one of the most circumstantial accounts. In December 1943, Ritchie, an army private, was in hospital in Texas with an upper respiratory infection. He began to spit blood, his temperature rose, and he lost consciousness. He woke up feeling confused, convinced that he had to catch a train to the medical school in Virginia; then he looked around and saw his own body on the bed. Outside in the corridor, a ward boy walked straight through him. He tried tapping a man on the shoulder and went through him; he leaned back against a guide wire and fell through it. Now finally convinced that he was insubstantial, he went to his own body and tried to get back into it; this proved to be impossible.

So far, Ritchie's account has been circumstantial and convincing; from this point on, it ceases to be either. He describes how the room suddenly became brighter—'like a thousand arc lights'—and a presence he identified as Jesus appeared. What follows sounds like a religious fantasy. Jesus took him on a flight through the air and into a great city; they walked through a red–light quarter, and Ritchie was able to witness the consequences of sin at first hand. They saw a bodiless alcoholic who kept trying to grab a bottle of whisky, but his hand went through it. Eventually, after more adventures of this kind, Private Ritchie was allowed back into his own body, a chastened and a wiser man.

Sceptics might be forgiven for concluding that this was a cynical and not-particularly subtle invention in the revivalist tradition of *Twelve Nights in a Bar Room*. But *prima facie* evidence makes it seem unlikely; Ritchie is a psychiatrist, with a position in a major hospital; if he wanted to invent a tale with a moral, he could easily have made it more convincing. If we find it impossible to accept the story as he tells it, the likeliest explanation is that his unconscious was setting out to divert and entertain. From which emerges an important and sobering lesson: that nothing is easier than to invent a story of paranormal experience that sounds circumstantial and convincing, and that if the conscious mind is too honest to do it, the unconscious will happily take the responsibility.

Does that mean that all such experiences must be dismissed as dreams? Such an attitude would not be as sensible as it sounds. Where 'proof' is concerned, every one of us has to rely on his own subjective judgment; and we exercise this judgment every day of our lives. If something strikes us as true, the best thing is to stand by that judgment, while bearing in mind that we *could* be mistaken. And if people I know believe that they have had a paranormal experience, then it is up to me to make up my mind (a) whether they are being totally honest, (b) whether they have been deceived by the unconscious mind.

I can illustrate this through an experience that happened to my mother. In 1955, our family doctor failed to diagnose a stomach pain as appendicitis; the appendix ruptured and she was rushed into hospital with peritonitis. For the rest of that year, she was in and out of hospital, having operation after operation. During this time I was writing my first book in London; on visits to the hospital in Leicester I saw her becoming steadily weaker. She says that she finally became convinced she was dying and felt quite resigned to it—even happy.

> Nothing else mattered. And suddenly I looked at the side of the bed, and there was this old fellow with a white beard, and he looked like a biblical character. I remember glancing down and noticing that he had sandals on. He'd got a kind of scroll in his hands, like those you see on a gravestone, and he unwound it, and started to talk to me. The words were most beautiful—I just wish I could remember the words, but I can't. He looked as though he was reading the words to me. Then he looked at me and said: 'Now look, you can't go yet, there's too much for you to do. You're needed here.' I felt ever so happy. I wish I could remember what he said. But he promised me something—he said I'd got to stay here for some reason. After he'd gone, I felt much better. And I knew I didn't have to die, if what he said was true. I *knew* it was true, because his voice was so gentle.

It is almost impossible to evaluate an experience like this. She is emphatic that it was not a dream. 'I was wide awake and I saw him. I thought it might have been your great grandad, but Aunt Con says he didn't have a little white goatee beard like this fellow.' Could he have been, as she suggests, some 'biblical character'? This seems unlikely, since his last words to her before he vanished were 'Shangri-la'—presumably pronounced as a kind of benediction—and it seems unlikely that a disembodied spirit would mention a place invented by the novelist James Hilton.[3]

On the other hand, the 'promise' came true; she was in hospital again the following May when my book *The Outsider* was published, and the nurse brought her in the early reviews, which launched it to best-sellerdom. After this, her life, like my own, changed considerably. The comment 'You're needed here', also proved to be prophetic; in the late 1960s, my father became ill with cancer and had to be nursed through the last seven years of his life.

Clearly, the experience with the old man meant a great deal to my mother. She has frequently said, ever since then, that she now has no fear of death. Although she agrees that it could have been some kind of hallucination, she nevertheless feels that it was sent to tell her something that was true. I am inclined to believe that her illness allowed her some precognitive glimpse of the future, and that the biblical figure was the method adopted by her subconscious mind to bring it to her attention and revive her will to live.

In 1960, Dr Karlis Osis, director of research at the Parapsychology Foundation in New York, decided to conduct a full-scale investigation into 'hallucinations' of this type. He decided that the people who would know most about 'crisis apparitions' would be doctors and nurses; accordingly, he sent out ten thousand questionnaires. From the replies, he obtained more than 35,000 observations of dying patients. One interesting point to emerge was that fear was not the most frequent emotion experienced by the dying, although there was a great deal of pain and discomfort. But in a large number of cases, the patient seemed to experience a state of great happiness, usually starting about two hours before death. And in many of these cases, the patient was convinced that he had seen something—frequently a deceased relative. In the majority of cases, the patient was fully awake and in an undrugged state; oxygen starvation to the brain was also ruled out as a cause.

In order to find out whether these 'hallucinations' were peculiar to Christian culture, Dr Osis began parallel studies of deathbed observations in America and India. The results were strikingly similar; the difference in culture made no difference. The other obvious possibility—that visions of dead relatives might be wish-fulfillment—was rejected because in many cases the dying patient strenuously objected to being 'taken away' by the unseen visitor.

In one interesting case, a woman died soon after childbirth in a Clapton hospital; she had not been told that her sister had died in the meantime. Shortly before her death, she stared in astonishment, and told the doctor that her deceased father had entered the room *with her sister* (whom she still believed to be alive). The case cannot be regarded as conclusive, since she may have learned of her sister's death telepathically, perhaps through the doctor or nurses. But here again, the most striking thing is the access to *true information* of someone on the point of death.[4]

Perhaps the real significance of the work of Dr Karlis Osis is that, by bringing together such a mass of deathbed observations, he has given the notion of life after death a new kind of statistical likelihood. Most people have heard of at least one dying person who thought he saw dead relatives; but such cases seem to be the exception. A volume describing the final moments of well-known people (i.e. sufficiently well-known to be written about) might also provide some interesting information. Wordsworth, on the point of death, thought he saw his dead sister Dorothy enter the room (although he may have been mistaking his niece for Dorothy). Emanuel Swedenborg predicted the exact date of his death many weeks in advance; a servant girl present at his deathbed reported: 'He was pleased, as if he was going to have a holiday, to go on some merry-making.' William Blake—as might be expected—'died in a most glorious manner'. Blake had always possessed the faculty of seeing disembodied spirits and 'elementals', and accounts by his contemporaries show that he meant he saw them literally, not through imagination. His friends Varley and Linnell used to sit beside him for hours as he stared into space and drew portraits of people he claimed to be able to see quite clearly. At Felpham, on the coast of Sussex, he remarked that 'voices of Celestial inhabitants are more distinctly heard, and their forms more distinctly seen'. Of his death, his wife wrote: 'Just before he died his countenance became fair—his eyes brightened, and he burst out in singing of the things he saw in heaven.'

Tolstoy seems to have recorded some similar insight at the end of his story *The Death of Ivan Ilyich*, describing a man's death from cancer: 'He sought his accustomed fear of death but did not find it . . . There was no fear because there was no death. In place of death there was light. "So that's what it is," he suddenly exclaimed aloud, "What joy!" ' The episode has the ring of a personal insight.

.   .   .

It would probably be true to say, then, that there is an impressive amount of evidence for 'survival', none of it watertight, yet convincing through sheer bulk. Why is it, then, that so many Christians remain unconvinced by the evidence offered by spiritualism?

It is, I think, basically a sense of the *irrelevance* of 'survival'. What is wrong with human existence is its dreamlike quality—what Camus called its absurdity. Death is simply the final absurdity. So it is no *answer* to believe that life continues on the other side of death. It may be true; but it is still no answer.

It is our fundamental instinct for evolution, for meaning, that produces this sense of absurdity. If I read a book like *War and Peace* or *The Old Wives' Tale*, I realise that I am drawn on by a desire to see the characters *fulfilling* themselves. But even this seems to be largely a matter of biological drives. A woman wants to see the heroine fall in love, marry the man of her choice, and become the mother of a contented family. A man wants to see the hero achieve success and sexual fulfilment, but not necessarily to become a married man with a family. So even the basic notion of fulfilment differs from person to person. Louisa M. Alcott and the Marquis de Sade might belong to different species as well as different sexes. And when, in a long novel, we have seen the various fulfilments take place, we still experience a desire to go on, to go further. Instead, the characters get old and die. It feels as if something important has been left out, as if human life ought to contain *another* element not present in a novel. But it doesn't. In life, as in the novel, we are left asking: What then?

A glimpse of something that *looks* like the answer occurs in the 'mystical experience', or even in sex. This is a new sense of power, of control. In the sexual orgasm—as described, for example, by D. H. Lawrence—everything seems to become more *real*, as if our feet were at last on some kind of solid ground. And *then* it suddenly becomes possible to see what is wrong with the notion of life after death that comes from study of the cross correspondence cases or the careers of famous mediums. For the question is precisely *what* survives death. These 'glimpses' seem to tell us that man is really a god. The personality is essentially a kind of illusion: *my* idea of what constitutes 'me'. This changes throughout the course of my own lifetime; so it seems absurd that the personality called F. W. H. Myers should still be communicating half a century after his death.

Again, there is a feeling that many people—perhaps all—contain a seed of destiny, of meaning, when they are born, and that their lives are an attempt to allow this meaning to emerge. A picture of Beethoven at twelve suggests that the Ninth Symphony is already inside him, waiting to get out. Even I, as a writer, feel that I have spent my life persuading something to emerge and that every word I have written has been an attempt to give it form, and existence in the light of consciousness. The notion of life after death seems meaningless except as a continuation of that purpose. I never cease to feel that human existence is like crawling through a very low tunnel, with hardly any freedom of movement. Sometimes, when we suddenly become aware of how little freedom we possess, we experience a panic that springs from a terrible claustrophobia. The ultimate fulfilment we can envisage is to emerge into the daylight. If *this* is what is meant by life after death, then it is certainly to be welcomed; but I find nothing about it in the cases reported to the Society for Psychical Research.

I woke up one night having a dream that seemed to summarise the problem of human existence. I was being wheeled along in a bathchair outside the British Museum, pushed by two attendants; I had no memory of how I'd got there. I turned around and asked: 'Would you mind telling me what we're supposed to be doing?' They looked at me in amazement, and one of them said: 'We thought *you* knew.'

The basic absurdity seems to lie in the notion of *time*; and this explains why we feel dissatisfied with the idea of life 'after' death; it still implies being trapped in time, and therefore stuck in the same narrow tunnel. The 'answer' we require is not to be assured of life after death, but to understand the nature of time, and to be able to stand above it.

An interesting clue was thrown off by Dr Steve Rosen in a paper on time delivered at the Parascience Conference in London in 1976;[5] he mentioned that we three-dimensional creatures perceive a line as stationary; but if we can imagine creatures who consisted of mere points, they would see the line as a succession of points, along which they had to move; it would be their equivalent of time. Perhaps, he suggested, our notion of 'moving time' is due to our 'dimensional inferiority'; creatures in a higher dimension would perceive time as a stationary line.

We have already glanced at this type of speculation earlier in this chapter. But expressed in this manner, it points the way to the next logical step. Human beings are apparently *both* types of creatures. On one level, we are trapped in time; in another, we are capable of precognition, which suggests that *we* see the line as stationary. Some higher rung of the ladder of selves sticks out into the timeless realm.

But since I am down here, on the time level, this realisation seems to be of no particular use to me. What can I *do* about it? This depends very much on my attitude towards my time-existence. And here again, Arthur Young's philosophy becomes relevant. Inanimate forms of existence, from light to inorganic molecules, are trapped in time; their existence *is* time. Plants and lower animals are obviously *more* trapped in time than human beings are. The plant's life consists of growing, performing its functions, and dying. Animals, too, are trapped in this world of necessity, responding to a perpetual present.

Human beings are also animals, but we have developed the ability to turn our heads slightly, so that we are no longer merely part of the process that goes on around us. Man has struggled for mental freedom and has ended by creating a whole world that exists on another level. It began by being a realm of the gods; and, according to Julian Jaynes, man did not even *need* consciousness to respond to this realm. But his aim was to create consciousness, to create a mirror in which he could see his own face. According to Sir Julian Huxley, one of the most important events in the history of humanity was the invention of art. The moment he learned to tell stories, man moved up to a level from which he could contemplate his everyday life as something separate, as another type of story. He learned to draw, to create music, to study nature scientifically; every new development enabled him to take another step backward from the mirror. Even the invention of wine, around 8000 BC, may have been crucial in his development, since it has the same power to enable us to contemplate our lives from 'above', to rise above 'contingency'.

But the creation of *self*-consciousness involved a basic danger. It introduced 'Hamlet's disease'. A simple, stupid creature, who plods on through life doing whatever has to be done, never loses a sense of movement, of freedom. The moment man learned to look at his face in a mirror, he lost this natural freedom. He was, admittedly, free to move forward; but he was also free to stand still, brooding on his own problems and unable to make up his mind. His new freedom brought a sense of inferiority; Hamlet may feel contempt for Rosenkrantz and Guildenstern, but he admires their lack of self-doubt, just as T. E.

Lawrence envied a soldier with his girl or a man patting a dog. We are now in the realm of the 'Outsider'.

Essentially, the power to create is the power to grasp the world in concepts; but we end by viewing the world *through* our concepts, as through the bars of a cage. They colour everything we see, as the world of a bad-tempered man is coloured by his anger. This is as true of men of genius as it is of idiots. Dante, Shakespeare, Balzac, were men enslaved by concepts. Dante's cage, admittedly, was a large one, as large as the Catholic Church. But Shakespeare, for all his creative genius, was a slave to a pessimism that regarded human existence as meaningless, a tale told by an idiot. We find the same contradiction in Balzac: a vast world, seething with vitality, yet poisoned by a philosophy of despair, in which the greatest men are doomed to the same defeat as the stupidest.

The same thing applies to our science and the philosophy we have modelled upon it. Concepts have made us master of the atom; they have also reduced us to a bundle of conditioned reflexes. Science shows us a meaningless world of mechanical forces.

This explains the 'existential dread' that has haunted the Western mind for the past two centuries. Trapped in a dark universe of his own creation, man's evolutionary drive is reduced to a hunger for security. This world around us may be meaningless, but at least it seems to be solid and stable. Perhaps death *will* snuff us out as if we had never existed; but we can bury our heads in the triviality of everydayness.

Philosophers have always recognised that the trouble lies in our concepts: that we live and breathe and see through them. Kant even thought that space and time were human creations, mere conditions of seeing. But Edmund Husserl was the first major philosopher to realise that concepts can enslave us only as long as we are unaware of their existence. As soon as the philosopher has identified and 'stained' them, as a biologist stains germs, they become harmless. Moreover, he recognised that the ability to be enslaved by concepts is a proof of the tremendous creativity of the human mind. And if we can once grasp that creativity, we can use our concepts to set us free. They may limit reality, but they can also help us penetrate deeper into reality—even to the realm of the 'keepers of the keys of being'.

Gurdjieff was another who recognised that our major problem is a totally false way of seeing and grasping the universe. He states in *Beelzebub's Tales to his Grandson* that man possesses two types of consciousness: one intuitive and direct, one based upon all kinds of false premises about reality of which we are not even aware. His own aim, he says, is to 'corrode without mercy all the rubbish accumulated during the ages'. But Gurdjieff also recognised that these false concepts' chief ally is the robot, which can be overruled by a sense of *urgency*. 'The sole means now for the saving of the beings of the planet Earth would be to implant again into their presences an organ . . . of such properties that every one . . . should constantly sense . . . the inevitability of his own death as well as the death of everyone upon whom his eyes or his attention rests.'

I had always recognised that this was the essence of the problem; that this was why 'Outsiders' subjected themselves to danger or hardship: to attempt to destroy the stultifying force of habit. But it was not until my panic attacks of 1973 that I suddenly grasped the precise nature of the mechanism that steals our freedom. From the moment we are born, our senses are continually being bombarded with meanings; I can recall, as a child, going for a walk on a sunny morning and feeling as if my senses were being *assaulted* by sights and sounds and smells. For the child, the whole world is an Aladdin's cave, a gigantic toyshop; he has only to smell newly-cut grass or autumn leaves to be convulsed by a kind of passion of longing.

It is not desirable to be so vulnerable; we develop 'filters' to cut out the meaning, like closing the windows of a classroom on a spring day to prevent the pupils from being distracted. As we get older, we become so accustomed to living in this sparsely furnished classroom that we keep the windows closed most of the time. Old people scarcely live in the real world at all; they stay inside their own heads. As a result they cease to experience the bombardment of meaning, until they also cease to feel desire.

My panic attacks came about because I was overtired and overworked. The result was that, quite unconsciously, I closed my windows and kept them closed. I ignored everything that was not connected with my work. The attacks were a form of suffocation, fainting spells due to lack of oxygen. They were triggered by a mechanism of self-consciousness, in the same way that thinking about itching produces a compulsion to scratch yourself.

As I slowly began to achieve insight into the process and to learn to reverse it, I realised that I had stumbled on a solution to the problem that had obsessed Gurdjieff and Husserl. I recognised, for example, that this could be the answer to the question posed by Bernard Shaw in *Back to Methuselah*, of how human beings could increase their lifespan. Most people actually die prematurely, of a kind of oxygen starvation. Meaning exists outside us; it is all around us, like the air. It stimulates our vitality and awakens our powers. Yet we allow ourselves to suffocate slowly, because we are unaware of the mechanism that opens the windows. If we could learn to control that mechanism, it would be the key to evolution.

It linked with a discovery I had made in my teens and then half forgotten. Through an essay by T. S. Eliot, I came upon the *Bhagavad Gita*, and through that, the whole Hindu and Buddhist philosophy of enlightenment and liberation. It produced a tremendous sense of mental relief after years of the usual adolescent fatigue and depression (complicated, in my case, by a kind of manic intellectuality). I learned to meditate—or concentrate—for an hour at a time, sitting cross-legged on the floor. And I instantly made a delightful discovery. My general level of vitality rose steeply, and I found myself constantly bathed in a kind of glow of meaning. Sights and smells and colours became somehow sharper. It was almost as if I had suddenly got rid of an oppressive catarrh that had destroyed my sense of smell. This intensified sense of meaning would fade as I became tired; but half an hour's meditation would quickly restore it. I found this new sense of meaning so fascinating that I decided to leave my home town and the office where I had worked and wander around England and France. It seemed absurd to live in such an astonishing world and stay in an office.

In the course of that *wanderjahre*, I developed another interesting trick. This consisted simply of looking at something and reminding myself that it contained immense depths of meaning: that if I could hear what it had to tell me, I would sit spellbound for hours. This would have the same effect as a piece of good news or good luck; a bubble of delight would rise in me, and a little of that vast, hidden meaning would overflow into my senses.

Then I married, begot a son, and settled down to the old routine of working at a regular job and trying to write books in my spare time. I never wholly lost the trick of inducing that inner expansion; but it became overlaid by practical affairs.

In the midst of my panic attacks, I realised that it was important to try to re-develop the trick of inner expansion. And as I re-learned it, I suddenly realised how closely it was connected with the central argument of my book *The Occult*, and with the notion of Faculty X.

I have already mentioned how, in a novel called *The Philosopher's Stone*, I had written a scene in which the hero sits on the lawn of an Elizabethan house, and allows himself to sink into a state of total serenity. He wonders idly what the house would have been like in the time of Shakespeare; and then, suddenly, *sees* the answer to his question. The Elizabethan parts of the house are still there; it is merely a matter of adjusting his perceptions to register them.

The episode was intended as fictional speculation; now I realised that it expressed the plain truth about Faculty X. We all possess the power to 'see' a house as it was a century ago; but it lies outside the range of our everyday senses. These create a kind of self-sustaining whole, which is called the personality, and which appears to have an independent existence. If anxiety causes me to narrow my senses still farther, a new—and less vital—personality will be formed. We have examined this phenomenon in the second Chapter of Part Two and seen how Janet could actually carry on a conversation with the 'wider' personality, while the narrower one heard nothing. In precisely the same way, the 'meanings' of the world around us carry on a conversation with our wider personality, while the person I think of as 'I' remains unaware.

So what is at issue in this present stage of human evolution is not simply a new scientific paradigm—although, God knows, that is needed urgently enough—but also a new, conscious ability to relax into that wider personality. Western man is in danger of suffocating himself with his drives and obsessions; he needs to learn the difficult trick of bringing them under control.

Again, my experience of panic attacks suggests the basic method. We spend too much of our time in a state of unproductive tension, as if expecting a blow; we are full of pockets of mistrust and negation. After my unpleasant experience on the night train, when I came close to total loss of control and inner chaos, I realised that the answer is to relax *beyond* normal relaxation. Anyone can go and lie in the sun, or sit in an armchair with a drink, and allow the superficial tensions to dissolve. But it is more difficult to press on beyond this point, into still deeper states of relaxation. And here I should point out again that it makes no difference whether we describe this process in terms of climbing or descending. We could speak of 'gliding', and of the attempt to get the glider off the ground, or of descent into oneself, as if in a kind of elevator, through layer after layer of meaning.

Now if we combine this insight with the recognition that 'man is a grandfather clock driven by a watch spring', we can see that the chief problem is to achieve the *power* to climb or descend. When I am tired and bored, I am stuck in the present, like a fly on flypaper, and I have no power to escape this time-trap. As soon as I become absorbed in anything, an inner dynamo begins to hum, and I can feel my strength increase. And the simplest way to cause that dynamo to turn is to focus on something I *want*: fame, sex, security, possessions, powers, whatever.

Man has discovered an interesting method of increasing his power to 'focus'; it is called art. We can see, for example, that Poe used his own peculiar obsession—the death of beautiful women—to escape the boredom and futility of his life as a hack journalist. But even hard pornography qualifies as a crude form of art, for its purpose is to focus sexual desire. Novels of violence focus our aggressions. Landscape painting focuses our longing for the impersonality of nature. A great painting or symphony may focus so many complex desires that it is impossible to express its aim in words; nevertheless, it is perfectly easy to recognise it as a means by which we *concentrate and intensify* our feelings. And, by so doing, descend more deeply into ourselves.

This leads to a further interesting recognition. *All* our drives and desires aim at this same 'concentration and intensity'. It is true that food and drink are basic necessities of life; but we prefer to eat a good meal or drink a fine wine because they bring the added pleasure of 'focusing'. The same is obviously true in the case of sex; biologically speaking, its purpose is the continuance of the species, but human beings have turned it into one of their most effective means of achieving 'intensity'. The desire for possessions springs from the need for security, but it is not security that makes a man buy an expensive sports car; it is a craving for the intensity of speed.

All this may seem obvious enough when it is pointed out; yet it is something that we normally fail to grasp. We imagine we want food or sex or possessions 'for their own sake'. In fact, we want them because, like a work of art, they enable us to focus and intensify our desires and thereby to raise the pressure of consciousness.

When human beings find themselves in a state in which they lack purpose, through boredom or frustration, they tend to look inside themselves for *any* form of desire, and to cling to this as their salvation. This leads to the psychological state known as obsession; James describes the case of a woman who had to eat all the time, another who had to walk all day, another who became a dipsomaniac, another who had to keep pulling out her hair. The need for motive, for desire, is so central to mental health that we cannot exist without it. And Maslow pointed out that when people are highly motivated, with plenty of desires and satisfactions, they become subject to 'peak experiences'—sheer overflows of vital energy.

In short, the common denominator of human desire is the need for heightened *pressure* of consciousness. This—and not sex or territory or aggression—is the key to the human evolutionary drive.

How does this recognition relate to the main theme of this book—man's 'paranormal' powers?

What I have tried to show is that the usual notion of evolution is mistaken. According to this view, man has taken several millions of years to reach his present position, and if he wants to evolve further, he can expect it to take another million years or so. Yet the evidence of paranormal research seems to show that he *already* possesses certain 'superhuman' powers, such as telepathy, psychokinesis, precognition. He is more 'evolved' than he realises.

If I were asked to draw a picture of a typewriter keyboard, with the positions of all the keys, I would be unable to do it. Yet my *fingers* know where all the keys are located. The knowledge, which began in my consciousness, has been passed on to an unconscious level. So it is quite conceivable that other kinds of knowledge have also been 'forgotten' by human consciousness, yet exist on deeper levels of the mind.

To activate these levels would require an immense amount of energy, a pressure of consciousness far higher than we possess at the present moment. The chief problem, then, at the present stage of evolution, is how to raise the pressure of individual consciousness.

The main problem with human beings is their lack of motivation. Because they think of themselves in terms of fairly simple desires, they are easily undermined by boredom. Yet the answer is simpler than it looks. It lies in a concept that could be called 'the feedback point'.

The feedback point is the stage at which the pleasure—or profit—from any activity is greater than the effort we put into it. So, for example, a child may have to be persuaded to learn to read; but, if he is intelligent, he is soon doing it for pleasure. Similarly, if I start a business, the feedback point arrives when I am making enough profit to start re-investing and expanding.

Before this point arrives, I may waste enormous amounts of money or energy and be dogged by discouragement. Under these circumstances, we have to be forced or persuaded to go on making an effort. If I try to force a child to learn something he hates, I may drive him to the point of exhaustion and rebellion and achieve only minimal results.

It should be clear that life on earth has still not reached the feedback point. Life has been driven to evolve largely by pain and inconvenience. And these are effective only up to a point. Beyond this, they produce discouragement and death, and nature has to begin all over again. This explains why evolution is such a murderous and wasteful process.

Yet there is at least one field in which nature has discovered a less wasteful method: reproduction. Giving birth to offspring and bringing them up to the point where they can look after themselves is a lengthy and exhausting process; yet most creatures seem to enjoy it. Sex is 'subsidised' by a deep and powerful instinct, which has turned it into a pleasure; consequently, nature has no need to use the big stick to persuade its creatures to reproduce. Sex has passed the 'feedback point'. And, as the human race has discovered, this can also involve certain problems, like overpopulation.

Consciousness has also been a response to pain and inconvenience. Like claws and fangs, it has developed as an aid to survival. And it has not yet reached its feedback point. On the contrary, most creatures seem to find it something of a burden. It separates us from our instincts and makes us clumsy and awkward.

But the past two or three thousand years have seen an important development in the history of consciousness. There came a point at which a few human beings realised that the pursuit of knowledge can be a self-rewarding activity. They discovered that thinking could be enjoyed 'for its own sake'—or rather, that the activity of thought could produce a sensation of *inner freedom*. Plato's dialogues show us young people enjoying the discussion of ideas as much as the food and wine. Even so, most Athenians remained suspicious of the value of 'pure thought', and Socrates was executed for trying to persuade the youth of Athens that it was a higher activity than fighting. Nevertheless, the human race had glimpsed an important discovery: that inner freedom can be increased by thought. Or, to put it another way, that we can use consciousness to increase consciousness.

All this brings us to the most interesting part of the story—and down to our own time. The nineteenth-century movement called Romanticism marked a new stage in the development of individual self-consciousness. Large numbers of poets, musicians and artists began to experience strange moods of godlike freedom which aroused enormous longing; this came to dominate their lives to the exclusion of comfort and security. The odd thing is that most of them had no great faith in the urges that drove them to turn their backs on society. They were tormented with guilt; many committed suicide or went insane, others died of various illnesses caused by exhaustion and discouragement. They raged against the apparent futility of existence and against the destiny that seemed to condemn them to failure and misery.

As far as these romantic Outsiders could see, this craving for freedom was impelling them towards self-destruction. Wagner thought art was an illness and went to a hydropathic establishment to be cured of it. Thomas Mann says of him: 'This nature felt itself every minute on the verge of exhaustion; only by exception did it experience the sensations of well-being.' Mann's own works are devoted to the proposition that the artist has turned his back on life and can expect nothing but loneliness and defeat.

All this shows a total failure to grasp what is happening to human consciousness. The romantics had stumbled on the discovery that the aim of human evolution is *increased pressure of consciousness* (or, as we would now say, expansion of consciousness). But the realisation remained on an intuitive level and was contradicted by all their conscious ideas and assumptions; hence the self-division and the high mortality rate.

The interesting thing is that romanticism has not died out. It is more alive today than it was in 1850. Moreover, it is no longer confined to a few hundreds—or thousands—of poets and intellectuals. Modern 'romantics' could be counted in millions. Many of them are not particularly intelligent; many are as self-destructive as their nineteenth-century counterparts. Some regard themselves as liberals, some as mystics and occultists, some merely as rebels who want to 'do their own thing'. All share a common recognition: that what really concerns them is freedom; not merely physical freedom, but inner freedom.

Does this mean that we are at a turning point in human history? I am inclined to doubt it. But it means that human consciousness is developing towards a new recognition: that the way ahead lies through *more* consciousness, not less. Modern man has a strong compulsion to fly back to nature, back to instinct. He is gradually learning that this is not the answer.

Man is approaching the 'feedback point' in the evolution of consciousness: the point where consciousness becomes self-sustaining. All my own work has been concerned with this contradiction: that in spite of the strange lightning flashes of inner freedom, which reveal that our basic aim is *more* consciousness, man continues to be suspicious of consciousness, suspecting that it will land him in a bleak and cold universe. So he continues to resist the movement of his own evolution.

Yet if the ecstasies of the romantics mean anything, they mean that man has a far greater control of his inner being than he ever realised. He is enmeshed in all kinds of curious misconceptions about himself and his fundamental nature: the chief of which is that he is a poor, helpless creature, born into a universe he fails to understand. The evidence we have examined in this chapter shows this to be untrue. The evidence of paranormal research shows that there is a part of our being that knows far more than the conscious mind. And the evidence of mystics through the ages suggests that there is a part of our being that knows even greater secrets than this.

Our natural tendency is to try to return to these intuitive depths; and in the chapter called 'Revelations', we have considered various methods of achieving this end. Yet most of these methods turn out to be ultimately unsatisfying, since all involve various degrees of loss of control. Only Gurdjieff recognised clearly that the answer must lie in increased control over the robot—'understanding the machine'.

This is precisely the kind of statement that worries us. Control seems to suggest some ugly, assertive will-to-power and ultimate breakdown. But we are forgetting what all the evidence of this book unmistakably suggests: that we already possess this control. It already exists, on deeper, or higher, levels of our being. How we have come to lose it is something of a mystery; the only thing that seems clear is that it has to do with the development of consciousness. 'Conscious' man is a pygmy, a mere fragment of his true self. That he once possessed such a conception seems clear from the occult traditions of alchemy and cabbalism. Our problem is that we know this intuitively and are inclined to suspect that the evolutionary excursion into reflective consciousness was a mistake. I am as much inclined to this instinctive mistrust as anyone. Yet the evidence tells me clearly that I am wrong. Consciousness is intentional; its destiny is to become more intentional. Through a gradual deepening of intentionality, it will re-establish contact with our 'lost' levels. The higher levels *are* there, as I discovered from the 'schoolmistress effect'. They can be summoned when we need them. But unless we know they are there, we make no attempt to summon them.

What will happen seems to me perfectly clear. Human beings will one day recognise, beyond all possibility of doubt, that consciousness *is* freedom. When this happens, consciousness will cease to suffer from mistrust of its own nature. Suddenly, the 'profits' will be clear and self-evident. Instead of wasting most of its energies in retreats and uncertainties and excursions into blind alleys, consciousness will re-cycle its energies into its own evolution. The feedback point will mark a new stage in the history of the planet earth.

When that happens, the first fully human being will be born.

Appendix

———◆———

Electromagnetic Induction of Psi States: The Way Forward in Parapsychology

By Peter Maddock

Judged according to acceptable standards of repeatability, the status of the evidence for parapsychological phenomena is still so poor that there remains considerable scepticism in the scientific Establishment concerning their reality.

Attempts to produce repeatable ESP in laboratory testing both by investigating the extent to which ESP might be affected by psychological parameters—personality characteristics, empathy, mood, heightened motivation, expectancy, or by belief in psi, etc.—and by using hypnosis, meditation, biofeedback, sensory deprivation, drugs and other methods to generate ASCs, have produced no consistent marked improvement in target-guessing scores. Moreover, it is impossible to ignore objections that once the controls are tightened, displays of PK phenomena ostensibly produced by Geller and other exponents seem not to manifest, in spite of their complaints that controls tend to inhibit psi ability. Because of these factors psi research is regarded by some investigators as having reached an impasse, and by many sceptics as an invalid field of enquiry.

But other researchers remain confident that the mass of anecdotal and experimental evidence so far obtained does warrant further systematic studies, and consider it reasonable to hope that certain essential conditions may be identified, which determine the occurrence of the phenomena and which could prove capable of being induced artificially in subjects.

The pursuit of this goal at Parascience Centre is necessarily a physics and biosciences oriented one.

Because it is an electro-chemical and bio-organism, the physical concomitants of thought and other brain processes are essentially electromagnetic in nature, and if psi exists, electromagnetism and psi must *couple* at a micro level within certain structures in the brain whenever phenomena occur. Since both spontaneous case and experimental evidence indicates that ESP and PK are generally speaking capricious, transient or intermittent in character, it may be inferred that such coupling must be delicately balanced, and usually unstable.

How then to enhance this coupling, and gain scientific control over the subject's capacity to undergo psychic processes?

An essential clue is provided by the correlation that has been established between ESP and memory, which indicates not only that telepathic psi must interact with the brain's memory system, but that because memory is encoded by nucleo-protein macromolecules in cortical neurons, these memory traces must be *psi-interactive biomolecules* (PIBs). If this is true it follows that the coupling of electromagnetism with psi will inevitably be governed by precise quantum energetic criteria, which immediately explains why telepathic receptivity as well as psi-interactive states in general are so critically balanced.

It also provides an insight into why the conventional methods of trying to improve ESP ability, mentioned above, have lamentably failed. They are evidently incapable of stabilising appropriate electroenergetic conditions in the cortex sufficiently to enable impinging patterns of psi information to keep on being transduced into corresponding patterns of neuron firing, so that subjects can undergo vivid, *continuous*, and fully dissociated ESP.

What then is the alternative? It would seem that the only way of bringing about truly stable psi-interactive states in the brain will be to employ an electromagnetic method of induction.

There is already empirical evidence to support this contention. For example, the case reported to the Parapsychology Foundation by a Washington electronics engineer who claimed: 'Working with high frequency machinery my colleagues and I have suddenly found we are on occasions telepathic.' Also, as long ago as 1924, the physician W. E. Boyd inadvertently discovered, while investigating electrical methods for diagnosing and treating disease, that impressively above-chance scores in target-guessing tests (as high as $P < 10^{-7}$) were consistently obtainable by connecting the subject's scalp to a damped oscillatory electrical circuit, tuned to resonate at about 100 Megahertz frequency, which therefore probably represented the first crude demonstration of a receiving system for cognitive psi. Unfortunately Boyd's results, which were carefully validated by a committee of government scientists under Sir Thomas Horder at the time, have remained virtually unknown, and so their immense importance has been overlooked by parapsychologists at large.

It must be emphasised these ideas do not imply that psi effects propagate by means of electromagnetic waves. This appears unlikely. It means, simply, that electromagnetic methods might nevertheless be developed as a physically precise and non-harmful way of manipulating the brain, for the purpose of stabilising either a telepathically receptive, or transmissive state in it, or indeed a state under which it can exert psychokinesis.

The technical details have been discussed more fully in papers I have presented at Parascience Conferences held at the City University and Imperial College of Science and Technology, London, respectively, in 1976 and 1977.

Hopes for a breakthrough on these lines are therefore well founded, and research has commenced at Parascience Centre, but progress has been greatly hampered so far by lack of adequate funds for this programme, and help is urgently needed.

Such a breakthrough would open up a dramatic new era in the history of man's control over nature, for when psi-energetic systems have been developed to a sophisticated stage it is expected that not only will repeatable psi be readily demonstrable, but that the capabilities of psychic subjects when subjected to electromagnetic induction will vastly surpass the performance of even the best natural medium or sensitive when working unaided, such as to make both telepathic communication and other forms of technological use a practical possibility.

It should not however be assumed, even if certain macro-molecular structures in the brain do comprise the interaction sites with psi, that this presupposes a naïvely monist view of reality, or that the concept of post-mortem survival is excluded, since it is conceivable that PIBs represent the interface between the material and non-material universe, or between the brain and *mind*, and it is precisely the study of phenomena associated with PIBs which will help modern science to probe into the nature and mode of propagation of psi, into the fundamental question of consciousness, and possibly throw light on the meaning of existence itself. Perhaps a great new knowledge-discipline, capable of encompassing facts about what we somewhat arbitrarily denote as the 'non-physical' world, and about man's own spirituality, will eventually emerge from this.

Notes

———————

INTRODUCTION: THE LADDER OF SELVES

1. See *The Occult*, Part 2, Chapter 8.
2. See *Twenty Cases Suggestive of Reincarnation*, p. 33 et seq.
3. For a more detailed discussion of these examples, see *The Occult*, pp. 58–62 and 555–6.

PART ONE

1   GHOSTS, GHOULS AND PENDULUMS

1. See *The Divining Rod* by Barrett and Besterman, pp. 260 and 267.
2. In fact, he later discovered that a man *had* committed suicide from the spot where Mina had felt the urge to jump.
3. See also Peter Underwood's *Gazetteer of British Ghosts*.
4. Lodge, *Man and the Universe*.
5. *Our Haunted Kingdom*, Wolfe Publishing Ltd., 1973, p. 200.
6. *The Power of the Mind*, Chilton Book Co., 1975, p. 165.
7. *Strange Powers*, 1973.

2   GIANTS AND WITCHES

1. Thames and Hudson, London, 1976.

3 THE PATH OF THE DRAGON

1. The anthropological technique known as Structuralism is based on the same notion. For example, in *The Raw and the Cooked*, Levi-Strauss analyses and contrasts 187 separate myths, attempting to glimpse their 'underlying structure'.
2. He is referring to the thirty uprights and their original lintels.
3. This view receives support from some recent experiments, which indicate that when the dowser's solar plexus is heavily insulated, the rod ceases to respond. Other insulation—like heavy gloves or thick shoes—made little or no difference.
4. If a weak electric current is passed through a fishpond, the fishes will swim towards the positive pole.
5. *Feng-shui* by E. J. Eitel (1873). Re-published in 1973 by Land of Cockayne Press, Cambridge, Foreword by John Michell.
6. *The Earth Spirit: Its Ways, Shrines and Mysteries*, Thames and Hudson, London, 1975.
7. Volume II.
8. Steve Moore, a British expert on leys, has made an interesting alternative suggestion: that the apparent conflict is simply the difference between the Chinese and the European mentality. Chinese religious lore insists that straight lines are 'arrows of misfortune'; good resides only in lines that curve and wander, following the natural contours of the earth. Europeans, with their logical and scientific outlook, have a preference for lines that run as straight as Roman roads. So in tracing earth forces, the Chinese emphasise the tendency to meander while Europeans minimise it. But European and Chinese geomancers seem agreed on a basic fact: that the lines of force are especially inclined to follow the edges of hills. (*The Ley Hunter*, No. 72.)
9. See p. 471 et seq.
10. *Fortean Times*, No. 17, August 1976, p. 12.
11. *Fortean Times* (The News), No. 3, March 1974, p. 20.
12. *Science and Society in Prehistoric Britain*, London, 1977.

4 THE TIMELESS ZONE

1. *The Strange Case of Dr M. K. Jessup*, edited by Gray Barker, Saucerian Books, Clarksburg, Virginia. Dr Manson Valentine's account, in *The Bermuda Triangle* by Charles Berlitz (p. 114), contains many inaccuracies.

PART TWO

1 THE CURIOUS HISTORY OF HUMAN STUPIDITY

1. In fact, subsequent research conducted in Pennsylvania by Dr Paul Taubman has demonstrated fairly conclusively that Burt's basic contention *is* correct: heredity *does* count for more than environment. (See *The Times*, May 13, 1977.)
2. See, for example, Fenton Bresler's account in *Scales of Justice*.
3. See p. 105.

2 HOW MANY ME'S ARE THERE?

1. Jung, *Collected Works*, Volume 1.
2. By Weir Mitchell (1888), cited extensively in William James's *Principles of Psychology*, Chapter 10.
3. Fischer was not her real name but a pseudonym chosen by Prince in writing about the case.
4. Prince complicates an already complex story by calling this 'spirit' 'Sleeping Margaret', to distinguish her from 'personality 3', also called Margaret. For the sake of simplicity I shall change the name.
5. See Part One, Chapter 4, p. 155. See also Part Two, Chapter 10, p. 476.
6. 'A Case of Possession and Modern Exorcism', *Bulletin de l'Université de Lyon*, cited in *Exorcism*, ed. Martin Ebon, NAL, 1974.
7. *The Dissociation of Personality*.
8. Berne, *Transactional Analysis in Psychotherapy*, New York, 1961.
9. *Sybil* by Flora Rheta Schreiber, Henry Regnery and Co., New York, 1973.
10. *The Psychology of Tension* by Björn Sjövall, Uppsala, 1964.
11. Polanyi, essay on 'The Structure of Consciousness', *Knowing and Being*, p. 217.
12. *The Three Faces of Eve* by Corbett H. Thigpen and Hervey M. Cleckley, New York, 1957. I have deliberately included no account of this case in the present chapter since the book is still generally available. Mrs Chris Sizemore—the 'Eve' of the title—established some kind of a record by manifesting no less than twenty-one separate personalities before she was cured.

3 IN SEARCH OF FACULTY X

1. L. L. Vasiliev, *Experiments in Distant Influence*, 1962 (British editions, 1963 and 1976), Chapter 4.
2. *Outcries and Asides*, 1974, p. 22.
3. *Psychic Explorations*, edited by Ed Mitchell and John White, New York, 1974, p. 185.
4. *Astral Projection, Magic and Alchemy*, edited by Francis King, p. 33.
5. *Magic, An Occult Primer*, by David Conway, Jonathan Cape, London, 1972.
6. *The Art of Memory*, London, 1966.
7. *Ars Reminiscendi*, 1583. The full Latin title of the book runs to nearly a hundred words; Francis Yates, to whom this account is heavily indebted, prefers to refer to it as *Seals*.
8. 'The Dangerous Prevalence of Imagination', *Rasselas*, Chapter XLIV.
9. I have explored the subject at length in *The Craft of the Novel* (1975), on whose arguments I have drawn heavily in the last two pages.
10. *The Serapion Brethren*, translated by Major Alex Ewing, London, 1896. In the interests of smoothness, I have taken the liberty of editing the translation.
11. Frederick Wertham, *The Shadow of Violence*, New York, 1949, Chapter 6.

4 THE REDISCOVERY OF MAGIC

1. Chapter 10.
2. See 'The Fight with the Shadow', *Collected Works*, Volume 10, p. 219.

3. *Memories, Dreams, Reflections*, p. 156.
4. Faber & Faber, London, 1944.
5. See p. 78.
6. *Collected Works*, Volume 8, paragraph 350. The critic of the unconscious is Guido Villa.
7. *Memories, Dreams, Reflections*, Chapter VI.
8. 'The Transcendental Function', 1916, *Collected Works*, Volume 8.
9. *Collected Works*, Volume 14, paragraph 749.
10. *Analytical Psychology, Its Theory and Practice*, p. 190 et seq.
11. *The Works of Wiliam Blake*, edited by Ellis and Yeats, 1893, Volume 1, p. 96.
12. 'Magic', in *Essays and Introductions*, p. 28.
13. 'Philosophy of Shelley's Poetry', ibid, p. 79.
14. *In Search of the Miraculous*, p. 265.
15. *Witness in Witchcraft*, Chapter 9.
16. *Wizard of the Upper Amazon* (1971), pp. 37–8, 156–9.
17. Quoted in Henry Summerfield's biography of Russell, *That Myriad Minded Man*, Colin Smythe Ltd., London, 1975, p. 27.
18. Grimble, *A Pattern of Islands*, Chapter 6; also quoted in *The Occult*, p. 74.
19. For a more detailed discussion, see Part 2, Chapter 9, p. 431.
20. A comparison between Janet's nine levels and Yeats's nine phases (2–10) shows an astonishingly close correspondence.
21. King and Skinner, *Techniques of High Magic*, p. 9.
22. G. K. Chesterton, *Autobiography*, London, 1936, p. 147.
23. *Isis Unveiled*, Volume 1, p. 315.

5 DESCENT INTO THE UNCONSCIOUS

1. See p. 223.
2. The 'ghost' was originally invented by the writer Frank Smythe and described on the back cover of issue No. 105 of *Man, Myth, and Magic*. Several workmen, Smythe alleged, had seen the ghost of the clergyman on Ratcliffe Wharf in Wapping, East London. It had been identified as the spirit of an evil old vicar who had also run a cheap lodging house and murdered sailors for their wages. After the story appeared, many people claimed to have seen the ghost, and a number of writers on ghosts repeated it without checking.
3. See *The Hedgehog and the Fox*. 'The fox knows many things; the hedgehog knows only one.' Berlin's distinction is between 'extraverted' writers like Shakespeare and 'introverted' ones like Tolstoy.
4. *The Presence of Other Worlds*, Harper, New York, p. 24.
5. *Recherches, Experiences et Observations*, Paris, 1811, and *Memoirs* (1809). See also E. J. Dingwall's *Abnormal Hypnotic Phenomena*, Volume 1.
6. p. 238. See also Dingwall, op. cit., p. 285.
7. *Abnormal Hypnotic Phenomena*, Volume 1, p. 158 et seq, and Volume 4, p. 94.
8. Macmillan and Co., 1932. This account is also heavily indebted to Henry Summerfield's biography of AE, *That Myriad Minded Man*, Colin Smythe Ltd., London, 1975.
9. *Candle of Vision*, London, 1918, p. 4.
10. p. 35.
11. *Candle of Vision*, pp. 5–6.

12. Ibid, pp. 8–9.
13. Ibid, pp. 72–4.
14. Ibid, p. 140.
15. Summerfield, p. 47.
16. *The Interpreters*, London, 1922.
17. *Imaginations and Reveries*, Dublin and London, 1915.
18. See *Scientific American*, February 1963. Also described by Robert Ardrey in *The Territorial Imperative*, pp. 327–9.

6 REVELATIONS

1. See *Altered States of Consciousness*, edited by Charles Tart, p. 367.
2. This essay is quoted at great length in *The Occult*, p. 555.
3. See Ouspensky's *In Search of the Miraculous*, pp. 82–9 and 122–140.
4. Ibid, p. 122.
5. Ibid, p. 40.
6. *The Fourth Way*, p. 415.
7. Ibid, p. 416.
8. *Venture with Ideas*, London, 1951, p. 148.
9. *Altered States of Consciousness*, edited by Charles Tart, p. 47.
10. *In Search of the Miraculous*, p. 120.
11. See *New Hope for Alcoholics* by Abram Hoffer and Humphry Osmond, New York, 1968; also my *New Pathways in Psychology*, London and New York, 1972, pp. 32 and 192.
12. See 'An End of An Adventure', *Encounter*, October 1976.
13. In the March 1977 *Encounter*, Cynthia Gladwyn also pointed out that in August—when the 'adventure' took place—Montesquiou, Mme Greffulhe and their friends would have been in the country, which would have excluded Versailles. In fact, Mme Greffulhe was in London on that day.
14. In an account written at my request.
15. See my *Strange Powers* (1973).

7 WORLDS BEYOND

1. Quoted by Joseph Campbell in *The Masks of God: Primitive Mythology*, p. 243.
2. *Gypsy Sorcery*, by C. G. Leland, London, 1891, p. 163.
3. 'A Study of Dreams', 1913, reprinted in *Altered States of Consciousness*.
4. Real name: Hugh Calloway.
5. See p. 115.
6. *The Romeo Error*, p. 132.
7. *To Kiss Earth Goodbye*, p. 90.
8. *Resurrection*, Cassell and Co., London, 1934, pp. 18–26.
9. The papers presented at the conference—including one on the tobiscope—are printed in *Galaxies of Life*, edited by Stanley Krippner and Daniel Rubin, New York, 1973.
10. The most exhaustive documentation of such cases is contained in Michael Harrison's book, *Fire from Heaven*, London, 1976.

11. Sybille Bedford's biography of Aldous Huxley, Volume 1, p. 224.
12. Published as *Magick Without Tears*, Llewellyn Publications, USA.
13. Paracelsus, *Selected Writings*, edited by Jolande Jacobi, 1959, pp. 133, 134.
14. I have spoken more fully of the meanings of the Sephiroths in *The Occult*, pp. 205–207.

8 ANCIENT MYSTERIES

1.   Walter Leslie Wilmhurst, Introduction to Hermetic Philosophy and Alchemy (1918).
2.   Under his 'magical name' Sapere Aude; published by the Theosophical Publishing House.
3.   I.e., *The Alchemists* by F. Sherwood Taylor, and *Alchemists Through the Ages* by A. E. Waite.
4.   For a fuller account, see *The Occult*, p. 243 et seq.
5.   Quoted in *Alchemists and Gold* by Jacques Sadoul, pp. 214–15.
6.   See p. 237 et seq.
7.   Its full title is *Historia von D. Johann Faustus*, Berlin, 1587.
8.   Some authorities have attributed it to Apollonius of Tyana, a well-known Cappadocian magician, born in the time of Jesus.
9.   *In Search of the Miraculous*, pp. 31–2.
10. *The Diary of a Modern Alchemist*, Neville Spearman, London, 1974, p. 27.

9 THE GREAT SECRET

1.   Volume 3, pp. 184–192.
2.   This interesting fact was brought to my attention by Mr John Sharp.
3.   'The insistence on preparing the herbal stone is because the *process* is akin to that of the magnum opus. And, incidentally, the production of the herbal stone is not as simple or mechanical as first reading might suggest.' Regardie in a letter to the author.
4.   *Grandmother's Secrets*, by Jean Palaiseul, London, 1973, is a comprehensive introduction to this aspect of the subject.
5.   Letter to the author.
6.   *In Search of the Miraculous*, p. 122.
7.   Ibid, p. 50.
8.   *The Occult*, p. 571.
9.   *L'Or du Millieme Matin*, Paris, 1969; English edition, 1975.
10. *The Works of Thomas Vaughan*, University Books, New York, 1968.
11. *In Search of the Miraculous*, p. 175 et seq.
12. See also p. 513.
13. See *The Cosmic Clocks* and other books by Michel Gauquelin.
14. *The Jupiter Effect*, London, 1974.
15. Oliver Marlow Wilkinson in *Men of Mystery*, edited by Colin Wilson, W. H. Allen, London, 1977.
16. *God is My Adventure*, Faber & Faber, London, 1935.

10 POWERS OF EVIL?

1. The term means to ignore and ostracise; it seems to have originated in Coventry, where girls who went out with soldiers were treated as outcasts.
2. See *The Occult*, pp. 225–7.
3. *The Werewolf*, London, 1933, p. 35. He is quoting from an article, 'Unlucky Possessions', by T. C. Bridges, *Occult Review*, March 1927, p. 159.
4. 'An Experimental Approach to the Survival Problem', *Theta*, Nos. 33–34, 1972. The lack of response in the rat may be due to the fact that rats, like humans, have no natural predators and have lost some of the 'sixth sense'.
5. *The Great Iron Ship* by James Duggan, 1953.
6. See p. 61.
7. Contribution to *Spuk: Wahrglaube oder Irrglaube?* (Ghosts: Reality or Delusion?) by Fanny Moser.
8. *The Cock Lane Ghost* by Douglas Grant, London, 1965. See also Andrew Lang's *Cock Lane and Common Sense*.
9. *Galaxies of Life*, edited by Krippner and Rubin, p. 6. See also Frank Edwards, *Stranger than Science*: 'High Voltage Humans', 1959.
10. Strindberg, *Inferno*, Chapter 6.
11. See 'Caesar's Lake' in *Unsolved Mysteries* by Valentine Dyall.
12. A summary of his information is as follows: Ley 1 runs from Beinn an t-Sithein (Headland of the Fairy Hill), through Ardachie, through the Cairn of the White Fox, Black Fairy Hillock of the White Stone and Fairy Loch. Ley 2 runs from the earthwork marked Fort at GR492236 near Loch Ness, through Ardachie Lodge, then on to Leitir Fheatna (Slope of the Alders) and the Crag of the Goat. Ley 3 runs from Benn Mheadhoin, through the Glen of the Horse, Ardachie, and Bald Hill of the Corrie of the Horse. Ley 4 runs from The Cailleach, GR82042, Corrie of the Horse, Cairn of the White Marshes, Ardachie, Corrie of the Birds and Headland of the Birds. Mr Jenkins points out that Loch Ness itself is seamed with ley lines.
13. From *Society, the Redeemed Form of Man*, p. 43. Also quoted in *The James Family* by F. O. Matthiessen, p. 161.
14. *Haunted Britain*.
15. See *Hypnosis and Suggestion in Psychotherapy* by H. Bernheim (1884) and *Hypnotism and Crime* by Heinz Hammerschlag (1956). Bernheim cites the records of the Draguignan Assizes for July 30 and 31, 1865. He gives the name of the village as Guiols.
16. Prince Felix Yussupov, *Rasputin, His Malignant Influence and Assassination*.
17. *Men of Mystery*, edited by Colin Wilson, W. H. Allen, London, 1977.

PART THREE

1 EVOLUTION

1. *Beyond the Outsider*, Appendix 1; also *New Pathways in Psychology*, pp. 248–9.
2. Cited by William James in *Varieties of Religious Experience*, Lecture VIII.
3. *The Riddle of the Pyramids*, 1974.
4. See p. 393.
5. See p. 262 et seq.

6. *The Ghost in the Machine* (1967), Chapter 16.
7. I wish to thank Stan Gooch, and his publishers Wildwood House, for allowing me to read the book in typescript.
8. *Beyond Biofeedback*, New York, 1977.
9. *The Psychology of Consciousness* (1972). I am grateful to Idries Shah for drawing this book to my attention.
10. *Arrow in the Blue*. See also *The Occult*, pp. 560–2.

2   MESSAGES FROM SPACE AND TIME

1. Jarrolds, London, 1930, p. 361.
2. At a press conference on May 10, 1971, reported in the *National Bulletin*. It is discussed in an article by Otto Binder, 'UFOs "Own" Earth', in *Saga* magazine for December 1971.
3. *Arigó, Surgeon of the Rusty Knife*, by John G. Fuller (1974).
4. *The Invisible College*, (1976), Chapter 9.
5. In a recent sighting—which took place only a few weeks before the present writing—the pilot of an aircraft flying to Portugal described watching the huge, cigar-shaped UFO hovering over the sea, and the smaller disc-shaped craft that came from it. Passengers and crew all watched the objects for several minutes.
6. Holiday also tells me that in 1976, Dr Robert Rines, the Loch Ness investigator, discovered a megalithic stone circle under sixty feet of water.
7. See *The Occult*, pp. 452–3.
8. In a paper, *Species Metapsychology, UFO Waves and Cattle Mutilations*, May 1977.
9. Published in *Oui* Magazine, April and May 1977.

3   THE MECHANISM OF ENLIGHTENMENT

1. *Watcher on the Hills*, London, 1959, p. 49.
2. Ibid.
3. Quoted from James's *Varieties of Religious Experience*, in which he quotes an earlier, pamphlet version; the later version is written in the third person.
4. Houghton Mifflin Co., 1976.
5. *Kundalini: The Evolutionary Energy in Man* (1967).
6. Santa Monica, 1967.
7. *Light*, Winter 1976, pp. 178–9. I am grateful to Mr C. L. Tilburn for sending me the article.
8. London, Stuart and Watkins, 1954. His full name was Rodney Collin Smith. He died in a curious accident—a fall from a tower—in Mexico in 1956.
9. Collin's 'correspondences' between planets and glands are as follows: the Sun—the thymus; Mercury—the thyroid; Venus—the parathyroid; Mars—the adrenals; the Moon—the pancreas; Saturn—the anterior pituitary; Jupiter—the posterior pituitary; Uranus—the gonads; Neptune—the pineal gland.
10. *The Role of Information Underload and Information Overload in Carcinogenesis*, by Augustin M. de la Pena, Ph.D., University of Texas Medical School. Dr de la Pena suggests that chronic information underload (i.e. boredom) has a promoting effect on cancer, while 'overload'—overstimulation—has a retarding effect. 'When the information deficit reaches some critical value, the central nervous

system sends a nonspecific signal to most somatic structure sites . . . indicating the need for novelty or information; carcinogenesis is the body's mode of providing "information novelty" . . .'

11. *Mysticism*, London, 1911, p. 301.
12. Conclusion of *Nanna, or the Soul Life of Plants*, quoted from *Religion of a Scientist: Selections from Fechner*, edited by Walter Lowrie, 1946.
13. Published privately in America by E. P. Dutton and Co., 1975.

4 OTHER DIMENSIONS

1. Pp. 55–6.
2. *Zettel*, paragraphs 45 and 46.
3. A friend has suggested plausibly that the words uttered may have been the Arabic greeting 'shalom aleikum'.
4. See p. 617. A detailed account can be found in *Death Bed Visions* by Sir William Barrett, pp. 11–14.
5. 'Self-Transforming Consciousness: The Bridge Between Dimensions?'

Bibliography

ALBERTUS, FRATER, *Alchemist's Handbook*, Routledge & Kegan Paul, London, 1960.

ALLEGRO, JOHN M., *The Sacred Mushroom and The Cross*, Hodder & Stoughton, London, 1970.

ARKLE, WILLIAM, *A Geography of Consciousness*, Neville Spearman, London, 1974.

ATWOOD, M. A., *Hermetic Philosophy and Alchemy*, The Julian Press Inc., New York, 1960.

BACHCHAN, H. R., *W. B. Yeats and Occultism*, Motilal Banarsidass, India, 1965.

BARBAULT, ARMAND, *Gold of a Thousand Mornings*, Neville Spearman, London, 1975.

BARRETT, FRANCIS, *The Magus. A Complete System of Occult Philosophy*, University Books Inc., USA, 1967.

BARRETT, SIR WILLIAM, *On the Threshold of the Unseen*, Kegan Paul, Trench Trubner & Co., London, 1920.

BARRETT, SIR WILLIAM and BESTERMAN, THEODORE, *The Divining Rod*, University Books Inc., USA, 1968.

BELOFF, JOHN, B.A., Ph.D., *New Directions in Parapsychology*, Elek Science, London, 1974.

BENNET, E. A., *C. G. Jung*, Barrie & Rockliff (Barrie Books Ltd.), London, 1961.

BENNETT, JOHN G., *Witness—Autobiography*, Turnstone Books, London, 1974.
—— *Energies*, Hodder & Stoughton, London, 1964.

BERNHEIM, M. D. H., *Hypnosis and Suggestion in Psychotherapy*, University Books Inc., USA, 1964.

BONUS OF FERRARA, *The New Pearl of Great Price*, Vincent Stuart Ltd., London, 1963.

BOZZANO, PROF. ERNEST, *Animism and Spiritism*, Arthur H. Stockwell Ltd., London.

BROWN, PETER LANCASTER, *Megaliths—Myths and Men*, Blandford Press Ltd., Dorset, 1976.

BUCHANAN, JOSEPH RODES, *Manual of Psychometry—The Dawn of a New Civilization*, Joseph Rodes Buchanan, Boston, 1885.

BUCKE, M. D., RICHARD MAURICE, *Cosmic Consciousness*, University Books, Inc., USA, 1961.

BURCKHARDT, TITUS, *Alchemy*, Stuart & Watkins, London, 1967.

BURR, HAROLD SAXTON, *Blueprint for Immortality*, Neville Spearman, London, 1972.

BUTLER, W. E., *How to Read the Aura*, The Aquarian Press, Northamptonshire, 1971.

CAPRA, FRITJOF, *The Tao of Physics*, Fontana/Collins, London, 1976.

CARLSON, RICK J., *The Frontiers of Science and Medicine*, Wildwood House Ltd., London, 1975.

CAVENDISH, RICHARD, *The Powers of Evil*, Routledge & Kegan Paul, London, 1975.
—— *The Black Arts*, Routledge & Kegan Paul, London, 1967.
—— *The History of Magic*, Weidenfeld & Nicolson, London, 1977.

COHN, NORMAN, *The Pursuit of the Millennium*, Granada Publishing Ltd., London, 1970.
—— *Europe's Inner Demons*, Sussex University Press, 1975.

COLQUHOUN, ITHELL, *Sword of Wisdom*, Neville Spearman, London, 1975.

COLLIN, RODNEY, *The Theory of Celestial Influence*, Stuart & Watkins, London, 1954.

COX, R. HIPPISLEY, *The Green Roads of England*, The Garnstone Press Ltd., London, 1973.

COXHEAD, NONA, *Mindpower*, William Heinemann Ltd., London, 1976.

CROOKALL, ROBERT, *The Supreme Adventure*, James Clarke & Co. Ltd., Cambridge, 1961.
—— *The Mechanisms of Astral Projection*, Darshana International, India, 1968.

CROWLEY, ALEISTER, *Gems from the Equinox*, (Edited by Israel Regardie), Llewellyn Publications, USA, 1974.
—— *Magick—In Theory and Practice*, Castle Books, New York.

—— *Magick Without Tears*, (Edited by Israel Regardie), Llewellyn Publications, USA, 1973.

—— *Magical and Philosophical Commentaries on The Book Of Law*, 93 Publishing, Canada, 1974.

—— *The Qabalah of Aleister Crowley—Three Texts*, Samuel Weiser, New York, 1973.

—— *The Book of Thoth*, Samuel Weiser, New York, 1972.

CUMMINS, GERALDINE, *Swan on a Black Sea*, Routledge & Kegan Paul, London, 1965.

DAMES, MICHAEL, *The Silbury Treasure—The Great Goddess Rediscovered*, Thames & Hudson, London, 1976.

DAUMAL, RENÉ, *Mount Analogue*, City Lights Books, San Francisco, California, USA, 1972.

DINGWALL, ERIC J., *Abnormal Hypnotic Phenomena, Volume 1: France*, J. & A. Churchill Ltd., London, 1967.

—— *Abnormal Hypnotic Phenomena, Volume 2: Belgium, Netherlands, Germany and Scandinavia*, J. & A. Churchill Ltd., London, 1967.

—— *Abnormal Hypnotic Phenomena, Volume 3: Russia, Poland, Italy, Spain, Portugal and Latin America*, J. & A. Churchill Ltd., London, 1968.

—— *Abnormal Hypnotic Phenomena, Volume 4: United States of America and Great Britain*, J. & A. Churchill Ltd., London, 1968.

DOUGLAS, ALFRED, *Extra Sensory Powers*, Victor Gollancz Ltd., London, 1976.

DOYLE, ARTHUR CONAN, *The Coming of the Fairies*, Samuel Weiser Inc., New York, 1975.

DUNNE, J. W., *The New Immortality*, Faber & Faber, London, 1938.

—— *Nothing Dies*, Faber & Faber, London, 1940.

EBON, MARTIN, *Exorcism: Fact Not Fiction*, The New American Library Inc., New York, 1974.

FIGULUS, BENEDICTUS, *A Golden and Blessed Casket of Nature's Marvels*, Vincent Stuart Ltd., London, 1963.

FLOURNOY, THEODORE, *From India to the Planet Mars*, University Books Inc., New York, 1963.

FODOR, NANDOR, *Between Two Worlds*, Parker Publishing Co. Inc., New York, 1964.

—— *Freud, Jung and Occultism*, University Books, Inc., New York, 1971.

FORT, CHARLES, *The Books of Charles Fort*, Henry Holt & Co., New York, 1941.

FOX, OLIVER, *Astral Projection*, University Books Inc., New York, 1962.

FULLER, JOHN G., *Arigó: Surgeon of the Rusty Knife*, Thomas Y. Crowell Co., New York, 1974.

GARDNER, GERALD B., *Witchcraft Today*, Jarrolds (London) Ltd., 1954.

GARFIELD, PATRICIA, Ph.D., *Creative Dreaming*, Simon & Schuster, New York, 1974.

GAUQUELIN, MICHEL, *The Cosmic Clocks*, Henry Regnery Co., Library of Congress, USA, 1967.

—— *The Scientific Basis of Astrology—Myth or Reality?* Stein and Day, New York, 1969.

GELLER, URI, *My Story*, Robson Books Ltd., London, 1975.

GREEN, CELIA and MCCREERY, CHARLES, *Apparitions*, Hamish Hamilton, London, 1975.

GREEN, CELIA, *The Decline and Fall of Science*, Hamish Hamilton, London, 1976.

—— *Out-of-the-Body Experiences*, Institute of Psychophysical Research, Oxford, 1968.

—— *Lucid Dreams*, Hamish Hamilton, London, 1968.

GREEN, ELMER and ALYCE, *Beyond Biofeedback*, Delacort Press/Seymour Lawrence, New York, 1977.

GREENHOUSE, HERBERT B., *Premonitions—A Leap into the Future*, Turnstone Press Ltd., England, 1972.

GUDJONSSON, THORSTEINN, *Astrobiology—The Science of the Universe*, Bioradii Publications, Reykjavik, Iceland, 1976.

GUIRDHAM, ARTHUR, *Beyond Jung*, Village Press, London, 1974.

GURDJIEFF, G. I., *Life Is Real Only, Then, When 'I Am'*, Triangle Editions Inc., New York, 1975.

GURNEY, E., MYERS, F. W. H. and PODMORE, FRANK, *Phantasms of the Living. Volume I and II*, Trubner & Co., London, 1886.

HADINGHAM, EVAN, *Circles and Standing Stones*, William Heinemann Ltd., London, 1975.

HAMILTON-JONES, J. W., *The Epistles of Ali Pauli (circa 1700 AD)*, John M. Watkins, London, 1951.

HARPER, GEORGE MILLS, *Yeats's Golden Dawn*, The Macmillan Press Ltd., London, 1974.

—— *Yeats and The Occult*, The Macmillan Press Ltd., London, 1975.

HAWKINS, GERALD S., in collaboration with JOHN B. WHITE, *Stonehenge Decoded*, Souvenir Press Ltd., London, 1966.

HEYWOOD, ROSALIND, *The Sixth Sense*, Pan Books Ltd., London, 1966.

HITCHING, FRANCIS, *Earth Magic*, Cassell & Co. Ltd., London, 1976.

HOFFMAN, ERNST THEODORE WILHELM, *The Serapion Brethren, Volume I*, George Bell & Sons, London, 1886.

—— *The Serapion Brethren, Volume II*, George Bell & Sons, London, 1892.

HOLMYARD, E. J., *Alchemy*, Penguin Books Ltd., Mddx., England, 1957.

HOLROYD, STUART, *PSI and the Consciousness Explosion*, The Bodley Head Ltd., London/Sydney, 1977.

HOWE, ELLIC, *The Magicians of the Golden Dawn—A Documentary History of a Magical Order 1887–1923*, Routledge & Kegan Paul, London, 1972.

—— *Urania's Children—The Strange World of the Astrologers*, William Kimber, London, 1967.

IVIMY, JOHN, *The Sphinx and the Megaliths*, Turnstone Books Ltd., London, 1974.

JACOLLIOT, LOUIS, *Occult Science in India and among the Ancients*, University Books Inc., NYUSA, 1971.

JAFFÉ, ANIELA, *From the Life and Work of C. G. Jung*, Hodder & Stoughton, London, 1972.

JONAS, HANS, *The Gnostic Religion: The message of the alien God and the beginnings of Christianity*, Beacon Press, Boston, 1958.

JUNG, C. G., *Analytical Psychology: its Theory and Practice*, Routledge & Kegan Paul, London, 1968.

—— *Memories, Dreams, Reflections*, Collins and Routledge & Kegan Paul, London, 1963.

—— *The Collected Works: Volumes 1–18*, Routledge & Kegan Paul, London.

KARAGULLA, SHAFICA, M. D., *Breakthrough to Creativity*, DeVorss & Co. Inc., Calif., USA, 1967.

KARLINS, MARVIN and ANDREWS, L. M., *Biofeedback: Turning on the Power of your Mind*, Garnstone Press, London, 1973.

KEEL, JOHN A., *Our Haunted Planet*, Neville Spearman, London, 1971.

KING, FRANCIS and STEPHEN SKINNER, *Techniques of High Magic*, The C. W. Daniel Co. Ltd., 1976.

KILNER, W. J., *The Aura*, Samuel Weiser Inc., New York, 1973.

KNIGHT, DAMON, *Charles Fort: Prophet of the Unexplained*, Victor Gollancz Ltd., London, 1971.

KNIGHT, DAVID C., *The ESP Reader*, Castle Books, USA, 1969.

KNIGHT, GARETH, *A Practical Guide to Qabalistic Symbolism. Volume I: On the Spheres of the Tree of Life*, Helios Book Service (Publications) Ltd., Cheltenham, Glos., 1976.

—— *A Practical Guide to Qabalistic Symbolism. Volume II: On the Paths and the Tarot*, Helios Book Service (Publications) Ltd., Cheltenham, Glos., 1976.

KRAMER, SAMUEL NOAH, *Mythologies of the Ancient World*, Doubleday & Co. Inc., New York, 1961.

KRIPPNER, STANLEY and DANIEL RUBIN, *Galaxies of Life: The Human Aura in Acupuncture and Kirlian Photography*, Gordon & Breach, New York, 1973.

KUHN, THOMAS S., *The Structure of Scientific Revolutions*, University of Chicago, 1970.

LAMB, F. BRUCE, *Wizard of the Upper Amazon: The Story of Manuel Cordova-Rios*, Houghton Mifflin Co., Boston, 1974.

LAPIDUS, *In Pursuit of Gold*, Neville Spearman, London, 1976.

LAURENCE, RICHARD, *The Book of Enoch The Prophet*, Wizards Bookshelf, Mn. 55378, USA, 1973.

LAYARD, JOHN, *The Lady of the Hare*, Faber & Faber, London, 1944.

—— *A Celtic Quest: Sexuality and Soul in Individuation*, Spring Publications, Zurich, Switzerland, 1975.

LEE, D. D. and FREDERICK GEORGE, *Sights and Shadows: Examples of the Supernatural*, W. H. Allen & Co. Ltd., London, 1894.

LEFORT, RAFAEL, *The Teachers of Gurdjieff*, Victor Gollancz Ltd., London, 1971.

LELAND, CHARLES G., *Aradia: The Gospel of the Witches*, The C. W. Daniel Company, London, 1974.

LESHAN, LAWRENCE, *Alternate Realities*, Sheldon Press, London, 1967.

—— *The Medium, the Mystic, and the Physicist*, Turnstone Books, London, 1974.

LETHBRIDGE, T. C., *Gogmagog: The Buried Gods*, Routledge & Kegan Paul Ltd., London, 1957.

—— *Ghost and Ghoul,* Routledge & Kegan Paul Ltd., London, 1961.

—— *Witches: Investigating an Ancient Religion*, Routledge & Kegan Paul Ltd., London, 1962.

—— *Ghost and Divining Rod*, Routledge & Kegan Paul Ltd., London, 1963.

—— *ESP: Beyond Time and Distance*, Routledge & Kegan Paul Ltd., London, 1965.

—— *A Step in the Dark*, Routledge & Kegan Paul Ltd., London, 1967.

—— *The Monkey's Tail: A study in evolution and parapsychology*, Routledge & Kegan Paul Ltd., London, 1969.

—— *The Legend of the Sons of God*, Routledge & Kegan Paul Ltd., London, 1972.

—— *The Power of the Pendulum*, Routledge & Kegan Paul Ltd., London, 1976.

LÉVI, ÉLIPHAS, *The History of Magic*, Rider and Company, 1957.

—— *Transcendental Magic*, Rider & Company, London, 1958.

—— *The Key of the Mysteries*, Rider & Company, London, 1969.

LINDSAY, JACK, *The Origins of Alchemy in Graeco-Roman Egypt*, Frederick Muller, London, 1970.

LONG, MAX FREEDOM, *The Huna Code in Religions*, DeVorss & Co., Calif., USA, 1965.

McINTOSH, CHRISTOPHER, *Éliphas Lévi and the Frech Occult Revival*, Rider and Company, London, 1972.

MATHERS, S. L. MACGREGOR, *The Kabbalah Unveiled*, Routledge & Kegan Paul Ltd., London, 1951.

MITCHELL, EDGAR D., *Psychic Exploration*, G. P. Putnam & Sons, New York, 1974.

MICHELL, JOHN, *The View Over Atlantis*, The Garstone Press Ltd., London, 1972.

—— *The Old Stones of Land's End*, The Garstone Press Ltd., London, 1974.

MOBERLEY, CHARLOTTE and JOURDAIN, ELEANOR, *An Adventure*, Macmillan & Co., London, 1911.

MONROE, ROBERT A., *Journeys out of the Body*, Souvenir Press Ltd., London, 1972.

MOSKVITIN, JURIJ, *Essay on the Origin of Thought*, Ohio University Press, 1974.

MOSS, DR THELMA, *The Probability of the Impossible: Scientific Discoveries and Explorations in the Psychic World*, J. P. Tarcher Inc., NY, 1974.

MULDOON, SYLVAN J. and CARRINGTON, HEREWARD, *The Projection of the Astral Body*, Rider & Company, London, 1968.

—— *The Phenomena of Astral Projection*, Rider & Company, London, 1969.

MURRAY, MARGARET ALICE, *The God of the Witches*, Anchor Books, NY, 1960.

—— *The Witch-Cult in Western Europe*, Oxford University Press, 1971.

MYERS, F. W. H., *Human Personality and its Survival of Bodily Death*, University Books Inc., New York, 1961.

NAUERT, CHARLES G. JR., *Agrippa and the Renaissance Thought*, University of Illinois Press, 1965.

OSTRANDER, SHEILA and SCHROEDER, LYNN, *PSI Psychic Discoveries behind the Iron Curtain*, Sphere Books Ltd., London, 1973.

OWEN, A. R. G., *Can We Explain the Poltergeist?* Garrett Publications, New York, 1964.

OWEN, IRIS M., and SPARROW, MARGARET, *Conjuring up Philip*, Fitzhenry & Whiteside, Ontario, Canada, 1976.

OWEN, ROBERT DALE, *The Debatable Land between this World and the Next*, Trubner & Co., London, 1874.

—— *Footfalls on the Boundary of Another World*, Trubner & Co., London, 1860.

PETERS, FRITZ, *Gurdjieff Remembered*, Samuel Weiser Inc., NY, 1971.

PHILALETHES, EIRENAEUS and others, *Collectanea Chemica: Being Certain Select Treatises on Alchemy and Hermetic Medicine*, Vincent Stuart Ltd., London, 1963.

PLAYFAIR, GUY LYON, *The Indefinite Boundary*, Souvenir Press, London, 1976.

POLLARD, JOHN, *Seers, Shrines and Sirens*, George Allen & Unwin Ltd., London, 1965.

PONCÉ, CHARLES, *Kabbalah*, Garnstone Press, London, 1974.

POWELL, A. E., *The Astral Body*, The Theosophical Publishing House, Ill., USA, 1973.

PRICE, HARRY, *Fifty Years of Psychical Research*, Longmans, Green & Co., London, 1939.

—— *Poltergeist Over England*, Country Life Ltd., London, 1945.

PRINCE, WALTER FRANKLIN, *The Mother Of Doris: Proceedings. A.S.P.R. 1923*, The American Society for Psychical Research, New York, 1923.

—— *Contributions to Psychology: The Doris Case of Quintuple Personality*, Richard G. Badger, Boston, 1917.

PUHARICH, ANDRIJA, *The Sacred Mushroom: Key to the Door of Eternity*, Victor Gollancz Ltd., London, 1959.

—— *URI: A Journal of the Mystery of Uri Geller*, Anchor Press, New York, 1974.

—— *Beyond Telepathy*, Doubleday & Co. Inc., New York, 1962.

RANDI, JAMES, *The Magic of Uri Geller*, Ballantine Books, New York, 1975.

RANDALL, JOHN L., *Parapsychology and the Nature of Life*, Souvenir Press, London, 1975.

REDGROVE, H. STANLEY, *Alchemy: Ancient and Modern*, E. P. Publishing Ltd., Yorkshire, England, 1973.

REGARDIE, ISRAEL, *A Garden of Pomegranates*, Llewellyn Publications, Mn., USA, 1970.

—— *The Tree of Life: A Study in Magic*, Thorsons Publishers Ltd., Northamptonshire, 1975.

—— *The Philosopher's Stone*, Llewellyn Publications, Minnesota, USA, 1970.

—— *The Middle Pillar*, Llewellyn Publications, Minnesota, USA, 1970.

REYNER, J. H., *The Diary of a Modern Alchemist*, Neville Spearman, London, 1974.

RHINE, J. B. and BRIER, ROBERT, *Parapsychology Today*, Castle Books, The Citadel Press, NY, 1968.

RICHET, CHARLES, Ph.D., *Thirty Years of Psychical Research*, W. Collins Sons & Co. Ltd., London, 1923.

ROBERTS, JANE, *The Seth Material*, Prentice-Hall Inc., New Jersey, USA, 1970.

ROBBINS, ROSSELL HOPE, *The Encyclopedia of Witchcraft and Demonology*, Peter Nevill Ltd., London, 1959.

ROLL, WILLIAM G., *The Poltergeist*, The New American Library, New York, 1974.

RULAND, MARTIN, THE ELDER, *A Lexicon of Alchemy*, John M. Watkins, London, 1964.

RUSSELL, EDWARD WRIOTHESLEY, *Design for Destiny*, Neville Spearman, London, 1971.

SADOUL, JACQUES, *Alchemists and Gold*, Neville Spearman, London, 1972.

SAGAN, CARL, *Communication with Extraterrestrial Intelligence (CETI)*, The Massachusetts Institute of Technology, 1973.

SCREETON, PAUL, *Quicksilver Heritage. The Mystic Leys: Their Legacy of Ancient Wisdom*, Thorsons Publishers Ltd., Northamptonshire, 1974.

SHAH, SAYED IDRIES, *Oriental Magic*, Octagon Press, 1970.

—— *The Sufis*, Doubleday & Co. Inc., New York, 1964.

—— *The Secret Lore of Magic*, Frederick Muller Ltd., London, 1957.

SHIRLEY, RALPH, *The Mystery of the Human Double: The Case for Astral Projection*, University Books Inc., New York, 1965.

SIDGWICK, ELEANOR MILDRED, *Phantasms of the Living*, University Books Inc., New York, 1962.

SILBERER, DR HERBERT, *Hidden Symbolism of Alchemy and the Occult Arts*, Dover Publications Inc., New York, 1971.

SJÖVAL, BJÖRN, *The Psychology of Tension*, Uppsala, 1964.

SMITH, SUSY, *The Enigma of Out-of-Body Travel*, Garrett Publications, New York, 1965.

STEINER, RUDOLF, *Ancient Myths: Their Meaning and Connection with Evolution*, Steiner Book Centre, Toronto, Canada, 1971.

STURGE-WHITING, J. R., *The Mystery of Versailles*, Rider & Co., London.

SWANN, INGO, *To Kiss Earth Goodbye*, Hawthorn Books Inc., New York, 1975.

SWORDER, MARY, *Fulcanelli: Master Alchemist. Le Mystère des Cathédrales*, Neville Spearman, London, 1971.

TART, CHARLES T., *Altered States of Consciousness*, Doubleday & Co. Inc., New York, 1969.

—— *States of Consciousness*, E. P. Dutton & Co. Inc., New York, 1975.

TAYLOR, F. SHERWOOD, *The Alchemists*, William Heinemann Ltd., 1952.

TEMPLE, ROBERT K. G., *The Sirius Mystery*, Sidgwick & Jackson, London, 1976.

THOM, A., *Megalithic Sites in Britain*, Oxford University Press, 1967.

—— *Megalithic Lunar Observations*, Oxford University Press, 1971.

THOMAS, THE REV. CHARLES DRAYTON, *Life Beyond Death With Evidence*, W. Collins Sons Ltd., London, 1930.

TOMPKINS, PETER and BIRD, CHRISTOPHER, *The Secret Life of Plants*, Harper & Row, London, 1973.

TYRRELL, G. N. M., *Science and Psychical Phenomena and Apparitions*, University Books Inc., New York, 1961.

VAN DUSEN, WILSON, *The Natural Depth in Man*, Harper & Row, New York, 1972.

—— *The Presence of Other Worlds*, Harper & Row, New York, 1974.

VAN OVER, RAYMOND, *Psychology and Extrasensory Perception*, The New American Library, New York, 1972.

—— *The Psychology of Freedom*, Fawcett Publications, Conn. USA, 1974.

—— *Unfinished Man*, World Publishing, New York, 1972.

VON REICHENBACH, KARL, *The Odic Force: Letters On Od and Magnetism*, University Books Inc., New York, 1968.

VALENTINUS, BASILIUS, *The Triumphal Chariot of Antimony*, Vincent Stuart Ltd., London, 1962.

VAUGHAN, ALAN, *Patterns of Prophecy*, Turnstone Books, London, 1974.

WAITE, A. E., *The Alchemical Writings of Edward Kelly*, Robinson & Watkins, London, 1973.

—— *The Turba Philosophorum*, Robinson & Watkins, London, 1973.

—— *The Hermetic Museum Volume 1*, Robinson & Watkins, London, 1973.

—— *The Hermetic Museum Volume 2*, Robinson & Watkins, London, 1973.

—— *The Works of Thomas Vaughan: Mystic and Alchemist*, University Books Inc., New York, 1968.

—— *The Secret Tradition in Alchemy: Its Development and Records*, Robinson & Watkins, 1969.

—— *The Book of Ceremonial Magic*, University Books Inc., New York, 1961.

WALKER, BENJAMIN, *Beyond the Body: The Human Double and the Astral Planes*, Routledge & Kegan Paul, London, 1974.

WALKER, KENNETH, *The Unconscious Mind*, Arrow Books Ltd., London, 1961.

WATKINS, ALFRED, *The Old Straight Track*, Garnstone Press, London, 1970.

WATSON, LYALL, *Supernature*, Hodder & Stoughton, London, 1973.

WEBB, JAMES, *The Age of the Irrational. Volume I: The Flight From Reason*, MacDonald, London, 1971.

WEIL, ANDREW, *The Natural Mind*, Jonathan Cape, London, 1973.

WEINER, HERBERT, *9½ Mystics: The Kabbala Today*, Macmillan Publishing Co., New York, 1969.

WEST, D. J., *Psychical Research Today*, Gerald Duckworth & Co. Ltd., London, 1954.

WOODROFFE, SIR JOHN, *The Serpent Power*, Ganesh & Co., Madras-17, India, 1974.

Index

Index